ENGLISH FRIARS
AND ANTIQUITY IN THE
EARLY FOURTEENTH
CENTURY

ENGLISH FRIARS
AND ANTIQUITY
IN THE EARLY
FOURTEENTH CENTURY

By BERYL SMALLEY

Fellow of St Hilda's College, Oxford

Author of *The Study of the Bible in the Middle Ages*

BASIL BLACKWELL
OXFORD
M CM LX

PRINTED IN GREAT BRITAIN BY
BILLING AND SONS LIMITED, GUILDFORD AND LONDON

TO
THE OLD SCHOOL HOUSE
MADEHURST

CONTENTS

PREFACE

THIS book originated in the Congress on Renaissance and Humanism held at La Mendola in August 1956. In a stimulating atmosphere, recalled with pleasure by all members, the Librarian of the Warburg Institute, Dr Otto Kurz, ordered me to turn a forty-minute paper into a book, and I obeyed him. The staff of the Warburg have helped me by answering my questions on the obscurest subjects. Dr R. W. Hunt of the Bodleian has continued to put his vast knowledge of medieval Latin literature at my disposal. He has offered ideas and criticism as well as information and has been unselfishly generous with his heavily occupied time: I owe him more than I can say. Dr A. B. Emden kindly let me use the material of his *Biographical Register of the University of Oxford to A.D. 1500* before it was published. Fr Thomas Kaeppeli O.P. gave me access to the rich store of *fiches* on fourteenth-century Dominicans collected by himself and his colleagues at the Istituto Storico of Santa Sabina. Others who have helped me in their special fields are Professor Guiseppe Billanovich, Miss G. M. Brereton, Dr L. E. Boyle and Dr D. A. Callus O.P., Miss R. J. Dean, Mr G. D. G. Hall, Mr N. R. Ker, Professors A. D. Momigliano and R. A. B. Mynors, Dr Otto Pächt who drew my attention to the picture reproduced in the frontispiece, and Professor F. Stegmüller. Mlle M. T. d'Alverny has given me much private help and advice as well as making it a pleasure to work in the Salle des manuscrits at the Bibliothèque Nationale. I should also like to thank Dr Burckhardt of the University Library at Bâle and Signora Anna Omooleo, who was Acting Librarian at the Laurentiana when I was working there. Many other librarians and their assistants have shown patience and courtesy. Mrs G. D. G. Hall has done the heavy work of indexing with her usual efficiency and zest. The editors of *Archivum Fratrum Praedicatorum* and *Medium Aevum* kindly allow me to reproduce material published in papers in their reviews. The Keeper of MSS at the Hunterian Library at Glasgow was good enough to arrange for the reproduction of the miniature shown in the frontispiece.

A travel grant made to me through the British Academy

from the Pilgrim Trust, for which I am deeply grateful,
enabled me to collect material in Continental libraries. My
tenure of a Special Lectureship in the Faculty of Modern
History has made it possible to take time off from teaching;
otherwise the book could hardly have got itself written. As it
is, the very nature of the subject has made for untidiness. I
have not begun to exhaust the material and have left many
loose ends in the hopes that some of my readers may put them
into order.

BERYL SMALLEY.

May 2nd, 1960
St Hilda's College, Oxford

ABBREVIATIONS

MANUSCRIPTS

B   Oxford, Bodl. 722 (2648)
C   Oxford, Balliol College 27
E   Oxford, Exeter College 27
L   Oxford, Lincoln College lat. 86
P   Cambridge, Peterhouse 210
R   London, Brit. Mus. Royal 4.A.i
S   Oxford, Corpus Christi College 186
T   Oxford, Corpus Christi College 187
U   Uppsala, University Library C.125 (7522)
V   Venice, Bibl. Marc. lat. 1790 (494)

Numbers in brackets after Bodleian MSS denote the number in the *Summary Catalogue*.

PRINTED SOURCES

Arch. FF. Praed.	Archivum Fratrum Praedicatorum
Arch. fr. hist.	Archivum franciscanum historicum
Archives	Archives d'histoire doctrinale et littéraire du Moyen Age
B.L.R.	The Bodleian Library Record
B.Q.R.	The Bodleian Quarterly Record
Charland	Th.M. Charland, Les *Artes praedicandi*. Contribution à l'histoire de la rhétorique au Moyen Age (Paris, Ottawa, 1938)
C.S.E.L.	Corpus scriptorum ecclesiasticorum latinorum
D.H.G.E.	Dictionaire d'histoire et de géographie ecclésiastique
D.N.B.	Dictionary of National Biography
E.E.T.S.	Early English Text Society
E.H.R.	English Historical Review
Forte	S. Forte, Thomas Hopeman O.P., *Arch.FF.Praed.* 25 (1955) 311-44
F.P.	A. G. Little, Franciscans Papers, Lists, and Documents (Manchester, 1943)
F.S.	Fritz Saxl. A volume of Memorial Essays, ed. D. J. Gordon (London, 1957)
Fulgentius metaforalis	H. Liebeschütz, *Fulgentius metaforalis*: ein Beitrag zur Geschichte der antiken mythologie im Mittelalter (Leipzig, 1926)
Glorieux	P. Glorieux, Répertoire des maîtres en théologie de Paris au XIIIe siècle, 2 volumes (Paris, 1933, 1934)
Herbert	J. A. Herbert, A Catalogue of Romances in the British Museum 3 (London, 1910)
Hinnebusch	The Early English Friars Preachers (Rome, 1951)

H.L.F.	Histoire littéraire de la France
I.M.U.	Italia medioevale e umanistica 1 (1958)
J.W.C.I.	Journal of the Warburg and Courtauld Institutes
Knowles	D. Knowles, The Religious Orders in England, 2 volumes (Cambridge, 1948, 1955)
Le procès	Th. Kaeppeli, Le procès contre Thomas Waleys O.P. (Rome, 1936)
M.A.R.S.	Mediaeval and Renaissance Studies
M.G.H.S.	Monumenta Germaniae Historiae. Scriptores.
O.R.	A. B. Emden, A Biographical Register of the University of Oxford to A.D. 1500, 3 volumes (Oxford, 1957-59)
Pantin	The English Church in the Fourteenth Century (Cambridge, 1955)
P.G.	Patrologia graeca
Philobiblon	Riccardo da Bury Philobiblon, ed. A. Altamura (Naples, 1954)
P.L.	Patrologia latina
Policraticus	Ioannis Saresberiensis Episcopi Carnotensis Policratici sive De Nugis Curialium et Vestigiis Philiosophorum Libri VIII, ed. C. J. Webb (Oxford, 1909)
Powicke	F. M. Powicke, The Medieval Books of Merton College (Oxford, 1931)
Q.E.	J. Quétif-J. Échard, Scriptores Ordinis Praedicatorum, 2 volumes (Paris, 1719, 1721)
Rech. Théol.	Recherches de théologie ancienne et médiévale
R.I.S.	Rerum italicarum scriptores
Robert Holcot	B. Smalley, Robert Holcot O.P., *Arch.FF.Praed*, 26 (1956) 5-97
Seznec	J. Seznec, The Survival of the Pagan Gods, translated from the French by B. F. Sessions (New York, 1953)
Stegmüller	F. Stegmüller Repertorium biblicum medii aevi, 5 volumes, in progress (Madrid, 1940-55)
Study of the Bible	B. Smalley, The Study of the Bible in the Middle Ages, 2nd ed. (Oxford, 1952)
Thomas Waleys	B. Smalley, Thomas Waleys O.P., *Arch.FF.Praed.* 24 (1954) 50-107
T.R.H.S.	Transactions of the Royal Historical Society
Welter	J. T. Welter, L'*exemplum* dans la littérature religieuse et didactique du Moyen Age (Paris, Toulouse, 1927)

The Trinity of Ancient Philosophers: see p. xv.

DESCRIPTION OF THE FRONTISPIECE

THREE ancient philosophers are presented according to the medieval iconography of the Blessed Trinity, which showed the Three Persons sitting in a row, the Father in the centre with the Son on his right and the Holy Spirit on his left. Seneca, the favourite moralist of the middle ages, here replaces God the Father; Plato and Aristotle come one on each side. They wear doctors' caps and fur-lined robes. Each holds an open book inscribed with a 'sentence' from his writings. Not only the men but their words, too, appear in medieval costume. Plato's book says:

> 'Genitorem et opificem universitatis tam est difficile invenire quam inventum digne profari.' (*Platonis Timaeus interprete Chalcidio*, ed. I. Wrobel, Leipzig, 1876, 24.)

Seneca's:

> 'Si vis Deo propinquare, bonus esto. Si vis habere honorem, dabo tibi magnum imperium impera(re).' (*Ep. mor. ad Lucil.* 95, 50: 'Vis deos propitiare? bonus esto.' ibid. 113, 30: 'imperare sibi maximum imperium.')

Aristotle's:

> 'Prima causa est nobilissima, que non alteratur nec mutatur, sed manet in sempiternum completa et perfecta.' (*De caelo* I, ix in the Arabic-Latin version, text 100, conflated with the commentary of Averroes.)

An inscription in a contemporary hand in the margin below the miniature has been partially erased, but can be read under an ultra-violet lamp:

> 'Philosophia est assimilatio operibus creatoris secundum virtutem humanitatis. Sumpta est ista diffinitio in secundo Platonis.' (From the neo-Platonist Jewish philosopher, Isaac Israeli, translated into Latin by Gerard of Cremona; J. T. Muckle, Isaac Israeli, *Liber de diffinitionibus*, Archives 11, 1938, 303.)

Each 'sentence' sums up the chief message of its author as transmitted to the middle ages. The inscription in the margin defines the purpose of philosophical studies, the most god-like of human activities, and explains the iconography of the miniature.

The setting is a compilation of extracts from moral, philosophical and religious pieces, written in England in the early fourteenth century, now MS Glasgow, Hunterian Library 231 (see J. Young and P. Henderson Aitken, *Catalogue of MSS in the Library of the Hunterian Museum*, Glasgow, 1908, 176-83). Other miniatures show a cleric called *Rogerus* kneeling and holding a scroll: he must have compiled the extracts and designed the illustrations. Dr R. W. Hunt has suggested that this Roger may have been the Roger Waltham, compiler of a *Compendium morale* which also shows admiration for ancient sages and for Seneca in particular. Waltham began his career as clerk and later as chancellor to Antony Bek, bishop of Durham, and worked in the civil service. He was a canon of St Paul's by 1309 and was still alive in 1330 (*O.R.* 3, 1974-1975). Respect for the ancients could hardly be carried further than it is in this miniature. Yet a reading of the compilation in the Hunterian MS gives the impression that 'Roger' was a devoutly religious man, who had no thought of belittling the Christian faith by his exaltation of 'good pagans'. Although he was a secular clerk and not a friar, he has put a contemporary attitude into pictorial form.

*   *   *

The dust jacket shows an ancient hero in contrast to ancient sages: King Alexander rides his war horse 'Bucefela'. He is reproduced from a photograph, kindly supplied by the Warburg Institute, of an early fourteenth-century copy of the miscellany called *Liber floridus*. This copy, now at Leiden University Library, MS Voss. lat. fol. 31 (the picture of Alexander is on fol. 211), was probably made in northern France or Flanders. On the *Liber floridus* see L. Delisle, Notice sur les MSS du 'Liber floridus', *Notices et extraits de la Bibliothèque nationale et autres bibliothèques* 38 (1906) 577-91.

INTRODUCTION

Some talk of Alexander,
And some of Hercules,
Of Hector and Lysander
And such great names as these.
The British Grenadier.

THIS book was born in an ambush. I meant to write a
continuation of *The Bible in the Middle Ages* to be called
The Bible in the Fourteenth Century. It seemed sensible to begin
with some leading English friars of the period who produced
voluminous biblical commentaries. They first lured me into
their midst by posing as commentators and then, throwing
off the mask, they surrounded me and barred retreat: they
wanted me to write about ancient gods and heroes instead
of the Bible. There was nothing for it but to comply with
their wishes. The ambush itself offered food for thought.
The friars who laid it formed an intriguing company, the
nature of which raised one question after another. The very
choice of terms to describe them has pitched their prisoner
into the sharpest of all historical controversies. How should
one define 'humanism'? What differentiated the medieval
from the Renaissance attitude to antiquity?

I decided not to prejudge the issue and to call the friars by
a colourless name. They will appear as 'the classicising
group': both words need explaining. 'Classicising' is a
clumsy, home-made adjective, but it has the advantage of
being noncommittal. It points to fondness for classical
literature, history and myth without suggesting that the
group played any special part in the rise of humanism.
Interest in the classics found its outlet in lectures on
Scripture and in sermons and aids to preaching. Two
members of the group commented on St. Augustine's *De
civitate Dei* as well. All worked within the limits imposed
upon them as teachers of pastoral theology and of patristics.

The 'group' counted seven members. I use the word
loosely to denote community of interests. Though younger
members read their elders' books and may have attended
their lectures, the friars did not form a school united by the

B   I

master-pupil relationship. They were divided between two mendicant Orders: John Ridevall and John Lathbury were Franciscans and the other five Dominicans. They even belonged to different universities: Thomas Waleys, John Ridevall and John Lathbury were Oxford men; Robert Holcot and William D'Eyncourt probably studied and taught at both Oxford and Cambridge; Thomas Hopeman and Thomas Ringstead were Cambridge men. The group's collective activity stretched over provincial towns in England. Thomas Waleys worked at Bologna and Avignon as well as at Oxford. Hence they never combined into a 'cenacle' like the pre-humanist one at Padua any more than they formed a school. Yet in spite of their loose ties they managed to produce writings of a distinctive genre admitting of no borderline cases. A friar doctor of the early fourteenth century either joined the classicising group or he kept clear of it. The first page of his lecture course on a book of the Bible will place him.

Manuscript copies of their works and medieval library catalogues justify the term 'group' from another point of view. Shorter pieces by several members were copied together so often that certain combinations become familiar. Works too long to go into a miscellany would normally be bound separately, but even these sometimes pair so that two of the seven friars go together. Medieval book-makers and librarians grouped them as representatives of a classicising type of pastoral literature.

Chronologically they fall into a period of some thirty years, about 1320 to about 1350. John Lathbury, the youngest of the seven, taught and wrote in the decade 1352-62. He marks the decline as well as the end of the movement. Of course the seven had forerunners in their love of the classics, but none quite like them. Classical studies continued in England when the last of them was dead and buried, but not among university friars. No more lectures of their characteristic type issued from friary classrooms.

The fact of forming a group makes them more significant than they would be as individuals. Their books, put together, would fill a wide shelf, which would hold some favourites of the later middle ages. Almost every good library in England and in the rest of Latin-speaking Europe had Holcot on Wisdom in one or more copies. Waleys, Ridevall, Ringstead and Lathbury produced one standard book each. Three of the seven, moreover, quote from lost books by other authors. In some cases not only the book but even the author quoted is quite unknown. Much of this lost literature seems to have been of a classicising kind such as would appeal to the friars, and so they point us to another shelf, which could be filled with more books if they were recovered and identified. As it is, the friars' quotations alone add up to a small volume.

While their joint effort impresses, each member of the group singly is worth knowing. We can admire Waleys and Ridevall as scholars. Their ghosts, the one rash, the other gentle, seem to haunt Bodley, eyeing the catalogues greedily. We can smile with Holcot and at Lathbury. D'Eyncourt, Hopeman and Ringstead have painted themselves in quieter colours, but each has his distinctive manner. A study of individuals, too, brings out the fact that 'classicising' covers two quite separate tendencies, which may be shown by the same person. Two or three members of the group produced pieces of solid scholarship or left traces of scholarly interests and intuitions. Some members went in for creative writing, as we should now call it; they indulged in fantasy, and it was fantasy presented as antique. As well as staging their clever ambush they carried me off into a far country. The landscape bristles with ruins, some genuine and some shams of the most extravagant sort. *Gesta romanorum*, a collection of tales which have nothing to do with ancient Rome, is the most famous sample. The author, an anonymous English Franciscan, drew on Robert Holcot.

Medievalists know that this strange country exists and have paid it visits, but so far they have missed the classicising friars as a group. Only John Ridevall has attracted attention to himself by writing a treatise which is honestly and obviously on mythology. The others hide behind deceptive titles. Who would look for evidence of Livy scholarship in a commentary on the Psalter? Waleys and Holcot, the two most distinguished members of the group, made names for themselves as theologians. Waleys has got into history by reason of his quarrel with Pope John XXII on the beatific vision; he figured as principal in a *cause célèbre*. Holcot has a place in the history of late scholasticism. Ringstead sat on the episcopal bench as bishop of Bangor. All three, therefore, owe their appearance in history books to causes other than their classical interests. D'Eyncourt, Hopeman and even Lathbury were obscure men except in their immediate academic circles. All seven have excluded themselves from literary history by writing in Latin instead of English. Their medium was the 'dog Latin' spoken and written in the schools. Their lectures read like tape-recordings and in fact originated in notes prepared by the master or 'reported' by a pupil. Their books, as distinct from their lectures, catered for readers who used Latin as a tool in the same practical way. So their language has no more appeal for the student of neo-classical Latin than it has for the specialist in Middle English. One can say in its defence that it brings us close to our authors, presenting no technical difficulties, since they wrote informally just as they would have spoken, and that Holcot, at least, contrived effects which can still please. But the friars are talkers rather than stylists. It is understandable that they should have been neglected.

I shall describe the seven in chronological order, considering those books which throw light on their classicising activities. Purely theological or scientific works will be set aside. On the other hand, I shall try to show each man in the round by collecting evidence for his outlook on current events and for his temper and mentality. The material is nearly all either in manuscript or in early printed editions which make recourse to the manuscripts necessary, with one exception: Dr. H. Liebeschütz provides a critical edition of Ridevall's *Fulgentius metaforalis* with a study of the genre and a useful list of parallels. Mr. A. B. Emden's *Biographical Register* makes it possible to stow away into footnotes much evidence for dates and identifications. Even so, I have had to introduce dry and technical details. These are organised in such a way that less patient readers will be able to skip them without losing the thread; at least I hope so.

Chapters V to IX describe the English friar doctors and form the core of the book. The chapters before and after discuss problems that they raise. Chapter I sketches their English public. The friars taught and wrote for the benefit of contemporary clerks and of lay men and women. What was the attitude of this public towards ancient history and myth? The friar doctors either shared it or at least took it into account; otherwise they could have made no contact with their readers and hearers. Chapter II outlines their means of communication with their public and explains why they chose to express themselves in biblical commen-

taries and aids to preaching. Chapter III connects them with
their forerunners of the thirteenth and early fourteenth
centuries. Chapter IV touches on the question of patronage.
Richard de Bury, the magnificent bishop of Durham, author
(or subject) of *Philobiblon*, collected books and befriended
scholars; he makes interesting comments on the state of
learning in England. Medievalists will recognise most of
the facts presented in these four chapters. The material is
simply rearranged in the form of answers to questions about
the aims and background of the classicising friars and of the
lost authors whom they quote.

Then comes the central block on the seven friars and then
we go over to France and Italy in search of parallels and
contrasts. The English friar doctors continue to look
eccentric, carefully as one may reconstruct their *milieu*. Did
French and Italian friars share the Englishmen's classicising
tastes? If they did, how far did they choose the same
medium of biblical commentaries and sermon literature?
If not, then what alternative methods of pleasing their
public did they use? The area of comparison could have
been extended over Germany and Spain, but it had to stop
somewhere, and my book is already overcrowded with
characters.

A last chapter on early Italian humanism broaches the
most delicate problem of all. We know nowadays that
Renaissance scholarship grew out of the medieval study of
the classics, but that it developed new features: the Trecento
passed into the Quattrocento. The classicising movement
in early fourteenth-century England had no such prospects.
It petered out. Humanism came later and as a foreign
influence. The story of its arrival in the fifteenth century
turns on the visits of Italians to England and on English
travellers in Italy. Some native scholarship indeed there was,
but it has to be looked for in abbeys, in great households and
even in grammar schools rather than in universities. The
classicising friar doctors seem to have had more readers
than imitators. Hence their movement may give the
impression of being a failed Renaissance. Why did it never
develop? It need not have been isolated, given the opportunities for meeting Italian scholars at the papal court at
Avignon: Richard de Bury met Petrarch there. The
mendicant Orders were still international, throwing their
network over Christendom. Thomas Waleys gained as a

classicist from having been sent to teach in the Dominican school at Bologna. These chances of learned contacts did not save the English friars from remaining provincial in their attitude. Apart from Waleys, they seem to have missed what was happening.

There is only one way to settle the question, if settled it can be, and that is to compare their activities with those of the early humanists. A comparison ought to show whether the English friar doctors and the early humanists started from the same point to achieve the same object or whether they were running on different tracks from the beginning. The dangerous words 'humanism' and 'Renaissance' have now slipped out. Before going any further I must explain in what sense I shall use them.

The concept of Renaissance is still being discussed relentlessly. *Ego neque pacificator historicorum neque collector omnium*, to quote Petrarch.[1] I shall simply state the one agreed conclusion: Italian writers of the Quattrocento themselves invented the idea of a Renaissance of antiquity. They believed that a 'middle age' of barbarism and ignorance had followed on the collapse of ancient culture. The classics had been suppressed and neglected, and therefore needed to be revived. Italian artists, poets and scholars brought about a revival by studying their ancient models in order to understand and imitate the glories of the past; ancient civilisation lived again. The Italian Renaissance existed in this sense as an idea in men's minds. We can treat it just as we do the Social Contract in the history of political thought. It is one thing to consider the historical importance of a theory and another to find it valid. The word 'Renaissance' can be used nowadays without submission to 'the tyranny of a metaphor' and without the implication that those who coined it had a good understanding of history.[2]

Recent studies on the origin of the word 'humanist' make it easier to use this term also in an objective way. *Humanista* began to denote a teacher of what we call 'the humanities' in the late fifteenth and early sixteenth centuries. *Studia humanitatis* to denote what he taught goes back to the late

---

[1] De viris illustribus, ed. G. Martellotti, *Prose, La letteratura italiana, studi e testi* 7 (1955) 220.
[2] For discussion and bibliography see W. K. Ferguson, *The Renaissance in Historical Thought* (Cambridge, Mass., 1948); F. Chabod, *Machiavelli and the Renaissance*, translated from the Italian by D. Moore with an introduction by A. P. D'Entrèves (London, 1958) 149-247.

fourteenth century. The 'humanist' was a professor of classical literature and its subordinate disciplines. The noun 'humanism' with its emotional overtones and its vague content is of quite modern origin.[1] The modern tendency is to use the term 'pre-humanist' for a small group of scholars and men of letters centred on Padua in the second half of the thirteenth and early fourteenth centuries. 'Early humanist' as distinct from 'pre-humanist' generally refers to Petrarch and Boccaccio and their friends and helpers. Dante is not often called either a 'pre-humanist' or an 'early humanist': his genius defies classification and he chose the *volgare* in preference to Latin. The pre-humanists all wrote in Latin; the early humanists, while admiring Dante and sometimes writing in the *volgare* too, still regarded Latin as a nobler medium. All these men lived before the terms *studia humanitatis* or *humanista* had gained currency, but they already agreed on the value of a literary formation and of literary pursuits. Hence 'humanism' in its historical context implies a preference for literary studies as against scholasticism. Humanists opposed declamation to disputation as a school exercise. The humblest professor of humane letters prided himself on teaching a better subject than the schoolmen with their logic chopping and their dog Latin, as he saw it. Grammar and philology were 'the great gods' of the early humanists. Their obsessive care for these disciplines enabled them to lay the foundations of a new culture. An emotional attitude to antiquity supplied the driving force behind their search for texts and their collation of manuscripts. Desire for better knowledge of the ancient world was compatible with wide interests; they were by no means blinkered antiquarians.[2] For purposes of comparison, however, I shall take a humanist to be a scholar who uses his learning consciously as an instrument for reviving the cult of *litterae humaniores*. Pre-humanist and early humanist will be used in their current sense. They are clear and precise terms and they save confusion with what I shall call classicism, mere interest in the classics.

The English friar doctors of the classicising group can go into the show-ring to compete with their Italian contemporaries as *érudits*. They may look rather lame, poor things,

---

[1] A. Campana, The Origin of the Word 'Humanist', *J.W.C.I.* 9 (1946) 60-73.
[2] See for instance Guis. Billanovich, Gli umanisti e le cronache medioevali, *I.M.U.* 103-38.

however hard I groom them; but the judge must accept their entry. They cannot compete as poets or as cultivators of *belles lettres*, since they were not men of letters, but scholars, teachers, preachers, and in some cases fantastics. My *Conclusions* will suggest reasons why their classicism failed to develop into humanism. Then, having finished with odious comparisons, I shall try to do them justice at last.

CHAPTER I

THE ENGLISH PUBLIC

Faire ben talcs in compaignye.
Kyng Alisaunder, line 4739.

'Once with Alexander, king of Macedon, we defeated the kings of the Medes and Persians and subdued the provinces of the East. Now, at the end of time, with great King Edward, we have borne a ten-year war with Philip, famous king of France; we have won back Gascony, taken by guile, with force of arms; we have got Wales by slaughter; we have invaded Scotland and cut down her tyrants at the point of the sword.'

THIS is said by the knights in a funeral panegyric on Edward I, written by a cleric called John of London soon after Edward's death on July 7, 1307.[1] The author makes each order of society, the Pope, kings, the queen mother, bishops, magnates, knights, clergy and laity, come forward in turn to praise the dead man's achievements. The knights take the opportunity to bring themselves into the picture. In doing so they give short and perfect expression to the medieval attitude to history. The knight, whatever his personal ancestry may have been, belongs to an undying order. He can appropriate the victories of Alexander or of any other hero, biblical, classical, legendary or medieval. John of London in his *Commendatio lamentabilis* makes the knights compare Edward, to his advantage, to Brutus the Trojan, King Arthur, King Edgar and King Richard as well as to Alexander. The bishops have already compared him

---

[1] Commendatio lamentabilis in transitu magni regis Edwardi, ed. W. Stubbs, *Chronicles of the Reigns of Edward I and Edward II* 2 (Rolls Series, 1883) 14: Olim cum Alexandro rege Macedonum reges Persarum et Medorum devicimus, et provincias orientales subegimus, nunc in fine temporum cum magno rege Edwardo contra illustrem regem Franciae Philippum guerram decennalem suscepimus; Vasconiam in dolo praepossessam recuperavimus vi et armis, Walliam hostili caede comparavimus, Scotiam truncatis eius tyrannis in ore gladii invasimus.

The *Commendatio* survives in five manuscripts and was widely known even before its publication by Stubbs. There is no evidence to identify the author, John of London, with any contemporary of the same name. We do not know whether he was a monk, a canon or a secular clerk.

to David, 'one-time king of the Israelite people'; the earls
and barons have found him as glorious in his wealth and
justice as Solomon.

The past, as presented in the *Commendatio*, seems vivid, but
lacking a third dimension. The speakers have an unsophisti-
cated approach to period and distance, barely distinguishing
between twenty and two thousand in years or miles. Though
we call the attitude 'medieval', it still lingers on in country
districts, where the last generation of farmers would describe
Cromwell's passage through the neighbourhood as though
their grandfathers had seen it. The attitude to space is
illustrated by the following conversation heard in a bus
which was crossing a wind-swept common in the High Peak.
An up-to-date passenger explained that the wind was cold
because it came from Siberia. An old man answered in his
Derbyshire drawl:

> 'When th'east wind blew over Fairfield they use to say
> it come from Tidser' (local name for a village five miles
> away); 'and now they say it come from further place.'

Chorus of passengers:

> 'But it cuts ye just the same!'

An audience with this mentality would see nothing funny in
a medieval fabrication such as the history of the foundation
of Tournai. Here Nebuchadonosor and Servius, king of
Rome, with allied contingents from Africa and Greece, lay
seige to 'the second Rome', Tournai, whose inhabitants turn
the tables by marching against Nebuchadonosor and taking
Jerusalem and Juda.[1] The British capture of Rome, as told
by Geoffrey of Monmouth, fades into plausibility in comparison.

The concept of anachronism can have no place in such
a view of history. Characters wear the costumes, speak the
idiom and follow the customs familiar to the story-teller
and his audience, irrespective of geography or date. King
Alexander in the Middle English poem rides 'a steed of
Narbonne' and his mother wears a mantle of Douai cloth.
He 'makes bailiffs and justices and takes fealty and services'
in the lands won from Darius. His single combat with King
Porus for the possession of India takes the form of a duel

---

[1] L. F. Flutre, *Li fait des romains dans les littératures française et italienne du
XIIe au XVIe siècle* (Paris, 1932) 60-85.

between two mounted knights. Demosthenes is 'a baron of price'. The poet and his audience knew that Alexander was not a Christian but a heathen king. He swears by Mohammed and sacrifices to idols 'Saracenwise'. Even so, 'the bishop' of the land of the Sun and Moon Trees 'shrives' him and his men before they go to the holy trees.[1] John of London's knights could have recognised themselves easily among the eastern marvels of the romance.

The sense of continuity expressed in the *Commendatio* is typical of the whole middle ages and not of any one period. John of London has also introduced an early fourteenth-century English *nuance*; it resulted from Edward I's reign. The old king, 'rex fortissimus, prudentissimus et sapientissimus', as Hemingburgh calls him,[2] seemed to have revived the age of heroism. Exaggerated and rhetorical as it sounds, the *Commendatio* only puts the chroniclers' judgments into phrases suitable to a funeral piece. Edward's contemporaries did not anticipate the criticisms made of him by modern historians.[3] They saw him as a great conqueror and law-giver. The literature of chivalry romanticised his wars. He vied with Alexander as a subject for mural decoration: Walter Langton, bishop of Lichfield 1296-1321, had scenes from Edward's life and campaigns painted on the walls of his magnificent new palace.[4] Whether the practical Edward, who fostered Arthurian romance from policy as well as from interest, saw himself in this chivalrous role is problematic:[5] his deeds fed posthumous hero worship. Further, they countered any sense of littleness that an English reader or hearer might have had when faced with antiquity. An Englishman could enjoy ancient stories and legends without feeling wistful. Glory could be won as easily now as ever. True, the losses of the following reign were deflating. The English advanced too rashly against the Scots at Bannockburn; even the high-spirited Alexander himself would have

[1] *Kyng Alisaunder*, ed. G. V. Smithers, I (*E.E.T.S.*, 1952) 61, 17, 265, 396-402, 175, 179, 325, 363.
[2] *The Chronicle of Walter of Guisborough*, ed. H. Rothwell (Camden Series 89, 1957) 379-80.
[3] G. Templeman, Edward I and the Historians, *Cambridge Historical Journal* 10 (1950) 16-35.
[4] Joan Evans, *English Art 1307-1461* (Oxford, 1949) 116; T. Harwood, *The History and Antiquities of the Church and City of Lichfield* (Gloucester, 1806) 288-9. I owe this reference to Mrs. Hester Jenkins. For paintings of Alexander, see P. Brieger, *English Art 1216-1307* (Oxford, 1957) 132.
[5] R. S. Loomis, Edward I, Arthurian Enthusiast, *Speculum* 28 (1953) 114-127; Sir Maurice Powicke, Edward I in Fact and Fiction, *F.S.* 120-135.

used a more cautious strategy.[1] But setbacks in Scotland
and Gascony or quarrels between Edward II and his earls
could be ascribed to personal causes. The chroniclers
explain that God humbles the proud. Soon Edward III's
victories in the first stage of the Hundred Years War renewed
his grandfather's tradition and raised fighting to a heroic
level again.

The knights of the *Commendatio* arc puppets, miming the
ideas of a clerk; they need not show how laymen imagined
their history. We ought, therefore, to find some real knight
to act as our control. Such a quest would be fruitless in the
early fourteenth century. Chronicles were still written by
ecclesiastics, though they sometimes had knights as informants and patrons. Geoffrey le Baker of Swinbrook
wrote for a knightly patron, Sir Thomas de la More, who
served on the deputation to ask Edward II to resign his
crown. Baker says that Sir Thomas drew up a report on the
proceedings in French: *sicut vidisti et in gallico scripsisti*.[2] Adam
of Murimuth and Robert of Avesbury reproduce despatches
written in French by lay commanders on the French
campaigns of 1346-7.[3] The knight or country squire of this
period had to be literate in so far as he was a man of
business. He managed his estates; he might act as steward
for his lord; he would serve on juries and commissions and
might represent his shire in parliament. This was the
routine background to hunting and fighting. He could make
a factual report as duty required. The more educated
knights and squires were probably too busy and unthinking
rather than too ignorant to try anything more ambitious.
They had to know two vernacular languages, since the
upper classes spoke Anglo-Norman French and the com-
moners English, which was working its way upwards. They
would normally be 'illiterate' only in the sense that they
knew little or no Latin.

[1] *Chronicon Galfridi le Baker de Swynebroke*, ed. E. M. Thompson (Oxford,
1889) 8: Ex adverso progredientis ab occidente exercitus Anglorum refulsit
sol oriens in scutos aureos et galeas politas, cuius radii micantes aspectus arma-
torum reverberantes movissent magnanimum Alexandrum ut illis loco et die
vel saltim hora diei congressum suspendisset, et solis meridiani, qui fuisset
illis dexter, iudicium expectasset.

[2] ibid. 27: on Baker and the de la Mores, see the editor's introduction, v-x.

[3] Adam of Murimuth, *Continuatio chronicarum* and Robert of Avesbury,
De gestis mirabilibus Edwardi Tertii, ed. E. M. Thompson (Rolls Series, 1889)
xliv, liii, 200-4, 388-90. The commanders were a baron, Bartholomew de
Burghersh, and a knight, Sir Thomas Dagworth. They may have dictated to
clerks.

Then, in the mid-fourteenth century, a Northumbrian knight, Sir Thomas Gray of Heaton, combined the skill, imagination and leisure to produce the first chronicle written by an English layman. The Scots held him prisoner in Edinburgh castle, thus forcing the leisure upon him. Here, in 1355 or soon after, he began his Anglo-Norman prose chronicle, the *Scalacronica*.[1] This authentic, flesh-and-blood knight sees eye to eye with the puppets invented by John of London.

Gray explains in his prologue how it happened that he came to write his chronicle. He belonged to a border family, constantly involved in war with the Scots. He got captured and whiled away the time in prison by reading chronicles in rhyme and prose in Latin, French and English. They made him wonder and wish that he had begun to study history earlier. In fact, he became so curious and thoughtful that having nothing else to do at the time he decided 'to treat and translate in short' the chronicles of Britain and the 'gestes' of the English. While he was thinking it over he had a dream, showing him how his chronicle should be written. The first part would necessarily take the form of a précis of earlier sources. His dream consists of a personified bibliography. There is nothing very original about it; Gray only pictures the main stages of historical writing as presented in the universal chronicles he was reading. As we might expect, he includes great chunks of legend together with political prophecy. But he describes it all with remarkable clarity and freshness.

The wise old Sibyl appeared to him in his dream and led him into an orchard, where he saw a ladder leaning against a wall. The Sibyl need not surprise us any more than the conventional dream about a garden or orchard. She was a well-known figure in chronicle, liturgy and drama; moreover, she had crossed the Channel and was sufficiently anglicised to prophesy against the Scots.[2] The ladder gives the book its title: a scaling ladder, used in seige warfare, also marked the arms of the Gray family. This ladder had five rungs and was supported by a Friar Minor, Thomas

---

[1] The *Scalacronica* has never been printed in full. The prologue and the part relating to the middle ages has been edited by J. Stevenson (Edinburgh, 1836); the part from Edward I's reign to the end has been translated into English by H. Maxwell (Glasgow, 1907).

[2] See the prophecy printed in appendix iii to *The Chronicle of Pierre de Langtoft*, ed. T. Wright, 2 (Rolls Series, 1868) 448-451.

Otterbourne, master of divinity and chronicler. His chronicle, which is lost in its original form, was to serve as a model; it may have listed and summarised Gray's other authorities.[1] The Sibyl explained to him that two books, which he saw underneath the ladder, were the Bible and the story of Troy. The wall represented the building of history and had in it windows on to the past. Gray climbed the first rung of his ladder and saw a great city with a house, where sat a master wearing a fur-trimmed gown.[2] The Sibyl said that this was Walter, archdeacon of Exeter, who translated the *Brut* into Latin.[3] On climbing the next rung, Gray saw a black monk writing in a study; it was Bede of Wearmouth, that reverend doctor who wrote *De gestis anglorum*. On the third floor of history he saw another black monk, with old grey head, writing in a cloister; it was the monk of Chester compiling his *Polychronicon*. Gray climbed the fourth rung and looked through the window at a strong castle with a townlet at its foot. There he saw a chaplain writing at a desk in his room, John of Tynemouth, author of the *Historia aurea*. Gray puts it on his fourth, and last accessible floor, because it begins at the Norman Conquest and so represents contemporary history. The Sibyl told him that he could not climb to the fifth floor, for there at the top of the building were Henry of Huntingdon and Merlin, wise men who had foretold the future.[4]

The scheme is a neat one, beginning with Scripture and antiquity and then listing the authors according to the period they wrote of. The mixture of fact and legend makes a fine prelude to his original contribution, when he stops compiling and records his own and his father's exploits on the Scottish border. The raids and forays of this military zone were as exciting as they were inconclusive. The Grays, like the knights of the *Commendatio*, might well suppose themselves to be continuing the heroic age. Yet Gray does not romanticise; he feels no need to. He can pass shrewd

[1] See: The Authorship of the Lanercost Chronicle, *F.P.* 51-4.

[2] *Scalacronica*, op. cit. 2: 'un mestre bien furre'. The *furre* may perhaps mean 'stuffed', i.e. very learned, and not 'trimmed with fur'. As Gray is reporting a visual impression, however, the second is more likely.

[3] Geoffrey of Monmouth says that Walter of Exeter offered him (optulit) the very old book on British history and claims to have translated it himself; see *Historia Regum Britanniae*, ed. A Griscom (London, 1929) 219. Gray has made a little mistake.

[4] See R. Taylor, *The Political Prophecy in England* (New York, 1911); and below, p. 139.

judgments on politics and describe a chivalrous adventure
in terms of commonsense. A certain knight called William
Marmion received a letter from his lady, sending him a
helmet and bidding him go to the most dangerous spot in
England, where the helmet should make him famous. His
friends decided on Norham, a town on the north-eastern
border, as the most dangerous spot available. Marmion
arrived there simultaneously with a Scottish raiding party.
The Scots laid seige to Norham castle, just as its defenders
were sitting down to dinner. Sir Thomas Gray the elder
saw him approaching on foot, 'all glittering with gold and
silver, marvellously finely attired with the helmet on his
head'. The story had come before him and Gray called him
to mount his horse: 'It is more fitting that deeds of chivalry
should be done on horse than on foot, *when this can be done
conveniently*'.[1] The knight errant in his fine array was soon
unhorsed and the old hand had to rescue him. But the
reservation in the saying on chivalry is the interesting point.
The mounted knight with all his chivalrous associations was
no longer the only force to be reckoned with in battle. The
victory of Flemish infantry over the French chivalry at
Courtrai in 1302 impressed contemporaries. Other
chroniclers beside Gray noticed the parallel between
Courtrai and Bannockburn: the Scots had taken a lesson
in warfare from the Flemish.[2] The Grays knew that knightly
behaviour was not always practical. They felt too sure of
themselves to want to gloss it over. They would engage
in chivalrous encounters when these could be done conveniently, and not otherwise.

Our knights, real and imaginary, have the same feeling
for antiquity. It touches their consciousness mainly in
the form of history, and 'history' means the story of battles,
conquests and adventures. The names of ancient sages mean
something too. Aristotle was Alexander's tutor and got
credit for his pupil's victories. Many names, anecdotes and
even theories of the philosophers must have filtered down
from the schools. The author of *Kyng Alisaunder* recommends
Ptolemy to those who would study natural science. One

---

[1] *Scalacronica*, op. cit. 146: 'Si est meutz seaunt chos qe chevalery en soit
fait a cheval qe a pee, ou convenablement ceo purra faire.'

[2] ibid. 142; *Vita Edwardi Secundi*, ed. N. Denholm-Young with a translation
(London, 1957) 56. The writer of the *Vita*, who used to be known as 'the Monk
of Malmesbury', was probably a secular clerk, perhaps John Walwayn, a
doctor of civil law; see xix-xxviii.

version of the poem refers to what Solinus, 'the good clerk men called Solim', has 'written in his Latin' concerning the hippopotamus, when fearsome beasts attack Alexander's army.[1] A school book of ancient proverbs and wise sayings called the *Distichs of Cato* had been translated into Anglo-Norman.[2] But ancient sages were predecessors of clerks, who communicated with them directly by means of 'clergy', their Latin learning, whereas the knights felt themselves akin to ancient warriors. The clerks for their part encouraged the distinction. The knight in spite of his growing literacy must fight with material weapons; the clerk fought the Evil One with books: 'Vos estis . . . arma militie clericorum, quibus tela nequissimi destruuntur', Richard de Bury wrote of books in his *Philobiblon*.[3]

Here legend entered in to give the unlettered layman a special sense of belonging to the ancient world. The *Historia Regum Britanniae* of Geoffrey of Monmouth and its derivatives did him this service. The *Historia* popularised the fiction that Brutus the Trojan conquered the giants who inhabited Britain, and was the first ruler of the island. At the price of bedevilling the problem of British origins, this tall story made British and English history part of ancient history, or perhaps the other way round. It gave the Englishman a new and personal interest in the tale of Troy and the Aeneid. Stories of Brutus and his heroic descendant, King Arthur, circulated in so many versions and translations that they became familiar to anyone with the smallest smattering of culture.[4] Antiquity appealed widely and directly for the very reason that it had combined with legend. The best way for the unlettered to study history was to listen to 'ancient romances'.[5] The two were indistinguishable. Wace's *Roman de Brut* equalled 'text book of British history'.

Not all could swallow Geoffrey of Monmouth whole, but

---

[1] op. cit. 5, 278.

[2] J. Vising, *Anglo-Norman Language and Literature* (London, 1923) 48; M. D. Legge, *Anglo-Norman in the Cloisters* (Edinburgh, 1950) 13-17.

[3] *Philobiblon*, 79.

[4] See P. Rickard, *Britain in Medieval French Literature 1100-1500* (Cambridge, 1956) 71-89 for a summary with bibliography on recent discussion of 'the matter of Britain', and J. Taylor, The French 'Brut' and the Reign of Edward II, *E.H.R.* 72 (1957) 423-37 for a recent study of the diffusion of the *Brut*.

[5] B. Woledge, La légende de Troie et les débuts de la prose française, *Mélanges Roques* 2 (Bade, Paris, 1953) 313-24. The paper refers to France in the twelfth century, but applies equally aptly to England in the early fourteenth.

few rejected him altogether.[1] The *Brut* filled a gap in the absence of authentic sources for the prehistoric and Celtic periods. Once the game had started, legend attracted legend to create an expanding pseudo-history. Modern historians see their subject as constantly widening, thanks to new discoveries and research work. In the same way, new medieval inventions added to what was believed about early Britain.[2]

It will prepare our minds for certain shocks to come in later chapters of this book if we consider *Des Grantz Geanz* as a sample. This Anglo-Norman poem on the Giants was probably composed between the middle years of the thirteenth century and 1333-4 (the date of an early manuscript).[3] The anonymous author wants to account for what happened before Brutus's conquest. He uses a mixture of biblical and classical sources which forge an even earlier link with antiquity. Thirty daughters of a king of Greece plotted to murder their husbands: none of them wanted to have a master and to be in subjection, but each to be her own mistress. The youngest sister told on the others; so they were punished by being set adrift in a boat. They arrived at length, very seasick, on the shores of a desert island. Albine, the eldest sister and *avouée* of the rest, took seisin of the land and it was called Albion after her. The sisters learned with much thought and cunning to supplement their vegetarian diet by setting traps for birds and deer. They recovered from their journey, grew 'big and fat' and began to want 'human company'. *Incubi* or 'bad fairies' came to satisfy their needs. *Incubi* had an advantage over human husbands for these prototypes of suffragettes in being invisible and undemanding. They bred children who founded a race of giants. These 'great giants' flourished in Albion until Brutus conquered them and changed the name of the island to Britain after himself.

Des Grantz Geanz was taken seriously enough to be copied

---

[1] L. Keeler, *Geoffrey of Monmouth and the Late Latin Chroniclers 1300-1500* (Berkeley, University of California Publications in English 17, 1946); T. D. Kendrick, *British Antiquity* (London, 1950); V. H. Galbraith, *Historical Research in Medieval England* (London, 1951). For criticisms of the Alexander legend in the fourteenth century see G. Cary, *The Medieval Alexander* (Cambridge, 1956) 233-43.

[2] For a summary of foundation stories, see H. Matter, *Englische Gründungssagen von Geoffrey of Monmouth bis zur Renaissance* (Heidelberg, 1922).

[3] G. E. Brereton, *Des Grantz Geanz an Anglo-Norman Poem* (Oxford, 1937) xxxii.

together with genuinely historical works; it is found beside Avesbury's *De gestis Edwardi Tertii* and the *Anonimalle Chronicle*, as well as prefacing the *Brut*.[1] Its fascination for a modern reader, apart from its merits as a story, lies in the author's offer of evidence to prove his reliability. He urges his hearers to listen carefully to what he has heard from

> un sage home
> Qi bien saveit les escriptures
> Des auncienes aventures.

Elsewhere he speaks as though his information came from a book. He authenticates his 'great giants' on the score of bones and teeth, which may still, he says, be dug up in many places and are too large to have belonged to ordinary men. Their huge walls are also to be seen, though many have been cast down by storms. Whether he had actual archaeological remains of any sort in mind or was just inventing them is uncertain. Finally he adduces oral tradition. Brutus saved the life of Gogmagog, the giants' lord, and got him to tell what he knew of the island's history. Brutus had it all remembered as a tale for the banquet hall:

> E Brut trestut fist remembrer,
> Qe autres aprés pussent saver
> La merveille de la geste
> Pur counter a haute feste,
> E qe hom puet aver en memoire
> La merveille del estoire[2]

Fiction is passed off as history so cleverly as to be indistinguishable except by an expert, and it is newly made fiction at that. The author, in fact, has improved on a current literary trick. One cited an authority, perhaps non-existent, as a source for one's story. Thus the German poet, Wolfram von Eschenbach, claims to have taken the tale of Parsival from 'Master Kyot, the Provençal': Master Kyot has so far eluded his seekers and seems to have subsided into fiction.[3] Vernacular writers perhaps felt a need to

---

[1] ibid. vi-xi; on the sources see xxxiii-xxxvii.

[2] 2, 14, 24-28. The author of the poem may have been working on an earlier version of the story, perhaps in Latin, which is now lost, xxxv.

[3] *Parz.* 416, 25: Kyot ist ein Provenzal,
          der dise âventiur von Parzivâl
          heidensch geschriben sach.

See B. Mergell, *Wolfram von Eschenbach und seine französischen Quellen* 2 (Münster in Westfalen, 1943) 1-12, 169-85.

imitate the schoolmen in arguing from authority, even to
the point of inventing what they could not otherwise have
put forward.

Listening to tales about the past of one's own country was
not only pleasant but praiseworthy. The clergy, as moralists,
condemned most secular pleasures, but they regarded the
study of history as eminently respectable. It belonged to the
best monastic tradition. History had a moral purpose,
teaching man by example to choose the good and avoid the
bad. Hence even its undoubted entertainment value could
not make it harmful. The reverend doctor Bede of Wearmouth himself had been 'skilled in our native songs'.[1]
Chronicles, moreover, had a useful public function in
substantiating the claims made by lawyers and politicians.
To compile chronicles was good patriotism. The fourteenth century has been described as 'the great age of
epitomes and popular histories'.[2] It will be worth our while
to consider the attitude to historical studies of three of these
popularisers, choosing Sir Thomas Gray's linguistic order,
'Latin, French and English'.

The Benedictine, Ranulf of Chester, begins his *Polychronicon* with a splendid defence of history. Sir Thomas
Gray set great store on the book, which became a favourite
of the later middle ages, both in Latin and in English
translations.[3] It is a universal chronicle with special
reference to Great Britain and England. Ranulf probably
finished his first draft about 1348. He won fame in his
lifetime and it was known that his abbey had a good
historical library. The government of Edward III sum-
moned him to a council to be held at Westminster on
August 21, 1352: he was to come 'with all your chronicles
and those in your charge, to speak and treat with the
council concerning matters to be explained to you on our
behalf'.[4]

Ranulf sets forth the claims of history in terms so eloquent
as to stand comparison with Richard de Bury's better-
known praise of books:

[1] Letter of Cuthbert, later abbot of Wearmouth and Jarrow, ed. C. Plummer
as an appendix to the *Historia ecclesiastica* 1 (Oxford, 1896) clxi: . . . erat doctus
in nostris carminibus.
[2] V. H. Galbraith, op. cit. 30.
[3] ed. C. Babbington and J. R. Lumby (Rolls Series, 1865-82) in nine
volumes.
[4] J. G. Edwards, Ranulf, Monk of Chester, *E.H.R.* 47 (1932) 94.

'Who, I ask, would know the Caesars, admire the philosophers or follow the apostles, unless the records of writers had made them known?'

History immortalises what would otherwise perish and fixes what would otherwise be forgotten. In the words of his fifteenth-century translator: 'Deeds that would die, story keepeth them evermore.'[1] He embarks on his plan as one entering the labyrinth of Daedalus and seems to marshal all the literary clichés at his command in order to justify his aim and method. True, he is a compiler, but compilation is useful and has excellent precedents; Ranulf quotes the *bon mot* of either Virgil or Horace (he isn't sure which of them it was) against the reproach of cribbing.[2] If he introduces heathen fictions, sayings of pagans and local marvels, at least they serve the Christian religion: it was allowable for Virgil to seek the gold in the dross of the poet Ennius,[3] and for the Children of Israel to spoil the Egyptians on their way to the Promised Land. Ranulf's apology has been rather pious up to this point; he has dwelt at length on the theme of history as a teacher of virtue. Now he lets out that it offers entertainment as well. He has employed his scissors-and-paste method (described in the twisted phrases of fourteenth-century Latin) so as to mix playful matter with serious, and heathen with religious by turns. He threshes out the difficulties and explains the outlandish so as to observe due sequence, and truth also, as far as possible: he does not vouch with equal certainty for everything that he tells.[4]

[1] op. cit. 1, 5-7: Quis, quaeso, Caesares hodie sciret, philosophos miraretur, apostolos sequeretur, nisi eos insignirent monumenta scriptorum? . . . Historia namque quadam famae immortalitate peritura renovat, fugitiva revocat, mortalia quodammodo perpetuat et conservat.
And see Trevisa's translation into English, printed ibid.
[2] ibid. 10, Virgil's answer to his detractors from Donatus, *Virgilii vita.* Ranulf found it ascribed to Virgil under the heading *conpilator* in Isidore's *Etymologiae* x, 44, and to Horace by Huguccio in the *Magnae derivationes;* I cannot find it in the thirteenth-century copy of the *Derivationes* in MS Oxford, Bodl. e Mus 96 (3582) under *compilo* or *commisceo;* Ranulf may have had an expanded copy.
[3] From Donatus, op. cit. Ranulf probably took the saying from *Policraticus* 1, 281.
[4] op. cit. 16: Quod si figmenta gentilium, si dicta ethicorum, si miranda locorum in hoc opusculo interdum interserantur, Christianae tamen religioni famulantur. Licuit enim Virgilio aurum sapientiae in luto Enniii poetae quaerere, et filiis Israel ad Terram Promissionis proficiscentibus Aegiptios spoliare. In quibus cunctis aliunde membratim excerptis, sed hic lineamentaliter concorporatis, ita seriosis ludicra, ita religiosis ethnica vicissim sunt admixta, ut succinctis tritis laxatisque exoticis processus series observetur, et integra

Happy chronicle, which could instruct, edify, amuse and serve Edward III's government simultaneously! The *Polychronicon* is a glorious jumble of fact, legend and marvel. Two older contemporaries of Ranulf made compilations with more restricted aims. Peter Langtoft, a canon of the Austin priory of Bridlington in Yorkshire, wrote a verse chronicle in Anglo-Norman, brought up to the death of Edward I in 1307. The author must have reached old age by that time, since he played an active part in the business and quarrels of his house in the years 1271-93. His chronicle with its northerner's anti-Scottish bias has been called 'an epic whose hero is Edward I'.[1] Langtoft, although a churchman, sees history in the same colours as the knights. From the very beginning, when 'le duk sire Eneas' escapes from Troy, he is leading up to the glorious wars of King Edward, especially against the Scots. Langtoft only shows a little disappointment towards the end, when Edward fails to get adequate backing for his conquest. Yet Langtoft feels himself to be writing in the ecclesiastical tradition. On reaching the Anglo-Saxon invasions he prays to his fellow Yorkshireman and predecessor, Father Bede, in a Latin rhyme, asking help for himself, Peter:

> Incipiunt gesta que sunt Anglis manifesta.
> Beda, pater, praesta Petro quod dicat honesta. . . .[2]

Robert Mannyng of Bourne in Lincolnshire gives the impression of being a graver person than either Ranulf of Chester or Peter Langtoft, less mellow than the one and less warlike than the other. This is rather to be expected, seeing that he belonged to the strictest Order of Canons Regular in England; he entered the Gilbertine priory at Sempringham, six miles away from his native Bourne, in 1288.[3] The Gilbertines were struggling with poverty and heavy debts, but do not seem to have been notoriously lax even in the early fourteenth century.[4] Mannyng spent some time at

---

pro posse veritas non vacillet; aequalis tamen utrobique per omnia teneri non poterit certitudo. . . .

The last phrase certainly refers to my translation of this passage! On the *topos seria-ludicra* see E. R. Curtius, *European Literature and the Latin Middle Ages*, translated from the German by W. R. Trask (London, 1953) 417-31.

[1] M. D. Legge, op. cit. 70-75.
[2] *The Chronicle of Pierre de Langtoft*, ed. T. Wright 1 (Rolls Series, 1866) 278.
[3] R. Graham, *S. Gilbert of Sempringham and the Gilbertines* (London, 1901) 158-159.
[4] ibid. 136-151.

Cambridge, where his Order had a house of study from
1290; they had been sending students to the university
earlier.[1] In 1338 he was at Sixhill, another Lincolnshire
priory.

Mannyng translated William of Wadington's *Manuel des
pechiez* into English as *Handlyng Synne* in 1303. This is a
handbook for priests with all the puritanism of its kind. It
condemns secular amusements in the shape of tournaments,
dances, carols and 'summer games'. Even miracle plays are
blamed except for those representing the Nativity and
Passion, if acted in church.[2] Yet in 1338 Mannyng translated
Langtoft's chronicle with additions from Wace's *Roman de
Brut* and other sources, giving as his reason that Englishmen
ought to know their history. Learning it, as he admits, will
provide a happy social pastime. The reprover of miracle
plays has written his verses in English for recitation to an
audience which understands neither Latin nor French on
occasions when men foregather for solace and game:

> Lordings that now be here,
> If ye will listen and hear
> All the story of England
> As Robert Mannyng written it found,
> And on English has it showed,
> Not for the learned but for the lewd,
> For those that in this land wone,
> That neither Latin nor French cone,
> For to have solace and gamen
> In fellowship as they sit samen.[3]

He goes on to explain the importance of understanding the
history of one's country. One should know who first inhabited the land, who ruled it, which kings were foolish and
which wise, which made war and which kept peace, and so
on. It is for this reason that he has translated Wace and
Langtoft into simple speech, 'that is lightest in man's
mouth'. Mannyng felt that his predecessors had made
history more difficult than it need be. Reciters, he says, tend
to spoil their stories by wanting to show off their cleverness.
The outlandish names in history also prove a stumbling
block. Hence people have begged him to turn his story into

---

[1] 44.
[2] *Robert of Brunne's 'Handlying Synne' and parts of William of Wadington's 'Manual des Pechiez'*, ed. F. J. Furnivall 1 (E.E.T.S., 1901) 154-6. I have slightly modern-
ised the spelling.
[3] *The Story of England*, ed. F. J. Furnivall 1 (Rolls Series, 1887) 1.

easy rhyme. He has done so for the sake of common men, who want to listen, and for love of the unlearned, 'to tell them of the chances bold, that here before were done and told'. He asks no reward but their prayers.[1]

The devout spirit of the translation appears especially when Mannyng reaches Langtoft's invocation of Bede. He makes a note of it and composes a prayer of his own in English for Bede's help and guidance, though he says that he feels unworthy even to open Langtoft's book and cannot imitate his 'fair speech'.[2]

The first part of the history has most interest for us, since Mannyng thought he ought to explain the causes of the Trojan war by introducing some pagan fables. He shirks nothing. We get the story of the Judgment of Paris in detail.[3] Juno, Minerva and Venus dispute as to which is the fairest, Juno beginning with royal bluntness: 'It am I!' They choose Paris as their 'domesman'. Mannyng does not see his goddesses as beautiful nudes. They are 'witches':

> There besides three witches were,
> Ladies were called and through the air did fare.

The lines would not conjure up a picture of old women on their broomsticks to Mannyng's audience, as they do today.[4] Nevertheless, his 'simple speech' must have clothed all his characters in home-spun. Helen has only a walk-on part. Paris entices her on to his ship to see his jewels and sails away with her on board. The author has no evidence as to her feelings:

> I cannot say of that lady
> Whether she was glad or sorry.

What does matter, from the point of view of the story, is that Menelaus, her husband, was angry.[5]

There is nothing naughty about pagan fables in Mannyng's matter-of-fact version. The author of *Handlyng Synne* finds them morally harmless, just part of the ancient record. He may well leave his readers wondering why the Fathers ever made such a fuss about them.

Antiquity therefore came to Englishmen as part of their

---

[1] ibid. 3.   [2] 2, 579-580.   [3] 1, 18-20.
[4] On the goddesses as sorceresses and demons, see F. von Bezold, *Das Fortleben der antiken Götter im mittelalterlichen Humanismus* (Bonn and Leipzig, 1922) 60-74; Seznec, 44-45, 48.
[5] Mannyng, op. cit. 25.

own history. As Christians they were linked to Rome and the Holy Land through the Bible and the lives of the saints. As Englishmen they were linked to Mount Olympus and Troy town. They could enjoy it all as 'a good yarn' without being scolded. Debates on the place of pagan fables in Christian education, which engaged the schoolmen, left this little corner in peace. To know his own past was every Englishman's birthright.

The only trouble from a moralist's point of view was that appetite for ancient tales grew to such proportions as to dull men's interest in religious history. The rivalry of secular stories was an old complaint, but it sounds with new urgency in the *Cursor mundi*. The author of the *Cursor*, a north-country priest, wrote probably in the first quarter of the fourteenth century and aimed at competing with the romancers. Men love to hear stories about ancient days, he says. To quote his well-known lines:

> Man yearns rhymes for to hear
> And romans read on manners sere,
> Of Alisaunder the conqueror,
> Of July Cesar the emperor,
> Of Greece and Troy the strong strife;
> There many thousand lost their life.

He goes on to list the *Brut* and the Arthurian and other romances, told in English, French and Latin.[1] Later in the poem he complains again that 'we' (for he includes himself) seldom go near a sermon, but when a secular tale is told we lock it fast in our hearts, making nought of Christ's word.[2] He plans a truly heroic counter-attack in the form of an English poem, presenting the Christian 'gestes' as an exciting and romantic story: set a romancer to catch a romancer. The story of salvation in the *Cursor mundi* has as much thrill and variety as legend and apocrypha can offer.

Perhaps the Holkham picture Bible had the same purpose as the *Cursor mundi*, to put sacred history on the same level as secular.[3] The book was commissioned by a Dominican friar to show to 'rich people'. He had in view 'a comfortable and educated, but not high-brow audience of laymen or ladies', rich but not noble. The date is about 1325-30. The

---

[1] ed. R. Morris 1 (E.E.T.S., London, 1874) 8.
[2] ibid. 5 (1878) 1362-3.
[3] W. O. Hassall, *The Holkham Bible Picture Book* (London, 1954). On its date and provenance, see 27-36.

artist tells the friar who orders the book that if God grant him long enough life, 'you will never see such another'. He carries out his promise; the book is artistically unique. The pictures, accompanied by an Anglo-Norman commentary, tell the story of salvation as enacted by 'a Chaucerian throng of real people'. Here, too, non-biblical matter has been pressed into service to enliven the story and fill in the blanks in the narrative.[1] Legend is part of the technique to be used in instructing laymen and women.

The poem and the picture book represent highly individual solutions to the problem of competing with secular tales. We shall see in the next chapter how preachers and homilists answered it.

How far did the taste for ancient romances go down the social ladder? The top and bottom present no difficulty. The nobility and gentry were steeped in 'gestes', as they were steeped in courtly love stories. They had no taste for classical names for their sons and daughters as yet; but one wonders what Earl Humphrey de Bohun had in mind when he called the youngest of his six sons 'Eneas'.[2] The peasantry at the bottom of the scale preferred stories of Robin Hood the Outlaw. The peasant waged an unceasing struggle against his lord, sometimes by legal means, sometimes by violence. It gave him more sympathy with robbers and rebels than with conquerors.[3] Yet Mannyng claims to be writing for common, ignorant men. We know little about the tastes of the townsman: England had developed no specifically bourgeois culture comparable to that on the Continent. The use of English provides our main clue in the absence of other evidence for the interests of the middle strata. Since the aristocracy spoke French, the increasing

[1] There are a few classical reminiscences. The birds of Juno and Minerva, the peacock and the owl, perch on the branches of a Jesse tree (fol. 2, p. 22). The nude bodies of the drowned in the Deluge scene recall late Roman pictures (fol. 8, p. 75).

[2] G. A. Holmes, *The Estates of the Higher Nobility in XIV Century England* (Cambridge, 1957) 20. Earl Humphrey was killed at Boroughbridge in 1322. Eneas died soon afterwards without heirs; so the name was not handed on. 'Aeneas' was the latinised form of 'Angus' and may have been chosen out of regard to the Bohuns' kinsmen in Ireland; see *The Complete Peerage*, ed. V. Gibbs and H. A. Doubleday 3 (London, 1913) 618. It may have shown some classical interest, nevertheless.

[3] The 'rhymes of Robin Hood' are first mentioned in the confession of Sloth in William Langland's Piers the Plowman, ed. W. W. Skeat. 1 (Oxford, 1924) 167. See R. H. Hilton, The Origins of Robin Hood, *Past and Present* 14 (1958) 30-44; Peasant Movements in England before 1381, *Economic History Review* 2nd series, vol. 2 (1949) p. 117-36.

use of English points to large sections of society between the magnates and the peasants as consumers of tales.

English-speaking audiences of the second quarter of the fourteenth century had *Kyng Alisaunder*, Robert Mannyng's *Story of England*, and a story of the siege of Troy to instruct them on antiquity. The third poem was probably composed by a minstrel of the north-west midlands between 1300 and 1325, though the earliest version has been lost.[1] All three point to the existence of an unlettered or half-lettered audience. The rhymes, which could be recited and memorised, brought them within reach of persons who either could not read or who preferred to listen. We should probably imagine country squires and squireens with their households, neighbours and dependents, reproducing the royal or magnate household in miniature. Of course, not all in any rank enjoyed so civilised a recreation as listening to stories. The author of *Kyng Alisaunder* notes that Philistines abound. Many there are, he says,

> That hadden liever a ribaldry
> Than hear of God and St Mary,
> Either to drink a cupful ale
> Than to hear of any good tale.[2]

The pub and bawdiness offered rival attractions to the minstrel as well as to the preacher.

This survey has sketched in the lay background to the development of scholarship in medieval England. The cult of story-telling was recognised and the stories included antiquity. The public was not passive but active. It had the clamorous greed of children. Indeed, from the point of view of imbibing classical culture, it was at the level of *Tanglewood Tales* and *The Heroes*. The lay attitude mattered to scholarship. Intellectually, clerk and layman belonged to distinct but interacting worlds, the scholars forming an élite within the clergy. Our scholars are all friars, whose job is teaching and preaching. On the one hand, the growth of an educated laity stimulated them. It was bound to do so, given the pupil-teacher relationship between priest and layman. On the other hand, it set a ceiling to their achievements. It would have been difficult to cultivate Petrarchan

---

[1] Some scholars would put it 1340-70; see J. E. Wells, *A Manual of the Writings in Middle English* 1 (Oxford, 1916) 106-9; 4th Supplement (1929) 1261; 5th Supplement (1932) 1346.
[2] op. cit. 3.

sensibility among these legend-hungry louts, as they would have seemed to Petrarch. A small group of patrons capable of appreciating scholarship, and a public wholly given over to sport and the 'cupful ale', might have provided a more propitious milieu for a classical revival than this half-and-half affair. But then early fourteenth-century scholarship would have lacked its distinctive characteristics. There would have been no Robert Holcot and later on no Chaucer.

CHAPTER II

TEACHING AND PREACHING

. . . . sic eloquentiae magister, nisi tanquam piscator
eam imposuerit hamis escam, quam scierit appetituros
esse pisciculos, sine spe praedae morabitur in scopulo.

Petronius, *Satiricon* iii.

THE mentality described in the last chapter presented
a challenge to the preacher. His congregations must
have been increasing in size, judging by the efforts which
were made in the late thirteenth and early fourteenth
centuries to enlarge the space available in mendicant
churches. The friars had worked out a type of architecture
specially adapted to the needs of the laity. The dimensions
of Santa Maria Novella and Santa Croce in Florence or of
the Jacobins' church at Toulouse must have enabled the
preacher to address almost as large a gathering in church as
out of doors; his voice set the only limit. The English
friary churches were not so vast, reflecting a less developed
urban concentration, but they catered for the same needs on
a smaller scale.[1]

Audiences were not only larger but more restive and
exacting than formerly. Stephen Langton, lecturing his
students at Paris around the year 1200 on their duties as
preachers, divided their future hearers quite simply into
clerical and lay. He thought of clerks as men trained in the
schools; they were sophisticated and dainty. Laymen, all
laymen, needed coarser fare. Preaching to the laity, therefore, as Langton impressed on his pupils, was less mentally
stimulating than preaching to clerks, but also more rewarding.[2] His distinction was perhaps too tidy even in the early
thirteenth century. A hundred years later it had ceased to
correspond with the facts of the social scene. Preachers still
observed a broad distinction between clergy and laity, since
only the former were literate in the sense of understanding
Latin, the language of the Church and of the schools. Most
laymen still depended on clerical instruction for anything
written in this medium. But sophistication had spread

---

[1] Hinnebusch, 135-48.   [2] *Study of the Bible*, 253-4.

outward and downward as literacy in the vernacular became more common. Important divisions grew up between various types of laymen. Preachers had to distinguish between peasants on the one hand and burgesses, knights or magnates on the other, with many intermediate grades of culture and learning. Congregations included the clergy gathered in universities and synods, convents of religious men and women, royal and noble households, townspeople and schoolchildren.[1] The sermon graced many social as well as liturgical occasions.

The educated and half-educated share the same traits in all periods, though fashions change. They are critical, eager for novelty and hopeful of entertainment, wanting to be stimulated or amused. A knight like Sir Thomas Gray must have been a tough customer to preach to. Women, probably leisured ladies and burghers' wives and daughters, seem to have formed a high proportion of lay audiences.[2] They had an appetite for romance and preachers knew it. Interest in theology was touching circles outside the schools. 'Laymen and old women' would tackle trained theologians on the question of freewill and contingency, William of Ockham noted in 1337-8.[3] The thoughtful author of the *Pearl* had forerunners in the earlier fourteenth century, who talked over deep matters, though they did not commit their views to writing.

What means of communication existed between friar doctors, teaching in university chairs, and their lay and clerical public? They acted upon it both directly and indirectly. Directly, because they would preach in person. The regency and its academic duties occupied a small part of their careers. In normal circumstances a friar doctor would resign his chair to a colleague after a year or two: the mendicants had a system of quick turnover in allotting their chairs, so as to train as many men as possible. The retired professor would then spend much of his life in contact with the people. He could instruct them in the home or on the

---

[1] J. A. Corbett, *The De instructione puerorum of William of Tournai O.P.* (Notre Dame, Indiana, U.S.A., 1955) 5-10.

[2] G. R. Owst, *Preaching in Medieval England* (Cambridge, 1926) 172-3.

[3] Tractatus contra Benedictum, iii, ed. H. S. Offler, *Guillelmi de Ockham Opera Politica* 3 (Manchester, 1956) 231: et ita omnia de necessitate eveniunt et nihil penitus contingenter, sicut quamplures infideles et antiqui haeretici docuerunt, et adhuc occulti haeretici et laici et vetulae tenent, saepe per argumenta sua etiam litteratos viros et in sacris litteris peritos concertantes. Robert Holcot complains that laymen demand reasons for their faith; see below, p.186.

road as well as in church. John of Wales O.F.M. compiled
matter which could be used as a conversation manual, 'the
evangelist at the breakfast table'.[1] Philip of Ferrara O.P.
produced the genuine article, a *Liber de introductione loquendi*,
1321/3-1347; he compiles improving remarks and *exempla*
for use at the table, at the fireside and on journeys.[2] But
the doctors were few in number in relation to members of
their own Orders and much more so to the total population.
They reached a wider public indirectly, through the
medium of their pupils and their readers. We shall begin
with the first stage in the transmission process, university
teaching.

The basic training for scholar preachers was given by the
doctor of divinity when he lectured on the 'sacred page'.
Attendance was compulsory for those reading theology. The
lecturer instructed his class on both the content and the
method of preaching. He taught what in modern jargon
we should call 'the ideology' of the medieval Church. He
put his teaching into a straightforward exposition of his text
or else expressed it by means of moralisation. He illustrated
his doctrine by *exempla* (moral stories), and he supported it
by quotation from sacred and secular authors. His pupils
therefore learned what to preach and how to illustrate
and support their statements. They were being prepared for
pastoral charge. The lecture course, when finished, would
circulate in copies either of the doctor's own version or of
notes taken by his students. Lectures on the *Sentences* and
disputations supplemented lectures on Scripture by grounding the student in dogmatic theology and in casuistry. There
was a slight overlap in that doctors lecturing on Scripture
would sometimes discuss theological questions of a controversial nature; but they generally kept off speculative
theology, which had its own place in the syllabus. They
limited themselves on the whole to restating safe, well-
established principles, such as could pass to wider circles
without any danger of being misunderstood.

The rate of output of these lecture-commentaries on
Scripture shows a suggestive fluctuation. There was a boom
in the late twelfth and very early thirteenth centuries,
followed by a slump lasting for about twenty years. Then

[1] Pantin, 147-8.
[2] R. Creytens, Le manuel de conversation de Philippe de Ferrare O.P.
Arch.FF.Praed. 16 (1946) 107-35.

came the peak period. The Friars Preacher and Minor had opened their *studia* at Paris and Oxford; they lectured on Scripture unweariedly. Output declined again in the period about 1280 to soon after 1310. Presumably lectures on Scripture continued during these three decades. University regulations required them. The reason why so little record of them has survived must be that they were poor in quality: contemporaries did not think them worth the trouble of copying. Pope John XXII wrote a scolding letter to the masters of arts and theology at Paris in 1317. Many masters, he had heard, began to lecture on their set texts, but were too frivolous and changeable to finish.[1] The decline in production of biblical commentaries, however, did not coincide with a decline in speculative theology, which prospered. Perhaps the great theological controversies of the late thirteenth century and the affair of Pope Boniface VIII absorbed all doctors' time and energy to the exclusion of their more humdrum duties. Then, quite suddenly, biblical commentaries begin to pour from the schools at a rate which will be maintained until about 1350. And now they come not only from Paris and Oxford but from the papal university at Avignon, from Cambridge, and from friary schools all over Christendom. Carmelite and Austin friars now share in the movement. The mendicant Orders have a second spring, corresponding to the first of a century earlier. Secular doctors hardly competed; none has left any solid volume of exegesis in this period.[2] Robert Holcot points to the contrast between the friars and the seculars in his inaugural lecture, given probably at Oxford in 1334. The mendicants, he complains, have to carry the main burden nowadays. As Christ entered Jerusalem riding on a lowly ass, so now he is borne through the theological faculty not by powerful rich men, but by poor religious.[3]

The revival of biblical studies must have owed something

---

[1] Denifle-Chatelain, *Chartularium Universitatis Parisiensis* 2, i, no. 741.

[2] Secular masters began to contribute in the late fourteenth century, when Wyclif taught at Oxford and d'Ailly and Gerson at Paris; see B. Smalley, John Wyclif's *Postilla super totam Bibliam, B.L.R.* 4 (1953) 186-204; Stegmüller, no. 6397-6412, 4483-4491; P. Glorieux, L'enseignement universitaire de Gerson, *Rech. Théol.* 23 (1956) 88-113.

[3] MS Brit. Mus., Royal 10.C.vi, fol. 137ra-b: . . . ita Christus immortalem Ierusalem, id est scholam theologicam, non per maiores, potentes et divites, sed per religiosos pauperes in maiori parte transvehitur hiis diebus.

The context is the old complaint that the lucrative sciences of law and medicine attract secular scholars away from theology.

to John XXII (1316-34): he reproved, directed, encouraged and rewarded.[1] It seems likely, too, that prodding from above was reinforced by increased demand from below. This also stemmed from papal policy. A new type of student was reading theology, swelling the numbers of friar students and of secular clerks, who hoped eventually to get benefices with cure of souls. The new men were already rectors of parishes. They had obtained licences authorising them to absent themselves from their churches for a term of years for the purpose of pursuing some recognised course of study, provided that they put in a suitable substitute. The system of licensing rectors and sometimes perpetual vicars to attend university courses was the papal answer to the problem of an ignorant parish clergy. The bishops, who bore the responsibility for granting leave of absence, seem to have welcomed it. A decree of Boniface VIII in particular, the *Cum ex eo* promulgated in the *Liber sextus* on March 3, 1298, gave force and precision to earlier papal concessions and made it easier for the diocesan to dispense a rector from residence. *Cum ex eo*, in England at least, brought 'a great exodus from the parishes to the universities'.

Seven years, the maximum time of absence allowed, would enable a rector to take his degree in arts and then to proceed to theology or canon law. Many could not stay long enough to qualify for the higher degree: either they could not afford it (they had to pay a vicar to serve the vacant church) or their diocesan refused to renew the licence. Moralists insisted that it did not matter. The rectors should learn to cope with their duties in the confessional and in the pulpit, which did not necessarily entail a full degree course.[2] Those who studied seriously would have found lectures on Scripture especially helpful for their purpose.

A number of monk students also were being sent by their

---

[1] J. R. Dean, Cultural Relations in the Middle Ages: Nicholas Trevet and Nicholas of Prato, *Studies in Philology* (Univ. of N. Carolina) 45 (1948) 548; B. Smalley, John Baconthorpe's Postill on St. Matthew, *M.A.R.S.* 4 (1957) 91-2. Another bit of evidence is the Pope's gift of thirty golden florins to Master Gregory of Lucca O.E.S.A. in December 1321, for his expenses during three months in preparing *quoddam opus super Moralia Iob.* It was probably a table or some kind of apparatus to St Gregory's *Moralia;* Notitiae ad Ord. FF. EE. S. Aug. spectantes ex Libris Introitus et Exitus Camerae Apost., *Analecta Augustiniana* 9 (1921) 82-3. On Gregory of Lucca see ibid. 19 (1943) 143; *Arch. FF. Praed.* 22 (1952) 233; Glorieux, no. 407.

[2] Fr. L. E. Boyle kindly gave me permission to quote from his doctoral thesis on William of Pagula, deposited in the Bodleian Library in 1955.

superiors to Oxford with the express aim of training them to preach. They lived in houses of study set up by the Benedictines to lodge their undergraduates and bachelors; but they were not reading for a degree. They were at Oxford in order to learn how to 'set forth God's word duly'. The rules drawn up for their guidance at the General Chapter of 1363 prescribe constant practice in preaching.[1] They must have attended lectures on Scripture, since these provided the necessary background to preparing one's sermons.

It seems likely that the parish rectors and the monk students of preaching would stimulate the friars to fresh vigour in their lecturing. The situation was full of irony. Both the monks and the secular clergy felt jealous of the friars and hoped to draw larger congregations to monastic cathedrals and parish churches. It may be supposed that they would dislike sitting at the friars' feet in a university. There was nothing else they could do. The only way to break the monopoly was to learn from their rivals. The friars for their part, always happily sure of their superiority, would welcome large classes. Secular clergy may also have attended the lectures given in friary schools in centres such as London, Northampton, Norwich and York.[2] Here they could get instruction on the spot without applying for leave of absence and far more cheaply.

The effects of the decree *Cum ex eo* have not been studied as carefully on the Continent as they have been for England, but the system seems to have operated in France too.[3] The principle behind the decree is referred to in *moralitates* given as a lecture course at Paris about 1325 by Pierre de Baume O.P. Just as the shepherds came to Bethlehem, which means 'house of bread or refreshment', and then returned to their flocks, so the shepherds of the Church should come to Paris or other *studia* to get the bread of heavenly doctrine (theology); then they should go home, as the shepherds did, to feed their sheep with the bread which they have gained

---

[1] W. A. Pantin, *General and Provincial Chapters of the Black Monks in England* 2 (Camden Society, 3rd series, 47, 1933): 75 ... necnon qui de monasteriis ad studium transmittuntur, non ut in theologia apicem magistralem ascendant aut gradum bacalariatus attingant, sed ut ibidem addiscant aliis debite proponere verbum Dei ... De hiis autem qui ad universitatem mittuntur, non ob aliam causam nisi ut ibidem addiscant aliis rite proponere verbum Dei ...
See also Knowles, 2, 24.
[2] See Pantin, 119. Holcot's lectures on Ecclesiasticus were probably given at Northampton, Hopeman's on Hebrews at London.
[3] L. E. Boyle, op. cit.

D

in study.[1] It sounds as though Pierre de Baume had some of these secular priests in his audience.

The lecture-commentary, when copied and circulated, would serve a public far outside the schools. It was now a source-book for sermon making at any reader's disposal. The doctor had woven the cloth which would later be cut to the pattern of the individual sermon. But the commentary, following the text of the Bible with many digressions, was so bulky as to need the services of a retailer. Annotators and indexers prepared it for the use of those who would draw on it. The manuscripts show that they followed three methods.

First, the annotator would guide readers by making marginal notes and headings to indicate the suitability of certain passages as themes for special days in the year or for special seasons or occasions. Sometimes the lecturer himself would have given the lead by referring to a feast day which occurred while he was going through his course. Thomas Hopeman did so consistently in his lectures on Hebrews: the reader can follow him round 'the whole scholastic year, three terms, from Michaelmas to Trinity'.[2] John Pecham, the Franciscan friar who later became archbishop of Canterbury, made practical suggestions for addresses at academic ceremonies, when he lectured on the Canticle at the papal Curia. *Thy breasts are better than wine* (i, 1) makes a theme for an introductory lecture in the faculty of theology, where theological wisdom is commended.[3] *The king has brought me into his storerooms* (i, 3) 'may be a theme for a *principium* of a doctor in theology. . . . He should not presume to dispense the ointments of the Gospels unless he has first been brought into the storerooms of both Testaments'.[4] Pecham also remembers the novice-master, offering him a theme for the instruction of novices.[5] Most passages of a commentary lent themselves to an improvised theme, which the annotator supplied where the commentator had made no specific suggestion.

---

[1] MS Bâle Univ. Libr. B.V.6, fol. 4vb: . . . et postea debent reverti ad propria, ut oves suas reficiant pane quem in studio acceperunt.

[2] Forte, 323-4.

[3] MS Florence, Laurent. Conv. sopp. 215, fol. 154vb: Thema pro lectione introductoria in theologia, ubi commendatur sapientia theologica simpliciter.

[4] ibid. fol. 158vb: Potest esse thema in principio doctoris theologici, cuius prima pars pertinet ad commendationem doctoris, qui presumere non debet dispensare unguenta (MS fluenta) evangelii, nisi ipse introductus fuerit in cellaria utriusque testamenti.

[5] ibid., fol. 156rb: Thema ad novitios informandos.

Secondly, the commentary would be fitted out with elaborate tables and indexes. A subject index guided the preacher who wished to speak of virtues or vices. He could turn up *Death* if he had to preach at a funeral. Another type of index linked the commentator's text to that of the liturgical year, so that one could find the text of the Gospel or Epistle of the day. A more complicated type puts in order those texts which the commentator had expounded while digressing from his main text. Thus Lathbury on Lamentations was indexed so as to supply matter for sermons on texts drawn from many other parts of the Bible.[1]

A vast amount of labour and ingenuity has gone into this kind of indexing. All kinds of devices were tried to make the index of one manuscript valid for other copies, where the leaves would not correspond. A careless scribe might frustrate every effort:

'The exemplar of my table was worth little, especially for the figures. Few of them are right, I think, after 100, but most are right below 100, as is clear. Believe if you will.'

So runs the warning of a student at Paris, who copied Holcot's Wisdom-commentary with a table.[2] A clerk and chaplain of Archbishop Arundel indexed another mammoth of exegesis, 'William of Nottingham on Clement of Lanthony', out of pity for students who fall into a decline or contract sickness worse than death by overworking.[3] We rarely find so personal a touch. Nearly all these patient tabulators have remained anonymous. At most they get mentioned as 'a certain deserving brother'.[4] A tabulator of Holcot on Wisdom refers to himself as 'ego simplex sine nomine'.[5] They put the preacher very much in their debt. Their labours enabled him to pick material for his sermons just as

---

[1] Appendix iii.

[2] MS Oxford, Bodl. Laud. misc. 562; see below, 137.

[3] B. Smalley, Which William of Nottingham? *M.A.R.S.* 3 (1954) 212-13.

[4] MS Padua, Anton. 476, fol. 193vb: Explicit tabula super postillam de Abbate, edita a quodam valenti fratre, ordinata et tabulata non per numerum foliorum, sed per numerum evangeliorum. Deo gratias.

The MS is a fourteenth-century copy of Francesco de Abbate O.F.M. on the Gospels for Sundays and Lent, which belonged to the Friars Minor of Padua; Stegmüller, no. 2295.

[5] MS Toulouse 39 has a table to Holcot on Wisdom ending: Explicit tabula postille memorate quam ego simplex sine nomine Dei adiutorio perfeci anno Domini m°ccc°octuagesimo 4° . . . It came from the Austin Friars. See *Cat. gén. des MSS des bibl. publ. des Départ.* 7 (Paris, 1885) 19.

one chooses a dress-length for summer or winter, or for a wedding or mourning.

The third and most drastic method of retailing was to break up the whole commentary and transcribe it again as matter for sermons according to the liturgical year. An 'exposition of the Gospels for the whole year according to St. Thomas, taken from his *Catena aurea*', circulated in Dominican libraries.[1] 'William of Nottingham on Clement of Lanthony' (a commentary on a Gospel harmony) was recast as matter for sermons on the Gospels according to the Use of Sarum.[2] Of course only expositions of the four Gospels or of the whole book of Pauline Epistles would lend themselves to such reorganisation. Some commentaries did not need it, having been arranged as lectures on the Gospels and Epistles for the year in the first place.

Sermons on their side sometimes show traces of having been adapted from commentaries. We can see Lathbury on Lamentations turning into sermons before our eyes. One set of manuscripts contains the original lecture course on Lamentations; another set contains part of it rearranged as excerpts. Some of these excerpts consist of passages from the commentary abridged and remodelled as skeleton sermons.[3] Robert Holcot's sermons probably derive from a lecture course on the Gospels.

As well as giving lectures which could be retailed as matter for sermons, the friar doctors prepared aids to preaching in the shape of *Artes praedicandi*, *exempla* collections and manuals of instruction on doctrine, the sacraments, social duty and virtues and vices. The *Artes* taught how to construct sermons according to the rules of ecclesiastical rhetoric, gave specimens and advised on the manner of delivery and choice of subject matter. The *exempla* collections provided the preacher with stories to point his moral. The manuals organised content in a systematic form.

Official training in preaching began at the university. Candidates for the degrees of bachelor and doctor in divinity had to give a specified number of sermons. The rule applied to seculars and regulars alike, though the Friars

---

[1] G. Meersseman, La bibliothèque de la Minerve au XVe siècle, *Mélanges Auguste Pelzer* (Louvain, 1947) 613. A set of expositions of the Epistles and Prophecies for Lent probably represent excerpts from the lectures of a fourteenth-century Italian Dominican; see A. Dondaine, La vie et les œuvres de Jean de San Gimignano, *Arch. FF. Praed.* 9 (1939) 148-50.

[2] B. Smalley, op. cit. 227-8.   [3] See below, appendix iii.

Preacher and Minor generally had charge of the administrative arrangements.[1] University sermons were formal academic occasions. We have seen how Pecham understood the needs of candidates for degrees and suggested themes suitable for inception in his lectures.

Material and pattern were stylised, but the sermon was supposed to have some touches of originality like a well-tailored suit. The preacher in a humble walk of life would make do with the secondhand and shoddy; the doctor had higher standards. Jordan of Saxony O.P. had to meet criticism for repeating his sermons. He answered sensibly that it would be wasteful to collect good matter and then throw it away.[2] Plagiarism was an even worse reproach than repetition. Detected, it put a master to shame and discredited his calling. The problem of conscience involved in safeguarding one's reputation as a preacher forms the subject of a *quodlibet* held at Paris between 1282 and 1291 by Gervase, Canon Regular of Mont-Saint-Éloi.[3] The *disputatio de quolibet* was an open discussion. The masters, bachelors and students attending it were allowed to ask any question they pleased, provided that it came under the heading of theology. They would seize on the chance to make the master commit himself on some burning question of the hour. Here the master's answer hints at current gossip or scandal. The question put to him was whether a doctor or bachelor committed mortal sin if he refused to lend a sermon to a colleague who wanted to borrow it, when he had reason to think that it would be returned to him undamaged. Gervase cites his own dilemma as an example. He has three sermons round his neck and he may be very busy. He's preached a sermon of his own making to the monks of a Charterhouse or some other small congregation. He sees no harm in keeping it prudently in reserve to preach again, in case he should have no leisure to prepare a fresh one. Suppose some persons, well provided with sermons for each day of the year, come and ask for it. If he lends it, he won't

---

[1] This holds good for both Paris and Oxford; see A. G. Little and F. Pelster, *Oxford Theology and Theologians* c. *1282-1302* (Oxford, 1934) 170-77.

[2] Gerardus de Fracheto, Vitae Fratrum Praedicatorum, ed. B. M. Reichert, *Mon. Ord. Praed. Hist.* 1 (Rome, 1897) 145: Idem magister in predicatione solebat eundem sermonem aliquotiens iterare. Quod cum obiceretur ei, respondit: 'Si aliquis collegisset bonas herbas et illas ad faciendum pulmentum cum studio preparasset, essetne conveniens illas abicere et pro colligendis aliis laborare?'

[3] Glorieux, no. 391,b: for a detailed discussion of the date, see his Les Quodlibets de Gervais du Mont-Saint-Éloi, *Rech. Théol.* 20 (1953) 129-34.

be able to use it himself afterwards, for fear of being re-
proached, as has happened to great masters. Someone might
say to him after his preaching: 'I'll show you the whole
sermon that you've just given, here in my notebook'. It
would dishonour the masters' professional standing if they
should preach sermons already current in notebooks.
Gervase, therefore, distinguishes between good and bad
motives in refusing to lend. It would be wrong to refuse out
of meanness, but there is no sin if the motive is human
foresight. A man is justified in hiding his sermon if to lend
it might bring discredit on his rank in his profession.[1]

Question and answer show what store the masters set on
originality and how jealously they protected themselves
against the smear of plagiarism. It was comforting to think
that a borrower would give himself away. Pierre de Baume
comments on the text: *A man shall be known by his learning:
but he that is vain and foolish shall be exposed to contempt* (Prov.
xii, 8); he says that some take a bundle of sermons or
quaestiones and preach or teach from it, but whether they
speak on their own account or not is known very well.[2]
These examples come from Paris. Robert Holcot of Oxford
makes the same point as Pierre de Baume, putting it more
elegantly. He quotes Martial's epigram on Fidentinus:

> The book is mine, Fidentinus, that you recite,
> So badly, you begin to make it yours.[3]

Originality, however sought after, could not show itself
in the basic content of sermons. This may seem surprising in

---

[1] See appendix i, p. 308.

[2] MS Eton College 79, fol. 23v-24: Nota de quibusdam accipientibus unum
rabanum sermonum vel questionum, et predicant vel docent, sed optime
cognoscitur utrum ipsi loquuntur a se ipsis.

Rabanum probably comes from the Netherlandish *raaband*, a naval term,
meaning 'rope-yard' and hence 'tie' or something tied, as we say 'a rope of
pearls'. The earliest known use of *raban*, the French form, is 1573, but it may
have been current much earlier; see O. Bloch and W. von Wartburg, *Diction-
naire étymologique de la langue française* (Paris, 1950) 502.

[3] Holcot is speaking against boastfulness, Sap. lect. ccxii, p. 695: Tales sunt
nonnulli pseudo-philosophi, qui sibi arrogant et attribuunt labores aliorum,
questiones, tractatus et compilationes studiosorum, quas vix intelligunt, in
quibus nichil habent proprium, nisi quod peius recitant talia, quam fuerant
ab auctoribus compilata, qualis fuit ille Fidentinus, quem lepide deridet Martialis Coquus, Epigr., lib. i. Iste Fidentinus libros quos Martialis ediderat, dum
recentes erant, subripuit et discipulis suis legit, at tamen eos perfecte non
intellexit. Reprehendens ergo eum super hoc Martialis scribit:

> Quem recitas meus est, O Fidentine, libellus,
> Sed male dum recitas, incipit esse tuus.

(Martial, *Epigr.* i, 38; cf. 29, 53, 72).

view of the fact that preachers worked against a background of rapid intellectual change. As schoolmen they joined in debates where the Thomist synthesis came under attack and where the tide of criticism and scepticism flowed strongly. But scepticism of a radical kind went with fideism, which was conservative. Theologians of all shades of opinion refrained from challenging traditional moral and social doctrine in their preaching.[1] Some were denying the metaphysical hierarchy of causes;[2] but sermons let out no hint of any such thing. Society still appears as a hierarchy. The preacher continues to prescribe the duties and denounce the sins of men on each rung of the ladder, with special reference to the duties and sins of prelates. It is all the old stuff again, little changed since the twelfth century. Moralists of the first half of the fourteenth century could not foresee the plagues, the wars, the Schism, the distress and the unrest which were coming. The world struck them as sad and bad, as it always had been, but they found it comparatively stable. Hence their teaching remained traditional, hackneyed even.

When statements degenerate into clichés they can be made interesting in one of two ways. Sincerity can give them new force. The traditional teaching of the Church came to life in the *Cursor mundi* and in the Holkham Bible. But this sort of presentation called for feeling and artistry. More important, both poet and designer had chosen media which favoured freshness, being free of polite conventions. St Francis, some hundred years earlier, had touched his hearers by preaching 'not according to the rules, but like a tub-thumper'.[3] Neither the lecturer nor the trained and licensed preacher of our later period enjoyed the Poverello's

---

[1] University sermons occasionally reflect current controversies; see Little and Pelster, op. cit., 171-2; but so far only twelfth-century sermons have been studied systematically from a theological point of view; M. M. Lebreton, Recherches sur les principaux thèmes théologiques dans les sermons du XIIe siècle, *Rech. Théol.* 23 (1956) 5-18.

[2] C. Michalski, La physique nouvelle et les différents courants philosophiques au XIVe siècle, extrait du *Bulletin de l'Académie polonaise des sciences et des lettres* (Cracow, 1928) 40-47.

[3] Thomas of Spalanto gives an eyewitness account of St Francis' preaching in 1222, quoted by J. R. H. Moorman, *The Sources for the Life of St Francis of Assisi* (Manchester, 1940) 56-7: Non modum praedicantis tenuit sed quasi contionantis.

The *contio* was a meeting of the people in an Italian city and the *contionator* a mob orator, who did not observe the rules of the trained rhetor, ecclesiastical or secular; see Boncompagni Rhetorica novissima, ed. A. Gaudenzi, *Bibliotheca iuridica medii aevi* 2 (Bologna, 1892) 296-7.

freedom; they had to follow school usage. The Franciscans had gone respectable and accepted the constraints of rhetoric, just as they accepted the discipline of scholarship. In an age of formalism people asked for a well-planned sermon from all but the greatest saints. The mystics, Richard Rolle and Master Eckhart, had something new to say, and said it: they, after all, were extraordinary.

Emotion then was excluded, save in small doses. There remained an appeal to reason, imagination and humour to make old sayings worth hearing. Reason could be used only sparingly: the preacher had to exhort the faithful, not argue with heretics. He felt all the more need to capture their imaginations and make them laugh now and then. New *exempla* and comparisons might brighten up stale advice. A joke might lodge it in the memory. A congregation with a taste for the classics would drink in eagerly any teaching with a classical flavour. The moral of the teaching remained constant. Why not choose a pagan example or a pagan setting for the story, 'just for a change'?

Here arise two related questions, neither admitting of a simple answer. First, how far could our friar doctors study pagan literature with a clear conscience? The answer is that it was a matter of where to draw the line. Some knowledge of pagan philosophy one must have; by the early fourteenth century no student in theology could complete his course without reading some passages at least from Aristotle, Avicenna and Averroes. It was impossible to distinguish between philosophers on the one hand and poets or men of letters on the other. They overlapped too much. The pagan pantheon had its historical, moral and physical inter-pretation, and so its study could be included in philosophy.[1] The writing of history, a legitimate activity, comprised pagan mythology. Latin literature contained much that a Christian could accept. The Fathers and Canon Law transmitted an attitude so ambivalent as to give scant guidance.[2] St Augustine's formula of 'spoiling the Egyptians' was perhaps the most elastic that has ever been invented. It really boils down to the proviso that a Christian, when studying the classics, must remember that he is a Christian. A strict or a wide interpretation alike involved compromise. Even

[1] Seznec, 11-147.
[2] Gratian, *Decretum*, d. 37. See G. G. Meersseman, *In libris gentilium non studeant. L'étude des classiques interdite aux clercs au moyen âge, I.M.U.* 1-14.

Giovanni Dominici in his *Lucula noctis*, written against the humanists, did not suggest that all pagan learning should be cut out of the school syllabus; he only advised that it be reduced to 'a bare minimum', an imprecise term. The ideal of an encyclopædic Christian culture is summed up engagingly in a bishop of Cambrai's epitaph on Gilbert of Tournai O.F.M. (d. 1284):

Christo servivit, qui totum scibile scivit.[1]

And yet the most broadminded interpreter of St Augustine had to reckon with limiting factors. The claims of his office and the commands of his superiors would interrupt his reading. No friar could devote himself wholly to the classics, with the best will in the world.

All allowed that some study of pagan literature was a necessary part of Christian education. Within this general agreement we find endless shades of difference. Further, we must remember that practice in the middle ages tended to be looser than theory. Where theory itself was loose, practice would vary even more. Many writers condemn pagan fables as mischievous, but sometimes the very man who does so proceeds to quote them as much as or more than the Scriptures. Vincent of Beauvais is an excellent example.[2] Blame of the poets satisfied the conscience and served as a passport rather than a barrier to travel in pagan country. It would be foolish to look for uniformity or consistency in the use of fables in preaching.

Our second question concerns the preacher's technique. How far was it permissible to introduce any light relief at all into lectures and sermons? Again, the answers vary. They range from blank refusal to unwilling consent. Pecham tells his friars to avoid all vanity and any mirth-provoking word.[3] Another Franciscan bows to necessity:[4] the preacher may tell a fictitious tale without committing mortal sin, if he sees his audience going to sleep.[5] Judging from his lectures, his students must have been in a constant state of torpor;

---

[1] Gilbert of Tournai, *De modo addiscendi*, ed. E. Bonifacio (Turin, 1953) 9.

[2] *De eruditione filiorum nobilium*, ed. A. Steiner (Cambridge, Mass., 1938) xv, 23, 35, 71.

[3] D. Douie, Archbishop Pecham's Sermons and Collations, *Studies in Medieval History presented to F. M. Powicke* (Oxford, 1948) 271.

[4] He was an early fourteenth-century commentator on Ecclesiastes, probably an Italian. The commentary is anonymous. The only copy is MS Padua, Anton. 227. See below, p. 277.

[5] fol. 4.

he has to rouse them by telling stories.[1] Most preachers held
to the maxim that prevention is better than cure. They tried
to forestall drowsiness by the use of *exempla* and other devices.
The *Artes praedicandi* sanction these as a concession to human
weakness:[2] listen to an English Dominican of the early
fourteenth century:

> Know that some story other than a Bible story may be
> brought forward; say, a tale from Augustine or Gregory or
> some such author, or from Helinand or Valerius or Seneca or
> Macrobius. A tale from Augustine, provided it be novel and
> unusual, is more acceptable than a tale from the Bible, and a
> tale from Helinand or some other writer who is rarely quoted
> than a tale from Augustine or Ambrose. And this for no other
> reason than men's idle curiosity.[3]

The desire for novelty in his audience pushes the preacher
ever further afield. Men prefer a story from the Fathers to
one from Scripture and a tale from a chronicler or a pagan
writer to either. Antiquity offered consoling precedents for
the use of tales in recreation. A scholar who admired the
restraint and gravity of ancient sages could read how Plato
encouraged his pupils to tell good stories in break.[4] Robert
Grosseteste, that pattern of Christian sagacity, had recommended historical and other tales about faith and morals as
suitable for the Sunday dinner table.[5] So again practice
varied. Some preachers, given an inch, would take an ell.

The result was inevitable. The sermon shared the tendency
of other contemporary art forms to become ever more
complex and decorated. Preachers noted it with alarm.
Pierre de Baume draws an apt parallel between the sermons
of his day and church music. In music the grave, clear

---

[1] He tells the story of Romulus and Remus with verses, fol. 2, and a long tale
of Alexander and his soldiers, fol. 2v; he interlards his commentary with the
sayings of ancient philosophers.

[2] Charland, 218. Not more than three jokes per sermon are recommended.

[3] ibid. 316.

[4] Et dixit discipulis suis: cum studere cessaveritis spaciemini in bonis ystoriis.
Et instruxit discipulis dicens: cum fessi a studio vacabitis, vacetis bonis ysto-
riis quod tedio careatis.
From Liber philosophorum moralium antiquorum, ed. E. Franceschini,
Atti del R. Istituto Veneto di scienze, lettere ed arti 91 (1931-2) 465, 487.

[5] *De decem mandatis*, MS Oxford, Bodl. Laud. misc. 524, fol. 91v: Interea
cenandi tempore debent esse salubres cogitationes vel commonitiones et edi-
ficantes ad vitam eternam, historice vel alie narrationes de fide et moribus et
vita eterna, tractatus et confabulationes.
Quoted by J. McCristal in a B.Litt. thesis on John Wyclif's *De mandatis
divinis*, submitted at Oxford in 1958.

plainsong of the earlier middle ages was being superseded by discant or 'pricksong', under the influence of the laymen who controlled the choirs in secular churches. The complaints of the clergy against these novelties grew louder until John XXII issued a bull in 1322 forbidding the use of discant in church services. The words of the bull make a good introduction to the comments of Pierre de Baume:

> 'Certain disciples of the new school', it runs, 'prefer to devise methods of their own rather than to continue singing in the old way. . . . Moreover, they truncate the melodies with hoquets, they deprave them with discants, sometimes they stuff them with upper parts (triplis et motetis) made out of secular songs.'

The Pope commanded that in future the integrity of the chant should remain unbroken.[1] Since Pierre de Baume lectured soon after the publication of the bull, his remarks on music must have sounded very topical.

They go to the root of the contrast between old and new methods. Both sermon and chant have lost their functional simplicity. The new techniques have a common drawback: they prevent the words of the Gospel and the liturgy from being distinctly heard. Instead of being expounded or sung consecutively, as they used to be, they are intermixed with foreign matter. Pierre says that Christ preached *the gospel of the kingdom* (Mt. iv, 23), not jokes, poems and philosophy. Then he launches his attack on the new ways of preaching and singing:

> It is the same with sermons today as it is with motets. In the old days chant was simple and plain. Then the tune and words and everything could be understood, because they could be distinguished. But now there are discants in the motets, so that only the tune can be followed. It charms the ear and has no other use. Similarly in the old days sermons were such as to profit the people. But now they have rhymes and curious comparisons, and philosophical subtleties are mixed with them; so many sermons do no good; they only please the hearers as oratory.[2]

[1] H. E. Wooldridge, *Oxford History of Music*, 2nd ed., revised by P.C. Buck (Oxford, 1929) 292-6.
[2] MS Bâle, Univ. Libr. B.V.6., fol. 46vb: *Predicans evangelium regni*, non trufas aut poetrias nec philosophiam. Sed de sermonibus dicitur esse hodie sicut de motetis. Antiquitus solebat esse cantus simplex et planus, et tunc intelligebantur melodia et voces vocabulorum et omia alia, sic quod poterant distingui. Sed nunc in motetis sunt confractiones, [sic] quod solum percipitur

Criticism failed to stem the tide. Love of elaboration and of secular themes, manifest in other spheres, was working in the sermon. Preachers, in spite of warnings to the contrary, had a human wish to please. They had to meet the cut-throat competition of professional entertainers, the minstrels and story-tellers. Each one disliked being outshone by a colleague and he lost face if he plagiarised. Circumstances combined to set a premium on being inventive and amusing. The precise form which amusement took would depend on the audience, in so far as the preacher could gauge its wishes. And so there might be 'talk of Alexander'.

---

melodia, que mulcet aures et nullam aliam facit utilitatem. Sic olim fiebant sermones unde populus proficiebat. Sed hodie fiunt rithmi (et) curiositatum concordantie, et immiscentur philosophice subtilitates, ita quod in multis sermonibus non est aliqua utilitas, sed solum oratoria complacentia auditorum. On Pierre de Baume and his commentary see below, 249.

CHAPTER III

FORERUNNERS AMONG THE FRIARS

Seneca Lucilio commendavit quedam
Que vix Evangelio postponenda credam.

Godfrey of St Victor, *Fons philosophie*.[1]

THE learned men of the school of Chartres soaked themselves in classical Latin literature. They read the original works available to them with three aims in view: they sought ancient wisdom, knowledge of the ancient world and models of style. Hence their letters and verse and prose-writings teem with erudite allusions and also strive after correct grammar and elegant diction. The *alumni* of Chartres, especially John of Salisbury, exemplify early twelfth-century classical studies in their purest and most engaging form. It was the culture of an intellectual aristocracy of clerks. A formation requiring so much time, love and patience, which had no obvious career value, could never have more than a limited appeal. Moreover, teachers of *litteræ humaniores* had to compete with the logicians. Logic was good for scholastic philosophy and theology and very bad for Latin. The tide swept over the pleasant little island where *belles lettres* had been cultivated in a Christian, but civil atmosphere. Laments of drowning men echo through the pages of twelfth- and early thirteenth-century satire: schoolboys no longer learn to express themselves correctly. The thirteenth-century revival of science proved to be incompatible with the Chartres ideal. At the same time an 'autonomous' literary culture developed, which no longer depended on imitation of the antique. The rhythmical Latin prose of *dictamen* for letter-writing and speech-making and medieval Latin verse for hymns and lyrics had their own rules. Classical rhetoric was not forgotten so much as absorbed into the new arts. Writers took what they wanted and left what seemed irrelevant.

A stimulating parallel has been drawn between the history of literary studies on the one hand and that of the visual arts on the other. French Romanesque differs from Gothic

---

[1] ed. P. Michaud-Quantin (Namur, 1956) lines 411-12.

in that the former incorporates morsels of genuine antiques and careful copies of antique models. The artist's inspiration is often Gallo-Roman. A pagan god leers out of classical foliage from the capital of a column in an abbey church. The antique, it is claimed, had more chance to be imitated in a centre where the clergy numbered enthusiasts for classical texts. Apart from a few survivals, it disappeared from Gothic art. Classical scenes and motifs continued to please the artists, proliferating merrily; but gods, heroes and philosophers look quite unlike their prototypes as represented by ancient and romanesque designers. They now wear medieval costumes and conform to Gothic rules of proportion and iconography. The increasing divergence coincides with and partly results from the contemporary neglect of literary values: 'la culture littéraire disparâit en quelques années sous l'assaut de la Théologie'.[1]

It is a useful comparison, so long as we realise that 'Theology', like a Gothic cathedral, admitted pagans, though theologians no longer wrote in polished Latin. Study of the classics continued, but students were more interested in matter than style. Their interest naturally affected their approach: it was less important to them to read the originals and more important to have their authors reduced to tabloid form. Philosophers appealed to them more than poets. Seneca had never enjoyed such prestige as he did in the thirteenth century, not even in the twelfth, which has sometimes been thought of as his peak period. He was given a kind of honorary baptism[2] and takes his place with the Church Fathers in the *Pharetra*, a collection of *auctoritates sanctorum*, ascribed to St Bonaventure and very popular as a handbook.[3] Still, the poets, though less appreciated as literature, were not banned by any means. They could teach philosophy and morals, if interpreted correctly. The friars as preachers gave both poets and philosophers a

---

[1] J. Adhémar, *Influences antiques dans l'art du Moyen Âge français* (London, 1939) 270. The antique continued to be copied on thirteenth-century gems and seals, however; see H. Wentzel, *Portraits 'a l'antique' on French Mediaeval Gems and Seals J.W.C.I.* 16 (1953) 342-50.

[2] Seneca was regarded as a pagan, not a Christian at this period; the mistaken idea that he was converted by St Paul is first found in Italy in the mid-fourteenth century; see A. Momigliano, Note sulla leggenda del Cristianesimo di Seneca, *Contributo alla storia degli studi classici* (Rome, 1955) 13-32. Walter of St Victor attacked Seneca as a pagan; see below, p. 294; n. 2.

[3] See the prologue and list of authors at the beginning of the *Pharetra*, *Opera S. Bonaventurae* 6 (Rome, 1596) 103-4. The *Pharetra* was compiled before 1264; the authorship is still doubtful; see Glorieux, no. 305 (bk).

currency unheard of in earlier centuries by using them as sources of *exempla* and wise sayings.

Thirteenth-century students of the classics pursued the first aim of the scholars of Chartres, to seek wisdom. They more or less rejected the third, to find models of style. The elusive middle term, 'knowledge of the ancient world', brings us to the heart of our problem. The seeker after knowledge wants information as well as instruction. Forbidden 'curiosity' enters in. Mid-thirteenth-century curiosity disguised itself as zeal for religion when it inspired the wideranging, all-embracing researches of the encyclopaedist. Ancient history and myth went shares with natural science and all other known branches of learning in their claims on his attention. Classical antiquity was fitted into an outline of universal history, beginning with Genesis. Never mind: the extraordinary industry of a medieval compiler will insert a volume under a sub-title.

Vincent of Beauvais O.P. was a king of compilers. He tells us that he started to collect material for an encyclopaedia with a team of friars to help him. Their joint efforts reached triple the size of a Bible. At this point their superiors understandably took fright at the expenses they were running into. Vincent was enjoined 'for the remission of his sins', begged by his brethren, and encouraged by his prior to cut it all down to a smaller manual, the size of one Bible only. He got round this publisher's verdict with enviable success. It seems that at first he showed willing and then protested that he had no time to abbreviate and that the cuts would spoil everything. So the *Speculum maius*[1] was published; a first edition, now lost, appeared before 1244[2] and the next about 1250.[3] It was divided into the *naturale*, the *historiale* and the *doctrinale*, and was followed by a *morale* which was compiled after Vincent's death.

His refusal to obey orders and abridge his *Speculum* had momentous results for medieval knowledge of history. The *historiale* offers an outline of universal history and is much more than a record of events: 'Attention is given to cultural history, after the latest and most improved fashion.' There is a section on the Hebrew religion, for instance, and an

[1] *Speculum maius*, Gen. prol. cap. vi (Venice, 1591) vol. 1, fol. 3.
[2] A. Dondaine, Le dominicain Jean de Mailly et la *Légende dorée*, *Archives d'histoire dominicaine* 1 (1946) 73-4.
[3] L. Thorndike. *A History of Magic and Experimental Science* 2 (New York, 1923) 459-61.

account of the ancient gods. 'Biographies of leading authors' of antiquity are followed by extracts from their books.[1] The bibliography impresses: Vincent assembled a big selection of ancient authors in the originals and in *florilegia*. He made a point of noting his sources, so that the *Speculum* gives the modern scholar a fair picture of what was liked and available in France in the mid-thirteenth century.[2]

The general prologue to the *Speculum maius* reads as a manifesto on the friars' attitude to the classics. John of Garland, a secular clerk and grammarian, working in the early thirteenth century, had lamented the passing of literary studies. Vincent, coming soon afterwards, has no wish to revive them from the grammarian's point of view, but he has his own use for ancient texts. His tone is hopeful and confident. He has seen in his own times a vast increase in the knowledge of secular and divine letters. All men, and the Dominicans in particular, busy themselves with expositions of Scripture in the historical and mystical sense and work out knotty questions of theology. Only Church histories, the 'milk which fed those simple men of old', have fallen into some neglect; yet they give pleasure as recreation and contain much that is edifying. He goes on to make the same claim for later ecclesiastical chroniclers and promises to copy long extracts from them, as being less well known than other types of author. Secular and religious history were so intermixed that Vincent's praise of the latter would cover the former. He defends himself for bringing in so much profane learning, again on the score that it is pleasing and useful: we honour the Creator by studying all his creatures, past and present. Vincent saw a bright future opening out to students and teachers of every subject. His *De eruditione filiorum nobilium* showed that he also believed in a liberal use of the classics in the education of upper-class laymen.[3] His hopes were fully justified: the heyday of Mendicant classicism began.

Oxford friars of the later thirteenth century made good use of the *Speculum maius*. They had had the further advantage of Robert Grosseteste's teaching and patronage of

[1] B. L. Ullman, A Project for a New Edition of Vincent of Beauvais, *Speculum* 8 (1933) 321.
[2] ibid., 312-22; Classical Authors in Certain Mediaeval *Florilegia*, *Classical Philology* 27 (1932) 1-42; E. Boutaric, Vincent de Beauvais, *Revue des questions historiques* 17 (1875) 5-57.
[3] ed. A. Steiner (Cambridge, Mass., 1938).

learning. The bishop of Lincoln, who died as a very old man in 1253, left a tradition of wide interests and bequeathed his excellent library to Greyfriars.[1] A mania for encyclopaedic lore, as one might almost call it, comes out in the lectures of Simon Hinton O.P. and of Thomas Docking O.F.M. Both friars crammed their biblical commentaries with miscellaneous information, much of it drawn from manuals and some of it in verse.[2] They were remembered at their respective convents: Holcot quotes Hinton and Lathbury Docking.[3] Roger Bacon O.F.M., a curious enquirer if ever there was one, must have had some influence, though it is difficult to assess in the absence of quotations. Docking admired and quoted him, but I have not found his name in biblical commentaries of the early fourteenth century. Bacon's activity as a book-hunter may have been as important for classical studies as the books he wrote. He hunted for rare texts and seems to have given wider currency to at least one of Seneca's.[4] We know that some thirteenth-century Franciscans anticipated later bibliographers by compiling a list of texts to be found in English libraries. It was mainly patristic, but included some classical authors. Boston of Bury, working in the early fifteenth century, used their ambitious, though unfinished, *Registrum librorum Angliae* as a basis for his *Catalogus*.

The interests of Grosseteste, Bacon, Hinton and Docking had lain in the fields of Scripture, patristic, ethics and natural science rather than in that of classical literature; but they taught the theologian to avoid narrowness. They prepared a porous soil, where classicism could flourish. The next generation had only to read a different type of secular book. The classicising group of friars began where their elders had left off. They always drew on natural science for many of their *exempla* and comparisons. Ancient history and myth infiltrated gradually. We shall watch the proportion between them changing in the lectures of Thomas Waleys, as he got more and more bitten by his classical authors.

---

[1] *Robert Grosseteste, Scholar and Bishop*, ed. D. A. Callus (Oxford, 1955) 121-45; below, p. 229.

[2] *Study of the Bible* 319-23; *F.P.* 98-121.

[3] See below, p. 229, Robert Holcot, 29.

[4] A. G. Little, Studies in English Franciscan History (Manchester, 1917) 188; C. H. Beeson, Roger Bacon and the 'Dialogues' of Seneca, *The Manly Anniversary Studies in Language and Literature* (Chicago, 1928) 243-53.

E

A thirteenth-century Cambridge theologian set an example in his religious verses, which contained many allusions to ancient philosophers and poets. This was Walter Wimborne O.F.M., lector to the Cambridge Franciscans between about 1263 and 1266.[1] He can claim to be an inspirer of the classicising group because Holcot and Lathbury quote extensively from a prose work of his. The original is lost, but their quotations suggest that it had the same tendencies as his surviving poems.[2] He composed them in honour of Our Lady and requisitioned a crowd of ancients to join in singing her praises. Wimborne describes himself as 'talkative' and correctly; he versifies interminably. He also presents himself as a scamp, who has put off repentance until late in life. A tavern has suggested one of his most daring comparisons.[3] The schools offer many others. The Virgin is a commentary and gloss on the Prophetical Books, revealing their hidden sense; she cheats the consequences of logicians. To call her 'columpna clinicorum' is a highly academic way of saying 'friend of the sick'.[4] The great writers of antiquity and even Minerva herself go dumb and pant in attempting to praise Mary. Wimborne makes out a list:

> Laudes tante matris Maro
> non araret celto claro
>   neque Titus Livius.
> Hic Homerus est elinguis
> et Minerva flatu pinguis,
>   hic est traulus Tullius.[5]

His best effort at making a synthesis of sacred and profane is where he describes the end of the Last Judgment: the blessed will hear a lecture from the Chair on Aristotle's Nicomachean Ethics. Wimborne prays Our Lady to see that he shall be placed with those,

---

[*] Eccleston, *De adventu Fratrum Minorum*, ed. A. G. Little (Manchester, 1951) 58; J. R. H. Moorman, *The Grey Friars in Cambridge* (Cambridge, 1952) 31, 144, 225. The bibliographs cut Wimborne in half, ascribing the verses to a fourteenth-century namesake, who may not have existed at all. Drèves saw no reason why the verses should not have been written in the thirteenth century. Their author gives his name and says that he belongs to the Order of St Francis; see G. M. Drèves, *Analecta hymnica* 50 (Leipzig, 1907) 630, 643.

[2] See below, appendix ii, 365.

[3] MS Oxford, Bodl. Laud. misc. 368, foll. 204ra, 205vb, 212rb, 215vb. Drèves, op. cit., ascribes this unpublished poem to Wimborne.

[4] *Encomium beatae Mariae*, ed. Drèves, ibid. 631, 632, 635.

[5] 637. *celto* and *traulus* are in the manuscript; I do not know what they mean nor how to emend them.

quibus doctor angelorum
legit librum ethicorum
in sublimi cathedra.[1]

Tender intimacy with the Holy Family, which we think of as typically Franciscan,[2] mingles with school learning in the oddest way.

Closer and more respectable forerunners than this Cambridge poet were John of Wales O.F.M. and Nicholas Trevet O.P.

John of Wales took his doctorate and was regent at Oxford Greyfriars about 1257-8 or perhaps rather later, having taken his bachelor's degree in theology before entering the Order. He is said to have joined the custody of Worcester.[3] This sounds quite plausible, since he must have come from Wales. He preached a university sermon at Paris in 1270 and two more in the spring of 1282. Archbishop Pecham chose him to send on an embassy to Prince Llewelyn in the autumn of the same year. The archbishop, a Franciscan himself, was doing his best to reconcile the Welsh prince with the king of England. It was tactful to send a distinguished Welsh friar as his envoy.[4] John is said to have been regent at Paris in 1282 and was certainly there in 1283, when he was appointed with three other doctors to examine the writings of Peter John Olivi. John of Wales died at Paris, perhaps as early as the spring of 1285. The dates of his works have not yet been established; it is not known whether they first appeared at Oxford or Paris or elsewhere. In any case, they soon became extremely popular both in England and abroad.

John compiled a long series of treatises which were called by rather fancy names all ending in '-loquium', *Communiloquium*, *Compendiloquium* and so on. The reason was that he intended them as manuals for conversation *ad omne genus*

---

[1] 643. Both poems are full of learned allusions; Cicero and Aristotle recur in the unpublished one, MS Laud. misc. 368, foll. 208va-211ra. Jesus, 'the first rhetor', is covered with 'the toga of flesh'; Drèves, 640.

[2] Mary plays with her Baby; Wimborne remains with the Holy Family when the Magi withdraw; MS Laud. misc. 368, foll. 204ra, 207va-b. These scenes are described in quite simple language.

[3] *O.R.* 3, 1960-1. He is entered under 'Waleys'. I have purposely been inconsistent in calling him 'John of Wales' as a way of differentiating him from his namesake, the Dominican, Thomas Waleys. It was a common surname, and does not necessarily imply a recent Welsh origin. Religious, however, took the name of their birthplace when they joined an Order; hence it is pretty safe to assume that John came from Wales.

[4] D. L. Douie, *Archbishop Pecham* (Oxford, 1952) 238-9.

humanum as well as for preaching and teaching. He thought that a good friar ought to know how to improve on any occasion, wherever he was and whatever type or rank of men he met, from the king down to the labourer.[1] Antiquity entered in because John wanted to show what pagans could achieve by the light of natural reason and virtue without those aids of revelation and grace which should enable Christians to do better. He filled page after page with specimens of good deeds and wise sayings ascribed to ancient statesmen and philosophers. A composite picture emerges of the ancient ruler, who listens to philosophic advice, as Alexander listened to Aristotle, and of the ancient sage, who exercises self-control in all things and preserves his independence by detachment: 'It is slavery to accept invitations from magnates.'[2] He welcomes poverty, but still remains urbane and enjoys good talk. He is grave and dignified, but witty.[3] John has armed his readers with a new Valerius Maximus brought up to date, vastly elaborated and expanded. It is all very edifying, but it is something else too. The reader learns about ancient customs and studies. He visits the ancient world under John's guidance. The most crying instances of curiosity as distinct from pure zeal for souls appear in a still unpublished treatise on the Ten Commandments, the *Legiloquium*.

John wrote this treatise as an aid to preaching and discourse like the others.[4] His subject here gave him a

---

[1] A. G. Little analyses and gives a brief résumé of *Communiloquium, Compendiloquium* and *Breviloquium* in *Studies in English Franciscan History* (Manchester, 1917) 176-86; see also Pantin, 147-8.

[2] *Compendiloquium* (Lyons, 1511) fol. 187vb: Servitus est acquiescere invitationibus magnatum et eas suscipere.

[3] ibid. foll. 189rb-212ra.

[4] The *Legiloquium* is contained with other works by John of Wales in MS London, Brit. Mus. Harl. 632, foll. 307v-318v. It is incomplete. John says in his prologue, fol. 307v-308: Ad manuductionem vero iuniorum in cognitione harum legum . . . colliguntur et scribuntur in hac collatiuncula, que potest dici legiloquium, auctoritates sanctorum de predictis legibus, adducendo et adiungendo dicta philosophorum gentilium que concordant cum legibus divinis sive preceptis. . . .
Later he underlines his purpose by saying that he will pass over points which pertain rather to disputation than to preaching, fol. 312v: De aliis vero multis que possent dici de die sabbati et que magis spectant ad disputationem quam ad predicationem supersedeo.
Cross-references show that this treatise came after his *Communiloquium* and *Monoloquium*, foll. 308, 313v-314. Other manuscripts of the *Legiloquium* are listed by Glorieux, no. 322(h) and by V. Doucet in his review of Glorieux, *Archiv. fr. hist.* 27 (1934) 552. The *Ars praedicandi* which has been plausibly ascribed to him by Charland, 58-60 (unpublished) seems to be severely technical in character

splendid opportunity to enlarge on his favourite theme, the virtues of good pagans: the heathen performed remarkable works, whether in hating vices, in so far as vices can be hated without the aid of justifying and purifying faith, or in helping the poor and afflicted or in doing justice or in undergoing fatigue and danger for the sake of the Common-wealth. Alexander fulfilled the natural law by doing as he would be done by; proofs are advanced from Valerius Maximus and Vegetius to show how Alexander considered his soldiers and subjects.[1] John was no snob and would bring forward the example set by peoples as well as by princes, and by barbarous peoples at that, the Bragmans and Scyths.[2] All could shame Christians for not living up to the law of the Gospel. So far so good! Did Christians also need to be told as much about idolatry as John proceeds to tell them? He pieces together excerpts from St Augustine's *De civitate Dei* and from Cicero's *De divinatione* and *De natura deorum* so as to describe its origins, its nature and the forms it took. That the men he admired should have been de-praved enough to worship idols pains him. He does his best for them: they were deceived by devils, and anyway sages such as Socrates, Anaxagoras and Epicurus scorned and mocked at idolatry.[3] John's enthusiasm has led him to stretch a point in favour of Epicurus, who had a reputa-tion for depravity in the middle ages; it is surprising to see him being driven into the sheepfold of good pagans on account of his disbelief. John would use his authors to prove the opposite of what they meant as a way of saving them from themselves. The profanation of a shrine, told as an example of impiety by Cicero and Valerius Maximus, shows 'how the heathen would laugh at the worship of idols'.[4] The

---

and does not bring in quotations from heathen philosophers or discuss their use. I have not read John's unpublished sermons. There is room for a much fuller study of his works and their sources than has yet appeared.

[1] ibid. fol. 308: Quam vero egregia opera fecerunt gentiles de operibus operatis sive exterioribus, sive in detestando vitia, sicut possunt detestari absque fide iustificante et purificante, sive in subveniendo miseris et afflictis sive in exercendis operibus iustitie, sive in sustinendis laboribus et periculis pro utilitate reipublice, patet in historiis . . . Satis enim Alexander magnus adimplevit legem naturalem faciendo aliis quod sibi vellet fieri. . . .

[2] fol. 309. [3] foll. 309v-310.

[4] fol. 310. John quotes Valerius Maximus, *Fact. et dict. mem.* i, i, externa exempla 3, and Cicero, *De natura deorum* iii, 82-4, on the sacrilege of Dionysius of Syracuse, copying the latter almost verbally, 'et ita ad impietatem in deos adiunxit iniuriam in homines', and ending: 'ex quibus patet qualiter gentiles deridebant cultum idolorum'.

most prophetic section of *Legiloquium*, however, is the little compilation on pagan cults. It anticipates in a modest way John Ridevall's fuller and more learned account of the pantheon in his commentary on *De civitate Dei*.

A treatise on penance is not an obvious place for quotations from classical authors; but we find them in John's. He composed his treatise in the form of short sermons or *collationes* for 'younger preachers'.[1] It begins with advice not to be 'curious' and to seek only what is necessary for salvation. Those who follow John's advice have the example of ancient philosophers set before them. The sages thought it blameworthy to neglect true wisdom for the sake of empty and useless studies. John justifies his statement by quoting Petronius' stricture on the schools of his day from the prologue to *Satiricon*.[2] Young preachers could find plenty of matter to enliven their exhortations to the faithful to come to confession in John's treatise. His lectures on St Matthew also contain quotations from philosophers.[3]

The success of his books shows that he understood the contemporary mood and that his repertoire came in useful. Both Thomas Ringstead and Robert Holcot quote him by name.[4] He offered a rich store of *exempla* and set an example, 'go and do likewise'. He also showed his imitators where they should look. His use of John of Salisbury's *Policraticus* links up the classicism of the twelfth century with that of the later middle ages. John of Wales popularised *Policraticus* by exploiting it as a mine of stories, precepts and facts about the ancient world. He drew on it for his big compilations[5] and for his lectures on St Matthew.[6] John of Salisbury had not meant his book to be used like this. He gave it a unified plan and addressed it to princes, courtiers and

---

[1] MS London, Brit. Mus. Royal 10.A.ix, fol. 2rb. Fr L. E. Boyle describes the treatise and gives a list of manuscripts in his doctoral thesis.

[2] MS Royal 10.A.ix, fol. 2ra: Unde et apud philosophos fuit culpabile, omissa veritate sapientiali et pertinentiis ad ipsam neglectis, vanis et superfluis vacare. Propterea ait Petronius in suo prologo: Ego, inquit, adolescentulos existimo in scholis fore [*sic*] stultissimos, quia nichil ex hiis que in usum habemus aut audiunt aut intelligunt.

The *Satiricon* was not often quoted in the thirteenth century. John may have found the famous criticism of Roman schools in a secondary source.

[3] MS Oxford, Magdalen College lat. 27, foll. 1-91; see Stegmüller, no. 4514.

[4] See below, pp. 151 and 218.

[5] A. G. Little, op. cit.

[6] MS Magdalen College lat. 27, fol. 72v: . . . ut enim ait Apuleius . . . sicut recitat Policraticus, lib. 6 in fine.

The quotation is from Apuleius, *De deo Socratis*, from *Policraticus* vi, 28; 2, 83.

churchmen as having a special message for them.[1] However, it could serve another purpose in other conditions. All the friar doctors of the classicising group followed John of Wales in prizing it as a *Golden Treasury* of excerpts. They used it as their gateway to antiquity, admitting to a knowledge of the classics a far wider circle than its author could have dreamt of reaching.

John of Wales, according to A. G. Little, is careful in giving his authorities, and generally, if not always, lets his readers know if he is quoting at second hand. John drew part of his matter from the originals. His quotations show wide reading; he must have taken pains to collect them. His love of books comes out in his praise of 'the efforts of men of old to form libraries'.[2]

'Libraries': these must keep us for a moment before we pass to Nicholas Trevet. He leads on into the early fourteenth century, when new facilities were being offered. We must consider what books giving first-hand information on ancient history and myth a serious student could find in England about 1300.

It is easy to point to the *spuria* and to the gaps on the shelves. Second-hand knowledge and misinformation were to be had in plenty. *Spuria* abounded, more especially in the form of didactic treatises ascribed to pagan moralists. Even John of Salisbury had quoted, if he did not actually compose, Pseudo-Plutarch's *Institutio Traiani*, supposed to be addressed by Plutarch to his pupil Trajan.[3] Two pieces may be cited by way of example because they had an irresistible appeal for the classicising friars. Walter Map, the twelfth-century wag, wrote a letter, full of classical allusions, recommending celibacy in preference to marriage. It was said to be written by Valerius to a friend called Rufinus, *Dissuasio Valerii ad Rufinum de uxore non ducenda*.[4] Map may have intended his title to pass as a joke, but it was taken seriously; readers got a vague impression that his fictitious Valerius was Valerius Maximus. The second piece was

---

[1] See H. Liebeschütz, *Mediaeval Humanism in the Life and Writings of John of Salisbury* (London, 1950) 23-33.
[2] A. G. Little, op. cit.
[3] H. Liebeschütz, John of Salisbury and Pseudo-Plutarch. *J.W.C.I.* 6 (1943) 33-9; A. Momigliano and H. Liebeschütz, Notes on Petrarch, John of Salisbury and the *Institutio Traiani*, ibid. 12 (1949) 189-90.
[4] R. J. Dean, Unnoticed Commentaries on the *Dissuasio Valerii* of Walter Map, *M.A.R.S.* 2 (1950) 128-50.

ascribed to Boethius and was a treatise on education called *De disciplina scholarium*. The author is unknown; he wrote in the early thirteenth century and had studied at Paris.[1] Moralists found both Pseudo-Valerius and Pseudo-Boethius extremely useful. Detection of forgeries depends on a critical appreciation of style, which did not interest the friars as moralists, on a sense of period, which they lacked, and on a dislike of being cheated. Medieval schoolmen could be hypercritical on points which really mattered to them and childishly credulous where they saw no reason to be otherwise. They did not mind if a good book were ascribed wrongly to a good author.

A serious student of the classics about 1300 was debarred from two primary sources of knowledge. First of all he had to limit his researches to literary texts; the science of archaeology was unborn. At most he could look at remains and inscriptions without knowing how to interpret them. Secondly, his texts had to be in Latin, since he could not read Greek. Neither the Greek studies of Grosseteste and Roger Bacon in the thirteenth century nor the decree of the Council of Vienne in 1312, ordering the establishment of chairs in Greek and oriental languages, succeeded in spreading a capacity to read it fluently.[2] Our 'serious student' had to make do with translations. The toil of older scholars had passed on to him a library of biblical, patristic, scientific and philosophical texts in Latin versions, but had left history and poetry almost untouched.[3] The driving force behind these versions had been either religious and missionary zeal or scientific rather than literary interest. Some historical material filtered through to tell of the Trojan war and of Alexander. The Latin versions of Aristotle provided scraps of information which meant little in the absence of background. The English scholar, Walter Burley, makes an acute and sensible confession of ignorance in his com-

---

[1] J. Porcher, Le *De disciplina scholarium*, traité du XIIIe siècle faussement attribué à Boèce, *Positions des Thèses de l'Ecole nationale des chartes* (Paris, 1921); Vincent of Beauvais, *De eruditione filiorum nobilium* op. cit., xxiv.

[2] See A. G. Little, *Studies in English Franciscan History*, op. cit. 215-18; R. Weiss, England and the Decree of the Council of Vienne on the Teaching of Greek, Arabic, Hebrew and Syriac, *Bibliothèque d'Humanisme et de Renaissance* 14 (1952) 1-9; The Study of Greek in England during the Fourteenth Century, *Rinascimento* 2 (1951) 209-39; *Humanism in England during the Fifteenth Century*, 2nd ed. (Oxford, 1957) 9-11.

[3] J. T. Muckle, Greek Works translated directly into Latin before 1350, *Mediaeval Studies* 4 (1942) 32-42; 5 (1943) 102-14.

mentary on the *Politics:* 'He frankly tells us that he has no knowledge of the history about which Aristotle talks. Besides, for the very reason that it is strange to him, it does not fulfil for him, he says, the function for which Aristotle introduces it, illustration. Hence he does not feel competent to comment on it.'[1] The texts of Plato available in Latin versions told more of philosophy than of life in Plato's Greece.[2]

The early humanists still suffered from the same disadvantages. Petrarch looked at ruins without much understanding and tried to learn Greek without succeeding. Both he and Boccaccio had great difficulty in finding even passable Greek teachers. Much effort was needed to put Greek studies on a sound footing in Florence in the late Trecento. The humanists' experience makes it easy to see why the decree of the Council of Vienne should have misfired.

Even the thirteenth-century section *MSS class. lat.* had some sad gaps. A medieval student would have found Tacitus difficult and unsympathetic, but he would have liked the gossipy *Historia augusta* which would have supplemented his Suetonius. The *Historia augusta* was unknown until its rediscovery in Petrarch's time.[3] Catullus was a very rare author. He could have been enjoyed and moralised to make him respectable. If the *Georgics* and the *Metamorphoses* could be equipped with their *moralitates*, why not poems about a boat and a pet sparrow?[4] Nevertheless, a good basic classical Latin library existed in England about 1300, after subtracting texts so rare as to be unobtainable. A reader of all the authors known to have belonged to English libraries could have emerged as a sound Latinist.

At this stage in the argument our typical scholar dissolves into air. Access to books depended on the resources of the local shops, if one could afford to buy, on one's convent or chapter library and on travel. The question of what books were available in a given library at a given moment is a

---

[1] C. Martin, Some Medieval Commentaries on Aristotle's *Politics, History* New Series, vol. 36 (1951) p. 38.

[2] The first part of *Timaeus* was known all through the middle ages, *Meno* and *Phaedo* from about 1156; see R. Klibansky, *The Continuity of the Platonic Tradition* (London, 1939).

[3] P. de Nolhac, *Pétrarque et l'humanisme* 2 (Paris, 1907) 79-80.

[4] See E. F. Wilson, The *Georgica Spiritualia* of John of Garland, *Speculum* 8 (1933) 358-77.

formidable subject. Professor R. A. B. Mynors has worked out a valuable guide to it in a recent paper: he has edited items relating to classical authors from the *Catalogus* of Boston, an early fifteenth-century librarian of the abbey of Bury St Edmund.[1] Boston made a list of authors with the *floruit* and book titles, quoting the incipits and the libraries in England where the books could be found, in so far as he had the information. The Franciscan *Registrum librorum Angliae* served him as a starting point. Professor Mynors also tells us on the basis of his intensive researches into medieval libraries and library catalogues whether each book was rare or common. This will do duty as an index, showing us what to expect and what to find surprising. I shall refer to it when we meet authors noted as 'rare'. Another approach to the same problem is to read the list of sources of *exempla* compiled by Welter, whose study of *exempla* collections shows roughly which authors were drawn upon and through which intermediaries.

Nicholas Trevet worked on a higher level than John of Wales. John had made 'select extracts' more readily available; Trevet made whole texts more intelligible. He was a true polymath, being theologian, biblicist, hebraist, historian and classicist. It is only in the last capacity that he concerns us here. Trevet's father was a Somerset knight, who served as itinerant justice. The son is said to have joined the Dominican Order in London. He was studying at Oxford by November 1297. He was regent probably between 1303 and 1307, and again for a second time in 1314. His studies at Paris probably fell in the intervening years, during which a dispute was going on between the friars and the University of Oxford. We hear of him at Oxford in the following year, 1315, and as lector at the London Blackfriars in September 1324. He was still living ten years later, aged well over seventy.[2]

Trevet commented on the following classical or pseudo-classical and late-antique texts: St Augustine's *De civitate Dei*, Boethius' *De consolatione Philosophiae*, Pseudo-Boethius' *De disciplina scholarium*, Livy's *Ab Urbe condita*, the *Declamationes* (the medieval title for the *Controversiae*) of the elder and the *Tragœdiae* of the younger Seneca; perhaps also on Cicero (text unspecified), on Juvenal, on Walter Map's

[1] The Latin Classics Known to Boston of Bury, *F.S.* 199-217.
[2] *O.R.* 3, 1902-3.

Dissuasio Valerii and on book vi of the *Aeneid*.[1] It is an impressive list, even when we realise that the scholastic method of expounding a text could be applied to different types of author without much modification. The method had developed from the late-antique period. The commentator discussed authorship, place, date, subject, purpose, etc., in his prologue and then ploughed along the lines, explaining the grammatical construction and amplifying his author's allusions. He did not have to bother about the literary or historical value of the work as a whole.[2] Hence Trevet inherited a ready-made procedure and had models to guide him when he chose a text possessing no apparatus. There were plenty of medieval commentaries on classical texts used as school books in the Arts course.

It is tempting to laugh at Trevet's scholarship. Take his commentary on the *Tragedies*:[3] he begins by quoting Pseudo-Boethius, *De disciplina scholarium* in praise of Seneca's doctrine; he fails to distinguish the younger from the elder Seneca; he admits to using only one text, and that defective; it was all he could get.[4] Then he makes a horrible mistake about the nature of ancient drama, concluding a series of muddles which had arisen since the deep understanding of the school of Chartres had given way to shallower studies.[5] The real interest of his commentaries lies in the fact that they were written at all, and were written because they were asked for.

No one had commented on *De civitate Dei* before, nor had any medieval scholar tackled the *Declamationes*, the *Tragedies*

[1] See ibid. for a bibliography of Trevet's works. His commentaries on Cicero and Juvenal are known only from a literary tradition; that on the *Dissuasio Valerii* is still in process of being sorted out of a number of manuscript commentaries on the same text; that on *Aeneid* vi is not certainly his and is any way a poor and derivative work: see J. R. Dean's review of E. Franceschini's studies on Trevet, *Medium Aevum* 10 (1941) 161-8. We are waiting for a fuller study of Trevet's life and writings, which Miss Dean has in preparation. At present the dates of his works are not sufficiently established to make possible an account of his intellectual development; this will be very interesting when it comes.

[2] H.-I. Marrou, *Saint Augustin et la fin de la culture antique* (Paris, 1949) 494-8; R. W. Hunt, The Introductions to the 'Artes' in the Twelfth Century, *Studia Mediaevalia in honorem R. J. Martin* (Louvain, s.a.) 85-112.

[3] ed. E. Franceschini, *Il commento di Nicolo Trevet al tieste di Seneca* (Milan, 1938).

[4] Boston of Bury lists the *Tragedies* but took his data from the register of the thirteenth-century Franciscans, suggesting that he had no first-hand knowledge of it; see *F.S.* 207.

[5] M. H. Marshall, *Theatre* in the Middle Ages: Evidence from Dictionaries and Glosses, *Symposium* 4 (1950) 1-39; Boethius' Definition of *Persona* and Mediaeval Understanding of the Theatre, *Speculum* 25 (1950) 471-82.

or *Ab Urbe condita*. *De consolatione Philosophiae* had already
attracted some earlier commentators, but the last of them
had lived in the twelfth century. This favourite late-antique
text needed an up-to-date apparatus after the long pause.
Trevet supplied it; his commentary became standard.[1]
Readers soon wanted more. An Italian Dominican cardinal
called Nicholas of Prato, Dean of the Sacred College, wrote
to Trevet to say that *De consolatione Philosophiae* had been his
companion ever since his youth, but that the commentary
had enabled him to read it with much more pleasure and
profit. He had heard that Trevet had also commented on
the *Declamationes* and asked that a copy should be sent as
soon as possible. Then he suggested the *Tragedies* as a new
subject. The cardinal explained that he wished to read
them. Alas! he found them too heavy going:

'Seneca's book of Tragedies is so full of difficulties and pitfalls,
with fables woven into its very texture, that it frightens off anyone who attempts to read it at the start.'[2]

It was an urgent plea for a classical text made easy. Trevet
sent his commentary to the cardinal in response to the
request about 1315. His newly discovered Livy-commentary
has an *explicit* stating that it was prepared at the command
of the pope himself. The correspondence relating to the
order has not survived; but John XXII instructed the papal
tax collector in England to make Trevet 'a gift of money to
help meet his expenses in composing a literary work commissioned by the pope' in January 1318. This may refer to
the Livy-commentary.[3] Its nature proves that Trevet wrote
it for the type of reader supposed by his commentary on the
Tragedies. John XXII, like the Dean of the Sacred College,
wanted access to a text which bristled with difficulties for
the uninitiated.

Classical studies were coming into fashion at Avignon.
Neglected texts were now being read and talked of. Seneca's

[1] P. Courcelle, Étude critique sur les commentaires de la Consolation de
Boèce, *Archives* 14 (1939) 97-100. Professor Courcelle puts Trevet's commentary
before 1307; for quotations of it in later writers, see below, pp. 157 and 206.
[2] The correspondence between Nicholas of Prato and Nicholas Trevet is
printed by E. Franceschini, op. cit. 1-4. The lines freely translated above read:
Tragediarum autem eiusdem memorandi viri liber tantis est obscuritatibus
plenus, tantis connexus latebris tantisque contextus et implexus fabellis, ut
statim temptantem se legere obscuritate sua deterreat.
[3] J. R. Dean, The Earliest Known Commentary on Livy, *Medievalia et
Humanistica* 3 (1945) 86-98.

Tragedies had circulated much less widely than his moral and philosophical books. Livy had lain right outside the school tradition; even John of Salisbury had not quoted him. Florus' *Epitome* and late compilations had done service instead. The average high-ranking churchman lacked the culture necessary to enjoyment of these new pleasures. Cardinal Nicholas of Prato (*c.* 1250-1321) had studied theology at Paris and had taught in houses of his Order in Italy before starting on his *cursus honorum* in the Church.[1] John XXII had the training of a canon lawyer and surrounded himself with lawyers. Well disposed to humane studies as they might be, these clever, sharp-witted men felt blank when faced with literary allusions couched in unfamiliar Latin. Their school education in theology or canon law had not prepared them for advanced study of the classics. Southern scholarship had not ripened sufficiently to offer the sort of guidance they needed. Petrarch was still a schoolboy in 1315; he remembered Cardinal Nicholas as a kind old man, who befriended him out of affection for his father's memory.[2] The Paduan circle was too small and exclusive to be applied to. Pope and cardinal turned to an Oxford friar with the same academic background as theirs. Trevet already had a reputation for scholarship throughout his Order and Nicholas of Prato may have met him in person when visiting England as a papal legate in 1301. It is not surprising that they knew and trusted him. The puzzling fact is that they sought in scholastic Oxford what they could not find in the *Midi*.

We should not antedate the split between humanism and scholasticism which developed in the course of the Trecento. Trevet approached the holy books of humanism in the same matter-of-fact way as he would tackle the Christian. He does not feel that he is 'turning a new page in history' or any such nonsense when he writes the first Livy-commentary. He might say with the Yorkshireman who was shown the water pouring down Niagara Falls that he saw 'nothing to hinder it'. Trevet cites St Jerome in praise of Livy in his prologue and then gets down to business without further talk. His prologue to his commentary on *De civitate Dei* shows that

---

[1] J. R. Dean, Cultural Relations in the Middle Ages: Nicholas Trevet and Nicholas of Prato, *Studies in Philology* (University of N. Carolina) 45 (1948) 541-64.
[2] ibid.

he made no sharp distinction between pagan and Christian texts and that he considered himself to be working in the framework of the Oxford Dominican tradition. He reminds readers that Robert Kilwardby O.P., archbishop of Canterbury and later cardinal, had divided the books of De civitate Dei into chapter with titles to facilitate reference, while he was studying sacred doctrine 'in our Order'.[1] Kilwardby's apparatus of chapters and titles had been part of an enterprise undertaken by the Dominicans and Franciscans in the thirteenth century to make the Fathers easier of access.[2] Trevet felt that still more apparatus was called for before students could profit from De civitate Dei:

> 'Augustine attacks the enemies of the City of God with their own weapons, sometimes introducing stories from the poets and heathen sayings, especially in the first ten books and in book xviii. This creates difficulties for readers who have less practice in such matters. Our purpose is to remove the obstacles to understanding and to make dark passages plainer to such readers, as our brothers have often urged us to do.'[3]

A manuscript title of Trevet's commentary expresses its function precisely:

> 'Incipit expositio historiarum extranearum dictorumque poeticorum que tanguntur ab Augustino in libro de civitate Dei.'[4]

In modern terms it 'gives the pagan background' to

---

[1] See H.-I. Marrou, La division en chapitres des livres de 'La Cité de Dieu', Mélanges Joseph de Ghellinck S.J. 1 (Gembloux, 1951) 235-49.

[2] On work by the English Friars, see D. A. Callus, The Tabulae super Originalia Patrum of Robert Kilwardby, O.P., Studia mediaevalia in honorem R. J. Martin O.P., op. cit. 243-70; New MSS of Kilwardby's Tabulae, etc., Dominican Studies 2 (1949) 38-45; R. W. Hunt, Manuscripts containing the Indexing Symbols of Robert Grosseteste, B.L.R. 4 (1953) 241-4; Chapter Headings of 'De Trinitate' ascribed to Adam Marsh, 5 (1954) 63-8.

[3] MS Oxford, Merton College 256 B, fol. ivb: Itaque frater Robertus de Kilwardbi, qui postea Cantuariensis erat archiepiscopus ac tandem Portuensis cardinalis, ut libri huius lectioni faciliorem redderet, dum in ordine nostro sacre doctrine intendebat, premissa singulorum librorum intentione etiam omnium capitulorum, ab olim brevibus titulis distinctorum, singillatim compendiose continentiam annotavit. Quamquam autem in omnibus libris istis beatus Augustinus studiosis quibuscumque utile ac delectabile exercitium prebeat, tamen nonnunquam interserendo gesta quedam, quorum historie sunt minus note, et quedam poetica aliaque dicta gentilium, precipue in primis decimis libris et in decimo octavo, ut hostes civitatis Dei ex propriis convincat, sepe exercitatis minus in talibus prestat offendiculum continue lectionis. Intentionis nostre est fratrum meorum [sic] frequenti pulsatus instantia hec impedimenta tollere et obscura huius lectoribus reddere clariora.
On this manuscript, see below, p. 88.

[4] MSS Oxford, Bodl. 292, fol. 119va, Merton 256 B, fol. 1ra.

St Augustine's polemic. Trevet provided the equipment needed by students whose education in the classics was too narrow to follow their author: 'Restat igitur ut, ignoratis poësibus, ignoretur Augustinus', as is pointed out in *Philobiblon*.[1] Trevet thought he was adding just one more apparatus to a patristic text.

The argument could be carried further; one wonders how far. Students need their 'pagan background' in order to understand *De civitate Dei*. How better can they acquire it than by reading Seneca's plays and *Ab Urbe condita* and any other text bearing on paganism? This was probably how Trevet reasoned.

Nor did the medieval encyclopaedic tradition distinguish sharply between pagan and Old Testament history. The two were normally put side by side, both manifesting the divine purpose. Another highly placed ecclesiastic and friend of John XXII, Master Hugh of Angoulême, papal nuncio and recipient of many benefices in England, wrote to Trevet begging him to finish his history of pre-Christian times. The Dominican's expertise on Livy, he suggested, would be most helpful to the undertaking. Trevet sent him the completed book.[2] Hence the study of classical authors and ancient history grew naturally out of the teaching of patristic as part of theology and out of the preparation of supplements to encyclopaedias. Enthusiasm did the rest: most teachers at one time or another have enjoyed getting up a fresh subject which proved congenial. Trevet's evidently fascinated him. He mastered classical Latin well enough to paraphrase his text, probably by dogged recourse to grammars and dictionaries. He read widely enough to explain those fables which drove the cardinal to despair, or at least he knew where to find them in reference books. He collected an assortment of histories and chronicles so as to compare them with Livy on the same events. In short,

---

[1] 116.

[2] J. R. Dean and *O.R.*, op. cit. Hugh of Angoulême, a member of the papal household in 1316, was appointed collector of papal taxes in England on July 29, 1323; he returned to Avignon in 1328. John XXII had used him as 'permanent diplomatic representative of the apostolic see in England' and rewarded him with the bishopric of Carpentras, where he ruled 1332-46. He is always given the title of *Magister* in papal letters relating to England. See W. E. Lunt, *Financial Relations of the Papacy with England to 1327* (Cambridge, Mass., 1939) 66, 501, 583, 623-4; *D.H.G.E* 11 (1949) 1113. Trevet's *Historia ab origine mundi ad Christum natum* was 'a Latin translation of a French chronicle' compiled by him 'for an English princess'.

he enabled a reader who did not know that 'Punic' meant 'Carthaginian' to delight in a tale as exciting as any romance about Troy or Alexander.

His work brought home to Trevet the defects in his library equipment. He was indeed a book-hunter, but of an embittered kind. He tried to tap the riches of English monastic libraries, only to find that they were poor in *originalia* and that their librarians were unhelpful. This particular complaint occurs apropos of his preparations for commenting on Scripture.[1] Sighs for the classical texts which he had sought unsuccessfully punctuate his commentary on *De civitate Dei*; he must have run into the same trouble in his pursuit of pagan authors. He had only one poor text of the *Tragedies*, as we have seen, nor could he find Livy's fourth decade. This was only to be expected in view of the rarity of Livy in England. Trevet must have had some difficulty in tracking down the first and third decades.[2] He achieved wonders in the circumstances. His pioneer work did not 'date' as quickly as such works generally do. Petrarch read his Livy-commentary; modern scholars are interested in his text of Livy; his writings had great success in early fourteenth-century Italy and remained popular in the home of the Renaissance for less sophisticated readers.[3] He acted first as high school master and then as 'prep school' master to the later middle ages.

Trevet's study of the *Declamationes* links him up with preaching as well as with teaching. He both commented on the text and moralised it, just as a contemporary French Franciscan moralised Ovid's *Metamorphoses*. The two moralisations helped preachers to brighten their sermons.[4] The *Declamationes* contained exciting material for *exempla*. A lawsuit turning on an heiress's capture by pirates might please better than a fairy story from Ovid. All landholders in the middle ages had some sort of legal experience; hence congregations would contain many amateur or professional lawyers.

[1] J. R. Dean, op. cit. 558.   [2] *F.S.* 205-6.
[3] R. Weiss, Notes on the Popularity of the Writings of Nicholas Trevet, O.P., in Italy during the First Half of the Fourteenth Century, *Dominican Studies* 1 (1948) 261-5; J. R. Dean, op. cit.
  Guis. Billanovich, Petrarch and the Textual Tradition of Livy, *J.W.C.I.* 14 (1951) 162. The writer considers that 'Livy editors should be persuaded to admit Trevet's citations into their apparatus without delay; especially in the case of the still doubtful chapters at the end of the third decade'.
[4] Welter, p. 347, n. 35; p. 363, n. 60.

It seems hard on Trevet to dispose of him as a mere 'fore-
runner' of the classicising group. I do not use the word in
any slighting sense. He did more for pure scholarship than
any member of the group, since he commented on Livy
and the two Senecas while they limited themselves to *De
civitate Dei* and to Fulgentius' *Mythologiae*. He was free from
the fantasy which infected them from Ridewall onwards.
Nevertheless, both Waleys and Ridevall surpassed him as
commentators on *De civitate Dei*, and the classicising biblical
commentary was not his invention but theirs. So 'fore-
runner' must do; he certainly made their activities possible.

The writing of books and commentaries, as distinct from
oral teaching, fell outside a friar's routine duties. He had to
work to order or get his superiors' permission. Questions
of time, expense and policy were involved. The Dominicans
would mobilise the whole Order for a worthwhile purpose;[1]
but they might well hesitate to allot money and man-power
to such marginal pursuits as commentaries on Seneca and
Livy, however widely they stretched their founder's intention. It must therefore be asked what 'outdoor relief'
a classicising friar might hope to get.

---

[1] See for instance A. Dondaine, *Secrétaires de saint Thomas* (Rome, 1956).
The whole Dominican Order was instructed to help Trevet compile his biblical
commentaries at the General Chapter of 1307; see *O.R.*

CHAPTER IV

PATRONAGE

The liberal are almost the most loved of all virtuous characters, since they are useful, and this depends on their giving.

Aristotle, *Nicomachean Ethics*, iv, 1.

TREVET was exceptional in receiving papal patronage;
but Thomas Waleys became chaplain to a Dominican
cardinal and resided at Avignon. The extent of patronage in
England itself is difficult to assess. Neither Edward II nor
Edward III revived the memory of Henry II as a patron
of scholars. Evidence for the bishops' share is necessarily
scrappy; we know that some bishops patronised some
scholars; a few bishops built up personal libraries.[1] Richard
de Bury stands out sharply against this cloudy background.
He befriended scholars and spent money on books, as other
bishops did on a smaller scale. He also advertised the fact,
erecting patronage into an ideal. He both was and saw
himself as being 'magnificent'. The see of Durham rivalled
the archbishopric of York in power and riches and had given
scope to showy occupants ever since the Norman Conquest:
Hugh du Puiset and Anthony Bek had impressed contemporaries by their display; but their ambitions took the form of
plans for enlarging their jurisdiction and privileges.[2] De
Bury had more in common with Clement VI, the most
generous and scholarly of the Avignon popes. 'Magnificence'
turned to learning.

De Bury had both an Oxford and a civil service background. He studied from about 1302 to 1312, though without
incepting.[3] He hoped to continue his studies later in life,
but was too busy. Many and varied employments in the
royal service occupied him both before and after his provision to Durham in 1333. He seems to have preferred to
act as a diplomat and *grand seigneur* and to have disliked

[1] K. Edwards, Bishops and Learning in the Reign of Edward II, *Church Quarterly Review* 138 (1944) 57-86; J. R. Dean, op. cit. 544.
[2] Roger Waltham (see frontispiece) was clerk and chancellor to Anthony Bek; but there is no evidence that the bishop encouraged him in his literary pursuits; *O.R.* 3, 1974.
[3] *O.R.* 1, 323-6.

routine administration; he resigned the posts of treasurer
and chancellor in rapid succession (1334-5); 'he never
leaves an office without getting a pardon for not accounting'.[1]
His own fortune was managed so badly that when he died
in 1345 his executors had to ignore his will and sell his
possessions to pay his debts. The scheme to endow a college
at Oxford to house his library fell through. His magnificent
carelessness has also prevented us from knowing what books
he had; no catalogue of his library has survived. There
are other tantalising problems, connected with his patronage.
We have a list of distinguished *protégés*, but we do not know
what form his encouragement took. Even his authorship of
Philobiblon has been questioned. The book is presented as
autobiographical and yet it is ascribed to Robert Holcot in
some manuscripts. According to others, Holcot 'edited' or
'composed' or 'compiled' it.[2] This has been taken to mean
that Holcot 'devilled' for his patron.[3] Holcot was no young
research student, but a doctor, when the book was finished
in 1344, and he was no hack, but a clever artist. He would
certainly have put something of himself into anything he
touched. We shall never know, therefore, how much of
Philobiblon is Holcot's and how much de Bury's.[4]

[1] N. Denholm-Young, Richard de Bury (1287-1345), *Collected Papers on Mediaeval Subjects* (Oxford, 1946) 1-25.

[2] Dr Altamura has described and listed the manuscripts in his edition 19-39. The most explicit statement on Holcot's authorship comes from a copy of about 1390 from the abbey of Bury St Edmund (now MS London, Brit. Mus. Royal 8.F. xiv, fol. 76): Incipit prologus in philobiblon ricardi dunnelmensis episcopi quem librum composuit Robertus holcote de ordine predicatorum sub nomine dicti episcopi.

[3] Pantin, 144-5. This seems to me to be more likely than Dr Altamura's suggestion that Holcot acted as De Bury's literary executor and published the book after his death: this would hardly account for the tradition that he edited, composed or compiled it in the bishop's name.

[4] I can see no answer to the question. No stylistic argument can be used. *Philobiblon* follows the rules of *dictamen* very strictly; Holcot, as was customary, published his lectures in the conversational Latin in which they were given: there is no reason why he should not have written according to the rules of *dictamen* or got help from one of the bishop's clerks in drafting, when he worked on a literary piece. It would be no use to compare sources and quotations, when we know that whoever drafted *Philobiblon* could have read Holcot on Wisdom, a very popular book, which came out in the early 'thirties. The most striking difference between *Philobiblon* and Holcot's lectures and sermons is that the former contains a number of words from Greek, such as *Theotokos* and the title of the book itself, and that the author recommends a study of languages, regarding Greece as the source of Latin culture. I have not found any interest in Greek in Holcot's writings. Whatever share we allow to Holcot, it is obvious that de Bury must have contributed *some* of the ideas expressed and have outlined his opinions, feelings and experiences to his assistant.

I shall refer to de Bury as the author, since the book is written in his name.

All the same, here is the book, 'finished in our manor
house of Auckland on the 24th day of January, in the year
of Our Lord 1344, the 58th year of our age being exactly
completed and the 11th year of our pontificate drawing to
its close'.[1] *Philobiblon* can be read and enjoyed irrespective
of its authorship. The bishop of Durham defends his
'ecstatic love of books' and his ardour in collecting them
against his critics. The latter accuse him of excessive
curiosity, greed, vanity and intemperate delight in literature.[2] His reply is a counterblast to the anti-intellectual
trend which gained force during the fourteenth century;
he ignored his critics 'as though they were yapping dogs'.
This was to make short work of current axioms:

> 'Qui magis intelligit, magis dubitat, et ille videtur plus
> sapere, qui plus desipit.'[3]

De Bury knew that in spite of man's 'wretched condition'
he can be happy in this vale of tears, at least when poking
about in Paris bookshops. *Philobiblon* describes how the
bishop bought and borrowed books, and accepted them as
bribes when in office, and how he kept a staff of scribes,
correctors, binders, menders and illuminators on his manors.[4]
We hear from another source that five carts were needed to
transport his library.[5] His agents scoured the Continent.
He preferred old books, but did not despise modern authors.
His spies also sent him copies of the latest good sermon
delivered at the Curia and notes of any *quaestio* recently
disputed.[6] The conversation of learned *protégés* in his
household supplemented his books, and he grieved, though
with a touch of paternal pride in his sorrow, when they had
to leave him on promotion to important posts.[7] He also kept
a team of friars at work after he became bishop: they were
set to correcting, expounding, tabulating and compiling.[8]

'The complaint of books' against war, neglect and the bad

[1] xx, 134; roman figures refer to the chapters and arabic to the pages.
[2] 73, 128-9.
[3] *Lotharii Cardinalis (Innocentii III) De miseria humane conditionis*, i, 12, ed. M.
Maccarrone (Verona, 1955) 18. This pessimistic little treatise enjoyed extraordinary popularity all through the thirteenth and fourteenth centuries.
[4] viii, 99-104; xvi, 122; xvii, 127.
[5] *Collectanea* 3, ed. M. Burrows (Oxford Historical Society, 1896) 9.
[6] *Philobiblon* viii, 102.   [7] 101.
[8] 103: De istis ad statum pontificalem assumpti nonnullos habuimus de duobus ordininbus, Predicatorum videlicet et Minorum, nostris adsistentes lateribus
nostreque familie commensales, . . . qui diversorum voluminum correctionibus,
expositionibus, tabulationibus ac compilationibus indefessis studiis incumbebant.

habits of their readers is original and timeless. The passage beginning 'In books I find the dead all but alive' has a sentimental interest for scholars. Nothing else of the same type came out of the schools and courts of early fourteenth-century England. Did *Philobiblon* get its inspiration from de Bury's friends at Avignon? Petrarch and de Bury met there in 1333. Petrarch judged the Englishman favourably: he was 'an eager spirit, not uninstructed, and a surprisingly inquisitive seeker after knowledge from his youth'. Petrarch questioned him as to the whereabouts of 'ultima Thule' and was disappointed that the bishop never fulfilled his promise to answer the query when he returned home to his books.[1] It seems that de Bury was also in touch with Petrarch's correspondent, Raimondo Subirani, an accredited representative of the English government at the Curia.[2]

The problem of early humanist influence on the writing of *Philobiblon* is worth considering, but the reply is elusive. Much can be accounted for by the English background, traditional and contemporary, without our looking for inspiration from abroad. We may begin with the literary form: *Philobiblon* is a letter, addressed to all the faithful. The letter was a favourite humanist genre. On the other hand, de Bury had collected correspondence early in his career. He had a formulary book into which he copied or had copied both 'useful' letters as specimens of diplomatic and 'fine' letters as models of style. The same book contained dictaminal material.[3] Hence the literary parent of *Philobiblon* lay on his desk. *Philobiblon* is written with strict regard to the rules of *dictamen*; de Bury was an expert in the *cursus*. He just adapted the form of a model letter or speech to a treatise on the love of books. Then there is John of Salisbury's vogue to be considered. De Bury bought a volume from St Albans which included the *Policraticus* and *Metalogicon*,[4] not to mention the fact that he quotes the former in his book.[5] John's obvious passion for learning and his personal tone may have affected his reader. The Greekish titles of his works may have inspired de Bury's.

---

[1] *Fam.* iii, 1.
[2] *The Liber epistolaris of Richard d'Aungervyle, Bishop of Durham*, ed N. Denholm-Young (Roxburghe Club, 1950) xii, 245.
[3] ibid.; see the whole introduction.
[4] We know this from a note in the manuscript (now MS London, Brit. Mus. Royal 13.D.iv) saying that it was resold to the abbey; see *O.R.* 1, 325.
[5] *Philobiblon*, xiv, 118.

Some scholars have pointed to the bishop's attitude to the Greek language and Greek culture. De Bury recommends the study of languages, especially of Greek, as an aid to learning, and says that he provided his scholars with Greek and Hebrew grammars. He regrets that the decree of the Council of Vienne of 1312 has not been carried out as it should have been.[1] He displays a little knowledge of Greek himself, sprinkling his book with words such as 'theotokos' for the Virgin. There is independent evidence that he had some instruction in Greek.[2] One passage in particular sounds 'humanist': de Bury points out that Latin culture derived from a Greek original; similarly, the Latin Fathers owed an inestimable debt to the doctors of the Greek Church:

'What would Virgil, the chief poet among the Latins, have achieved, if he had not despoiled Theocritus, Lucretius, and Homer, and had not ploughed with their heifer? What, unless he had read again and again somewhat of Parthenius and Pindar, whose eloquence he could by no means imitate? What could Sallust, Tully, Boethius, Macrobius, Lactantius, Martianus, and in short the whole troop of Latin writers have done, if they had not seen the products of Athens or the volumes of the Greeks? . . . As Rome, watered by the streams of Greece, had earlier brought forth philosophers in the image of the Greeks, in like fashion afterwards it produced doctors of the orthodox faith.'[3]

Echoes of Grosseteste and Roger Bacon! Both had set an example, not wholly forgotten in Oxford, of studying and of urging the study of Greek on others.[4] Bacon had written a Greek grammar. He had argued with passion that knowledge of Greek was vital to Latin scholars. One of his favourite arguments was precisely that Latin culture de-

[1] x, 110-11.
[2] Walter Burley, dedicating his translation of the *Ethics* and *Politics* to de Bury, says that the latter 'being *sufficienter in isto ydiomate instructus*, had helped him'; see N. Denholm-Young, *Collected Papers on Mediaeval Subjects* (Oxford, 1946) 18.
[3] *Philobiblon*, x, 110: Quid fecisset Vergilius, Latinorum poëta precipuus, si Theocritum, Lucretium et Homerum minime spoliasset et in eorum vitula non arasset? quid nisi Parthenium Pindarumque, cuius eloquentiam nullo modo potuit imitari, aliquatenus lectitasset? Quid Sallustius, Tullius, Boëtius, Macrobius, Lactantius, Martianus, immo tota cohors generaliter Latinorum, si Athenarum studia vel Grecorum volumina non vidissent? . . . Cuius rivulis Roma rigata, sicut prius generavit philosophos ad Grecorum effigiem, pari forma postea protulit orthodoxe fidei tractatores.
I have used E. C. Thomas's translation (London, 1902) 74-5.
[4] Dr Denholm-Young points this out, op. cit. 18.

rived from Greece; he instanced grammar, philosophy, theology, medicine and law.[1] Bacon's thesis, at first or second hand, could easily lie behind the thought of *Philobiblon*. De Bury has grafted it on to the current theory of *translatio studii*, which he mentions in the book. Learning had passed from the orient to Greece, thence to Rome, thence to Paris, and thence (if one were English) to Oxford;[2] next time it would move to barbarous peoples, far to the West.[3]

Something remains unaccounted for, nevertheless. Grosseteste and Bacon were not much interested in historians and poets. They could not have suggested the names of Theocritus, Lucretius and Pindar. The careful chronology of the list of Latin writers who were indebted to the Greeks, with only Boethius out of order, makes a medievalist stop to reread this passage in *Philobiblon*. The author goes on to make a fascinating comparison between the Greek and Latin genius. Here, perhaps, we have a reminiscence of some literary talk among scholars at Avignon or perhaps some remark may have set a train of thought going.

Original pieces of this kind shine out from the commonplaces. The sub-structure of *Philobiblon* is conventional enough. Criticism of careless and ignorant prelates and clergy and complaints that religious disgrace their respective founders belong to the moralists' stock-in-trade. De Bury was as deeply 'clerical' as any medieval bishop could be.

---

[1] *Compendium studii*, viii, ed. Brewer (Rolls Series) 646-8; *Operis maioris pars septima seu moralis philosophia* ii, 2, ed. E. Massa (Turin, 1954) 42: Et certum est quod Latini a Grecis habuerunt iura et leges, scilicet a libris Aristotelis ac Theophrasti, eius successoris, preter leges duodecim tabularum, quas primo transtulerunt de legibus Solonis Athenensis.

[2] ix, 108: Minerva mirabilis nationes hominum circuire videtur, . . . Indos, Babylonios, Egyptios atque Grecos, Arabes et Latinos eam pertransisse iam cernimus. Iam Athenas deseruit, iam a Roma recessit, iam Parisius preterivit, iam ad Britanniam, insularum insignissimam, quin potius microcosmum, accessit feliciter, ut se Grecis et barbaris debitricem ostendat.

[3] An anonymous poem of about 1356-7 on the riots between town and gown at Oxford on St Scholastica's day makes the University complain that she has 'cast aside, one after the other, for their shortcomings, the great empires of the ancient world, Assyrians, Medes, Persians, Greeks and Romans, and then the Gauls and Germans. She came to England and long flourished at Oxford, but now sees that she is despised:

> O si respiciam plagas occiduas,
> Et sic preficiam gentes residuas;
> He forsan salient in vires strenuas,
> Ad tempus capient laudes precipuas.

Printed in *Collectanea* 3 (Oxford Historical Society, 1896) 177-8.

Laymen he thought unworthy to share in book-learning or even to handle precious parchment. Books are for the clergy, who should love them for the sake of their privilege; ability to read the Psalter saves one from the jurisdiction of secular courts. He dwells on the career value of literacy and learning and on their function in refuting heretics.[1] He defends profane studies with the age-old argument that we need them as an instrument for the understanding of Scripture. The argument is pushed a little further to include patristic with Scripture: how can we read the Fathers intelligently without knowing the poets whom they quote so often?[2] De Bury may have had contemporary commentaries on *De civitate Dei* in mind at this point.

His method of presenting his case is wholly traditional. He proceeds by reason and persuasion. The former is backed by argument, the latter by *exempla*. The sayings and tales from antiquity might have been drawn from any contemporary manual. We move within the framework of Vincent's *Speculum maius*. De Bury's passion only stopped short of law books.[3]

Either he or Holcot or the two jointly, as seems most probable, produced a basically conventional work which yet had a personal touch and a rare sparkle. The original part of the argument may derive from John of Salisbury, Grosseteste, Bacon, talk at Avignon and the bishop's own 'star', his private, compelling demon: 'We have, under the aspect of Mercury, entertained a blameless pleasure in books, which under the rule of right reason, over which no stars are dominant, we have ordered to the glory of God's supreme Majesty.'[4] Aristotle, not the dry Aristotle of our text-books, but the living gentleman scholar, the anti-puritan, has inspired *Philobiblon* from first to last. De Bury's veneration for him breathes through the book. The magnificent patron of the bishop's dream is described in the *Ethics*.[5]

Philobiblon is informative on the background of the

---

[1] iv, 84-9, 1, 77, 79, viii, 101.   [2] xiii, 115-16.   [3] xi, 112-13.

[4] xviii: . . . cecidit circa libros nostre mercurialis species voluptatis honeste, quam ex recte rationis arbitrio, cuius nulla sidera dominantur imperio, in honorem ordinavimus maiestatis supreme. . . .

[5] On meanings ascribed to *magnificentia* in the medieval schools and the effect of the *Ethics*, see R. A. Gautier, *Magnanimité. L'Idéale de la grandeur dans la philosophie païenne et dans la théologie chrétienne* (Paris 1951). St Thomas, after some hesitation, chose the aristotelian definition of magnificence, 'munificence dans les dépenses', in preference to the Abelardian, 'heureux achèvement des grandes choses'; see ibid., 312.

classicising friars. The Mendicants come in for their share of reproach with the other clergy,[1] but when the bishop describes his experiences as a book-hunter, he changes his tune. The monks who sold or gave him books brought them out of mouldy cupboards in shocking condition;[2] evidently a rich bishop had better luck with them than poor Trevet. The Mendicants, on the contrary, entered into the spirit of the chase, putting the resources of their international Orders at his disposal. All gave him valuable help; the Friars Preacher, in particular, were useful and generous.[3] This smacks of Holcot, but it also faithfully reflects the distribution of the classicising group; there were five Dominicans as against two Franciscans; all were bibliophiles. Another significant fact to emerge is de Bury's pride in Oxford. Paris struck him as sleepy and conservative from an academic point of view. Oxford with its new logic was forging ahead.[4] The humanist opposition of literary studies to scholasticism did not enter into his mind. The medieval encyclopaedic tradition had room enough for all; he did not see why any studies should be mutually exclusive.

Two secular scholars patronised by de Bury contributed to classical studies, though their fame rests on other achievements. Thomas Bradwardine became a household word for his views on predestination; he was also a great mathematician. Bradwardine brings numerous quotations from the Latin classics into his theological *De causa Dei*. He may also, it has been suggested, have been responsible for the more humane character of the books acquired by his college of

---

[1] *Philobiblon* vi. De Bury's account of the friars' teaching of Scripture will be discussed below, pp. 107-8 and 156.

[2] viii, 99-100.

[3] 101-3. He says of the Dominicans: Sane quamvis omnium religiosorum communicatione multiplici plurimorum operum copiam tam novorum quam veterum assecuti fuerimus, Predicatores tamen extollimus merito speciali preconio in hac parte, quod eos pre cunctis religiosis suorum sine invidia gratissime communicativos invenimus, ac divina quadam liberalitate perfusos sapientie luminose probavimus non avaros sed idoneos possessores.

[4] 102: . . . si parisiensis soliditas, que plus antiquitati discende quam veritati subtiliter producende iam studet, si anglicana perspicacitas, que antiquis perfusa luminaribus novos semper radios veritatis emittit, ...

ix, 107: . . . parisiense palladium nostris mestis temporibus cernimus iam obscuratum. . . . Quiescit ibidem iam calamus omnis scribe, nec librorum generatio propagatur ulterius, nec est qui'incipiat novus auctor haberi'. Involvunt sententias sermonibus imperitis et omnis logice proprietate privantur; nisi quod anglicanas subtilitates, quibus palam detrahunt, vigiliis furtivis addiscunt.

The *anglicane subtilitates* in this context can only refer to Oxford logic.

Merton in the twenty years or so after his death (1349), by his influence on younger scholars.[1] Walter Burley, better known as a philosopher and especially as a commentator on Aristotle, wrote a treatise called *De vita et moribus philosophorum*. It consists of biographies of the leading sages of ancient times, with excerpts from their writings and sayings. He drew on John of Wales and Vincent of Beauvais, but added new material. A recent study of the manuscripts has proved that Burley wrote his treatise on the Continent; he taught at Toulouse and Bologna and spent some time at Avignon. *De vita et moribus philosophorum* quickly became a classic in France and Italy, but was much less read in England.[2]

Summing up the results of these two chapters, one can say that Englishmen played a surprisingly large part in popularising a knowledge and understanding of the Latin classics. John of Wales, Nicholas Trevet and Walter Burley are international figures. Richard de Bury or Robert Holcot for him wrote a book which is still read for pleasure on love of books and patronage of scholars. It was not at all an insular movement. John of Wales and Walter Burley both taught abroad as well as at Oxford. A pope and a cardinal commissioned works from Trevet. De Bury not only had his symbolic meeting with Petrarch at Avignon, but toured the Continent as a royal servant and diplomat. Clerical Europe in the late thirteenth and early fourteenth centuries was still a family with its centre at the Curia. The Hundred Years War, especially in its later stages, and the Great Schism made contacts more difficult. The classicising group of friars were among the last members of a united, if quarrelsome, household.

---

[1] On Bradwardine see *O.R.* 1, 244-6; on Merton Library see Powicke, 25, 126-61. The books in question are a Marco Polo and a treatise on the East, a Palladius, a Caesar (*De bello gallico*), Seneca's *Quaestiones naturales*, and Trevet and Waleys on *De civitate Dei*. The history and geography make a change from the strictly professional scholastic works which formed the bulk of the collection up to about 1350. See also *Archives* 25 (1958) 295-329.

[2] On Walter Burley, see *O.R.* 1, 312-13; J. O. Stigall, The Manuscript Tradition of the *De vita et moribus philosophorum* of Walter Burley, *Medievalia et Humanistica* 11 (1957) 44-57; J. N. Hough, Plautus, Student of Cicero, and Walter Burley, ibid. 58-68.

CHAPTER V

THOMAS WALEYS

... Crispo Sallustio, e seco a mano a mano
un che già l'ebbe a schifo e l'vide torto:
ciò è l'gran Tito Livio padovano.

Petrarch, *Triumphus Fame*, iii, 40-2.

I.—LIFE

THOMAS Waleys had the most dramatic career of the classicising group.[1] He entered the Dominican Order when he was fifteen or sixteen years old and studied at the Oxford Blackfriars. The long dispute between the friars and the university interrupted his academic exercises, preventing him for three years from reading the *Sentences* as a bachelor and proceeding to the master's degree. The parties reached a *modus vivendi* in 1314 and a final settlement in 1320. Both sides appealed to the pope.[2] Waleys, still a bachelor, got 'letters of commendation from the king on going to the Roman Curia' on April 4, 1318, and again in the same year on November 28. He must have been appointed to serve on a delegation on behalf of his Order in connexion with the appeal. On April 27, 1318 he was presented with other Friars Preacher to the bishop of Lincoln and licensed to hear confessions in the diocese. Presumably he went to the Curia at Avignon later in the year. Nicholas Trevet's admirer, the old Dominican cardinal, Nicholas of Prato (d. 1321), was still dean of the Sacred College in 1318: Waleys perhaps made his first contacts with patrons of classical learning when on his delegation. The settlement enabled him to read the *Sentences*, incept and teach as regent master. As he was still a bachelor in 1318 his regency would fall at least two years later, probably about 1321. Later on in his life, when he had to defend his orthodoxy, Waleys stated that he taught as master for as

---

[1] *Le procès*; B. Smalley, Thomas Waleys O.P., *Arch. FF. Praed.* 24 (1954) 50-57; *O.R.* 3, 1961-2. Mr Emden's discovery of the letters of commendation, calling Waleys B.Th. in 1318, makes it necessary to revise the date of his regency, which I put tentatively about 1317 in my paper.

[2] *Rashdall's Medieval Universities*, ed. F. M. Powicke and A. B. Emden 3 (Oxford, 1936) 72-4.

long as he wished; he resigned his chair freely to a pupil of his, as the custom was, to the regret of many, both masters and scholars, who would have liked him to hold it longer. Short regencies were the rule in the Dominican Order. Moreover a long queue must have formed in consequence of the stoppage of official university teaching at Blackfriars during the quarrel. Hence Waleys would probably have been rationed to one or two years' tenure of his chair.

His superiors then assigned him to a lectorship at the Dominican *studium* at Bologna. It was customary to post an English friar to the important Italian teaching centre, and Waleys, having visited Avignon, must have seemed an obvious choice. We do not know in what year he went out. He attended a council there in 1326-7 and was replaced as lector by another English friar at the General Chapter of 1331. The next post he held was a chaplaincy to the Dominican cardinal, Matteo Orsini. He was in the cardinal's household at Avignon at the beginning of January 1333; hence he must have held his chaplaincy for a little over a year, from late in 1331 to the New Year of 1333. The years at Bologna and in Orsini's household were the most fruitful of his life. He showed learning enough at Bologna to draw to himself the notice of those who interested themselves in classical studies. We have seen already that these were in vogue at Avignon. Cardinal Orsini, a student in canon law in his secular days, a doctor of theology in the Order, and a truly magnificent benefactor, may have picked him out as a promising subject.[1]

Waleys seemed to have his foot on the ladder, but now came his tragedy. The years of his lectorship at Bologna had coincided with a stormy period in papal politics. John XXII antagonised the Franciscans by his decision against their doctrine on apostolic poverty. The Order split: an orthodox party accepted the papal ruling, though disgustedly; a dissident group refused; its members went over to the

[1] Q.E., 1, 596. Matteo Orsini was created cardinal in December 1327, after holding the post of lector of the sacred palace (the *studium* in the papal household) for a short time, and other preferments. He died on August 18, 1340. His benefactions to his Order earned him a recommendation to its prayers in all the General Chapters up to the eighteenth century; see *Arch. FF. Praed.* 10 (1940) 341, 369; 17 (1947) 234n; 22 (1952) 200; 26 (1956) 312. On the chapel he built at Santa Maria sopra Minerva, see ibid. 26, 343n. On his academic career before 1326, see ibid. 8 (1938) 28-35. Unfortunately we have no catalogue of his books and Fr Th. Kaeppeli tells me that they are not mentioned in his unpublished will.

emperor, Louis of Bavaria, and his anti-pope. The pope's enemies, religious and political, combined against him in 1328. The Dominicans generally supported him on the doctrinal question. Moreover he had befriended their Order, canonising St Thomas and showing special favour to the Oxford Friars Preacher in their conflict with the university. It was natural, therefore, that Waleys should have worked actively for the papal cause: Bologna was the headquarters of the papal party in northern Italy. He tells us himself that he preached at Bologna and Arezzo against the heresy of the Friars Minor on the poverty of Christ. He must have made many enemies before ever he came to Avignon.

Then John XXII raised a new storm by publicly teaching a disputable thesis on the nature of the beatific vision. He explained that he propounded it as a personal view and not *ex cathedra*; he withdrew it on his deathbed and his successor pronounced against it officially. At the time, however, it caused heated discussion and ill feeling. Those theologians who argued for the pope's thesis, sincere as they may have been, incurred the reproach of 'flattery'. The Orders disagreed among themselves. On the whole, unfortunately for Waleys, positions tended to be reversed, so that John found more acceptance for his view among the orthodox party of the Franciscans than among his former allies, the Dominicans. It happened that the Franciscans staffed the Inquisition at Avignon. Waleys believed that the pope's view was heretical. He declared as much in a sermon preached at Avignon on January 3, 1333. While refraining from a personal attack on the pope, he denounced his supporters in violent terms.[1] Waleys said afterwards that he had not meant to speak so strongly, but that he got carried away. He was impulsive and imprudent. His language about 'flatterers' must have cut the Friars Minor to the quick. Further, he misjudged the pope's character if he relied on past friendship to protect him. John XXII was the last man to forgive a thrust at himself in the person of his adherents.

Waleys received a summons to answer charges of heresy. The inquisitors ignored his views on the beatific vision, since this doctrine awaited definition, and impugned other heads

---

[1] The sermon is printed in *Le procès* 93-108, with all the documents relating to the case.

of his teaching. He appealed from the Inquisition to the apostolic see and was transferred from the inquisitors' to the papal prison. Here he remained while his case dragged on. The records of his interrogation suggest that Waleys had a quick temper but a rather slow-moving mind, an unlucky combination in the circumstances. Nothing definite was proved against him, but John's successor, Benedict XII, had not released him by August, 1338. He probably owed his freedom to the next pope, Clement VI, who was elected in 1342. Clement, as archbishop of Rouen, had sat on the commission appointed by John XXII to examine the charges. He took a more favourable view than the other members and tried to soften the verdict. The new pope was also a famous doctor of theology, liberal, generous, and well disposed to the Dominicans. The case had created a stir in Christendom. The king of France had written to John XXII to express interest and concern.[1] The Order would not forget its doctor and would try again at an opportune moment. Waleys spent his last years free in England.

His last work, a treatise on preaching,[2] can be dated soon after his release, say a few years after 1342. It is dedicated to Teobaldo Orsini, archbishop of Palermo (1336-50), a cousin of Waleys' former protector, Cardinal Matteo, who had died in 1340; Waleys had reason to be grateful to the family. The treatise, in spite of its dedication, envisages a public of English clergy. Waleys makes no reference to his troubles and seems to have come through with his spirit unbroken.

Then we have petitions from Waleys to Pope Clement VI, asking for benefices for two friends. The pope granted both. The first petition, answered in the autumn of 1348, asks for provision for a Spanish clerk, whom Waleys may have known at Avignon. The second, answered in the spring of 1349, asks that a Master Lambert of Poulshot may be provided to the church of Bishopstone in Salisbury diocese. Waleys gives as his reason that he is 'broken with age and gravely stricken with paralysis'. It sounds like a stroke. He therefore pleads for a benefice for his special friend, on whom he depends above all others. Master Lambert cares for him

---

[1] For an account of the inside of a papal prison about 1350, see J. Bignami-Odier, *Études sur Jean de Roquetaillade* (Paris, 1952) 20-3.

[2] Charland, 307-403; B. Smalley, op. cit. 52-3. The proof that Waleys wrote for English clergy is that he followed the Sarum Use and did not expect them to know about Italian customs in preaching.

freely and without any civil obligation. The petition implies that Waleys is living near his friend, and hence that he is at Oxford or perhaps somewhere in Wiltshire: Lambert of Poulshot, rector of Donhead St Mary in Wiltshire, got leave of absence to study from the bishop of Salisbury on various occasions between October 31, 1342 and November 10, 1353. He was certainly at Oxford in 1352 and probably off and on from the autumn of 1342. His title of *Magister* signifies that he had already qualified in arts; he probably aimed at a higher degree in theology or canon law.[1] It seems surprising at first sight that Waleys, a friar, should have relied on a secular clerk to procure him the bare means of life; but 1348-9 was the year of the Plague, which hit convents particularly hard. Waleys either failed to survive it or else lingered on for a few years afterwards, leaving no trace in the records.

II.—BIBLICAL COMMENTARIES

Waleys left *Moralitates* on a number of Old Testament books, Exodus to Ruth inclusive, Ecclesiastes and Isaias, and a much longer commentary on part of the Psalter. The *Moralitates*, as we have them, represent excerpts from notes of his teaching. They form a set, which sometimes appears complete in the manuscripts and may be combined with other works of a similar type. They have never been printed.[2] It is not certain whether the lectures lying behind the *Moralitates* were given at Oxford or Bologna. Waleys may have taken his Oxford notes abroad with him and used them again, or he may have begun the lectures at Oxford and finished them at Bologna.[3] If he did finish the whole

---

[1] B. Smalley, op. cit. 53-5, *O.R.* 3, 1508-9.

[2] The *Moralitates* represent excerpts from full commentaries, which contained both literal and moral exposition. Some exist in two *reportationes*. See the description and analysis of manuscripts in B. Smalley, op. cit. 58-66; Stegmüller, no. 8237 (correct Maz. 193 to 183)-8243, 1; 8249-51. There is still room for study of the manuscript tradition.

[3] The evidence is inconclusive. In the first place, the *Moralitates*, in whole or in part, survive in nine MSS in England, of English provenance; six copies are recorded in English libraries, which are now lost. There are only five on the Continent and one or two recorded. It is suggestive that the number of copies of the Psalter-commentary, which we know to have originated at Bologna, are reversed; there are nine on the Continent and five in England. On the other hand, Waleys localises an *exemplum* 'in Anglia' in his *Moralitates* on Josue, which might imply that he was lecturing in Italy; in Oxford the country would have been taken for granted, especially as he says that he heard it himself; see below, 82. An argument for his having begun them at Oxford and finished

course at Oxford (which would be surprising in a short regency) he must have brought a copy to Italy, since it circulated there very early: the prior of the Dominican convent at Treviso left Waleys' '*Moralitates* on Exodus and many other books of the Bible' to the convent in a will dated May 22, 1347.[1] The Psalter-commentary came after the *Moralitates*, wherever they were given, and certainly originated as a lecture course at Bologna.[2] It makes a fat volume even though it breaks off unfinished on Ps. xxxviii, 2. The Psalter-commentary got into print and ran into three early editions.[3]

English preachers used both the *Moralitates* and the Psalter-commentary. John Sheppey, the Benedictine prior of Rochester, later bishop of Rochester (1352-60), an Oxford graduate in theology who had incepted in 1332, quoted the *Moralitates* on Numbers in a sermon preached in 1343.[4] An *exemplum* from the Psalter-commentary, vouched for by Waleys as paralleled in his own experience, reappears in *Gesta romanorum*[5] and again, ascribed to Waleys, in a sermon

---

them at Bologna would be that lectures covering so many biblical books could hardly have been compressed into one tenure of a chair. It seems more likely that they would be spread over two. I have used two Oxford MSS for purposes of quotation, New College 30 (late-fourteenth century) and Bodl. Laud. misc. 345 (late-fourteenth or early-fifteenth century).

[1] C. Grimaldi, Due inventari domenicani del secolo xiv tratti dall' Archivio di S. Nicolò di Treviso presso l'Archivio di Stato in Venezia, *Nuovo archivio veneto* (R. Deputazione veneta di storia patria) 1918, 147.

[2] This is proved by the explicit of MS Rome, Bible. apost., Vat. lat. 5888, fol. 80ra: Expliciunt moralitates lecture facte in Bononia per magistrum Thomam anglicum dum legeret ibidem.

[3] London, 1481, Rome and Venice, 1611. For a list of MSS see B. Smalley, 66-9; Stegmüller, no. 8245-7. MS Vat. lat. 5888 contains the moral exposition only and in a *reportatio*; other copies and the printed editions give a literal and moral exposition in a second, fuller *reportatio* or Waleys' own notes. I have used the copy in MS Oxford, Exeter College 39, a fourteenth-century copy written in England. Since the volume is not foliated, I refer to the *locus*. The edition made in London, 1481, is very difficult to use, since the psalms are not numbered and the text is not underlined.

[4] MS New College 92, fol. 142v. The quotation has been added to the sermon in the margin in Sheppey's hand: 'et nota in Waleys, cap. 12 . . .' . The quotation (from Bartholomeus Anglicus *via* Waleys) can be verified exactly from Waleys on Numbers, MS New College 30, fol. 29. The sermon can be dated 1343, but Sheppey may have made the addition later. Mr G. Mifsud kindly allows me to quote this information from his unpublished Oxford B. Litt. thesis, *John Sheppey, Bishop of Rochester, as Preacher and Collector of Sermons* (submitted in 1953). See also *O.R.* 3, 1683.

[5] On Ps. xi, 5 Waleys tells a story of a lunatic who believed himself to be headless. A doctor cured him by making him wear a heavy leaden cap. Waleys himself had seen a man who firmly maintained that he lacked a heart and other internal organs. See Herbert, 220.

preached by the Franciscan friar Nicholas Philip, 1431-36.[1]
John Lathbury quotes Waleys on the Psalter three times in
his *Alphabetum morale*, a collection of sermons and material
for sermons.[2]

A personality shows through all these commentaries. The
lecturer has the same combative, self-assertive spirit as the
Avignon preacher. He says 'ego dico' and 'audeo dicere',
even when he is going to make an incontrovertible point.
On the other hand, he shows the underlying good sense
and power of observation of the older Waleys, who wrote
the *Ars praedicandi*. Thus he criticises current abuses in as
measured a way as your professional moralist could be
expected to do. Instead of joining in the current attack on
papal provisions, he merely complains of graft in the filling
of vacancies; appointments become a matter of luck rather
than merit.[3] The sinner who rouses him most to wrath is
the deceitful scribe. We hear a cry from the heart of a
scholar as Waleys draws a lesson from the need to control
one's copy. His text is *Inspice, et fac secundum exemplar* (Exod.
xxv. 40):

> 'The scribe is given an exemplar in order that he may trans-
> fer what is in it to another parchment or book without adding
> or subtracting anything, since scribes are not commonly
> expert enough to make changes except by mistake. Neverthe-
> less, the deceitful scribe, being paid according to the number
> of lines or stops in his exemplar, wilfully skips things, hoping
> that his trick will not be found out until after he has got his
> pay. Hence it often happens that he deserves no pay, but a
> penalty instead, because the parchment he wrote on is quite
> wasted. The prudent man, therefore, will inspect the work
> carefully before returning it to the scribe (for the next instal-
> ment), in case he should be cheated.'[4]

Waleys was observant enough to pounce upon a new
invention as a subject for moralisation. Eyeglasses came
into common use in the early fourteenth century and

---

[1] MS Oxford, Bodl. lat. th. d. 1, fol. 117; Welter, 415-16. Philip refers to
Waleys by name.
[2] MS London, Brit. Mus. Royal 11. A. xiii, fol. 24v: Item caritas est in
tunica Christi inconsutili, secundum quod recitat Wallensis super vi ps., versus
7 ... (a legend about Pontius Pilate follows); fol. 47v: Auctor de naturis rerum,
ut recitat Wallensis super illud psalmi *Insidiatur ut rapiat pauperem* etc dicit quod
vulpis primo ludit cum lepore, deinde dentibus eum temptat, sed in fine rapit
et mordet; fol. 168: Wallensis super illud psalmi *In laqueo isto*. . . .
Quoted verbally from Waleys on Ps. vi, 7; ix, 32 and ix, 16.
[3] B. Smalley, op. cit., 71-3.   [4] See appendix i, p. 308.

G

tradition has connected the discovery with certain Italian Dominicans.[1] Waleys mentions the eyeglass which has enabled old men to read what they otherwise could not by enlarging the letters, 'at least as they appear to the reader'.[2]

One of his tales of rural life would have delighted the heart of the economic historian W. Ashley, since it illustrates his thesis that the English peasant had a strong preference for coarser types of bread: according to Ashley, white flour replaced bean, rye and barley only in consequence of the industrial revolution.[3] Waleys had heard that a certain bishop wanted to construct a fishpond on one of his manors in England. He had many peasants set to work on it and ordered that they should be provided with good wheat and good foods, hoping to strengthen them and hearten them to work harder. It had quite the opposite effect. After three or four days they began to work slackly and slowly. When the bishop rated one of the peasants, he objected that he had no bread and therefore was unable to work. On the bishop's saying that he had ordered his steward to give them wheaten bread every day, the peasant answered: 'That bread's not for the likes of us; I don't call it bread. Let bean bread be given us and then we shall be able to work.' And so they did, when the wheaten bread was withdrawn from them.[4]

The main interest of Waleys' lectures is that they represent a development in technique. A tendency showed itself in the early fourteenth century to give more space to *exempla* and to moralised items of natural science. Commentators married the *exempla* collection to the biblical commentary, using their text as a thread on which to string non-biblical stories. They offered their hearers and readers an *exempla* collection arranged in relation to the biblical text. Waleys was one of the first systematisers of this new kind of lecture course.[5]

The method was traditional and lay ready to hand.

---

[1] A. C. Crombie, *Robert Grosseteste and the Origins of Modern Experimental Science* (Oxford, 1953) 151.
[2] On Ps. xiii, 3: Non potuerunt (senes) scripturam legere, unde indigerent ad legendum oculo vitreo, quia enim vitrum litteram facit grossiorem saltem aspectui legentis; ideo mediante vitro legit quod aliter non possit.
[3] *The Bread of our Forefathers* (Oxford, 1928) 164-5.
[4] See appendix i, p. 309.
[5] He may have imitated Jacques de Lausanne; see below, p. 248.

St Gregory the Great had used it especially in his *Moralia* on Job. He praised the custom of digression where it would satisfy the hearers' spiritual needs. The lecturer on Scripture should turn aside from his main text to expound a second text, suggested by the first. St Gregory assumed that lecturers would choose, as he did, the second text from the Bible by association of word or idea. It did not occur to him that the choice might fall on a quotation from some secular book.[1] Commentators of the thirteenth and fourteenth centuries followed the tradition of digressing, but they took the second text from a non-biblical source, often pagan, with increasing frequency. Waleys systematised. Suppose that his text of the Bible refers to a *bird*; he turns to the *Historia animalium* of Aristotle or to some encyclopaedia, and moralises what he finds about the nature and habits of birds. Or he goes to an ancient historian. Two stories from Frontinus' *Strategematon* illustrate the text *as a bird fleeing away, . . . so shall the daughters of Moab be* (Isa. xvi, 2). Frontinus tells of two generals who detected ambushes by noting the flight of birds from the spot where the enemy lay hidden. Waleys moralises the story to make the birds signify holy men, who flee from the ambush set by the world. As the birds' flight warned the generals, so Christians must learn from example to beware of worldly temptations. He supports his lesson by quoting another scriptural text: *And they shall fly away like a bird out of Egypt* (Os. xi, 11).[2] *Egypt* always signified the world, and the Israelites good Christians who fled from its dangers. Waleys has sandwiched Frontinus between two texts from Old Testament Prophets, a savoury morsel between two slices of bread: it was neatly done.

His systematic procedure opened up new possibilities. The lecturer on Scripture from now onwards could indulge his secular interests and perform his statutory duties at one and the same time. A friar doctor who enjoyed reading the classics or indeed any other sort of secular literature no longer needed any special grace from his superiors. It ceased to be necessary to take time off from routine teaching. One could prepare one's lectures and pursue *paganica studia* concurrently. Waleys had not found an ideal solution; no compromise can ever be that. The type of lectures that he favoured resulted in a quaint mixture of sacred and profane; on the other hand, it stimulated browsing and book-hunting.

[1] See *Study of the Bible*, 33-4.   [2] See appendix i, p. 309.

Lecturers prided themselves on their many and varied quotations. The records of their teaching suggest some sort of game of scoring off one's colleagues by quoting more and rarer secular authors than the other man.

Waleys could hardly have foreseen the full consequences of his invention. He was no Machiavellian schemer. His *exempla* collection disguised as a biblical commentary left the lecturer free to choose whatever secular literature he liked. Hence it did not lead to the classicising type inevitably. The content of Waleys' lectures has even more importance than their form because he chose the classics as the source for his *exempla*. Here again he blundered along, beginning with a preference for natural history and marvels and gradually developing a taste for ancient history and mythology. The change is perceptible in the course of his *Moralitates* and Psalter-commentary.

The *Moralitates* at first relies mainly on the lore of encyclopaedias or on such books as St Albert's *De animalibus*, Pliny's *Historia naturalis* and Solinus' *De mirabilibus mundi*. Waleys varies them with an occasional story from Valerius Maximus or Vegetius. Both were well-known authors, proving no special interest in the classics on his part. We also find a reference (inexact) to *Quintus Curtius de Alexandro Magno*,[1] a tale from an *antiqua gesta romanorum* and others from Eusebius and *De civitate Dei*. None of them promises anything unusual. The *Moralitates* on Isaias marks a change. Waleys tells stories from Frontinus' *Strategematon* on Isa. xvi, 2 and goes on to quote a dozen more passages from it within the space of nine leaves.[2] He quotes twice from Justinus' abridgment of Pompeius Trogus,[3] as well as continuing to use his old favourite, Valerius Maximus. Ancient history had begun to attract him. Was it because he had just come to Italy?

The Friars Preacher of Bologna had collected a first-class library by 1386, the *terminus ad quem* of their earliest surviving

---

[1] MS New College 30, fol. 63: Unde narrat Quintus Curtius de Alexandro Magno quod periculosissima quandoque ingrediebatur et ubicumque fortissimos hostes acerrime conspexisset, eo se semper ingerebat periculum, quia suum non militum valebat.

See Quintus Curtius Rufus, *Historia Alexandri Magni* ix, 4: Rex non sua sed militum sollicitudine anxius . . .

[2] MS New College 30, foll. 8, 10v-19. Frontinus appears in a number of medieval English library catalogues, *F.S.* 210.

[3] MS New College 30, foll. 11, 16v. This book, too, was well represented in medieval England; *F.S.* 206.

catalogue; and there were others in the neighbourhood.[1] We do not know how these libraries were built up, but it may be supposed that Waleys found a good nucleus when he arrived at the *studium*. *Introduxit me rex in cellario suo*; Waleys got drunk on books. Quotations of writers from Aristotle to Marco Polo rolled off his tongue: 'What next?' his pupils must have wondered. A full list of authors quoted in his Psalter-commentary would be out of place here. It will suffice to give samples indicating his tastes and his library facilities. He preferred the Fathers to medieval theologians and shows a particular affection for St Ambrose,[2] anticipating humanist tastes in this. He had the Pseudo-Aristotelian *Oeconomica*, translated in the second half of the thirteenth century,[3] as well as the better-known works of Aristotle and Pseudo-Aristotle available at the time, also Proclus' *De decem dubitationibus circa providentiam*, translated in 1280.[4] His shelf of medieval encyclopaedias contained not only *Policraticus* and Vincent's *Speculum*, but Walter Burley's *De vita et moribus philosophorum*.[5] Burley's book circulated earlier and more widely on the Continent, especially in Italy, than it did in England.[6] This makes Waleys' use of it significant, confirming one's impression that he found new riches at Bologna: Burley supplied him with the latest *compendium* of lore

[1] M.-H. Laurent, Fabio Vigilii et les bibliothèques de Bologne au début du XVIe siècle, *Studi e testi* 105 (1943).
[2] Waleys quotes St Ambrose on the Hexaemeron, on St Luke, on Ps. cxxxviii, and the *Apologia prophetiae David, De bono mortis, De fide, De Iacob et vita beata, De Ioseph, De Isaac, De officiis, De virginibus, De viduis, Epistula ad Simplicianum,* and Pseudo-Ambrose, *De moribus brachmanorum* and *De Salomone.* All these he could have read in the Dominican library at Bologna. The *De Salomone* is listed with the ascription to Ambrose in the pre-1386 catalogue; see M.-H. Laurent, op. cit. 83.
[3] He quotes *Oecon.* i, 2 on Ps. xvii, 5 and 1, 3 on Ps. xxx, 4; see *Aristoteles latinus*, ed. G. Lacombe (Rome, 1939) 75.
[4] He quotes stories of three philosophers who restrained their anger on Ps. ii, 12 and a passage explaining the moral value of punishment on Ps. ix, 25; both sets of quotations come from *De decem dubitationibus* viii. Waleys quotes it as *Proclus, Liber de providentia* which is the title of another minor work of Proclus. He probably read the two works in the same volume where, if they were copied consecutively, he may have taken them as one. On the translation and diffusion of Proclus, see M. de Wulf, *Histoire de la philosophie médiévale* 2 (Louvain, 1936) 48.
[5] On Ps. xxx, 7: Narratur in libro de vita philosophorum quod Solon (MS Salomon), unus de septem sapientibus . . . Waleys tells how Solon left Athens when the city became subject to tyrants from Burley, ed. H. Knüst (Tübingen, 1886) 13-14. This is certainly taken from Burley; the story does not appear in a more popular compendium, the *De dictis philosophorum* (see below, p. 152).
[6] See J. O. Stigall, op. cit.

relating to pagan sages. Like most contemporaries, he was taken in by Walter Map's *Dissuasio Valerii* and quoted it as frequently in his Psalter-commentary as he had in his *Moralitates*.[1]

The appetite for ancient history grows keener. Stories of Alexander and Hannibal multiply at the expense of *exempla* from natural science; so do allusions to classical mythology. A vacant benefice, causing envy and discord, reminds Waleys of the golden apple of the Hesperides.[2] *Who shall ascend into the mountain of the Lord?* (Ps. xxiii, 3) prompts him to tell the story of Icarus and Daedalus. *See my abjection and my labour* (Ps. xxiv, 18) suggests, even less appropriately, the twelve labours of Hercules.

Sallust comes to join Maximus, Frontinus and Justinus: Waleys quotes the saying, that Cato won the more glory the less in his modesty he sought it, to illustrate the text *Who is this King of glory?* (Ps. xxiii, 10).[3] A story from Aulus Gellius about Aristippus' wish for survival in a shipwreck answers the question: *Who is the man that desireth life, who loveth to see good days?* (Ps. xxxiii, 13).[4] Waleys brings forward Suetonius on the text *They spoke indeed peaceably* (Ps. xxxiv, 20): Augustus Caesar refused to make war unless it offered more prospect of gain than of loss, comparing war to fishing with a golden net.[5] Sallust, Aulus Gellius and Suetonius provide evidence for a growing taste for ancient history, but are not in themselves out-of-the-way authors. Livy, however, has begun to permeate the commentary by now. Waleys quotes *Ab Urbe condita* eleven times on Ps. xxiii-xxiv. His quotations are mostly long and they follow the text of Livy quite closely. It looks like a sudden discovery of the pleasure of reading a new book on Roman history. Then Waleys seems to ration himself to an occasional quotation: we find one on Ps. xxvi, 3 and another on xxxvi, 39: the commentary stops at Ps. xxxviii, 2. All his quotations come from either the first or third decade as might be expected. The fourth was still a rarity; Trevet could not find it when he wrote his Livy-commentary. Waleys entered

---

[1] On Ps. xxxi, 6; see also MS New College 30, fol. 44v. On *Valerius ad Rufinum*, see above, p. 55.

[2] On Ps. xxi, 18.

[3] Unde dicit Sallustius in Catelinario [*sic*] de Catone: quominus petebat gloriam et magis illum sequebatur.
From *Coniuratio Catilinae* liv, 6.

[4] From *Noct. attic.* XIX, i, 10.　　　　　[5] From *De vita Caesarum* II, xxv, 4.

into the spirit of the tale, as appears from his little addition
to Livy on the meeting between Scipio and Hannibal. Livy
says of the two generals:

> 'They were not only the greatest of their age, but the equals
> of any king or emperor of all peoples previously remembered.'

Waleys finds even this praise too weak. He quotes the
passage, adding after *equals*: 'Supply *or greater than* . . .'.[1] Few
words, but evoking the breathless hush of the meeting as
Petrarch imagined it:

> ' . . . Sileant michi cuncta priorum
> Nomina! Non alias nullo consistere campo
> Maiores Fortuna duos visisse negabit.'[2]

The school tradition knew almost nothing of Livy.
Vincent of Beauvais and John of Salisbury were Waleys' two
favourite encyclopaedists; neither of them could have
introduced him to *Ab Urbe condita*. Vincent does not quote
it at all;[3] John of Salisbury, while recommending Livy to
students, may not even have read him.[4] Waleys, moreover,
had a much better grounding in Livy than had later
members of the classicising group at Oxford and Cambridge.
We shall see that their knowledge of *Ab Urbe condita* was
slight compared to his, although they all belong to younger
generations. It is possible that he owed something to
Trevet, who commented on the first two decades. If Trevet
wrote his Livy-commentary 1316-19, as has been suggested,[5]
Waleys could have seen it before he left England; but the
date is still uncertain, and all the evidence points to Bologna
as the place where he began to get interested in Livy. It
was close to the Livy country at Padua; Waleys could have
made friends who would communicate their enthusiasm.
Personal contacts in Italy rather than school tradition provide the most satisfying reason for his study of *Ab Urbe
condita*.

To Titus Livius from Valerius Maximus is a long stride.
Maximus produced an *exempla* collection 'avant la lettre': his

---

[1] On Ps. xxiii, 10: . . . *non sue modo etatis maximi duces, sed omnis ante se memorie,
omnium gentium cuilibet regum sive imperatorum pares*. Supple vel maiores.
From *Ab Urbe condita* XXX, xxx, 1.
[2] *Africa* vii, 160-80.　　　　　　　　[3] E. Boutaric, op. cit. 56.
[4] John of Salisbury puts Livy in his list of recommended historians but does
not quote him; see *Policraticus* 2, 364.
[5] J. R. Dean, The Earliest Known Commentary on Livy, op. cit. 92.

Facta et dicta memorabilia might have been written especially to suit the taste of the middle ages. Its vogue increased with the use of *exempla*; it was commented on and translated into the vernacular.[1] Maximus stands beside Aristotle and Seneca in a picture showing three pagan with three Christian philosophers (Ambrose, Augustine and Aquinas) in a fourteenth-century *Compendium moralis philosophiae*.[2] The student of Livy needs a tougher digestion than the reader of Maximus' potted stories. He must love the history of Rome, as distinct from liking tales of the Romans. Waleys had this love. Livy's sudden irruption into the Psalter-commentary betrays love at first sight.

III.—THE COMMENTARY ON *De civitate Dei* I-X

This commentary represents Waleys' main contribution to classical scholarship. A fourteenth-century English copy puts the date of completion in 1332.[3] Finished it must have been by January 3, 1333, after which date he was in prison. It seems probable, therefore, that he wrote part, at least, in the household of Cardinal Matteo Orsini. Perhaps he began it at Bologna and took it with him to Avignon. We shall see that he was collecting material for it both in England and at Bologna. The inspiration came from Trevet in the first place, since Waleys knew Trevet's commentary on *De civitate Dei* and meant to improve on his senior. My guess at his evolution would be that he returned to England from Bologna for a long vacation and took the opportunity to collate manuscripts of his text and to inspect the two

[1] R. Sabbadini, *Le scoperte dei codice latini e greci ne' secoli xiv e xv* 2 (Florence, 1914) 37-44.
[2] T. Kaeppeli, Luca Mannelli e la sua *Tabulatio et expositio Senecae*, Arch. FF. Praed. 18 (1948) 244-6.
[3] MS Oxford, Merton College 256B, fol. 75ra: Expositio fratris Thome Waleys doctoris sacre theologie O.P. super libros Augustini de civitate Dei facta anno Domini m°ccc°xxx°ii.

See Powicke no. 362. The volume was given to Merton by John Grandison, bishop of Exeter (d. 1369), and the flyleaf has an inscription in a hand identified by Mr N. R. Ker as Grandison's. It contains Trevet on *De civitate Dei* (foll. 1ra-74vb), followed by Waleys on books i-viii, 1 (foll. 75ra-208vb). The date 1332 cannot refer to the copying of the manuscript, since the hand is later. The scribe was copying a defective exemplar of Waleys' commentary. There are a number of gaps; most of the prologue is missing and the text breaks off at viii, 1. A comparison with the more widely known text shows that even where the scribe left no blank space in the manuscript many passages have been omitted and others have been abridged. A few passages, however, are fuller here than in the more widely known text. Miss Dean kindly pointed out the incipit of Waleys' commentary contained in this copy.

decades of Livy known to Trevet. Waleys' commentary stems from Trevet's example and from his own Italian-born enthusiasms.

The project offered wonderful scope. St. Augustine's wealth of allusions to events, traditions and books, which were familiar to fifth-century readers, needed much research work before they could be understood and expounded by a fourteenth-century commentator. What better occasion could Waleys have found to delve into sources and enlarge his knowledge of ancient history? *Ab Urbe condita*, forced into his Psalter-commentary, imposed itself as an object of study to a commentator on *De civitate Dei*. Waleys decided to cover the first ten books and go no further; he tells us so. He chose them for study because they stood in especial need of explanation. A fourteenth-century catalogue says correctly that Waleys expounded 'the sayings and *exempla* alleged by St Augustine from the poets'.[1] His success is proved by the fact that his commentary became a classic. It was preferred to Trevet's for the books which it covered, but since Waleys stopped towards the end of book x, he was supplemented by Trevet on the remaining books. The combined apparatus, Waleys on books i-x, Trevet on books xi-xxii, was often copied and went into a number of early editions. The first translator of the text into French, Raoul de Praelles, drew on it largely for his French commentary.[2]

Waleys shows in his prologue that he aimed at improving on Trevet. He, 'Brother Thomas, Englishman, of the Order of Preachers', will remove, at least in part (understand 'as Trevet had not done at all'), the obstacles confronting students of *De civitate Dei* by explaining the first ten books, since they are the most difficult on account of their many histories and fables, known to few readers. He will skip the

---

[1] P. Auer, *Ein neuaufgefundener Katalog der Dominikaner Schriftsteller* (Paris, 1933) 109: Exponit dicta et exempla poetarum per beatum Augustinum allegata.

[2] A. de Laborde, *Les MSS à peintures de la Cité de Dieu* (Paris, 1909); the editions of the combined Trevet-Waleys commentary are listed here, 139-46. Miss Dean will give a list of manuscripts in her forthcoming study of Trevet. I have used the edition made at Louvain, 1484, checking selected passages from MS Auxerre 243, a copy made at Pontigny in 1358; see B. Smalley, op. cit. 86-7. The edition is not foliated; I therefore refer to the *locus* of *De civitate Dei*. My references will be to the edition, checked from MS Auxerre 243, unless otherwise stated. I quote from MS Merton College 256B where the text is fuller. I have used the modern chapter system.

easier passages in order to concentrate on the harder, and will begin with a general introduction to the aforesaid books.[1] The last promise is fulfilled by an account, drawn from Isidore, Orosius and Paul the Deacon, of the origin and nature of the Goths and of their effect on Roman opinion. Thus, at the very beginning, Waleys offers better guidance than Trevet, who had not attempted to give a historical background, compressing his history into a few lines of his prologue.

As Waleys proceeded, he kept Trevet's commentary before him. Trevet complains that he has been unable to find certain books; Waleys on the same passage boasts of his better luck and mentions books which Trevet had not even tried to find, but which he, Waleys, has read. Trevet sometimes slips up on a bibliographical point; Waleys corrects him, anonymously but unmistakably. He shows just that smugness which all feel, though some try to hide, when they go one better than a distinguished elder.

Here are four examples. First, St Augustine cites Apuleius (*De civ. Dei*, iv, 2). Trevet says in his commentary that Apuleius wrote *three books*, the *De moribus et vita Platonis*, which Trevet has seen, and the *De deo Socratis* and *De mundo*, which he has not seen.[2] 'Apuleius', says Waleys,

> 'wrote *five* books, which I have seen, that is to say, *De dogmate Platonis*, *De deo Socratis*, *De mundo*, which is called the *Cosmographia* of Apuleius, also *De magia*, where he defends himself against his accusers, who said that he used magic art, a book mentioned by Augustine, below, book viii, chapter 19, also the book *De asino aureo*, which is also called *Metamorphoses*, where he relates his marvellous transformations. Augustine mentions this book below, book xviii, chapter 18.'[3]

Waleys might well take pride in having seen five books by Apuleius. Trevet had seen one only, though he knew of three; Vincent of Beauvais had found two only, the fairly

---

[1] See appendix i, p. 309.

[2] MS Bodl. 292, fol. 132rb: Scripsit autem Apuleius libros tres, unum de moribus et vita Platonis, quem ego vidi, alium de deo Socratis, tertium de mundo, de quo fit mentio.

[3] On iv, 2: Scripsit autem libros quinque, quos vidi, scilicet de dogmate Platonis, de deo Socratis, de mundo, qui vocatur cosmographia Apulei, item de magia, in quo se defendit contra accusatores suos, qui eum uti arte magica dicebant, de quo libro fecit Augustinus mentionem infra, lib. viii, cap. 19, item librum de asino aureo, qui et metamorphoseos appellatur, in quo narrat mirabiles transmutationes factas arte magica, . . . de quo libro facit Augustinus mentionem infra, lib. xviii, cap. 18.

common *De vita et moribus Platonis* and *De deo Socratis*.[1]
Waleys had seen in addition the Greek work on cosmography
translated into Latin and ascribed to Apuleius, which Trevet
had heard of but had not seen, and the *De asino aureo* and
De magia; he quotes their alternative titles as well and shows
knowledge of their contents. The last two books were
almost unknown until their discovery by Zanobi da Strada
and their transcription by Boccaccio. The fourteenth-
century catalogue of the Dominican library at Bologna lists
one book only by Apuleius, the *De deo Socratis*. No library is
known to have possessed all five books. Waleys must have
looked for them intensively. He was lucky to have had
access to a copy of the rare *De asino aureo* and *De magia*;[2]
perhaps he saw it at Avignon.

Secondly, Augustine (*De civ. Dei*, v, 2) refers to a passage
in Cicero's *De fato*, iii, 5. Trevet thought it came from
Cicero's *De divinatione*, book ii, or from *De fato*, but he had
not seen complete copies of either and had not found the
story in question.[3] Waleys writes that it comes from *De fato*,
making clear that he has seen it there.[4]

Thirdly, Augustine quotes from a lost work of Sallust
(*De civ. Dei*, ii, 18) which disappeared during the middle
ages and is known only in fragments today: the *Historiae*.[5]
Trevet did not even know of its existence. He tried to find
the quotation in Sallust's *Bellum Catilinae* and succeeded
in discovering a rough parallel; but he was puzzled because
the copy of *Bellum Catilinae* which he used struck him as
a good text; and yet it did not contain St Augustine's

[1] E. Boutaric, op. cit. 44.
[2] Of thirty-eight surviving manuscripts of *De asino aureo* only two and a fragment of a third are before about 1300 and only four are early fourteenth-
century. The two earliest manuscripts of *De asino aureo* include the *Apologia*,
but there are no surviving early fourteenth-century copies of the latter; see
D. S. Robertson, Manuscripts of the *Metamorphoses* of Apuleius, *Classical
Quarterly Review* 18 (1924) 27-9; *Apulei Apologia*, ed. Butler and Owen (Oxford,
1914) xxxiii-xlix; M. Manitius, *Handschriften antiker Autoren in mittelalterlichen
Bibliothekskatalogen*, (Beiheft zum Zentralblatt für Bibliothekswesen, Leipzig,
1935) 149-50; Guis. Billanovich, *I primi umanisti e le tradizioni dei classici latini*
(Fribourg, 1953) 33, 40.
[3] MS Bodl. 292, fol. 134va: Ponit quandam narrationem Ciceronis, quam
puto positam vel in secundo de divinatione vel in libro de fato, quos ego com-
pletos non vidi, in hoc quod de sortibus multa disputat de geminis; sed hanc
narrationem ibi non vidi.
[4] On v, 2: Fit autem in hoc capitulo mentio de Possidonio cuius etiam dicta
aliqua de fato recitat Tullius in libro de fato. . . .
[5] B. Maurenbrecher, *C. Sallusti Crispi Historiarum Reliquiae* (Leipzig, 1891)
4-6.

quotation exactly.[1] He looked for it carefully without result.[2]

'Some', says Waleys, 'think that this book [the *Historiae*] is the first book of the *Catilinarium*, because Sallust wrote it before the *Iugurtinum*, and no historical works other than the *Catilinarium* and the *Iugurtinum* are found today; and so they look in the *Catilinarium* for the passage alleged by Augustine from Sallust's *Histories*. They labour in vain, for they will not find it.'

He then explains that Sallust wrote a book of *Histories* which is now lost, as is proved by the fact that St Augustine ascribes to Sallust material not to be found in either of Sallust's surviving works, *Catilinarium* and *Iugurtinum*. Aulus Gellius quotes from the fourth book of the *Histories*, too.[3] Waleys had better information on bibliography than Trevet had, as well as more books at his disposal.

Fourthly, Trevet's defective knowledge of Livy provokes Waleys to make the most arresting statement in his commentary: he tells us not only what books he read, but who lent them. Trevet says on a quotation from Livy (*De civ. Dei*, ii, 24) that Livy, according to tradition, left thirty decades, of which he, Trevet, has seen two only, on the foundation of Rome and on the Second Punic War.[4] His commentary on Livy in fact covers only these two decades, the first and third. The fourth must have been unobtainable in England at the time. It was hardly known anywhere

---

[1] MS Bodl. 292, fol. 123va: In libro tamen quem habui, qui michi videbatur bene correctus, non potui ista verba invenire. Quedam tamen hiis consona inveni circa medium Catilinarii, qui est primus liber historie eius.

[2] ibid., fol. 126va (on iii, 16): Ponit Augustinus verba Salustii, que in libro quem habui, licet diligenter exquisierim (MS exquisierint), invenire non potui; tamen sententiam forte ex verbis Salustii extrahi possibile (est).

Note that in both passages Trevet uses the past tense. He no longer had the *Catilinarium* beside him and was relying on his notes.

[3] On ii, 18: Hic credunt aliqui quod iste liber sit primus liber Catilinarii, et hoc quia Sallustius prius scripsit Catilinarium quam Iugurtinum, nec plures libri historici quam Catilinarium et Iugurtinum modo ab eo inveniuntur conscripti, et ideo querunt in Catilinario ea que in isto capitulo allegat Augustinus de historiis Sallustii, et frustra laborant, quia non invenient. Scripsit enim Sallustius unum librum historiarum, qui iam non invenitur, quod ex hoc patet, quia hic aliqua ponuntur tamquam Sallustii, que nec in Iugurtino nec in Catilinario inveniuntur, et Agellius, libro v et libro ii, introducit quartum librum historiarum Sallustii.

Waleys seems to be referring to Aulus Gellius, *Noct. attic.* XVIII, iv, 3 and II, xvii, 7.

[4] MS Bodl. 292, fol. 124va: Hoc dicit narrare Livium, quem prenominamus Titum, qui de gestis romanorum fertur scripsisse 30 decades librorum, de quibus tantum vidi duas decades, unam ab Urbe condita et aliam de secundo bello punico.

until the second quarter of the century; we know that it reached Verona before 1329 and Naples before 1332.[1] Waleys could pride himself on having had access to a rare copy. He quotes Jerome's praise of Livy from the prologue *Frater Ambrosius*, prefixed to the Vulgate, and continues:

'He was a very great historian, for he is supposed to have written thirty decades, that is volumes, on Roman history, of which each contained ten books. Of these I have seen two in England, that is to say, one from the foundation of the City and the other on the Second Punic War. I have seen the third together with these two at Bologna, and I had it a long time for inspection, from the lord bishop of Modena; it was on the Macedonian War. I have not seen any more decades nor have I been able to discover where they may be found.'[2]

Waleys makes good his claim to have read the fourth decade by quoting it copiously on *De civitate Dei*, as well as using the more common first and third.[3] More, he had pondered the problem of the missing decades and had compared the traditional number thirty with Florus' abbreviation of *Ab Urbe condita*. This made him think that the traditional number had been exaggerated: Florus abridged 142 books only, going from the origin of the City to the death of Augustus' stepson, Drusus, whose funeral Augustus attended.[4] Waleys knew Florus' *Epitome* well; he

[1] Guis. Billanovich, Petrarch and the Textual Tradition of Livy, *J.W.C.I.* 14 (1951) 169-70; Dal Livio di Raterio, *I.M.U.* 2, 103-78.

[2] MS Merton College 256B, fol. 103vb-104ra (I have underlined the words not found in the printed edition): Istud vero quod hic recitat Augustinus dicit Livium scripsisse. . . . Fuit autem iste Livius de quo dicit Hieronimus in prologo biblie sic: Ad Titum Livium lacteo eloquentie fonte manantem etc. Fuit etiam maximus historiographus. Fertur enim quod 30 scripsit decades, id est volumina, de historiis romanorum, quorum quodlibet decem libros continebat, ex quibus *duas vidi in Anglia*, videlicet unam de origine Urbis et aliam de secundo bello punico; tertiam *cum istis* vidi *Bononie* (MS ronon.) *et habui diu ad inspectionem a domino episcopo mutinensi* (MS mitinensi) et fuit de bello macedonico. Plures non vidi, nec scire potui ubi invenirentur.

[3] Where Augustine refers to the beginning of luxury at Rome (iii, 21), Waleys quotes a long passage from *Ab Urbe condita* on the same subject: *Demum tunc primum*. . . . Unde Titus Livius, de bello macedonico lib. viii, loquens de exercitu Manlii Volsconi, qui gallogrecos, id est galathas subiugavit, dicit sic: Luxurie peregrine origo ab asiatico exercitu invecta vel inventa est . . . future luxurie.

From XXXIX, vi, 7-8. The alternative *invecta vel inventa* must refer to a variant noted in the margin or to a barely legible word in Waleys' text of the fourth decade. He quotes it in many other places, but this will serve as an illustration.

[4] On ii, 24: Plures non vidi, nec scire potui ubi invenirentur, nec credo tamen quod tot decades scripsit, quia eius abbreviator, Anneus Florus, tantum abbreviat (c) xlii libros Titi Livii ab origine Urbis usque ad mortem Drusi, privigni Cesaris Augusti, cuius obsequiis Augustus interfuit. See below, p.108.

searched it for St Augustine's elusive Livy quotation.[1] He was versed in Livy scholarship.

The two decades seen by him in England were probably the same copies as Trevet's. The two at Bologna may have been at any of the great libraries in the city. He implies that he saw the fourth decade separately, telling us that he had it thanks to the bishop of Modena. This would explain why he did not quote it in his Psalter-commentary, as he would have done, we may be certain, had he been able, to show off, if for no other reason. He must have had access to the first and third only at that period; he read the fourth towards the end of his stay at Bologna, when he was working on *De civitate Dei*.

The fourth decade was a treasure to be gloated over by a chosen few. The bishop of Modena, Guido de Guisis, puts himself among their number by the fact of his having lent it to Waleys. He will also introduce us to Waleys' learned friends at Bologna. His epitaph in the Franciscan church at Udine made Guido de Guisis a native of Reggio, a doctor of canon law, and bishop of Modena and Concordia successively.[2] A career of this kind with its Italian political background would provide material for a thesis, but the details which I have hastily assembled fit into pattern as if by magic.

Guido de Guisis, archdeacon of Reggio, was elected bishop of Modena in the spring of 1318. He was then teaching canon law at Bologna as professor *ordinarius*. University regulations forbade him to leave the city territory without licence, which it would have taken him at least eight days to obtain. John XXII solved the problem by summoning him to Avignon.[3] He then quashed the election

---

[1] ibid.: *ut scribit Livius:* Titus Livius, in aliquo libro suo quem non vidi, quia ut alias dixi, tres decades eius vidi, nec quod hic allegatur de Livio ponit Anneus Florus, eius abbreviator, in aliquo libro Titi ab ipso abbreviato.

[2] F. Ughelli, *Italia sacra* 5 (Venice, 1720) 356. The Franciscan church at Udine, dating from 1236, was largely restored in the eighteenth century; see *Encyclopaedia italiana* 34 (1937) 603.

[3] *Lettres communes*, ed. G. Mollat, 2 (Rome, Paris, 1905) 167-8, no. 7302, May 26, 1318: Guidoni de Guizzis, archidiac. Regin., D.D. vacante nuper eccl. Mutinen., capit. et nonnulli praelati civitatis et diocesis de Mutinen. ad quos episcopi pertinet electio, eundem Guidonem, in minoribus ordinibus constitutum, in episcopum postularunt. Guido autem legendi ordinarie in decretis ministerium in studio Bononien. assumpsit, et rectoribus et universitati scolarium iuris canonici dicti studii non licet a finibus Bononien.abire; haec vero licentia, quam ultra viii dies rectores concedere non possunt, praefato Guidoni elargitur . . . ut ad A.S. se conferat et ibidem moretur, postulationis praefatae ad episcopatum Mutinen. negotium prosecuturus.

and provided de Guisis to the see himself. That was on September 9, 1318.[1] Since Waleys probably went to Avignon late in the year, it is possible that he met de Guisis at the Curia. The latter got letters testifying to his consecration on April 17, 1319.[2] A bishop of Modena could keep in touch with friends at Bologna, but we know something more definite. The troops of the emperor Louis of Bavaria occupied Modena and intruded a schismatic bishop in the last months of 1329. Bishop Guido had gone to join the papal legate at Bologna, the rallying point of the Guelfs.[3]

His rival kept possession of the see until July, 1330.[4] We may picture the bishop escaping from Modena to Bologna with the fourth decade in his baggage, determined to save it from the 'furor teutonicus'. Waleys was nearing the end of his stay at Bologna in 1329-30, since he was replaced as lector in 1331. His appetite for Livy was by now well developed. De Guisis' exile of nine months or so from Modena would give Waleys plenty of time for reading the fourth decade, as he claims that he had. Whether the book belonged to the cathedral library at Modena or was the bishop's own property must remain uncertain for the present.[5]

De Guisis was translated to the bishopric of Concordia in Venetia on September 16, 1334, and died on June 17, 1347, after working actively as legislator and reclaimer of the rights of his see.[6] No less a person than the canonist Giovanni d'Andrea executed his will. D'Andrea tells us so in the preface to his account of the functions of executors in his

---

[1] ibid. 279, no. 8405. Another clerk was collated to the vacant archdeaconry of Reggio; ibid., 318, no. 8801. There seems to be no record of teaching at Bologna, but this may be explained by the lack of documents available for the period. Ughelli makes him a nephew of the canonist Guido da Baiso, known as the 'Archdeacon', but gives no evidence; he also says that Giovanni d'Andrea quotes Guido de Guisis' *quaestiones*, here confusing the two Guidos; op. cit. 2, 129.

[2] ibid., 364, no. 9275.

[3] Bonifacio Morani, *Chronicon mutinense*, ed. Muratori (R.I.S. 11, 1727) 120-21. The emperor Louis deprived Guido, 'privato prius, publica etiam sententia, Guidone vero episcopo, Bononiae tunc Bertrando legato apostolico adhaerente'.

[4] ibid., 125; Giovanni da Bazano, *Chronicon mutinense*, ed. G. Carducci and U. Fiorini, (R.I.S. 15, iv, 1919) 103; see F. Bock, *Reichsidee und Nationalstaaten* (Munich, 1943) 275-80.

[5] A copy of all three decades was made at Modena in 1405; see Guis. Billano-vich, Un altro Livio corretto dal Valla, *I.M.U.* 275 n.

[6] *D.H.G.E.* 13 (1956) 422; Ughelli, op. cit. 5, 347-56.

commentary on the *Speculum iuris canonici*. He has just been engaged, he writes, as executor for three testators, who, he had hoped, would not need him so soon. The second and third were his son-in-law, Azzo, and his own wife. The first was 'the lord Guido, bishop of Concordia, a father very close to my heart, whose affairs involved me in business at Bologna, Modena and Reggio.'[1]

The two canonists were probably colleagues at Bologna before Guido's election to Modena. Politics also brought them together: both were allies of the cardinal legate, Bertrand du Poujet, a canonist himself, to whom d'Andrea dedicated his *Novella*. D'Andrea's papalism and his mission to John XXII are too well known to need references.[2] The evidence for de Guisis' politics appears in the papal letters. John XXII associated him with Cardinal Bertrand du Poujet and the bishop of Mantua as papal representative to negotiate with the Ghibellines, Cane Grandi de la Scala and Passerino of Mantua, in 1323; he was present at a meeting between the parties in the bishop's palace at Mantua.[3]

After his expulsion from Modena the pope tried to compensate him for the damage done to his property by the Germans and Ghibellines.[4] This was probably also in recognition for his services to the papal legate while Modena was occupied. De Guisis, as a supporter of John

---

[1] *Gul. Durandi Episcopi Mimatensis Speculum Iuris Ioan. Andreae, Baldi reliquorum-que . . . doctorum theorematibus illustratum* 1 (Bâle, 1574) 690-1: Istius vero partis praeeligendae causam dedit quia ultra praeteritas, quarum aliquae adhunc pendent, novissime simul occupor tribus executionibus voluntatum certorum, quos nec dispositionis executores fore sperabam, scilicet domini Guidonis Concordiensis episcopi, cordialissimi mihi patris, propter quem Bononiae, Mutinae et Rhegii mihi hoc onus incumbit: item domini Azonis dilectissimi generi, post cuius funus mihi coniugem charissimam dies quarta subtraxit.

D'Andrea finished his commentary on the *Speculum* late in 1346 or early in 1347, but he must have made additions to it later; he died in 1348. His son-in-law is said to have died on August 24, 1347; Schulte thought that it must have been earlier, to fit in with the date of the *Speculum:* see *Die Gesch. der Quellen und Literatur des kanon. Rechts* 2 (Stuttgart, 1875) 210-12. It seems however, quite natural that d'Andrea should have referred to Guido's death in June and Azzo's in August, followed four days later by his wife's. He certainly refers to Guido de Guisis. The Bishop Guido who died on March 23, 1333 was a Camaldulian monk, formerly abbot of Vangadizza, Venetia, who had no known connexions with Bologna, Modena and Reggio; see J. B. Mittarelli and A. Costadoni, *Annales Camaldulenses* 5 (Venice, 1760) 337, 345. He was translated to Concordia from Pola; see *D.H.G.E.*

[2] See B. Tierney, *Foundations of the Conciliar Theory* (Cambridge, 1955) 199-219; *D.H.G.E.* 2 (1914) 1735-6; 8 (1935) 1070-74.

[3] *Jean XXII, Lettres communes*, op. cit. 4 (1910) 347, no. 18159.

[4] ibid. 7 (1919) 289, no. 41512; 10 (1930) 185, no. 53224.

XXII and of the pope's favoured legate, would have much in common with d'Andrea.[1]

Waleys therefore adds a bishop, a former canonist of Bologna and friend of John XXII, who had visited Avignon, to the circle of Livy readers of the pre-Petrarchan period. Waleys discloses at the same time one of his own contacts with the circle. He probably had others, which may appear through some chance find in a manuscript or record.

Another book in his repertory takes us away from Bologna to the papal library at Avignon. He uses Festus Rufus' *Breviarium* for a comment on Augustine's reference to the size and duration of the Roman empire, because Festus gives a list of provinces subject to Rome. The *Breviarium* would have been unobtainable in England; Boston of Bury did not know of its existence; and it was rare on the Continent. The catalogue of the papal library of 1375 lists a *Breviarium Festi dictatoris, magistri militis*;[2] Waleys quotes the book in similar terms, calling it 'Liber Festi, dictatoris romanorum'.[3]

Apuleius' novel and *Apologia*, Festus' *Breviarium* and Livy's fourth decade make an impressive list of book-hunter's trophies. They mingle with the standard medieval dictionaries, chronicles and lives of saints. Waleys lacked the discrimination which Petrarch would show in his choice of authors. At the same time it must be said in the English friar's favour that he was sober in comparison with many of his contemporaries. His imagination could work without the stimulus of such books as the *Mirabilia Urbis Romae*. He had an instinctive preference for history as against medieval legend. Ancient monuments had impinged on his consciousness, as appears from his account of Roman theatres; he describes them on *De civ. Dei*, i, 31:

'Theatres are places specially organised for watching plays of this kind. All can sit and see them clearly and distinctly,

---

[1] D'Andrea knew Petrarch, but their personal friendship probably began in 1345; see F. Lo Parco, *Revue des bibliothèques* 16 (1906) 301-18; Francesco Petrarca e Tommaso Caloiro all'Università di Bologna, *Stud. e mem. p. la st. dell' univ. di Bol.* 11 (1933) 87; Petrarch *Fam.* v, 7-9. Hence there is no reason to postulate any connexion between the poet and de Guisis through their mutual friend d'Andrea.

[2] See M. Manitius, op. cit. 191.

[3] On v, 1: *tam magnum tamque diuturnum* . . . de cuius magnitudine certum est quod tota Europa et Africa et tota fere Asia pro aliquo tempore fuerunt ei subiecte. Patet autem expressius eius magnitudo ex provinciis ei subiectis, de quibus est liber Festi, dictatoris romanorum, in quo patet quod nunquam habuit dominium simpliciter totius orbis.

H

since nobody blocks another's view as is plain from the theatres built in ancient times, which are still visible in the City and elsewhere.'[1]

This rather suggests that Waleys had visited Rome. He could also have inspected ruins in northern Italy and have seen Arles and Nîmes during his stay at Avignon: he probably would not know the difference between a theatre and an amphitheatre.

Waleys approaches his text as a scholar, who has collated manuscripts and collected variants. One passage, he says, is discrepant and corrupt 'in many books'.[2] He has looked at various copies 'in England and also in Bologna' to verify a reading that worries him.[3] He makes a great effort to disentangle the persons and events described by his author. Augustine (i, 5) ascribes to Cato a speech which Sallust actually puts into the mouth of Caesar. Waleys, puzzled by the discrepancy which appeared when he looked up the reference to Sallust, decided that scribes must have made the mistake. It was the custom, he explained, to give the initial letter only in writing names; thus Augustine wrote C for Caesar and it was wrongly transcribed as Cato.[4] Augustine mentions a Marcus Drusus (iii, 26). Trevet failed to identify him, but Waleys discovered that he was Marcus Livius Drusus. The nature of the feast called *Fugalia* (ii, 6) intrigued Waleys. According to modern scholarship Augustine was alluding to the feast of *Regifugium*, celebrated to commemorate the flight of Tarquin.[5] Waleys did not know of this and guessed that *Fugalia* was the feast of the mother goddess, Berecynthia, who came to Rome from Phrygia, and had been referred to in a previous chapter (ii, 4). Her feast, Waleys suggested, might have been called *Frigialia* or *Frigalia* after Phrygia, just as other feasts were called after the patron deity; *Fugalia* might represent a corruption of the text. He admits with engaging honesty, however, that he has never in all his researches found any reading but *Fugalia*. This leads on to an even more ingenious

---

[1] On i, 31: Theatra autem sunt loca sic ordinata specialiter ad ludos tales spectandos, quia omnes sedere possunt et ludos istos clare et distincte videre, quia nullus alterius aspectum impediat, sicut patet in theatris antiquitus constructis, que adhuc in Urbe et alibi apparent.

[2] On v, 10: Est autem littera Augustini que sequitur, scilicet *quidquid autem aliorum hominum etc*, obscura et in multis libris discordans et vitiata.

[3] See below, p. 99, n. 1.   [4] See appendix i, p. 310.

[5] J. G. Frazer, *The Fasti of Ovid* 2 (London, 1929) 499-502.

speculation. Jerome in his commentary on Galatians says that all the poets call Phrygians timid, that is 'ready to flee'. Hence *Fugalia*, if this were the correct reading, would still refer to the Phrygians and would be an ironic allusion to their national character, which would account for Augustine's pun on the word: he says that the feast was 'indeed a flight from modesty'; this would have been beside the point, had the word been originally *Frigalia* or *Frigialia*.[1]

Waleys even reflected on the similarity or difference between ancient institutions and those of his time. He comments on *salario publico* (i, 3):

> 'Note that among the Romans of old doctors received their stipend from the public, that is from the funds of the community, and this obtains up to the present day in many cities of Italy, as appears at Bologna and in many other cities.'[2]

As a matter of fact the commune of Bologna began to pay professorial stipends only in the late thirteenth century and the system established itself gradually.[3] Waleys observed with northern eyes, accustomed to separation between town and gown; seeing the likeness to the municipal schools of ancient Rome, he supposed that the practice had been continuous. The Roman legion, on the other hand, had no fourteenth-century parallel. Hired companies bore the brunt of fighting. Mercenaries might be disbanded at the end of a campaign and had no permanent attachment comparable to the legionaries'. Waleys cast around for an illuminating comparison and hit on an abbey of canons regular:

> 'Since this man is said to have been a *soldier of the sixth legion*, it should be known that the Romans had many legions in permanent service; but they were so distinguished and organised that one was called "first" and another "second". Soldiers

---

[1] See appendix i, p. 310.

[2] On i, 3 (words in brackets added from MS Merton College 256B, fol. 77vb): *et salario publico*: notandum est hic quod olim apud romanos doctores receperunt salarium suum de publico, id est de bonis communitatis, et hoc usque ad presens in multis Italie civitatibus observatur (sicut patet Bononie et in civitatibus aliis muiltis).

It might be suggested that the specific allusion to Bologna proves that Waleys was living there at the time of writing and had not yet gone into Orsini's household. It is really no proof at all: the allusion to Bologna and other Italian cities would have been just as apt and comprehensible elsewhere, and Waleys was writing, not lecturing to an audience which needed local allusions.

[3] S. Stelling-Michaud, *L'Université de Bologne et la pénétration des droits romain et canonique en Suisse aux XIIIe et XIVe siècles* (Geneva, 1955) 44.

were allocated to them in such a way that, wherever they might be, they always belonged to the same legion, just as the canon of an abbey, even if he be absent, is always said to belong to it. A legion bore a certain resemblance to a college of soldiers. The legion enlisted first was called "first" and the next "second" and so on, according to the order of seniority.'[1]

Waleys had found a very apt likeness, when he pointed to canons regular rather than to monks or friars. The monk took vows of stability and was less likely than the canon to be away from his abbey on lawful business. The friar joined an international Order and might be transferred from one convent to another. An abbey of canons or a collegiate church was just right for his purpose. He showed perception, too, in realising that the Church provided an example of corporate organisation which was lacking in contemporary armies.

Petrarch, like Waleys, remarked on the difference between 'modern' troops and Roman legions; but it was the moral aspect which interested him. He stressed the superior discipline and hardiness of the Romans without giving any technical explanation of the different methods of recruiting.[2] Waleys showed greater acuteness and objectivity on the subject. The professional moralist, when he took a holiday, had better insight than the amateur.

Waleys surpassed Trevet as a commentator on *De civitate Dei*. This was easy, given his facilities at Bologna and Avignon and his friendship with a book-loving bishop of Modena; but he also surpassed himself. He learned to prefer ancient history to natural science and marvels, he steeped himself in primary sources and he gave exact references. The inquisitors cut short a promising career when they charged him with heresy soon after his coming to Avignon.

---

[1] On ii, 24: Quia vero dicitur iste fuisse miles *sexte legionis*, sciendum est quod cum romani continue habuerunt multas legiones, erant tamen sic distincte et ordinate ut una esset prima et alia diceretur secunda, quibus ascribebantur sic milites quod ubicumque essent, semper erant de illa legione, hoc modo quo canonicus abbatie alicuius, licet absens sit, tamen dicitur esse de illa abbatia; nam legio habuit quendam similitudinem collegii militum, et que primo scripta fuit prima vocabatur, et que secundo secunda, et sic deinceps secundum ordinem antiquitatis sue.

[2] 1. *Fam.* xxii, 14, written in 1360.

IV.—'DE MODO COMPONENDI SERMONES'

This treatise interests us in so far as it shows us Waleys after leaving his prison. He had been there for at least five and probably some nine years. He presents his book as the fruit of a lifetime's experience, writing as one 'brought up in the Order of Preachers from my boyhood, and a dweller in diverse *studia generalia* and provinces'.[1] No trace of bitterness appears in it, but rather reflection and maturity. Waleys was an enemy of formalism in a more personal and original way than the writers of other *Artes praedicandi*, who tend to repeat the same clichés. English preachers, he thought, could learn from the more conservative Italians. The northern method was to detach a text from the gospel of the day and expound it in isolation from its context. According to 'the old way', still current in parts of Italy, the gospel for the day was read and expounded as a whole. Waleys found this preferable.[2] He disliked the formal structure of sermon described in the *Artes*: why introduce the theme (i.e. the main text of the sermon) by a pro-theme, when the theme should suffice? The preacher should break through the conventional form of procedure if the spirit moves him: *The word of God is not bound.*[3] Waleys had forgotten, it seems, the consequences of his impulsive outburst in his Avignon sermon; he still believed in spontaneity.

His advice to preachers is practical and sensible and he drives it home by a fund of good stories. The beginner should practise his delivery in a lonely place, just as Vegetius tells the raw recruit to the army to practise his drill. A preacher will lose all count of time, because what he says is so interesting to himself, however tiresome to his audience. He should ask a friend beforehand to signal to him when to stop.[4] The text of the sermon must be checked to see which version of the Bible or liturgy it comes from, since the wording may differ; here the scholar speaks.[5] Waleys allows concessions to a congregation of clergy. The preacher will find it blasé and inattentive. He may therefore introduce cadences and rhetorical colours, so long as he does not sicken his hearers by overdoing it. Laymen are easier to please.[6]

Whatever his thoughts in prison may have been, Waleys

[1] Charland, 328.   [2] 344.   [3] 329, 355-7.
[4] 339-41.   [5] 347.   [6] 373-5.

did not revise his opinion on the value of the classics: he remained unrepentant. Part ii of his treatise contains model sermons to illustrate his account of technique. One of them compares redeemed humanity to the ancient Romans. The latter rightly judged themselves superior to other peoples on account of their world empire. So Christian men may judge themselves superior to the angels; *God hath not subjected unto angels the world that is to come* (Hebr. ii, 5); the 'empire and kingdom of heaven' surpasses even that of the Romans on earth.[1] The text *Behold thy king cometh to thee, meek* (Mt. xxi, 5) suggests Virgil's 'parcere subiectis et debellare superbos'.[2] Waleys quotes his old favourites, Sallust,[3] Vegetius, *Policraticus*,[4] and Walter Burley's *De Vita et moribus philosophorum*.[5] Among the last things the old man wrote was a quotation from Ovid, *De remedio amoris*.[6]

V.—WALEYS' ATTITUDE TO THE CLASSICS

Waleys carried further the classicising biblical commentary and he used the text of *De civitate Dei* as a basis for the study of antiquity. He not only quoted pagan writers, but praised them lavishly. They tell fine tales finely.[7] Sallust was 'an excellent'[8] and Livy 'the greatest' Roman historian. Such tributes flow as naturally from his pen as the praise of the psalmist:

'*Blessed is the man* (Ps. i, 1) . . . Finely and reasonably does the psalmist set blessedness and virtue foremost before us at the beginning of his book.'

[1] The sermons have not been printed. MS London, Brit. Mus. Royal 8. E. xii, fol. 2v: Si ergo romani se digniores ceteris nationibus se reputabant, et merito, quia apud eos erat imperium orbis terre, idem poterit humanum genus reputare de se per comparationem ad angelos, apud quod remanet imperium celi et terre. Unde ipsius est imperium et regnum celeste magis quam unquam fuerit terre imperium romanorum.

[2] ibid.

[3] fol. 37v, a verbal quotation from *Catilinae coniuratio*, xiv, 4.

[4] foll. 42, 13v.

[5] fol. 19: Narratur in libro de moribus philsophorum. . . . Waleys tells the story of Thales' answer to a question from Burley, op. cit. 10. This is interesting in view of the scarcity of copies of Burley's books in England; see above, p. 74. Perhaps Waleys had brought a copy home with him from Avignon, or had notes from it.

[6] fol. 15; he quotes lines 651-2.

[7] On *De civ. Dei* i, 3: . . . quam describit Ovidius pulchre et diffuse; on i, 13: . . . de quo pulchre dicit Ovidius; on iii, 17: . . . Eutropius, lib. ii, narrat historiam satis pulchram; on viii, 12: Pulchra de ipso narrat Valerius.

[8] On i, 5: . . . ut per Sallustium patet, excellentem historiographum romanorum.

Waleys' comments on St Augustine go far beyond what was wanted for understanding of the text. Readers did not need to know all that their guide could discover about Archimedes in order to follow an account of the Roman capture of Syracuse (i, 6). The question arises whether his attitude differed from that of John of Wales or of Nicholas Trevet.

He shared their blindness to the beauties of style, although, like Trevet, he could explain the difference between medieval and classical Latin. He does not try to imitate his authors, which was only commonsense in view of his purpose as a teacher. But he never shows any awareness of literary graces and this contrasts strongly with his praise of their subject matter.

The difference in his attitude to pagans is really one of degree. Waleys follows John of Wales in admiring their virtues, but he loves them even more dearly. His remarks gain in point and daring by reason of their setting in a commentary on St Augustine. Waleys' author engaged in anti-pagan polemic: pagan cults are shown to be false and hollow in comparison to Christianity. Waleys, on the contrary, would rather explain their likeness and teach Christians to emulate the fervour of pagan worship. When Augustine mentions Berecynthia (ii, 4), Waleys introduces and comments on a story from Valerius Maximus to illustrate the Romans' reverence for their mother goddess. He makes a parallel between Berecynthia and the Blessed Virgin. Then he deliberately suggests the continuity of pagan and Christian cults by telling how the Pantheon was rededicated in Mary's honour:

'Here it should be known that this goddess, whom they called the mother of the gods, meaning the earth, was held by the Romans in such reverence that before her image was translated[1] to Rome from Pessinunte, as Valerius tells, book i: *Very often the emperors*, that is those who had command, such as consuls, praetors and so forth, *partakers of victory*, that is after winning victories, *went to Pessinunte to fulfil the vows they had made*. Christians should reflect on the great distance between Rome and Pessinunte so as to see what reverence they owe to the Mother, not of false gods, but of the one true high God. Domitian built the temple at Rome in honour of this goddess and it was called the Pantheon. Pope Boniface hallowed it in

---

[1] 'Translation' normally referred to the ceremonial transfer of relics from one shrine to another.

honour of blessed Mary, as is told in the Legend of All Saints. Now it is called the church of Santa Maria della Rotonda.'[1]

The parallel between pagan and Christian worship recurs. Waleys explains the difference between *sacella* and *sacrae aedes* (*De civ. Dei* vi, 3) by pairing them with private chapels and public churches. The *sacella* corresponded to private chapels, each serving one house or family, since the Romans worshipped their *Penates* in their *sacella*, choosing or making their domestic gods according to individual devotion.[2] *Genius* in the singular denoted a nature god; *genii* were gods allotted to men in the same way as 'we Christians' hold that two angels, one good and one bad, are assigned to each man.[3] Already, in his commentary on Isaias, Waleys had compared heathen and Christian signs and miracles. He says on the prophecy *Behold a Virgin shall conceive* (vii, 14):

'The Virgin's conception was the most certain sign of the liberation of mankind. Although marvellous, it was not incredible, for Pliny tells that in the year when Hannibal was defeated trees brought forth corn. Pliny means that this was a sign or portent of victory. Hannibal was the greatest enemy of the Romans; such another they never had. So to our purpose: the devil is the greatest enemy of mankind. . . . '[4]

He shows some critical sense in distinguishing between what is credible and what is not, in telling his pagan stories. The practice described by Livy (VII, iii, 6) of driving nails into the wall of the temple of Jove to ward off pestilence was

---

[1] See appendix i, p. 311.

[2] On vi, 3: Differentia fuit inter sacella et sacras edes, que modo inter capellas privatas, que deserviunt uni domui vel familie et ecclesias communes, nam in sacellis colebant deos penates, quos quilibet secundum devotionem suam sibi elegit aut fecit. Dicit autem Trebatius, lib. ii de religionibus, quod sacellum est locus deo sacratum cum ara.

See Aulus Gellius, *Noct. attic.* VII, xii, 5.

[3] On vii, 7: Genius vero dicitur deus nature, sed genii alios deos signant, qui deputantur hominibus eo modo quo nos ponimus duos angelos, unum bonum et alterum malum, hominibus assignari.

[4] MS Oxford, Bodl. Laud. misc. 345, fol. 172va: Certissimum signum liberationis generis humani fuit conceptus virginis, qui licet sit mirabilis, non tamen incredibilis. Narrat enim Plinius, lib. (xv)iii, quod anno quo superatus est Hannibal in arboribus nota (MS nata) produntur frumenta. Innuit autem Plinius, lib. (xv)iii, quod hoc fuit signum seu portentum eius victorie. Fuit autem Hannibal maximus hostis romanorum, qualem nunquam habuerunt. Sic in proposito, nam diabolus est hostis maximus humani generis. . . .

The reference is to Pliny, *Nat. Hist.* xviii, 18. MS Oxford, New College 30 gives the number correctly, though the text is corrupt in other respects. Both MSS have *nata* for *nota* (also MSS Oxford, Magdalen College lat. 203 and Merton College 196). It may have been in Waleys' text of Pliny.

'superstitious'.[1] The changes of sex, regarded by Livy and Aulus Gellius as portents, were either delusions of the devil or else just natural.[2] Arion's dolphin did not really get turned into a constellation in reward for its service; that was a poetic fiction. On the other hand, the ancients give plenty of evidence that a dolphin could carry a man on its back.[3]

'Poetic fiction' or myth traditionally had a historical, a physical and a moral interpretation, which rationalised and justified its 'fables'.[4] Waleys brought forward the tradition to prove that poets hid truth behind their fictions; their function was to relate truth under a certain veiling. He used all three interpretations. The moral suited his biblical commentaries. He turned more towards the historical and physical in his commentary on De civitate Dei. His difficulty here was that he had chosen to expound an author who aimed at discrediting pagan mythology. Augustine ridiculed the justification of myth as figuring some natural process. He instanced as an absurd example the interpretation of Saturn, devouring his sons, as a figure of all-consuming time. Waleys deals with the ridicule by simply ignoring it; he gives the traditional interpretation of the Saturn myth and adds a historical interpretation for good measure.[5] He had already referred to it in his Psalter-commentary, pointing out its resemblance to the cycle of fortune's wheel. The myth of earth-born Titans, who fought against the gods and were overcome by Jove, recalled the cycle and struck him as 'not wholly fabulous'.[6]

---

[1] On Ps. xxiv, 12:

[2] On De civ. Dei iii, 31: Non credo tamen istas predictas mutationes feminarum in masculos fuisse veras, sed potius vel fuisse illusiones diabolicas; vel que sic videbantur converse erant hermafrodite, in quibus prius dominatur sexus femineus et postea masculinus.

[3] On De civ. Dei i, 14: Licet autem illud de translatione delphini in celum sit fictio poetica, non propter hoc credendum est quod illud quod narratur de Aryone portato a delphino sit fictum, quia quod delphini homines susceperunt in mari ad portandum patet per Solinum, qui de pluribus hoc refert. . . .

[4] Seznec, 11-121.

[5] On vi, 8: Est autem hic sciendum quod omni poetice fabule subest aliquid veritatis secundum intentionem poete fabulam fingentis. Unde secundum Isidorum, viii Etymol., officium poetarum est veritatem ipsam sub quibusdam tegumentis enarrare. Unde alique fabule habent expositionem phisicam, alique historicam, alique moralem. Expositio vero fabule de Saturno filios devorante, quam hic ponit Augustinus, est expositio phisica. Habet et aliam expositionem historicam, quia scilicet Saturnus, rex Crete, pater Iovis, in veritate fuit erga filios suos multum crudelis.

The reference to Isidore's Etymologies is to VIII, viii, 10.

[6] On Ps. ii, 2: Ideo non videtur totum fabulosum quod dicunt poete, sicut recitat Isidorus, ix Etymol., videlicet quod terra, irata contra deos, produxit

Augustine charged the Roman poets with immorality on the score that they excused Romulus' murder of his brother Remus. Waleys took the charge as being levelled particularly against Ovid's version of the tale in his *Fasti*. Here not Romulus but Celer hits Remus on the head with a shovel. Waleys thought that Celer personified anger. He therefore interpreted Ovid to mean that Romulus killed Remus unintentionally in a passion. Ovid, according to Waleys, was clothing the truth in poetic dress; and so, he implies, Ovid did not excuse the murder. St Augustine's commentator has defended 'the poets' against his author's charge.[1]

Waleys even tends on occasion to adapt Christian teaching to pagan ethics. A passage of his Psalter-commentary marks an attempt to retell the Gospel in Aristotelian terms. *For thy magnificence is elevated above the heavens* (Ps. viii, 2) is first explained according to its traditional meaning as a prophecy of the Ascension and secondly according to Aristotle's definition of 'magnificence'. In order to see what Waleys meant we must know what he read in his *Nicomachean Ethics*:

'Magnificence also seems to be a virtue concerned with wealth; but it does not like liberality extend to all the actions that are concerned with wealth, but only to those that involve expenditure on a fitting scale. For, as the name itself suggests, it is a fitting expenditure involving largeness of scale. . . . It is what is fitting, then, in relation to the agent, and to the circumstances and the object. The man who in small or middling things spends according to the merits of the case is not called magnificent. . . . For the magnificent man is called liberal, but the liberal man is not necessarily magnificent. . . . Hence a poor man cannot be magnificent, since he has not the means to spend large sums fittingly: . . . it is the *right* expenditure that is virtuous. But great expenditure is becoming to those who have suitable means to start with, acquired by their own efforts or from ancestors or connexions, and to people of high birth or reputation, and so on; for all these things bring with them greatness and prestige. . . . Of *private* occasions of expenditure

---

quosdam gigantes, scilicet titanes, qui pugnarent contra deos, quos tamen dicunt a Iove fuisse superatos.

See Isid., *Etymol.* IX, ii, 135.

[1] On *De civ. Dei* ii, 14: Sciendum est tamen quod Ovidius sub tegumento poetico expressit facti veritatem, nam per Celerem, quem dicit Remum occidisse, intelligit impetum ire quo Romulus movebatur ad occidendum fratrem suum celeriter, id est indeliberate, ita quod secundum intentionem Ovidii Romulus hoc fecit ex impetu passionis, non ex iudicio rationis.

See *Fasti* iv, 837-44.

the most suitable are those that take place once for all, e.g. a wedding or anything of that kind, or anything that interests the whole city or the people of position in it, . . . for the magnificent man spends not on himself but on public objects.'[1]

Waleys quotes the passage with its distinction between magnificence and liberality. Then he explains how it can be applied to the Gospel story. Christ on earth could practise the virtue of *liberality*; indeed he gave liberally such gifts as were becoming to his station in earthly life, and told the Apostles also to give as they had received, freely. But he was too poor on earth to practise the virtue of *magnificence*. After the Ascension, however, he appeared as his Father's Son, noble and glorious. Then he showed his magnificence on the two occasions described by Aristotle as fitting. The first was a wedding: Christ brought into his house human nature as his bride, and gave her that greatest of gifts, the Holy Spirit. The second occasion fitting for a display of magnificence was the public welfare: the gift of the Holy Spirit falls into this category; it was truly for the public welfare, since it confirmed the whole Church in grace and in virtue.[2]

Here Waleys proclaims himself to be a follower of St Thomas, who had discussed the meaning of the word *magnificence*, and had ended by adopting its Aristotelian definition. Both St Albert and St Thomas, expounding the *Ethics*, responded to its challenge: they revived within a Christian framework 'the Greek ideal of the grandeur and dignity of man'.[3] Waleys expressed the same concept in his more naïve fashion. His classical studies had bitten so deep as to affect his judgment as well as his interests. He liked to picture the Saviour in the guise of some ancient hero. It was not enough to be poor and 'liberal'; Christ must appear also as well-born and 'magnificent'.

Waleys gives content to certain reproaches which might otherwise seem vague and uncalled for. The Franciscan visionary, Jean de Roquetaillard, wrote from his prison (1345-9) that the Church, the bride of Christ, was adorning her chamber with paintings, silks and 'pagan fables full of turpitude'.[4] To be sure, he was an *exalté*, but Richard de Bury, who cannot be accused of narrowness, felt that his

---

[1] iv, 2, translated W. D. Ross (Oxford, 1940) 1122a, 19-1123a, 5.
[2] See appendix i, p. 311.   [3] R.-A. Gautier, op. cit. 443-66.
[4] J. Bignami-Odier, op. cit. 54, 69.

contemporaries were underrating the Bible. He accused the Friars Preacher, whose Order was founded expressly for the study of Scripture, of neglecting their duty:

> 'The Holy Scripture is not expounded, but is set aside and treated as though it were commonplace and known to all, though very few have touched its hem . . . '[1]

French Franciscan and English bishop anticipate the theme of *Lucula noctis*, where Giovanni Dominici O.P., writing about 1405, complains that Christian books lie in sordid neglect, while pagan go clad in covers of silver and gold.[2] Dominici wanted to reverse a trend which, ironically enough, had been started by members of his own Order some eighty years earlier. Waleys, however well-meaning, must have scandalised the puritans.

The two Englishmen, Trevet and Waleys, mark successive stages in the history of classical studies. A pope and a cardinal turned to Trevet in England for help in understanding Seneca and Livy. Waleys, working at Bologna and Avignon a few years later, learned enough to put Trevet in the shade. Italian humanism had begun to develop. Waleys travelled as far along the path to humanism as a friar could go while remaining true to his vocation. He showed unexpectedly what an Oxford Thomist could achieve in a southern *milieu*. The mixture was unusual and impermanent. Waleys put zeal for Catholic doctrine before the joys of book-hunting; otherwise he would have kept quiet at Avignon and not taken sides so rashly in a theological quarrel. The south had overtaken the north in classical studies and would hold the lead for two centuries.

---

[1] *Philobiblon* vi, 93: Sacra scriptura non exponitur, sed omnino seponitur, quasi trita per vicos et omnibus divulgata supponitur; cuius tamen fimbrias vix paucissimi tetigerunt. . . . De hac mille moralis discipline sententias enucleare poterit qui indulget assidue, si tamen ostium aperire dignetur ille qui condidit spiritum pietatis, que et recentissima novitate pollebunt et sapidissima suavitate auditorum intelligentias refovebunt.

[2] ed. E. Hunt (Notre Dame, Indiana, 1940) 122: Negliguntur sacra, squalent libri fideles, et gentilium sericis tecti, auro argentoque muniti, ut pretiosi leguntur. . . .

Addendum to p. 93, n. 4: Guis. Billanovich points out that Waleys is here referring to the rare *Periochae*, often ascribed to Florus; *I.M.U.* 2, 158.

CHAPTER VI

JOHN RIDEVALL

She has done what she could.

Epitaph on a stone in a country churchyard.

I.—DATES

RIDEVALL, in contrast to Waleys, passed through life almost unrecorded. There are three firm dates: he incepted in theology at the Oxford Greyfriars about 1331 and was fifty-fourth lector about 1331-2; he attended the council of his Order at Bâle on October 28, 1340.[1] His works are as follows: (1) a treatise on mythology for use in preaching, *Fulgentius metaforalis*; (2) a *Lectura* on the Apocalypse, which survives in excerpts; (3) a newly discovered critique of Trevet on *De civitate Dei*; (4) a commentary on *De civitate Dei* of which we have only that on books i-iii and vi-vii; (5) a commentary on the *Dissuasio Valerii de uxore non ducenda*; this is lost but may perhaps be found and identified (6) perhaps a commentary on the *Confessions* of St Augustine, known only from a reference by Robert Holcot.[2]

The surviving works can be grouped into rough chronological order. Holcot quotes *Fulgentius metaforalis* in lectures given at Oxford probably in the academic year 1333-4. He also quotes the *Lectura in Apocalypsim* in the same course: Ridevall must have given the *Lectura* during his regency at Greyfriars 1331-2. *Fulgentius metaforalis* is a treatise, not a lecture course, and so may have come before the regency. The critique of Trevet on *De civitate Dei* came before Ridevall's own commentary, since he refers to the matter as forthcoming.[3] He did not know of Waleys' commentary on *De civitate Dei* when he wrote the critique of Trevet nor when he commented on books i-iii. He used it, however,

---

[1] See *O.R.* 3, 1576. The name is spelled in a number of ways.
[2] See Robert Holcot, 53.
[3] Fr Kaeppeli has kindly communicated his discovery to me. He publishes an account of Ridevall's critique of Trevet in *Arch. FF. Praed.* 29 (1959).

in his commentary on books vi-vii. It seems that Waleys finished his commentary, covering books i-x only, in 1332 at Avignon. It would have taken a little time to reach Ridevall in England. We can deduce that Ridevall began his commentary before 1333 and that he had Waleys' in or soon after 1333, when he had reached book vi. His interest in *De civitate Dei* must have been of long standing. He began by discussing the failings of Trevet and then embarked on an exposition of it himself. He probably started to think it over and to collect material before his regency of 1331-2 and wrote before, during and after his regency. I shall take his commentary on *De civitate Dei* as being the latest in chronological order, because, although he may have begun it first, he was still at work on it in 1333 or later. Thanks to Holcot, we know that *Fulgentius metaforalis* and the *Lectura in Apocalypsim* came before 1333-4, when he quoted them.

Ridevall's use of Waleys and Holcot's use of Ridevall have helped to date his work: but the inter-relationship has another significance. The Minorite has wedged himself firmly between the two Friars Preacher. Moreover he shows two tendencies, blending but distinguishable. As a scholar he continues the work of Trevet and Waleys, also of John of Wales, a member of his own Order. As a fantastic he stimulated Holcot to go further.

II.—'Fulgentius Metaforalis' and the Apocalypse-Commentary

Ridevall's treatise on mythology is a 're-moralisation' of parts of Fulgentius' *Mythologiae*, a book written at the end of the fifth century, which told the principal myths of Greco-Roman antiquity with their physical, allegorical and moral interpretations. The original has been judged harshly: 'Among the remnants of an effete and expiring classicism none are more pretentious, yet essentially trivial, than the three treatises which bear the name of Fulgentius'. Yet the mythographer provided the middle ages with a precious school book, where students could find guidance to their reading of the poets in a form acceptable to the Christian. Indeed, Fulgentius transmitted the myths as they had been understood in late antiquity. The spiritualising interpretations wanted little remodelling in a Christian sense to adapt them to medieval needs. The *Mythologiae* served Carolingian scholars well.¹ A twelfth-century mythographer, who was probably 'Master Alberic of London', known as *Mythographus Tertius*,² produced an enlarged Fulgentius, presented in the contemporary idiom. Master Alberic and his predecessors used Fulgentius mainly as a textbook for the study of the liberal arts, that is, for grammar and rhetoric. He enabled one to follow the allusions in one's authors and he offered a choice of rhetorical figures for one's own compositions. Ridevall could have given his version a distinctive sub-title, *Mythologia praedicabilis*. Just as lecturers on Scripture had moralised their text in order to prepare it for preachers, so Ridevall turned the *Mythologiae* into a preacher's handbook. Fulgentius passed from the arts course to theology.³

Ridevall begins according to tradition with a prologue explaining the origin of idolatry and hence of the worship of heathen deities. Then he describes in turn the chief gods and goddesses with their associates and their attributes. Each one personifies a virtue or its component. Saturn stands for prudence, his son, Jupiter, for benevolence, which proceeds from prudence, his daughter, Juno, for memory, which is a part of prudence, his third child, Neptune, for understanding, his fourth, Pluto, for providence. Their various partners and offspring again represent dependent virtues. Ridevall takes 'the venerable Fulgentius' as his starting point and draws largely on Alberic of London, but he adds details from other sources on the cult of the gods and on ancient customs, such as the garb of philosophers and the Roman triumph.⁴ He elaborates on his predecessors especially in working out the moralisation of the myths: each makes the text of a homily, with supporting quotations and *exempla* from Christian and pagan authors. The homiletic matter brings out a trait in Ridevall, which we shall notice again. Religious sincerity shows through his commonplaces. He is really interested in following through the stages of repentance.⁵ The spiritual writers of the twelfth century

---

¹ M. L. W. Laistner, *The Intellectual Heritage of the Early Middle Ages* (Cornell, 1957) 202-15.
² E. Rathbone, Master Alberic of London, 'Mythographus Tertius Vaticanus', *M.A.R.S.* 1 (1941) 35-8.
³ See *Fulgentius, Mythologiae*, ed. R. Helm (Leipzig, 1898); Mythographus Tertius, ed. G. Bode, *Scriptores rerum mythicarum latini tres Romae nuper repertae* 2 (Celle, 1834); *Fulgentius metaforalis*.
⁴ *Fulgentius metaforalis*, 74, 82.   ⁵ ibid. 88-93.

appeal to him. We need not be surprised at his copious quotations from St Bernard and the Victorines, who were universally popular; but he draws our attention by quoting the *De spirituali amicitia* of the twelfth-century English Cistercian, Ailred of Rievaulx.[1] An older Franciscan professor had turned in the same direction, showing fondness for English monastic writers of the twelfth century.[2] Ridevall's classicism did not prevent him from following suit. He compares the attitudes of the Christian and the good pagan as despisers of the world. The former wept at man's malice; the latter smiled. Ridevall prefers Christian tears to the pagan philosopher's ridicule.[3]

He prepares his myths for the use of preachers by a mnemonic device, rewriting Fulgentius in rhythm. The mythographer's description of Saturn, 'Opis maritus, senior, velato capite, falcem ferens; cuius virilia abscissa et in mari proiecta Venerem genuerunt', becomes:

> Opi maritatus, senio gravatus,
> capite velatus et falce sceptratus,
> vultu desolatus, pudendis orbatus
> et prole cibatus.[4]

He goes on to moralise each phrase of the easily remembered sentence.

What immediately strikes a modern reader of these descriptions is that Ridevall calls them 'pictures' and introduces them by the word 'pingitur'. Any notion that he was referring to real paintings or carvings is dispelled when he ascribes his 'pictures', as I shall call them, to the poets. He writes 'poetica pictura', 'secundum poeticam imaginem' and 'pingitur a poetis'. He had literary precedents. Fulgentius occasionally writes 'pingitur' as when he gives Neptune a trident and Mercury a helmet. 'They paint Venus naked,' he says; 'she is painted as being carried in a seashell.'[5] Alberic of London uses 'pingitur' more often than Fulgentius, and Ridevall never omits it. A deeper interest in the pagan deities led to the production of illustrations to *Fulgentius metaforalis*.[6] Ridevall's 'pictures'

---

[1] 85-6.
[2] B. Smalley, John Russel O.F.M., *Rech. Théol.* 23 (1956) 277-320. Russel flourished at the turn of the thirteenth century; he was lector at the Cambridge Greyfriars, but visited Oxford and used the Franciscan library there.
[3] *Fulgentius metaforalis*, 76-7.   [4] ibid. 73.
[5] Fulgentius, *Mythologiae*, op. cit. 19, 29, 40.
[6] See the plates and discussion in *Fulgentius metaforalis*, and Seznec, passim.

did not lend themselves to visual representation and the results were as clumsy as might have been expected. The illuminator could only draw a figure surrounded by and loaded with its attributes. Ridevall described Juno as 'redolent of unguents'. The poor artist could only set an open flask beside her head. The Blessed Virgin is shown in late medieval art as surrounded by her symbols, the 'garden enclosed', the 'tower of David' and so on. Ridevall's illuminator produced rather the same effect. The starting point was unpromising even from a literary angle. Ridevall's deities lack grace and sex appeal. Robert Mannyng's three goddesses in his vernacular history are at least hearty English ladies;[1] the Oxford friar desiccates them by his scholastic formulae.

'Without doubt our most curious monument of the application of Christian allegory to mythology', writes Seznec of *Fulgentius metaforalis*. So it is, because the modern reader imagines the gods in their ancient or Renaissance setting; a medieval sermon-book seems the wrong place for them. All the same, I would class *Fulgentius metaforalis* among Ridevall's scholarly works. He takes pains to collect authentic details about the pagan deities and their cult. He tries to reconcile divergent accounts of their origin.[2] Fulgentius ascribed the origin of idol worship to the Egyptians, Peter Comestor in the *Historia scholastica*, and his source, Isidore, to the Babylonians. Isidore also told the myth of Prometheus to explain the beginnings of idolatry among the Greeks. Ridevall solves the problem by considering Fulgentius' purpose in compiling his mythology. The mythographer was writing a book of fables with their interpretations, organised according to the description of virtues and vices. He did not mean to trace the history of idol worship, and therefore it did not matter to him which people invented the practice. He only wanted to demonstrate that it sprang from the disorderly passions of man. Another solution to the problem would be that the Egyptians were the most ancient race in the world, as appears from Plato in the *Timaeus* and from other old histories. The Babylonians, in that case, were not the first idolators, but the first known to their neighbours, which is why Isidore gives them precedence over the Egyptians and Greeks. Abstract the scholastic form of Ridevall's argument, and you have a

---

[1] See above, 23.   [2] *Fulgentius metaforalis*, 69-70.

I

sensible historical approach to discordant authorities. He
takes account of their intentions as writers instead of treating
them as all on the same level. Literary sources were the only
ones available, and they were limited. Ridevall had to use
them as he could. He had no means of checking their
statements. The only way out was to scrutinise their purpose
in writing. His choice of authors shows wide reading and
catholic tastes. He likes quoting poetry and treats his
readers to verses from Juvenal and the twelfth-century
Archpoet. The latest literary fashion had impinged on his
mind; we see it in quotations from 'Seneca's first tragedy'
(*Hercules furiens*) on Cerberus and on the Furies.[1] Ridevall
may have been indebted to Trevet, who popularised the
Senecan *Tragedies*.

So far, all is scholarship and sobriety, given the medieval
context. Fantasy pure and simple plays on the end of the
prologue. Ridevall has just been discussing the origin of
idolatry; he now personifies her. She is a woman of ill
fame, eyeless, deaf, proclaimed by trumpet (as criminal),
defaced and disease-ridden:

> Mulier notata, oculis orbata,
> aure mutilata, cornu ventilata,
> vultu deformata et morbo vexata.

Ridevall uses the same technique for Idolatry as he will do in
describing his gods and goddesses. Each of her traits is
explained. She 'is painted' as an ill-famed harlot because
idolators leave the true God to fornicate with idols. Her
blindness and deafness refer to Fulgentius' account of the
historical origin of idolatry. According to him, the first idol
had been made by a father in his dead son's likeness and his
slaves had worshipped it in order to please him. Idolatry
is shown as blind and deaf because she sprang from flattery,
which blinds and deafens its object. The remaining traits
illustrate the same group of ideas.[2]

Personification was a common device, inherited from
antiquity and familiar to all schoolmen from the ladies
representing liberal arts in Martianus Capella's *Nuptiae*.
Similarly Prudentius had personified virtues and vices in his
Psychomachia. Ridevall's Idolatry is a natural development.
The really fantastic part of the composition appears in its
presentation. Ridevall begins:

[1] ibid. 103, 109.   70-71.

'It can be noted how the ancient poetic picture of this greatest of sins, idolatry, agrees with Fulgentius' procedure in his series of myths. This was the picture of Idolatry according to the poets.'[1]

An ancient poetic picture! Idolatry passes herself off as a member of the panthcon as painted by the poets. Ridevall's deities belie their parents, it is true, but they are legitimate, if ugly, children of the Olympians. Idolatry has no such descent. Ridevall incurs grave suspicion of being her father: I know of no earlier example of this kind of 'picture'. The nearest approach to it is in a commentary on Isaias by St Albert, belonging to the late thirteenth century. He says on *Make bare thy legs* (xlvii, 2) that such is the custom of harlots; then he adds:

'For this reason Venus used to be painted with her skirt slightly raised, showing her leg, to incite men to lust.'[2]

The mythographers all represent Venus as naked; so Albert's goddess had some other source. Curious and of an observant turn of mind, he may have seen or read some study of her wearing a dress. Maybe he simply invented her as a personification of harlotry. Ridevall knew something of St Albert's commentary on Isaias:[3] the little sketch of Venus 'as she used to be painted' may have caught his fancy.

He has tried to sell us his first 'genuine' sham-antique. Idolatry is by no means the last. Liebeschütz noted that the *Lectura in Apocalypsim* contained more 'pictures'.[4] Prophetic

---

[1] ibid. 70: Notari autem potest qualiter antiqua pictura poetica huius maximi peccati, scilicet ydolatrie, concordat cum processu Fulgentii in serie istius mithologie. Hec enim fuit apud aliquos ydolatrie pictura: . . .

[2] Postilla In Isaiam, *Opera* 19 ed. H. Ostlander (Münster, 1952) 474: *Revela crura*, quod meretricum est, quae revelatione crurium ad libidinem provocant. Propter hoc etiam Venus pingebatur, quod veste aliquantulum elevata crus revelavit, ut ad libidinem provocaret.

[3] Below, 125.

[4] Excerpts from Ridevall on the Apocalypse survive only in MS Venice, Marc. lat. 1790 (494) (=V), foll. 90ra-99va (medieval foliation). The hand is English, fourteenth-century. The title is: Extracta de lectura fratris Iohannis Ridevaus super Apocalipsim O.M.
Incipit: Nota quidam philosophi dixerunt quod revelare futura non pertinet ad Deum Iovem, sed ad Apollinem . . .
Explicit: Pluto sceptrum inferni, Neptunus sceptrum aquarum . . . The extracts come from a commentary on Apoc. i-iv. The volume contains a miscellany, including Holcot's *Convertimini*, Thomas Waleys on Isaias, Trevet's *Declamationes Senece moralisate* and Ridevall's *Fulgentius metaforalis*, used by Liebeschütz for his edition; see J. Valentinelli, *Bibliotheca manuscripta S. Marci Venetiarum* 1 (Venice, 1865) 262. I have worked on a microfilm, kindly sent me by the Librarian. I quote according to the medieval foliation, because this is

Revelation, 'as the philosophers painted her', appears on the first page. The philosophers, according to Ridevall, endowed her with twelve attributes. She was the daughter of Apollo, god of divination. She lay on a sick-bed, heavy with sleep, bereft of goods, condemned to exile and charmed by music. She was a purified virgin, wounded in the liver, crowned with laurel, kissed on the face, and watched over by guards. Ridevall backs up his description by quotations from pagan, Jewish and Christian authors on the subject of divination and prophecy. Laurel was a tree sacred to Apollo, hence the laurel crown. 'Kissed on the face' refers to pure begetting: Prophetic Revelation was conceived in a kiss and not in carnal desire. The eyes surrounding her represent her insight into past, present and future. Guards watch over her lest quacks, the pyromancers and geomancers, should steal her.[1] Ridevall evidently thought it fitting that just as Idolatry headed the train of pagan gods and goddesses, so Prophetic Revelation should introduce the Apocalyptic visions.

Hard on her heels come Grace as painted by the poets, Sophia or Wisdom as painted by the philosophers, Death as painted by the poets, and then Sloth, Faith and Hope. Holcot, quoting from an unabbreviated version of the *Lectura*, adds Truth and Sweetness (*Suavitas*). Traits drawn from ancient sources, after the manner of Prophetic Revelation's laurel crown, mingle with others, no doubt freshly invented. Grace includes a genuinely ancient and pictorial theme in the description of the three maidens; it comes from Servius on the *Aeneid* and we shall meet it again:

'Three maidens are painted, one with her face turned away, and the others looking at her.'[2]

Two sketches of Time also derive from ancient literature and representational art. Time's picture was called Saturn among the ancients, because he was said to have devoured his sons. Time was also painted as a snake with its tail in its mouth, continually devouring itself. Death, on the other hand, does not recall classical motifs. Ridevall says that the

---

clearly marked and much easier to make out on a microfilm than the modern numbers.

[1] See appendix i, 312.

[2] V, fol. 90va: quia depinguntur tres virgines, quarum una habet vultum aversum; alie due resdiciunt ad eam.

See below, 171.

poets painted her as a wrinkled old woman, set in the south, lying in bed, bound in chains, secured with bolts, bereft of light, widowed, voiceless, black-legged, thin, dry-boned and broken-limbed.[1] It is probable that he did quote classical sources in evidence; but his abbreviator has cut them out, and they must have been strained to produce this 'picture'.

Sophia has a mixed parentage, partly ancient and partly medieval. The philosophers called her Sophia because she was painted with whitened head and gilded breast.[2] She was bounded by a circle and lovely in the sunlight. They painted her as the goddess of wisdom with a sundial close by. She was painted with a star according to the various characteristics of wisdom. Some put the seven Pleiads in her right hand; others put the seven planets, on account of the various characteristics of wisdom. *Sancta Sophia* has a long and complex literary and artistic history.[3] Ecclesiasticus connects her with heavenly light; Platonic doctrine makes rationality akin to the stars. Her attributes were transferred to the Virgin from the twelfth century onwards. Our Lady was also the woman of the Apocalypse, *clothed with the sun . . . and on her head a crown of twelve stars* (xii, 1). Ridevall could have seen a miniature showing *Sancta Sophia* holding a sceptre with a seven-rayed star. Another miniature shows her seated with her head in the celestial sphere, adorned with the seven planets.[4] The tiresome abbreviator has cut out Ridevall's quotations in support of his 'picture' of Wisdom; but he had many reasons for connecting her with stars and sunlight.

He goes on to say that the philosophers painted her with a speaking countenance. Fortunately his reason for this trait of Wisdom has survived the abridgment of his commentary: 'Aulus Gellius in his *Attic Nights* says that the ancients put an image of wisdom before all their temple doors, and made words issue from her mouth:

> Usus me genuit; peperit memoria.
> Sophiam me vocant greci, vos sapientiam.'

---

[1] See appendix i, 312.   [2] See appendix i, 312.
[3] Melle M. T. d'Alverny kindly sent me these suggestions from her forthcoming book on *Sancta Sophia*.
[4] A miniature showing Sophia holding a seven-rayed sceptre illustrates an allegorical poem containing a eulogy of Sapientia-Philosophia, which was presented to King Robert of Naples; Sapientia with her head in a sphere adorned with the seven planets occurs in an eleventh-century manuscript from S. Martial de Limoges.

Aulus Gellius says only that a certain philosopher *thought that
the verse ought to be written over temple doors.* He mentions no
image of wisdom.[1] Ridevall construed him to mean that
the ancients set up a most peculiar and unclassical figure
before their temples. Presumably it had its mouth open as
if to speak, and the verse was inscribed beside it!

Another lightly sketched 'picture' shows the same imagina-
tive process at work, on a patristic text this time. St
Augustine says that Epicurus brought in the virtues as
handmaidens to pleasure. Ridevall makes him say that the
Epicureans fancied Pleasure 'sitting in a chair with all the
virtues serving her as handmaidens'. He adds on his own
account that the Stoics painted Honour presiding and a
troop of virtues serving her. The Peripatetics painted
Honour presiding, seated in a chariot, guiding another troop
of virtues. The faithful, however, think that Charity (not
Honour) is mistress in the hierarchy of virtues, and holds
sway as their queen.[2] Ridevall has started from a single,
restrained metaphor of St Augustine and has covered
'pictures' of Pleasure, Honour and Charity with patristic
authority. A few learned allusions to ancient philosophers
have been thrown in to make it sound still more plausible.

All this fancy is verbal, not visual; the 'pictures' will serve
as aural aids to preaching. Their many abstract and sometimes conflicting traits could hardly be illustrated. The
most enterprising artist might pause before he tried to put
Prophetic Revelation on paper. Not one but a whole row
of miniatures would have been needed to represent her.
Ridevall did not intend it, any more than he intended his
gods and goddesses to be truly painted. Holcot borrowed
Ridevall's technique and improved on it, being both a more
skilful and a more productive craftsman. Some of his
'pictures' of virtues were actually illustrated in the fifteenth
century and come off better than Ridevall's gods and
goddesses. It seems sensible, therefore, to defer any further
consideration of Ridevall's 'pictures' until we come to
Holcot and see how he quoted and added to them. Meanwhile, I shall say something of the *Lectura* in which they
appear. They look even odder in a biblical commentary
than Idolatry does in *Fulgentius metaforalis.*

Ridevall on the Apocalypse must have resembled Waleys
on the Psalter in the unabridged version. As far as one can

[1] *Noct. attic.* xiii, 8.   [2] See appendix i, 313.

judge from the surviving excerpts, he gave a literal exposition of his text, describing, for instance, the heresies mentioned there.[1] He makes it more actual to students by calling the letters to the churches 'bulls'; they were used to papal bulls. He tells stories of the lives and sayings of philosophers and myths, such as that of Icarus.[2] Like Waleys, he draws on a great variety of sources.

The rarest known book that he quotes is the Greek lexicon, *Suidas*, in a Latin translation. Explaining why Prophetic Revelation is 'condemned to exile on account of her separation from men', Ridevall brings forward the case of the legendary seer and sorcerer, Hermes Trismegistos, who studied in deserted, lonely places, and so gained the spirit of divination or prophecy. He progressed so far in knowledge of divine matters as to propound something like the doctrine of the Trinity; hence he was called 'Hermes Trismagister'. Ridevall gives as his authorities for the story 'the book *Suda*' and 'the book which is called *On the Twelves*'.[3] Robert Grosseteste translated a number of items, 'mainly of historical and biographical interest', from *Suidas*, a copy of which he possessed. Ridevall found part of his tale under the item *Hermes*: the seer was called 'Trismagister' because he had an intimation of the Trinity.[4] Since Grosseteste left his personal library to the Oxford Greyfriars,[5] Ridevall would have access to the translation from *Suidas*. We can hardly call him a 'book-hunter' on the strength of it; but at least he knew how to profit from Grosseteste's bequest. The mysterious book of *Twelves* must have contained an account of Hermes' solitary life, which is not in Grosseteste's *Suidas*. Ridevall probably had an astrological work on the

---

[1] He takes the opportunity to attack later heresies too, discussing the views of Mahomet, V, fol. 92va.

[2] V, fol. 93ra.

[3] V, fol. 90ra: Unde in libro Suda et in libro qui dicitur de dodec?r? [the word is abridged and barely legible] dicitur quod Hermeis [*sic*] divinator studivit in locis derelictis, ab hominibus separatis, et ideo optinuit spiritum divinationis vel prophetie, et in tantum profecit in cognitione divina quod posuit tres personas maximas et unum totum, et ideo vocabatur Hermes Trismagister.

[4] MS Oxford, Bodl. Digby 11 (1612), fol. 33: Vocabatur autem Trismagister, quasi diceret maximus, quia de Trinitate locutus est, dicens in Trinitate unam esse deitatem. . . .

On Grosseteste's translation of items from Suidas and his copy of the Greek text, see S. H. Thomson, *The Writings of Robert Grosseteste* (Cambridge, 1940) 63-4; *Robert Grosseteste Scholar and Bishop*, ed. D. A. Callus (Oxford, 1955) 45. We do not possess all the items translated by Grosseteste; the only two known copies are defective.

[5] ibid. 121-45.

Dodekaoros, or Twelve Houses, ascribed to Hermes, which contained some biographical data on the supposed author; a vast body of Hermetic literature was circulating.[1]

Two *exempla* deserve a *Nota bene* as being typical of what we shall find in Holcot. Plato merited in virtue of his virginity to have a revelation of Christ himself. Hence a medal was wont to be found on the philosopher's breast bearing the inscription: 'I believe in Christ, Son of God, to be born of the Virgin, to die on the Cross and to rise again on the third day.' Ridevall calls this an 'aphorism' and says that he found it in a commentary on Boethius, *De disciplina scholarium*, on the words (*Platonis*) *probata virginitas*. He got the word *aporisma* from a neighbouring passage in the text of Pseudo-Boethius. His commentator was probably the Stamford master, William Wheatley, who compiled an *apparatus* to *De disciplina scholarium* in 1309; Wheatley tells the story in a slightly different version: the inscription was found in golden letters in Plato's tomb. Ridevall may have been quoting from memory or he may have heard the text expounded at school by some other master, drawing on a common stock of material.[2]

His second story gives 'one reason' why the emperor Nero had Rome set on fire: he disliked the street-lighting system, because it frightened evildoers off the streets at night, when he wanted to prowl himself. Ridevall refers to a commentator on Boethius, *De consolatione Philosophiae*, on the subject. The commentators all describe Nero's burning of Rome on *De consol. Phil.* ii, metr. 6, *Novimus*; but they give as the reason that he wanted to see what the spectacle of burning Troy would have looked like. Ridevall perhaps refers to his commentator for a general account of the episode and found his 'reason' for it somewhere else. Alternatively, his story may have been added to the text of the commentary in the copy he used.[3]

Both stories in their mad improbability make fine specimens of the sham-antique genre. The good pagan is gilded and the bad blackened. The story of Nero also suggests the wonder of ancient Rome; her brightly-lit streets

---

[1] A Greek treatise on the dodecatemories was ascribed to Hermes; see A. Festugières, *La révélation d'Hermès Trismégiste* 1 (Paris, 1944) 105. See also W. Gundel, Neue astrologische Texte des Hermes Trismegistos, *Abhandlungen der Bayerischen Akademie der Wissenschaften*, Phil.-hist. Abt. N.F. 12 (Munich, 1936) 135, 229, 310.

[2] See appendix i, 313.   [3] ibid. 314.

contrasted with the dark alleys of medieval cities. The provenance is equally typical. Ridevall claims to draw both tales from commentaries on late antique or apocryphal texts. He points us to a busy centre of the sham-antique market.

The *Lectura in Apocalypsim* develops the fantastic side of Ridevall, which is only hinted at in *Fulgentius metaforalis*. He enlivened his teaching with a mish-mash of genuine and pseudo, the latter made up of some pure fantasy. Waleys' diffuse type of scriptural commentary must have influenced him; but he went further than Waleys in his pre-Livy period had ever gone. It seems most unlikely that Idolatry's inventor could have submitted himself to the discipline of scholarly research; and yet the first part of the prologue to *Fulgentius metaforalis* suggests that he could. The commentary on *De civitate Dei* will prove it.

III.—THE COMMENTARY ON 'DE CIVITATE DEI'

Trevet inspired Ridevall's commentary directly, just as he had inspired Waleys'. Ridevall read Trevet and found him insufficient, just as Waleys had done. He began by writing a critique of the older scholar. His tone was gentle and respectful, however, as though he realised that Trevet had put younger students of *De civitate Dei* in his debt. Ridevall had less reason to be cocky than Waleys: working in England, he had no better facilities than the object of his criticism; but he also had a more patient temperament than his fellow critic and made it a principle to do justice to all his authors. His essay on Trevet's mistakes suggested to him the idea of writing a better commentary of his own. Hence the project, when it materialised, represented earlier thought and study.

Alas! it was doomed to neglect from the first. The combined Trevet-Waleys *apparatus* to *De civitate Dei* got in ahead and drove off competitors. Ridevall's had no chance; it is a tribute to his scholarship that his work had even a limited circulation. The commentary survives in two manuscript copies, both incomplete. One copy fills two square, fat volumes, written in English hands of the middle or third quarter of the fifteenth century, now MSS Oxford, Corpus Christi College 186-7.[1] MS 186 contains a prologue

[1] =S, T. The medieval provenance of these two manuscripts is unknown; see B. Smalley, John Ridevall's Commentary on *De civitate Dei*, in *Medium Aevum* 25 (1957) 144-5.

to the whole text, followed by a commentary on books i-iii. MS 187 has a commentary on books vi-vii. A third volume, which is now lost, would have contained the missing part on books iv-v. The prologue supposes an intention to comment on all twenty-two books, but we do not know whether Ridevall ever got further than the end of book vii.

The Corpus manuscripts witness to an interest in the commentary during the fifteenth century. A contemporary annotator has gone through both volumes making marginal headings and comments, which show that he not only read them but followed every line with rapt attention: 'Nota bene'; 'Nota valde horrenda'; 'Nota bonum exemplum contra otiositatem'. He supplements Ridevall from his own stock of knowledge, taken, for instance, from John of Wales' *Breviloquium*.[1] He draws pointing fingers and illustrates the text by crude sketches of gods and goddesses; two-faced Janus and Ceres figure in the margin.[2] Unusual emotion prompts him to break into English and write 'Loke ye' instead of 'Nota'. Curiosity combines with caution when he writes against an account of pagan orgies: 'Lok heyre sed cave'![3]

The second copy of Ridevall on *De civitate Dei* was found recently by Fr T. Kaeppeli in MS Berlin, Theol. lat. Fol. 581. It is anonymous here and is written in a fourteenth-century hand, but is more fragmentary than the Corpus copy. It represents the commentary on books vi-vii, as found in MS Corpus 187, without the beginning.[4]

Ridevall expresses the same purpose as Trevet and Waleys. He wants to make St Augustine's allusions intelligible, first to himself and secondly to his readers.[5] As we might expect from the author of *Fulgentius metaforalis*, he is particularly interested in the pagan deities and sets out 'the mythological background' to *De civitate Dei*. In default

---

[1] ibid. 145, S, fol. 69v.   [2] T, foll. 113, 150.   [3] ibid. fol. 152.

[4] This manuscript is not in Rose's catalogue of the Berlin collection. I have not seen it and owe the description to the kindness of Fr. Kaeppeli.

[5] S, fol. 3v: . . . quia in hoc volumine tanguntur plures poeses extranee et antique historie, que fortasse passim omnibus non sunt note, ideo ad clariorem notitiam talium ignotorum ponitur in sequentibus expositio brevis secundum exigentiam materie et facilis, tam de dictis poeticis quam de de gestis historicis contentis in serie presentis voluminis, ut sic lectorum fastidio caveatur et auctoris intentio citius et facilius ab ipsis legentibus capiatur.

Ridevall does not acknowledge the desire to educate himself; but it leaps to the eye in his painstaking researches.

of our convenient formula, 'background', he finds a plan which enables him to describe the pantheon. St Augustine aims at confuting idolators, 'magnum opus et arduum'. Ridevall argues, therefore, that each of the twenty-two books will attack the cult of a special sort of god or goddess. It was a 'great work' indeed to confute the pagans, because they 'magnified' their gods, calling them 'great' for a number of reasons. So Ridevall divides pagan deities into twenty-two classes, each corresponding to a book of *De civitate Dei*, according to the pagans' reasons for magnifying them. The first class of gods were called great on account of their priority in time, e.g. Saturn and Cybele, the second on account of their dignity, e.g. Jove and Juno, his wife. Ridevall gives *Hercules furiens*, which he had quoted in *Fulgentius metaforalis*, as his authority for this statement. The third-class gods were 'great' by reason of their strength and fierceness, e.g. Mars and Bellona, and the fourth by reason of their 'universal perfection'. Pan represents this fourth class because the poets figured him as the god of perfection of all the universe, 'as appears from his picture or description, which Augustine touches on and others too, that is, Isidore, Raban and Huguccio in his *Derivations*'.[1] The fifth-class gods owed their greatness to domestic affection, e.g. *Lares* and *Penates*. And so we go through Ridevall's *catalogue raisonné* of the ancient gods, ending with the goddess Fama of glory and renown in class twenty-two.[2]

Having finished his prologue, he begins on his text. He checks nearly every one of his author's references; he compares his author's account of events with other versions; he notes where they differ and tries to make them agree. Trevet's commentary lay beside him and he criticises it respectfully but firmly. He could not add to Trevet's bibliography, as Waleys could, but he paid more careful attention than Trevet to the available sources. Trevet failed to identify the Marcus Drusus mentioned by Augustine, iii, 20; he could find no reference to Drusus in Orosius. Ridevall emends:

---

[1] Augustine only mentions *Panes* in *De civitate Dei* and does not describe them, but Ridevall found a full description with the etymology, 'pan, id est omne: fingunt enim eum ex universali elementorum specie . . .' in the *Etymologiae* of St Isidore VIII, xi, 81-3. This is repeated by Raban in *De universo* xv, 6 (*P.L.* 111) 432, and substantially by Huguccio in his *Derivationes*, MS Oxford, Bodl. e Mus. 96 (3582) p. 318.

[2] See appendix i, 314.

'Augustine gives a third example to prove his point concerning Marcus Drusus. Orosius makes no mention of this man, however; or so it seems to a worthy doctor, who wrote on this volume of St Augustine; but I do not think that the doctor is right here or in many other places, and here especially.'[1]

Ridevall's fifteenth-century annotator recognised the 'worthy doctor' and wrote 'Contra Triveth' in the margin. Ridevall then explains that Marcus Drusus should be identified with the Marcus Livius Drusus referred to by Florus and Valerius Maximus; and Orosius does mention him, although 'the doctor' says the contrary.[2] Waleys corrected the same mistake, but Ridevall worked it out quite independently; he does not use Waleys for this early part of his commentary.

Evidence of borrowing from Waleys begins on book vi; perhaps his book had just been brought to England. Ridevall treats him with less respect than he shows to Trevet. He calls Waleys 'aliqui' and quotes his rather surprising view that pagan genii corresponded to Christian angels without comment.[3] On the other hand, he jumped at the chance to read extracts from Livy's fourth decade *via* Waleys. He reproduces some of Waleys' quotations, not mentioning his intermediary, but covering himself from any charge of inaccuracy which might be brought: a long quotation from Livy on the introduction of Bachanalia to Rome *via* Waleys is said to come 'roughly' from Livy's history.[4]

The first and third decades were available to Ridevall and he exploited them thoroughly. He also had a copy of Florus' *Epitome*. His handling of Florus illustrates both his limita-

---

[1] S, fol. 148: Tertium exemplum ad probandum propositum suum ponit Augustinus de Marco Drusio, de quo tamen non facit Orosius mentionem, sicut videtur uni doctori valenti, qui scripsit super istud volumen beati Augustini, sed in isto dicto non credo hic nec in aliis multis, doctorem istum bene sensisse, et maxime in proposito.
Trevet says (MS Bodl. 292, fol. 130rb): De Marco Druso, tribuno plebis, nichil inveni de Orosio.

[2] S, fol. 148v; Patet ergo quod Orosius facit mentionem de isto homine, de quo loquitur Augustinus in littera, licet doctor ille dicit [*sic*] oppositum.
Ridevall quotes Florus, *Epitome* ii, 5, Maximus, *De dict. et fact. mem.* IX, v, 2, and Orosius, *Hist. adv. pagan.* V, xviii, 2-7.

[3] On vii, 6, T, fol. 111v: Immo dicunt aliqui quod sicut nos christiani credimus quod per Dei ordinationem sit cuilibet homini ordinatus ad custodiam unus angelus bonus . . . et unus angelus malus . . . sic isti pagani et infideles credebant quod quilibet homo haberet duos deos genios.
See above, p. 104.

[4] T, fol. 66v, Ridevall quotes *Ab Urbe condita* XXXIX, viii-ix from Waleys' summary of it on *De civ. De*, vi, 9, ending: Hec sparsim et sententialiter ex historia Titi Livii.

tions and his acumen. His copy of the *Epitome* was anonymous. He did not know who wrote it and calls it 'a certain
history of the Romans', giving the incipit, or 'another history
of the Romans'.[1] He set store by his 'other history' and was
pleased to find that it agreed with Livy, as well it might.
Modern research, however, has shown that Florus depended
on other sources besides Livy: the *Epitome* is not a mere
abridgment of *Ab Urbe condita*.[2] Ridevall, knowing neither
the author nor the customary title, made a meticulous
comparison between Florus and Livy on the Gallic sack of
Rome and gleaned an extra detail: Livy tells how the
senators looked 'as though they were gods', where 'the
history' (Florus) says 'as though they were gods *and genii*'.[3]

His lack of basic library facilities drove Ridevall to tainted
sources in his quest for knowledge. The *Mirabilia Urbis
Romae* offered him a description of the golden palace on the
Capitol, containing statues of all the provinces with magic
bells round their necks. He swallowed it whole apparently.[4]
He found a strange account of the image of Priapus, as set up
in pagan temples, in St Albert's postill on Job; so he says.
St Albert mentions the temple of Priapus, though not the
image, in his postill on Isaias.[5] Ridevall may have had an

---

[1] S, fol. 39v: . . . quedam historia romanorum, que sic incipit: Populus
romanus a rege Romulo . . . ; fol. 163v: . . . quedam romanorum historia, prius
pluries allegata . . . ; fol. 148: Patet enim evidenter quod una alia romana historia, quam prius pluries allegavi, facit mentionem de Livio Druso. . . .

[2] P. Zancan, *Floro e Livio* (Padua, 1942) 32-69.

[3] On iii, 29, S., fol. 156v: Unde notandum est quedam historia [*sic*] de
reverentia quam fecerunt galli senones senatoribus, quam etiam historiam
tangit Titus Livius, et cum eo concordat illa historia quam prius pluries allegavi, et fuit etiam de isto in precedentibus tactum. Dicit etiam Titus Livius
quod imminente gallorum adventu . . . ceperunt eos revereri tanquam deos
genios, sicut dicit quedam historia, et post exhibitam senatoribus reverentiam
ceperunt galli recedere de domibus senatorum.

Ridevall is quoting with considerable verbal exactness from *Ab Urb. cond.*,
V, xlvi and interpolates from *Epitome* I, vii, 14. He then goes back to Livy for
the story of how a Gaul stroked a senator's beard, which is not told by Florus.

[4] On ii, 29, S, fol. 87v: Unde sicut dicitur in tractatu quodam, intitulato De
mirabilibus Rome, infra arcem capitolii fuit palatium quod erat pro magna
parte aureum et lapidibus pretiosis ornatum, quod dicebatur valere tertiam
partem mundi. Ibi tot statue erant quot sunt mundi provincie, et quelibet
statua habebat tintinabulum ad collum. . . .

See R. Valentini and G. Zucchetti, *Codice topographico della Città di Roma* 3
(Rome, 1946) 34.

[5] On vi, 7, T, fol. 44: Nota ad litteram, sicut recitat dominus Albertus in
postilla sua super librum Iob, infideles faciebant in templis imaginem poni deo
Priapo in hac forma. . . .

See St Albert on Isa. xix, 16 in Opera 19, op. cit. 245. The 'Iob' in the text
may be a copyist's mistake for an abbreviation of Isaias, or Ridevall may have
made it himself. St Albert does not refer to Priapus in his postill on Iob.

annotated copy. The reference illustrates his knack of unearthing details in out-of-the-way places.

In spite of his limitations, he succeeds better than Waleys as an interpreter of his author. The strongly Christian turn of mind which we have noted before and a certain sympathy interested Ridevall in the *mens Augustini*. Waleys tended to ignore the writer except as a gateway to antiquity; his references to St Augustine's purpose are perfunctory. Ridevall does not lose sight of the polemical purpose of *De civitate Dei* and brings out the relationship between the allusions and the polemic. He asks what type of source St Augustine used and why. Augustine lays himself open to criticism by quoting legends as though they were historically true, when they are not. Thus he quotes Virgil, who was a poet rather than a historian. Ridevall explains that his author argued sometimes *ad hominem* and sometimes *ad rem*. He quoted Virgil according to the former type of argument because the Romans admired him. Fiction and exaggeration moving to pity belong to the craft of poets and rhetors, which the Romans held to be practised by Virgil. When he argued *ad rem*, Augustine proved his competence in true history as distinct from legend by quoting the respectable historian, Sallust.[1] Ridevall used the same technique in discussing the chronology of the servile and civil wars. A comparison between *De civitate Dei* and Orosius' history shows much disagreement. Ridevall answers that St Augustine did not intend to narrate history nor to be a historian; he meant rather to refute idolators by proving the worthlessness of pagan cult in preserving the Roman commonwealth; he therefore refers to events as it suited his purpose and did not bother to put them in chronological order.[2]

We recognise the method which Ridevall has used in discussing the various accounts of the origin of idolatry in his prologue to *Fulgentius metaforalis*. He considers his authors' intentions in an even more remarkable way in handling the sources on Julius Caesar. The first Roman emperor has provoked controversy through the ages. Was he right to seize power or was he a tyrant? Were his assassins justified? Many writers, ancient, medieval and modern, have been unable to make up their minds and have adopted an ambivalent attitude. Dante, it has been pointed out, held

---

[1] Appendix i, 314.   [2] Appendix i, 315.

Caesar's foundation of the empire to be providential and put Brutus and Cassius with Judas into Satan's mouths. Yet he also put the man who advised Caesar to cross the Rubicon into Hell as a Sower of Discord, and in *De monarchia* he sympathises with Cato, who preferred suicide to life without liberty. It amounts to 'an extraordinary series of contradictions'.[1] Ridevall felt bound to tackle the problem because Augustine counts Caesar's murder among the disasters which befell pagan Rome (iii, 30). Another tradition, represented in the chronicles of Marianus Scotus and Paul the Deacon, blamed Caesar as a tyrant. Ridevall submits that, if so, his murder would have been a benefit rather than a disaster to the commonwealth. Augustine would have erred in his judgment; he could not argue against the idolators that Caesar's death was a disaster, and hence that the pagan gods had failed to protect the Roman state from calamity. The problem is resolved partly by a scholastic distinction: to kill a tyrant (supposing that Caesar was a tyrant) may be good for the commonwealth 'simply and absolutely'; but it may be bad in a particular case owing to the circumstances: Caesar's murder led to civil war. Augustine meant that it was bad in this second way. Diverse authors agree with him. Ridevall quotes various judgments on the consequences of the murder.

Then he moves forward and confronts the divergent opinions on Julius Caesar. According to some, Caesar won power by violence, but afterwards corrected himself and ruled mercifully. The Roman people did not regard him as a tyrant, witness their rage at his murder, their symbolic cremation of his body and their building of a column to his memory. Ridevall quotes Richard of St Victor, Orosius and Martin of Troppau in support of this view. How then, he asks, can we accept the words of Marianus Scotus and Paul the Deacon, who say that Caesar was killed on account of his tyranny and insolence? Ridevall has recourse to what we should now call the 'class bias' of his authors. The senators and other potentates of the republic regarded Caesar as a tyrant because he struck at their power, and so they plotted to kill him. But the Roman people did not hold this opinion of him. Hence, says Ridevall, the histories sometimes speak of Caesar according to the senators' point of view; then they say that he behaved tyrannically and

[1] E. Schanzer, Dante and Julius Caesar, *Medium Aevum* 24 (1955) 20-22.

insolently. Sometimes they speak according to the people's point of view; then they say that he acted kindly and mercifully; Augustine agrees. Ridevall seems to have 'merited a revelation', like Hermes Trismegistos or Plato. True, he quotes late chronicles instead of going back to the primary sources. True, it does not occur to him that several may derive from the same source and may therefore be discounted as evidence. But this would not affect his reasoning, which is that the histories reflect different points of view. It followed that the student must interpret them accordingly. Ridevall grasped this principle of method, without, apparently, realising how new it was.

He goes on to condemn the conspirators for their motives, quoting Florus on their 'envy'. Their wickedness constituted a disaster in itself. John of Salisbury praises Caesar's popularity and military prowess; this indeed represented the most widely held estimate of him in the middle ages. Weighing up his soundness and valour in warfare, considering his honourable character, and measuring the ills and strife which befell the citizens of the Roman state after his death, we may be sure, says Ridevall, that it would have been better for the public good for Caesar to have remained alive than that he should have been killed by a plot. Consequently, Augustine makes his point: Caesar's death brought disaster to the material prosperity of the commonwealth.[1] Ridevall's political theory is not original. He believes tyranny to be a 'bad thing', but he dreads the possibly worse disorders which may result from tyrannicide. St Thomas argues on the same lines in his *De regimine principum* (i, 3 and 6). Ridevall's freshness lies in his mode of justifying St Augustine.

Supporting his author against the pagans and investigating their antiquities at the same time involved some conflict of loyalties. He held the balance very nicely. While defending Augustine's argument with all the force at his command, he still did his best for those good pagans so dear to the heart of a classicising friar. Ridevall seizes on any praise of their doctrine. Augustine quotes Persius on the truths which a man ought to know (*Sat.* iii, 66-72). When, he asks, did the gods teach such wholesome morals? The pagan poets held better opinions than the gods they worshipped (ii, 6). Ridevall lists and expounds the twelve notable

[1] Appendix i, 315.

truths in order to show that Augustine also taught all of them in various books of *De civitate Dei*. Thus he proves to his own satisfaction the basic agreement between the pagan poet Persius and the Church Father.[1]

Then Augustine quotes Varro as saying that the philosophers wrote for utility and the poets to give pleasure (vi, 2). Ridevall hurries to defend some at least of the poets against the charge that they wrote only to please. Varro did not mean to say that there was no pleasure in philosophy and no utility in poetry. Philosophy offers wonderful pleasures, as Aristotle proves. The Roman satirists did not only give pleasure: they were strong and sharp reprovers of vice and carnal indulgence, as appears in the books of Juvenal, Persius and of the poet Horace, as well in his Satires as in his Odes and Epistles. Varro meant to say that the end intended by the philosophers in their civil theology differed from that intended by the poets in their poetic theology. The philosophers aimed at utility or the attainment of truth. This indeed is of the greatest utility to the speculative intellect, as being its highest perfection. They also taught honour or moral virtue, which is of the greatest utility to the practical intellect. It was not so with the poets. Many poets made many songs inciting men to carnal pleasure, such as Ovid and many another, though others, such as the satirists, reproved the vices of the flesh. Some poets aimed at utility and others at pleasing, as Horace says:

aut prodesse volunt aut delectare poetae.[2]

Ridevall saw the satirists as his own spiritual ancestors. They ridiculed Roman society just as he might ridicule his contemporaries in his preaching. He defends them as moralists without regarding poetry as equivalent to 'natural theology'.[3]

We found that Waleys made shrewd comparisons and contrasts between ancient and medieval institutions. Ridevall equals him in insight. Varro's approach to religion perplexed Ridevall. It seemed strange that the Roman writer should dare to criticise fables about his gods, while upholding the civic cults which were based on such fables.

---

[1] ibid. 318.   [2] Appendix i, 319.

[3] St Augustine's quotations from Varro made a *locus classicus* for defence of poetry; see Guis. Billanovich, Pietro Piccolo da Monteforte tra il Petrarco e il Boccaccio, *Mediævo e Rinascimento. Studi in onore di Bruno Nardi* (Florence, 1955) 18-19.

K

Ridevall solved the contradiction in Varro's attitude by distinguishing between poetic fables and the legally established religion of ancient Rome. Worship of the gods and its procedures had been established by the emperors and *senatus consultus*. Specific penalties had been decreed against transgressors, as we learn from Valerius Maximus. The poets' sayings and fables, on the other hand, were not held as authoritative; it was permissible for anyone to think the opposite, to contradict freely or even to reject them. Varro, therefore, could condemn poetic theology, but he did not dare to attack political or civil. Ridevall looked for an illustration to show how this could happen. A thought struck him; he pointed to the medieval Church. 'Among us Catholics', as he puts it, there are many questions which the Church has not yet determined. Men may lawfully hold contrary opinions concerning the truth of such questions and may refute one another by argument and reason. But, once the Church has decided, no one may go against her sentence or contradict her. It was the same in the Roman commonwealth. The poets' authority obliged no man to refrain from saying what he liked; but no one could lawfully disobey what was decreed by *senatus consultus* and the emperors.[1] In each case, as Ridevall understood it, freedom of discussion depended on a legal decision.

His most striking contribution to scholarship was made rather by the way. Discussing St Augustine's use of Virgil to rebut the pagans, Ridevall asks himself whether the story of Dido and Aeneas is historically true. He decides on chronological grounds that it is not true, but a mere legend. All his guidance came from Papias' *Vocabularium*, a standard dictionary, and the chronicle of Marianus Scotus. Yet these two sources convinced Ridevall that Aeneas could never have met Dido, foundress and queen of Carthage, because he lived more than three hundred years earlier: 'If we go to history, therefore, it is not true that Aeneas saw Carthage or Queen Dido.'[2] Petrarch prided himself on being the first to expose as a legend the story that Dido killed herself for love of Aeneas: the historical Dido was true to her husband's memory. He claims to have made the discovery early in life.[3] Even so, he can hardly have anticipated Ridevall, working about 1332 or earlier, and he certainly did not publish it until much later. An Oxford Franciscan, grubbing

---

[1] Appendix i, 319.   [2] ibid. 320.   [3] Below, 293.

in medieval compilations, had already had the strength of mind to reject the most famous of Virgil's stories. Petrarch of course had no suspicion of this. Ridevall was too little read for anyone in Petrarch's circle to have noticed him. The commentary on *De civitate Dei* as contrived by Trevet and enlarged by Waleys and Ridevall had proved its value as a tool of research. A tool of some sort was indispensable before history and antiquities achieved the status of autonomous disciplines. Roman history became one in the late Renaissance; even then it was taught in the form of commentaries on Livy and Tacitus; a set text remained basic.[1] Late fifteenth-century commentaries on Virgil show a certain similarity to early fourteenth-century commentaries on *De civitate Dei* in providing scope for new interests which could find no outlet elsewhere:

> 'The text of Virgil is made a pretext for a historical review, aided and at the same time called for by the discovery of new sources. Curiosity pushes further back into the distant shadows of classical antiquity . . . and fastens on men and things of a time buried in oblivion, whence the new philology has the task of rescuing them.'[2]

This appreciation of Martino Filetico and his friends at Rome about 1470 describes what our friars were doing in their humbler way. They started as teachers of uneducated clergy and ended as scholars in their own right.

Ridevall at first strikes us as less successful than Waleys. He was thrown on his own resources and enjoyed none of the facilities that Waleys had at Bologna and Avignon. And yet Ridevall looked even further ahead. His scholastic training had shown him how to expose and confront divergent opinions in his authors. The scholastic mode of expounding texts taught him how to sift them with scrupulous care. Ridevall used this method to work on problems of ancient history. Florus' *Epitome* was a nameless old book to him, but he read it to good purpose.

There remains one puzzle about Ridevall. How could the self-same person be a forger of fancies, disguised as antiques, and a scholar of sound sense and critical ability? The answer, I think, is that every schoolman had a dual personality; Ridevall's was just an extreme case. A *Sentence-*

---

[1] A. Momigliano, *Contributo alla storia degli studi classici* (Rome, 1955) 75.

[2] C. Dionisotti, Lavinia venit litora, *I.M.U.* 289.

commentary had to be sober and unrhetorical. A sermon, on the contrary, was expected to be flowery and entertaining. Ridevall was in the second vein when he lectured on the Apocalypse, training his pupils to be preachers. Alone in his study, poring over St Augustine and his sources, Ridevall was a research worker of an austere type. Would it have distressed him to know that in the long run his fancies would have more effect than his scholarship?

CHAPTER VII

ROBERT HOLCOT

Straight mine eye has caught new pleasures . . .

Milton, *L'Allegro*.

I.—CAREER AND ACTIVITIES

'Bells ringing over the water make sweeter music and carry more strongly to greater distance.'

A Flemish Dominican, Michel du Four, used this charming comparison for the theme of his prologue to the Fourth Gospel: *The word of the Lord was made unto John* (Lc. iii, 2).[1] It expresses the aim of many early fourteenth-century commentators. They hoped that their teaching would have more effect if they presented it gracefully. Du Four based his lectures on St Thomas's commentary on the text, making them more popular and illustrating the moral teaching by nature lore. Robert Holcot marks the extreme of this tendency, though he differed from the Fleming in thinking in terms of sight rather than of sound. He represents a 'Decorated period' in the history of exegesis, preferring decoration to decorum. No medieval moralist, and it is a large claim, ever had a stronger sense of humour.

Holcot was the most celebrated and the most diversely gifted of all the friars in the classicising group. Specialists have found him interesting from various points of view. Historians of scholasticism know him as an intellectual sceptic, who rejected the traditional and Thomist proofs for the existence of God and who was one of the 'Pelagians' attacked in Bradwardine's defence of predestination. The complement to this position was fideism.[2] He enters into the history of science in virtue of his 'bonus tractatus de stellis', a book dealing with astronomy and geography and

[1] Quoted by T. Kaeppeli, Der Johanneskommentar des Michael de Furno O.P., *Arch. FF. Praed.* 4 (1934) 225-8: Secundum naturam verbum super aquam delectabilius in loco distantiori auditur, unde campane pulsantes super aquam delectabiliorem faciunt melodiam et ad loca distantiora virtuosius se diffundunt.

Du Four was assigned to read the *Sentences* at Paris in 1318.

[2] This is not the place for a full bibliography on Holcot as a scholastic; see *O.R.* 2, 946, and G. Leff, *Bradwardine and the Pelagians* (Cambridge, 1957) 216-27.

touching on astrology; it amounts loosely to a commentary on Aristotle's *De coelo*.[1] Holcot probably wrote it for use in teaching students in his Order: friars had to learn enough science to prepare them for a university course in theology in their own *studia*. The most personal and typical trait in the treatise is an opening question 'of a somewhat sensational and sophistical sort, perhaps intended to catch the attention of the lecturer's audience'. It was like Holcot to provoke his pupils by maintaining 'paradoxical positions' with his tongue in his cheek. We have met him already as a helper of Richard de Bury.[2] This side of him interests students of medieval book-hunting and of early humanism. Lastly he has a place in the history of preaching. The artificial, over-ingenious and pagan element in his *Moralitates* has been noted,[3] and he has an important role in the evolution of the *exemplum*.[4] It may be added as a sub-section in the history of preaching that Holcot has also intrigued the art-historians. His *Moralitates* contain curious, emblemlike 'pictures', akin to Ridevall's, but lending themselves more readily to illustration.[5] Fritz Saxl found actual miniatures in two German picture-books of the early fifteenth century. He could find no earlier illustrations and wondered why the 'pictures' had waited so long for an artist.[6]

Holcot fits into this book as a member of the classicising group. He played a key part in the movement, if we can speak of a 'movement'. The turning from scholarship to fantasy dates from Holcot's writings. He is linked to his more sober forerunners in two ways: Ridevall introduced him to the pleasures of fantasy or at least gave a dazzling show of its possibilities; Trevet, Waleys and Ridevall in his learned mood gave Holcot's fantasy much genuine classical lore to play upon. Holcot may be perverse; he is neither illiterate nor ignorant as a classicist.

His theological opinions would not have concerned us had he chosen to keep them in a watertight compartment. On

---

[1] L. Thorndike, A New Work by Robert Holcot (Corpus Christi College, Oxford, MS 138), *Archives internationales de l'histoire des sciences* 2 (1957) 227-35.

[2] See above, 67.

[3] G. R. Owst, *Preaching in Medieval England* (Cambridge, 1926) 301; *The Pulpit and Literature in Medieval England* (Cambridge, 1933) passim; see index.

[4] Welter, 360-66.   [5] *Fulgentius Metaforalis* 39.

[6] Aller Tugenden und Laster Abbildung, *Festschrift für Julius Schlosser* (Vienna, 1927) 116-21; A Spiritual Encyclopaedia of the Later Middle Ages, *J.W.C.I.* 5 (1942) 99-103, 115-17.

the contrary, he made no secret of his views on the burning
topics of the day, but taught them in his biblical commentaries, which were intended to train students as preachers.
I shall sum up his teaching on current problems in so far as
he brings it into his homiletics. A composite Holcot will
emerge, incomplete indeed, but at least uniting in himself
the several persons known to different types of specialist.

'Robert' means 'strength' and 'Holcot' 'cot in the rock';
so he tells us in a pun on his texts, *The Lord is my rock, and my
strength* (II Reg. xxii, 2) and *My dove in the clefts of the rock*
(Cant. ii, 14). Therefore his strength is in the Lord.[1]
Holcot is a village in Northamptonshire.[2] Robert probably
made his profession at the Dominican priory at Northampton,
an important midland centre which had been settled by the
Friars Preachers as early as 1233.[3] He was sent to study at
Oxford and was there from about 1326 to about 1334.[4] He
received licence to hear confessions in Lincoln diocese in
March 1332 (Oxford was in the Lincoln diocese). He
probably incepted in theology in the same year. His *Sermo
finalis*,[5] delivered when he resigned his chair to his successor,
Roger Gosford O.P.,[6] can be dated by its references to the
disturbances at Oxford caused by riots between northern
and southern students, which led to the migration to
Stamford in the spring of 1334;[7] he refers to the troubles
and not to the actual migration. This puts his Oxford
regency between the dates 1332 and 1334. It had lasted
a year. Holcot says that he won his chair in competition
against a certain Crathorn,[8] who had a special grace from
the university, whereas he himself had followed the normal
course of study. His professorship had been laborious: he
refers to his commentary on the *Sentences*; and owing to some

[1] He makes the pun in the prologue to his Wisdom-commentary, C, fol. 3rb-va:
Hec sunt autem foramina domuncule sive case, in quibus iuxta cognominis mei
sensum debeo conversari. Ita cognomen habeo a foramine case datum, et ideo
sicut nomen meum in robore, ita cognomen meum intueor in foramine petre.

It was a common practice to hide one's name in the text of one's opening
lecture; see D. Trapp, Augustinian theology of the fourteenth century, *Augustiniana* 6 (1956) 269-72.

[2] It means 'cot in the hollows'; see E. Ekwall, *The Concise Oxford Dictionary
of English Place-names* (Oxford, 1940) 233. Holcot's later connexion with
Northampton shows that he took his name from the Northamptonshire Holcot
and not the Bedfordshire.

[3] Hinnebusch, 495.   [4] *O.R.* 2, 946-7.

[5] J. C. Wey, The *Sermo finalis* of Robert Holcot, *Mediaeval Studies* 11 (1949)
219-22.

[6] *O.R.* 2, 794.

[7] *Victoria County History of Oxfordshire* 3 (1954) 8.   [8] *O.R.* 1, 511.

unspecified emergency he had had to lecture in hired rooms instead of at Blackfriars. Though weaker than others, he had persevered in his pursuit of wisdom.

It is possible that Holcot was sent from Oxford to Cambridge and had a second regency: two manuscripts of his Wisdom-commentary described him as a doctor of Cambridge. Our next definite date for him is given by a licence to hear confessions in Salisbury diocese before 1342. He was probably attached to the Dominican house at Salisbury.[1] Further licences prove that he was at Northampton between February 10, 1343 and October 21, 1348. This would support the tradition that he caught the plague while ministering to the sick and died at Northampton in 1349. His grave was remembered in a will as late as 1536, the very eve of the Reformation. A certain Mary Middleton made a bequest of vestments and plate to Northampton Blackfriars and asked to be buried in the church 'next to Holcott'.[2]

We have no exact date for his connexion with Bishop Richard de Bury. If he was ever attached to the bishop's household as his confessor or in some other official capacity it must have been after his Oxford and possibly Cambridge regencies and before he was licensed to hear confessions in Salisbury diocese, that is before 1342. They may have kept in touch when Holcot moved to Northampton and he may have acted as the bishop's literary executor after his death on April 14, 1345. Holcot's experience seems to have been purely English. There is no evidence that he ever went abroad.

[1] The priory at Wilton, founded in 1245, probably became a cell of Salisbury after 1281; see Hinnebusch, 56, 495.

[2] R. M. Serjeantson and H. I. Longden, The Parish Churches and Religious Houses of Northamptonshire, *Archaeological Journal* 70 (1913) 446. Fr G. Anstruther of Santa Sabina kindly sent this reference.

II.—BIBLICAL COMMENTARIES, SERMONS AND 'MORALITATES'[1]

Holcot left commentaries on three books of the Old Testament, Wisdom, Ecclesiasticus and the Twelve Lesser Prophets. All three bear unmistakable signs of having originated as lecture courses. It is important from the point of view of his mental development to discover if possible when and where they were given. For simplicity's sake it seems better to start from the end. The Ecclesiasticus-commentary breaks off after chapter vii. A tradition expressed in three different explicits held that he died before he could finish.[2] The fact that he made more use of Nicholas of Lyre here than in his other commentaries also suggests that it came later in his career.[3] Therefore Holcot must have been lecturing on Ecclesiasticus at Northampton, where he spent the last six years of his life and where he died. A close

---

[1] On the manuscripts and editions of these works of Holcot, see Stegmüller, no. 7411-25; Robert Holcot, 9-27. My quotations are from the following: (i) Twelve Prophets: MS Oxford, Bodl. 722 (2648)=B. The numbers in brackets refer to the Summary Catalogue, where a description will be found. It is an early fifteenth-century English copy. The earliest of the four surviving MSS is London, Gray's Inn 2, foll. 1ra-72ra, late fourteenth-century, which I have used for checking. The text is in a poor condition in all copies of this commentary. (ii) Wisdom: MS Oxford, Balliol College 27=C, written in England in the mid-fourteenth century by a scribe who seems to have had the 'liber magistri' (Holcot's own copy?) before him. The text is good, though already it has some mistakes; the original may not have been perfect. C also lacks a quire, involving the loss of *lectiones* lxxii-lxxxii, in whole or in part. I refer to the Bâle edition of 1586 for the lost part and for passages where there is no great difference in the text. This will enable readers to look up the context. My references to the *lectio* will enable other passages, quoted from C, to be looked up in print, if the reader wishes. (iii) Ecclesiasticus: I refer to the edition made at Venice, 1509, and have checked it from MSS Bâle, Universitätsbibliotek B.V.11 and London, Brit. Mus. Royal 2.F.vii. (iv) Moralitates: I refer to the numbers and text printed at the end of the Wisdom-commentary in the Bâle, 1586 edition. There are too many MSS of the *Moralitates* for a thorough survey. I have looked at a number of MSS and have reached the conclusion that although the order differs, the text of the Bâle edition is good enough for my purpose. A new edition of the *Moralitates* is desirable. (v) Sermons: I quote from MS Cambridge, Peterhouse 210=P, the sole surviving copy. See also *Arch, FF, Praed*, 29, (1959) 95.

[2] MS Braunschweig, Stadtbibl. 26, fol. 292v: Morte preventus nichil aliud de dicto libro exposuit.

MS London, Brit. Mus. Royal 3 A. xiv, fol. 67rb: Morte preventus residuum non complevit. This copy, fourteenth-century, from Reading Abbey, may well represent an early tradition.

ed. Venice, 1509, fol. 62vb: Clarissimi sacre theologie professoris magistri Roberti Holkot Anglici O.P., viri doctissimi, super prima capitula Ecclesiastici postilla eruditissima explicit. Quam doctor ipse preclarus a Deo vocatus ac morte preventus explere non potuit.

[3] See below, 150.

scrutiny leaves the impression that the teaching in it is just a little more elementary than that in the Wisdom-commentary, which represents a university course; otherwise there is no difference in technique. Hence the lectures on Ecclesiasticus bear interesting witness to the teaching activities of the friars in their 'extra-mural' schools up and down the country.

The commentary on the Twelve Prophets may have been the earliest of the three. Unlike the other two, it survives in four manuscript copies only and has never been printed. No wonder! It was copied and circulated from a set of very rough lecture notes, which refer to the actual quires of the master's notebook and contain allusions to points that he intended to make, the kind of personal shorthand used by all lecturers in a hurry. Holcot for some reason never prepared the completed course for publication. The four surviving copies, three of them prettily illuminated, show that even his untidy sheaf of notes found readers. Two Oxford *exempla* suggest that the place was Oxford, though this is not quite conclusive.[1] The *terminus a quo* is 1332, since Holcot refers to his *Sentence*-commentary.[2] Veiled allusions to current events point to a date not long after the deposition of Edward II in 1327. Holcot complains of bishops, perhaps of one in particular, who stir up the people and clergy, flee from the country's enemies and ruin their lord through opportunism and bribery.[3] The passage goes further than the moralists' stock-in-trade under the heading 'bad prelates'; it hints at specific treachery. Holcot would have been agreeing with many of his contemporaries if he blamed the conduct of the English bishops in the crises of Edward II's reign, attacking more especially those who went over to Mortimer

---

[1] B, fol. 56: Nota quomodo quidam scolaris Oxonie doluit dentes. The story breaks off here.

fol. 86: Nota quomodo quidam magister Oxonie consumpsit omnia bona sua in meretrice quadam, et cum non haberet plus ad tribuendum, ipsa caute eum occidit.

Oxford *exempla* may occur in a lecture given elsewhere. See Forte, 329.

[2] B, fol. 94: Da hac materia require diffuse in questionibus quas tractavi super quartum Sententiarum.

fol. 94v: De istis dixi super secundum Sententiarum.

fol. 115: De ista materia dixi super primum Sententiarum.

[3] B, fol. 58: Constat autem quod prelati cupidi faciunt perturbationes in populo et in clero. Homo impavidus expavescit, quando aliquis pomposus, audax et strenuus inter pauperes sibi subiectos, debiles et egenos, fugit hostes regni, vel ductus tempore, accipiens pecuniam, perdit dominum suum regem, et hoc facit perturbationem.

and Isabella to their own profit.[1] The deposed king had
been a good friend to the Dominicans and Holcot may well
have shared the sympathies of his Order for Edward.[2]
Another allusion to the defeat of the English at the hands of
the Scots shows that he taught when the reverses of Edward's
reign still rankled.[3] The English are compared to owls,
because all nations despise and mock at them.[4] The fall of
Mortimer and the beginning of Edward III's personal rule
in October 1330 may have inspired Holcot's thanksgiving
that the English now have a king to hearten them and lead
them to victory; the great shame of the country, in his
opinion, is the lack of wise barons and earls.[5] All this puts
the lecture course soon after the *terminus a quo* in 1332. The
year of the Oxford regency, 1333-4, is indicated.

If we fill up this year with lectures on the Twelve
Prophets, we shall have to put the Wisdom-commentary
a little later. It was the custom at Paris, and probably also
at Oxford and Cambridge, for the doctor to lecture on a
book of the Old and a book of the New Testament concurrently. We know in fact that Holcot at least began a
course on the Gospels during his Oxford regency. He could
hardly have run three courses together. The lectures on

[1] For contemporary opinion and modern criticism of it see K. Edwards,
The Political Importance of the English Bishops during the Reign of Edward
II, *E.H.R.* 59 (1944) 311-47; J. L. Grassi, William Airmyn and the Bishopric
of Norwich, ibid. 70 (1955) 550-61.

[2] Knowles, I, 169.

[3] The twelfth-century English chronicler Henry of Huntingdon tells how a
certain holy man prophesied that the English would be defeated by the French
and even by the Scots, whom they despised, as a punishment for their sins;
Historia Anglorum (Rolls Series) 173. The English defeats at the hands of the
Scots in Edward II's reign brought this prophecy into circulation. The Canon
of Bridlington recalls it apropos of the Scottish invasion of 1322; Gesta Edwardi,
Chronicles of the Reigns of Edward I and Edward II (Rolls Series) 2, 80-81. Holcot
tells it, quoting Henry of Huntingdon, B, fol. 57.

[4] Holcot is comparing the English to monkeys, owls, asses and peacocks, on
account of their various vices; B, fol. 94v: . . . bubonibus propter aliorum contemptum et irreverentiam, quia communiter omnes nationes contempnunt
anglicos et derident.

[5] Holcot tells a story, ascribed to Trogus Pompeius, which he may have taken
from John of Wales (*Communiloquium*, op. cit., fol. 59va), of how the Macedonians
were defeated by the Illyrians, because they had no king to lead them; but
when their infant king was carried on to the battlefield, they won a victory.
B, fol. 15v: . . . Hec ibi. Ex istis accipitur quod ipsi (macedones) dixerant se
prius victos quia non defuit animus, sed dominus . . . Benedictus Deus! Anglici
modo possunt dicere: nunc habemus animum et regem etc. Verumptamen
credo quod una de maioribus ignominiis Anglie est paucitas baronum et
comitum sapientum.
He tells the same story on Wisdom (lect. cxx, p. 404), but without making
any comment on current events.

Wisdom, moreover, spread over two academic years, beginning about Michaelmas. This commentary, unlike that on the Twelve Prophets, is divided into *lectiones*, 212 in all.[1] In *lectio* liv he refers to the feast of the Conversion of St Paul (January 25) as to be celebrated tomorrow.[2] He had reached the first Sunday after Easter by *lectio* lxxxiii, according to a marginal note, 'i post Pascha' (C, fol. 127ra), and he was looking forward to next day's break for Whitsuntide by the end of *lectio* c.[3] Supposing that he gave six more lectures between Whitsuntide and long vacation, he would have divided the course evenly, 106 lectures per year. The second set, *lectiones* cvii-ccxii, contain no evidence as to the season when they were given, but this is not surprising; the evidence for the first set is quite casual.

Two references provide a rough *terminus a quo* for the whole course. Holcot quotes a 'wisecrack' against subtle questions by Simon Mepham, archbishop of Canterbury June 5, 1328-October 12, 1333.[4] Since this is the type of story which circulates after the subject's death, Holcot would probably have started the second year of his course (we are at *lectio* cxvii) in or after the autumn of 1333. The other reference is more general and comes in the prologue. Holcot says that canon and civil law should follow theology, as a maid follows her mistress, not walk beside her. It is dangerous, unsuitable and absurd that lawyers should determine in their legal terms concerning the articles of the faith, the sacraments

---

[1] The commentary on the Twelve Prophets in the manuscripts is divided according to the chapters of the biblical text; there is no separate division into *lectiones*. Perhaps the original lecture course comprised one lecture on each biblical chapter, but it does not seem safe to calculate the total length of the course on this assumption.

[2] C, fol. 89va: et sic fuit sanctissimus predicator, sanctus Paulus, splendor ecclesie, cuius cras conversationem celebrabimus, instructus tam in moralibus quam scientialibus ad pedem Gamalielis doctoris.

[3] C, fol. 153va: quia ergo Spiritus iste intelligentie est nobis ita multipliciter necessarius, dignum est cessare, et circa huius cultum istis diebus vacare antequam ulterius procedamus.
Holcot has just devoted a lecture to the text vii, 22-3, which he has interpreted of the Holy Spirit. Further evidence that the course covered two years is given by Stegmüller, no. 7416, from a Naples manuscript.

[4] Sap. lect. cxvii, p. 393: Nota dictum Simonis de Mepham, Cantuariensis archiepiscopi. Ista, inquit, valent in urbe, non in orbe, loquens de subtilitatibus questionum.
The only work of a literary kind ascribed to Mepham is the Speculum Regis Edwardi; see L. E. Boyle, The *Oculus Sacerdotis* of William of Pagula, *T.R.H.S.* 5th series, vol. 5 (1955) pp. 104, 107. Since this saying does not occur in the Speculum, it must have been remembered from his talk. It agrees with his reputation for holy simplicity; see *D.N.B.* 13, 260-3.

of the Church, the beatific vision and the gravity of sins. This turns Catholics into schismatics, the faithful into heretics and doctors into flatterers. The outburst ends with an open allusion: 'as has happened to you recently, and as you have just seen by experience'.[1] Holcot is referring to the beatific vision controversy, started by Pope John XXII in December 1331. It had not died down by the time of his death on December 4, 1334. Thomas Waleys had been arrested and imprisoned for heresy on account of his sermon preached at Avignon on January 3, 1333. He was still in prison and was not released by John's successor. Waleys had attacked as 'flatterers' those theologians who supported the Pope's opinion. John's views had certainly caused scandal, if not schism in Christendom.[2] He was a lawyer rather than a theologian by training, a point which Holcot's audience would not miss. Holcot himself would have felt strong resentment at the fate of his fellow Dominican. The reference, coming at the beginning of the course, suggests the autumn of 1333 or a year or two later.

Given that the lectures on the Twelve Prophets belong to the Oxford regency, 1333-4, and that the lectures on Wisdom cannot have been started in the same year, it would make sense to send Holcot to Cambridge for a two-year regency, 1334-6. This would explain why manuscripts of the Wisdom-commentary seen by Echard called Holcot a Cambridge man. The lectures on Wisdom contain nothing to suggest that they were given in Oxford, but their whole atmosphere is that of a university. They contain no obvious allusions to current English politics. The lapse of a few more years would explain why the civil war and defeats of Edward II's reign had ceased to weigh on his mind. Further, the Wisdom-commentary represents Holcot's *chef d'œuvre*. It made him 'famous overnight', as Fr Wey has put the matter. Holcot on Wisdom became a standard part of the equipment of every good theological library in the later

---

[1] C, fol. 2vb: Et signanter dicitur quod ista famula dominam sequebatur. Nimis enim periculosum est, inconveniens et absurdum quod cum sua domina pariliter passu procedat, quod ipsa de fidei articulis, de ecclesie sacramentis, de visione beatorum vel pondere peccatorum determinet iuxta verba legum in terrenis negotiis usitata (MS visitata). Hec enim catholicos in schismaticos, fideles in hereticos et doctores in adulatores convertit, sicut recenter vobis occurrit et nuper experimento vidistis.

[2] *Le procès* 7-63. Waleys accused the supporters of John XXII's opinion of being weak-kneed and said that the whole church was scandalised, ibid. 105, 108.

middle ages. His popularity is reflected in the extraordinary number of manuscripts both in England and on the Continent and in the number of early printed editions. If the Wisdom-commentary were later than that on the Twelve Prophets, it would show that Holcot had found his feet. He had not polished his notes on the Twelve Prophets enough to make them presentable. He did get the lectures on Wisdom into publishable form and they succeeded brilliantly.

A fragmentary commentary on Ecclesiastes may perhaps be ascribed to Holcot. It has been copied into a volume with abridgments of his commentaries on Wisdom and Ecclesiasticus in a fourteenth-century English manuscript, London, Brit. Mus. Royal 2.D.iv, foll. 90-159v. Whether the original was a complete commentary cannot be known, since the text here breaks off at iii, 20, the rest having been lost. Local allusions place it in England and it is in Holcot's classicising style.[1] Hence it is more likely to be his than the commentary ascribed to him in some continental manuscripts, which differs in technique from his authentic works.[2] I have not studied the incomplete commentary closely enough to say whether it has any indications of place or date or any proof that Holcot was the author. It might represent notes which were never written up and which did not achieve even the limited circulation of the lectures on the Twelve Prophets.

Holcot intended to lecture on St Matthew and got as far as giving his inaugural in the form of a *principium*.[3] Here he apologises to his hearers, 'socii reverendi, qui in hac universitate lectores biblie sunt hoc anno', for deferring it so long. He pleads distracting business and broken health as the reason. Now, however, the feast of the Purification (February 2) has passed. He dares not delay any further and he performs the scholastic act appropriately on St Scholastica's day (February 10).[4] The university was probably Oxford.

---

[1] See Robert Holcot, 9-10. The script is so rough as to be barely legible in places.

[2] Stegmüller, no. 4936; see below, 278. Stegmüller ascribes yet another anonymous commentary on Ecclesiastes to Holcot, but without giving his reasons, no. 7414.

[3] The *principium* is Fr Wey's discovery, kindly passed on to me; see Robert Holcot, 24.

[4] MS London, Brit. Mus. Royal 10.C.vi, fol. 136vb: Ego autem, occupatione temporali distractus et dispositione corporali confractus, exilem illam oblationem, quam volui facere, non valui usque modo. Iam autem, postquam illa Virgo, cuius semper spero presidium, cuius semper imploro subsidium, cuius habitum semper geram, cuius regnum queram, puerum Iesum presentavit in

Manuscript tradition has attached the *principium* to Holcot's *Sentence*-commentary, which belongs to Oxford together with his *Sermo finalis*. He makes the same complaints about health and business in both *principium* and *Sermo finalis*. The date would therefore be February 1334. The *principium* promises a lecture course on St Matthew to follow. Holcot plays on the number thirty in the text: *I will give you thirty shirts and as many coats* (Iud. xiv, 12). *Thirty* corresponds to the lectures of his projected course, twenty-eight chapters of St Matthew plus a prologue and 'today's lecture'. Holcot will give his audience thirty lectures corresponding to the thirty coats. The thirty shirts, of thinner stuff than the coats, signify his literal expositions of the Gospel text, which will be very thin in his lectures. In other words, he meant to concentrate on *moralitates*.[1]

The remaining twenty-nine lectures are lost, if Holcot ever carried out his promise to give them. But some of their *moralitates* may have passed into his sermons. These are preserved in a single manuscript which is now no. 210 of Peterhouse, Cambridge.[2] The attribution to Holcot is in a later hand, but its genuineness is attested by the authentic excerpt from his Wisdom commentary which follows and by the contents. The homilist was certainly English: he follows the Sarum Use[3] and occasionally uses English

---

templo, quem attulit et intulit et optulit, attulit in Ierusalem, intulit in templum et optulit Deo Patri, iam, inquam, ultra proscrastinare non audeo, sed statim *Ierusalem evangelistam dabo*, actumque istum scholasticum die Scholastice virginis, que tunc valde convenienter evenit, inchoabo.

The *Ierusalem evangelistam dabo* (Isa. xli, 27) is the opening text of the *principium*.

[1] ibid., fol. 137ra: De hoc autem meo offertorio faciendo exponere possum illud Iudicum xiv: Dabo vobis triginta sindones et totidem tunicas. Cuius ratio est quod quia evangelium Mathei habet 28 capitula, que cum uno prologo et lectione hodierna faciunt 30, ecce triginta tunice; sed triginta sindones, qui sunt panni tenues, signant litterales expositiones, que per me super illas tunicas valde tenuiter apponuntur. Dabo ergo vobis triginta sindones et totidem tunicas.

[2] Echard mentions the Peterhouse MS and another collection of Sunday sermons, now MS Oxford, Bodl. 687 (2501), op. cit., 632. The second has a different incipit and is ascribed clearly elsewhere to John Waldeby; see *Summary Catalogue* under no. 2501. Since Peterhouse 210 is not foliated all through, I shall refer to the numbers of the sermons, marked throughout the MS in red. They are short enough to make it possible to trace a reference easily. See M. R. James, *A Descriptive Catalogue of the MSS in the Library of Peterhouse* (Cambridge, 1899) 251-2.

[3] The Lenten sermon, no. xlv, which will be quoted frequently, refers to the prayers said before the blessing of the ashes on Ash Wednesday, according to the *Sarum Missal* (ed. J. Wickham Legg, Oxford, 1916) 49: sed certo modo est tempus gratie, misericordie et indulgentie, sicut ecclesia canit. The Gospels and Epistles follow the Sarum Missal.

phrases.[1] He quotes the same type of classical and pseudo-classical source as Holcot does and tells one characteristic story, also found in the Wisdom commentary.[2] He attacks the doctrine of predestination.[3] Sermon no. xlvii, for the first Sunday in Lent, has an Oxford setting, referring to the system of loans from university chests. Private benefactors from the late thirteenth century onwards had been establishing chests from which loans might be made to poor scholars on deposit of a pledge, usually in the form of a book.[4] The homilist describes the procedure carefully and mentions the bedels, university officials responsible for routine duties, 'in this university'.[5] He points out in the same sermon how evil spirits vex the university especially in the holy season of Lent. There are rows at night and riots, blows, slaughter, homicide and wicked conspiracy by day.[6] Medieval universities were never orderly, but this suggests something worse than usual. It could refer to events in the spring of 1333, which led to a royal commission of inquiry into disturbances at Oxford, appointed on May 6 of that year, or to the troubles of the year following.[7] In that case we are near to Holcot's Oxford regency of 1333-4.

It need not be assumed that all the 119 sermons of the collection are Holcot's, but they all seem to come from his milieu. I shall refer to them as Holcot's to avoid clumsy phrasing.

The title of the collection, 'Sermons for Sundays and weekdays', does not mean that each Sunday and weekday

---

[1] *Sermo* xxiv: Anglice, bond of buxumnesse, lif of bysynesse, stat of worthyness. *Sermo* lviii has an *exemplum* about three devils called Hardhert, Lokepors and Stoppemouth. *Sermo* lxv has an *exemplum* about a girl called Lothe, who changes her name to Rosa. The same story has already been told in *Sermo* xviii, but here the names are Feda and Honesta, i.e. Latin instead of English.

[2] See below, 334.

[3] See below, 190.

[4] *Victoria County History, Oxfordshire* 3 (1954)9.

[5] *Sermo* xlvii: Karissimi, scholares in universitate ista, qui nimis diligunt delicate vivere, patiuntur penuriam pecunie in expensis, et causa est quia non ad necessitatem expendunt, sed ad superfluitatem consumunt. Ex hoc enim contingit interdum quod libros suos et alia pretiosa iocalia impignerare coguntur communibus cistis. Sed receptor pecunie nomen suum scribit diligenter in principio libri sui, ne liber alienetur ab eo in perpetuum, et bedellus proclamat quod quicumque veniat die assignato; aliter cautionem perdat.

[6] ibid.: Et nota quomodo spiritus nequam hanc universitatem temptando magis modo infestant hiis sacris diebus. Iam de nocte oriuntur perturbationes, de die seditiones et verbera, trucidationes et homicidia, prave confederationes. Et non est dubium quin sit temptatio diaboli ad impediendum sanctas occupationes que deberent modo isto tempore fieri.

[7] See above, p. 135, n. 7.

has its sermon. Christmas Day, the Epiphany, Easter Sunday and Sundays 8-17 after Trinity Sunday are omitted. Yet the feast of the Circumcision (January 1) is included. Two sermons towards the end are headed 'Sermo ad curatos' and 'Sermo ad religiosos' respectively,[1] while the last sermon of all has no heading. It is not for preaching on a text for the liturgical year, but is intended for a clerical congregation, perhaps a synod.[2] There are sometimes two or more sermons for the same day; Passion Sunday has as many as seven (no. lxvii-lxxiii) of which no. lxxii is addressed to religious. The tone of all supposes a university audience or at least an audience of clergy. Most of them start from the Gospel for the day, but some take their text from the Epistle. The construction varies. All begin 'Dearly beloved' and end with a prayer. Within this framework we find fully worked out schemes, as recommended in the *Artes praedicandi*, and simple *moralitates*, which might have been lifted straight out of a lecture on Scripture.

A possible explanation would be that Holcot assembled notes or drafts of sermons, which he had given or thought he might give, and put them into order. The gap of ten Sundays for the summer months suggests long vacation. If he had unpublished lecture notes on New Testament books by him, he might well use them for his sermons.

The *Moralitates*, a series of moralised *exempla* for the use of preachers, are printed at the end of the Bâle edition of the Wisdom-commentary (pp. 709-48). J. Th. Welter has published a list of manuscripts and has compared the manuscript traditions. He found that the edition put the items in a more logical order than that of the earlier manuscripts and that the number of items varied slightly.[3] J. A. Herbert lists and summarises the *exempla* in the British Museum manuscripts of the *Moralitates*, giving sources and analogues where possible.[4]

The date depends on the relationship between the *Moralitates* and the *Gesta Romanorum*, a compilation which

---

[1] The sermons get out of order towards the end: no. cvi, 7th Sunday after Trinity; no. cvii, 4th Sunday in Lent (omitted in its proper place); no. cviii, 18th after Trinity; no. cix, 'sermo ad curatos' (not on a text of the year); no. cx, 19th after Trinity; no. cxi, 'sermo ad religiosos'; no. cxii-cxviii, 20th after Trinity up to Advent.

[2] The text is *Apprehendite arma et scutum* (Ps. xxxiv, 2). Bishops and priests are urged to acquit themselves well in the spiritual warfare.

[3] Welter, p. 360, n. 63. See also Stegmüller, op. cit.

[4] 106-16.

L

seems to have originated in a Franciscan milieu in England. The earliest manuscript of the *Gesta Romanorum*, now at Innsbruck, is dated 1342; it represents a version which was later altered and expanded.[1] Welter argued that the compiler borrowed from Holcot and not vice versa. A comparison of the *Gesta Romanorum* with Holcot's biblical commentaries bears out his argument. Only a few of Holcot's *exempla* are common to his *Moralitates* and his commentaries. The *Gesta Romanorum* contains many *exempla* from the *Moralitates*, but none, as far as I can see, from the commentaries. This suggests very strongly that the compiler of *Gesta Romanorum* borrowed from the *Moralitates*, where he had all the *exempla* collected together. Had Holcot borrowed from *Gesta Romanorum* he could have used it for his commentaries as well as for his *Moralitates*. This would give a *terminus ad quem* for the *Moralitates* of a few years before 1342, to allow time for the compilation of *Gesta Romanorum* before the writing of the first copy known to us. I think that the *Moralitates* came after the commentary on the Twelve Prophets. Here Holcot uses the 'picture' technique which characterises many items of the *Moralitates*, but it strikes me as much less effective and developed in the commentary than it is in the *Moralitates*.[2] Hence the *Moralitates* would come after *c.* 1334, the date of the commentary on the Twelve Prophets, and before 1342, by which time the compiler of *Gesta Romanorum* had used them.

The extraordinary success of the *Moralitates* is proved by the large number of manuscripts, widely scattered, and by quotations. Some items reappear in an *exempla* collection of the later fourteenth century, MS Brit. Mus. Harl. 7322.[3] Some are quoted with or without acknowledgment to Holcot in a continental collection, anonymous, but known from the incipit as 'Prudentia depingebatur' or 'Prudentia secundum aliquos depingitur'. This is a collection of 'pictures' of virtues, vices and concepts, such as Human Nature, Wisdom,

---

[1] Ed. W. Dick (Erlangen-Leipzig, 1890). The later version was edited by H. Oesterley, Berlin, 1872. He gives the parallels with the *Moralitates*. On the date and origin of *Gesta Romanorum* see Welter, 367-75. For an account of it, see below, 183.

[2] See below, 179. Welter thought that the *Moralitates* came after the Wisdom commentary, because the latter does not use the 'picture' technique at all: but neither does the Ecclesiasticus commentary, which probably belongs to the end of Holcot's life. He may have regarded it as more suitable to the exposition of the Prophets than to that of Wisdom literature.

[3] See Herbert, 166-79.

Foolish Love, True Love, Flattery and Prayer.[1] The compiler has borrowed with express reference to Holcot on
Temperance and Prayer, and without acknowledgment on
Flattery, Mercy and Piety.[2] Later still, some 'pictures' from
the *Moralitates* were illuminated in two independent compilations containing descriptions of virtues and vices and
other didactic material, lavishly illustrated, MSS Rome,
Casanatensis and London, Wellcome Museum. Both
picture books come from Germany and were made in the
early fifteenth century.[3]

   Another aid to preaching prepared by Holcot, the
Convertimini, need not detain us here.[4] It contains many
exempla, but only one 'picture' of the type found in the
Moralitates, a 'picture' of Justice. This would put its composition in the same period of Holcot's life as the *Moralitates*,
that is after the lectures on the Twelve Prophets. Otherwise
there is no indication of date.[5]

   Summarising an admittedly hypothetical scheme, we get
the following order: the lectures on the Twelve Prophets
belong to Holcot's Oxford regency, 1333-4; the lectures on
Wisdom belong to a Cambridge regency, after the academic
year 1333-4 and before 1342, perhaps 1334-6. The
Moralitates, which do not represent a university course, came
after the lectures on Wisdom. The lectures on Ecclesiasticus

---

   [1] Liebeschütz gives a list of MSS and analyses the content from MS Rome,
Vat. Palat. lat. 1066, foll. 231v-234v, in *Fulgentius Metaforalis*, 49-53, 115. I
have worked on the copy in MS Paris, Bibl. nat. lat. 590, foll. 177-89. Holcot's
Moralitates have been copied into the same volume, foll. 73-99v; the two are
often found together. One of the 'pictures' is ascribed to a chancellor of Paris,
fol. 185: 'secundum cancellarium parisiensem depingitur sic. . . . ' This seems
to have led to the ascription of the whole collection to the same man: 'Tractatus
de vitiis et virtutibus datus per reverendum magistrum nostrum cancellarium
parisiensem, sacre pagine professorem' is the title in the Paris MS. This in turn
has led to the identification of the Paris chancellor with Jean Gerson, though a
recent study of his works does not include the treatise; see P. Glorieux, La vie et
les œuvres de Gerson, *Archives* 18 (1951) 149-92. It would be difficult to decide
between the eight Paris chancellors who held office between 1336 (the earliest
date for Holcot's *Moralitates*, which are quoted in the treatise) and 1395, the
palaeographical *terminus ad quem;* some MSS of the treatise are late fourteenth-
century.
   [2] MS lat. 590, foll. 180v (sicut optime declaretur in moralitatibus Holcoth,
moralitate 4a); 187; 183; 186; 187. The corresponding items in Holcot's
Moralitates are no. 4, 2, 39, 15, 8 in the same Paris manuscript, no. XXXVIII,
XIX, LXIII, X, III of the Bâle edition, where the order is different.
   [3] See above, p. 134, n. 6.
   [4] Described by Welter, p. 366, n. 63, and analysed by Herbert, 116-55. The
Convertimini has never been printed.
   [5] For the *Tractatus de septem vitiis*, wrongly ascribed to Holcot, see Robert
Holcot, 27-8.

belong to Northampton, 1343-9, the last six years of his life. The fragmentary lectures on Ecclesiastes, if genuine, could be fitted into the last period at Northampton. They might even have been given at Salisbury around 1342. The collected sermons probably represent a life-time of preaching and teaching, though one at least suggests 1333-4.

III.—METHOD AND SOURCES

Holcot follows the scholastic method of exegesis: he starts with a general introduction to the book or group of books;[1] he divides his text; he explains the literal sense; he treats questions (*quaestiones* or *dubitationes*) on theology or casuistry arising from it; he draws out its allegorical or moral significance; this offers him his opportunity to train his pupils as preachers. As he warned his hearers in his *principium* on St Matthew, his literal exposition of the text was 'very thin'. In his lectures on the Twelve Prophets it is very thin indeed and nowhere does he bother with scholarly investigation into Old Testament history or into textual problems. The Wisdom literature raised less intractable difficulties than did the Twelve Prophets in respect of the literal sense. He explains to his pupils the allusions to earlier scriptural history made by his authors and he clarifies their argument as best he can. The books of Wisdom and Ecclesiasticus suited him. His prologues glow with emotional pleasure, rare in medieval commentaries, as he enters with gusto into the praise of wisdom and of moral conduct. The Wisdom Books appealed to Holcot and his contemporaries as the biblical equivalent of the didactic literature on political and moral science and of the philosophical 'sentences' which they loved so well. Some manuscript copies of Holcot on Wisdom have a note following the explicit, summarising the content of the book of Wisdom: 'Although wisdom is found in each part of Holy Scripture, it is contained especially and in a particular form in this book, where kings and princes are instructed on the worship of God and on right conduct.'[2]

---

[1] The lectures on the Twelve Prophets begin with a division and have no set prologue; but this lecture course has come down in a rough set of notes and may have lost its prologue.

[2] MSS London, Brit. Mus. Add. 31,216, fol. 175va, and Cambridge, Pembroke College 181, fol. 138vb: Quamvis ista sapientia in qualibet parte scripture sacre valeat inveniri, specialiter tamen et quadam peculiari forma in libro sapientie continetur, in quo reges et principes de cultu Dei et bonis moribus informantur.

It was here that the pious reader could find most easily those 'thousand lessons of moral teaching' promised him by Richard de Bury. While the Wisdom literature had gained in popularity with the Paris masters of the thirteenth century, the book of Wisdom itself had received no satisfying treatment. Holcot's lectures on the biblical *Governance of Princes* came at the right time. He equipped it with a compendium of sacred and secular learning. Pierre Ceffons, who aimed at the same kind of amalgam as Holcot, describes him admiringly as: 'Magister Robertus Holcot, qui scripsit super librum Sapientiae, vir notabilis litteraturae et in doctrinis theologicis plurimum eruditus.'[1] The Ecclesiasticus-commentary had an appeal similar to that on Wisdom and it won only a little less success: it is unfinished and not quite so exuberant.

Holcot uses an informal, conversational tone in all three commentaries. It is most marked on the Twelve Prophets, where he will break off a discussion saying: 'I leave you to work that out.'[2] In the Wisdom-commentary he will address his audience as 'viri scholastici',[3] but he speaks to them more lightly after a lecture devoted to the dangers of female society for young men:

> 'And so let me end at last with Valerius and say: "May God almighty grant that you be not misled by woman's wiles and enlighten your heart, lest you turn where I fear." '[4]

He says when discussing *libido* in marriage that such questions may seem low and very remote from holy contemplation, but they shouldn't be unknown to preachers and pastors, whose business is always to be general practitioners of souls.[5]

His *quaestiones* correspond to his special type of teaching. They are miscellaneous in content and often bear no obvious relationship to the literal interpretation of the text under discussion. They are scholastic in form, but not so developed or so advanced as those in *Sentence*-commentaries, *quaestiones*

---

[1] D. Trapp, Peter Ceffons, *Rech. Théol.* 24 (1957) 113.
[2] B, fol. 94: Relinquo vobis argui.   [3] Sap. lect. xcvi, p. 323.
[4] ibid., xxxviii, p. 136, C, fol. 63rb: Concludam igitur finaliter cum Valerio et dicam: Det vobis Deus omnipotens femine falaciis non falli et illuminet cor vestrum, ne tendatis quo timeo.
Holcot refers to the *Dissuasio Valerii de uxore non ducenda.*
[5] ibid., xliv, p. 158, C, fol. 73rb: Licet ista videantur vilia et a sancta contemplatione valde distantia, non tamen debent esse incognita nec predicatoribus nec pastoribus, quorum interest semper esse generales medicos animarum.

ordinariae or *quodlibets*. They were spoken by the master, not disputed as a scholastic exercise. Holcot follows the custom of not going too deeply into theological problems in his lectures on Scripture and of quoting theologians of the last generation rather than contemporaries.[1] The place for speculative theology was in lectures on the *Sentences* and in disputations. Why then did he introduce *quaestiones* at all? He was training his schoolmen, specialists in theology, to be general educators. As well as preaching, they might have to lecture on theology in priory or in cathedral schools to clergy who would never get to a university. Holcot's *quaestiones* and *dubitationes* would help them to give simple instruction within the framework of a lecture or sermon. His lectures on Ecclesiasticus, if they were given at Northampton, were catering for precisely this type of non-university man. These theological sections are interesting in that Holcot puts forward his personal views on questions of the hour more clearly and shortly than he could do in the intricacies of scholastic argument. Pagan writers press in even here. When Holcot discusses the question whether it is lawful to kill infidels in order to recover the Holy Land, he cites the so-called letter of Aristotle to Alexander, dissuading him from bloodshed, among the Christian authors *contra*.[2] The sermons resemble the lectures in containing theological discussion in some places as well as *moralitates*.

Holcot's personal interests are reflected in his choice of sources. His quotations from exegetes are limited for the most part to standard authorities, the latest being Pierre Auriol's *Compendium litteralis sensus totius Bibliae* and Nicholas of Lyre, whose famous *Postilla litteralis* was just coming on the market. Holcot quotes him on the Gospel in his lectures

---

[1] Duns Scotus is the latest theologian to be quoted by name, B, fol. 117. On the cautious and elementary character of theological *quaestiones* in biblical commentaries of the late thirteenth century, see B. Smalley, A commentary on the Hexaemeron by Henry of Ghent, *Rech. Théol.* 20 (1953) 86-99. Holcot discusses the question whether the damned in hell will be punished by burning in material fire apropos of Sap. xvii, 5, lect. clxxxix, p. 621, and ends cautiously: In ista dubitatione non est querenda nova fictio, sed cum reverentia recitanda sunt dicta sanctorum. Volo igitur recitare quid de igne inferni, quid de loco et igne purgatorii senserint doctores antiqui.

[2] Sap. lect. lxvi, C, fol. 107vb: Item Aristoteles in quadam epistola ad Alexandrum sic dicit: O Alexander, noli sanguinem effundere, quia quotiens creatura creaturam occidit, virtutes celorum moventur ad divinam vindictam.

Holcot has just quoted Mt. xxvi, 52: omnes enim qui acceperint gladium, gladio peribunt. The 'letter' is Pseudo-Aristotle, Secretum secretorum, ed. R. Steele, *Opera hactenus inedita Rogeri Baconi* 5 (Oxford 1920) 55. Holcot makes a rough quotation.

on the Twelve Prophets (once only) and four times on Kings in his lectures on Ecclesiasticus. Lyre's postills on the Twelve Prophets, Wisdom and Ecclesiasticus probably appeared too late for him to use in his lectures.[1] His choice of non-exegetical sources makes a strong contrast in its range and variety. A complete study of them would keep a team of research students busy for several years. To turn the pages of the Wisdom-commentary in the Bâle edition, where the verse quotations are printed as verse, is to see it in its true light as a vast *florilegium* of verse and prose. The other commentaries and the sermons would look similar if we could read them in a more modern presentation.

Two problems face the student from the beginning. Holcot's classicism baffled his scribes and the text is sometimes hopelessly corrupt: '. . . fabula de Pigmaleone pictore' (C, fol. 241va) has turned into 'de pugna leonis contra pictorem' in the Bâle edition (p. 540). Even C, which is close to 'the master's book', can have 'Cithon' for Cicero.[2] We have nothing as good as C for the other texts. Then there is the problem of Holcot's intermediaries. He quotes mainly at second hand, as was customary. We have a better chance of understanding him if we can find the compilation in question. The *Speculum* of Vincent of Beauvais seldom left his side. He quotes from it constantly both with and without acknowledgment. He naturally used the *Policraticus*[3] and he quotes John of Wales by name twice at least:[4] this probably does not exhaust his debt to the *Communiloquium*.[5] He took sayings of ancient philosophers

---

[1] Robert Holcot, 29-32.

[2] C, fol. 242ra: De multiplicatione vero idolorum dicit Cithon et ponitur hic in glosa Lactantii quod optimi quique virorum deorum honore consecrabantur.

The reference is to a quotation from Cicero in Lactantius, Divinae institutiones, i. 15 (*C.S.E.L.* 19, 56). Lactantius calls him 'Cicero'; a medieval scribe, accustomed to 'Tullius', might not recognise the name. The corruption may have been in Holcot's copy of Lactantius already, or more likely in the excerpt through which he knew the passage.

[3] His quotations include 'Iohannes in Enthetico', the verse prologue to *Policraticis*, B, fol. 91v, see *Policraticus*, vol. 1, p. 11, lines 7-8.

[4] Sap. lect. cxcvii, p. 650: Talis dux fuit Iulius Cesar, qui nunquam dixit militibus suis: ite; sed semper: venite; et subiunxit causam: labor, inquit, participatus cum duce videtur militibus esse minor, sicut de eo scribit Iohannes Galensis.

John of Wales describes Caesar's regard for his soldiers, though without giving this example; *Communiloquium* xvii, op. cit., foll. 30vb-31ra.

Ecclus. lect. x, fol. 9vb, a definition of the virtue of patience 'secundum Valensem', from *Breviloquium* iv, ed. cit., fol. 257va.

[5] See below, 324.

from the *Liber philosophorum moralium antiquorum*, a very popular translation from the Arabic.[1] But to give an illustration of the difficulties involved, he also quotes from a *Liber de vita philosophorum*, which is neither Walter Burley's nor John of Wales' *compendium*, and which I have not identified.[2] His verse quotations cover almost all the field of classical and Christian poets and versifiers currently used in his day, from Virgil and Ovid and the poets of the silver age through medieval writers, including 'Alan the Great' (of Lille), as Holcot calls him,[3] to preachers' jingles.[4] He had a special liking for the verse sections of Boethius' *De consolatione Philosophiae*. Reading out poetry evidently gave him pleasure. He checks himself after quoting a long piece from William Brito's *Vocabularium*. 'There are many other elegant verses,' he says, 'which I pass over, lest I should seem to have quoted the poets more copiously than the prophets.' But the temptation is too strong. Just a bit more! Brito 'adds verses about a certain type of priest and curate, which you should have heard once at least'.[5] Perhaps the rarest medieval poem to be quoted is the comedy *De Babione*. The author was probably an Englishman writing towards the end of the twelfth century. His good knowledge of antiquity would have pleased the classicising friars.[6]

[1] ed. E. Franceschini, *Atti del R. Istituto Veneto di scienze, lettere ed arti* 91 (1931-2).

[2] *Sap. lect.* xcv, C, fol. 143vb: In cuius signum antiqui philosophi philosophiam vocaverunt matrem suam, sicut Plato et Demosthenes dixisse leguntur in libro de vita philosophorum. Unde isti duas matres se fatebantur habere, videlicet naturam et philosophiam, de quibus matribus ista fuit eorum sententia: natura nos genuit mortales et rudes, sed philosophia nos genuit divinis virtutibus informatos.

[3] C, fol. 194ra: Contra istud vitium fecit Librum de complanctu nature Alanus magnus, metro et prosa compositum curiose.

For a recent study of this poem with a bibliography see R. H. Green, Alan of Lille's *De planctu naturae*, *Speculum* 31 (1956) 649-74.

[4] On this type of verse see L. Thorndike, Unde versus, *Traditio* 11 (1955) 163-93.

[5] *Sap. lect.* xlix, C, fol. 82va: Multi alii versus ibi ponuntur, quod transeo, ne videar poetas allegasse diffusius quam prophetas. Tamen de presbiteris et curatis subiungit versus quos expedit saltem semel audisse, et dicit sic: . . .

The verses come from the Aurora of Pierre Riga; see P. Beichner, *Non Alleluia ructare*, *Mediaeval Studies* 18 (1956) 140. They are quoted by Brito in his *Vocabularium*, art. Presbyter, MS Oxford, Bodl. Rawl. C. 896, fol. 237-237v.

[6] *Sap. lect* xxxviii, p. 136, C, fol. 63rb: . . . teste Babione qui in fine comedie sue dicit sic: Babio testis adest, hec ultima verba tenete: Sunt incredibiles, uxor, alumpa, cliens.

See E. Faral, *De Babione*, poème comique de XIIe siècle, *Bibl. de l'École des Hautes Études* 293 (Paris, 1948) lines 483-4; pp. xxxvi-xxxix, lviii-lx. Faral notes Holcot's quotation. Thomas Hopeman quotes the same lines, MS London, Brit. Mus. Royal 4.A.i, fol. 18va. He must have taken it from Holcot on Wisdom.

J. Th. Welter has listed the sources for the *exempla* in Holcot's Wisdom-commentary. It appears from this that he used nearly all the story books available in his day: the list is almost co-extensive with Welter's enumeration of all the sources used in medieval *exempla* from the twelfth century onwards.[1] I shall concentrate here on special aspects of the subject, referring readers to Welter for a general picture of Holcot's prose sources. The Wisdom-commentary does not differ greatly from his other homiletic productions.

It is natural to compare him as a classicist with Thomas Waleys. Holcot, too, was a book hunter. He tells us that he 'found' 36 of Seneca's *Epistulae morales*, additional to the better known 88.[2] The *Epistulae* were divided into two parts in the manuscript tradition, and of these nos. 1-88 were copied more often than nos. 89-124.[3] Holcot had a copy of the rarer second part. He takes pains to refer to the numbers in *integri libri* in contrast to those in *communes libri*.[4] We are close to the adventures in bookshops described in *Philobiblon*. Aulus Gellius' *Noctes Atticae* is said to have been a rare book in medieval England.[5] Holcot, like his patron, sometimes quotes from it. He may have been able to use Richard de Bury's copy.[6]

Perhaps another bibliographical triumph lies behind his quotations from what he calls 'Palefatius, *De incredibilibus*'. Palaephatius on the rationalisation of Greek myths was used as a textbook in the Greek-speaking world right down into the Byzantine period,[7] but there seems to be no record of his having been translated into Latin in the middle ages, apart from one quotation in the *Historia scholastica*. This quotation refers to the story of Ulysses' escape from Scylla and the sirens. It does not correspond to the text of *De incredibilibus* but might conceivably derive from it.[8] Holcot

---

[1] 95-101, 360-1.

[2] Sap. lect. xv, C, fol. 26rb: Item epistola 14, que tamen communiter non habetur, quia inveni 36 epistolas preter illas 88 que communiter habentur.

[3] Schanz-Hosius, *Geschichte der römischen Literatur* 2 (Munich 1935) 704.

[4] Sap. lect. xcvi, p. 323; cl, p. 503; clxxx, p. 594; ccvii, p. 684.

[5] *F.S.* 211.

[6] See *Philobiblon* 82, 97, 106. Holcot tells the story of how Herodes Atticus exposed a false philosopher from *Noct. attic.* ix, 2 (B, fol. 83).

[7] Pauly-Wissowa, *Real-Encyclopädie*, 18, Stuttgart, 1942, 2449-55. The Greek text is edited by N. Festa, *Mythographi graeci*, 3, ii, (Leipzig, 1902). There is a Latin translation in *Opuscula mythologica physica et ethica, Graece et Latine* 1 (Cambridge, 1671).

[8] *P.L.* 198, 1290: Palefatus in libro Incredibilium tradit Ulyssem in trierim syrenorum fugisse Scyllam, spoliare hospites solitam. Syrenes quoque mulieres

quotes Palaephatius twice, in the first of his sermons. Neither quotation bears the slightest relationship to anything in *De incredibilibus*.[1] The first gives a theory of man's life after death, ascribed to a philosopher called 'Lucreon': man's life on earth depends upon a lamp, which each has allotted to him in the underworld; man dies as his lamp goes out. His body returns to the earth whence it came; his soul returns to his creator; and his shade enters the underworld when Queen Proserpina signifies that the time has come. The second quotation tells the story of Orpheus and Eurydice. The genuine Palaephatius refers to it much more briefly. Holcot, therefore, must have had a collection of myths and fables going by the wrong name. Lathbury probably used it too; he quotes a Pseudo-Palaephatius for the same type of *exemplum*. It is surprising that so rare a book should have been known even by its title in the early fourteenth century.

Alike in their pursuit of books, Waleys and Holcot differ in the use which each makes of his quarry. Waleys as a scholar had the advantage of contacts in Northern Italy and Avignon and of a more studious temperament. He developed an interest in ancient history and antiquities for themselves. Holcot valued them more for their moral content. Good pagans, lacking the aid of revelation, could put Christians to shame. Some preachers keep the sword of reproof in its sheath, while others speak out boldly, teaching how to avoid sin and to walk in God's paths, 'in the manner of certain satirists, such as Flaccus, Persius and Juvenal'. Would that Christians might exercise the same self-control in speaking evil as certain pagans! The pagans were punished for neglecting to consult their false gods in time of crisis; how much more should Christians have recourse to the true God in all their business, if they wish to obtain what they seek?[2]

Waleys seldom made a mistake. Holcot could be wildly wrong in his references. He claims to be quoting from Sallust against Cataline when he is really quoting from

---

fuisse, que decipiebant navigantes.

This quotation is mentioned by Seznec, p. 17, n. 16. The chapter on Scylla in *De incredibilibus* does mention Scylla, sirens and a trireme; but the version in the *Historia scholastica*, if it really derives from this passage, gives a very garbled account of it.

[1] See appendix ii, 360.
[2] Ecclus. lect. lii, fol. 43ra; lect. lv, fol. 44vb; lect. xlix, fol. 39vb.

Cicero's *Pro M. Caelio*.[1] Worse, he cites Livy as an authority
on the history of the Roman emperors. He tells two stories
about Nero's extravagance, both deriving from Suetonius,
as Holcot could have discovered, had he looked carefully at
his *Speculum historiale*.[2] He gives John of Salisbury and
Orosius as his authorities, correctly, since each has one of
the stories. But then he throws in Livy to make good
measure.[3] The Ecclesiasticus-commentary has a fantastic
tale about the promulgation of imperial laws. When the
Roman emperor promulgated a law relating to the whole
empire and not to one part of it only, he had a vein opened
and let his blood fall to the ground, in order to signify that
those who disobeyed would be touching his very blood and
deserved to be put to death. The most startling point in this
rigmarole is that Holcot fathers it on Livy 'in his book on
the origin of the City'.[4]

We shall now take a slow-motion film of Holcot manipu-
lating his sources, to see how he mixes sacred and profane
and how he assembles detail. An excellent example will be
found in his praise of good women in a moralisation of the
word 'water' (Wisdom xvi, 19). He begins with good
Christian women. Our Lord found greater constancy and
devotion in his women disciples than in Peter, John or
James, and may well say in the words of Boethius that no
fright could stay them at least from sharing his journey; he
showed himself first to women after his resurrection. Holcot
goes on to good pagan women. The *locus classicus* for his
theme was St Jerome's defence of chastity against Jovinian.
Jerome listed Penelope, Portia, Lucretia and Dido as
examples of faithful wives. He deliberately chose the older
version of the Dido story, according to which she killed
herself to avoid marrying again. Holcot takes over the list
and embroiders by quoting Ovid's letter from Penelope to

---

[1] Ecclus. lect xv, fol 13vb: Contra varia vitia Cataline fecit Sallustius, magnus
rhetor, unum librum, quem Catalinarium appellavit, ubi de eo sic dicit: . . .
secundo, subiungit Sallustius: . . . tertio, subdit Sallustius de moribus Cataline.
All three quotations come from *Pro M. Caelio*, 14. Holcot probably took them
from Vincent of Beauvais, *Speculum historiale* vi, 31, (Venice, 1591) fol. 63ra.
Vincent ascribes them correctly to Cicero, not to Sallust.
[2] ibid., ix, 7, fol. 109ra; Suetonius, *De vita Caesarum* vi, 30.
[3] B, fol. 20: Item de Nerone dicitur in Policratico, lib. 6, cap. 14, quod nullam vestem bis induebatur, ut in aliquo pre ceteris singulari gloria preluceret,
et piscebatur retibus aureis, secundum Orosium, De ormesta mundi, et Titum
Livium.
See *Policraticus*, 2, 40: Orosius, *Adversus paganos*, (*C.S.E.L.*) 5, 453.
[4] Appendix i, 321.

Ulysses. Anxious to call as many witnesses as possible, he ruins the effect, when he comes to Dido, by adding a reference to the *Aeneid*. Virgil's Dido was only too anxious for a second marriage; but Holcot does not notice what he has done. The Sabine women join his company, because he has found them coupled with Lucretia in the *Letter of Valerius to Rufinus*. Martial supplies him with lines on Portia, and on another faithful Roman, Arria, wife of Paetus. He also takes from Martial the name of Caesar's daughter, Julia, and of Sulpicia. He ends with 'Alcyone, Calyce and countless other women'. Alcyone and Calyce belong to Ovid's *Epistle* from Hero to Leander; Hero mentions them as women who were loved by the sea-god. They have no relevance as examples of faithful wives. Holcot perhaps liked their names and hoped that no one would investigate the context.

Holcot next explains woman's place in the home. A house without women is a house without order. Marriage is not only for the purpose of begetting children, but for good husbandry, which cannot be achieved without a woman, as Aristotle teaches and as it is said in Genesis: God made woman as a helpmeet for man. Hence all man's goodness and stability is founded on the gracious support of good women.[1]

The piece looks forward to Boccaccio's *De claris mulieribus*. Boccaccio mentions Penelope, Lucretia and Sulpicia in his prologue, though he illustrates the new selectiveness by omitting all the women of Scripture except for Eve, the common mother, on the ground that the two types, scriptural and pagan, do not meet. But the passage has even more interest as an illustration of Holcot's method. How wilfully slapdash he is! And we can see the reason. He must have drawn on notebooks, compiled by himself in the course of his reading or by assistants. The page before him on this occasion would have had excerpts from Ovid's *Epistulae heroides*. This would explain how Alcyone and Calyce got in with Penelope. One remembers Richard de Bury's team of tabulators and compilers. Useful as they were, they had much to answer for.

De Bury's helpers also busied themselves with *expositiones*.[2] By the early fourteenth century not only the Bible, Canon and Civil law and medical texts had acquired their glosses

---

[1] Appendix i, 321.   [2] *Philobiblon*, 103.

and commentaries, but also every widely-read literary text. Holcot drew much of his classical and pseudo-classical material from this type of source. Sometimes his commentaries are known and can be checked easily. His *expositor super eclogam Theoduli*, who gave him the story of Licaon, corresponds to the standard commentary printed with the early editions of Theodulus' *Ecloga*, an often-expounded ninth-century school text.[1] Even the names of the commentators are known in some cases: Remigius on the *Nuptiae* of Martianus Capella was a favourite.[2] Nicholas Trevet produced what became the standard fourteenth-century commentary on *De consolatione Philosophiae*; Holcot refers to him frequently as 'the commentator', though he may occasionally slip in something which is not in Trevet, *more suo*.[3] He also quotes William of Aragon, another fourteenth-century commentator, perhaps earlier than Trevet, on the same book. Holcot calls him 'Willelmus Medicus'. Aragon is in fact known as a scientist, author of *De somniis et visionum prognosticationibus*.[4] He may have commented on the *De somno Scipionis* of Macrobius, also. Holcot quotes a William who expounded Macrobius for a medical detail on the death of prematurely born babies.[5] He may mean William of Aragon.

Research on medieval commentaries on classical texts is not far enough advanced to make it possible to check Holcot's more obscure sources. If Holcot gives a true account of them, the research student in this field will be entering into fairyland. He quotes four *exempla* from 'little notes' and a 'little gloss' on Cicero's *Philippics*, *De senectute* and *De amicitia*. Three of them contain an element of the marvellous. All illustrate the author's meaning in concrete and striking

[1] Ecclus. lect. lii, fol. 42ra: Lichaon, qui fuit rex Archadie, invitavit Iovem ad hospitium suum cum ceteris diis. Lichaon, volens experiri utrum Iuppiter esset verus deus an non, porrexit ei venenum, ob quam rem Iuppiter eum mutavit in lupum.
The story can be found almost verbally in *Ecloga Theoduli cum commento* (Cologne, 1495) fol. 13v. On medieval commentaries on the Ecloga, see M. Manitius, *Geschichte der lateinischer Literatur des Mittelalters* 1 (Munich, 1911) 572-4.
[2] See, below, 172. On Remigius as a commentator see C. E. Lutz, Remigius' Ideas on the Classification of the Seven Liberal Arts, *Traditio* 12 (1956) 65-86.
[3] Robert Holcot, 37-8.   [4] ibid. 38-41.
[5] Sap. lect. lxxxix, p. 302: Quicumque autem nascuntur ante septimum mensem communiter moriuntur, sicut dicit Guilelmus de mortibus, exponens Macrobium, De somno Scipionis.
The quotation does not refer to William of Aragon's *De somniis* in MS Oxford, St John's College 172, foll. 140-152v.

terms. The *exemplum* on the *Philippics* (II, iv, 7), illustrating
the value of friendship, is the strangest. An old man gives
a beryl stone to someone who feels that the sun has been
withdrawn from him. The gem attracts sunlight and the
man sees reflected in it himself in a pit, with a lion trying to
devour him and 'worms' (dragons?) ready to press upon
him. A long-absent and neglected old friend comes to the
rescue.[1] The *exemplum* on *De senectute* describes four serpents
breathing out four flames, corresponding to the four kinds
of worldly desire which inflame mankind. Of the two on
De amicitia, one tells how the invader of a kingdom prepared
for its defeat by fomenting discord among the royal counsellors, the other how two friends felt sympathy for each
other at a distance.[2] The four stories come from Holcot's
commentary on the prophet Joel, suggesting that he had
glossed copies of Cicero beside him while he was preparing
his lecture, or else that he had opened his notebook at a page
giving excerpts from them, which he had made: he claims to
have 'seen' for himself the first and most fantastic tale.

Some madly circumstantial scraps of pseudo-history come
through the same channel. One passage shows us the
beginning and end of a legend. Commending Scripture in
the customary manner in the prologue to his Wisdom-commentary, Holcot says that it follows the precept of Horace
on 'mixing grave and gay', and he quotes the tag, a favourite
of Stephen Langton in the late twelfth century: *Omne tulit
punctum qui miscuit utile dulci* (*Ars Poetica*, line 343).[3] He then
proceeds to describe how a Roman poet's work would be
read publicly before the five orders of the Roman People.

---

[1] B, fol. 43v: Hic potest adduci historia quam vidi in quadam notula super
primum librum Tullii in Philippicis, super illud: *quid est aliud quam tollere a vita
vite societatem, colloquia amicorum absentium*. Quidam videns solem sibi subtractum,
multum dolens a quodam sene accepit berillum, qui ad se trahit radium solis.
Vidit (ibi?) leonum (eum?) devorare volentem. Erat in puteo profundo et
ascendere non potuit, ubi a vermibus, nisi citius recederet, premeretur. Hec
dicit illa notula, quia non habuit bonam societatem. Venit ergo quidam senex
socius, qui diu absens fuerat et quem ille reliquerat, et dat ei libellum (sic)
contra leonem.
[2] These three *exempla* need not be transcribed in full. B, fol. 44: Iterum super
illam litteram, *ante faciem eius ignis vorans* (Joel i, 3) adduci potest quod dicitur in
quadam notula super Tullium, De senectute, quod quidam vidit quatuor
serpentes quatuor calores emittere . . . ; fol. 44v: Unde dicitur in quadam notula
super Tullium, De amicitia, quod quidam volens regnum cuiusdam invadere,
qui(a) rex per tres consiliarios regebatur unanimes et concordes, caute inter
istos consiliarios discordiam procuravit . . . ; fol 46: Dicit enim glosa parva super
Tullium, De amicitia, quod inter duos homines . . .
[3] *Study of the Bible*, 256; and see E. R. Curtius, op cit. 417-28.

If it won general approval, each order would put a mark
(punctum) at the end of the writing, after which the poem
would be held to be 'authentic' (we should say 'to be a
classic'). It is a charming picture!

The beginning must be sought in Pseudoacron, the fifth-
century glossator of Horace, who says on the line in question
that *puncta* means the people's votes. He has just mentioned
centuriae seniorum and *equites*. The Roman People, elders and
knights, have been brought together with a reference to
voting by *puncta*. Any scholar who knew of the five orders
and of the ancient custom of reading one's books aloud,
often referred to in classical poetry and still practised in the
middle ages, could have invented the scene of a public
reading before the five orders. Heaven knows through what
stages the story had passed between Pseudoacron and
Holcot.[1]

'A certain expositor on Juvenal's first *Satire*' gave him a
detailed account of a morning in the life of noble Romans.
It began with an early visit to the monuments, where young
men were edified by the sight of their forbears, weapons in
hand, depicted on the triumphal arches. The full tale of this
Roman morning will come better in a study of Holcot's
views on education.[2] Another reference to an 'exposition
of Juvenal' sounds more sober: the story of Numa and the
ancile shield is told apropos of the second *Satire*.[3]

His false quotations from classical authors may sometimes
derive from their commentators; he may have confused the
commentary with the text or found it already confused in his
scrapbook. He can quote correctly from Aristotle's *Poetics*,[4]
but he tells two stories which have no place there. One takes
the form of a dialogue between a poet and a deserted palace,[5]
the other of a saying to dissuade poets from taking gifts: to
put oneself under an obligation is to go in fetters. Aristotle
is supposed to have quoted it from Arabian poets![6] All the

---

[1] Appendix i, 322.   [2] Below, 193, and appendix i, 333.
[3] ibid. 336.
[4] Sap. lect. clxiv, C, fol. 241vb: Sicut enim dicit Aristoteles in Poetria, homo
naturaliter delectatur representatione.
From *Poet.* iv, 1448b, 8.
[5] Sap. lect. xvii; see below, p. 169.
[6] Sap. lect. xcii, C, fol. 140ra: Recitat Aristoteles in Poetria sua quod poete
arabici vocaverunt dona compedes, quia sicut compeditus non potest pro-
cedere sicut vellet et possit secundum virtutem motivam (MS nocivam)
corporis sui, sed constringitur et retrahitur ad ambulandum secundum mensu-
ram quam compedes sibi limitant et concedunt (MS conceduntur), ita reci-
pientes dona, quantumcumque sint discreti et fortes in iustitia, sentiunt se

same, even the most charitable explanation will not save Holcot's scholarship. We cannot blame a commentator for 'Livy's' tale about imperial laws. Holcot could have read only one commentary on *Ab Urbe condita*, since only one existed. That was by Trevet, who was a scholar, not a romancer.

We now turn to Holcot's quotations from medieval prose sources as distinct from his use (either real or alleged) of medieval commentaries on classical or early medieval texts. Not all can be traced to surviving works or even to known authors. The interest of these bibliographical puzzles is that they seem to lift a curtain, behind which we see an unsuspected throng of writers with classicising or 'pictorial' tendencies.[1]   Holcot drew on the Franciscan, Walter Wimborne's lost treatise, *Tractatus moralis de elementis*, which contained some sort of 'picture' of *amor*. He cites Hugh Sneyth O.P. for a moralisation of a pseudo-classical 'law'. He took many 'pictures' from John Ridevall's commentary on the Apocalypse as well as one from *Fulgentius metaforalis*. Holcot had the Apocalypse-commentary in full or at least in a more complete form than has come down to us. It is possible that he also had a lost and unrecorded commentary by Ridevall on St Augustine's *Confessions*. He uses a writer referred to as 'Boralensis', who is neither Walter Burley nor Simon of Boraston, for pseudo-classical stories, wise sayings and 'pictures'. 'Boralensis' is a mystery man at present. So is 'a certain postillator called Peter', the source for an elaborate *exemplum* involving a long series of mottoes and inscriptions; it belongs to the same *genre* as the pseudo-law and 'picture' type of story. A *Liber Lebeonis* is even more intriguing. The name looks like a textual corruption going back to an early stage in the manuscript tradition. Holcot quotes it as his source for a rather poetic story, containing an allusion to Jupiter holding up the sky to prevent its falling. Can 'Lebeon' be the same as the philosopher 'Lucreon' quoted by Pseudo-Palaephatius? Of the known writers, Wimborne and Sneyth are late thirteenth-century; Ridevall was contemporary with Holcot. 'Peter the postillator',

---

restrictos et retentos et quasi quodammodo compeditos, ne libere exerceant quod iustitia eis suadet.

It sounds as though a warning to judges not to take presents had been applied to poets.

[1] See appendix ii.

'Boralensis' and the writer of the *Liber Lebeonis* cannot have been much earlier, judging from the samples we have; their late medieval tone is unmistakable. Holcot begins to resemble the leader of a chorus.

His allusions to persons and events of medieval history show another mixture of fact and fancy. Some of his *exempla* come from Henry of Huntingdon, Geoffrey of Monmouth and Gerald of Wales.[1] Some represent anecdotes which might have a basis in hearsay or record. A certain archbishop of England refused to obey the king, who said to his intimates: 'Our father the archbishop has a lion's heart; he'll soon have a sheep's tail.' The king then ordered his temporalities to be confiscated and, sure enough, he came round.[2] William (II?), king of England, introduced luxury to the country, sending round to all parts for magnificent and marvellous recipes for his table. A king, whose name is not given, said that he would rather lose his kingdom than miss a good drink. Holcot adds to the pious sayings ascribed to King Henry III of England found in *exempla* collections. He repeats a remark made by a bishop of Chichester, who had formerly practised in the court of Arches, that he used to 'sell his silence' at a high price, in the manner of Demosthenes. This must refer to Gilbert of St Lifard, bishop of Chichester 1288-1305. The goings on of an incestuous priest in the diocese of Chichester were 'known to the whole countryside'. Brother Richard the Shoemaker's vision of an apostate to Judaism in the reign of Edward I, who died without renouncing his errors, almost certainly refers to the Dominican, John of Reading; he was circumcised and married a Jewess. Holcot's story about the priest of Frome (in Somerset?), catching his neighbours' geese on autumn nights with two corded and weighted rods called 'reason and justice', is so charming that its truth does not matter: at his parishioners' request, the priest excommunicated all and sundry who had stolen geese '*without* reason and justice'. The plague of flies in Norfolk, which ruined the crops and had the words 'ira Dei' written on their wings, may reflect a local legend.[3] The story of the Oxford scrivener, misled by sorcery, who claimed to be the eldest son of Edward I and was executed as a traitor at Northampton, might sound fictional if its truth were not vouched for by contemporary chronicles.

---

[1] Robert Holcot, 44. [2] For all these stories, see appendix i.
[3] Sap. lect. ccvi, p. 681.

M

Even the fantastic tale that the king of France, doubting his son's legitimacy, had him exposed to a lion, and that the lion proved the child's true birth by frisking gaily round him, must derive from a real scandal at the French court. Holcot says that it happened 'recently'. Three princesses were arrested and accused of adultery in 1314. One of them, Jeanne de Bourgogne, wife of Philip V, was exonerated. Her eldest son died in infancy on February 18, 1317. The birth of this child, whose father reigned from 1316 to 1322, may have given rise to Holcot's story: there had been a lot of gossip about it.

He says *narrant historie* when he tells the story of William the Conqueror's introduction of French into England. In fact it was a legend: the Conqueror took no steps to suppress English; the victory of French among the upper classes happened naturally as a result of the Conquest and was not 'planned'.[1] Holcot voices an anti-Norman version of the Conquest which was shaping itself in England in the later middle ages. Both Robert of Gloucester and Ranulf Higden regret the substitution of French for English among the aristocracy.[2] Holcot makes the picture more concrete, presenting the change from English to French as a stroke of conscious policy on the part of William the Conqueror. William pondered how to abolish the 'Saxon speech' in order to assimilate the two peoples one to another. He therefore decreed that no one should plead in the royal court except in French and that each boy to be taught his letters should learn French, and Latin by means of French, which continues 'to the present day'. The moralisation gives bite to the story. William I represents the devil, king of the realm of falsehood, as opposed to Christ, the king of truth. Like William, the devil has no hereditary right to his kingdom, but rules by might alone; hence he is no true heir, but a conqueror. His own language in his infernal province is the language of lies. To assimilate the world to this infernal province, he has decreed that lies should be used in all secular business. Just as the schoolboy begins by learning

---

[1] On the unhistorical nature of the legend and the gradual recovery of the English language, see W. H. Stevenson, The Introduction of English, *An English Miscellany Presented to F. J. Furnival* (Oxford, 1901) 421-9; V. H. Galbraith, Nationality and Language in Medieval England, *T.R.H.S.* 4th series, vol. 23 (1941), pp. 113-28; H. Suggett, The Use of French in England in the Later Middle Ages, ibid., vol. 28 (1946) pp. 61-83.

[2] *Metrical Chronicle*, ed. W. A. Wright (Rolls Series, 1887) 2, 543-4, *Polychronicon*, op. cit. 2, 156-8.

French, so the youth, starting on his career in the world, by toil and study learns to tell lies. Holcot does not work out his parallel any further, but he implies a contrast between honest Englishmen and deceitful French. He begins, moreover, with a sharp distinction between the two peoples; a man is known as French or English by his speech.

Probably his need to moralise led Holcot to exaggerate. We can hardly suppose that he meant his parallel between William and the devil, Normandy and the infernal regions, to be taken too literally. If pressed, it would make Edward the Confessor into a type of Christ and the truth. Holcot certainly thought of the Confessor as a model king. After listing the qualities of a good ruler, he says he is sure that St Edward had them all, and that his land was not lacking in government and dignity, for the reason that his feast is kept with great ceremony in England.[1] Still, we must not run away with his passing ideas. The importance of the passage is that Holcot goes further than Robert of Gloucester or Higden in judging the linguistic effects of the Conquest and that he anticipates the *Historia Croylandensis* in his anti-Norman bias. The latter, written probably in the late fourteenth century, adds changes in customs and laws to changes in language and ascribes it all to the Normans' hatred of the English.[2] Hence the Wisdom-commentary shows us a legend in evolution.

Holcot draws many *exempla* not from history but from the life around him. Whether his scenes are observed directly or borrowed from earlier writers (always a moot point in medieval homiletics), he chooses pretty ones and he presents them freshly. He has an artist's touch in adding detail. The rascally priest of Frome and his clerk go hunting the neighbours' geese on *autumn* nights: Holcot has suggested Michaelmas dinner without a word too much. Two samples of his contemporary scenes will be given here, selected for their Arcadian flavour, though he may not have intended it. The apple harvest supplies one *exemplum*. Children are allowed to pick fruit in magnates' orchards and eat as much as they can, but the gardener examines each one separately

---

[1] B, fol. 14v: Certus sum quod sanctus Edwardus omnes conditiones habuit gratiose et terra sua non fuit sine rege nec sine solempnitate, quia die suo magna est solempnitas anglicorum.

[2] ed. T. Gale, *Rerum Anglicarum Scriptorum Veterum*, 1, (Oxford, 1784) 70-1. On the date of Pseudo-Ingulf, the author, see C. Gross, *The Sources and Literature of English History*, 2nd ed. (London, 1915) no. 1371.

as he leaves and sometimes even unbelts him to see that he takes no fruit away in his jacket. Clever boys, when they notice this, arrange to throw their pickings over the wall or fence to some comrade who afterwards goes shares, so that they can eat with more enjoyment and peace of mind. Similarly rich men must strip themselves for their friends and relatives on their deathbeds and are sometimes robbed of the very clothes and beds they lie in. Prudent men share their goods with the poor in their lifetime, unknown to their relatives, and so store up treasure in heaven, as the boys store up their pickings.[1] Another *exemplum* describes a game which shepherds play in country places. One shepherd draws a circle with his staff and makes lines inside it, in which he puts 'a great family' of sticks called wooden men, with one bigger than the rest, called their king. His opponent, standing outside the circle, aims with his staff at the 'men' in the circle, striking them now from one point, now from another. But so long as they fall within the circle, and not outside it, the master of the game comes and replaces them. If he can knock them down outside the circle he snatches them freely as his own; and so he wins the game and is delighted. The sticks nearest the circumference of the circle and furthest away from their king are the most vulnerable. So it is in the world, etc.[2]

Holcot can give a personal flavour to an old story. He repeats from Alexander Nequam's *De natura rerum* the tale of the adulterous swan, whose mate called the other swans on the lake to deplume and kill her,[3] with the observation that perhaps the female swans were called first because women tend to be harder on their own sex than they are on men.[4] He has the knack of making what he says memorable. Some writers achieve the same end by reason of their passion and sincerity. Holcot is the antithesis to these earnest spirits. He wins his readers by his tolerant amusement.

A study of his sources has proved conclusively that Holcot did not aim at exact scholarship after the manner of Trevet, Waleys and Ridevall in his sober mood. One does not

---

[1] Ecclus. xliv, fol. 36va.

[2] The game seems to be a simple version of Loggats, said to have been played at sheep-shearing feasts and forbidden by the statute 33 Henr. VIII, cap. 9; see W. C. Hazlitt, *Popular Antiquities of Great Britain*, 2nd ed. 3 (London, 1870) 317. Miss Nancy Forman kindly sent me the reference. See appendix i, 329.

[3] *De natura rerum* (Rolls Series) 112-13.

[4] B, fol. 4: . . . quia communiter mulieres contra mulieres sunt crudeles et quandoque sauciabiles vel minus crudeles contra virum.

examine a historical novel as though it were submitted as a doctoral thesis. Holcot chose the role of romancer and *raconteur*. He reflected his countrymen's attitude to ancient history in his own Latin medium. We shall reach even higher flights of fancy when we come to his 'pictures'.

IV.—THE 'PICTURES'

The 'pictures' in the *Moralitates* raise the problem of Holcot's sources again in an acute form. Five persevering scholars, Oesterley, Herbert, Welter, Saxl and Liebeschütz, have failed to find them. The 'pictures' have an ancient setting, but every line betrays their origin in the middle ages. Here is

'The likeness of Penance, which the priests of the goddess Vesta painted, according to Remigius. Penance used to be painted in the form of a man, his whole body naked, who held a five-thonged scourge in his hand. Five verses or sentences were written on it.'[1]

The inscriptions on the five-thonged scourge follow. If the student turns trustfully to Remigius of Auxerre on the *Nuptiae* of Martianus Capella, he will find nothing of the kind. It would be extraordinary if he did: no *locus* of the Nuptiae could have suggested the subject of penance to Remigius. Holcot gives no authority for the next 'picture' of penance:

'Penance was also painted in the temple of the goddess Vesta in the likeness of an armed knight, to show that we must fight against the devil.'[2]

Purity is painted in the form of the goddess herself:

'The goddess Vesta used to be painted with a lily having five leaves, and a verse written on each, which the priests of the temple would expound in the concourse of people in the goddess Vesta's temple.[3]

Vesta represented chastity; so much was commonplace; but where did Holcot read that her priests gave sermons on it to their pagan congregations? 'Theodosius in vita Alexandri' tells of Alexander's reception by a king of Sicily, who invited him to sleep in a bed with four curtains, each bearing

[1] *Moral.* XXII, p. 728.   [2] XXIII, p. 729.   [3] XXXII, p. 736.

the picture of a beautiful woman with an inscription.[1] Neither Theodosius nor this story of Alexander conveys anything to an expert on the medieval Alexander legend. 'Romulus in annalibus indorum', who tells an equally medieval type of story, is another question mark.[2]

Holcot 'found' in an exposition of Cicero's *Academica* that Varro depicted Sin in the form of a goddess, with three other likenesses, of God, of the devil and of man respectively. She was holding out to each of them a letter or charter, containing inscriptions, which are then given.[3] The word *peccatum* occurs in the *Academica* (i, 37) as a possible *locus* for the story. Holcot has already repeated *exempla* from glosses or expositions of other works of Cicero in his lectures on the Twelve Prophets. *Exempla* might just pass; the description of Varro's portrait of Sin in an exposition is difficult to swallow! 'Fulgentius' vouches for a story which is not in the works of the mythographer.[4] 'Livy's' account of a golden table and of an image of the goddess of Fortune at Rome is not in *Ab Urbe condita*.[5]

The 'pictures' raise another problem which exercised Saxl: had the author any actual pictures in mind or did he regard them as purely literary productions? Did he even intend them to be presented as illuminations or in any other visual form? The absence of illuminations in manuscripts of the *Moralitates* before the fifteenth century inclined Saxl to think that they were purely literary. We have seen that Ridevall's 'pictures' derived from literary sources and that he described them in such a way as to make them quite unsuitable for miniatures. Saxl's guess about Holcot was certainly correct in Ridevall's case. Holcot, however, had a different type of mind from Ridevall; his 'pictures' are worth examining separately.

His lectures and sermons help to answer the problems raised by his *Moralitates*. There are no elaborate 'pictures' in his commentaries on Wisdom and Ecclesiasticus; but they show him referring to visual aids. He points to paintings

---

[1] I, p. 709.   [2] V, VI, XXIV, pp. 712-13, 729.

[3] XXXI, p. 734: Tullius in Academicis questionibus, questione quarta, commendat Varronem eo quod ipse tradidit iura deorum, ubi in expositione inveni quod Varro depinxit peccatum ad similitudinem dee, cuius ponebantur tres imagines. Prima fuit imago Dei; secunda fuit imago diaboli; tertia fuit imago hominis. Et ista dee imago unicuique imagini unam litteram sive cartam porrigebat . . .

[4] XXVI, p. 731.   [5] XXI, XLIV, pp. 727, 744.

and carvings by way of example. The painting on a building indicates its function: a chapel has different kinds of painting from a tavern: the one is painted with the deeds of saints, the other with the deeds of fools.[1] Tombs of the wealthy are covered with carvings and paintings, which show weeping and praying figures, in contrast to the corruption within.[2] He illustrates the vice of self-importance from the painted carving of a grotesque or 'babwen' on a corbel, pretending to support the whole weight of the building to its heavy fatigue, with neck, shoulders, arms and face jutting out.[3] Painting is used as a symbol. The devil paints vices in the shape of animals in the sinner's soul.[4] The illuminator's technique of mixing his colours suggests moral lessons.[5] Painters design very well the eyes, feet, hair and all the members of their likenesses and omit nothing, not even the folds of the garments.[6] Charlemagne is said to have had all the liberal arts painted in his palace 'miro modo', when he 'transferred study' from Rome to Paris.[7]

The Ecclesiastes-commentary in MS Royal 2.D.iv, which may be by Holcot, and is anyway in his *genre*, describes a picture with inscriptions, 'at Paris, in the house of certain Lombards'. It illustrated the Aristotle-Phyllis legend, popular in the middle ages, and frequently represented in art from the late thirteenth-century onwards. The scene is recorded in a fresco in a fourteenth-century house at

---

[1] Sap. lect. lxvii, p. 239.

[2] Sap. lect. xii, p. 44, Ecclus. lect xv, fol. 13va. Holcot may have seen the weepers on the tomb of Archbishop Pecham (d. 1292) at Westminster Abbey. The author of the *Commendatio lamentabilis*, op. cit. 6, praises Edward I's magnificent piety to his dead relatives: 'Sepulchra eorum artificiosius cunctis mortalibus decoravit, et curiosius sculpi fecit.' For early representations of weepers on tombs, see E. Mâle, *L'art religieuse de la fin du Moyen Âge en France*, 5th ed. (Paris 1949) 417.

[3] Sap. lect. clxvi, C, fol. 245vb: ... omnino similes sunt babbewyno, depicto et sculpto, qui collo, humeris et brachiis et facie prominens, totam fabricam cum onerosa fatigatione se simulat supportare.
Dante describes a corbel in much the same way, *Purgatorio*, x, 130-4.

[4] Ecclus. lect lii, fol. 42rb-va. The seven deadly sins were associated with animals; M. W. Bloomfield, *The Seven Deadly Sins* (Michigan, 1952) 245-9.

[5] Ecclus. lect. vii, fol. 8rb; lect. lxxxi, fol. 58vb. This was a traditional comparison; Robert de Monte says in his chronicle, *P.L.* 149, 880: Sicut enim pictores ferrugineum colorem substernere solent, ut rubeis superpositis magis elucescat ...

[6] P, sermo cviii: Pictores enim optime oculos, pedes, capillos et omnia membra imaginum formant et nichil eorum omittunt, nec plicas vestium.

[7] Sap. lect. lv, p. 196. See the chronicle of Pseudo-Turpin, ed. C. Meredith Jones, Paris 1936, 220-8; R. Hinks, *Carolingian Art*, (London, 1935) 152-3; E. Mâle, *L'art religieuse du XIIIe siècle en France*, 8th ed. (Paris, 1948) 80-89.

Constance, where it formed part of a 'domination of women' series.[1] The Philosopher was so besotted by the charms of a pretty girl as to let her ride on his back, while he crawled on all fours. The rider in the Paris painting is described as 'a wretched woman', which does not sound like Phyllis, but it may be a reflection on her character and not on her looks. The inscriptions give her speech to Aristotle and his reply to her in some kind of French verse.[2]

Holcot loved inscriptions as well as pictures as a subject for his *exempla*. He mentions devices on shields[3] and verses on the tomb of Fair Rosamund[4] and of Julius Caesar.[5] He tells a well-known story of a statue with inscriptions concealing buried treasure, and another of inscriptions written on circles, found underneath the house of a wealthy Roman.[6] 'A certain postillator called Peter', whom I have not identified, supplied him with the tale of a runaway slave, whose master, pitying him, wrote to him in the form of an inscription:

'Voco. Expecto. Agnosce. Remitto. Ignorans contempnis. Punio. Accipe. Redde. Adiuvo. Premio.'

The slave on returning received presents from four friends with which to cover his nakedness. Each piece of clothing bore inscriptions of the same type, admonishing him with

---

[1] A. Borgeld, *Aristoteles en Phyllis* (Groningen, 1902) 78-9; D. J. A. Ross, Allegory and Romance on a Medieval French Marriage Casket, *J.W.C.I.* 11 (1948) 118-20.

[2] MS Royal 2.D.iv, fol. 158v: . . . ita se male humiliavit (Aristoteles) et tam de sapiente infatuatus erat, quod captivatus amore cuiusdam mulieris, permisit eam equitare se ipsum. Unde sicut vidi scriptum Parisius in domo quorundam lombardorum ibi hec historia depicta erat. Mulier misera super philosophum equitans dixit sic: Aristote, sire veillard, qe tant savez d'augni et de arte, portez me suef par courtoisie, on vous aurez del seorgorie. Cui miser Aristoteles respondit: Dame, ieo faco tut mon poer pur acomplier vostre volire, e chose qa vous a talent pur tost venir a mautent.

Miss M. Dulong kindly transcribed this very difficult passage for me. The French does not correspond to the conversation between Aristotle and Phyllis in the *Lai d'Aristote of Henri d'Andeli*, ed. M. Debouille (Paris 1951).

[3] Sap. lect. xxxvi, p. 127.

[4] Ecclus. lect. xv, fol. 13va. See A. Kelly, *Eleanor of Aquitaine* (Cambridge, Mass., 1950) 395.

[5] B, fol. 119: Nota hic quod dicitur in sepulchro Iulii Cesaris:

Si lapis est unus, qua nunc sit arte levatus?
Si duo sunt lapides, dic ubi contigui.

The rhyme is found in other contexts and versions; see J. Werner, *Beiträge zur Kunde der lateinischen Literatur des Mittelalters*, 2nd ed. (Aavan, 1905) no. 145; J. W. Spargo, *Virgil the Magician* (Cambridge, Mass., 1934) 229-30.

[6] B, foll. 23, 36v; Herbert, 127, 240.

wise counsels.[1] There is a story of a snobbish senator who built himself a very fine castle and wrote the following rhyme over the doorway:

> 'Decretum detur, ne dormiat aut epuletur
> Hic gens villana, sed Achilles, Plato, Diana.'

He meant that no one should come to stay the night or have dinner who was neither a knight nor a philosopher nor a lady. Having been converted by a dream, he substituted the following:

> 'Muta decretum; sanctorum suscipe cetum,
> Nudum Martinum, Lazarum, Iacobum peregrinum.'[2]

A stranger tale tells how a Jew saw the Incarnation of Christ prophesied in a dream. He beheld a silver statue, standing between two valleys, having a golden head and a crown of flowers with the Tetragrammaton inscribed on it.[3]

In the intervals of describing pictures or quoting mottoes and verses, Holcot shows himself to be a conscious artist in words. He tries to convey atmosphere and to bring out the poetry in his fables and metaphors. A touching instance is his treatment of the theme *sic transit gloria mundi*. The passage of time induces in him a mood of pleasant, gentle melancholy. He expresses it first by various similes for human life found in Scripture, all representing its transitory nature, and then by a fable, which he ascribes wrongly to Aristotle's *Poetics*: a poet addresses a palace, now old and deserted, on its former glory, and the palace, taking pity on his tears, answers that all temporal things must pass away. Lastly, Holcot compares man's life in this world to a fox, crossing a frozen river. She listens to the current of water running under the ice and will not trust herself to the ice, if the current flows too strongly. The glory of the world resembles fair, shining ice, and is just as brittle. Now a king, now an earl, now a bishop, now a knight passes. Take heed! A topic which might be as banal as it is gloomy acquires grace and charm in Holcot's phrasing:

> 'Notandum est quod sacra scriptura vitam humanam comparat multis rebus, sed nunquam vel raro alicui rei permanenti

---

[1] B, fol. 39: Ut autem homo curetur ab omnibus infirmitatibus est advertendum quod quidam postillator, nomine Petrus, finxit . . .
See Robert Holcot, 58, for the full text.
[2] Sap. lect. ccx, C, fol. 311va-b.
[3] B, fol. 63.

vel stabili, sed semper rebus transeuntibus et caducis. Comparatur autem vita humana quandoque herbe, quandoque rori, quandoque hospiti, quandoque cursori. Omnia autem ista transitoria sunt, momentanea et caduca. . . . Sic ergo patet quod vita nostra semper rebus transitoriis comparatur, iuxta responsionem quam quoddam vetus palatium desertum dicitur respondisse; unde Aristoteles in Poetria inducit fabulam cuiusdam poete quoddam palatium desertum deplora(n)tis in hiis verbis: Domus egregia! compungor ad lacrimas, tuam intuens solitudinem. At illa contremuit, compassa michi propter lacrimarum multitudinem. Cui inquio: Ubi, queso, sunt qui quondam in te habitaverunt et iocundam vitam cum securitate et temporis amenitate duxerunt? At illa: temporales, inquid, exeuntes temporaliter cum tempore, et me quoque sub sorte temporis quandoque transituram dimiserunt. Res nempe nulle stabiles, que cum fluxu huius temporis fluxibiles fluunt. Hec responsio palatii. Vulpecula, transitura glaciem, apponit aurem ad glaciem et si audit aquam currentem et fluentem fortiter sub glacie nullo modo confidit de illa glacie, quia est nimis tenuis ad supportandum eam. Ista cautela debemus nos uti. Gloria mundi est quasi quedam pulchra et splendens glacies, quia delectable est honorari ab hominibus, pasci et potari et vestiri delicate et habere magnam familiam, cui possit imperare; sed cavendum, quia glacies illa est valde fragilis. Ausculta diligenter et audies murmur aquarum transeuntium sub ista glacie. Apocalipsis: Aque multe, populi multi.[1] Advertas et audies, quia modo transit unus rex in mortem, modo unus comes, modo episcopus, modo miles, et sic de aliis; et ideo de illa glacie non est confidendum (Sap. lect. xvii, C, foll. 29vb-30va)'.

We now draw nearer to the technique of the 'pictures'. Holy Scripture is personified with the seven liberal arts kneeling round her, each with the instrument of her trade.[2] Holcot had probably read a description of Philosophy surrounded by the seven liberal arts; it may have been adapted to Scripture in his source. Then we have descriptions of pagan gods and goddesses with their attributes. Holcot took a great interest in the pagan deities. He takes a leaf from the book of his predecessors, John of Wales, Thomas Waleys and John Ridevall. The reproval of idolatry in Wisdom gave him his opportunity to describe the

---

[1] From Apoc. xvii, 15.
[2] Ecclus. lect. i, fol. 2vb: Unde imaginandum est quod septem artes, quasi septem ancille ad arcem domine saptientie imperatricis, provolutis genibus, obtulerunt suum ancillarium famulatum. . . .

pantheon.[1] He describes in other contexts Minerva, Mercury, Apollo, the goddess of Fortune[2] and the three Graces,[3] using as his sources Servius on Virgil, Fulgentius, Isidore, Remigius on the *Nuptiae*, Peter Comestor's *Historia scholastica* and Mythographus Tertius.[4] His sources are as literary as Ridevall's; but when he describes the three Graces he suggests that they might have a truly pictorial aspect: Servius tells that Grace used to be painted as follows 'among the heathen, who had pictures of the virtues in books'. He then describes the three maidens. Did Holcot imagine this 'heathen picture-book' of the virtues as having miniatures? It sounds like it.

He often moralises his deities after the manner, but independently of Ridevall. This makes a bridge to the 'pictures' in his *Moralitates*. His Wisdom-commentary has a 'picture' of Drunkenness in the form of a god, who is obviously Bacchus:

> 'Someone imagines that the likeness of Drunkenness was painted thus: it had the likeness of a child, having a horn in his hand and a crown of glass on his head.'

The child signifies that a drunkard becomes speechless and infantile, the horn that he keeps no secrets, and the crown that he thinks himself rich and glorious, when he really has nothing.[5] The first words of the passage, 'Fingitur a quodam

---

[1] Sap. lect. clv, pp. 518-19.

[2] Sap. lect. cxiii, p. 380; lect. cxli, p. 473; Ecclus. lect x, fol. 9rb; lect. lxxii, fol. 54rb.

[3] P, sermo xlv: In cuius signum Servius super primum librum Eneidarum refert quod apud gentiles, qui picturas virtutum habebant in libris, isto modo gratia pingebatur. Fuerunt tres puelle, quarum una habebat faciem aversam et vultum torvum, alie vero due facies conversas ad populum et iocundas, ad docendum quod gratia amissa, id est a nobis perdita, duplex redit.

Servius on Virgil, *Aen.* i, 720 (editio Harvardiana, 2, Lancaster, Penn., 1946): quod vero una aversa pingitur, duae nos respicientes, unde et supra (548) nec te certasse priorem paeniteat.

[4] Mythographus Tertius was probably Master Alberic of London; see E. Rathbone, op. cit. The book was often ascribed to Alexander Nequam. Holcot refers to it as *Alexander Nequam in scintillario poetarum* and *Alexander in mythologiis suis*.

[5] Sap. lect. xxi, C, fol. 36ra: Fingitur a quodam ebrietatis imaginem sic fuisse depictam, imago puerilis, cornu habens in manu et in capite coronam de vitr(e)o. Puer erat in signum quod facit hominem elinguem et insensatum, more pueri. Cornu habebat in manu in signum quod nullum celat secretum, sed clamando et clangendo revelat. Coronam habebat vitream, quia reputat se gloriosum et divitem, quia est ebriosus, cum nichil habeat.

The *vitro* and *vitream* may perhaps be corruptions of *viteo* and *viteam*. In that case the crown was of vine-leaves instead of glass, and the figure looked more bacchic.

ebrietatis imaginem sic fuisse depictam' let the cat out of the bag. Someone in the present tense imagines or pretends that the likeness of Drunkenness used to be painted in the past tense.

All this is a child's toy compared to the 'pictures' in the commentary on the Twelve Prophets. Here Holcot opens the door of his workshop and lets us see him fabricating his queer objects. I have counted twenty-six of them. None is identical or even similar to any 'picture' in his *Moralitates*. Holcot introduces them in exactly the same way as Ridevall introduced 'pictures' into his Apocalypse-commentary. He puts them into preacher's rhythm; he lists the attributes of his subject and supports each one with a string of quotations to show its moral significance; sometimes, but not always, he gives his source for the 'picture' as a whole, or at least explains where he started from.

I shall transcribe all twenty-six 'pictures', reducing each to a catalogue of its details and omitting the supporting texts, unless they point to an interesting source. The 'pictures' become tiresome as soon as the initial surprise has died down; but it is impossible to discuss their genesis without having them spread out on one's table. They are numbered according to their order in the commentary.

1. *Fornicatio*, on Os. i, 2

Fornicatio pingitur esse una mulier, lecto reclinata propter desideria . . . 2° pingitur ut stomacho gravata . . . 3° depingitur pice denigrata . . . 4° pingitur ut dextra mutilata . . . 5° depingitur ut cornu ventilata . . . 6° pingitur ut oculis orbata . . . 7° item pingitur cremata . . . 8° pingitur ut corpore vitiato . . . 9° pingitur ut fame fedata . . . 10° pingitur cede cruentata . . . (B, foll. 3-4).

2. *Cupido*, on Os. ii, 3

Super illam litteram, *Ne forte expoliem eam nudam*, potest (esse) descriptio Cupidinis, dei amoris. Pingitur enim puer pharetratus, facie ignitus, nudus et pennatus, adamantinis nexibus alligatus. Ultimam conditionem ponit Remigius super Martianum, De nuptiis Mercurii et Philologie (B, fol. 6, 6v).[1]

[1] The whole description comes from Remigius on the *Nuptiae;* I have used the twelfth-century copy in MS Oxford, Merton College 291 : '*In potentiam pharetrate* Cupidinis dicit, ut malum demonstret esse Cupidinem filium Veneris, qui depingitur puer nudus, alatus et pharetratus . . . *Adamantinis nexibus*, id est fortissimis et insolubilibus (fol. 3va)'.
'*Micat*, id est splendet tibi Cupido flagrans, id est splendore ore, id est aspectu . . . (fol. 11rb)'.

3. *Rex*, on Os. iii, 4-5

Rex enim debet esse protectio et solatium subditorum, terror adversariorum. In signum istorum et aliorum secundum Boralensem rex pingitur esse talis, scilicet oleo linctus, sole vestitus, anulo insignitus, virgis sceptratus, iride coronatus, luna calciatus, in throno collocatus, baltheo zonatus, leonibus armatus, ut sic per istas decem descriptiones possit pervenire ad regnum celorum (fol. 11, 11v).

4. *Terra*, on Os. iv, 1 (against worldly riches)

Potest dici quod terra tunc potuit esse descripta sub specie cuiusdam statue habentis buccas grandes, bovinas linguas, et caudas serpentinas, in manu sinistra gladium, in dextra manu Mercurium,[1] cum oculo chimerino[2] et pede vulpino, et hoc dico correspondenter ad litteram istam (fol. 16v).

5. *Caritas sive dilectio*, on Os. vi, (the whole chapter)

Hic dicendum est secundum Augustinum super Iohannem, sermone 7: Qualem faciem habet dilectio, qualem formam, qualem staturam, quales manus, quales pedes habet, nemo potest dicere. Habet tamen pedes, quia ipsi ducunt ad ecclesiam.[3] Unde ex ista imagine potest caritas sive dilectio describi sicut una regina in throno collocata, statura elevata, figura quadrata, Phebo maritata, prole vallata, melle cibata, cum facie quadriformi et veste auriformi, manus habens stillantes et porrectas, aures apertas et directas, oculos flammeos et uxorinos et pedes caprinos (fol. 21).

6. *Liber*, on Os. vii, 5 (against drunkenness)

Ex istis[4] apparet quod Liber, id est deus vini, depingitur quasi iuvenis, hyans, hirsutus, exprimens et cornutus, a Merone nutritus, victor solis calore, sedens in tigribus (MS tegribus), vallatus (MS vallata) menadibus, id est ministris; cum defectibus depingitur, nudus seu nudatus, membratim divisus, de femore Iovis natus, edere adornatus (fol. 25v).

7. *Idolatria*, on Os. ix, 1

In fine capituli, super illam litteram *Noli letari*, ubi loquitur de idolatria, pono picturam antiquorum de idolatria. Depinge-

---

[1] Explained later as: 'Iterum 4° describitur terra quasi statua cum Mercurio et hoc propter furtum . . . Mercurius enim dicitur deus mercatorum et furum (fol. 17v)'.
[2] 'Chimera enim interpretatur idem quod fluctuans in amore (fol. 18)'.
[3] From Augustine, *In Epist. Ioh.* tract. VII, cap. iv (*P.L.* 35) 2034. The personification is further worked out by Augustine: 'Habet manus, nam ipsae pauperi porrigunt . . . Habet oculos . . . Habet aures . . . '.
[4] Holcot found all these attributes in Mythographus tertius, ed. G. H. Bode, *Scriptores rerum mythicarum* (Cellis, 1834), 245-6. He refers to it in his explanation as 'Alexander in mythologiis suis'.

batur enim quasi mulier notata, oculis orbata, aure mutilata, cornu ventilata, vultu deformata, morbo vexata[1] (fol. 30).

8. *Puer*, on Os. xi, 1 (on innocence)

Super illam litteram, *Quia puer Israel*, dicitur quod puer depingebatur sine (sic, cum?) specie floris, modice stature, forme pure, vultu letatus, lacte satiatus, paratus ad ambulandum, extendens manus ad dandum et os ostendens ad osculandum (fol. 32).

9. *Amicitia*, on Joel ii, 18

Iterum super illam litteram, *Zelatus est Dominus*, dicitur quod Dominus amore punivit eos, quia ipse est enim amicus noster specialis . . . Secundum fictionem poeticam et partim per auctoritatem sanctorum ponitur quod amicitia pingebatur in forma cervi, alterius cervi capud supportantis,[2] in forma cordis in duobus corporibus existentis, in forma anime duo corpora vivificantis, in forma papardi et camaleonis colorem mutantis, in forma panis recreantis, in forma lucis et solis letificantis, in forma pueri ortum custodientis, in forma ferri ferrum acuentis (fol. 45v).

10. *Pigritia*, on Mich. iv, 5

Super istam litteram, *Omnes populi ambulabunt unusquisque in nomine dei sui*, dicitur quod hoc est contra habentes pigritiam, qui torpent et iacent, que pigritia depingitur quasi vetula rugosa, in lecto soporata, pede vulnerata, manu mutilata, fame attenuata, veste lacerata, igne concremata. . . . [3] Unde secundum quendam grammaticum depingitur pigritia cum spinis acutis in signum quod homines ferventer et acute laborant pro temporalibus divitiis adquirendum, et iste spine lacerant vestem caritatis et pietatis. . . . Nota secundum Remigium quod pigritia pingitur habere visum obscuratum, auditum gravatum, tactum ebetatum, pallentem in colore, tristem in merore[4] (fol. 74, 74v).

---

[1] From John Ridevall's *Fulgentius metaforalis*, 70. The rhymed description is the same. Ridevall prefaces it by the words: 'Notari autem potest, qualiter antiqua pictura poetica huius maximi peccati, scil idolatrie, concordat cum processu Fulgentii in serie istius mithologie. Hec enim fuit apud aliquos idolatria' . . .

[2] In justifying this description, Holcot cites Augustine's story of deer helping one another across a river by supporting one another's heads, on Gal. vi, 2, *De divinis quaestiones* lxxxiii, quaestio 71 (*P.L.* 40), 81.

[3] Based on *Accidia* in Ridevall's *Lectura*, V, fol. 94vb.

[4] I have not identified the 'quidam grammaticus' or the passage in Remigius. The latter may be wrongly ascribed, since there is no obvious *locus* for a picture of 'pigritia' in the *Nuptiae*.

11. *Patientia*, on Nahum i, 3

Super istam litteram, *Dominus patiens*, describit Boralensis patientiam, dicens quod est homo sedens, ditatus, vilibus cibatus, vultu letatus, omnibus inclinatus,[1] purpura vestitus, hostibus munitus, cum manu arida et alia extenta, sine pedibus, sine lingua et auribus (fol. 82v).

12. *Impatientia*, on same text

Impatientia fuit descripta quasi pauper splendide cibatus, mestitia respersus, omnibus adversus, vestibus nudatus, aculeis vallatus, cum manibus leprosis et pedibus vulpinis, cum lingua serpentina et auribus leoninis. Expositio istius picture pateri potest ex dicta descriptione patientie. Ideo transeo (fol. 83).

13. *Luxuria*, on Nahum iii, 4

Notandum quod secundum aliquos luxuria fuit depicta mulier plena sorde, sine corde, excecata, spoliata, ignita, columbis custodita, cum dampno de mari nata, Vulcano maritata, concha marina honorata, rosis adornata[2] (fol. 85v).

14. *Fides*, on Habuc. ii, 19

Quintum peccatum fuit idolatria, ibi, *Ve qui dicit ligno etc.* Nota quod dicit Augustinus, 4 De civitate Dei, cap. 20: Fides, inquit, dea credita est et accepit illius (sic) templum et altare inter deos;[3] et quidam dicunt quod cum deo Iove fides apud antiquos fuit depicta quasi virgo delicata . . . 2° pingitur fides vultu venerata . . . 3° pingitur fides purpurata . . . 4° pingitur fides fronte signata . . . 5° depingitur manu dextra, utens utraque manu pro dextra . . . 6° pingitur fides ornata . . . 7° scribitur (sic) fides anulo arrata . . . 8° pingitur fides in equo locata . . . 9° pingitur fides hostibus vallata . . . 10° armis velata . . . 11° scuto gemmata . . . 12° telis infestata . . . 13° formata caritate . . . (foll. 89-90).[4]

15. *Fortuna*, on Habuc. iii, 4

Notandum quod Moyses dicitur fuisse cornutus et divites dicuntur cornuti propter fortunam, que depingitur quasi mulier delicata, in rota celata, cum facie duplata, vultu variata, visu excecata, cornibus vallata (fol. 91v).

---

[1] MS *ab omnibus*, but *homo omnibus inclinatus* below.
[2] The 'picture' of *Luxuria* slides into a description of Venus.
[3] *De civ. Dei.* iv, 20.
[4] From Ridevall's *Lectura*, V, fol. 95ra. Holcot has taken the attributes from Ridevall, but added his own *exempla*, quotations and explanations.

16. *Spes*, on Soph. iii, 2

Super istam litteram, *In Domino non est confisa*, potest adduci quod in parte ait Prudentius de pictura spei et magister Iohannes Ridevalis addit, et ego alia supcraddam. Pingitur enim spes in forma matris seu matrone, stature erecte, scuto protecte, decore commendate, vultu letate, hostibus vallate; galea firmata, suaviter dicitur pennata, nam applicata,[1] in pulvere collocata, pacifice conversata.[2] Depingitur in forma matrone quando agitat hastam vibrantem (MS vibrantis), auro coronate, lanceo sceptrate (fol. 96).

17. *Suavitas*, on Ag. 1, 10

Potest dici quod fingunt poete de pictura suavitatis, scilicet quod erat imago sexus virilis, infacilis, cor madens cruore, oculis [sic] amore; os spirat dulcorem, manus fundunt rorem. Dicit magister Iohannes Ridevalensis quod est imago sexus virilis ad designandum quod suavitas debet carere mollitie feminee . . . [3] (fol. 98).

18. *Pax*, on Ag. 1, 12

Notandum autem quod Iesus est rex pacificus et pax secundum quosdam depingitur esse una domina ex Minerva generata, statura elevata, facie iocundata, gladio reparata, olivis honorata, care comparata, tubis proclamata, (?) res sociata, lucidi coloris, validi vigoris (fol. 98).

19. *Misericordia*, on Zach. 1, 16

Super illam litteram, *Revertar ad Ierusalem in misericordiis*, fingitur quod misericordia erat picta quasi mulier de Phebo generata, pellicano confortata, oleo coronata, aquis irrigata, in sinistra sex lilii foliis adornata, in dextra sex lucernis illustrata, cum sinistra plena et dextra serena, cum vultu iocundato et vestitu variato, cum ore ebrioso et latere diviso . . . in medio egentium collocata, sanguissuge sociata . . . ore obriso (fol. 101v).

20. *Gratia*, on Zach. iv, 7

Notandum est propter litteram *Exequabit gratia gratie* ponitur depictio gratie quod dicitur esse talis secundum Fulgentium et alios. Recitat magister Iohannes Ridevalis quod gratia depingitur dei Iovis nata, nectare cibata, ore dulcorata, sensu

---

[1] Something has dropped out here.
[2] Also from Ridevall's *Lectura*, V, fol. 95vb. Holcot has added the last attribute and much of the explanation. The *Psychomachia* of Prudentius has suggested only the *suaviter dicitur pennata*; '. . . praestringens aêra pinnis in caelum se virgo rapit' (*C.S.E.L.* 61) 183. The *stature erecte* may perhaps echo the *Peristephanon*: 'spem non iacentem' (ibid. 383). The *Spes* of Prudentius is a virgin, not a matron.
[3] Holcot is referring to a part of the *Lectura* now lost.

approbata, lumine lustrata, flore decorata, facie letata, vultu variata, veste nudata, serto coronata, lingua lunata, manu colligata, numero sacrata, sp(h)erice sceptrata, musis comitata[1] (fol. 107v).

21. *Avaritia*, on Zach. v, 7: *Ecce mulier sedens in medio amphorae*

Notandum quod amphora dicitur esse avaritia et avarus etiam describitur secundum Chrysostomum super Mat., omelia 28, esse homo ab oculis ignem emittens, niger, ab alterutris humeris dracones habens (loco) manus dependentes. Fit autem ei os pro dentibus gladios acutos habens infixos, pro lingua autem veneni et pestiferi formati fortem [sic] emanantem, habens etiam ventrem caminum; pedes sunt subalati; facies ipsa a lupo et cane constructa, et loquitur nichil humanum sed sonitum habet non delectabilem, sed terribilem, et in manibus flammam habet. Terribilia esse videntur que dicta sunt, sed nondum secundum quod est avaritie formavimus. Hec ille[2]. Ex istis dictis posset dici quod avarus pingitur esse homo denigratus in cute, gladio transverberatus, cum fonte venenato et oculis igneis cum flamma in manibus, ex humeris draconibus dependentibus, cum vultu lupino, habens os pro dentibus cum subalatis pedibus et sonis terribilibus (fol. 109).

22. *Veritas*, on Zach. viii, 19

Iterum super illam litteram, *Veritatem et pacem diligite*, ponit picturam veritatis quam tangit Ieronimus in suo dialogo inter Atticum et Actabolon [sic], ut dicit magister Iohannes Ridevalis.[3] Pingitur enim esse in forma virili, etate senili, veste lacerata, fronte rugata, corpore fedata, pedibus nudata, onere gravata, armis infestata, onere captivata, morte dampnata, capite truncata, sed in sede revocata. Hec omnia patent in Christo (fol. 114v).

23. *Devotio*, on Zach. x, 2

Ratione istius dicti pone (MS post) descriptionem devotionis quam fingit Boralensis posse dici talem. Ergo describitur esse quasi imago pallida, sp(h)eris coronata, Iovis consecrata, nectare nutrita, podere vestita,[4] fontibus irrigata, hostibus impugnata, sensibus sopita, facibus ignita, balsamo intincta,

---

[1] From Ridevall's *Lectura*, V, fol. 90va. Ridevall gives seven attributes of *gratia*, Holcot fifteen.

[2] *Hom. xxviii in Mt.* (*P.G.* 57) 356. Holcot has copied this description of a monster faithfully from Chrysostom, who ends: 'Hoc monstro deterior est avarus'.

[3] This comes from a lost part of Ridevall's *Lectura*. Atticus says to Critobulus in St Jerome's *Dialogus adversus Pelagianos*: 'Veritas amara est, rugosae frontis, offenditque correptos'. (*P.L.* 23) 520.

[4] Cf. Apoc. i, 18.

N

vario precincta, oleo lincta, Hercule munita. Hec ille (fol. 117v).

24. *Superbia*, on Zach. xi, 2

Nota quod superbia describitur vel depingitur esse quasi rex coronatus, ut aquila exaltatus, vestibus laceratus, capite infirmatus, cum dentibus aprinis et pedibus taurinis, colore denigratus, familia stipatus, magnam habens prolem et impugnans solem, vermibus infestatus, in fetibus collocatus, tenebrescens et intumescens[1] (fol. 120v).

25. *Mansuetudo*, on Zach. xiv, 3

Ideo dico quod hec virtus mansuetudo describitur sive depingitur quasi una domina regina, divitiis ditata, in pace locata, orti servativa, ferri attractiva, cum pulchra comitiva, Iovis placativa, viliter despecta et fortiter protecta, in auribus ornata, honorifice exaltata (fol. 128).

26. *Paupertas*, on Malach. ii, 2: *Mittam in vos egestatem*

Dicitur quod paupertas describitur quasi una domina, vultu letata, philosophis maritata, deliciis refecta, Iano despecta,[2] quasi aqua clara et pura, ut castrum secura, sedens quietata, recte dimensionata, hostibus infestata, auro coronata, armis immunita, bisso vestita, mercibus honorata, in sublimi collocata (fol. 136v).

Our list shows that Holcot had predecessors in the invention of 'pictures', John Ridevall (7, 10, 14, 16, 20, 22), the mysterious Boralensis (3, 11, 23) and perhaps an unnamed grammarian (10). He ascribes the semi-classical 'pictures' of Luxury (13) and Peace (18) to 'aliqui' or 'quidam'. Once the technique had been discovered, mass-production could begin. The same attribute, such as 'vultu letatus', could serve for more than one 'picture'. Those looking for material could find it in the Fathers, not to mention Prudentius and Boethius. Love had hands and feet according to Augustine (5), Truth a wrinkled forehead according to Jerome (22); Chrysostom described the avaricious man as a fantastic monster, which needed only slight rearrangement to turn it into a 'picture' (21). The study of rhetoric contributed 'poetic fictions' as a source (9, 17); the list of figures for Friendship (9) suggests a series

---

[1] Ridevall's 'picture' of superbia in his *Lectura* (V, fol. 97ra) is quite different from Holcot's.

[2] Holcot supports this attribute by Horace, *Epist.* I, i, 53 (fol. 137), quoting the inscription in the temple of Janus.

of emblems rather than a single 'picture' of the usual type. The *distinctio* was another precursor of the 'picture'. Holcot's Child (8) could be re-written as a *distinctio*; he lists and moralises the properties of a child.[1] The development lies in his disposition of the properties. Instead of remaining a mere list, as they would do in a *distinctio*, they create the image of a real live baby. For the most part, however, the 'pictures' do not lend themselves to reproduction in colour and line. They are just as 'verbal' as Ridevall's. They consist of qualities which are sometimes hardly capable of representation, such as 'fame fedata' (1), and sometimes incompatible; Luxury is both 'spoliata' and 'rosis adornata' (13). The gods and goddesses as represented in medieval art have more attributes than they know how to carry.[2] It is even more difficult to imagine Faith with her thirteen qualities (14). They would tax the most resourceful artist.

Holcot so far has borrowed an existing technique. The *Moralitates* show an advance in method. There are three main changes. He reduces his cumbersome set of attributes so as to present a single image, fanciful indeed, but easily grasped and capable of being drawn or painted. This makes room for verbal inscriptions in the 'picture', helping to point its moral. They appear on or besides the central figure or on scrolls which are part of the design. Thirdly, he seems to insist much more on the antique setting. To see the difference, one may compare the incisive 'picture' of Mercy, as 'the pagans' used to paint it, in the *Moralitates* with the corresponding muddle in the commentary (19); a man holds a cloven heart inscribed with messages of mercy:

'The pagans imagined that there were as many gods as there were virtues, which virtues were called after them and appropriated to them. The god of piety and clemency used to be painted in the likeness of a man, who held in his hand a heart split in two pieces.'

Messages of mercy and promise of forgiveness to the repentant sinner were written in letters of gold around and on each piece of the heart.[3] Friendship has ceased to be a mere

---

[1] *Study of the Bible*, 246-8, 258-9.   [2] Seznec, 149-83.
[3] *Moral.* III, p. 710: Finxerunt pagani tot esse deos, quot sunt virtutes, quibus diis virtutes appellate et appropriate sunt. Deus autem pietatis et clementie depingebatur ad similitudinem hominis, qui tenebat in manu sua cor scissum in duas partes; et in circuitu cordis scribebatur litteris aureis sic: Pietas et misericordia tota die expectant, quando peccator a suo peccato recedere curet.

catalogue of symbols, as he is in the commentary (9). He
has become a handsome youth dressed in green, bareheaded
and with his side open to show the heart within. Inscriptions
appear on his head, on the fringe of his dress, and on the
heart.[1] Compare also the 'picture' of Devotion ascribed to
Boralensis (23), whence no clear figure emerges, with the
very paintable Prayer of the *Moralitates*. A man turns his
head and heart heavenward. Four angels surround him,
each bearing a scroll inscribed with encouraging verses.[2]

The 'laws' in the sermons, lectures and *Moralitates* make a
helpful parallel: they seem to be just as fictional as the
'pictures'. A 'law' concerning marriage or inheritance will
be quoted with a case arising from it, which will then be
moralised.[3] The Ecclesiasticus-commentary contains an
imaginary story about the method of promulgating imperial
laws ascribed to Livy, as we have seen.[4] An *exemplum* of the
same type is ascribed to Hugh Sneyth O.P., who was
teaching at Oxford between 1287 and 1296.[5] Nicholas
Trevet may have invented this kind of moralisation in his
Declamationes Senece moralisate; he certainly made it popular.
Holcot quotes the book without acknowledgment in one of
his sermons.[6] The *genre* originated in the moralisation of laws

---

In una parte cordis scriptum erat litteris aureis sic: Nisi esset peccatum, non
esset misericordia. Si venia petatur, cito habetur. In altera parte cordis scribebatur: Ibi est misericordia, ubi est peccatum. Ibi nulla est misericordia, ubi
nulla est peccatum.

[1] XXVI, p. 731: Narrat Fulgentius in quodam libro de gestis romanorum quod romani verum amorem sive veram amicitiam hoc modo descrip-
serunt, scilicet quod imago amoris vel amicitie depicta erat instar iuvenis cuiusdam valde pulchri, induti habitu virido. Facies eius et capud disco-operta
erant sive nudata, et in fronte ipsius erat scriptum: Hyems et estas. Erat latus
eius apertum, ita ut videretur cor, in quo scriptum erant hec verba: Longe et
prope. Et in fimbria vestimenti eius erat scriptum: Mors et vita. . . .
The enumeration continues.

[2] XIX, p. 725: Unde oratio depingebatur ad modum hominis, qui habuit
capud et cor conversum ad celum. Imago vero fulciebatur quatuor angelis;
et quilibet tenebat rotulum in manu sua, cuius pictura erat iste versus: Terris,
igni, mari, vento peto predominari. Secundus angelus tenebat in manu sua
rotulum aliud, in quo (erat) iste versus: Vir, pete. Sum presto. Si plangas,
cominus asto. Tertius angelus tenebat in manu sua aliud rotulum, in quo
scriptum erat iste versus: Cum petor, accedo. Non postulor; inde recedo.
Quartus angelus tenebat in manu sua quartum rotulum, in quo scriptum erat
iste versus: Adiuvo constanter. Non desero. Pugno libenter.

[3] V, p. 712: Narrat Romulus in Annalibus Iudeorum, quod in India
fuerunt leges. . . .
The 'Iudeorum' should be corrected to 'Indorum'. The laws of the Indians
described here come from the Pseudo-Aristotle, *Secretum secretorum*, ed. R. Steele,
Opera hactenus inedita Rogeri Baconi 5 (Oxford 1920) 49.

[4] Appendix i, 321.   [5] Robert Holcot, 52.   [6] Appendix i, 329.

and cases found in Seneca and Quintilian.[1] The moralist then proceeded to invent his own. He would ascribe them to some ancient writer or else use a formula such as *Lex erat apud antiquos*. It was pushing the technique a stage further. Other contemporary influences occur to the mind. A literary starting point might be the interior decoration of a palace: 'An interior, decorated with motifs from the medieval system of knowledge' was 'one of the favourite subjects for description in vernacular poetry'.[2] English illumination could have suggested the inscriptions so typical of Holcot's 'pictures'. William de Brailles, an artist who worked almost certainly at Oxford soon after the middle of the thirteenth century, puts scrolls bearing inscriptions into his miniatures in a distinctive manner.[3] He was a famous illuminator, whose work Holcot may have known and admired. The *Somme le Roi*, compiled in 1279 by a French Dominican for King Philip III, to whom he was confessor, had collected a fixed cycle of miniatures before 1294. These show virtues personified with their attributes. The Parisian artist Honoré, working 1288-93 (he died before 1318), painted them seated on animals and holding shields bearing devices.[4] 'Force' holds a lion painted on a shield; a stream flows from beneath her feet. Humility holds a mirror, because the first degree of humility is to know oneself, in one hand and a rod in the other, and stands on a unicorn. Prowess is 'seated on a bull with a large ring through its nose and holds a pink medallion on which is a lion passant'.[5] Vices are generally shown performing the appropriate actions or in historical scenes; King Ochozias falls 'through the lattices of his upper chamber' (IV Reg. i, 1), signifying pride. But one Paris miniature shows Luxury holding a cloth and chains.[6] There are no exact parallels to our 'pictures' and the symbolism, since it has to fit into the scope of a single miniature, is less multiple than it is in Ridevall's and in Holcot's early efforts. The underlying concept, however, is strikingly similar, especially in the simpler 'pictures' of the *Moralitates*.

[1] Holcot moralises a passage from Seneca, *Controv.* i, 6 in P, sermo xxiii, and a passage from Quintilian, *Declam.* ix, ibid. sermo xcvii.
[2] G. V. Smithers, op. cit., 2, 29.
[3] G. Pollard, William de Brailles, *B.L.R.* 5 (1955) 202-9; P. Brieger, *English Art 1216-1307* (Oxford, 1957) 85-93.
[4] E. G Millar, *An Illuminated Manuscript of La Somme le Roi, attributed to the Parisian Miniaturist Honoré* (Roxburghe Club, 1953) 2-3, 12-14. The *Somme* was very well known and was translated into English as *Ayenbyte of Inwyt*.
[5] Plates VI, VII, VIII, X.　　　　　[6] Plate XXVI.

Nevertheless, I agree with Saxl in thinking that the genesis of the 'pictures' was literary. Ridevall's 'painters' were not artists working with the brush, but poets and philosophers, as hc tclls us. Holcot came closer to seeing what he described in his mind's eye, and he evolved a clear image from a mess. Looking at miniatures may perhaps have helped him to simplify his 'pictures' and may have suggested the use of inscriptions. But his 'pictures' resemble his 'laws' in having literary sources, wherever sources can be traced. It is very doubtful that hc mcant them to be illustrated. The 'pictures', like all the other *exempla* in his *Moralitates*, were aids to preaching. An image which could be grasped easily, complex enough to intrigue without confusing, projected back into antiquity and supplied with inscriptions to intrigue still further, this made first-class preaching material.

We already have an answer to our other problem: who were Holcot's unknown ancient authors? Where did he find his 'Fulgentius in quodam libro de gestis romanorum', 'Romulus in annalibus indorum' and 'Theodosius in vita Alexandri'? A study of the *genre* will have shown that Holcot either made them up or picked them up in some contemporary forgery. Lathbury quotes a Pseudo-Fulgentius, who provided him with apocryphal stories of ancient Rome.[1] Romulus and Theodosius are known only from Holcot. We have seen him attach *exempla* to real authors without any justification or read into a text far more than is there, as Ridevall had done earlier. Ridevall had also ascribed his 'picture' of Idolatry to the ancient poets. It was just a step further to invent the author along with the story or 'picture' or 'law'. Vernacular poets and romancers, perhaps borrowing from the schoolmen their habit of quoting authority, had been known to invent their authors. Now a schoolman borrows a custom of the romancers. Theodosius and Romulus fall into place beside Master Kyot and the 'wise man' and many another literary fiction. Holcot not only pillaged antiquity and improved on it, but fitted out his stories with authors' names. He anticipates the novelist who finds his tale 'in an old manuscript', hidden in a secret drawer or in a chest in the lumber-room. A novel beginning in this way may be pretty enough; it will shock the stickler for historical accuracy as much as it thrills more romantic readers.

[1] Below, 230.

The anonymous Franciscan who compiled *Gesta impera-torum*, later called *Gesta Romanorum*, improved on Holcot. He drew on the *Moralitates* and added many tales of the same type. The title was a stroke of genius. The book tells of romance rather than of Romans, but the public it was designed for tended to identify them. It had a long life, and so had the illusion, as sub-titles of English translations will prove: *The famous book intitled Gesta Romanorum, or a record of true ancient histories* (1789); *Gesta Romanorum, or forty-five histories originally (t'is said) collected from the Roman records* (1703). Even the moralisation kept its appeal: an abridged version was offered as *A Young man's Guide to a Virtuous Life* in 1698. Finally a translation appeared in 1824, which was re-edited in 1905 under the title: *Gesta Romanorum, entertaining moral stories invented by the monks as a fireside recreation and commonly applied in their discourses from the pulpit whence the most celebrated of our own poets and others have extracted their plots*. Thus Holcot, *via Gesta romanorum*, lived on into the twentieth century as an entertainer.

V.—THE MIND OF HOLCOT

Holcot admitted as an exegete to the scepticism that he professed as a theologian. He did not parade it. The text of Ecclesiasticus and of the Twelve Prophets gave him no occasion to discuss proofs for the immortality of the soul or for the existence of God, and he did not raise the matter. Wisdom, on the contrary, offered a challenge which he felt bound to meet. Chapter ii puts forward the arguments of the ungodly, denying the immortality of the soul and drawing the consequence:

> 'We do know what we have here; we don't know what we shall get hereafter; and so let's have a good time.'[1]

Can one prove to such persons by rational arguments that the soul is immortal and hence that they must expect rewards and punishments in the afterlife? Holcot answers that the immortality of the soul can be inferred in three grounds, God's goodness (assuming here his existence), his equity in rewarding and punishing, and his truth in fulfilling his promises. But the argument is qualified:

[1] Sap. lect. xx, C, fol. 34ra: Hic scimus quid habemus; nescimus quid habebimus in futuro; et ideo ducamus letos dies.

'Although perhaps it cannot be proved by natural reason, as appears plainly enough from the weakness of the reasons put forward by saints and philosophers alike, yet it's most important to believe it, just as many other things are true, which we cannot prove. For one of these two statements is necessary: the world began to be, or the world did not begin to be (i.e. it was not created, but is eternal); and yet neither proposition can be demonstrated by proof. . . . Similarly, the squaring of the circle is certain, but its demonstration was not discovered in Aristotle's time.'[1]

Nor does he accept rational proofs for the necessity of a resurrection of the body. St Thomas's argument that man's natural desire for bliss cannot be fulfilled in this life, and yet requires the union of soul and body, does not meet the case of the damned. Richard of Middleton argues that no natural tendency is in vain; but every rational soul has a natural tendency to rule and govern the body; therefore every rational soul will be re-united to the body. This does not meet the case of the damned either. Their natural desire for well-being will be frustrated; and we know by faith that 'many are called and few chosen'. Holcot falls back on Scripture, on revelation to the holy Fathers and on miracles, such as the miracle of the seven sleepers in the *Legenda aurea*.[2]

He had less difficulty with a further contention of the ungodly: not only man's soul but even his name will perish and be forgotten, so that nothing remains either of his person or of his reputation: *And our name in time shall be forgotten, and no man shall have any remembrance of our works* (ii, 4). This was soon disposed of by one who 'talked of Alexander' and admired the ancient heroes. Holcot points out that the fame of great men does not perish. Public figures are better remembered than private. Some men have even been treated as gods and have been sung by the poets. He goes on to argue that desire for good fame is a necessary stimulus to goodness, though the virtuous man should not care excessively for his reputation.[3] All the same, he did not think the prospect of future glory or shame in men's remembrance on earth an adequate substitute for rewards and punishments after death as a deterrent to evil doers. He admits as much. If our hope lay only in the present, we should be the most miserable of men:

[1] Appendix i, 329.   [2] See below, p. 326.
[3] I summarise the gist of lect. xviii.

'Given that there is no future penalty, I don't see why one shouldn't enjoy the charms and pleasures of this life.'

One *must* believe in a future life![1] But he had renounced any hope of convincing the ungodly by reason.

Chapter xiii raised the question, even more fundamental, whether natural reason sufficed to prove the existence of God. The author of Wisdom argues that the pagan philosophers might have attained to a knowledge of his existence by contemplating his works: *But all men are vain, in whom there is not the knowledge of God: and who by these good things that are seen could not understand him that is. Neither by attending to the works have acknowledged who was the workman* (xiii, 1). Holcot asked how the philosophers could attain to a knowledge, which, as he thought, was not accessible even to Christians by the light of mere reason. He answered that God would always reveal himself to true seekers:

'But how is it that the philosophers should be expected to prove that God exists, when even Christians, who have knowledge of the one true God, are not able to do so? On this it should be said, as I think, that it has not been proved by any reason up to now that God is or that God is the Creator of the world; but to all who bear themselves innocently in God's sight and use their natural reason to enquire, putting no obstacle in the way of divine grace, God will communicate sufficient knowledge of himself, in such a way as to suffice for their salvation. We have examples of this in Cornelius, to whom Peter was sent, and in Paul, to whom Ananias was sent: these two so inclined themselves as to receive revelation or inspiration concerning the one God; and so it should be said that the man who uses his natural reason blamelessly will never lack knowledge of God, at least in so far as is necessary for his salvation.'[2]

Verses 3-9 continue the argument that the philosophers might have deduced God's existence from the grandeur and beauty of created things. Holcot explains it in all fairness to his author, adding to it the consideration that Aristotle 'tried to prove' the existence of God from the need

---

[1] lect. xx, C, fol. 33vb: De ista conclusione primo videndum est de consequentia; et sine dubio videtur bona et satis consulte et prudenter illata, quia si in hac vita tantum sperantes essemus, miserabiliores sumus omnibus hominibus ... Unde dato quod non foret pena futura, non video quin fruendum esset illecebris et delectationibus huius vite, sed hoc antecedens est falsum.

Holcot then argues that earthly goods are not ends in themselves, but his argument depends on faith, not reason.

[2] Appendix i, 327.

for a prime mover. But he has to point out that his author seems to contradict himself, having said previously: *And hardly do we guess aright at things that are upon earth. . . . But the things that are in heaven, who shall search out?* (ix, 16). Again Holcot helps his author to make his case by adducing a current distinction: it is one thing to understand *that* God is, another to understand *what* he is. Supporters of this distinction say that the philosophers could have reached the former but not the latter grade of understanding (i.e. they could have realised that God is, without rising to a knowledge of him such as Christians have). Holcot then gives his own opinion. He repeats what he has said before, and is even more categoric: he has not so far found it proved that God is. He therefore falls back on another approach to the question, basing himself on St Augustine's teaching that a primitive revelation made knowledge of God's existence possible to all. He goes on to suggest that not only knowledge of God but all science came from a primitive revelation rather than from human reason. The Master of the Histories tells us that the patriarch Noe had a son called Ionith, who received the gift of wisdom from God and discovered the science of astronomy. As sages learnt to measure the size of the earth, sun and moon, so they might have learnt to worship the true God, because he would have revealed himself to them, had they been worthy.[1]

Lectures on Wisdom were not the place for Holcot to justify his rejection of intellectual proofs for God's existence. He had done so in his *Sentence*-commentary. He simply states his position. His scepticism appears all the starker for the absence of scholastic arguments. No one, pagan or Christian, had produced a rational argument for the existence of God or for the immortality of the soul that satisfied him. He doubted whether the unaided human intellect could reach certainty even in human science. If we remember the wide diffusion of his Wisdom-commentary, we realise the importance of this simple statement. How many readers were introduced to the scepticism of the schools through Holcot's plain speaking?

He did not keep his scepticism in a closed compartment of his brain: far from it. He drew consequences for the function of theology. Thus he felt some irritation against the 'laymen of modern times', who expected theologians to give

[1] Appendix i, 327.

reasons for their faith. A good theologian who had heard heretics arguing against it without succumbing was worth more than such laymen.[1] His attitude is summed up in an *exemplum*, which he tells at least twice, and which represents his best effort to persuade the unbeliever. A simple Dominican lay brother converted a heretic, where good clerks had tried and failed. The heretic, 'a great clerk' himself, persisted in refusing to believe in the immortality of the soul, until the lay brother put it to him that one had better 'play safe'. One would lose nothing by believing, even if one's belief were unfounded; one would gain eternal bliss if it should prove to be true.[2] This is real scepticism. It goes with fideism. Holcot tells the story to urge the advisability of belief in the absence of rational proof.

His *Sentence*-commentary shows a formidable power of criticism in such abstract questions as proofs for the existence of God. We shall now watch him training it on to historical and literary evidence. He does so fitfully, but to good effect, passing from romance to history as easily as *vice versa*. He attacks the claims of the rival Orders of Carmelites and Austin Friars to have originated in Old Testament times, and so to have senior status *vis à vis* the Dominicans and Franciscans. The Carmelites claimed to have been founded by the prophet Elias on Mount Carmel, and regarded St John Baptist as a member of their Order. The Austin Friars claimed to have St Augustine as their founder; he had grouped the hermits of his day into an Order and had given them a rule. Holcot sets forth the claims of the Carmelites on the text: *the top of Carmel is withered* (Amos i, 2). Then he makes fun of them. He points out that if religious existed at that time, they must have belonged to the sect of the Pharisees, the Sadducees or the Essenes, according to Josephus,[3] and that these were the chief conspirators against Christ, and that for envy. So if the Carmelites' supposed ancient foundation were genuine, it would be nothing to boast about. The knights of today would hardly boast of their descent from those who crucified Christ. As for the dream of Elias' father, that he saw men clad in white,

---

[1] Sap. lect. xxix, C, fol. 48ra: . . . ideo multo plus meretur bonus theologus, qui vidit et audivit rationes hereticorum contra fidem, et tamen assentit (fidei), quam laici moderni temporis, qui putant nos theologos habere scientiam subalternantem ad fidem eorum, quasi nos demonstrare possemus illa que ipsi tantummodo fide tenent.

[2] Appendix i, 330.   [3] *Antiquit.* XIII, v, 9.

greeting one another[1], it does not follow that they signified the Carmelites, as is claimed: millers and shepherds might just as well be Carmelites on this argument. Then it is the turn of the Austin Friars. Holcot says that if St Augustine received the habit and organised them into an Order at the age of eighteen, according to their story, then he received the habit while still a Manichee and unbeliever, and he had a son afterwards; St Augustine was thirty years old at the time of his conversion, as is plain. Holcot implies that the Austin Friars' claim has its dangers as well as the Carmelites', if they make it a subject for boasting.[2]

He tells us elsewhere, very acutely, that St Augustine made a rule concerning a common life for clerks, which many religious adopted later on, among them the Order of Friars Preachers. The Hermits of St William and of St Augustine[3] received it long afterwards, precisely when they ceased to be hermits and came to live in urban communities. The Rule of St Augustine is not for hermits at all and St Augustine himself never was one, as appears from his own words in the *Confessions*, describing how he contemplated withdrawing into the wilderness and how God restrained him from doing so.[4] The rivalry between the Orders for precedence has sharpened Holcot's tongue on this occasion and he gives free rein to his critical sense. The discussion continued after his death. Some of the points he made were remembered, but the protagonists tended to dwell on legal arguments and did not show Holcot's feeling for first-hand historical evidence.[5]

We sometimes see flashes of the same critical spirit when he considers questions of bibliography. Petrarch is supposed to have been the first scholar to expose as spurious the *De*

---

[1] It was part of the Carmelite legend that Elias' father had seen the Order foretold in a vision before his son's birth.

[2] Appendix i, 330.

[3] On the origins of the Carmelites, Austin Friars and Guillemites, see *D.H.G.E.* 5 (1931) 499-502, 11 (1949) 1073-4.

[4] Appendix i, 331.

[5] A Cambridge Dominican, John Stokes, must have used some of Holcot's arguments in a *Determinatio* of 1370, which is now lost. A Cambridge Carmelite, John Hornby, replied to Stokes in 1374, in his *Defensorium sui ordinis*, which preserves his opponent's criticisms of Carmelite claims. Stokes had made Holcot's point that an order founded by Elias must have belonged to one of the Jewish sects mentioned by Josephus. Hornby answers by distinguishing between *secta* and *religio*; MS Oxford, Bodl. MS e Mus. 86, fol. 197va-b. On the controversy see B. Jarrett, *The English Dominicans* (London, 1921) 16; B. Xiberta, *De scriptoribus scholasticis saeculi XIV ex ordine Carmelitarum* (Louvain, 1931) 172; Knowles, op. cit. 2, 52.

vetula, a poem ascribed to Ovid and believed to have been found in his tomb. Roger Bacon had accepted it as genuine. Its charm lay in the 'prophecies' of the coming of Christ contained there.[1] Holcot quotes these so-called prophecies, adding:

'But whether the book is Ovid's, God knows. . . . Agreed, that if the book was really his, it was a very fine prophecy. But that's by the way.'[2]

He tried to verify the legend that the Venerable Bede had paid a visit to Rome.[3] He has not found it in any authentic work. Some say yes, some no. Perhaps what one man has seen in the original text, another hasn't. Holcot himself has not seen it and neither have the monks, who claim to have all Bede's books. He shrugs his shoulders.[4] Ancient myths, he thinks, should be taken with a pinch of salt. After telling of the giant Titon, who covered nine acres of ground when he lay down, Holcot says that he wouldn't have written it unless he had found it in Isidore. If you work out the measurements, 'you'll get a solemn lie, I think'.[5] Some of the miracles currently reported in England may be either superfluous or fictitious.[6] Many a preacher brings the faith

---

[1] P. Lehmann, *Pseudo-antike Literatur des Mittelalters* (Studien der Bibliothek Warburg, Leipzig 1927) 13-14; F. Ghisalberti, Medieval Biographies of Ovid, *J.W.C.I.* 9 (1946) 36-7.

[2] Sap. lect. lxi, p. 216: An sit liber Ovidii, Deus novit . . . Unde constat quod si liber veraciter suus erat, fuit pulcherrima prophetia; sed hoc est extra propositum.

[3] On the origin and growth of the legend, see C. E. Whiting, The Life of the Venerable Bede, *Bede, his Life, Times and Writings*, ed. A. Hamilton Thompson (Oxford, 1935) 11-14. William of Malmesbury refuses to vouch for its truth in his *Gesta Regum*, ii, 57.

[4] B, fol. 61: Istud non vidi in aliquo auctentico, sed dicitur sic fuisse. Utrum autem Beda fuerit Rome vel non, nescio. Quidam dicunt quod sic, quidam quod non. Ideo historia predicta valeat quantum valere potest. Forte quod unus non vidit in originali, alius vidit; ideo non est sic arguendum. Ego hoc non vidi in libris Bede, nec monachi, qui dicunt se habere omnes libros Bede. Ergo non est in ali(qu)o libro Bede.

[5] Sap. lect. cxxxii, C, fol. 200ra: Monstrum etiam fuit ille Tition, qui iacens novem iugera occupavit, sicut Homerus testatur. Hoc non scriberem, nisi in Isidoro invenissem. Est enim iugerum quantum aratrum arare potest uno die, et continet in longitudine secundum Papiam ducentos quadraginta pedes, et in latitudine medietatem, quod spatium, si multiplicetur per novem, et dicatur quod homo tantum spatium occupaverit iacendo, fiet sollempne mendacium, sicut credo.

[6] Ecclus. lect. xlvii, fol. 38ra: Ex hiis videtur quod si tot sunt miracula in Anglia, sicut dicitur hiis diebus, vel radix fidei adhuc non est firmata in Anglia, sed infirma, vel si sit firmata, tunc quando dicuntur miracula vel sunt superflua vel sunt ficta.
This occurs in a *quaestio* on why miracles should have occurred more frequently in the early Church than later.

into contempt by trying to prove what is true with the help
of fictions, such as the marvellous properties of stones and
herbs, which experience disproves. This is the reason why
his hearers do not believe him and despise all his teaching;
he intermingles the false with the true.[1]

Holcot did not practise what he preached in avoiding the
marvellous. He understood contemporary taste too well.
He was equally erratic in his scholarship. The inconsistency
becomes understandable if we imagine a critical sceptic
turned loose among the authoritative texts of his time. The
rejection of rational arguments to prove God's existence left
faith and Scripture to bear the whole weight of Christian
theology. Holcot of all men needed to refrain from casting
doubt on revelation as contained in the Bible.[2] He could
hardly have engaged in criticism when dealing with secular
texts without at some stage applying the same technique
to the text standing on the lectern before him in his class-
room. He could not afford to. Perhaps this accounts in
part for his preference for *moralitates* and for the admitted
thinness of his literal exposition. They absolved him from
any serious consideration of historical evidence. *Moralitates*
and 'talk of Alexander' were safe as well as amusing.

Holcot was a 'Pelagian' in the fourteenth-century con-
notation of the term. He belonged to the opposite camp to
Bradwardine, who taught the doctrine of predestination
in an extreme version.[3] One of his sermons shows him
concerned with the moral implications of Bradwardine's
doctrine. He starts from the theme that man has free will
to accept or reject God's grace, putting it very simply in the
form of a metaphor. All men are called to heaven and to

---

[1] ibid. lect. liii, fol. 43ra: Tertio, verbum predicatum debet esse probabile,
ut illud quod suadetur et docetur secundum fidem appareat esse verum . . . Sic
multi allegant virtutes lapidum et herbarum, naturas rerum diversarum; et
tamen experientia docet oppositum. . . . Et hec est causa quare frequenter non
credunt omnes homines predicanti et aliis, quia doctrinam totam parvipendunt,
quia ad probandum vera interserunt quedam falsa.

[2] The question of God's knowledge of future contingents, as debated in the
schools, raised the problem of the infallibility of revelation. Was God's knowledge of the future limited by the truth which he had revealed? Those who
would not accept Bradwardine's doctrine of necessity had to answer it. One
line of argument was to make God's knowledge of the future itself contingent:
his omniscience covered future contingency; but in that case, revelation itself
would be contingent. Holcot took quite another line: the whole of his discussion
on future contingents was directed to preserving the infallibility of revelation,
even though at the expense of God's omniscience. See G. Leff, op. cit. 224-39.
Thus Holcot clung to the absolute certainty of Scripture.

[3] G. Leff, op. cit. 127-39, 216-27.

the Last Judgment. God gives them their expenses for the journey and the help of his grace, by means of which they may make it, if they will. If this were not so, then it would follow that sinners could not be blamed for their evil deeds, such as killing father or mother or any other sin against God or man. Indeed, they might justify themselves at the Last Judgment, reasonably imputing their guilt and damnation to God himself, who had denied them his grace. Without going into the deep theological problems involved, which would have been out of place in homiletics, Holcot takes every opportunity to dwell on God's love and mercy to sinners, if only they will exercise their freedom to respond. God offers the means of grace through the sacraments. A certain patriarch of Jerusalem made himself a throne at the doors of the church, where he sat every Wednesday and Friday to hear poor men's cases, that grace might be denied to none. Christ is even more generous. Desiring to confer his grace on each individual, he sits enthroned in his vicars in each church and awaits penitents, that they should come to confession trusting that grace will be conferred.[1]

The doctrine of predestination as taught by Bradwardine had obvious drawbacks from the point of view of a preacher and confessor, anxious to drive home the lesson of moral responsibility and the need to frequent the sacraments. Bradwardine himself never developed the practical consequences that his doctrine would have for the sacramental system of the Church. Holcot did so for him, as a method of refutation. That he was temperamentally averse to its ruthlessness is certain. The theme of hope for repentant sinners constantly informs his pages. The preacher, he says, must never drive wretched men to despair by his scorn, but must rather teach them the truth gently, sympathising with them in their sin and peril.[2] Only long intercourse with Holcot will make the reader aware of his consistency in this direction. He follows his own advice to preachers here at least. The prodigal son *motif* becomes especially familiar. But the gentle side of his nature emerges most clearly of all in his views on the education of youth.

[1] Appendix i, 331-2.
[2] Ecclus. lect. liii, fol. 43rb: Verbum predicatum debet esse suave, ita quod non nimis amare contempnat predicator nec detestetur miseros peccatores, quia sic ad desperationem et contemptum misericordie possent faciliter excitari. Sed . . . cum suavitate debent docere veritatem fidei, de peccatis et periculis eorundem compatiendo, non turpiter condempnando.

Holcot is more humane and progressive than Vincent of Beauvais, or William or Gilbert of Tournai in their standard books on the subject.[1] True, he brings out the brutal old *clichés*, but always softens them, sometimes jokingly. He moralises the command to St Peter (John xxi, 15-17) so as to inculcate the need for strictness. Christ said 'Feed my lambs' twice and 'Feed my sheep' once, in order to signify the difference between the types of teaching required for youths and adults. Simple admonition suffices for adults; youths need blows as well as words if they are to be properly taught. 'Tam verbis quam verberibus' was a common pun; but Holcot adds that 'a certain novice' is said to have expounded the precept to St Peter otherwise. It meant, the novice argued, that young friars ought to have two meals a day, whereas fasting was suitable for their elders: this was how he interpreted the command to prelates to feed the lambs twice and the sheep once.[2] Holcot insists on the need for affection in the master-pupil relationship, though here he is original only in his emphasis.[3] Pupils listen eagerly to a clever master, as he advances from elementary to more advanced lessons. Holcot illustrates this from the big letters of the alphabet fixed to the board and the smaller letters, later to be learned from books. Children also appreciate kindness in their teacher and love to be taught with kindness. Continuity and application are important, too. That is why magnates having sons to be educated arrange to have resident masters for them.[4] Students should learn one thing at a time. If they try to work at a number of difficult subjects simultaneously they thrive no better than a child fed on the milk of different foster-mothers. They know a bit of everything.[5]

Lecturing on Wisdom, he gives his hearers a complete scheme of education, addressing them as adults, who will have charge of youth. He divides his talk into four parts,

---

[1] Vincent of Beauvais, *De eruditione filiorum nobilium*, ed. A. Steiner (Cambridge, Mass., 1938); J. A. Corbett, *The De instructione puerorum of William of Tournai*, O.P. (Notre Dame, Indiana, 1955); Gilbert of Tournai, *De modo addiscendi*, ed, E. Bonifacio (Turin, 1953).

[2] Appendix i, 332.

[3] Thomas Docking makes the same point; see *F.P.* 121.

[4] Appendix i, 332.

[5] P, sermo xcvii: Notandum quod pueri pasti lacte diversarum mulierum non bene crescunt, nec scolares simul dati diversis artibus et difficilibus possunt ad aliquid (MS aliud aliquid) perfectum attingere. Sciunt tamen aliquid parvum de quolibet.

each of which is illustrated by classical stories and quotations.[1] Youth needs character training, sharp correction, moderate diet and lenient judgment.

Holcot illustrates the type of character training that he thinks desirable from the methods of ancient pagans, who used books, pictures and symbols. Incidentally, he is justifying his own use of verbal pictures and symbols, here disguised as the visual aids of antiquity. The nobles of old sought out the best philosophers as tutors for their sons to teach them both letters and character. Trajan had Plutarch, Nero Seneca and Alexander Aristotle. Pictures of noble deeds corrected the possible defects of tutors. Holcot found an account of the Roman use of pictures in an exposition of Juvenal's first *Satire*, or so he tells us. It forms part of a morning in the life of the ancient Romans. All together would pay an early-morning visit to the triumphal arches, where their forbears were represented with the arms and knives with which they had conquered their enemies, so that the young men, seeing them, would be stimulated to virtue in imitation of their deeds. Then they would visit the temple of Apollo, who was the god of wisdom. After that, the judges went down to the forum and the senators to the Capitol, the judges to hear cases and the senators to deliberate on the common weal of the republic; and so they passed their time until noon. To prevent the young men from being hindered in their useful employments the whole forenoon, it was ordered that prostitutes were not on any account to leave their stews before noon, lest the youths be disturbed in their studies and the men in their counsels for the republic by voluptuous pleasures in any way. This, according to Huguccio, is the reason why prostitutes were called *nonarie* among the Romans; they were allowed to go out in the afternoon and not before.

The Roman day was getting less edifying as it proceeded. Holcot lost interest in it and passed on to the Roman use of symbol. He describes from Macrobius the *bulla*, an amulet worn with the pretextile robe by noble Roman boys. The purple colour of the robe reminded them that *noblesse oblige*, while the heart figured on the *bulla* taught them, as they looked at one another, that all were human.

He illustrates the need for 'sharp correction' from the story of Heli and his sons in the Bible and from the misdeeds

[1] Appendix i, 333.

o

of Lucretius' son from Pseudo-Boethius, *De disciplina schola-rium*. St Augustine tells how his mother refused to let the girls in her household drink even water between meals. Her object was to teach them sober habits, lest they should get into the way of tippling, when they were married ladies with the key of the wine cellar at their disposal. This illustrates the need for moderation in diet. Finally, youth must be judged leniently: 'Don't despair of them if they sin frequently.' Holcot points to the conversion of St Paul, whose feast will be celebrated on the morrow, as an appropriate and topical example to hearten discouraged teachers.

His sympathy extended from children to their mothers. He discusses marriage, adapting Aristotle's teaching on friendship to the relations between husband and wife. Friendship in marriage is incompatible with the choice of a wife for the sake of beauty or riches. It is rare and of slow growth. He recommends kindness and consideration for the wife from her husband.[1] Injustice in moral values moves him. An outburst against current venality in the Church ends with the remark that the traffic in benefices in the Curia and in the king's court is much worse than the petty theft which goes by the name of sacrilege:

> 'What justice is it to call the man who steals a chalice or holy book from a church a sacrilegious robber and not him who steals the church itself with all its goods?'[2]

He has the medieval preacher's distrust of the effects of wealth. Riches drive away freedom, jollity and confidence. Every rich man is suspicious. If he sees a poor man he judges him to be a thief; if he sees a rich man, he thinks him a robber.[3]

Perhaps this gentle strain in Holcot explains his dislike of ecclesiastical endowments. He spoke strongly against the Donation of Constantine, who was supposed to have endowed Pope Sylvester I with temporal power in the West. Holcot accepted the fable of the Donation in common with his contemporaries, and with it another: when Constantine endowed Sylvester, a voice from heaven cried: 'Today

---

[1] Appendix i, 336.

[2] Sap. lect. cxxxii, p. 446: Que justitia est vocare illum sacrilegum latronem, qui furatur calicem vel sacrum librum de ecclesia, et non illum qui furatur ipsam ecclesiam et omnia bona eius?

[3] ibid. lxv, p. 222: Auferunt ergo divitie ab homine libertatem, hilaritatem et securitatem, quia omnis dives est suspiciosus. Si videt pauperem, estimat esse furem; si videt divitem, putat eum esse predonem.

poison has been poured into God's Church!' He introduces
it into his 'picture' of Poverty to illustrate the drawbacks of
riches. The Church, he says, was better off when she was
ruled by poor fishermen. Nowadays religious are too busy
looking after their temporal wealth to attend to their spiritual duties as they should. He then tells another current
exemplum:[1] Holy Mother Church appeared to 'a certain saint'
in the form of a lady, who was beautiful to look at from behind, but ugly in front. She told him that it signified her
beauty in times past, as seen in the Fathers, and her ugliness
today as seen in modern prelates.[2]

Holcot blames the Donation for the litigation which vexes
and distracts the Church. This age of the world corresponds
to the sign of the Archer in the zodiac, when the arrows of
litigation fly. The Donation has caused lawsuits, pleas and
quarrels among the clergy as to which of them should seem
greater. There are royal supplications to the Curia and
accusations and defamations in inferior courts. Hence the
Church is full of lawyers, to defend her against wrongs.
Were she as poor now as she was in the days when Christ
lived on earth, she would need no pleaders, having no
aggressors. A poor young merchant has no fear of robbers
and suffers no insults; but when he's made money, even
those who formerly strove to enrich him now try to despoil
him. So it is with the Church: she throve on poverty; now
she seeks wealth and the archers shoot at her.[3] Holcot's
silence can say as much as his criticism. He hardly mentions
the Pope in his lectures, except for a papal action of which
he naturally approves, the support of Thomist doctrine.[4]
He does not dispute papal claims directly; neither will he
argue in their favour.

A glance at his background is necessary in order to
establish the precise shade of his politics. The legend that
Constantine's Donation had evoked a divine warning against
the pouring of poison into the Church appears first in a poem
of the German minstrel, Walther von der Vogelweide, in the
early thirteenth century.[5] It became a commonplace of

---

[1] See Herbert, 662.   [2] Appendix i, 336.   [3] Appendix i, 337.
[4] The withdrawal of the Paris condemnations as touching the doctrine of
St Thomas, Sap. lect. clxxxix, p. 623.
[5] On the first appearance and spread of the legend, see J. Döllinger, *Die
Papst-Fabeln des Mittelalters*, 2nd ed. (Stuttgart, 1890) 113; K. Burdach, *Vom
Mittelalter zur Reformation* 2, i (Berlin, 1913) 226-7; A. Borst, *Die Katharer*
(Stuttgart, 1953) 215.

anticlerical satire. We find it in a treatise of Remigio Girolami of Florence O.P.,[1] in a sermon of Durand de Saint-Pourçain O.P.,[2] and in Higden's *Polychronicon*.[3] It was acquiring a heretical flavour in Holcot's day, notwithstanding its use by men of undoubted orthodoxy. The Valdensians had 'made it a dogma'. The Spiritual Franciscans relied on it in their struggle with John XXII. Later on it would be adopted by Wyclif and the Lollards. Holcot was lecturing in the lifetime of John XXII or very soon after his death (Dec. 4, 1334). John upheld the views of Boniface VIII on the relations between Church and State. To attack the Donation after the issue of the Bulls *Ad conditorem canonum* and *Cum inter nonnullos* was to make one's sympathies tolerably clear. Holcot's words, if reported at Rome, must have irritated.

The logical step to take after regretting ecclesiastical endowment was to exalt the power of the State and *raison d'état*. The Church would never despoil herself; hence the advocates of apostolic poverty for the clergy turned to the temporal power as the one hope for reform. Marsilio of Padua and Wyclif both did so. Holcot drew no such conclusions. There is no evidence that he would have subscribed to any scheme for disendowing the Church by force. He was merely expressing a mood of nostalgia for the pure and primitive past, which spread throughout Christendom as a reaction to the prevailing legalism.[4] Yet his scattered remarks on politics add up to a stress on the power of the State in the person of its ruler. Taken separately, they do not pass beyond generalities on the duties of kingship, and echoes of Aristotle's *Politics*: the effect is cumulative. That he had a certain understanding of *raison d'état* appears in his admission that the ruler may extort taxes from unwilling subjects for the good of the Commonwealth. He goes on to warn his students that this applies to the king only and not to lesser lords; confessors must realise that there is a big difference between them.[5] He also taught that bishops had a

---

[1] C. T. Davis, *Dante and the Idea of Rome* (Oxford, 1957) 85.

[2] MS Paris, Bibl. nat. lat. 14,799, fol. 140vb: Nota quod dolium vacuum melius sonat quam plenum; sic vacui a bonis ecclesiasticis melius resonant laudes divinas . . . Unde tempore Constantini audita fuit hec vox manifeste, dicens: Hodie infusum est venenum in ecclesia.

[3] op. cit. 5, 130.

[4] Y. Renouard, *La Papauté à Avignon* (Paris, 1954) 116-22.

[5] Sap. lect. xxiii, C, fol. 38va: Ad tertium dicendum quod aut principes extorquent quod est necessarium reipublice defendende, et tunc, licet subditi

duty to the State. The author of Wisdom addresses them directly, saying: *For they that have kept just things justly shall be justified: and they that have learned these things shall find what to answer* (vi, 11). Holcot deduces from his text that prelates must preach political sermons on occasion. It is not enough to preach generalities, when they have cure of souls; they must descend to particulars should bad reports or rebellion make it necessary.[1] Most significant of all is his linking of the Donation to the greediness and *disloyalty* of prelates. He repeats the story of the voice from heaven crying that poison had been poured into the Church, and goes straight on to say, as a kind of gloss on the words:

'It is obvious that greedy prelates make disturbances among the people and the clergy. The brave man panics when someone who is pompous, daring and active enough among his poor subjects, weak and needy as they are, flees the enemies of the realm or yields to the pressure of the moment and takes money, ruining his lord the king thereby. This makes disturbance.'[2]

Holcot here touches lightly on a chord which would reverberate in the polemical works of Wyclif: endowment causes treachery and sedition. Holcot was probably thinking of a particular case, but their inference was identical.

John Baconthorpe O.Carm. was lecturing in the same decade as Holcot; he violently defended both the Donation and the claims of John XXII in regard to Church and State.[3] Perhaps our Dominican inspired the defence of the Donation by his criticism. He certainly explains the Carmelite's

---

invite solvant, ipsi non sunt in periculo, aut extorquent quod non est necessarium, et tunc sunt oppressores et raptores . . . Unde ad restitutionem tenentur; et hic caveant dominorum confessores, quia longe aliter est loqui de regibus et de dominis istis parvis.

[1] Sap. lect. lxxx, p. 278: Et datur exemplum prelatis quod non est satis generalia predicare, cum curam habeant animarum, sed necesse habent in casu ad particularia descendere, quando infamia seu rebellio compellit.

This *lectio* is missing from C owing to the loss of several leaves.

[2] B, fol. 58: Ideo dicitur in magna vita Constantini quod cum Constantinus ecclesiam dotaverat, audita est vox de aere, dicens: Hodie venenum tenentur in ecclesia Dei est infusum. Constat autem quod prelati cupidi faciunt perturbationes in populo et in clero. Homo impavidus expavescit, quando aliquis pomposus, audax et strenuus inter pauperes sibi subiectos, debiles et egenos, fugit hostes regni, vel ductus tempore, accipens pecuniam, perdit dominum suum regem; et hoc facit perturbationem.

On the political circumstances which may have inspired Holcot's remark, see above, p. 138.

[3] B. Smalley, John Baconthorpe's Postill on St Matthew, *M.A.R.S.* 4 (1958) 121-39.

warmth on the subject. We can sum up his position *vis à vis* Baconthorpe as follows: he disliked ecclesiastical wealth and power on the score that it led to litigation and distracted the clergy from their spiritual and pastoral duties; Baconthorpe held that endowment was an essential condition of the Church's mission to the world. Holcot emphasised the duty of the Church to the king and feared that temporal possessions might tempt to disloyalty; he kept silence on the subject of the papacy. Baconthorpe, on the contrary, saw the clergy first and foremost as soldiers of the papacy to defend the claims of the Church; he kept silence on the subject of the State as a focus for duty and obedience. Many cross-currents of opinion existed in an English university in the early fourteenth century.

They could coexist in the same breast. Consistency was not Holcot's outstanding virtue as a thinker, unless it may be that he was true to his scepticism in being inconsistent. Scepticism makes it difficult to hold a clear-cut theory in politics as in theology, witness William of Ockham. If endowment had really 'poured poison into the Church', it would seem that the whole body was poisoned and that a purge was the only remedy. Far from holding this pessimistic view, Holcot saw the bright side of the contemporary Church. Indeed he is one of the few medieval moralists who let slip occasionally that not all is wrong. Surprisingly, he has a good word for modern prelates. In one passage he compares them to eagles, which are said to have one claw bigger than the other. The two claws signify two affections, the right the care for souls, the left the seeking for tithes. Instead of blaming prelates for neglecting the former for the sake of the latter, Holcot says that by God's grace the right claw is much bigger than the left. The clergy plead in the courts for churches, offerings and tithes, but they do so as a means to guarding Christ's sheep.[1] Common sense tempers his dislike of worldliness. He admits in a *quaestio* on the acceptance of persons that there may be some justification in preferring a canon and civil lawyer to a theologian in collating to a vacant bishopric, where the liberties of the church are in danger through litigation; the lawyer will defend them better.[2] It was a significant admission from a

---

[1] Sap. lect. lxv, p. 230.
[2] Sap. lect. lxxix, p. 277: . . . isto modo forte non est acceptio personarum in collatione episcopatus, dimittere unum bonum theologum et promovere unum

theologian, given the violence with which they used to denounce the promotion of lawyers to benefices with cure of souls. Holcot seems to have felt that the Donation was a *fait accompli*, however regrettable, and that one might as well act accordingly. He joins in the general complaint against graft in the giving of benefices, but he also sees that the Church provides a career open to talents:

'We commonly see that the sons of the rich and powerful do not learn, and that the sons of simple poor men are raised to the highest ecclesiastical dignities by reason of their character and science.'[1]

The interpretation of medieval moralists is such a tricky business that one can only consider the mind of the writer, while distrusting his picture of the state of society; this will normally be overdrawn and second-hand. Holcot gives us a valuable sample of a state of mind. He criticises, but not bitterly. He has no sense of impending crisis. 'The world is so full of a number of things, I'm sure we should all be as happy as kings' sums up his attitude to life. He stands out in sharp contrast to a later English moralist, Thomas Brinton O.S.B., bishop of Rochester 1373-89.[2] Brinton made a collection of sermons, some composed by himself, others earlier. At least five of the moralised fables from classical sources contained there derive from Holcot on Wisdom or from some common source. The identity of the fables brings out the difference in temperament of the homilists. We shall compare two cases, to illustrate the variety in treatment, the fables of Atalanta and of Narcissus.[3]

The Atalanta story appealed to Holcot so much that he told it at least four times (in sermon no. cxvi, in the *Sermo*

---

bonum iuristam et canonistam, ubi negotia ecclesie sint litigiosa, ut ille per iura sua defendat melius libertatem ecclesie.

This *lectio* also is missing from C.

[1] B, fol. 19v: Videmus communiter quod filii divitum et potentum non addiscunt, et filii simplicium pauperum propter mores et scientiam promoventur ad maximas ecclesiasticas dignitates.

[2] *The Sermons of Thomas Brinton, Bishop of Rochester* (1373-1389), ed. M. A. Devlin O.P. (Camden Society, 3rd series, vol. 85-6, London, 1954). See the review by H. G. Richardson, *Speculum* 30 (1955) 267-71; he has shown that Brinton did not compose all the sermons in the volume. For our present purpose, it is enough that he or another had them copied together, and I shall refer to the author as Brinton.

[3] The three other parallels are (i) Hercules kills the snakes sent to his cradle by Juno; Holcot, Sap. lect. xxiv, pp. 86-7; Brinton, p. 56 (ii) the sacrifice of Numa Pompilius; Holcot, Sap. lect. xcviii, p. 653; Brinton, p. 107 (iii) Ulysses and the sirens; Holcot, Sap. lect. lxiv, p. 226; Brinton, p. 312.

finalis, in the *Moralitates* and in the Wisdom-commentary),
giving it different applications. In the fourth telling Atalanta
signifies the human soul, which is of wondrous beauty, being
created in God's image, and of great swiftness. Our thoughts
and emotions are now in Rome, now in Paris, now in heaven,
now on earth and now in hell. The soul has to race on the
course of this present life to win a prize at the Last Judgment.
Atalanta's suitor signifies another very fast runner, the devil,
who tries to race with us and throws down golden apples,
the sinful joys of the world, to distract us on the course.
Holcot ends on a note of encouragement, reminding his
hearers of St Paul's brave performance in the race for salvation.[1] Brinton tells the story in almost the same words and
moralises it in the same way. But he has the late medieval
fixation on decay and death. His conclusion is very different.
Instead of holding out hope, he recommends meditation on
death, when the devil tempts us. Think how abominable
your corpse will be. Our flesh is compounded of the four
elements, and yet when dead it is committed to neither
water, air nor fire, for fear of stench and corruption, but is
hidden in earth as so much vile poison. 'Behold the glory
of flesh, how it ends!'[2]

Holcot tells the Narcissus myth with his inimitable light-
ness and grace, drawing the moral that those who glory in
their fragile beauty and delight only in their good looks in
youth will fade. When they ought to be men, they become
useless flowers. He then passes from heavenly to earthly
beauty without losing sight of his main theme, the beautiful.
He misses out the death of the body and turns to heaven.
Aristotle teaches in the *Ethics* that no earthly pleasure can
satisfy man with his human craving for change. God, on

[1] Sap. lect. xiv, pp. 52-3: Virgo ista velocissima est anima humana, que est
mire vetustatis, quia creata ad Dei imaginem, et nimie agilitatis, quia affectionibus et cogitationibus nunc est Rome, nunc est Parisius, nunc in celo, nunc in
terra, nunc in inferno. Itsa habet currere per stadium vite presentis ad bravium
finalis iustitie. Sed unus agillimus, qui simul cum ea conatur currere, videlicet
diabolus, qui cursor velocissimus est, . . . habet tria poma aurea, id est tres
peccatorum delectationes, . . . Et ideo necesse habemus certare viriliter et per
virtuosam continentiam a talibus abstinere . . . Sic enim certaverat et cucurrerat
Paulus, sicut ipsemet recitat. . . .

[2] op. cit. 41-2: Si te invadat hostis antiquus per carnis lasciviam, recole
diligenter qualiter caro tua in vita delectabilis ita erit in morte abhominabilis
quod quamvis sit compacta ex quatuor elementis, scilicet ex igne, aqua, aere,
et terra . . . ipsa tamen mortua in aquis non proicitur ne aque inficiantur, in
aere non suspenditur ne aer corrumpatur, in igne non comburitur ne fetor
sentiatur, sed tanquam venenum vilissimum sub terra absconditur ne amplius
videatur. Ecce gloria carnis, quali fine clauditur.

the contrary, being simple and unchanging in his nature, ever rejoices in the one simple delight which he has in the contemplation of himself.[1] And so man may look forward to unchanging bliss after his glorious resurrection.[2] Brinton's treatment of the same theme shows again how the ugliness of death fascinated him. He gives a gruesome description telling how beauty fades in sickness and death: 'Behold the glory of your shape, how it ends!'[3] This is his repeated warning.

We have heard Holcot on the topic 'quali fine clauditur'. He can speak of it as well as Brinton, but he does so with a gentle sadness, not with Brinton's horror and gloom.[4] Even sudden death may wear a serene aspect, as in this tale of a scholar, who died at his studies:

'It is read of a certain man, holy and learned, that he was found dead among his books in his chair, having an open book on his knee. When his friends, pitying, found him, and would have grieved at his sudden death, they looked more carefully and found his hand lying on the book and his finger pointing to the text of this lecture: *But the just man, if he shall be prevented with death, shall be in rest.*'[5]

It symbolised the passing of an era that Holcot himself should have perished in the plague of 1349. Artistic, cul-

---

[1] *Ethic. nicom.* vii, 14, 1154b, 20-30.

[2] Sap. lect. clvi, pp. 519-20: Iste puer, propter speciem nimiam elatus in superbiam, designat vane gloriantes de fragili decore corporis, qui tantum delectant de sue pulchritudinis venustate, quod totaliter evanescunt. Ubi homines esse deberent, inutiles flores fiunt . . . Sic per oppositum dicit Aristoteles: quia Deus est natura simplex et invariabilis, semper gaudet una et simplici delectatione, quam habet in contemplatione sui ipsius. Cum ergo ad statum divinum devenimus, per gloriosas dotes corporis et anime, erit delectatio nostra semper una et uniformis et perpetua.

[3] op. cit. 220: Tales propria pulchritudine decepti non attendunt proprie fragilitati quo(u)sque ad modum florum fuerunt commutati. Sicut verum flos primo virescit, deinde marcescit, et tandem evanescit, sic venustas corporis virescit dum quis est iuvenis, marcescit asperitate febre vel alterius infirmitatis, et tandem evanescit per resolutionem in cineris vilitatem. . . . Quisque igitur superbis de pulchritudine corporis, attende quomodo morte accedente nasus frigescit, dentes nigrescent, vene et nervi rumpentur, et cor pre nimio dolore dividetur. Immo corpus tuum nunc apparens pulchrum et delectabile ita in morte erit abhominabile quod tanquam venenum pessimum sub terra abscondetur ne amplius videatur. Ecce forma glorie tue, quali fine clauditur.

[4] Above, 169.

[5] Sap. lect. xlviii (on Sap. iv. 7), C, fol. 79rb: Legitur de quodam viro sancto et litterato, quod mortuus inventus fuit, sedens inter libros suos in cathedra et habens in gremio suo librum apertum. Cumque alii compatientes eum adinvenerunt et multum de subita morte tristarentur, consideraverunt diligentius et invenerunt manum suam super librum iacentem et indicem extentum ad textum huius lectionis: *Iustus autem si morte preoccupatus fuerit, etc.*

tured, smiling, perhaps rather flippant and inconsequent too, he closed the period of literary interests among the English Dominicans. Ringstead, D'Eyncourt and Hopeman carried on the tradition for a few years longer, but they had less standing and less personality. The chime of the bells 'ringing sweetly over the water' died away. The future of theology in England lay with grimmer, narrower men.

CHAPTER VIII

WILLIAM D'EYNCOURT, THOMAS HOPEMAN AND THOMAS RINGSTEAD

Interrogatus quid sibi ex philosophia acquisivisset,
ait: 'Posse cum omnibus hominibus fabulari.'

Walter Burley, *De vita et moribus philosophorum*
xxxi (Aristippus).

I.—CAMBRIDGE

CAMBRIDGE never rivalled Oxford until the reformation period, but in the early fourteenth century she
lagged behind the older university less than used to be
thought. Cambridge was beginning to make a mark on the
episcopate. Cobham of Worcester, one of Edward II's
bishops, had studied and taught theology there.[1] An analysis of the bench under Edward III shows that although just
over half were Oxford graduates, 'the handful of Cambridge
men, probably only seven, were nevertheless, despite their
numerical inferiority, a very interesting set of scholars and
statemen'.[2] Two were Dominicans, Thomas de Lisle of Ely
and Thomas Ringstead of Bangor. The Friars Preachers
had a flourishing house of studies at Cambridge, founded in
1238; it numbered fifty-five friars in 1325 and sixty-one in
1328.[3] It is a curious fact that Robert Holcot had no 'classicising' successors in his own Order at Oxford, but three at
Cambridge. This would be more understandable if, as is
suggested by other evidence, he had passed on from Oxford
to give his most popular lecture course to a Cambridge
audience.

His three Cambridge imitators (if not pupils) belong to the
backwash of the classicising movement: they took over an
existing technique. Being out of touch with developments
on the Continent, they did not find any new classical sources.

---

[1] K. Edwards, Bishops and Learning in the Reign of Edward II, *Church
Quarterly Review* 138 (1944) 62, quoting *Annales Paulini*, *Chronicles of the Reigns of
Edward I and II*, op. cit. 1, 273-4.

[2] J. R. L. Highfield, The English Hierarchy in the Reign of Edward III,
T.R.H.S., 5th series, vol. 6 (1956) p. 128.

[3] Hinnebusch, 89, 493.

Their works are still interesting as showing how the movement spread and how it could be interpreted differently by individual teachers. Thomas Hopeman stands closest to Holcot. William D'Eyncourt and Thomas Ringstead look back to the more sedate tradition of Thomas Waleys, though they do not reach his level of scholarship. The last of the three, Thomas Ringstead, has the added importance that he multiplies quotations from medieval authors. The dearth of fresh discoveries in the classics made it necessary, if the lecturer wished to compete with his colleagues, to enlarge the range of medieval literary works to be quoted. All three friars wanted to 'go one better'. It was not their fault that they lacked Waleys' opportunities and Holcot's touch of genius.

II.—WILLIAM D'EYNCOURT

This Dominican came from the north of England: he received licence to preach and hear confessions in the diocese of Carlisle on May 4, 1331 and again about 1344.[1] He may have been related to Oliver D'Eyncourt O.P., who was prior of the Oxford convent in 1274 and 1275; Oliver mediated between the northern and southern students at Oxford and persuaded the archbishop to entertain the Dominicans when they held their provincial chapter at York. A secular priest of the same name, who lived in the late thirteenth and early fourteenth centuries, was a graduate of Oxford and a chancellor and benefactor of Cambridge. William D'Eyncourt may have studied first at Cambridge and then at Oxford. He may have been regent at Cambridge about 1340.[2] He thus makes a link between the two universities. He may have heard Holcot lecture on Wisdom at Cambridge and a stay at Oxford would have brought him into touch with the classicising tradition among both Dominicans and Franciscans. His only surviving work is a lecture course on Ecclesiastes.

D'Eyncourt on Ecclesiastes survives in two copies only. One follows Holcot on Wisdom in the fourteenth-century manuscript now at Balliol.[3] The second, also fourteenth-

---

[1] See O.R. 1, 576-7 for all three D'Eyncourts.

[2] W. Gumbley, *The Cambridge Dominicans* (Oxford, 1938) 18.

[3] C, foll. 317ra-383vb. For a description of C see Robert Holcot, 11-12. The title, *Lectura Willelmi Dencourt super Ecclesiasten* (fol. 317ra), is written in a different hand from the text, but is roughly contemporary. We can accept the ascription to D'Eyncourt for two reasons. A work would not be ascribed to a

century, belonged to the Dominicans of Klosterneuburg.[1] Both copies break off just before the comment on Eccles. vii, 1 (*Aut quis ei poterit indicare etc.*), indicating that the commentary ended unfinished. It must have had a very limited circulation, but at least one reader appreciated its points. He wrote approving notes in the margins, such as 'Bonus processus de bello' against D'Eyncourt's exposition of *tempus belli* (Eccles. iii, 8).[2]

The commentary was given as a lecture course, as appears from the form of words used in the prologue.[3] There is one piece of evidence for dating it. D'Eyncourt says:

> 'We see with our own eyes that there is always a very good (i.e. cheap) market for goods gained in war, especially while the war lasts.'[4]

It sounds as though he had actual conditions in mind. The first campaigns, or rather plunder raids, of the Hundred Years War would begin to bring looted goods on the English market sometime after the summer of 1339. This fits in with the date which has been suggested for his regency, about 1340, before his second licence to preach at Carlisle about 1344.

The commentary includes literal and spiritual exposition of the text and certain *dubitationes* arising from it. D'Eyncourt began with the resolve to do justice to the claims of the literal sense, quoting the expert on biblical scholarship, Andrew of St Victor; but the resolve soon melted. By the end of the first chapter he has dropped Andrew and turned to Alexander Nequam on Ecclesiastes instead. Nequam's

---

little-known scholar by accident; C came from Holcot's circle; the copyist of Holcot on Wisdom, contained in the volume, was working from a 'liber magistri'.

[1] Stegmüller, no. 2885. This copy is now MS 760 of the Municipal Library of Klosterneuburg, foll. 1ra-81ra. I have been able to study it in a microfilm through the Librarian's kindness. This copy is anonymous. The text resembles that of C, except that it has an additional prologue, not in C. Both prologues have the same incipit: 'Vanitati enim creatura subiecta est, Rom. viii.' Then they diverge from each other. Both are introductory to Ecclesiastes. I think that D'Eyncourt wrote only the second (i.e. the second in the Klosterneuburg MS, the only one in C). The extra prologue has none of his characteristic quotations from classical sources.

[2] C, fol. 342rb.

[3] C, fol. 318ra: *Verba Ecclesiastes.* Iste liber quem pre manibus habemus. . . . Accedamus igitur ad expositionem tituli.

[4] C, fol. 339ra: Videmus ad oculum quod de bonis acquisitis in guerra semper fit optimum forum, et maxime dum durat guerra. . . . Dicitur enim communiter quod bonum forum extrahit denarium de bursa.

classical allusions, rhetorical style and pious asides pleased him better than Andrew's astringent manner. D'Eyncourt's preference for Nequam sums up the whole attitude of the classicising group in England.[1] Other quotations show Dominican learning stretched out in successive layers. D'Eyncourt's 'postillator authenticus' is Hugh of St Cher[2] and his 'doctor communis' St Thomas.[3] 'Dominus Albertus' appears frequently, especially in connexion with natural science; and he knows his Vincent of Beauvais. He quotes much from Nicholas Trevet on Boethius, hardly distinguishing between the text and its commentary.[4] Holcot's influence proclaims itself in his tastes and method. He probably borrowed the dialogue between the poet and the deserted palace ascribed to the *Poetics* from Holcot on Wisdom.[5] A reading of Waleys on the Psalter may have put him on to Livy. He quotes *Ab Urbe condita* seven times. All but one of the quotations are genuine, and have references; the exception, which has no reference, probably derives from Livy through an *exempla* collection; it is not a fake, but rather an elaboration on what Livy tells of Scipio's virtue.[6] D'Eyncourt's use of *Ab Urbe condita* marks him out as more of a scholar than Holcot. Needless to say, he knew only the first and third decades. The fourth had not reached England by the date of his regency. Apart from quoting Livy, D'Eyncourt ranged over the common run of classical and medieval authors. He had a special addiction to the *De dictis philosophorum*, which he quotes at least forty times.[7] The book appealed to him as being well suited for use in a lecture on Ecclesiastes. His philosophers expressed the same scorn for worldly vanity as the Preacher.

---

[1] Quotations from Andrew, C, foll. 318ra-319vb, correspond to the original, G. Calandra, *De historica Andreae Victorini expositione in Ecclesiasten* (Palermo, 1948) 3-10. On Andrew's method see ibid. xliv-lx and *Study of the Bible*, 138-9. I checked sample quotations from Alexander Nequam's commentary in MS Oxford, Corpus Christi College 45, foll. 121ra-123ra.

[2] Quotations from Hugh of St Cher, C, foll. 322rb-324ra, 337rb-368ra and *passim*, correspond with Hugh's *Postilla in Ecclesiasten ad loc.*; see Stegmüller, no. 3679. D'Eyncourt sometimes refers to him by name as *Dominus Hugo*.

[3] C, fol. 322vb: Hunc occasum adorabant Iudei, sicut docet doctor communis, prima, q. 102, art. 4, ad quartum argumentum.
   See *Sum. theol.* Ia IIae, q. 102, art. 4 ad 5.

[4] Quotations from Trevet on Boethius, C, foll. 332rb, 351vb-352ra, correspond to Trevet in MS Oxford, Bodl. Auct. F.6.4. (2150), foll. 101v, 204v-205. D'Eyncourt quotes verbally with some abbreviation.

[5] C, fol. 380va: Aristoteles in Poetria narrat fictionem cuiusdam poete deplorantis ruinam cuiusdam palatii. . . .

[6] Appendix i, 337.   [7] ed. cit.; I checked sample quotations.

D'Eyncourt took little interest in the mind of his author except where it coincided with his own ideas. He palliates the scepticism and passes over the doubts in the manner of all but the most perceptive and original of medieval exegetes. Hence he makes his contribution mainly in padding. *Tempus occidendi* (iii, 3) suggests an excursion into history: he lists some of the most notable Christian martyrs with the names of Roman emperors under whom they suffered.[1] We have seen that *tempus acquirendi* (iii, 6) brings him up to modern times and the sale of goods looted in warfare. So, too, the Preacher's reflections on the fruitlessness of human effort makes him think of the different rates of pay for skilled and unskilled labour: stone-cutters, set to work on building a palace, are paid not according to how hard they work, but according to their skill.[2]

Two gems are buried in this uninspiring matter. One is a pseudo-classical rarity. Warning his class that immoral love is punished, D'Eyncourt quotes a verse which he says is written on the tombstone of 'Ganymede the Neapolitan', exiled from his native land for the love of the prince (of the gods). It is a garbled version of an epigram found in a fourteenth-century English collection, Pseudo-Martial. Here Ganymede is called *chrysopolita*; the lines scan, as D'Eyncourt's do not; there is no mention of a tomb.[3] D'Eyncourt or his source has made an airy fancy yet more fanciful by bringing it nearer home and adding a concrete detail:

> . . . sicut patet de Ganimede, in cuius sepulchro tale scribitur epitaphium:
> Hic ego iaceo Ganimedes neapolita,
> Quem procul a patria principis egit amor.
> Talia perpetuis compenso gaudia penis.
> Talia consequitur premia talis amor.[4]

The second surprise is the ascription of the *Quaestiones*

---

[1] C, fol. 335rb.

[2] C, fol. 320vb: Videmus enim quod isti latomi qui positi sunt ad edificandum aliquod palatium non plus lucrantur secundum quod plus laborant. Non enim ille (MS illi) qui plus laborat maiorem recipit mercedem; quia illi qui percutiunt lapides et parant cementum plus laborant quam subtiles latomi, et tamen non recipiunt equalem mercedem; sic in mundo. . . . *Latamus* for stone-cutter is found in 1366, *latomus* occurs later; see Baxter and Johnson, *Medieval Latin Word-List* (Oxford, 1934) 242.

[3] Edited from MS Digby 172 by R. Ellis, *Texts, Documents and Extracts chiefly from MSS in the Bodleian and other Oxford Libraries* (*Anecdota Oxoniensia, Classical Series*, vol. 1, part 5, Oxford, 1885) p. 20.

[4] C, fol. 341vb.

naturales of the twelfth-century scholar Adelard of Bath to 'Alfred, king of the English'.[1] This error at least has nothing mysterious about it. Late copies of the *Quaestiones naturales* give a number of variants for Adelard's name, including 'Aluredus', a common spelling for 'Alfredus'.[2] D'Eyncourt or his source had jumped to the conclusion that the 'Aluredus' was King Alfred, the great Anglo-Saxon promotor of learning and 'rerum ignotarum investigator'.[3] D'Eyncourt or indeed any reader of Trevet on Boethius would learn that King Alfred had translated *De consolatione Philosophiae* into English.[4] What more probable than that he should have written a popular and reputable, but by now old-fashioned, work on natural science as well? The English in the early fourteenth century were building up an image of a ruler of their own, wise and devoted to his people, who founded universities and patronised scholars and who could stand comparison with Charlemagne.[5] D'Eyncourt shows us a stage in the development of this Alfred legend. It had more basis in historical fact, after all, than many which chase one another through the pages of Holcot and his colleagues. And D'Eyncourt gives evidence of sobriety by using no 'pictures'.

[1] On Eccles. iii, 19: *nihil habet homo iumento amplius*, fol. 353va: Supple: quantum ad corpus. Imo plures defectus corporis habet homo quam iumentum, de quo valde admiratur Aluredus rex anglorum in libello suo qui intitulatur Dialogus Aluredi de naturalibus questionibus, ubi cap. 15 querit talem questionem: cum multe nature a Deo producte habeant robur eis innatum, ut aper dentes, leo ungues . . . destitutum est. Hec ille.

A roughly verbal quotation from Adelard's *Quaestiones naturales*, which is in the form of question and answer and has varying titles in the MSS, ed. M. Müller, *Beiträge zur Geschichte der Philosophie und Theologie des Mittelalters* xxxi (Münster, 1934) 19-20.

[2] ibid. 72.

[3] Ranulf Higden, *Polychronicon*, ed. cit. 6, 358.

[4] On iv, metr. 3, MS Oxford Bodl. Auct.F.6.4. (2150), fol. 205: Inhabitavit autem hec maga quandam insulam secundum veritatem historicam, que ad regnum Tracie pertinebat, cuius rex erat Ulixes, ut (MS ubi) dicit Aluredus rex in anglico.

In King Alfred's English version of the *De consolatione Philosophiae*, translated into modern English by W. J. Sedgefield (Oxford, 1900) 134, Circe 'was said to be mighty in witchcraft and dwelt in the island upon which the king we spoke of was driven'. King Alfred's version was not translated into Middle English, so far as is known, and it is not at all clear whether Trevet or his informant would have been able to read Old English. King Alfred does not say exactly what is ascribed to him by Trevet, i.e. that Circe's island belonged to the kingdom of Thrace, whose king was Ulysses, but only that Ulysses was driven on to it.

[5] See B. A. Lees, *Alfred the Great* (New York, London, 1915) 450-1, for the Alfred legend in the fourteenth century.

III.—THOMAS HOPEMAN

Fr. S. L. Forte has recovered Thomas Hopeman from the confused notices which enmeshed his memory, and has made him a living figure.[1] Hopeman probably graduated at Cambridge and was regent 1344-45. He was appointed penitentiary for the diocese of Ely (in which Cambridge was situated) between 1345 and 1348. The Dominican bishop of Ely, Thomas de Lisle, confirmed him in his appointment on September 15, 1348. The General Chapter of the Order assigned him as lector to the house of studies in London in 1350. De Lisle again confirmed him in his office of penitentiary for Ely diocese on March 11, 1351, although he was still in London. The last we hear of him is that a royal warrant was issued for his arrest on August 10, 1355; he had gone abroad without royal licence. It seems very likely that Hopeman had gone to Avignon in connexion with the dispute between de Lisle and Edward III. The bishop himself went to Avignon in 1356. Hopeman may have stayed abroad until his death at a date unknown.

His only surviving work seems to be his commentary on Hebrews. Here he refers to a lecture on Tobias, and bibliographers have ascribed to him commentaries on Genesis and on the Epistle of St James, as well as that on Hebrews. The missing works may come to light one day. Meanwhile an immensely long set of lectures puts him squarely in the classicising group, though, strangely enough, he is the least famous of its members. The only copy known to survive belonged to a Dominican called Nicholas Waleys.[2] The script is mid-fourteenth-century, that is, contemporary with Hopeman. Nicholas Waleys is probably the Dominican of this name who got papal permission to choose a confessor 'to give him plenary indulgence in the hour of death' on June 10, 1352. It would follow that Hopeman's commentary was soon forgotten. His contemporary and colleague in the Order, Nicholas Waleys, preserved the one sample of his teaching that we have.

The lecture course spread over two academic years, as did Holcot's on Wisdom. Hopeman seems to have started in the autumn of 1344 or of 1350. If the former, he gave

---

[1] I have not added anything to Fr Forte's paper except for a comparison between Hopeman and Holcot and the two other Cambridge friars.
[2] MS London, Brit. Mus. Royal 4. A. i (=R).

P

it at Cambridge, if the latter, at London. Cambridge, as a university town, might be thought to be the more likely place, but London cannot be excluded, seeing that Holcot probably gave his lectures on Ecclesiasticus at Northampton.

Hopeman's commentary resembles Holcot's more closely than D'Eyncourt's, containing the same kind of mixture of theology[1] and moralisation; D'Eyncourt's theological pieces are shorter and fewer. Hopeman is more personal than D'Eyncourt. He tells us his name in his prologue, just as Holcot does in his. We hear that *Thomas* means *totus means* and *Hopeman spei homo*. So *Thomas Hopeman* means 'the whole, that is the happy or perfect man, in motion towards God through the virtue of hope'.[2] He was frail in physique, but energetic. Men marvel, he says, at the capacity for excessive and tiring work in one so fragile. His secret was hope in the Lord.[3] Hopeman must have belonged to the same type as Holcot, who also complained of being weaker than others and yet got through a large amount of work. Further, he had read Holcot on Wisdom: he quotes the dialogue between the poet and the deserted palace,[4] as D'Eyncourt does, and also the lines from *De Babione*, clearly lifted from Holcot.[5] He begins in the spirit of an admirer of Holcot by praising Scripture with the help of all sorts of mythological comparisons. It binds man to God with invisible but sensible chains, like the net cast by Vulcan over Mars and Venus. It resembles the chain which bound Ulysses to the mast when he passed by the sirens, the chain which was thrown around Protheus to make him answer, and the gordian knot, whose untying brought a man to the throne.[6] Later on he compares Moses to Neptune and St

---

[1] Fr Forte has printed Hopeman's discussion of the Immaculate Conception, apropos of the feast of the Conception of Our Lady on December 8, 334-44.

[2] R, fol. 2ra: Que verba tam nomen quam cognomen meum implicite complectuntur. Thomas enim dicitur quasi totus means, quod est nomen. Et cognomen componitur ex spe et homine. Totus pertinet ad beatitudinem, quia totum et perfectum idem; means ad ultimum verbum cum dicitur 'in te'; fol. 138rb: Est enim cognomen meum spei homo, scilicet hope man.
The first passage refers to the text: *Beatus homo qui sperat in te* (Ps. lxxxiii, 13). See Forte, 311-12.

[3] R, fol. 138rb: Homines solent mirari quomodo, cum ego ipse sim exigui roboris modiceque virtutis, tam indefatigibiliter insisto laboribus excessivis et ultra vires; et si diligenter considerarent non deberent mirari: nam habeo cum spe magnam et antiquatam connexionem ex cognomine. . . .

[4] R, fol. 145ra.   [5] R, fol. 18va.

[6] R, fol. 6rb: Sic et sacra scriptura . . . est nexus inviolabilis amicitia coniungens Deum et hominem, similis cathenis adamantinis, quibus ligavit Vulcanus Martem cum Venere, id est Deum cum homine in unitate, suppositis

Thomas Aquinas to Minerva.[1] He attempts something like Holcot's 'pictures': Holy Scripture, like the virtue of hope, resembles a sphere, a rounded foot, an anchor and a shield or helmet;[2] Venus, symbolising carnal pleasure, swims naked in the sea with wings on her shoulders and her head crowned with roses.[3] Hopeman uses the moralised 'law' type of *exemplum*. All this recalls Holcot and so does a certain carelessness in giving references.[4]

The likeness to Holcot in method goes with a difference in tone between the two friars. Hopeman had hope of a supernatural kind; we miss Holcot's natural gaiety. The younger Dominican felt more pessimistic about the state of the contemporary Church; he says nothing new, but his pages convey an impression of gloom. He and D'Eyncourt both show that the classicising technique could become mechanical in the hands of less gifted lecturers.

IV.—THOMAS RINGSTEAD

Ringstead ended life as a bishop and hence his career is better documented than that of most friars. He seems to have come of a north-east-midland or East Anglian family. His will, dated December 3, 1365, tells us that his mother was buried at Huntingdon in the Austin Friars' church, and that he had a grandmother still living at Littleborough in Nottinghamshire.[5] *Blomefield's History of Norfolk* gives Ringstead

---

invisibilibus cathenis, sensibilibus tamen. Est etiam felix ligamen, quo Ulixes ad malum ligatus sirenarum dulces cantilenas illesus pertransiit. Est et vinculum quo Protheus, nisi ligatus, responsa non dabat. . . . Est et nodus gordianus, propter cuius solutionem quis ad regni solium sublimatur.

[1] R, fol. 79rb, quoted by Forte, 314.

[2] R, fol. 3va: Sacra nempe scriptura ad modum spei reddit ad virtuosa motabilem, inter laboriosa infatigabilem, inter scelerosa incontaminabilem et inter timorosa insuperabilem. Quo ad primum tenet similitudinem corporis sp(h)erici, quo ad secundum pedis circimi (*sic*; circularis is demanded by the context); quo ad tertium tenet typum anchore, quo ad quartum clipei, scuti (MS scutum) sive galee.

Holcot's 'picture' of Hope has a helmet (above, p. 176); otherwise Hopeman's attributes are independent.

[3] R, fol. 145rb, from Mythographus Tertius, under the name of *Alexander in scintillario*; see above, p. 111, n. 2.

[4] R, fol. 32rb: Dicit quidam auctor, estimo quod Giraldus, De scrophagis Hibernie, quod Apulie et Sicilie partibus sunt cicade quedam alate. . . .

From Gerald of Wales, *Topographia hibernica* i, 21, *Opera* 5 (Rolls Series, 1867) 53-4. Hopeman got it right, but did not look it up: *estimo quod Giraldus*.

[5] Mr J. R. L. Highfield has kindly given me an abstract of the will from the unprinted register of Archbishop Islip, fol. 245v. Fr Walter Gumbley gives a short account of Ringstead's career in *The Cambridge Dominicans* (Oxford, 1938) 18. The *D.N.B.* notice is not very helpful. I have restricted my study

Parva in Norfolk as his birthplace and suggests that he belonged to an old landed family of the county.[1] There is another Ringstead near Oundle in the north-east of Northamptonshire. Men of the same surname appear in the records as holding benefices and taking part in county business 1343-59.[2] Whichever Ringstead gave him his name, it was natural for Thomas to go to Cambridge as the nearest university town.[3] He had a brother called Master Ralph, who probably also went to Cambridge; Thomas named him as executor and legatee.

Master Ralph Ringstead was highly successful. He petitions the pope for the vicarage of Sutton, Exeter diocese, in 1350 as 'Ralph Ringstead M.A., B.C.L. of Lincoln diocese'.[4] He witnesses a document as canon of Exeter cathedral in 1362.[5] He wrote to Archbishop Langham, October 10, 1366, giving an account of the benefices he held in accordance with the canon law rule against pluralism. Ralph describes himself as a Master of Arts and Law, of Lincoln diocese, now and for some time past staying in Exeter diocese on account of the benefices he holds there. His benefices are the perpetual vicariate of Sutton (for which he had successfully petitioned in 1350), a canonry and prebend at Exeter, a canonry and prebend at Bangor (obtained, one supposes, through his brother, Bishop Thomas Ringstead) and a canonry and prebend at Heytesbury, Sarum diocese. Should it be necessary to renounce all but two benefices which might lawfully be held together, he would choose to keep those at Sutton and Exeter.[6] He stayed on at Exeter,

---

to the obvious printed sources. Our knowledge could be enlarged in all probability by a wider search which would include unprinted notices. His executors and other persons mentioned in his will could be traced.

[1] 10 (London, 1809) 347. Ringstead was quite a common Norfolk surname; see the index volume to *Blomefield's Norfolk*, 260.

[2] A John Ringstead was parson of Harpole; *Calendar of Patent Rolls*, 1354-58, 284; *Calendar of Inquisitions under Edward III*, 10, 304, 355. A Thomas Ringstead acts as mainperner and acknowledges or claims debts of the order of twenty marks, subsequently paid; *Calendar of Close Rolls*, 1343-46, 479, 490, ibid., 1346-49, 47, 420, 590; ibid., 1349-54, 66. We shall see that our Thomas's brother Ralph was of Lincoln, not Ely, diocese.

[3] A John and a Robert Ringstead are found at the Franciscan house at Cambridge in the early fourteenth century (1306 and 1347); see J. R. H. Moorman, *The Grey Friars in Cambridge* (Cambridge, 1952) 203-4.

[4] *Calendar of Papal Petitions relating to Great Britain and Ireland*, 1342-1419, 205. His estate as vicar of Sutton was ratified by the Crown on February 7, 1366; *Calendar of Patent Rolls*, 1364-67, 220.

[5] *The Register of John de Grandisson Bishop of Exeter* 1327-1369, ed. F. C. Hingeston-Randolph 3 (London and Exeter, 1899) 1241.

[6] ibid. 1251-2.

being keeper of the spiritualities of the see in the vacancy of 1369-70.[1] The next bishop appointed him Official-Principal in 1370,[2] but he died soon afterwards: the executors of his will were acquitted of their administration of his goods in September 1371.[3]

Ralph and Thomas had an uncle, 'Dominus' Roger Ringstead, who was buried in the Dominican priory church at Chichester. He may have been a person of some consequence and have helped to launch his nephews on their careers. Thomas seems to have felt special love and gratitude to him. He left 'a coverlet of scarlet silk to put on his uncle's tomb on anniversary days', and he made a number of bequests at Chichester, Huntingdon and London and to individuals for Masses and prayers to be said for Roger's soul: only one bequest concerns the soul of Thomas's father. Another uncle mentioned in the will as already dead is a 'Brother William Ringstead'.

Thomas is first mentioned in the register of Bishop Thomas de Lisle in an entry dated September 15, 1348. The bishop revokes the appointment of penitentiaries for Ely diocese excepting for five men, among whom are Thomas Hopeman and Thomas Ringstead O.P. He reserves certain cases to himself and two others, one of them Master Thomas Ringstead.[4] The latter, therefore, had joined the Order and had taken his master's degree in theology before the date of the entry. He was at Avignon by 1353, when he petitioned the pope for a benefice for 'Thomas Henrici' of Chester, a clerk who was serving him in his office of 'penitentiary of England.'[5]

---

[1] *Registrum Simonis de Sudbiria, 1362-1375*, ed. C. T. Flower and M. C. B. Dawes (*Canterbury and York Society*, 1938) 2, 74, 76, 80, 85-6.

[2] *The Register of Thomas de Brantyngham Bishop of Exeter 1370-1394*, ed. F. C. Hingeston-Randolph 1 (London and Exeter, 1901) 140.

[3] ibid. 242. The terms of the will are not given.

[4] J. Crosby, Ely Episcopal Registers, *Ely Diocesan Remembrancer* no. 110 (1894), p. 275.

[5] *Calendar of Papal Petitions*, 1342-1419, 249. Fr. L. E. Boyle has kindly sent me a fuller extract: Reg. Suppl. 25 (olim 23), fol. 209v (olim 211v): Supplicat frater Thomas Ryngsted penitentiarius Anglie . . . pro Thoma Henrici dicti de Cestria clerico ac servitori suo in penitentia. . . .

Fr Boyle also points out that a Thomas de Anglia is mentioned as a papal penitentiary in the Introitus and Exitus Register for May 25, 1353, quoted by E. Goeller, *Die päpstliche penitentiarie* 1, i (Rome, 1907) 133n. He explains that Ringstead would call himself 'penitentiarius Anglie' on the ground that minor penitentiaries assisted their major, who was generally a cardinal, and that 'the ideal was to have all the chief nations and languages represented among the minor penitentiaries'. Ringstead, being a minor, would regard himself as representing England.

He left money for Masses to be said for the soul of the same Thomas of Chester, formerly his clerk, at Chichester Dominican priory in his will. He petitioned for a benefice for his relative, Thomas Danvers, clerk of Lincoln, as papal penitentiary in 1355.[1] Thomas de Lisle's influence may have helped him to obtain his post. Pope Innocent VI sent him to Edward III as papal nuncio to make peace between England and France in 1356, and provided him to the bishopric of Bangor in the following year.[2] He received his faculty to consecrate as bishop on September 17, 1357. The details of his career as bishop fall outside the scope of this study. He died in January 1366.[3]

His will, as Mr Highfield points out, shows Ringstead as a scholar and patron of scholars. He left £5 for five poor students of his diocese to study canon or civil law at Oxford or Cambridge at three marks a year for as long as the money should last. Holcot, it will be remembered, admitted that lawyers might be preferred to theologians for promotion when the business of the church was litigious; Ringstead had had experience at Bangor which would prove to him the value of a legal training. He left his missal and large breviary to the Cambridge Dominicans. Three masters of theology, Brothers Parcons, Richard Wyn and William Husee, were to have £2 each. The soul of his patron, Thomas de Lisle of Ely, was remembered. Ringstead wished to be buried at the church of the Friars Preachers of London, to whom he left his hangings and a gift of £20.

This member of the classicising group gives the impression of having come of a more substantial and distinguished family than the others. His relatives, though not aristocratic, were probably landed, and they made their mark on the Church.

The fruits of his teaching period were a little-known commentary on the *Sentences*[4] and lectures on Proverbs. The latter succeeded nearly as well as Holcot on Wisdom or

---

[1] ibid., 285, 290: Reg. Suppl. 28 (olim 26), fol. 52: Supplicat Sanctitatem Vestram humilis et devotus orator vester frater Thomas de Ryngstede penitentiarius Sanctitatis Vestre et sacre theologie magister, Anglicus, quatenus in persona dilecti consanguinei sui Thome Danvers, clerci Linc., gratiam faciens specialem. . . .
   I owe this reference also to the kindness of Fr Boyle.
[2] *Calendar of Papal Letters Relating to Great Britain and Ireland*, 3, 620, 581, 584.
[3] F. M. Powicke, *Handbook of British Chronology* (London, 1939) 196.
[4] F. Stegmüller, *Repertorium commentariorum in Sententias Petri Lombardi* (Wurzburg, 1947) no. 907.

Ecclesiasticus. Twenty surviving manuscripts have been listed, widely scattered, and an edition appeared in 1515.[1] A classicising commentary on Proverbs had been needed to complete the series. Edmund Lacy, bishop of Exeter, who died in 1455, left his copy of Ringstead on Proverbs to his cathedral church, where it was chained next to Holcot on Wisdom in the great library.[2] This must have been a common sight on the shelves of a library of the later middle ages. Lincoln College, Oxford, had one copy kept in the library and a second circulated among the fellows.[3]

Ringstead covered chapters i-xxix, perhaps having no time to finish. He calls himself *lector* and addresses his hearers[4] in the prologue, and his exposition is divided into *lectiones*. The usual number is 176; at least one copy has 181. References to seasons are lacking, but a story about the English siege of Calais gives a year. Ringstead tells how a messenger from the King of France was captured by the English and kept his secret under torture.[5] This puts the lecture course in the academic year 1347/8 or a little later. It fits into his regency at Cambridge, which would fall sometime between 1347/8 and 1353, when he had left for Avignon.

Ringstead's membership of the classicising group appears in his first lines. He begins with a long quotation from *Policraticus* in praise of letters.[6] Then he uses a verbal picture

---

[1] Stegmüller, no. 8172. The edition, François Regnault, Paris, 1515, is ascribed to 'either Robert Holcot or Thomas Waleys', an easy mistake, given an anonymous copy; the technique is similar in all three friars. The edition omits many passages found in the MSS and is very bad. I have used MSS Oxford, Bodl. 829 (2720) and Lincoln College lat. 86 (=L), both fifteenth-century. The Lincoln College MS was given by John Forest, Dean of Wells, a great benefactor. The Bodleian MS has the advantage of giving names of authors in the margins, but the text is rather worse than that of L. My survey of Ringstead on Proverbs has been hasty: much more work could usefully be done on it.

[2] *Summary Catalogue* no. 2720.

[3] R. Weiss, The Earliest Catalogues of the Library of Lincoln College, *B.Q.R.* 8 (1937) 343-59.

[4] L, fol. 12va: Hiis de causis, confisus in Christo, cuius eloquium semper parabolicum fuit, exorsus sum os meum in hiis Salomonis parabolis aperire, ut et de me exili lectore et vestrum quolibet auditore iterem quod premisi: *In absconditis parabolarum conversabitur*.

[5] L, fol. 263va: . . . de quo audivi quod in obsidione regis Anglie circa Kaleys missus ad urbem ex parte regis Francie et captus ab anglicis, cum penis gravissimis urgeretur ad extorquendum secreta sibi commissa, post multa tormentorum genera elegit cum silentio mortem magis quam loquendo proditiosam vitam conservare.

[6] L, fol. 12ra, from *Policraticus*, Prol., 1, 12-13: Iocundissimus . . . docet inscriptio.

in comparing the wisdom of Proverbs to the wonderful tree described in Prudentius' *Psychomachia*:

> 'I contemplate with Prudentius in his *Psychomachia* the temple of marvellous design, supported by a sevenfold column. In the midst grows a tree whose top is green.'[1]

The exposition of the tree's wonders interweaves itself into a commentary on the famous verse of *Didascalicon* giving the requirements for serious study, humility, enquiry, quiet, silence, poverty and a foreign land.[2] The six rules for study lend themselves to illustration by *exempla* and parallels. When Ringstead has finished his prologue and reached his text, his commentary becomes even more of a *florilegium* in character than Holcot's.

The choice of extracts is less fanciful than Holcot's or Hopeman's and shows more resemblance to D'Eyncourt's. Ringstead even debunks a pseudo-classical 'image' of Peace, found in a 'book of descriptions'. The book must have been some sort of 'picture' collection, such as Holcot's *Moralitates* or 'Prudentia depingebatur'.[3] Ringstead seems to doubt whether the image of peace actually existed and traces the inscriptions which were said to surround it to a medieval Christian source:

> 'It is said in books of descriptions and at least is pretended that the image of peace was surrounded by these inscriptions: "I avoid quarrels, hurt none, ignore injuries and conquer by patience." And this description is taken from the last words of St Bernard, when he was happily drawing near to his death.'

Ringstead then quotes the rules for a peaceful life ascribed to St Bernard in the *Vita secunda:* they could certainly be epitomised in the little jingle said to have surrounded the

---

[1] L, fol. 12va: Quantum ad materiam sapientie scientieque pretacte, contemplor cum Prudentio, Sichomachie sue, modicum ante finem, templum quoddam mirande fabrice columpna septemplici supportatum, in cuius medio crescit arbor viridis verticis (MS vertice).

From *Psychomachia* 868-87, ed. Bergman (*C.S.E.L.* 61) 209-10.

[2] L, foll. 12va-14vb. Ringstead recommends eager study with the condition that it should bear fruit in good works: Secunda clavis apperiens est assiduitas studii inquirendo, dum modo tamen ad Christum per opera fructuosa ipsa studii aviditas referatur.

See Hugh of St Victor, *Didascalicon* iii, 12, ed. C. H. Buttimer (Washington, D.C., 1939) 61.

[3] See above, 146.

image.[1] He makes sparing use of this type of *exemplum*, preferring straightforward tales and quotations. His classical repertoire makes no advance on D'Eyncourt's. The Livy quotation that I have noted is a very loose one. Ringstead tells the story of the eagle's swooping down to snatch the hat off Tarquin's head as he was driven into the City. Though he gives a reference to *Ab Urbe condita*, he does not reproduce it verbally.[2] Two references to Quintus Curtius Rufus' *Historia Alexandri Magni* are worth mention. English homilists quote this author less often than they do Valerius Maximus, Suetonius, Vegetius or Sallust. Ringstead quotes the speech of the Scyth to Alexander in a shortened form, beginning: 'Quintus Curtius tells of someone who said to Alexander . . . '.[3] The second quotation comes in a typical string of tales illustrating the importance of observing one's religion. First, Fabius carries the sacred objects through the enemy lines to the Quirinal during the siege of the Capitol by the Gauls. This is from Valerius Maximus.[4] Next comes 'the most Christian king Alfred', according to William of Malmesbury's account of his conduct in the Danish invasions.[5] The third story is ascribed to Quintus Curtius and would have dumbfounded him. Ringstead makes him say that the Greeks always carried before them into battle the god of their cult, that is fire, enclosed in a coal, so that religion need not be neglected in prosperity; in

[1] L, fol. 80va: Dicitur in libris descriptionum et fingitur saltem quod pacis imago talibus erat titulis circumscripta: Rixas fugio, neminem ledo, Iesus ignosco, patiens vinco. Et sumitur hec descriptio ex verbis beati Bernardi ultimis, quando morti feliciter appropinquavit. Tria, inquid, vobis, fratres, custodienda relinquo, que in stadio vite presentis quo cucurri pacifice me memini observasse. Nemini scandalum facere volui, et si quando feci, sedavi meliori modo quo potui. Minus meo sensui quam alterius semper credidi. Iesus de ledente vindictam nunquam expetii.
See *S. Bernardi vita secunda auctore Alano (P.L.* 185) 520. Ringstead makes a free quotation.
[2] L, fol. 44ra: Narrat Titus Livius anno ab Urbe condita [*sic*], libro primo, quod cum Priscus rex superbus curru in urbem veheretur de superis aquila cadens de capite pilleum Prisci tulit.
From *Ab Urb. cond.* I, xxxiv.
[3] L, fol. 33vb: Unde recitat Quintus Cursius de quodam qui sic ait Alexandro: Quid? tu ignoras arbores magnas diu crescere, una tamen extirpari hora? Stultus est qui earum fructus propter earum altitudinem expectat. . . .
From *Historia Alexandri Magni* VII, viii, 14-16.
[4] From *Fact. et dict. mem.* I, i, 11.
[5] L, fol. 37rb: Simile de christianissimo rege Alfredo Malmesburiensis narrat. Ringstead perhaps meant to expand the reference. He had in mind *Gesta Regum Anglorum* ii, 122 (Rolls Series, 1887) 1, 129: Licet enim, ut quidam ait, leges inter arma sileant, ille (Alfredus) inter fremitus armorum leges tulit, quibus sui et divino cultui . . . assuescerent.

adversity they found help in calling upon the *numen*. The tale may derive from a reference to the Persian (not Greek) cult of Sol or Mithras. There is nothing about a *carbunculum* in the text, however.[1] Ringstead probably drew on a *florilegium* with incorrect headings. The Children of Israel, carrying the Ark of the Covenant, bring up the rear of a mixed procession. 'Possidonius in libro de romanorum superstitionibus' catches the eye and raises expectations. It disappoints us by boiling down to a deduction from a passage in *De civitate Dei*. St Augustine describes Possidonius as a great astrologer and philosopher. Ringstead or his source concluded that Possidonius must have written a book on Roman superstitions.[2]

He compensates for the lack of new classical sources by exploiting the riches of rarer medieval books, though he does not neglect old favourites, such as the *Communiloquium*.[3] It will be enough to describe the least familiar medieval author, 'Helias Tripolanensis'. Ringstead quotes copiously from him under two titles, *De vita scholarium atque sua* and *Contra nobilitatem*. The only other writer to quote Elias of Tripoli (if that is the right way to translate it) is John Whethamstead, abbot of St Alban's 1420-40. His *Pabularium*, a book of quotations arranged alphabetically under subject headings, quotes 'Helias Tripolanensis, *De sua suorumque scholarium vita*'. He give us extracts under many headings.[4] Some verses under the heading 'Stema' (Ancestry) have 'contra nobilitatem' as their theme, arguing that ancient lineage without wealth is valueless. This suggests that *Contra nobilitatem* was an alternative or sub-title to *De sua suorumque scholarium vita* and not the title of a separate work. Elias and his book or books would have gone down unknown to history, but for Ringstead and Whethamstead. Their

---

[1] L, fol. 37rb: Unde et de grecis narrat Quintus Cursius quod deum quem coluerunt, ignem videlicet, inclusum carbunculo, proficientes ad bellum semper previum habuerunt, ut et in prosperis nichil religionis deesset; et si quando casus adversus contingeret, numen invocantes subsidium (et) auxilium invenerunt.
See *Historia Alexandri Magni* IV, xiii, 12. MS Bodl. 829, fol. 12rb, has 'solem' instead of 'ignem'.
[2] MS Bodl. 829, fol. 14rb. Ringstead refers to *De civitate Dei* as his only authority for Possidonius' book (v, 2 and 5). Neither Trevet nor Waleys had deduced its existence from the text of *De civitate Dei*.
[3] L, fol. 183vb: Unde refert Gallensis, parte ultima libri sui. . . .
Ringstead tells a widespread *exemplum*, 'bad custom in the world; the young die', from John of Wales, *Communiloquium* VII, i, 3, ed. cit., fol. 158va.
[4] See below, appendix, ii, 351.

quotations and references show that he wrote in alternative verse and prose. He worked in the didactic, classicising genre, but was no fantastic. Ringstead had chosen a staid and sober author.

Modern *exempla* in the lectures include a story about Prince Edward of Carnarvon, later King Edward II. The prince's father, King Edward I, had cast him off under the influence of evil counsellors. He bore the injury patiently and came to his father's help on a winter's night, when the king was riding along a muddy, dangerous road. Fearing for his safety, Prince Edward took the horse's bridle and walked beside him until the danger was over. The king did not know who had come to his rescue. Prince Edward signifies Christ in the moralisation of the story.[1] It must have originated in memories of the quarrel between Edward I and Prince Edward in 1305. The prince, being short of pocket money in consequence, wrote to the earl of Lincoln that he intended to follow his father round wherever he went until he should be received back into favour. His household accounts show that he actually did so. The quarrel started in the summer and the reconciliation took place in mid-October.[2] The story must be apocryphal, since it is set in the winter. It probably circulated in connexion with the cult of the murdered king at Gloucester Abbey. Edward II had befriended the Dominicans and they cherished his memory.

Ringstead reserves his harshest criticism as a moralist for kings and great lords who oppress the poor to satisfy their greed for vainglory and 'novelties'; the worse gangster is counted as the wiser king and lord. He tells an amusing story of a priest who played dice with the patron of a fat living, then vacant. The priest wagered twenty pounds that the lord would win the game and would not give him the benefice. The lord, seeing his cleverness, lost the game intentionally and conferred the church on him, thinking to avoid simony by means of the trick.

The lecturer has his feet firmly on earth and can vary his classical allusions by a homely metaphor from the cloth industry. Colour dyed in the wool or in manufacture stays fast, but if cloth is dyed after making up it stains very easily, should any liquid be spilt on it. So with promotion: virtue must be

---

[1] For this and the following pieces, see Appendix i, 338-9.
[2] H. Johnstone, *Edward of Carnarvon* 1284-1307 (Manchester, 1946) 96-103.

dyed in the wool and not assumed afterwards; otherwise it will not take the responsibilities of office. Ringstead here reminds us of Waleys' and Holcot's moralisation of the new invention of eyeglasses; all three friars show an interest in technical skills. They recall the early nineteenth-century moralisation of the railway, which serves as an epitaph in the south porch of Ely Cathedral, dated 1845:

> God's Word is the first Engineer,
> It points the way to Heaven so dear,
> Through tunnels dark and dreary here
> It does the way to Glory steer.
> God's Love the Fire, his Truth the Steam,
> Which drives the Engine and the Train
>
> .   .   .   .   .   .
>
> Come then poor Sinners, now's the time,
> At any Station on the Line.
> If you'll repent and turn from sin
> The Train will stop and take you in.

Ringstead has something for everyone. His lectures build up a picture of a future diplomat and bishop.

I have lingered too long in the daylight from reluctance to turn to the dusky phantasmagoria of Lathbury on Lamentations.

CHAPTER IX

JOHN LATHBURY

Congregavit plurimam multitudinem, et obturaverunt cunctos fontes.

II Paralipomenon, xxxii, 4.

I.—LIFE AND WRITINGS

JOHN probably took his name from the village of Lathbury in north Buckinghamshire near Newport Pagnall. He was ordained subdeacon as a Friar Minor in the diocese of Coventry and Lichfield on April 22, 1329.[1] Then we lose sight of him until 1342, when he was licensed to hear confessions in Sarum diocese for one year. He attended the Provincial Chapter of his Order held at London in 1343 and studied at Oxford both before and after this date. On November 11, 1352 he was licensed again to hear confessions for one year, this time in the archdeaconry of Buckingham. He died at Reading in 1362 as an old man (*senex*), according to Bale.[2] His Oxford regency must have fallen soon after 1350: the precise date is not known. The medieval list of Franciscan regents at Oxford ends about 1350 and does not include him; but if he was old or elderly at his death in 1362 he must already have been older than was normal for a regent master in a mendicant Order by 1350; so we cannot defer his regency too long. The prologue to his commentary on Lamentations takes the customary form of an inaugural lecture, praising the Scriptures. The task of lecturing has been enjoined on him, he says. He chooses the book of Lamentations for the present in contrast to his 'reverend predecessor' in the chair, who has been lecturing on the Canticle;[3] unfortunately this does not help to identify the

---

[1] *O.R.* 2, 1104-5. [2] *Index*, op. cit. 225.

[3] MS Exeter College, Oxford 27 (=E), Prol., V (for my method of referring to passages in this MS, see below): Dicebatur enim michi *lege*, quando in meritum obedientie iniungebatur michi legere, et ideo liber sacre scripture seu potius pro nunc liber Trenorum Ieremie prophete michi datus est *nescienti litteras*. Illum enim librum, Deo docente, intendo legere, quia sicut predecessor meus reverendus legit Canticum Canticorum, sic per oppositum ego legam Lamentationes Lamentationum.

Lathbury is referring to the text Isa. xxix, 12: *Et dabitur liber nescienti litteras diceturque ei: Lege.*

unnamed colleague or to fix the date of the regency. Bale
gives the incipit of a commentary on Acts by Lathbury.
He may also have lectured on the Psalter or part of it; but
neither commentary has been identified.[1]

According to Bale, John Lathbury the elder, that is our
John Lathbury, gave Ridevall's commentaries on *Valerius ad
Rufinum* and Fulgentius, that is his *Fulgentius metaforalis*, with
many other books to John Lathbury the younger in 1348.
The books were kept at Reading Greyfriars.[2] His possession
of books by Ridevall puts Lathbury into the direct line of
the classicising friars. He prolonged their movement into
the 'fifties and brought it to a sad end. The history of *Lathbury on Lamentations* proves that it was a successful end, however. The commentary fills a folio volume in manuscript,
even though it stops after chapter iii and leaves out most of
chapter ii of the biblical text. It has survived, more or less
intact, in seven copies in England, written in the fifteenth
century, most of which have illuminated title-pages and
present a handsome appearance. One was drawn up in a
fishing net from the sea bottom. Excerpts were copied into
two fifteenth-century English miscellanies, one mainly on
grammar and *dictamen*, the other devotional, compiled by
John Dygon, the recluse of Sheen. It was reorganised into
distinctiones and drafts of sermons by Lathbury himself, and
circulated as an *Alphabetum morale*. Finally it was chosen as
one of the first books to be published by the Oxford Press in
1482. The edition included a larger number of copies on
vellum than was customary: the expense may have been
'covered by subscriptions from members of the university and
from colleges'.[3]

MS Merton College 189, one of the seven English copies,
dated 1406, has an index on the flyleaf which suggests a
reason for Lathbury's appeal to readers and shows how carefully he was studied. Most copies include elaborate tables
of texts and subject matter; but this did not satisfy some
anonymous fifteenth-century scholar. He wrote in his own
hand a list of all the authors quoted by Lathbury with the
number of the leaf. The commentary must have impressed
him as a rich mine of quotations. The most extraordinary

---

[1] *O.R.* 2, 1105. Stegmüller lists a commentary on Acts with this incipit,
no. 4763, but it is too early for Lathbury, being thirteenth-century.
[2] *Index*, op. cit. 242. On the younger John Lathbury, another Franciscan,
who died in 1375, see *O.R.* 2, 1105.
[3] See appendix iii.

evidence comes from Padua. The *Antoniana* has a copy, anonymous and lacking the prologue, written in fifteenth-century Italian humanist script and prettily illuminated. A coat of arms on the first page shows that it was prepared for some Italian gentleman. He, too, may have been beguiled by the authors quoted. It is comic to see in this Renaissance setting an English friar who justifies every rude remark ever passed on the culture of 'the waning middle ages'.

I have chosen MS Oxford, Exeter College 27 (= E), to quote from. It is beautifully clean and legible, and the chapters of the commentary are in order, whereas in the Merton copy they are sometimes misplaced. All the copies which I have seen are so corrupt that it would be difficult to choose between them; the editon of 1482 is worse. Since E is incompletely foliated, I shall quote according to the chapter divisions of the commentary. Each chapter is subdivided by letters of the alphabet. Chapters exceeding the division A to Z start again with double letters, AA, etc. This system of reference has its advantage in that it is common to a number of manuscript copies and to the printed edition. The chapters are easily turned up and are manageable in size; there are over a hundred of them.

II.—Personality and Tastes

The lecture course on Lamentations gives a general picture of the mind of its author. We get to know Lathbury less well than Waleys or Holcot, but better than our other friars. He was conscious of his English background, quoting a popular saying: 'England is called "Mary's dower" ', and playing on 'Angles and angels'.[1] In a list of the various ways in which kings are made he says that hereditary succession by the son is the custom in England.[2] A special attachment to the Midlands may show itself in an addition which he makes to the account of the chief rivers of the country in *Polychronicon*. Here the three chief rivers are said to be Thames, Severn and Humber, into which flow Trent and Ouse. Lathbury promotes the Trent to the rank of fourth river, explaining that it rises in the West of England near the abbey called Trent (Burton-on-Trent) from a

---

[1] E, 99, C: Dicitur enim vulgariter quod terra Anglie est dos Marie, unde anglici quasi angelici.

[2] E, 107, D: Secundo, fiunt reges ex hereditaria filii successione, sicut consuetum est in Anglia.

beautiful fount, flows on to Nottingham and falls into the Humber further north.[1] That he felt himself to be a son of St Francis appears from a number of pious references,[2] and he sets his Founder besides St John Baptist as an example of 'voluntary poverty'.[3] None of the allusions implies any sympathy with the Spirituals: Lathbury was carefully orthodox, like the vast majority of English Franciscans; he was even a keen papalist.[4]

The lectures begin with a *reductio ad absurdum* of the practice of quoting an introductory text. Lathbury chose *In nomine Patris et Filii et Spiritus sancti. Amen.* This enabled him to dilate on the virtues of the holy names. He gives a further reason for his choice, explaining that the prophet Jeremias used the threefold alphabet in order to signify the three Persons of the Trinity. This illustrates Lathbury's uncertain attitude to the literal interpretation of Old Testament prophecy. He quotes copiously from St Jerome on Jeremias, Paschasius Radbertus, the *Glossa ordinaria* (mainly excerpts from Paschasius with additions by Gilbert the Universal), Andrew of St Victor on Jeremias and Nicholas of Lyre. All these authors are juxtaposed without any suggestion that they contradict one another. Nicholas of Lyre in particular reacted against the older commentators' mystical approach, teaching that the alphabet of Lamentations originally carried no mystical significance. The text, he held, could be understood best if it were read as a lament: his predecessors had complicated it too much. Lathbury turned the deaf ear to Lyre's warning.[5]

---

[1] E, 57, EE: Scribitur enim in historia polychronica, lib. i, quod fluunt in Britannia quatuor famosa flumina, scilicet Tamisia, Sabrina, Humbria et Trenta . . . Trenta vero, ut notum est, in occidente Anglie iuxta abbatiam que dicitur Trenta ex fonte pulchra orta est, que defluens usque ad Nothyngam et ultra ad boriales partes cadit in Humbriam.

See *Polychronicon*, ed. cit. 2, 48-52. Lathbury may have found the addition in his copy of *Polychronicon*. The Trent does not *rise* by the Benedictine abbey of Burton-on-Trent, but flows past it.

[2] E, Prol., X; 46, D; 57, XX.

[3] E, Prol., AA: Videbis in Iohanne Baptista victus abstinentiam et vite austeritatem et in fideli Francisco temporalium indigentiam et voluntariam (MS ultimatam) paupertatem.

[4] B. Smalley, Flaccianus, *De visionibus Sibyllae*, *Mélanges offerts à Étienne Gilson* (Toronto, Paris, 1959) 551-3.

Lathbury does not introduce theological *quaestiones* into his commentary, but he mentions in passing that he does not accept the doctrine of the Immaculate Conception, giving as his reason that all doctors, apart from St Anselm, agreed that Mary was conceived in original sin, E, 99, D. On discussion of the question in the fourteenth century, see Forte, 329-34.

[5] Appendix i, 339.

His lack of critical sense comes out again in his use of New Testament apocrypha and in his choice of *exempla*. The former had normally been excluded from school lectures, as distinct from popular instruction. Some lecturers even warned their pupils against apocryphal tales.[1] Lathbury broke with custom in quoting Pseudo-Melito's *Assumption of the Virgin* and a 'Gospel of Nicodemus'.[2] Three personal *exempla* tell of marvels in foreign lands. Lathbury vouches for his informants' good faith; he had swallowed their yarns eagerly.

A certain trustworthy man, to whose word Lathbury holds as he would to his book, firmly stated that he had seen the sorrowful picture of Mary grieving at the foot of the Cross, painted by St Luke. She had a clear complexion and a fair countenance. Streams of tears rolled down her cheeks to her chin, so that the prophecy *Her tears are on her cheeks* (Lam. i, 2) corresponded very well to her portrait.[3] Lathbury's friend must have seen a picture of the Madonna ascribed to St Luke. There were many in Italy. One, at least, represented her weeping by the Cross.[4] It suited Lathbury's description of the scene. He wallowed in tears and swooning.

A venerable knight, whose holy life gave credence to his words, devoutly related to Lathbury a vision that he had seen on crusade. A heavenly host had appeared in the air to help the Christians by paralysing the infidels with terror.[5] Lathbury may well have met a returned crusader: he could have talked in his boyhood to some very old man who had accompanied Prince Edward to Acre in 1271. The story was a traditional crusaders' tale.[6]

'Brother Herman of Cologne' told him a different type of marvel. He heard it from Brother Herman when they met

---

[1] *Study of the Bible*, 239; B. Smalley, John Russel, op. cit. 318-19.
[2] E, 31, I, on the brightness of the Virgin's corpse; see M. R. James, *The Apocryphal New Testament*, new ed. (Oxford, 1955) 213.
   E, 41, X: Item in evangelio Nicodemi, visus est angelus Domini cum rumphea ignea velum templi in duas partes a sursum usque deorsum divisisse per medium, qui etiam sic clamabat: Testis sum Passionis.
   This is not in the *Acta Pilati*, sometimes called the *Evangelium Nicodemi*; see M. R. James, op. cit. 94-5.
[3] Appendix i, 340.
[4] E. von Dobschütz, Christusbilder, *Texte und Untersuchungen zur Geschichte der Altchristlicher Literatur* N.F. 18 (1899) 28, 67, 84, 267*-80*.
[5] Appendix i, 340.
[6] It appears already under the year 1098 in *Anonymi gesta francorum*, xxix, ed. B. A. Lees (Oxford, 1924) 67.

at the Chapter of the Order at London in 1343, and many times before and after while they were both studying at Oxford. A town in Herman's native country called *Engere* (Engers to the south of Cologne), whence the word England is derived, had near it at a mile's distance an enormous old oaktree. It used to bear a wonderful crop of acorns every Christmas at midnight. The local people would flock there, and Herman with them when he was a boy. They brought lights and lanterns, and sticks and sacks, and picnicked, played or slept until the acorns appeared. Then they gathered the crop, since the tree never yielded at any other time of year. The distribution of the acorns on the oak forecast which regions would have the best harvest that season.[1] Lathbury unsuspectingly recounts the performance of a heathen rite, thinly christianised, under the sacred tree of German mythology.[2]

He resembled his predecessors in his taste for a mixture of sacred and profane authors. But they had handled their sources with a certain grace; Lathbury seems to be working a mincing machine. The pretentious and yet mechanical nature of the process may be illustrated from his comment on *How doth the city sit solitary* (Lam. i, 1). He compares the mourning city to the *Mater dolorosa* of the Crucifixion scene, collecting all the instances he can find from biblical or profane history and myth where anyone sat anywhere, either rejoicing or grieving. He pairs or contrasts them with Mary. His copyists have piled on the bathos by turning some of the names into puzzles:

> Quomodo igitur sedet?
> Non sedet cum sublimato Salomone in throno dignitatis,
> sed sedet cum excecato Samsone in carcere dedecoris et deformitatis.
> Non sedet cum Midride in solio regalis otii,
> sed sedet cum Appollo(ne) in pulvere servilis opprobrii.[3]
> Non sedet cum Tantalo in cathedra studii perfamosi,[4]
> sed sedet cum Ovidio in terra aliena exilii lacrimosi.

---

[1] See A. G. Little, *The Grey Friars in Oxford* (Oxford, 1892) 236.

[2] H. Bachtold-Staubi and E. von Hoffman-Krayer, *Handwörterbuch der deutschen Aberglaubens* 2 (Berlin, Leipzig, 1929) 646-59.

[3] Lathbury refers to Apollo's exile from Olympus. I cannot identify *Midride*. Can it mean Mithridates?

[4] Tantalus was sometimes regarded as a philosopher and Lathbury may have misread St Jerome, *Ep.* 53 (*P.L.* 22) 541, prefacing the Vulgate Bible: . . . ut Hiarcam in throno sedentem aureo et de Tantali fonte potantem . . . audiret docentem.

Non sedet cum Sardanapallo in camera virginis delicate,
languens ex amore,
sed sedet cum Appollonio in provincia mortis elongata [*sic*],
lugens ex dolore.[1]

A similar comparison begins with the prophet Jeremias
squinting at the Blessed Virgin; he 'raises one eye to her
virtues and the other eye to her misfortunes'.

Sed pro dolore levando unum oculum ad Marie preconia
et alterum ad Marie infortunia sub cruce patibulo, Ieremias
ex stupore, ex amore, ex dolore sic plangit et plorat, quasi
diceret: *Quomodo sedet sola civitas plena populo*, quasi diceret:

Non sedet sicut Thamar in bivio voluptatis,
sed sicut Isis mestissima sub legibus languoris.
Non sedet sicut Pallas in radio claritatis,
sed sicut plorans Passis in tenebris meroris.[2]
Non sedet sicut Susanna delicata sub umbra iuniperi,
sed crurore prolis conspersa sub umbra patibuli.
Non sedet sicut Antigua, lasciviens super montis declivium,[3]
sed sicut Agar, lamentans iuxta arborem filium suum
semivivum.
Non sedet sicut Ruth ad latus messorum,
sed cum misera Martia in medio luporum.[4]
Non sedet cum regina Vasti in convivio,
sed cum Proserpina in misere mortis gremio.
Non sedet cum Ixion in musicorum consortio,
sed sicut innocens Daniel in septem leonum medio.
Non sedet sicut Diana stipata deliciis,
sed sicut Axa plena singultibus et suspiriis.[5]
Non sedet sicut Barsabe prope regis solium iuxta filium
suum imperantem,
sed prope crucis nidulum iuxta Filium in patibulo palpi-
tantem.

That will do, though Lathbury has not finished.[6]

[1] See *Historia Apollonii regis Tyri*, ed. A. Riese (Leipzig, 1893).
[2] *Passis* is the spelling in all the MSS I have seen, but Lathbury probably
wrote *Saffo* for *Sapho*; he mentions *Saffo mulier* in an account of Sapphic verse,
E, 1, L. The *f* and *s* are easily confused in fifteenth-century script. A scribe
confronted with *Sasso* would be apt to corrupt it still further. Lathbury could
have read of the poetess's grief in Ovid's *Epistula Sapphus*.
[3] I cannot identify Antigua.
[4] Is Martia 'Mrs Mars'? Lathbury may have meant the Vestal Virgin who
bore Romulus and Remus to Mars. Wolves surround her because a she-wolf
suckled the twins!
[5] Not appropriate as an example of sorrow: Axa sighed as she sat upon her
ass because she wanted to wheedle her father into increasing her marriage
portion and succeeded, Ios. xv, 18.
[6] E, 4, B; 6, O.

Holcot offered the same sort of mix-up in his praise of good women.[1] But what a difference there is between him and Lathbury! Holcot had not only better taste; he had something to say. The same contrast appears if we watch Lathbury trying to produce a visual image. Holcot could convey a scene; his junior gets cloudy and muddled. For instance, he imagines the Church as God's house. Four painters, signifying the apostles, martyrs, confessors and virgins respectively, depict stories on the walls. Each painter has a special colour and each paints a special type of story. Lathbury misses his effect by leaving each painter to manage with only one colour.[2] Fortunately, he does not attempt 'pictures'. Scholarship, artistry, humour, all these traits of the classicising group are conspicuous by their absence in the youngest member.

Yet Lathbury had positive qualities, to give him his due. First of all he showed courage in fighting a rearguard action against the enemies of pagan learning. MS Merton College 189 has a *quaestio* added to the end of the commentary, asking whether Christian theologians should make use of the sayings of heathen poets and philosophers. It is written in a hand contemporary with the text (1406). It may represent Lathbury's teaching or it may have been suggested by his use of poets and philosophers in his commentary. In either case, it justifies and defends his classicism. Four arguments are put forward against the objection that the theologian should use only what is suitable and useful, which the sayings of the heathen are not. Three of the arguments in favour of heathen sayings are trite: heathen poets and philosophers support and adorn the teaching of the faith; they are instruments of divine wisdom and eloquence; they represent the spoils of the gentiles, which should be stripped off and shared out to Christians. A fourth is more original: the poets and philosophers provide a subtle means of bringing teacher and pupil closer together, because they offer matter of common interest.[3] Presumably the pupil has come fresh from the arts course and has to be broken in to theology gently.

Lathbury collected books as eagerly as any member of the group. An anthology of Latin religious verse could be assembled from his commentary. Versification interested him so much that he gave a short lesson on the subject in

---

[1] Above, 155.   [2] Appendix i, 340.   [3] Appendix i, 341.

connexion with the metre of Lamentations. The gist of it comes from Jerome and Isidore, but he illustrates their argument by quoting his own examples. He makes a list of biblical and classical heroes to explain the subject matter of heroic poetry and he compares Lamentations to a Latin poem about Edward the Confessor. Needless to say, he puts classical and medieval poetry on the same level, choosing his examples mainly from medieval.[1]

Like Ridevall he exploited Grosseteste's bequest to Grey-friars. It included the bishop's unpublished papers, mostly in the form of marginalia in his books. Lathbury quotes a gloss in Grosseteste's copy of Albumasar's *Introductorium maius*, a treatise on astronomy; it was written beside the description of the sign Virgo, which was thought to signify the Virgin and the child Jesus.[2] He had a lost work of Thomas Docking, either a commentary on Genesis or more probably a biblical grammar. Robert Crichlade's abridg-ment of Pliny's *Historia naturalis*, an uncommon book, may well have been at Greyfriars,[3] also Joachim of Fiore on the Apocalypse and Pseudo-Joachim's *De semine litterarum*.[4] The library would have needed to be phenomenally rich, however, to have possessed every rare book quoted by Lath-bury. He must have visited others. We know from Bale that he made a big private collection and we know that he acquired the treatise on husbandry ascribed to Walter of Henley for Reading Priory.[5]

The remainder of the chapter on Lathbury will be con-cerned with his quotations from lost or unrecorded works. Some of the authors are quite unknown. I have restricted the list to authors who give the impression of being late medieval. There is plenty of pseudo-patristic, pseudo-Anselm and pseudo-Bernard; but all this must be omitted. The following authors share the trait of being medieval

---

[1] Appendix i, 342.

[2] For quotations from lost or unrecorded works, see appendix ii. On the use of Grosseteste's papers at Greyfriars, see B. Smalley, John Russel O.F.M., op. cit. 309-10. It is interesting to note that Lathbury refers to the sermons of St Augustine as though he or his readers could consult an actual volume on the shelves; E, 34, S: Augustinus, sermone 13, volumine primo . . . 34, P: Similiter Augustinus, sermone 8, volumine secundo.

For similar types of reference, see 39, B and 40, A.

[3] E, 6, L; Crikeladensis in historia naturali, lib. 1, cap. 43 . . . (a description of the city of Meroe).

This corresponds with the passage in Crichlade in MS London, Brit. Mus. Royal 15. C. xiv, fol. 14rb. On Crichlade see *O.R.* 1, 513.

[4] B. Smalley, Flaccianus, op. cit.   [5] *O.R.* 2, 1105.

and making no bones about it; they have no pretensions to antiquity. Lathbury's *auctor de proprietatibus elementorum* was probably the Cambridge Franciscan, Walter Wimborne. Holcot ascribes a very similar type of book to Wimborne. They were probably quoting the same book, which was anonymous in Lathbury's copy. A grammar book ascribed to 'Landaf' is very intriguing. Unhappily, he quotes it only as agreeing with Isidorc's *Etymologies*. Two devotional books quoted are a 'libellus qui intitulatur *Pentasse* (or *Pentase*)' and a *De corde sive musica amoris*. The *Pentasse* was written in mixed prose and verse; it compared the mercy of the glorious Virgin to the ark, which saved men from the flood. The *De corde* compared the soul to love's castle. The three letters COR, inscribed on the gate, have a mystical significance. Lathbury ascribes this book to 'Carnotensis'. It is possible that he thought the author was John of Salisbury, who died as bishop of Chartres, since he also quotes 'Carnotensis' as the author of *Policraticus*. If so he was wrong. *De corde* reads like a florid work, abounding in rhetorical cries and questions. It was probably written later than the twelfth century.

III.—The Collector of Forgeries

We turn from the authors presented as medieval to those labelled 'ancient,' and what an outrageous collection they make! Lathbury doted on forgeries. Ridevall and Holcot liked them too, but they were capable of putting the tongue in the cheek, and they joined in the game. Lathbury takes it all seriously, or so it seems. He reminds us of some wealthy, trusting amateur who has fallen into the clutches of a dishonest dealer.

His most prolific forger took the name of Fulgentius and masqueraded as a 'Roman senator'. Lathbury seems to have identified him with the mythographer.[1] Pseudo-Fulgentius is credited with the following: *De ornatu civitatis, De parvo lapide, De secretis Virgilii, De tribus serpentibus, de vita Virginis gloriose* and a *Numerale*. The first book is introduced with the words: 'Sic ergo tradidit ille senator romanus, scilicet

---

[1] Lathbury quotes Fulgentius' *Mythologiae* as follows, E, 110, B: . . . ut patet per Fulgentium in libro de ortu deorum et per Augustinum . . . infinitis erroribus circa Creatorem et creaturam infideles pagani mundum repleverunt.
He does not differentiate the true from the Pseudo-Fulgentius when he quotes them.

Fulgentius . . .'. It gave an account of an ideal city, with illustrations from ancient Rome. Pseudo-Fulgentius drew on the *Mirabilia Urbis Romae*, but added details as circumstantial as they were imaginary, such as a kind of Chelsea Pensioners' Hospital for retired knights in the Trastevere. *De parvo lapide* is quoted as the source of a tale of Alexander. The citizens of a marvellous town in lower India offered Alexander a fair maiden as tribute, telling him that her merit lay in prudence and wisdom. Alexander, 'being a philosopher himself', questioned her. She answered by making a number of cryptic claims, which pleased him so much that he accepted her, raised the siege, and withdrew, placated. This tale is introduced by the respectful words: 'tradit auctor ille . . .'. *De secretis Virgilii* told of Virgil the wizard. Stories of his marvellous constructions at Naples and Rome had been circulating north of the Alps for several centuries. Pseudo-Fulgentius could have collected walls of air, magic books and magic mirrors from current legends;[1] but he painted the lily; none of his marvels is described so elaborately elsewhere. He tells us that Virgil built a palace of clotted air, which reflected absolutely everything in the world. Virgil also found a book in the temple of Apollo. It had four leaves. The master spirits of the four points of the compass would appear to him according to which leaf he read; the spirit of the North would obey him in all things. Then Virgil contrived seven mirrors 'with stupendous art'. Each had a different effect, though all were marvellous. The mirror of pleasure, for instance, showed the spectator all that his heart could desire.

The most revealing of the Virgil stories tells how the poet built an underground room 'for love of Augustus' son'. The room produced a new prodigy at each of the seven hours. At the hour of noon the noise of drunken revelry was heard, though nobody could be seen. At the hour of Mercury anything thrown into it would be burnt. The hour of Venus was marked by stench, that of Phoebus by litigious voices, that of Mars by shouts and groans, and that of Jove by thunderbolts. It was quiet in the house at Saturn's hour, but whoever entered would be vexed inexplicably by

---

[1] J. W. Spargo, *Virgil the Necromancer* (Cambridge, Mass., 1934) 8-19, 62, 64, 67, 134-5. See also D. Comparetti, *Virgilio nel medio Evo*, new ed. (Florence, 1946) and G. Pasquali, *Vecchie e nuove pagine stravaganti di un filologo* (Florence, 1952) 18-20.

melancholy. Virgil called his marvel 'the house of grief,' and dedicated it to Pluto. Now we know! *De secretis Virgilii* was a preacher's book. The secret room signified the soul, the seven hours the seven sins and Pluto the devil. The seven magic mirrors signified the seven sins, too. The maiden with her cryptic claims who was sent to Alexander in *De parvo lapide* signified the Virgin. *De ornatu civitatis* must have had the same purpose as *De secretis Virgilii* and *De parvo lapide*. Pseudo-Fulgentius wrote in the *genre* of *Gesta romanorum*.

His *De tribus serpentibus* was a biblical work, called after the serpents which plagued the Israelites in the wilderness (Num. xxi, 6). It seems to have had a section concerning Jeremias, and so presumably was an aid to Bible study. Lathbury quotes once only from *De vita Virginis gloriose*. The passage describes her physical beauty. He mentions the *Numerale* in the same breath as William de Montibus' better-known book of the same title. William de Montibus (d. 1213) made a compendium of theology, arranged according to numbers, three for the Trinity, and so on. Pseudo-Fulgentius must have chosen a similar lay-out. Lathbury quotes from a section on seven.

Is his 'Fulgentius' the same as Holcot's? The latter ascribes a *Liber de gestis romanorum* to 'Fulgentius'.[1] Boston of Bury credits him with a *Liber de rebus signatis*.[2] It is conceivable that *De secretis Virgilii*, *De parvo lapide* and *De ornatu civitatis* might circulate under alternative titles and that the same writer is meant. Or perhaps Pseudo-Fulgentius produced a *De gestis romanorum* (not the same as the more famous *Gesta romanorum*) and a *De rebus signatis* in addition to the six books ascribed to him by Lathbury. Alternatively, one or more others may have borrowed the name 'Fulgentius' from the first forger.

Pseudo-Aulus Gellius, *De bellis Armenie*, was another preacher's book; the forger had collected tales of Alexander's conquest of Armenia, or perhaps he invented them. Aulus Gellius (Agellius to the middle ages) refers to Alexander's conquests in his *Noctes atticae*, a favourite book among the classicising friars. Hence a *De bellis Armenie* might be

---

[1] Above, p. 180, n. 1.
[2] *F.S.* 212. Boston refers to Fulgentius in his section on Apuleius, whom he confuses with Plato: . . . item *De republica* secundum Fulgentium libro *De rebus signatis* (?) ad Calcidium.

ascribed to him with some show of reason. We do not depend solely on Lathbury for our knowledge of it. Stories
from it appear in *exempla* collections and Boston of Bury
couples it with *Noctes atticae* under *Agellius*, though he had
not actually seen a copy.[1] Lathbury quotes a long, elaborate
story about the seven deadly sins, signified by heraldic
devices. Pseudo-Agellius had cashed in on the contemporary
love of heraldry and had chosen the Alexander legend as his
setting. He must have hoped to impress an aristocratic
congregation. Faking coats of arms for disguised knights in
tournaments was quite common, but it is doubtful whether
Pseudo-Agellius' efforts would have satisfied a herald.
The Persians, according to his story, had seven twin brothers
as their army leaders. Each one carried a royal shield,
bearing a motto and curiously painted. The seven devices
stand for the seven sins. My favourite is *gula*, represented by
an ocean whirlpool with three mouths, and inscribed:
'Per tria monstrata devorabo cuncta creata.' Alexander,
on hearing of the brothers' demeanour, had a counter device and motto set on his shield. He defeated the brothers and
subdued their kingdom. Alexander signifies the victorious
Saviour.

We have seen that Holcot quoted a Pseudo-Palaephatius,
De incredibilibus. Lathbury tells several myths from the same
source. Pseudo-Palaephatius cannot have been a sound
mythographer if he thought that Niobe was a 'maiden'
and conflated her story with that of Echo; but Lathbury
may have misquoted him in order to make Niobe signify the
weeping Virgin. He throws some light on the nature of the
compilation by quoting an account of the darkness reported
by pagans on the day of the Crucifixion. Pseudo-Palaephatius
was therefore a Christian, collecting or inventing supposedly
pagan witnesses to the gospel story.

Lathbury's account of darkness at noon as recorded by
Pseudo-Palaephatius includes a reference to 'Berosus, historian of Athens'. Berosus is said to have reported the same
prodigy of darkness, which 'confounded the wisdom of the
Athenians'. The Babylonian chronicler Berosus was known
to the West by name at least through Josephus and Eusebius.
Pliny also mentions him, telling that the Athenians set up a
statue to Berosus in the gymnasium; they gilded the tongue
as a compliment to his skill in making astrological predic-

[1] *F.S.* 211.

tions.[1] This was quite enough to set a forger to work on a history of Athens ascribed to Berosus. Lathbury had no doubt that a genuine history of Athens by Berosus existed; he gives a precise reference. Judging by the context, however, it seems probable that he had before him some list of pagan witnesses to the darkness of the Crucifixion noon, and that the list included a reference to Berosus' history of Athens. Such a list would have corresponded to the *Liber de testimoniis gentilium de fide christiana*, a collection of pagan prophecies on the Incarnation. The *Liber de testimoniis gentilium* is ascribed both to Roger Bacon and John of Paris. Lathbury had a copy and quotes it anonymously.[2] A parallel collection of *testimonia* to the Passion may well have been circulating and would have had an equal appeal for contemporaries. The witnesses to the Incarnation come from well-known sources, the Sibyl, Virgil, Pseudo-Ovid, etc. The witnesses to the Passion may have improved on the former by including new forgeries.

This Pseudo-Berosus has a more famous namesake, on whom he throws a faint ray of light. Giovanni Anni or Nanni of Viterbo, a Dominican orientalist, printed a set of hitherto unknown chronicles with his own commentary on them at Rome in 1498; a 'Berosus' figures in Anni's *Antiquitates*. It is now generally accepted after much controversy that the chronicles are spurious. Moreover, the text and commentary hang so closely together that they must have been produced by the same author. Anni's Pseudo-Berosus lived 'before Alexander's monarchy' and had read Tacitus' *Germania*.[3] He cannot, therefore, have been the same as Lathbury's: the latter's Pseudo-Berosus was supposed to have lived in the first century A.D., since he witnessed to the Passion, and the forger could not have read Tacitus' *Germania*, which was only rediscovered in the fifteenth century. However, it has been claimed on Anni's behalf that he may have started from earlier forgeries and

---

[1] *Nat. hist.* vii, 123: . . . astrologia Berosus, cui ob divinas praedicationes Athenienses publice in gymnasio statuam inaurata lingua statuere. . . . On Berosus see Pauli-Wissova, op. cit. xxxi, 309-17.

[2] B. Smalley, *Flaccianus*, etc., op. cit.

[3] I have used the edition of Antwerp, 1552, published as *Berosi sacerdotis chaldaici antiquitatum Italiae ac totius orbis libri quinque, commentariis Ioannis Annii Viterbensis illustrata.* See C. Gotthelf, *Das deutsche Altertum in den Anschauungen des sechzehnten und siebzehnten Jahrhunderts* (Berlin, 1900) 6; O. A. Danielsson, *Annius von Viterbo über die Gründungsgeschichte Roms, Corolla archaeologica principi Gustavo Adolpho dedicata* (Lund, 1932) 1-16.

embroidered on them. Echard stated that he had seen a chronicle compiled about 1220-70, containing names of various authors used by Anni, among them Berosus.[1] Lathbury's Pseudo-Berosus lends credit to Echard; he suggests that medieval forgeries under the name of the Babylonian chronicler were in circulation. Anni must be held responsible for his particular forgery; but it seems now that Echard was right in thinking that he had medieval precedents. He was less preposterously original than it might appear.

A chapter in Josephus, *Antiquities of the Jews*, supplies the key to another of Lathbury's favourites. Josephus tells us that Hiram king of Tyre sent to King Solomon tricky riddles and enigmatic sayings; Solomon was clever enough to solve them all. Menander, says Josephus, 'who translated the Tyrian records from the Phoenician language into Greek speech, also mentions these two kings'. According to Menander they sent each other riddles and each paid a fine if he could not answer his correspondent's.[2] A rich literature accumulated round 'the wisdom of Solomon'; so it is not surprising that Lathbury should have found a book called 'Menander' on the riddles of Kings Hiram and Solomon. *De figuris regum Hiram et Salomonis* by Pseudo-Menander was a collection of riddles, divided into books, parts and chapters. The riddles began: 'Si legis, lege!' They ranged from questions concerning natural science, such as why those mountains most exposed to sunshine are the most damp and fertile, to the mutability of human affairs. Lathbury tries to answer them himself, giving them a moral or allegorical significance; the mountains represent the souls of the righteous, burning in the rays of God's love. This suggests, though it does not prove, that Pseudo-Menander left his readers to guess at Solomon's answers.

Nor was medieval Jewry neglected. Lathbury quotes 'Rabi Salomon, de lege legenda' and uses it as an aid to Bible study. No work of this title is known to have been ascribed to the Jewish commentator Rashi (d. 1105). It consisted of some easily accessible rabbinic lore, but also contained a rhetorical passage, quite alien to Rashi's succinct style, where 'Rabi Salomon' accused the Greeks of mispronouncing *Alleluia* and the Latins of omitting the *s* in 'the holy name of our father Israel'. Pseudo-Rashi knew

---

[1] Q.E. 2, 4-7; *D.H.G.E.* 3 (1924) 383-6.   [2] *Antiqu.* viii, 5.

'just enough Hebrew to misread the language'. *De lege legenda* was obviously a forgery, not translated from the Hebrew, but originally composed in Latin. It was probably inspired by Nicholas of Lyre's *Postilla litteralis*, which had popularised the name and learning of the great Jewish commentator. A compendium of Hebrew lore of a showy but painless kind would enable teachers and preachers to quote 'Rabi Salomon' without knowing enough Hebrew to read him, and without even taking the trouble to study Lyre's quotations from him in the *Postilla litteralis*. Lathbury for one was taken in. He quotes Rabi Moses (Maimonides) and Pseudo-Rabi Salomon in the same breath, feeling sure that he has coupled together the twin lights of Jewish scholarship.

The gem of his collection was a book of pseudo-sibylline prophecies ascribed to 'Flaccianus'.[1] The historical Flaccianus was a friend of St Augustine and proconsul of Africa in 393. Augustine tells how Flaccianus, 'a distinguished, learned and eloquent man', showed him the sibylline prophecies of Christianity in a Greek manuscript and convinced him that they were genuine.[2] Among the pseudo-sibylline prophecies circulating in the middle ages was Pseudo-Bede on the Roman senators' dream. Pseudo-Bede's prophecy was assembled from various sources and originated in the eleventh century. His story goes that a hundred Roman senators all had the same dream on the same night. They saw nine suns in the sky, each sun having a different appearance. They reported to the emperor Trajan, who fetched the Erythrean sibyl to Rome in order that she might interpret the dream. She explained that the nine suns signified the nine ages of the world.[3] Pseudo-Flaccianus took up Pseudo-Bede and made a vast elaboration. He copied out Pseudo-Bede as his prologue and then gave the sibyl a number of visions, some based on the nine suns, others original. Her visions incorporate the stock features of pseudo-prophecy, natural disasters such as heat and drought and symbolic animals; a maiden tames a lion, which follows her round as a pet; a woman bewails the bitterness of her soul in a wilderness for seven nights. Other features are unusual. *Imagines* weave themselves into complicated patterns. The sibyl saw a glass image set 'in the valley of the

---

[1] B. Smalley, 'Flaccianus etc', op. cit.,   [2] *De civ. Dei*, xviii, 23.
[3] E. Sackur, *Sibyllinische Texte und Forschungen* (Halle, 1898) 117-77.

boxers'. It was large and comely and had the words *agyos oux* written on its breast in shiny gold letters. Lathbury was puzzled. He knew that *agyos* meant holy, but *oux* defeated him: Flaccianus did not explain what it meant. The original of the puzzling word may have been *aux* from the Arabic *awj*, meaning apogee. A mixture of Greek and Arabic would have increased the mystery of the vision.[1] Voices sounded from above, from below and from all sides, questioning the image as to what it was, where it came from, and so forth.

A later vision showed the glass image surrounded by six others. Each of the six varied in its composition according to its provenance: a starry image came from heaven, an iron one from earth, a fiery one from the east, an airy one from the west, a watery one from the south and an earthen one from the north. Each in turn cried out against the glass image in their midst, addressing it with a command; each command began with the cry 'Alpha', followed by a word beginning with *a*. This vision was one of a series, seen by the sibyl on seven successive days or nights. Lathbury does not quote them all, but he has told us enough to indicate the extraordinary fancy which could devise seven times six *imagines* in addition to the first one, made of glass.

Both prophets and pseudo-prophets generally prophesy against someone or something. The medieval sybil became a mouthpiece for religious and political propaganda. It would be strange if Pseudo-Flaccianus had been an exception; he must surely have intended his sibyl to denounce the Pope or a king or emperor according to his point of view. Indeed, it is hard to see what else could have moved him to take so much trouble over his forgery. *De visionibus sibille* was not suitable for preaching as were *De secretis Virgilii* and *De bellis Armenie*. The good Lathbury, however, chose to quote only passages which could be taken as predicting the spread of Christianity. His attitude of devout admiration for the forgery prevents us from finding out its true purpose. Nor does he help us to guess at the date. It was probably early fourteenth-century, since it is not quoted except by Lathbury, as far as we know. The use of *imagines* also points

---

[1] The *aux* is one of the two points of the elliptic orbit of a planetary body, at which it is respectively at its greatest or least distance from the body about which it revolves; see Roger Bacon, *Opus maius* IV, iv, 4, ed. J. H. Bridges I (Oxford, 1900) 137, quoted by A. Altamura in a note to *Philobiblon* 145.

to the period of their vogue in preaching. Some *exempla* collection may have suggested them to the forger. Lathbury, however, saw *De visionibus sibille* as coming straight from St Augustine's Africa. He refers to it reverently. The holy sibyl spoke more subtly than he could grasp, as 'Flaccianus', writing in beautiful figures, recorded in his book on her visions.[1]

One more forgery must be mentioned, though it does not belong to Lathbury's collection. Another Pseudo-Flaccianus appears in connexion with a *Gesta grecorum*. The original book is not known to have survived; but certain *exempla* in fourteenth-century compilations are ascribed to 'Flaccianus in gestis grecorum'.[2] *Gesta grecorum* must have been modelled on the highly successful *Gesta romanorum*. The forger went one better by assuming an ancient name instead of leaving his book anonymous. St Augustine's learned proconsular friend could read Greek, as the saint clearly indicates. Who had more qualifications to compile a *Gesta grecorum*? This forger may have borrowed the name from the writer of Lathbury's *De visionibus sibille*, or he may have been the same person, writing as moralist instead of pseudo-prophet. He raises the same kind of problem as Pseudo-Fulgentius.

The two books ascribed to Flaccianus make a fine climax to my list of *spuria*. Each marks the highest peak of absurdity in its own *genre*. *De visionibus sibille* is the strangest of Lathbury's collection of forgeries; no more need be claimed for it. *Gesta grecorum* brings the preacher's contempt for pedantic accuracy to its extremest degree: the Carthaginians, surprised at their defeat by the Romans, sent to the oracle at Delphi to ask the reason. The reply being too oracular for them, they asked Duke Hannibal to go to Rome and fetch the poet Virgil. He did so and Virgil interpreted the oracle in the light of verses which had been written on the gates of Carthage![3]

---

[1] E, 2, D; 58, A.

[2] P. Lehmann, *Pseudo-antike Literatur des Mittelalters* (Leipzig, 1927) 25-6; B. Smalley, Flaccianus, op. cit. 554-6. It is an open question whether either or both Pseudo-Flacciani should be connected with the Flaccus Africanus quoted in medieval treatises on astrology as the author of a treatise on seven herbs related to the seven planets; see L. Thorndike, Engraved Astrological Images, *Melanges Auguste Pelzer* (Louvain, 1947) 243.

[3] A late addition to Walter Map's *De nugis curialium*, ed. M. R. James (Oxford, 1914) 260-61. It is ascribed to *Flaccianus in historiis carthaginensium* here, and in a slightly different form to *Flaccianus in gestis grecorum* in a fourteenth-century *exempla* collection; see Herbert, 3, 179.

Lathbury found nothing new in the way of classical texts, but he enriches our knowledge of forgeries. That he saw no difference between them will reflect on his scholarship and on his taste, but not on his zeal and curiosity. He collected as keenly as any humanist. His takings in the hunt for books show painfully how far the paths of northern and southern learning had diverged. Petrarch could talk and write to Richard de Bury: Lathbury would have struck him as childish.

CHAPTER X

COMMENTATORS AND PREACHERS IN FRANCE

> ... in sermonem huiusmodi rex prorupit, "Inter
> cetera vero regna de Francia quoque nil dicetur!"
> Statimque subiungens, "Et nos certe panem," inquit,
> "habemus et vinum et gaudium."
>
> Gerald of Wales, *De instructione principum* iii, 30
> (Rolls Series, 8, 318).

THE comparison to be attempted in this and in the next chapter will be narrow in scope. To study the history of early humanism in general would tax the strength of a giant. The question to be considered is whether interest in the classics took the same form in French and Italian schools as it did in English. Here its typical though not its happiest medium was *moralitates*. The friar doctors of France and Italy offer ground for comparison, since they too produced *moralitates* in plenty. Did they insert as many quotations from classical or pseudo-classical authors? If not, what other kind of illustration of their teaching did they choose? Paris, Avignon, Bologna, Florence and Padua seem to have been the main centres of production. A distinction between France and Italy will of course be arbitrary: the mendicant Orders worked on an international plane; friars travelled over Christendom and mixed at Avignon. But the material demands a distinction of some sort to make it tractable. My survey is impressionist and incomplete in any case. Nevertheless, certain conclusions emerge from it. *Moralitates* fall into three main types, if we include the English classicising type. They make an overall pattern without corresponding exactly to regional divisions or to divisions between Orders.

I shall begin with the Franciscans and start at the top of the ladder. There are two French doctors and cardinals: Vital du Four (d. 1327) and Bertrand de la Tour (d. 1332). Vital studied at Paris, but taught at Montpellier 1295-96 and then at Toulouse.[1] His *Speculum morale totius*

---

[1] Stegmüller, no. 8309. P. Glorieux, Maîtres franciscains régents à Paris. Mise au point, *Rech. Théol.* 18 (1951) 329-32.

sacrae Scripturae was finished in 1305 and probably belongs to his teaching period, since he did not serve as Provincial for Aquitaine until two years later. The *Speculum* resembles the *Summa* of John Bromyard in being a compendium for the use of preachers arranged as *distinctiones* on words listed in alphabetical order. Vital illustrates his *distinctiones* by scriptural texts, which he generally expounds in a moral sense; the *Speculum*, therefore, consists largely of *moralitates* arranged as a dictionary. The number of surviving manuscripts prove that it was thought to be useful; it even ran to five printed editions.

Vital offers a good example of an ambivalent attitude to secular learning. He says of *Doctores* that they need a little in order to refute error *ex propriis*, but he criticises them for seeking too much. Devotion, he says, is better than learning. Yet a little further on he tells them to imitate the bee in sucking honey from suitable flowers, quoting from Macrobius, Seneca and Virgil. The four animals of Ezechiel's vision represent the four parts of philosophy which serve the study of Scripture.[1] Vital tells a few stories from the lives and sayings of philosophers,[2] as well as quoting from classical sources. One 'howler' in bibliography exposes his scholarship. A famous story, the pirate's answer to King Alexander, had reached the middle ages in two versions. The shorter was told by St Augustine in *De civitate Dei* (iv, 4), the longer by John of Salisbury in *Policraticus* (iii, 14); John either found it in a lost source or expanded the shorter version himself. Medieval moralists noted the difference. Robert Holcot, for instance, gives the story according to St Augustine and adds that it is told in *Policraticus* more fully.[3] Vital had correct references for the two versions of the tale, but he thought that St Augustine had read it in *Policraticus*![4] John of Salisbury's book was often quoted by its title or sub-title, *De nugis philosophorum*, without the author's name. Vital must have used a compilation and supposed that *De nugis philosophorum* was an ancient work.

---

[1] ed. Venice (1600), foll. 114-16, 120v.
[2] foll. 113v, 159, 194, 237. A saying of St Francis is quoted, fol. 297. Vital is fond of St Bernard and Pseudo-Dionysius.
[3] Sap. lect. iii, p. 12.
[4] *Speculum morale*, ed. cit., fol. 127: Unde sicut recitat Augustinus, iv de civitate Dei, cap. 4, et accipit de tertio libro de nugis philosophorum. . . .
I checked the edition from a good fourteenth-century manuscript copy MS Oxford, Bodl. Laud. misc. 255, fol. 159ra.

R

His picture of St Augustine thumbing the pages of *Policraticus* in search of *exempla* is very engaging.

Bertrand de la Tour was a more outstanding personality than Vital. His teaching at Paris won him the title of *doctor famosus*. After his regency, 1311-12, he followed Vital as Provincial of Aquitaine, and was promoted to be an archbishop and then a cardinal, 1320-23. He died in 1332. As a compatriot and protégé of John XXII Bertrand was intimately involved in the struggle against the rebel Franciscans; he had the fame of a great agent of the Papacy as well as of a Paris doctor.

His *Summa* of sermons and *collationes* for the liturgical year had more success than any other contemporary work of the kind, judging by the number of manuscript copies, of early editions and of abridgments and excerpts. John Lathbury quoted it.[1] Bertrand finished the *Summa* before 1327 and it goes back to his regency, at least in part.[2] The notice in the *Histoire littéraire* gives it low marks: 'morne suite de citations encastrées dans le grillage de l'argumentation.' Further, it is said to have no personal touch and no originality of content; Bertrand refuses to commit himself on any of the burning questions of the hour. How to explain the success of so wretched a book? Considering his delicate position *vis à vis* his Order and the Papacy, his refusal to discuss controversial questions was natural. The *Summa* may have succeeded by reason of its essentially 'safe' character. Other factors suggested in the notice are its pedagogical qualities, its completeness and its convenient arrangement. The last two points are convincing. A preacher with access to the *Summa* would find himself armed with one or more discourses for any day of the year, easily turned up by reference to the liturgical cycle. A smaller collection of sermons for the dead, which circulated separately, illustrates still more clearly the comprehensive nature of Bertrand's plan.[3] Its

---

[1] B. Smalley, Flaccianus, op. cit.

[2] *H.L.F.* 36, 202-3; Glorieux, no. 349. MS Toulouse 326 seems to represent a version close to the original lectures. It is a scholastic type of book; the title is: Incipit postilla super evangelia dominicalia et ferialia totius anni compilata per fratrem Bertrandum de Turre [*sic*] O.F.M. sacre theologie doctorem.
It therefore dates from before his cardinalate. The exposition takes the form of a commentary rather than of sermons, though it already follows the liturgical year. The versions in MSS Toulouse 327-8 look like later stages of revision, where the commentary has been worked into sermon form. There are still other versions. The sermons on the Epistles, MSS Toulouse 324-5, seem to represent the same stage as MSS 327-8 on the Gospels.

[3] MS Bodl. Laud. misc. 410, foll. 95-113v.

possessor could preach from it on All Souls Day and at the funeral of any great person, ecclesiastical or secular, theologian or jurist. He had a sermon for the funeral of a great lady, whether countess or abbess (though said to be more appropriate for an abbess), who had befriended some particular religious Order or convent. The commoner is not forgotten. One sermon is for the death of 'any good woman', more especially if her name were Mary.[1]

However, it seems that something more is needed to explain Bertrand's popularity as a homilist. He must have appealed to certain circles by reason of his consistency and singleness of purpose. He states his intention at the very beginning of the volume on the Gospels. He will expound the Gospels for the year according to the use of St Gregory and of the Roman Church, not in ornate speech, but in raw homilies for the benefit of simple folk.[2] And he keeps his word. He introduces no light relief, apart from an occasional homely comparison. Classical lore is shunned. He makes sparing use of *exempla* of any sort. *Moralitates* occur, as they would in any fourteenth-century sermons, but they are traditional in make and do not wander far away from the text to be expounded; he has them well under control. At the same time he links his teaching to the liturgy of the Roman Church, as he is careful to explain. A preacher who would make no concession to secular tastes, but wanted to ground his flock in the faith, as the liturgy gave him occasion, would find a safe guide in the *Summa*. It is heavy going, but only a genius, which Bertrand was not, can make puritanism other than drab.

He stuck to his principles even when preaching to the scholars of Paris. An isolated sermon has survived, given 'at Paris in the Minorites' convent to the scholars on the feast of St Clement'.[3] The scholars heard an address on the virtue of clemency, with no trimmings. Bertrand, therefore, set the seal of his authority as a great doctor and churchman

---

[1] foll. 107v-110.

[2] MS Toulouse 326, fol. 1va: . . . non sermone falerato, sed rudibus omeliis ad utilitatem simplicium exposituri sumus evangelia singulis dominicis et temporibus secundum ordinationem beati Gregorii et sacrosancte ecclesie ordinarium. . . .

[3] MS Oxford, Bodl. 46 (1877) foll. 298ra-299rb. The title is: 'Sermo factus Parisius in domo minorum scolaribus in festo beati Clementis per fratrem B' de Turre.' The sermon has been written on a blank page of the manuscript in a fourteenth-century hand; see Glorieux, no. 349, i, 3. As Bertrand is called simply 'frater', the sermon must belong to his regency or earlier.

on a type of morality which we may classify as 'plain'. It avoids jokes and pagan fables in practice as well as in theory. It stands at the opposite pole to the classicising type found in England.

Then we have an Apocalypse-commentary by a successor of Vital and Bertrand as Provincial of Aquitaine. Dominique de Bartha was lector at the Franciscan *studium* at Avignon in January 1333.[1] He taught theology in the Order continuously for thirty years; apart from his lectorship at Avignon, we do not know where. Later in 1333 he was appointed Provincial of Aquitaine. He died while still holding the office in September 1342 at Montpellier, when returning from the Curia.[2] He was remembered for his 'welcome postill on the Apocalypse'.[3] This survives in one copy only, so far as is known.[4] It belonged to the Franciscans of Santa Croce and is now in the Laurentian Library at Florence. Dominique gave his commentary as a lecture course[5] some time after 1319, since he quotes the *Compendium litteralis sensus* of Pierre Auriol,[6] and presumably before he became Provincial in 1333. He intended it especially for the consolation and instruction of his dear brethren, the sons of St Francis.[7] They

[1] The Inquisitor at Avignon consulted him on January 17 with other theologians in connexion with the case against Thomas Waleys; he was then lector at Avignon; *Le procès* 118.

[2] *Chronica XXIV Generalium Ordinis Minorum, Analecta franciscana* 3 (Quaracchi, 1897) 505, 537. He appointed procurators for his Province in a document dated February 24, 1339; F. M. Delorme, Les Cordeliers dans le Limousin, *Arch. Fr. Hist.* 32, 1939, 256.

[3] *Chronica XXIV Generalium*, ed. cit., 537: Qui XXX annis continuis in Ordine legerat theologiam et fecit gratam postillam super Apocalypsim.
The *Compendium chronicarum, Arch. Fr. Hist.* 3 (1910), 298, expands the notice: . . . qui in sacra Theologia eruditis, 30 annis continuis super Sententias legit et scripsit, et gratam postillam super Apocalipsim fecit, et alia plurima dictavit.
No works other than the postill on the Apocalypse survive, though Dominique de Bartha could hardly have taught theology for thirty years without leaving some writing on the *Sentences*.

[4] Stegmüller, no. 2163.

[5] MS Florence, Laurent. Plut. XII. dext. 11, fol. 1ra: . . . liber Apocalipsis, cuius lecture habemus intendere, . . . ; fol. 2ra . . . in presenti volumine, cuius lecture habemus intendere, Christo duce, . . .

[6] fol. 7ra: Docet namque decem modis scriptura sacra disciplinam Dei, sicut in suo scripturarum compendio ponit ille venerabilis doctor P.
fol. 101rb: . . . Et ideo sto cum sensu litterali secundum dominum P.
fol. 116rb: . . . et ideo sicut prius secundum dominum P. compendium [sic] est littera exposita.
On the date and editions of Pierre Auriol's *Compendium litteralis sensus totius sacre Scripture*, see Glorieux, no. 351(h).

[7] foll. 227vb-228ra: Utique vobis carissimis meis fratribus, patris beati Christi vexiferi, pauperis Francisci, filiis, ad quorum consolationem et aliqualem eruditionem specialiter ego ineruditus volui laborare, vobis opto ego gratiam domini nostri Iesu Christi, etc.

must have welcomed it, as the chronicler implies that they did, for the very reason that it was safely non-controversial. This was all the more acceptable in a commentary on the Apocalypse. Joachite speculation had made St John's revelations dangerous to handle. The lecturer walks warily in explaining the literal sense. Armed with his *Compendium*, he tries to distinguish it from the spiritual, but sometimes gives up the attempt, exclaiming: 'God only knows!'[1] However, the literal exposition need not keep us. Its interest is that it shows an orthodox and not very incisive mind.

Dominique imitates Bertrand in providing *moralitates* of a plain and humourless kind. The absence of jokes and fables does not clear the commentary of foreign bodies. The Franciscan pushes to its furthest limits the practice of inserting themes for sermons. His lectures consisted of a set of rhetorical pieces arranged in the framework of the commentary, just as Thomas Waleys' consisted of *exempla* in the same framework. Both developed a current fashion to absurdity. Dominique's themes, moreover, tend to slide over the borderline between purely religious and ceremonial or official occasions. There are themes for sermons on St Francis and on St Louis of Toulouse, academic themes, such as *principia* and thanksgiving for the end of term, themes for the reception of a novice and for a great man's funeral, a *collatio* in defence of the faith when heretics are condemned, and a farewell address, to be given when some notable person leaves a college or a concourse of people among whom he has dwelt.[2]

Pope Benedict XII (1334-42) introduced the use of *collationes* at the Curia in ceremonies for the reception of legates and the creation of cardinals.[3] His well-meant effort to give curial procedure a more spiritual tone favoured just the kind of development to be seen in Dominique's commentary. It points the way to a treatise on clerical rhetoric of the type found in MS Paris, Bibl. nat. lat. 2584, foll. 166ra-192vb:[4] *Tractatus brevis quo datur sapienti occasio proponendi cum*

---

[1] fol. 138ra: Utrum autem hic sit sententia litteralis Deus novit, quia nec hic nec alibi in toto illo libro postillando ipsum [sic] intendo pertinaciter defendere, nec volo esse defensor pertinax, sed recitator compendii supradicti.

fol. 163ra: Si sit intellectus et sensus litteralis huius littere novit Deus.

fol. 168rb: Si iste sit sensus litteralis huius textus novit Deus, quoniam hic liber est mortalibus satis occultus.

[2] Appendix i, 344.   [3] *H.L.F.* 37, 521.

[4] Italian, fourteenth century; see Ph. Lauer, *Bibl. nat. cat gén. des MSS latins* 2 (Paris, 1940) 531-2.

gratia oportuna negotia cum responsis dignis. The writer addresses himself to ecclesiastical diplomats, sent on missions concerning church business, such as collecting tenths and negotiating with secular rulers on all kinds of matters. He advises them always to begin a speech with some scriptural texts; nothing makes a better impression, as he calls on St Bernard to witness.[1] Several of Dominique's themes would fit well into such a treatise.

The unctuous tone of his commentary makes them stand out from their background in bizarre contrast. The effect is almost as comic as when Thomas Waleys brings the labours of Hercules to bear on the psalmist's prayer. Rejection of fables in favour of 'plain' *moralitates* gave no guarantee of relevance.

Guiral Ot gives us an opportunity to compare 'figures' invented by a Franciscan for use in preaching and meditation with Holcot's 'pictures'. Ot was another Friar Minor of Aquitaine. He is said to have been a bachelor before 1315, but did not read the *Sentences* at Paris until 1326. At some stage in his career he taught at Toulouse before being appointed Minister General of the Order to replace the rebel Michele da Cesena on June 10, 1329. Guiral Ot is remembered best as a supporter of orthodoxy against the Spirituals in the period of the Franciscan revolt. Clement VI raised him to be patriarch of Antioch and gave him the revenues of the church of Catania in Sicily on November 27, 1342. He died there of the plague in 1349.[2] His *Figure* survives in the Paris manuscript, Bibl. nat. lat. 590 (foll. 1-73) which also contains a copy of Holcot's *Moralitates* and of the treatise on virtues and vices, *Prudentia depingebatur;* the *Figure* was evidently felt to belong to the same genre. It was indeed a current type. The phrase *una figura brevis predicabilis* crops up in contemporary commentaries, in

---

[1] fol. 166ra-b: Ea propter presenti memoriali cogitam inserere auctoritates scripture cum processibus paucis et brevibus, que possunt valere ad talia. Nichil enim prorsus tam reddit gratifica proponentis intenta et sua verba tunc proponenda, sicut verba sapienter assumpta et ordinate premissa de veneranda scriptura, cuius propositum omnino est auctoritatem prestare, negotio gratiam prebere eloquio et efficatiam parare proposito, sicut habetur in libro Proverbiorum, xxii, et aliis multis locis. Nichil etiam tam manifestam facit veritatem, sicut, premissa scripture auctoritate congruente, materia brevis et pura ad propositum propositio, sicut dicit beatus Bernardus, primo De consideratione.'

It is not clear to which passage of the *De consideratione* the writer alludes; he may merely mean that St Bernard was a good stylistic model.

[2] *H.L.F.* 36, 203-25; Stegmüller, no. 2466.

Dominique de Bartha's for instance.[1] We do not know when Ot assembled his 'figures', except that it was probably not in the last seven years of his life.[2]

His biographer in the *Histoire littéraire* prints an excerpt and breaks off in disgust: 'Mais nous n'avons pas, en vérité, le courage de continuer.' Tediously involved the *Figure* may be, but some items in it show an attempt to stimulate the visual imagination. The fourth 'figure' recommends the rainbow as a subject of meditation for the devout soul at Christmastide. The bow of the Old Testament promise prefigures the Nativity:

> 'The devout soul must envisage and try to contemplate mentally as if in riddles many things in the most holy canon at the Nativity of Our Lord Jesus Christ. . . . Know that this arch is God's blessed Son, appearing in the flesh to whomsoever contemplates devoutly. The arch is coloured, figured, brought forth and shown forth. . . .'[3]

Figure no. 11 concerns the 'image of memory'. Seven points are to be commended. There are seven methods of producing a likeness: Nature uses propagation, painting colours, sculpture carvings, impress seals, stamping dies, designing sand, reflection mirrors.[4] Ot moralises the seven methods. Like Holcot he plays with the idea of artistic representation, but timidly, and wholly avoiding classicism.

We must go to the bottom of the Franciscan ladder to find moralised fables. French preachers owed their *Ovide moralisé* to an anonymous Friar Minor. He wrote at the request of a Queen Jeanne, who was probably the wife of Philip V,

---

[1] MS Laurent. Plut. XII dext. 11, fol. 92va: De isto textu posset colligi una figura brevis predicabilis, quia in toto textu isto pro sensui mistico colligendo occurrit meditandum.

[2] MS lat. 590, fol. 73: Expliciunt figure fratris Gerardi Odonis sacre pagine professoris de ordine fratrum minorum necnon ministri quondam generalis eorum.
This may indicate that the *Figure* belongs to the period before November 27, 1342, since the title of patriarch is not mentioned.

[3] ibid., foll. 14-15: Incipit figura quarta de incarnatione domini nostri Iesu Christi. Debet videre anima devota et attemptare contemplari in sacratissimo canone multa in nativitate domini nostri Iesu Christi. . . . Sciendum quod iste archus est benedictus Dei Filius apparens in carne cuilibet devote contemplanti, quo coloratur, figuratur, generatur, declaratur. . . .

[4] ibid., fol. 26: Incipit figura undecima de imagine memorie. Circa imaginem memorie septem sunt commendanda, ut luculenter apparet, que sunt videlicet: Natura, pictura, sculptura, impressura, percussura, collatura, speculatura, ut patet. Iste filiis, coloribus, sculptilibus, sigillis, monetariis, pulveribus, s(p)eculis.
There is no verb in the last sentence because the composition is schematic.

Jeanne de Bourgogne (d. 1329). His book can be dated 1316-28.[1] The translator-moralist must have had his superiors' permission to write, but it may be significant of their attitude to classical learning that we know so little about him: the Franciscans did not regard him as a star. His *Ovide moralisé* was popular, however. It may be noted in passing that he inserted 'pictures' of gods and goddesses in the mythographers' manner.[2]

We turn next to the Dominicans.[3] Jacques de Lausanne, Pierre de Baume and Armand de Belvézer bring us much closer to *moralitates* of the English type, with a significant difference. Jacques de Lausanne,[4] who took his name from his birthplace,[5] was the eldest of the three. He must have been adult in 1303, since he attended a chapter of the Order at Paris in that year. He was 'bachelarius biblicus' in July 1314. He received his master's degree in 1317 through the intervention of the king of France and the Pope. He became Provincial for France in 1318 and probably died about 1322, when another friar was appointed. Jacques had already made his name as a preacher when he was still *bachelarius biblicus*; his works most probably belong to this period of his life. He left sermons for Sundays and holy days and *moralitates* on many books of the Bible. The latter seem to represent excerpts from full commentaries. They circulated widely both as *moralitates* on the biblical text and as a *compendium moralitatum* in an abridged, alphabetical form.

Jacques proceeds as systematically as Bertrand de la Tour, but in the opposite sense. Whereas Bertrand is uniformly grave, Jacques, to quote the notice in the *Histoire littéraire*, 's'est fait un système d'être constamment jovial, même en discourant sur les choses qui prêtaient le moins à rire': he indulges in burlesque. The method he followed in reaching his end was to turn his *moralitates* on the text into an *exempla* collection. Many another commentator had introduced *exempla* into his *moralitates*. What distinguishes Jacques is that he excludes almost all other matter. We have a paral-

---

[1] Welter, p. 347, n. 5; J. Engels, *Etudes sur l'Ovide moralisé* (Groningen, 1943) 46-62.

[2] ibid. 69.

[3] Three commentators must be mentioned here as having left *moralitates* of a traditional type, neither classicising nor specialised in any other way: Nicholas of Lyre O.F.M., Dominique Grima O.P. and Pierre de la Palu O.P.

[4] *H.L.F.* 33, 460-79; Welter, 49, 385, 405; Stegmüller, no. 3887-3969.

[5] B. Smalley, Thomas Waleys O.P., p. 62, n. 13.

lel in Thomas Waleys' *Moralitates*, but Jacques de Lausanne's probably came first: he was teaching as a bachelor before 1317 and there is no proof that Waleys started at Oxford any earlier; his *Moralitates* may all belong to his Bologna lectorship in the mid 'twenties. Jacques may therefore have invented the new type of commentary.

The likeness in form and purpose between the two Dominicans only sharpens the contrast in their choice of sources. The Paris friar prefers natural history and bestiary lore, the herbal and lapidary, and travellers' tales. Animal stories please him since they lend themselves to shrewd comparisons between men and beasts. He supplements traditional stories by personal anecdotes and by his observations on everyday life. Thomas Waleys began in this way, but branched off later into exploration of the classics. Jacques' successors developed his style in a different direction. The Fleming, Michel du Four, who followed him at Paris in 1318, keeps to his technique.[1] Pierre de Baume and Armand de Belvézer go off on their own, each independently.

Pierre de Baume came from the same eastern border region as Jacques de Lausanne; he made his profession at Besançon. Like Jacques he made himself useful in the Order as a preacher and administrator rather than as a scholar.[2] He was assigned to read the *Sentences* at Paris in 1322, and had the title of master on March 7, 1325.[3] The Chapter at Dijon, 1333, appointed him Provincial of France. In this capacity he preached a sermon at the papal court at Avignon.[4] He was appointed vicar to the Master General of the Order in 1342 and Master General in the following year. He died on March 1, 1345. Apart from the sermon at Avignon, he left a lecture-commentary on Proverbs, given while he was 'bachelarius biblicus' and before the canonisation of St Thomas, July 18, 1323, lecture-commentaries on three of the Gospels, probably dating from his regency,

---

[1] Above, p. 133, n. 1.

[2] *H.L.F.* 36, 180-90; Stegmüller, no. 6735-6741.

[3] A sermon in MS Paris, nat. lat. 14799, fol. 147ra, is headed: Dominica 2 adventus et fuit festum beati Nicolai, a fratri I de Palma O.P. The 'I' is probably a mistake for 'P'. The feast of St Nicholas, December 6, fell on the second Sunday of Advent in 1321, 1327 and 1332. 1327 seems to be the most probable year. A more detailed study of the collection might decide; it might also tell us whether the 'P. de Pal' ', mentioned in the titles of other sermons, is Petrus de Palma or Petrus de Palude.

[4] T. Kaeppeli, Predigten am päpstlichen Hof von Avignon, *Arch. FF. Praed.* 19 (1949) 389.

1325 or soon after, and some undated homilies. The lectures on Proverbs include brief notes on the literal sense, but are mainly *moralitates*; those on the Gospels consist of *moralitates* excerpted from what were originally full commentaries.[1] Langlois in the *Histoire littéraire* notes the resemblance between Pierre de Baume and Jacques de Lausanne. The younger Dominican probably came to Paris too late to attend his senior's lectures; but he must have drawn his inspiration from reading them and have taken them as a recipe for popular preaching.

His lectures show no interest in the classics. Two texts of Proverbs would have sent the English friars yelping down the trail: *in acervum Mercurii* (xxvi, 8) and *cum senatoribus terrae* (xxxi, 23). De Baume explains them as shortly as was necessary for an understanding of the sense.[2] He has the same leaning to animal lore as Jacques de Lausanne, and produces startling effects, as when he compares Jesus' cry from the Cross to the peacock's cry.[3] His approach is more personal, however; he feels that he has a contribution to make: the *pauperes moderni doctores*, following the *maiores*, could still expound some things in Scripture by their own talents.[4] He explains the Gospel in current terms, comparing St Matthew, receiving his mission to write, with a schoolmaster's deputy, a newly made knight, and a jurist who is given a book in token of his doctorate. Martha and Mary, types of the active and contemplative life, signify two sorts of brethren in a convent. Martha represents 'the administration'. Obedientiaries must not domineer over the others nor *vice versa*. All must behave as children of one Master and of one mother, their Rule.[5]

Illustrations from everyday life become more closely observed. De Baume exploits the interest we all take in eating and drinking. The taverner gives leavened bread and salt meat to his customers free of charge to make them

---

[1] Pierre de Baume showed his interest in the literal sense by acquiring postills of Nicholas Lyre for his Order; *H.L.F.* 36, 361.

[2] MS Eton College 79, fol. 67v: Mercurius deus est mercatorum secundum gentiles; fol. 84v: Senatores a senatu et diurnitate temporis dicti sunt, et fuerunt primo electi a Romulo custodes et provisores reipublice.

Probably from Huguccio, *Magnae derivationes*, MS Oxford, Bodl. e Mus. 96, p. 377.

[3] Because it drives off poisonous animals; MS Bâle B.V.6, fol. 37vb. De Baume mentions Holy Week services in his account of the Passion (fol. 37ra), but most of the matter is in a light vein.

[4] ibid. fol. 24vb.   [5] Latin texts, appendix i, 344-5.

thirsty, so that he can sell more wine. It is wasteful to crumble bread with one's fingers; better use a knife. We read of wine, vintners, viticulture, savoury smells from the kitchen, good and bad digestions, cheesemaking and barrels brought up from the cellar.[1] A lily in a window pot, which needs watering often, makes a pleasant touch.[2] We go shopping. Drapers dress their windows with fine pieces to deceive us, but make us buy inside in the dark and won't allow us to bring their goods to the light; so we buy coarse instead of fine cloth.[3] We pass castles with narrow little windows and wary porters and through toll-gates built by princes. We enter the hall and see paintings which display arms of beaten enemies and Saracens falling in battle with Christians. We visit the fairs of Champagne[4] and the Paris schools, where we watch the rector's election and hear the master coaching his favourite pupil for responsions. De Baume hands out sound advice: read only one book at a time; don't let dissension arise in a college because someone wants to be promoted over the heads of other members; clip his wings. Our friar knows human nature: a father gives his son a good hiding, but protects him against anyone else who tries to beat him. He takes us to the deathbed of a lawyer who told Brother Pierre de la Palu (a contemporary) that he trusted to one good deed to save his soul; he handled the case of a poor client against a great clerk, who was trying to disinherit him, and won it.[5]

Reading his lectures, one soon comes to like the sensible, wideawake friar. His unpublished sermons show him distributing the same salty lessons, lavishly sprinkled with popular proverbs; he preached just as he lectured.[6]

Armand de Belvézer was a Provençal from the neighbourhood of Millau.[7] There is no record of his having taken a degree or studied at Paris, though he may have been there; he refers to it as a small city in proportion to the number of

---

[1] MS Bâle B.V.6, foll. 1va, 2ra, 2va, 3ra, 8ra, 8vb; MS Bâle B. IX. 21, fol. 116v; *H.L.F.* 36, 187.
[2] MS Eton College 79, fol. 24.
[3] ibid. fol. 49v: Vendentes vero pannos parant fenestras pulchris pannis, ut tollant iudicium visus ementium, et vendunt in tenebris, nec permittunt pannos portari ad lucem, et dum illi credunt emere pannum bonum et subtilem, dum veniunt ad lucem, inveniunt quod emerunt pannum grossum et rudem.
[4] ibid. foll. 26v-27v; *H.L.F.* 36, 187-8. [5] Appendix i, 345.
[6] MS Paris, Bibl. nat. lat. 14799, foll. 147ra-149rb, 177ra. Two of his remarks on contemporary preaching have been quoted above, 33, 42-3.
[7] *H.L.F.* 36, 265-95; Stegmüller, no. 1430-32, 1.

inhabitants.[1] We hear of him first in 1313, when Clement V sent him to Lombardy on an embassy to the Emperor Henry VII. He was lector at the Dominican convent at Montpellier in 1326. In this year John XXII granted him the title and licence of master in theology and promoted him to be lector at the papal university at Avignon, a post at this time normally held by a Dominican.[2] It was an uncomfortable chair in the period of the beatific vision controversy. John XXII inevitably consulted his *lector sacri palatii* on the nineteen propositions extracted from the works of Thomas Waleys and impugned as heretical. Armand was charged under threat of excommunication to examine them and to give his opinion before Christmas (1333). A committee of theologians had already pronounced against their orthodoxy in September; hence Armand found himself caught between the Pope on one side and his own Order on the other. He did his best for his fellow Dominican by putting a favourable interpretation on the impugned propositions wherever possible, stating that he based his opinion on 'authorities such as St Thomas Aquinas'.[3] The irony here, which would not have been lost on John XXII, was that the Pope himself had canonised St Thomas and had supported his doctrine. A new man had been appointed to the lectorship by about November 1, 1334. Armand may have fallen ill; but John XXII did not like opposition. Armand's predecessor had been promoted to a bishopric. Armand, unrewarded, must have ended his life quietly in some house of his Order. The rubric of his commentary on St Matthew reads: . . . *lectura cum postillis Magistri Armandi, quondam lectoris sacri palatii.*[4] It sounds as though the original rubric had been written when Armand was still living, but retired from his chair. We hear nothing more of him.

The writings of Armand which interest us here are his lectures on a part of the Psalter, reported from his teaching at Avignon in 1328, a set of sermons and *collationes*, also deriving

---

[1] He compares Bethlehem to Paris in commenting on Mt. ii, 6: *Et tu Bethlehem . . . minima es*; MS Uppsala 7522, fol. 14: . . . potius laudatur locus, ut si dicerem de villa Parisiensi quod esset parva civitas respectu inhabitantium, qui ibi sunt multi, tunc magis commendarem ipsam respectu numerorum magnorum.

This may well have been a conventional comparison and does not necessarily indicate a personal knowledge of Paris.

[2] On the papal university see R. Creytens, Le *studium Romanae Curiae* et le maître du sacré Palais, *Arch. FF. Praed.* 12 (1942) 1-83.

[3] *Le procès*, 28-31.   [4] Stegmüller, no. 1432, 1.

from his teaching, but chosen by himself and dedicated to his compatriot, Cardinal Raymond de Mostuéjouls, soon after December 18, 1327,[1] and a recently discovered lecture-commentary on St Matthew.

Armand transposed the method of Jacques de Lausanne and of Pierre de Baume into his native idiom, quoting Provençal proverbs *in nostro vulgari* and referring to scenery, custom, flora and fauna of his country, *in terra mea*. Provençal patriotism has earned him better treatment in the *Histoire littéraire* than is meted out to his northern colleagues. He taught at a time when southern culture was giving way before northern penetration. A few lines preserved from troubadour songs, quotation from an otherwise unknown version of *Solomon and Marculf*, and local colour combine to make him 'un témoin aussi intéressant qu'interéssé de la civilisation du midi'. He writes of the snail and its habits 'in terms which recall La Fontaine'. In fact this is just the same type of natural history as we find in Jacques de Lausanne and in Pierre de Baume; Armand's snail has the distinction of being Provençal. Closer acquaintance shows him to be less shrewed and forceful than de Baume, dismissed as scarcely worth reading in the *Histoire littéraire*; but he handles pleasing matter pleasantly and takes his readers for a holiday in Provence. We see orange trees and towns perched on rocky hills; we negotiate windy mountain passes and a region noted for its savage dogs.[2] Armand tells his anecdotes of the country so vividly that one sees his gestures and hears the laughter of his audience.

[1] See the very full descriptions of the two Vatican MSS Borgh. 101 and 341 by A. Maier, Codices Burghesiani Bibliothecae Vaticanae, *Studi e testi* 170 (1952) 131-3, 386-9; for other MSS Stegmüller, no. 1432. Unfortunately the date 1328, found in the explicit of the *reportationes* in MS Borgh. 101, fol. 35, is given in the notice in *H.L.F.*, 273, as 1338, and this has given rise to the assumption that Armand was still living in 1338, for which there is no proof. The relationship between Armand's lectures, *quaestiones* and *collationes* on the Psalter needs sorting out. A complete record of his teaching on Scripture would also have to include his *Collatio super Scripturam sacram*, probably a *principium* or inaugural lecture, and his prologue to the Psalter; see Stegmüller, no. 1430-31. These are scholastic works which need not be considered here. The sermons and *collationes* were printed at Lyons, 1525, with the dedicatory letter. Since Armand writes to the Cardinal *in novitate vestre assumptionis* (fol. 3v), the date must be soon after his promotion at the consistory of December 18, 1327; he died on November 12, 1335; see Eubel, *Hierarchia*, etc., i, 15. The printed edition contains 98 *collationes*. Manuscript copies contain sometimes more and sometimes less; thus MS Borgh. 341 has only 42 and in a different order; for others not included in the edition, see *H.L.F.* 272-4.

[2] *Sermones etc* (Lyons, 1525) foll. 101, 104v, 108v-109; *H.L.F.*, extracts quoted 287-95.

His comparisons have a concreteness rarely surpassed even in fourteenth-century homilies. Preaching on the feast of St Thomas, 'God's close counsellor and secretary', he compares detractors to the donkey who tried to start a concert which would rival the nightingale's.[1] The feast of St Peter in Chains suggests a comparison between Christ and some great baron, who builds a fine church with a tall belfry beside it and furnishes it with bells. He then tests their notes and puts the best bell on top, just as Christ, when St Peter confessed him, saying *Thou art the Christ*, recognised his note as the deepest and best and set him over the other apostles. Someone might object, says Armand, that St Peter's note was not so good: he rang false and denied his Lord at the pull of one little servant girl. Armand answers that women in general, let alone servant girls, don't understand bell-ringing.[2] A *collatio pro mortuis* will illustrate his light touch and his use of proverbs. 'Every saint wants his candle': how much more does God, Holy of Holies, want candles and offerings? It is commonly said that 'St Giving' has entry everywhere. As priests never close the church door, but open gladly to those bringing gifts, so St Peter, *claviger ethereus*, opens to those who knock, when they bring the gifts of good deeds, and ushers them into God's presence with glory.[3] We seem to be dancing 'sur le pont d'Avignon'. Changes of mood only strengthen the illusion, since contrasts marked the gay society of the time. A sermon for All Souls Day shows Armand preaching under the influence of ideas associated with the Dance of Death and with the meeting between three living and three dead, so prominent in late medieval culture. He experiments with the macabre.[4]

Lectures on the Psalter and Gospel, delivered to the students of the papal university, might be expected to read more heavily than *collationes* and sermons. The Psalter-commentary at least is more sedate in tone and less transparently simple, though even here Armand uses proverbs and animal stories and applies familiar terms, *bursarius Dei* for

---

[1] *Sermones*, foll. 11v, 121.
[2] ibid. foll. 131v-132: . . . Respondeo: si ad pulsationem ad verbum unius ancille ista campana male sonuit, non est mirum, quia non dicam de uno ancilla, sed communiter mulieres nesciunt pulsare campanas, et ideo non est mirum si ancilla pulsante Petrus male sonuit, quia Petrum pulsare nescivit, immo nec ad eam pertinuit.
[3] ibid. fol. 112.   [4] *H.L.F.*, 285.

a generous man, for example.[1] The lecture course on St Matthew is fuller and throws new light on the author.[2] It seems to belong to the period of the beatific vision controversy, December 1331 to Armand's resignation of his chair before about November 1, 1334. The text *Blessed are the clean of heart: for they shall see God* (Mt. v, 8) forced him to touch on the subject, but he keeps off the problem raised by John XXII, saying openly that he will stop at this point.[3] Even to shelve the question, when lecturing at the Curia, implied disagreement with the Pope's view, and demanded courage.

This is a long commentary, including literal and moral exposition. The former interests us as showing that Armand was no classicist. Ancient history made no appeal to him: when the devil tempted Christ on the very high mountain by pointing out to him *all the kingdoms of the world* (iv, 8), Armand makes him say: 'That's the kingdom of the Romans and over there of the Franks, and so for the rest.'[4] The anachronism might serve as an illustration; it would have pained a purist like Thomas Waleys. Nor did Armand feel veneration for pagan philosophers. Instead of holding them up as examples to Christians, he says that *Blessed are the poor in spirit* (v, 3) excludes the 'vain' poverty of philosophers; Socrates despised money for study's sake, not for God's sake.[5] Armand's *moralitates* contain no *exempla* nor allusions drawn from the classics.

Light relief is again provided by proverbs taken from country lore: a foal will never carry a good load unless he learns to trot early. Armand applies this to the Holy Child, who had to carry the sins of mankind, and whose troubles

---

[1] MS Borgh. 101, foll. 3v, 68, 76.

[2] MS Uppsala 7522 (=U), written in several fourteenth-century hands, probably of North Germany or the Netherlands. A late hand has written across the top of fol. 1: Liber Bibliothecae Varmiensis (Ermeland, East Prussia). There are many marginal notes in various hands. Stegmüller, no. 1432, 1, transcribes the introductory note and incipits and explicit. I have read about half of this very long commentary in a microfilm, kindly sent by the Librarian.

[3] Appendix i, 346.

[4] U, fol. 39v: . . . sicut mundus totus poni solet in mappa, que est quedam pictura dicta mappa mundi; sed alii verius (dicunt), scilicet quod secundum diversas regiones et diversa regna monstravit, puta digito, ostendendo: ad partem illam est regnum romanorum, ibi francorum, et sic de aliis.
Armand is only repeating what he found in his sources, but he has not thought fit to alter them.

[5] U, fol. 53: . . . ut excludatur paupertas ficta, sicut in ypocritis, et vana, sicut in philosophis, secundum quod Socrates contempsit pecuniam propter studium et non propter Deum.

began early with the flight into Egypt; he and his Mother had to trot.[1] There are several good stories. One turns on a pun on the name of a judge called Burlata: he gave an unjust sentence and the lawyer said to him: *Burlata bene burlavit*, that is, 'has mocked us'. Armand tells it apropos of King Herod's anger at being tricked by the magi, adding that in this case the mockery came from the Holy Spirit.[2]

The precept against praying 'as the hypocrites do' (Mt. vi, 5) is illustrated by an elaborate 'framed' story. Armand is attacking those who pretend to pray in corners, but who choose places where they can be seen, so as to look humbler than if they were to pray in public. The 'frame' of the story is that a learned but ambitious man, hearing that a church had fallen vacant, went there and prayed, choosing corners where some of the brethren would be sure to pass, and remained standing, as though he wished to be inconspicuous. This made such an impression that some of the brethren in chapter said he would be a good man to have as their prelate: he was not only learned, but also, as they had seen, devout and humble, for they had seen him praying devoutly in secret. Thereupon, one who knew him better said that he wanted 'to sell them his donkey'. Here begins the inner story: a peasant wanted to sell a wretched old donkey, of no use whatsoever. He couldn't sell it in the market, because he looked so lecherous that nobody would trust him. At last he went to a fair in distant parts where he wasn't known. He chose a quiet corner near the market place, where many persons would be sure to pass him. There, standing by his donkey, he began to say his *Pater noster*, devoutly and somewhat raising his voice. In answer to a passer by, who questioned him, he said that he'd be glad to sell his donkey, but was so simple that he was afraid of being cheated in the market; nor did he wish to leave off his usual prayers until some good man should pass, who would pay him a fair price, without cheating. Meanwhile

---

[1] U, fol. 8v: *Dicitur vulgariter quod pullus natus de asino vel equo nisi mox trottet et etiam irascatur nunquam portabit bonum onus.* . . . *Mox in ortu suo scivit (Christus) trottare, nam tres reges ab oriente fecerunt et ipsum et matrem trottare cum magna festinantia.*
Armand used the same proverb for a sermon, *H.L.F.*, 283.

[2] U, fol. 17v: *Iratus est valde* et dicit(ur) *illusus* (MS illusum), non sicut dictum fuit de quodam iudice Burlata nomine, qui tulit iniquam sententiam. Ei dixit advocatus: Burlata bene burlavit, id est illusit: sed hec irrisio fuit per Spiritum sanctum.
Burlare and the Old French *borler* mean 'to mock'.

he kept repeating *Pater noster qui es in celis* and the rest.   The questioner was taken in, so much so that he paid twenty shillings for a donkey which was hardly worth five.   The peasant took his money, went off, and was never seen there again.   'And so', said the brother, 'this ambitious man aspires to our prelacy with his feigned simplicity.   He wants to "sell us his donkey".'

Armand agrees with the creator of Tartuffe:

> 'les plus beaux traits d'une sérieuse morale sont moins puissants, le plus souvent, que ceux de la satire; et rien ne reprend mieux la plupart des hommes que la peinture de leurs défauts.'

He had chosen the right fault to paint for an Avignon audience, accustomed to the scramble for preferment. Successful hypocrisy must have been the most hated vice. A moment's reflection will suggest that he had another reason for his choice of allusions.   The papal university assembled clergy from all over Latin Europe.   Residence in the *midi* was one of the few things they had in common.   He pointed to scenes which all could observe in their excursions out of town.   Armand also reproaches clerics who prefer preaching in towns rather than villages, unlike their Master: Jesus preached through *all Galilee* without respect to place.[1] By concentrating on rural themes the papal lector was equipping his pupils to preach to countryfolk.

Pierre de Baume and Armand de Belvézer developed the 'Lausanne' type of *moralitates* in the direction of the picaresque.   Not for them the pretty tale or 'picture' in its pseudo-classical setting or the weird visions of the sibyl. French realism confronted English romanticism.   De Baume had a background of French urban culture.   He preached to burghers whose *fabliaux* show a taste for broad, down-to-earth humour, and who enjoyed miracle plays specialising in street and tavern scenes: Cliquet, Pincedé, Rasoir and their successors diced and pitted their wits against dishonest innkeepers.[2]   De Belvézer adapted the manner to his native Provence.   Both resembled Robert Holcot in being novelists, but their novels are 'contemporary' instead of 'popular

---

[1] On Mt. iv, 23: *Et circuibat Iesus totam Galileam*, U, fol. 48v: Non per unum locum, sed ubique, sicut multi faciunt, qui libentius predicant in civitatibus quam in villis et plus apud pingues ecclesias quam apud pauperes; sed Christus sine loci acceptatione ivit per totam.

[2] See Grace Frank, *The Medieval French Drama* (Oxford, 1954).

S

historical'. Both recall Louis VII's modest saying, according
to Gerald of Wales: 'We French have bread and wine and
gladness as our portion.'

The French friars affected two types of *moralitates*, the plain
and the picaresque. The former relied on serious piety, the
latter agreed with the English classicising type in aiming
at entertainment. Franciscans preferred the plain type
and Dominicans the picarcsquc. Possibly rivalry between
the Orders led their members on to accentuate the contrast
and to reprove or shock their colleagues. Our textbook picture of jolly Franciscans and grave Dominicans has reversed
itself. Agonising conflicts among the sons of St Francis will
explain the sadness and fear of scandal which already drove
Pecham to forbid the preacher 'any mirth-provoking word'.
They could copy one aspect of their founder's character,
when they had to refuse his poverty. The English province
suffered from the quarrel much less. Hence Ridevall and
Lathbury after him made no fetish of bareness in their aids
to preaching. The Dominicans for their part, whether
French or English, enjoyed that freedom from inhibitions
which goes with unity of purpose. Both types of *moralitates*,
however, resemble each other and differ from the English classicising type in ignoring *paganica studia*.

If we venture outside our general terms of reference and
ask whether interest in the classics existed apart from
moralitates in the mendicant Orders, the answer seems to be
'No'. The *Ovide moralisé* is an exception and it goes no further
than popularisation. Vincent of Beauvais and Gilbert of
Tournai do not seem to have had successors in the early
fourteenth century.

Classicism appears around the middle of the century
in representatives of the old monastic Orders. Pierre Ceffons[1]
was a white monk of Clairvaux, who was studying at
the Cistercian college at Paris at the time of the Black
Death, 1348; he describes its horrors vividly. He returned to Clairvaux about 1353, after taking his bachelor's
degree in theology, but probably not as a fully fledged doctor.
Ceffons adds to the bewildering variety of fourteenth-
century classicism. He had an extravagant personality and
an urge to express himself. Obstacles such as snooping,
heresy-hunting, legalism and unnecessary regulations

---

[1] My information on Ceffons all comes from D. Trapp, Peter Ceffons of
Clairvaux, *Rech. Théol.* 24 (1957) 101-55.

aroused his fury. Personal characteristics apart, the fact that he belonged to a monastic rather than to a mendicant Order brought its own *nuance*. Cistercians contributed to scholastic theology at Paris; the austere monk who reigned as Pope Benedict XII (1334-42) left a long compilation on the Gospel of St Matthew.[1] Ceffons, therefore, was not peculiar in being a writer, though he had to defend himself for being a classicist. He had an advantage over the friars as a student of classical literature. They were tied to their 'dog Latin', being educators and popularisers. Ceffons composed rhetorical pieces for himself and a few monastic friends, casting his thoughts in the form of various letters and of a dream, which he describes. His essays in fine writing are hardly Ciceronian, but he tried to do more than quote copiously from the ancients. He seems to have distinguished between questions which could only be debated in current scholastic terminology and questions which had been discussed in ancient times. He explains jokingly that he would have liked to use rhetorical colours in his *Sentence*-commentary, combining logic with rhetoric. His friends advised him not to, and it would have made the whole thing too long. The expense of copying would have been prohibitive; it would have weighed enough to break the backs of Alexander's charger, Bucephalus, and Hector's Galatea, another famous war-horse. Problems discussed by the Stoics, on the other hand, could and should be argued in their own idiom. Ceffons apparently collected classical words and phrases and experimented with them:

> 'He first jots down a possibly complete classical dictionary for each idea-complex he happens to deal with. He uses each word he knows—and treasures—in a short sentence; he plays with classical words as a musician would play with tones to find a satisfactory and pleasing tune.'[2]

In some respects he was even more elaborately silly than his English contemporary, John Lathbury, which is saying a lot. He improves, and one would have thought it impossible, on Lathbury's theme, *In nomine Patris et Filii et Spiritus Sancti*, by taking the single word *O*. We are not surprised to hear that some critics at Paris objected to his choice. His

---

[1] Stegmüller, no. 3882, 2; 5690. I have looked at the beautiful fifteenth-century copy in MS Rome, Bibl. apost. vat. Barb. lat. 600. It shows no classicising tendencies.
[2] Trapp, 120.

fantasy went further than the Englishmen's. He wrote a letter, ascribed to Lucifer, beginning with the salutation:

'Lucifer, prince of darkness, ruling the sad realms of deep Acheron. . . .'

The prince of darkness addresses Pope and bishops, praising their conduct. Our Lord Jesus Christ, through Ceffons, his official stenographer (*notarius*), replies in a letter to Pope Innocent VI and the Roman Curia to warn them against Lucifer. His refutation takes the form of a verbal commentary on the first letter. 'Our Lord quotes freely not only Holy Scripture but also Church Fathers, many pagan authors and poets, and even Ceffons himself.'[1]

The satire covers a defence of the ancients which is more outspoken than anything we have heard in England. 'All that the pagans have said is Ours', writes Ceffons' Christ. Ceffons argued in public for the use of pagan writers by theologians[2] and followed them even when they led him into difficulties. He maintained publicly at Paris that it was impossible to disprove Stoic fatalism by natural reason; a great company of ancients, including Livy, reinforced by Alan of Lille and John of Salisbury, is adduced to back the opinion. Ceffons held that faith alone, not reason, could refute them.[3] His scepticism and fideism resemble Holcot's and go with classicism in each case. But the mainspring of Holcot's scepticism was logic, which had no necessary link with his classicism. Ceffons' scepticism seems to grow out of his classicism. The latter affected his theology more directly than it did Holcot's; their relationship is clearer and more causal. Ceffons also advances towards a view of history and a metaphor which come close to the idea of Renaissance. Truth is divine and all truths flow from a wisdom constantly rediscovered. Christ says:

'Let truth which seems to be hoary with age have a second, more eloquent youth in the minds of our faithful.'[4]

It would be ungrateful to ask Ceffons for 'pictures'; his fancy does not run that way. But he does offer the *topos* of a

[1] 118.
[2] ibid. Our Lord's arguments in the letter take up Ceffons' *quaestio* in his lecture on the *Sentences*: Utrum theologis liceat allegare dicta philosophorum gentilium aut etiam poetarum.
[3] 107.
[4] 119: et quae prospicitur veritas velut iam senii respersa canitie fidelium nostrum dissertius iuvenescat in mentibus.

decorated interior. His Sentence-commentary should have been adorned like the space inside 'an amazing hall, glittering proudly with many images'.[1]

For 'pictures' we must go to the Benedictine, Pierre Bersuire,[2] whose descriptions of gods and goddesses bridge the gap between Ridevall's *Fulgentius metaforalis* and Petrarch's *Africa*. Bersuire entered the Franciscan Order when very young, but soon transferred to the Benedictine; he was at the abbey of Maillezais in Poitou by 1317.[3] The change is understandable in view of the negative attitude to classical learning which marked the French Franciscans.[4] Bersuire slipped out of the cramping routine of the cloister by getting to Avignon and finding a patron in the papal vice-chancellor, Cardinal Pierre des Prés. He went to the Curia before 1328 and received a number of preferments in the 'thirties. His stay at Avignon coincided with Petrarch's. Bersuire also visited the poet at Vaucluse to ask his advice on classical studies sometime between 1337 and the spring of 1341. The French monk then accompanied his cardinal patron on a diplomatic visit to Paris, and stayed there or near from about 1342 until his death in 1362. In 1351 he was imprisoned by the bishop of Paris on the charge of engaging in 'forbidden sciences, evil and smacking of heresy'. We do not know what they were. His classical studies were vouched for by a king and a cardinal and the suggestion that he suffered for his satires on the upper clergy does not hold water; every moralist was *ipso facto* a satirist. It is far more likely that Bersuire was accused, whether truly or falsely, of dabbling in magic of some sort. He had a bad time in prison, but was free by 1355. The university would protect him, since Bersuire had inscribed himself as a student. King John the Good nominated him as a royal secretary while the case was in progress and rewarded him for his literary work by appointing him to be prior of Saint-Éloi. His old friend

---

[1] 131: Sic quod redderetur Sententia velut aulae stupendae multis superbiens imaginibus refulgans amplitudo.

[2] The best account of Bersuire's life and works, pending the notice in a forthcoming volume of the *Histoire littéraire*, is F. Ghisalberti, *L' "Ovidius moralizatus" di Pierre Bersuire* (Rome, 1933). See also J. Engels, op. cit. 23-45.

[3] On Maillezais see Cottineaux, *Répertoire* (Mâcon, 1935) 1709.

[4] The Benedictine Pierre Roger, Pope Clement VI (1342-52), was a learned doctor and great patron of learning, but he seems to have been more interested in natural science than in the classics; see Stegmüller, no. 6835; A. Maier, *Der literarische Nachlass des Petrus Rogerii (Clemens VI)*, *Rech. Théol.* 16 (1949) 86-96.

Petrarch visited Paris on an embassy the year before Bersuire's death. They met and talked. Petrarch wrote to Bersuire on the journey home, but news of his death came soon afterwards.

Bersuire's most valuable contribution to classical studies was probably his translation of Livy into French at King John's request. His moralisation of Ovid's *Metamorphoses* in Latin has more interest for us here, since he prefaces it with a set of 'pictures' of gods and goddesses. His *Ovidius moralisatus* formed part of a vast design to compile *moralitates* which should embrace the whole universe, including the Bible. Pagan divinities and fables belonged to the encyclopaedist's universe by a tradition going back to the *Etymologies* of St Isidore. The *Metamorphoses*, 'a gentile Bible', was an obvious focus for their moraliser.[1] The great *Reductorium*, dedicated to Cardinal Pierre des Prés with a wealth of classical allusions, made Bersuire famous, and proved useful to preachers and homilists, as he intended.[2] The section on Ovid enjoyed even greater popularity than the rest. It had a separate existence and survives in a number of recensions, of which only two need concern us. The first was made at Avignon before 1342 and the second in 1342 at Paris.

At Avignon Bersuire read the standard mythographers, Fulgentius, Rabanus and Mythographus Tertius (Alberic of London). They left him unsatisfied; and so he consulted Petrarch:

'I shall therefore begin with the first book of Ovid, God permitting, but first of all I shall add something on the forms and figures of the gods. Since I could nowhere find their images described or painted systematically, I had to consult the venerable Master Francesco Petrarca, the poet and famous orator, learned alike in moral philosophy, in history and in poetics. He describes the aforesaid images in a certain work of his in elegant verse.'[3]

---

[1] Ghislaberti, op. cit. 27.

[2] For the *Reductorium* see Stegmüller, no. 6425-6429, who quotes the prologue.

Bersuire moralised the encyclopaedia of Bartholomew the Englishman for natural history. In addition to moralising certain parts of Scripture in the *Reductorium*, he compiled a moralised dictionary of biblical words with the purpose of making each *predicabilis*; see Stegmüller, no. 6427. His *moralitates* are sober in content in the sense that he does not add classical or pseudo-classical elements, but limits himself to moralising his subject.

[3] Ghisalberti, op. cit. 89-90: A primo igitur libro Ovidii Deo permittente incipiam. Sed ante omnia de formis figurisque deorum aliqua super addam. Verumptamen quia ipsorum deorum ymagines ordinate scriptas vel pictas

Bersuire refers to Petrarch's account of the gods and goddesses as they were represented in the palace of Syphax (*Africa*, iii, 128-264). Petrarch began his poem at Vaucluse about 1338 and showed a first draft of the beginning to King Robert at Naples in 1341. He tried to keep it private, but he could make an exception for so eager a student as Bersuire. In fact a comparison has shown that Bersuire owed part of his general plan and certain words and details to the description of the 'images' in *Africa*.[1] Some years later at Paris he came across two recent books which he had not heard of before, the *Ovide moralisé* and Ridevall's *Fulgentius metaforalis*. He added quotations from them to a second recension of his *Ovidius moralisatus*.

Bersuire, therefore, composed his first recension of the 'pictures' independently of Ridevall and in consultation with Petrarch. The poet, it has been said, 'was the first writer to compose a sequence of pictorial descriptions of pagan divinities freed from interpretative incrustations and designed solely for the purpose of adornment'.[2] In pursuit of his aim he 'retains only the pictorial elements, the visual details indicative of the pose, costume, and attributes of each god', and 'preserves only those details which have the value of images'.[3] His *species deorum* shining with gold, whether wall-paintings or 'gilded bas-reliefs', certainly suggest visual images. Petrarch with his 'elegant and precise hand' has traced them free of some at least of those cumbersome attributes in which Ridevall delighted. Bersuire reset them in a framework of *moralitates*. Even so, a comparison between Bersuire and Ridevall brings out the influence of the visit to Vaucluse. Bersuire describes a pictured scene. 'The sea was painted before Saturn, in which his daughter, the fair maid Venus, was being born.' Ridevall does not mention a painted sea.[4] Bersuire throughout tries to organise

---

alicubi invenire non potui, necessarie habui consulere venerabilem Franciscum de Petrarco poetam utique et oratorem egregium in omni morali philosophia nec non et historica et poetica disciplina eruditum qui prefatas ymagines in quodam opere suo eleganti metro describit.

Libros etiam Fulgencii Alexandri et Rabani necessarie habui transcurrere, et de diversis partibus trahere figuram vel ymaginem quam diis istis ficticiis voluerunt antiqui secundum rationes historicas vel philosophicas assignare.

[1] E. H. Wilkins, Descriptions of Pagan Divinities from Petrarch to Chaucer, *Speculum* 32 (1957) 511-19.

[2] ibid., 513. The motif of a decorated interior was not new in itself; it went back to *Aen.* i, 453-93; and see above, p. 181, n. 2.

[3] Seznec, 173-4.

[4] Ghisalberti, op. cit. 90-91; *Fulgentius metaforalis*, 73.

his details in true pictorial form. He also conveys emotion; Ridevall does not. Compare Pluto in *Fulgentius metaforalis* with Bersuire's 'picture' of the god of Hades:

> A poetis ergo pingitur iste deus:
> Ligno coronatus, opibus ditatus,
> inferis prelatus, Cerbero delatus,
> Etati ligatus, Furiis armatus,
> et Fatis vallatus.[1]

Bersuire writes:

'Quampropter ipsi Plutoni, id est in inferno vel virtute sua inferna gubernanti, suam imaginem depinxerunt, et eum tenebrarum deum vocaverunt. Erat igitur imago eius homo terribilis in solio sulphureo sedens, sceptrumque regium in manu tenens; et (? MS scilicet) Cerberum sub pedibus eius calcabat; et iuxta eum et Furias et Parcas et Harpias habebat. De throno sulphureo et flumina manabant, que Cohitum, Flegetontem (et) Acherontem (MS Iacetontem) dixerunt. Stigem autem pallidum iuxta ista flumina assignabant.'[2]

He evokes the image of a frightening deity enthroned among the flames. The classical Hell is sensed more immediately than it is in Ridevall's jingle for preachers.

Ceffons and Bersuire differ individually as two bizarre and versatile persons always will; but they differ from their mendicant compatriots even more. If we compare them with the classicising group in England, we find another contrast. Neither can be called 'early humanists' by any stretch of imagination, but they come closer to it than the Englishmen, except for Waleys.

---

[1] *Fulgentius metaforalis*, 100.

[2] Ghisalberti does not include the 'picture' of Pluto among his excerpts from Bersuire. I have used MS Oxford, St John's College 37, fol. 13. It is written in a fifteenth-century English hand and is ascribed to Trevet, a common error: Incipit Tryvet super Ovidium Metamorphosios, primo de diis et eorum picturis atque figuris (fol. 1). An inscription on the flyleaf shows that it was used for preaching: Liber quondam magistri Thome Eyburhale datus magistro Roberto Elyot anno Domini 1472 ad terminum vite sic quod non vendatur sed post eius mortem detur alicui volenti predicare (fol. iv).

On Thomas Eborall and Robert Elyot see *O.R.* 1, 622, 638.

COMMENTATORS AND PREACHERS IN ITALY

Varietas delectat.

Proverb.

ITALY produced at least one classicising biblical commentator. He was an Austin Friar called Michele da Massa Marittima, belonging to an Order whose members in Italy helped and befriended the early humanists.[1] He came of the Beccucci family of Massa Marittima, a town subject to Siena in the south-west of Sienese territory. It had a small convent of Austin Friars. Michele would probably join the Order there; the library acquired a copy of his *Sermones ad populum*.[2] His academic career is mysterious.[3] He was a bachelor of theology at Paris 1325-6. When next heard of he is attending the Chapter General of his Order at Venice as diffinitor in 1332. He died on May 10, 1337, perhaps at Paris, but still a bachelor. Why did he never incept in theology and why were his works so little known and quoted in his Order? Doctrinal differences have been suggested as the answer: Michele happened to be on the losing side among the Austin Friars and was condemned to die without ever receiving the *magisterium*. There is a story of a popular riot at his funeral at Siena (conflicting with the tradition in his Order that he died at Paris); the people showed their sympathy for him by putting a master's cap on his tomb.[4] His own prologue to his Gospel-commentary suggests that he went from Paris to teach at some other *studium*; he lectured 'at Paris' (as a bachelor) on the Bible *cursorie* 'last year', when he gave a general *principium* on the Old Testament. He will now, he says, begin his lectures on St Matthew

---

[1] R. Weiss, Notes on Dionigi da Borgo San Sepolcro, *Italian Studies* 10 (1955), gives a full bibliography.

[2] De antiquis ordinis Heremitarum S. Augustini bibliothecis, *Analecta Augustiniana* 23 (1954) 213.

[3] The latest study is by D. Trapp, Augustinian Theology in the Fourteenth Century, *Augustiniana* 6 (1956) 163-75.

[4] The title of master given him in the title of his Gospel-commentary in the copy at Rome, MS Bibl. Angelica 369, may support this popular rumour.

by praising the New Testament.[1] This implies that he is teaching somewhere else. There is nothing to indicate the place.

Michele left a large number of writings, theological, moral, devotional and biblical. He did not comment on any classical texts,[2] but showed his interest in the classics in other ways. His personality, as shown in his works, is as mysterious as his career. He emerges as a bizarre but elusive figure. I shall limit myself to a quick glance at his treatise on the seven virtues and vices, his treatise on the Passion and his surviving biblical commentaries, on St Matthew and St Luke.

A comparison of these three works shows either a developing interest in the classics or else a reaction away from them. Our lack of dates makes it impossible to say which. I shall describe them in the order suggested by a developing interest. The treatise on virtues and vices is quite conventional.[3] Seneca is the only ancient writer to be quoted.[4] The *Tractatus de Passione Domini* became very popular.[5] It is a book for devotional reading from the Friday before Passion Sunday to the end of Holy Week. Michele guides his readers through a conflated Gospel story, stimulating devotion by means of asides and digressions. He writes in a vein of tender domestic piety, telling much of the story in the form of a soliloquy by the grieving Mother. Our Lady addresses St James as 'my Son's secretary' and St Peter as *pontifex ecclesie*. She would have told Judas the steward, she cries, that had she guessed his wicked purpose she would have gone out to work or even sold herself into slavery to

---

[1] MS Paris, Bib.. Arsenal 1032, fol. 1rb-va: . . . quam quidem arborem (Scripture) . . . tractavi aliqualiter in generali principio super bibliam, quando cursorie legi eam Parisius . . . quia in anno preterito feci principium generale super totam scripturam, applicando aliqualiter in speciali ad scripturam veteris testamenti. . . . Quia tamen anno preterito inchoaveram, non tamen adhuc totum perfeci, sed eum perficiam post, stante opitulatione divina, et quia per tunc non haberem opportunitatem faciendi solempniter, sicut deceret, principium super novum testamentum, . . . incipiam Deo dante novum testamentum a capite. . . .

[2] D. A. Perini, *Bibliographia Augustiniana* 2 (Florence, 1931) 191-2. A *Summarium in Ethicam Aristotelis* is not certainly his.

[3] MS Oxford, Bodl. Canon. pat. lat. 86, foll. 50-88v. There is another copy in MS Bordeaux 267. The late Mgr A. Pelzer kindly gave me these two references. The treatise is cast in the form of a commentary on the names of the halting places of the Israelites on their journey through the wilderness (Num. xxxiii, 1-49).

[4] From *De ira*, MS Canon. pat. lat. 86, fol. 59v.

[5] Stegmüller, no. 5636. There are eight MSS at Munich alone.

earn him his thirty pieces of silver, rather than let him win them at such cost.[1] Michele already shows a certain extravagance. He piles on the agony, quoting an apocryphal book on the life of the Virgin and dwelling on her tears: she shed as many as would have sufficed to wash two bodies; the angels in charge of her restored her natural moisture by a miracle.[2] He cites marvels, such as nine magic springs, which he compares with the nine orders of angels and with the nine streams gushing from the side of Our Lord.[3] An *exemplum* mixes pseudo-antique and Christian elements. Michele refers to the well-known legend that the leopard is only to be tamed by the sight of lambs' blood,[4] and adds that Julius Caesar, in his zeal for mercy, kindliness and piety, had two images designed on his crown: a leopard and a lamb showing the leopard its blood. Christ 'figured' this design on his Cross.[5] The good pagan's crown is brought into relation with the symbol of Redemption.

Michele expounded Scripture on an English scale. His Gospel-commentaries would have stood comparison for sheer bulk with Lathbury on Lamentations; it is no wonder that they have survived mainly in fragments and excerpts.[6] His commentary on St Matthew in MS Paris, Arsenal 1032, is prefaced by (i) a general prologue or *principium* to the New Testament, (ii) a *divisio librorum*, (iii) a prologue or *principium* to St Matthew, (iv and v) commentaries on the two prologues of the Vulgate. Each one of these pieces represents a separate lecture, ending with a prayer. Even the *divisio librorum* or classification of the New Testament books has fanciful comparisons. Michele likens the divisions to colours according to those vices which they teach us to avoid: green is the colour worn by hunters, so as to catch their game

---

[1] MS Oxford, Bodl. 758 (2670), foll. 59v-62, 27.

[2] ibid. fol. 2-2v: . . . sicut narrat sanctus Iacobus in quodam libello quem fecit de vita Virginis gloriose, pluribus vicibus die Mercurii ante diem eius passionem cecidit profecto semiviva ante conspectum dilectissimi filii sui flendo.

fol. 30v has the passage on the tears, which is too long to quote. The *libellus* must have been an expanded version of the apocryphal infancy gospel ascribed to St James. The *Meditationes* ascribed to St Bonaventure and the *Vita Christi* of Ludolf the Carthusian both describe the Virgin as weeping and swooning, but they do not mention the book of St James as a source or give so many marvellous details.

[3] ibid. foll. 6v-16v. [4] See Vincent of Beauvais, *Spec. nat.*, xix, 76.

[5] MS Bodl. 758, fol. 30: Et ideo Iulius Cesar, quia ipse erat zelator clementie, benignitatis ac pietatis, describi fecit in sua corona duas imagines, scilicet leopardum et agnum sibi ostendentem sanguinem suum. Revera hoc bene figurabat in cruce Christus.

[6] See appendix iii.

more easily, and so on.[1] Commentators normally explained the Vulgate prologues in a brief and businesslike fashion, however much they intended to spread themselves in their lectures on the text. Not so Michele: he introduces *exempla* and sayings of philosophers even at this stage.[2] It seems, moreover, that the commentary, as we have it, represents his notes and that the actual lecture would have been expanded. In the lecture on the second prologue he refers to Julius Caesar's crown in terms which would be incomprehensible if we had not read the full account of it in his *Tractatus de Passione Domini*.[3] Later on, when he is lecturing on the text, he notes that a *quaestio* is to be inserted which he does not write out.[4]

The text receives a theological, a literal and a moral exposition. On the genealogy, for instance, Michele first proves that Christ was the true Messias; then he discusses the names and histories of the patriarchs, using Nicholas of Lyre, without mentioning his name;[5] thirdly he moralises the text with the aid of many *exempla*. The most complete copy of the commentary, including prologues and going up to Mt. xxvii, fills 348 leaves. The others break off unfinished at earlier stages. A copy which omits the prologues, and stops at Mt. viii, 26, fills 136 leaves. It will be easier to tackle the colossus in a set of extracts mainly from the *moralitates*, in MS Rome, Angelica 369, going up to xxv, 24. They occur in an interesting compilation, which includes two sets of excerpts from Michele on St Luke. The original of this commentary, too, may have been on a very large scale; it has been lost, with those on the other Gospels.

The dates of both commentaries (on St Matthew and St

---

[1] MS Arsenal 1032, fol. 9ra. On the correspondence between the seven deadly sins and seven colours, see M. W. Bloomfield, *The Seven Deadly Sins* (Michigan, 1952) 23, 438.

[2] There is a story about elephants (fol. 14ra), a reference to the Four Monarchies (fol. 18vb) and a story from the *Historia Brittonum* (fol. 19rb); the philosopher 'Symphons', asked why he did not lament at the burning of his house and goods, replied that he kept all his goods in his head (fol. 14va). Gerard of Liège in his *Doctrina cordis* tells the same story beginning 'Unde Seneca refert de quodam. . . .' (ed. Paris, 1506, sig. i, 5v).

[3] MS Arsenal 1032, fol. 17rb: Narratur de dispositione corone Iulii Cesaris secundum beatum Matheum etc.

[4] ibid. fol. 21va: Sed dubium est circa hoc, utrum in Christo sint due filiationes distincte; et arguo primo etc. Deducas hanc questionem.

[5] The discussion of the question why Rahab the harlot should be listed in the genealogy depends on Nicholas of Lyre on the same text, Mt. i, 5. This does not help to date the commentary, since Lyre's Gospel-commentaries in a first recension were among his earliest works.

Luke) must be after Michele's teaching as a bachelor at Paris, that is after 1326. According to his prologue, already quoted, he began the year after reading the Bible *cursorie* at Paris. The commentary on St Matthew certainly and that on St Luke probably, judging by the surviving excerpts, were so long as to have run over lecture courses lasting several years each. He may have gone on adding pieces afterwards. It would be rash to put a *terminus ad quem* before his death in the spring of 1337.

The MS Angelica 369 is a beautiful, carefully prepared copy made in Italy in the fourteenth century. Whoever made or ordered the compilation has revealed his interests in the incipit to the extracts from Michele on St Luke:

> 'Incipit prima expositio super Lucam ad litteram secundum magistrum Michaelem de Massa Maritime ordinis fratrum heremitarum sancti Augustini, moraliter et exemplariter multum utilis et plena documentis plurimorum philosophorum et poetarum ac gestis romanorum secundum Valerium Maximum.'

. . . *plus in Valerio quam in Christi evangelio* . . .[1]: Michele verifies this puritan reproach to the letter. The incipit gives a fair enough account of his commentary. Whoever composed the title thought it no reproach, but a splended advertisement. Two items in the volume, not ascribed to Michele, put the miscellany squarely into its class:

(i) Notes for preachers in the form of saying of philosophers and of writers on natural science; they include quotations from Vegetius, Valerius and the tale of Alexander. There is a story of the temple of Jove, the god of merchants and coiners, at Rome in the days 'when Rome ruled over the whole world'. Two jars, one containing a sweet drink, the other a bitter, stood at the gates and a similar pair at the doors of the temple. A *lex scripta et constituta* decreed that no one might enter without first drinking. Each entrant had to taste at the doors of whichever drink he had omitted at the gates, so that he could not avoid drinking both sweet and bitter before going into the temple.[2] This is the sham antique law type of *exemplum*. The setting in ancient Rome suggests that it may have occurred in Pseudo-Fulgentius' *De ornatu civitatis* or something of the sort.

---

[1] Heinrich von Langenstein on Genesis, quoted by F. W. Oediger, *Uber die Bildung der Geistlichen im späten Mittelalter* (Leiden, 1953), p. 39, n. 5.

[2] Appendix i, 347. For an account of MS Angelica 369, see appendix iii.

(ii) Holcot's *Moralitates* with additions from the collection *Prudentia depingebatur* and a few similar items.

Michele, therefore, takes his place in a company of amateurs and collectors of sham antiques.

His commentaries display a familar procedure. They are *exempla* collections or miscellanies of prose and verse. Writers on natural science and marvels predominate. Michele has a special affection for Ratus (Rhazes or al Razi), the Persian physician who flourished in the late ninth and early tenth centuries, whose works were well known in translation.[1] Otherwise we meet old friends, Valerius, Frontinus, Vegetius, Seneca, Virgil, Ovid, medieval compilers, John of Salisbury and Vincent of Beauvais, 'histories of the Romans' and many others. Michele is a keen talker of Alexander. We also find a 'picture' of Saturn as the ancients represented him[2] and a 'picture' of Iustitia according to the ancient philosophers.[3] The words *antiquitus depingebatur* and *depingebant* make the student of Holcot feel at home with the Italian Austin friar.

I have not found any Livy quotations or any other evidence that Michele interested himself in classical scholarship except as a collector of *exempla*. But his devotion to tales of ancient heroes went deep, so deep indeed as to colour his attitude to the Gospel story. He draws a parallel between the genealogy and birth of Christ according to St Matthew and those of other great kings and emperors of history, Cyrus, Alexander, Julius Caesar and Charlemagne. All peoples, he says, tell of marvels concerning the generation, and the manner, time and circumstances of the birth of their first rulers (the founders of their dynasties). He runs with evident pleasure through the wonderful tales he has found concerning the births of these great conquerors. Among them is the legend that the name 'Carolus' referred

---

[1] Thorndike, *History of Magic* op. cit. 1, 667-71.

[2] MS Angelica 369, fol. 13rb: Saturnus antiquitus depingebatur senex et macilentus atque tristis. Item Saturnus naturaliter habet mortiferas qualitates.
The 'picture' occurs in a passage on astronomy and does not seem to depend on the mythographers.

[3] MS Rome, vat. lat. 382, fol. 72vb: . . . ubi videre oportet quomodo antiqui philosophi depingebant iustitiam. Dicebant quod iustitia debet (depingi in) figura regine, (alii) quidem (non) in forma mulieris, sed viri etc.
Biblical comparisons follow, beginning with Noe. This passage probably represents one of Michele's notes for his own use when lecturing, and would have been expanded. It has not been copied among the excerpts from the commentary (on Mt. v. 20) in the Angelica MS. I cannot find the source for this 'picture'.

to Charlemagne's conception in a cart.[1] There was all the more reason, Michele concludes, why St Matthew, the public notary of the Christians, should describe the generation, and the manner and circumstances of the birth of Christ, who is emperor not only of an earthly but of a heavenly kingdom.[2] The evangelist's role as 'public notary of the Christians' reminds us of Michele's modernisation of his characters in his treatise on the Passion; but the secular parallels and the aristocratic values in his commentary go beyond anything he attempted in the *Tractatus*.

The tremendous bulk, the classicising technique and even the content point to English influence on Michele. He tells *exempla* from the *Historia Brittonum*. He compares the British King Arthur with the English King Richard I as zealous champions of Christendom against the Saracens.[3] He seldom gives his source for current *exempla*; so it is all the more significant that 'many men worthy of credence' have told him the story of a fasting woman, now living in England.[4] Further evidence: he could not have found his model for a classicising biblical commentary within his own Order in Italy. Agostino Trionfo (d. 1328), a prolific biblicist, is soberness personified.[5] Nor could Michele have heard a

---

[1] On this legend and the stories of Peppin and Bertha, see R. Folz, *Le souvenir et la légende de Charlemagne dans l'Empire germanique médiéval* (Paris, 1950) 472. Michele goes beyond his sources in making Charlemagne illegitimate. He may have been influenced by the medieval Alexander legend.

[2] Appendix i, 347.

[3] MS Arsenal 1032, fol. 19rb (in prologue no. ii): Legitur in historia Brittonum . . .
The story of the building of Canterbury was quite common in English *moralitates*.
MS Angelica 369, fol. 4ra (on Mt. i, 1): Legitur in historia Brittonum . . .
The origin of the dragon on the standard was also a common theme.
MS Vat. lat. 382, fol. 43vb continues after the story of Aurelius Ambrosianus, Arthur and the dragon: Et hic ideo quia ille illustrissimus rex Ricardus zelo fidei Christi plurimam et maximam stragem de saracenis in partibus ultramarinis (fecit).

[4] MS Arsenal 1032, fol. 6rb: . . . audivi etiam a plurimis fidedignis quod nunc vivit in Anglia quedam mulier, que nec comedit nec bibit per annos 30, et de hoc solempnia experimenta sunt habita. . . .
The story of a fasting woman, located now in Italy, now in Germany, circulated in the fourteenth century; see R. Creytens, Le manuel, op. cit. p. 116, n. 36; Petrarch *Rerum mem.* iv, 121. It may, however, point to special relations between Michele and England, since he vouches for it personally.

[5] B. Ministeri, De Augustini de Ancona O.E.S.A. († 1328) vita et operibus, *Analecta Augustiniana* 22 (1952/3) 148-262, revises the chronology of his life and gives a bibliography of his works. His *Lectura in evangelium S. Mathei* is said to have been finished at Venice in 1326 and he may have taught at the *studium* of his Order at Padua at about that time. His commentaries on the Canonical Epistles and St Paul may belong to his regency at Paris, 1313 or

classicising biblical lecture course in Paris. How the cross-Channel influence reached him cannot be known; but he may have met Waleys at Bologna in the late 'twenties; Holcot on Wisdom may have arrived on the Continent in time for Michele to read it before his death in 1337. His own Order provided a background of general interest in the classics, and would make him receptive to English methods. Italian influence on the Oxford Austin Friars is well established.[1] Perhaps the exchange could work the other way round.

Michele's type of commentary failed to take root in Italy, as we shall see when we look at a cross-section of Italian homilists, beginning with the Friars Preachers. The obvious starting point is Florence. The school at Santa Maria Novella reached its fullest development in the later fourteenth century, but it received the impress of a strong personality at the turn of the thirteenth. Remigio Girolami, a theologian and preacher, who had studied at Paris, died there at an advanced age in 1319.[2] Remigio's sermons and his postill on the Canticle constitute something of a test case. He was sympathetic to classical studies, annotating a work of John of Wales and the *Moralium dogma philosophorum* in his own hand with verses of his own composition.[3] He admired the civic virtues of the ancient Romans: his teaching on the subject may have influenced Dante, who may have been his pupil (it is a much-discussed problem among Dante scholars).[4] He held up good kings of pagan times as an example to the Florentines in a sermon.[5] But the sermons, though full of topical allusions and interesting for their political theory, are not classicising in Holcot's manner. The postill on the Canticle yields a few quotations from Ovid[6] and a

---

1315. I have examined his biblical commentaries to see of what type they are. Agostino expounds at length, but he does not introduce classical material as a rule; he is mainly interested in bringing out the theological content of his text.

[1] A. Gwynn, *The English Austin Friars in the Time of Wyclif* (Oxford, 1940) 42; Knowles, 1, 242.

[2] The fullest notice on Remigio and the school at Santa Maria Novella is by S. Orlandi, *Necrologio di S. Maria Novella Firenzi* (Florence, 1955) 1, 276-307. For his biblical works, see Stegmüller, no. 7249.

[3] Orlandi, 1, 301-5.　　　　　　　[4] See C. T. Davis, op. cit. 80-86.

[5] MS Florence, Naz. conv. sopp. G. 4.936, fol. 4ra: . . . et exempla de regibus antiquis gentilibus, scilicet de Calanto, de Theodosio, de Alexandro, de Tito, de Traiano, etc.
On Remigio's sermons see also G. Salvadori and V. Federico, I sermoni d'occasione, le sequenze e i ritmi di Remigio Girolami fiorentino, *Scritti vari di Filologia* (Rome, 1901) 455-508.

[6] MS Florence, Laurent. conv. sopp. 362, foll. 103rb, 104vb, 105ra, 115vb.

line from the medieval poet Enrico da Settimello, whom Remigio would have read as a good Florentine.[1] Otherwise it has no strictly literary allusions. Remigio's mental outlook was coloured by his reading and his reflections on ancient history and ethics, yet he did not think of the classics as front-line ammunition in his sermons and lectures on Scripture.

Giovanni di San Gimignano (d. after May 6, 1333) was another Tuscan, professed at Siena, who specialised in preaching. He may have studied at Barcelona; otherwise his teaching and administrative functions in the Order fell in Tuscany and Rome.[2] Giovanni offers us the most pointed contrast to his confrères Waleys and Holcot. He talked not of Alexander but of the great saints and doctors of his Order; their names and praises were constantly in his mouth. He used *exempla* and allusions to historical events in his sermons and compiled a book of *exempla* and analogies for use by preachers, but without taking any special notice of the classics. His favourite opening to a sermon was a generalisation based on common knowledge or experience: 'we see that a rose is pleasant and useful . . .'. The agreed proposition will then be applied to the subject of the sermon.[3] Significantly Giovanni has been described as 'one of the most representative preachers in the Dominican pulpit at the beginning of the fourteenth century.' His contemporary, Antonio Azaro of Parma, also had great success as a preacher.[4] Indeed, his influence lasted longer; the balanced character and general applicability to any audience of his sermons may have kept them from dating. Here again the preacher observes moderation in his choice of stories and allusions. Both friars lend themselves to a direct comparison

---

[1] ibid., fol. 91vb: Per nigritudinem autem intelligitur infamia iuxta illud Arigetti: Quem semel horrendis maculis infamia nigrat.

From Enrico da Settimello, *Elegia*, ed. G. Cremaschi (Bergamo, 1949), p. 26, line 19. Settimello is a village near Florence. William of Aragon also quotes from the *Elegia* in his commentary on Boethius, MS Cambridge, Gonville and Caius College 309, fol. 97: Bene dixit *oportet*; est enim oportunum et utile valde cito remedia querere, ut dicit Arrigetus: Nam nequit antiquum medicina pellere morbum; Quodque diu crevit durat in esse diu.

From the *Elegia*, op. cit., p. 62, lines 23-4.

[2] A. Dondaine, La vie et les oeuvres de Jean de San Gimignano, *Arch. FF. Praed.* 9 (1939) 128-83.

[3] See Charland, 143-4 for this device.

[4] G. Meersseman, Le opere di Fra Antonio Azaro Parmense O.P., *Arch. FF. Praed.* 10 (1940) 20-47. Very little is known of Antonio's career, apart from his connexion with Parma. He entered the Order in 1259 or 1260 and is said to have been still alive in 1314.

T

with Holcot on the Sunday Gospels. Their sermons took the form of homilies or postills preached through the liturgical year, so that the contrast in illustration and stories comes out plainly. Two attractive vernacular homilists, Aldobrandini da Toscanella and B. Giordano da Rivalto (d. 1311), can also be eliminated. They were earnest and artistic enough to discard anything which would spoil the effect of limpid sincerity conveyed by their sermons.[1]

These Tuscan Dominicans lived too early to have been influenced by Waleys or Holcot. Since Waleys taught at Bologna and his works found a place in Italian Dominican libraries, it is possible that he may have had imitators. Naples may have been a centre for his kind of preaching. King Robert the Wise (1309-43) had a passion for composing sermons and *collationes*. Laymen were not encouraged to preach, but Robert was a king and an exception; so his taste was indulged. He inserted many quotations from the classics into his addresses to lay and clerical audiences. One theme comes from Sallust. His address to the Sienese ambassadors contains praise of ancient philosophers.[2] Robert preached 'passing well for a king', it seems. For that very reason it is unlikely that he showed much originality; he probably borrowed the technique in vogue among the clergy of his kingdom. Boccaccio's friend, Pietro Piccolo da Monteforte, sent a copy of the *De genealogia deorum* to the Naples Dominicans and reported that they found it *valde praedicabilis*, very useful for preaching.[3]

Still, the evidence so far collected shows that the Friars Preacher of central Italy steered a middle course. They admitted a few jokes and allusions; but they did not go in for the classicising English type nor for the French picaresque.

---

[1] Th. Kaeppeli, La tradizione manoscritta delle opere di Aldobrandini da Toscanella, *Arch. FF. Praed.* 8 (1938) 163-92. Aldobrandini falls just outside our chronological limits; he did not live long, if at all, after 1300. B. Giovanni da Rivalto of Pisa entered the Order about 1280. He taught at Pisa and Perugia and was lector and preacher at Santa Maria Novella between 1303 and 1309; see G. Meersseman, Les confrères de S. Dominique, *Archiv. FF. Praed.* 20 (1950) 32; S. Orlando, *Necrologio*, op. cit., i, 280, 495. A. Galletti in his study of Giordano's vernacular sermons and their transmission, Frà Giordano da Pisa, predicator del secolo XIV, *Giornale storico della letteratura italiana* 31 (1898) 1-48, 193-243, 33 (1899) 193-264, notes the absence of classical quotations (33, 288). See also R. Davidsohn, *Geschichte von Florenz* 4 i (Berlin, 1927) 36-8.

[2] W. Goetz, *König Robert von Neapel* (1309-43) (Tübingen, 1910) 34, 63-6.

[3] Guis. Billanovich, Pietro Piccolo da Monteforte tra il Petrarca e il Boccaccio, *Studi in onore di Bruno Nardi* (Florence, 1955) 18, 48-9.

My cross-section of Franciscans comprises four who left postills or sermons on the liturgical year. Landolfo Caraccioli of Naples was the most distinguished. He studied at Naples and Paris and then taught at Naples, spreading the teaching of Friar John Duns Scotus in southern Italy. He became bishop of Castellamare in 1327 and archbishop of Amalfi in 1331, and died in 1351.[1] It is not known where or when he wrote his sermons and *collationes* on the Sunday Gospels.[2] They are rather scholastic and academic in tone. Landolfo arranges his material in a complicated manner; a résumé of the whole story of salvation gets into his exposition of the text for the first Sunday of Advent. He always begins with an authority, who is quoted immediately after his text; but his authors are mainly theological, patristic or medieval. An occasional classical quotation or allusion does not disturb the general impression of sobriety.[3]

None of the other three friars was a master of Paris. Francesco degli Abbati of Asti belongs to 'the first half of the fourteenth century'. His *Postills on the Gospels for Sundays except in Lent* have a livelier air than Landolf's.[4] He brings in animal lore and comparisons from everyday life and uses the same technique as Giovanni di San Gimignano in beginning each sermon with a generalisation drawn from common experience: 'We see that a wise king, if he sees wars threatening his people, will assemble strong, loyal knights to protect them. Since he wishes to test the knights' strength and loyalty, he employs three means to do so.' The preacher then describes how the knights will be trained and tested.[5]

---

[1] *D.H.G.E.* 11 (1949) 980. I have not seen the commentary on Zacharias ascribed to him; it is not listed by Stegmüller, no. 5365-7, who mentions his work on the Gospels but gives no MSS. Bibliographies for these four Franciscans will be found in Stegmüller. I have noted only those MSS which are not given there.

[2] I have seen copies in MSS Florence, Laurent. Plut. viii dext. 12, foll. 56ra-109va and Padua, Anton. 468, foll. 1ra-161rb. The Dominicans of Bologna had his *expositio evangeliorum* and the Austin Friars his *Sermones in variis festis*; see M.-H. Laurent, Fabio Vigili, op. cit. 98, 134. I have not seen the edition of his sermons on the Gospels.

[3] For instance, MS Anton. 468, fol. 13rb: Hannibal's troops were overcome by luxury after crossing the Alps. He does not quote Livy.

[4] *D.H.G.E.* 1 (1912) 29; Stegmüller, no. 2295. I used the copy in MS Padua, Anton. 476, foll. 1ra-193vb. There is another at Burgo; see *Arch. fr. hist.* 46 (1953) 486. The Dominican library at San Eustorgio, Milan, had a copy; see Th. Kaeppeli, La bibliothèque de Saint-Eustorge à Milan, *Arch. FF. Praed.* 25 (1955) 27.

[5] fol. 32vb, on the Fourth Sunday after Epiphany, *Ascendente Iesu in naviculo* (Mt. viii, 23): Videmus quod rex sapiens diversa bella videns suo populo minere aggreget sibi milites fideles et fortes, qui gentem suam ab hostibus suis

He varies his procedure by quoting proverbs: 'It is written that everyone opens his door gladly to three sorts of men, the doctor, the friend and the master.'[1] The only classical author that I have noticed is Boethius.

The title to fame of Giàcomo di Bianchi of Alessandria is his abridgment of Aristotle's natural and moral philosophy for King Robert of Naples. This puts his *floruit* in the king's reign, 1309-43. Otherwise little is known of him.[2] His sermons and *collationes* on the Sunday Gospels survive only in one Paduan manuscript, as far as I know. In spite of his work for King Robert, he does not enliven his sermons with Aristotelian references. He uses the current technique of starting from a generalisation and commenting on it, but still keeps close to the Gospel story. A personal note following the explicit states that he compiled his expositions for the benefit of novices and students to help them to understand the Gospel; he has stated nothing which is not to be found in the original works of the saints or in authentic glosses.[3] Bianchi gave his readers a model of plain exegesis.

Filippo di Montecalerio (Moncaglier) was lector at Padua in 1330 and papal penitentiary 1336-44.[4] His sermons on the Sunday Gospels and his Lenten sermons had considerable success.[5] I have seen the former, in two Paduan manuscripts.[6]

possint defendere et tueri; et experiri volens utrum milites sint fortes et probi tripliciter erga ipsos se habet. . . . Et hec tria in hoc evangelio continentur, scilicet grossa navigatio, . . . submersionis pericula, . . . et virtuosa sedatio.

[1] fol. 6ora, on the First Sunday after Easter, *Cum ergo sero esset* (Ioan. xx, 19): Scribitur quod tria genera hominum consuevit quilibet in domo sua recipere libenter, scilicet medicum, amicum et magistrum.

[2] A. Pelzer, *Cat. cod. Vat. lat.* 2, i (1931) 292-6; M. H. Laurent, op. cit. 119-20; Stegmüller, no 3866-7. Stegmüller gives no MSS.

[3] MS Padua, Anton. 491, fol. 209rb. The text is so corrupt or ungrammatical that I have not tried to emend it: Explicit postilla super evangelia dominicalia. Suprascriptas expositiones dominicalium evangeliorum ego, frater Iacobus de Alexandria quantum Deus tenuitati mei ingenii largitus est compilare studui. Primum quidem ad ipsius largitoris gloriam et Virginis Marie est honor et ad sanctum Franciscum reverentia cuius regule professor sperans quod hoc opus michi cedat ad novitiis et studentibus esse intelligendum evangelium ad profectum. Intelligat autem qui legerat me nichil in expositionibus affirmasse quod non vel in orginalibus sanctorum vel in glosis auctenticis inveniantur expressum.

[4] J. B. Sbaralea, *Supplementum ad scriptores trium ordinum S. Francisci* 2 (1921) 381.

[5] Stegmüller does not mention them. Both works were at the library of San Eustorgio; see Th. Kaeppeli, op. cit. 29, 31. The Dominican and Franciscan libraries at Bologna each had a copy of his Sunday Gospels; see M.-H. Laurent, op. cit. 97, 248. The Austin Friars of Padua had his *solemne opus quadragesimale*; see *Analecta Augustiniana* 23 (1954) 246. His introductions to the Sunday Gospels, i.e. the opening of his sermons, were combined with the postills on the same Gospels of Antonio Azaro O.P. in MS Clm. 26660; see G. Meersseman, Le opere di Fra Antonio Azaro, op. cit. 37.

[6] MSS Anton. 448 and 467.

One reason for its popularity may be that Filippo expounds the whole text and not only the opening words of each Gospel for the Sunday. The tone is more rhetorical than that of the others; he has a trick of introducing his authorities with 'audi!': 'Hear Chrysostome!' 'Hear Leo in his sermon!' His authors include a frequent mention of 'Grecus', which suggests a scholarly approach, even if he were merely using the Greek fathers quoted in St Thomas's *Catena aurea*.[1] He shares the liking for a general statement as an opening, with a preference for serious philosophical remarks. One gets the impression of a work of unusual solidity for its *genre*.

The four Franciscans are not at all standardised. Each has his own personality and manner. Nevertheless they form a group which may be compared collectively with the French Franciscans on the one hand and with Ridevall and Lathbury on the other. The Italians are less determinedly 'plain' than the Frenchmen, showing some willingness to 'flatter' the ears of their audiences; but they differ from the English friars as chalk from cheese. Both Franciscans and Dominicans in Italy bear out Thomas Waleys' statement in his *De modo componendi sermones* that sermons in Italy kept closer to the text of the Gospel than was customary in the north.

The nearest approach to the English classicising type that I have found among the Italian Franciscans is an incomplete lecture course on Ecclesiastes (on i, 1-8). It was given at Vicenza or Parma or perhaps at both places by an anonymous fourteenth-century Franciscan and is now at Padua.[2] He produced a gay little commentary. A mention of Rome in the Vulgate prologue to Ecclesiastes induced him to tell the story of Romulus and Remus with verses.[3] He talks of Alexander and his soldiers and quotes sayings of philosophers on every page. Valerius Maximus and John of Salisbury's *Policraticus* are quoted.[4] This anonymous fragment, surviving by chance in a scholar's notebook, shows that it is dangerous to generalise. But at least it has the weight of numbers against it.

---

[1] His quotations of *Grecus* on Lc. ii, 8, *Et erant pastores*, MS Anton. 467, fol. 26vb, are taken straight from the *Catena aurea, ad loc. Opera S. Thomae* 15 (Venice, 1593) foll. 140vb-141ra. I do not know if this is so in all cases.

[2] MS Anton. 227, foll. 1-28v, *lecta Vincentie Parmense*. The MS belonged to a Master Lorenzo de Capeelis O.F.M. in 1409.

[3] fol. 2v.

[4] foll. 4, 19v. For the lecturer's remarks on preaching, see above, 41.

Finally, there are many scholastic lectures to be found at Assisi, Florence and Padua, given by Franciscan friar doctors. I have not found any classicising tendencies in those I have seen. One very widely spread postill on Ecclesiastes, belonging to the early fourteenth century and probably written at Paris, electrified me by quoting *Titus Livius*. The commentator cites him as a writer on natural science! This postill is still in search of an author. Both Dominican and Franciscan Orders are suspect.[1]

Michele da Massa Marittima O.E.S.A. was the only Italian friar to give full-blooded classicising lectures on Scripture, and he shows traces of English influence. The French picaresque did not spread to Italy either. Moralists in Italy as elsewhere blamed preachers for introducing subtleties and novelties;[2] but the reproach seems to have been less well-founded than it was in the north. Homilies in northern and central Italy at least seem to have been less secular in content than one would expect from a study of Dominican preaching in France and of the classicising group in England.

It sounds like a paradox, when Italy was drawing ahead to become the chief centre of classical studies in Europe, and when Boccaccio was about to produce the superb entertainment of his *Decameron*. Really it is no paradox at all, but a measure of the advanced character of lay culture in Italian cities. The educated layman had his own approach to the classics and did not need a children's hour version. He could provide his own amusement without laughing at pulpit jokes and stories. On the contrary, he was sophisticated enough to prefer his religion plain. A friar, if true to his calling, should set an example of gentle simplicity instead of meddling with polite letters. Boccaccio's friars are either knaves or holy fools. His 'frate antico, di santa e di buona vita, e gran maestro in Iscrittura, e molto

---

[1] Stegmüller, no. 4936, acribes it to Giovanni da San Gemignano O.P. on the strength of the ascription in MS Florence, Bibl. Naz. conv. sopp. 513.A.2. Other copies are anonymous or ascribed to other authors. The Pseudo-Livy quotation is on fol. 222vb of the Nazionale MS, on the text Eccles. i, 6: Titus Livius, lib. 2, sol est stella regalis, mundi lumen, et oculos reddit formosos (et) vivificatos, et sic de multis aliis effectibus quos ibi enumerat secundum opinionem gentilium.

Intrigued, I verified the text from MSS Florence, Laurent. Plut. vii. dext. 12, fol. 144ra and Paris, Maz. 233, ad loc. It is the same in all three. The writer has just been quoting Martianus Capella and Macrobius on the heavenly bodies. It is a mystery how Livy got into this company.

[2] A. Galletti, op. cit. 31, 196-8.

venerabile uomo', was diddled by ser Ciappelletto; another well-meaning confessor, of celebrated piety, acted as an innocent go-between for a Florentine lady and her lover.[1] A literary convention need bear no relation to historical fact, but it denotes an attitude. Religious in Italy were expected to be other-worldly, hence the support for Franciscan Spirituals and for extremist movements. Rhetoric in the pulpit was desired and demanded only in so far as it was sacred rhetoric and not a graceless bastard.

The friar doctors of the Italian cities understood the mind of their hearers. This emerges both from sermons and from lectures, which were designed to train students to preach in their turn. The preacher refrained from bringing coals to Newcastle in the shape of classical allusions, but offered a pathetic contrast instead. The Gospel, pure and simple, stirred the emotions and appealed to the aesthetic sense more immediately than the Gospel seasoned with Pliny or Maximus. In the same way Petrarch avoided quoting from profane authors in his devotional pieces. Italian friars who were versed in classical learning would share his taste. Not ignorance but sophistication may explain the absence of an Italian Holcot.

[1] *Il Decam.* i, 1; iii, 3.

CHAPTER XII

EARLY ITALIAN HUMANISM

Le corps de Rome en cendre est devallé,
Et son esprit rejoindre s'est allé
Au grand esprit de ceste masse ronde.

Joachim du Bellay, *Les Antiquités* v.

THE pre-humanists and early humanists were nearly all lawyers and sons of lawyers, notaries, jurists or professors of law.[1] Even Boccaccio, who was exceptional in being a merchant's son, studied canon law at Naples. Petrarch studied civil law and could have made a great success of it had he chosen; or so he tells us. The country people round Vaucluse regarded the prophet of humanism as a clever lawyer and pestered him for advice on their little affairs.[2]

That lawyers could form a professional aristocracy and build up dynasties within it resulted from the nature of city life in Italy. Medieval systems of land tenure and the litigiousness of landlords and vassals or tenants encouraged and enriched the lawyer everywhere. Add trade disputes and agreements, rapidly developing business methods of banking, insurance and credit facilities, and inter-state relations demanding a knowledge of international law, and you have the conditions in which notaries and lawyers will thrive. All need training in order to qualify, which puts a premium on teaching. The Italian law schools, especially Bologna with its proud tradition and long-established pre-eminence, attracted students from all over Europe. Since Italian universities were secular, not clerical as they were further north, the teachers, students and practitioners of law did not normally take orders unless they preferred to make their career as canonists and looked to the Church for advancement. The *domini* of Bologna, as the professors of civil law liked to be called, were married men with families. They possessed fine houses and estates in the country. Many received the honour of knighthood. The civilian had a part to play in the internal and external politics of his city.

[1] R. Weiss, *The Dawn of Humanism in Italy* (London, 1947) 5-6.
[2] *Poster.* 17; *Metr.* 55-60.

He would serve as a magistrate, go on embassies, sit on commissions and perhaps be elected Podestà of a neighbouring city government: the Italian communes appointed 'foreigners' as their presiding chief magistrates. Incidentally service as an ambassador to or as a magistrate in a foreign commune corrected the parochialism of civic life. Lovato Lovati (1241-1309), besides taking part in the government of Padua, lived for a time at Vicenza as Podestà. Here he had frescoes representing historical scenes with his own Latin inscriptions on them painted on the walls of the town hall. Here, too, he probably met the Vicenzan notary Benvenuto Campesani, who was in touch with pre-humanist circles in both Padua and Verona. Campesani is best known for his epigram on the return of the Catullus manuscript to Verona, printed in some of the older editions and in the most recent edition of Catullus.[1]

The universities provided some elements of a liberal education. The civilians handled Roman law texts, which must have given them a feeling for antiquity: Petrarch described the civil law as 'absque dubio magna ... et romane antiquitatis plena'.[2] From the time of its first revival its professors had seen themselves as champions of civilised procedure against barbarous old customs.[3] The conflict between Roman and Lombard law kept this sense of mission alive at least in the kingdom of Naples.[4] More important perhaps, the law students had to have graduated in arts before proceeding to the higher faculty. This involved the study of Latin grammar and rhetoric, which at worst would convey a smattering of literary culture. At best it meant sitting at the feet of a versifier or poet.[5] A doctorate at law necessitated a capital outlay on account of the length of the course and the expenses of the final examination and graduation ceremony. The notaries, who were much more numerous than the doctors, followed a shorter and more strictly technical course.

---

[1] R. Weiss, Lovato Lovati (1241-1309), *Italian Studies* 6 (1951) 3-28; *Benvenuto Campesani* (1250/55 ?-1323), Estratto dal 'Bolletino del Museo Civico di Padova' 44 (1955) 3-17.

[2] *Poster*. 17.

[3] H. Kantorowicz and B. Smalley, An English Theologian's View of Roman Law: Pepo, Irnerius, Ralph Niger, *M.A.R.S.* 1 (1943) 246-52.

[4] W. Goetz, *König Robert von Neapel (1309-43)*, (Tübingen, 1910) 42.

[5] On the school tradition of grammar and poetry, see P. H. Wickstead and E. G. Gardner, *Dante and Giovanni de Vigilio* (London, 1902); P. O. Kristeller, Humanism and Scholasticism in the Italian Renaissance, *Studies in Renaissance Thought and Letters* (Rome, 1955) 553-84.

The *ars notaria* belonged to the arts course and did not count as a higher faculty, but it included training in grammar and *dictamen*, that is the drafting of letters and speeches according to certain stylistic rules.[1] The qualified notary, therefore, possessed a good working knowledge of civil law and he had been trained to be style-conscious. True, dictaminal Latin was very unclassical; it had developed at the papal Curia and was a highly original medieval language. Nevertheless, a person whose ear has been sharpened to detect cadence and artifice in his text and to mark any lapse in fine writing will notice the style of any author he reads.

Material conditions favoured professional men with literary interests. A cenacle, whether Mussato's or the Verdurins', supposes town life and *villegiatùra* so that friends can pass their spare time together. Political turmoil brought stimulus as well as interruption and danger, and sometimes the enforced leisure of exile. Mussato like Dante wrote his greatest work as a refugee.

Humanism then developed in a professional lay society, whose members tended to be rich or at least of moderate means. They were experienced in worldly matters, full of civic pride and yet able to communicate with likeminded men in other centres. Nowhere outside Italy could one find families where the men had a tradition of university degrees, of personal libraries and of browsing and scribbling as a hobby. Why this secular domestic culture should have turned to humanism is another problem. It has to be remembered that a middlebrow culture persisted in Renaissance Italy, devouring the old medieval favourites and even swallowing Lathbury on Lamentations. The encyclopaedists Vincent of Beauvais and John of Wales kept their appeal. Tales of chivalry remained popular. This public got its classics in translation, sometimes through the French. The early thirteenth-century chronicle *Li fait des romains* was translated into Italian in the early fourteenth century or perhaps earlier. There are six different versions of the translation all belonging to the fourteenth and fifteenth centuries.[2] It evidently stood up to the competition of the

---

[1] S. Stelling-Michaud, *L'Université de Bologne et la pénétration des droits romain et canonique en Suisse aux XIIIe et XIVe siècles* (Geneva, 1955) 66, 71, 187-91.

[2] L. F. Flutre, *Li fait des romains dans les littératures française et italienne du XIIe au XVI siècle* (Paris, 1932) 189. On Italian translations of John of Wales, see A. G. Little, *Studies in English Franciscan History* (Manchester, 1917) 175; see also J. O. Stigall, op. cit. 51.

new humanist translations of Livy.[1] Yet somehow or other at the turn of the thirteenth century highbrow groups split away from the middlebrow. The process has been observed and described for Padua and Arezzo and reconstructed with many gaps in the evidence for Florence.[2] No one has explained just why it happened.

The pre-humanists elude us partly because so many of their works are known only by their titles. A treatise or poem existing in a small number of copies intended for passing round among a few friends could disappear very easily. Such writings had little interest for the later humanists, who soon outstripped and forgot their predecessors. What did survive lay hidden until modern scholars in their search for origins found it out, too late to do more than collect bits and pieces. This does not apply to Albertino Mussato: he gained more than local celebrity and has left an imposing body of writings. And yet it is still difficult to understand the inspiration moving his cult of antiquity. He was indeed *engagé*, taking part in affairs as soldier and statesman as well as being a lawyer and man of letters. He wrote his tragedy, the *Ecerinide*, as propaganda against tyranny; it was acted in public with this purpose. But he would have convinced a wider circle had he written it in easier Latin. The guild of notaries urged him to use more intelligible and less refined language in his poetry. His choice of an esoteric medium hardly suggests that the pre-humanists had a definite programme or that they thought of their studies in terms of a battle of ideas, however much they were involved in politics as individuals. They seem on the contrary to have resembled the eighteenth-century physician, whose epitaph in Bath Abbey says that he had 'an uncommon genius for Historie Painting (An Amusement worthy his enlarged Mind)'. Pre-humanism started in the leisure hours of busy but cultured men.

If we cannot penetrate their secret we can at least compare

---

[1] On these translations see Guis. Billanovich, Il Boccaccio, il Petrarcha e le più antiche traduzioni in italiano delle decadi di Tito Livio, *Giornale storico della letteratura italiana* 130 (1953) 311-37.

[2] H. Wieruszowski, Arezzo as a Center of Learning and Letters in the Thirteenth Century, *Traditio* 9 (1953) 374-83; R. Weiss, Lineamenti per una storia del primo umanesimo fiorentino, *Rivista storica italiana* 60 (1948) 349-66. There is no general study of pre-humanism at Padua, but its rise can be followed in accounts of Lovato and Mussato; R. Weiss, *The Dawn of Humanism*, op. cit.; Guis. Billanovich, *I primi umanisti e le tradizioni dei classici latini* (Fribourg, 1953) 14-24; N. Sapegno, *Il Trecento*, 2nd ed. (Milan, 1955) 151-6.

them with the English classicising friars. The *Compendium moralium notabilium* of the Paduan lawyer Geremia da Montagnone will make a fair starting point for comparison. It is a compilation and therefore belongs to the same literary genre as the English lectures: we have seen that the latter are largely chains of *exempla* and excerpts. Montagnone put his material together after 1295, continuing to work on it and to make additions until his death in 1320/1; so that the framework is early fourteenth-century. His collection of moral sayings from biblical, classical, patristic and medieval writers follows a long tradition and his preface keeps to the rhythmical *clausulae* of *dictamen*. But he arranged his authors in a new way and gave them titles designed to distinguish between the classical and the post-classical. Isidore of Seville (d. 636) seems to mark his dividing line between the two eras.

Only the ancients are allowed the title of 'philosopher'; later writers on philosophical subjects are called 'religiologus', like the authors of the Bible and the Fathers. Only the ancients are 'poets'; after the classical period we find 'versifiers'. The distinction shows that Montagnone regarded ancient thought and ancient literature as superior to 'medieval'. Robert Holcot, who classed Pierre Riga among the poets and called Alan of Lille 'Alanus Magnus', would have sighed to see his favourites downgraded. Montagnone also tried to put his authors into chronological order under each of his subject headings. In doing so he managed to weed out some of the spurious, though by no means all. He knew that the *Distichs* ascribed to Cato were late antique and that the *De quattuor virtutibus* ascribed to Seneca belonged to the period between Priscian and St Ambrose; he could not place it more precisely, not realising that the author was St Martin of Braga. His exceptionally wide range of books includes many by Cicero, the humanists' lodestar; Montagnone quotes from the rare *Topica*. Modern scholars find the *Compendium* of special interest on account of its quotations from 'Catullus poeta'. Catullus had been neglected during the middle ages, but began to be read again in Italy in the early fourteenth century. This was one manifestation of the new taste in classical poetry. Montagnone probably added quotations from him in the later drafts of the *Compendium*, thus marking himself out as a member of the *élite* who had access to the rare *Liber Catulli*, and who could appreciate his luck.[1] Montagnone died only a year or two after Thomas Waleys had begun his career as a doctor and before Ridevall or Holcot had qualified. Yet he already had better equipment and a more sophisticated standard.

His *Compendium* reflects the Paduans' main interests. Lovato made a systematic search through the old abbey library of Pomposa looking for purer copies of well-known texts and copies of rare ones. He found a good, early text of Seneca's *Tragedies* and had all three decades of Livy. The Paduan group also exploited the rich collection in the cathedral library at Verona, which contained Catullus and Tibullus. It was a promising start on the resources close at hand. They studied their texts from the point of view of style; Lovato worked on the metres of Seneca's *Tragedies*,[2] Mussato summarised the plots.[3] The next step was to imitate. Mussato wrote history after the manner of Livy and Sallust, rejecting both the style and the arrangement of the typical medieval chronicle. He dramatised the legend of Ezzelino da Romano and his family after the manner of Seneca. The reign of terror under this late thirteenth-century tyrant and his horrible end had made an unforgettable impression on the Paduans. Mussato's *Ecerinide* puts the tragedy of the 'demon brood' in a neo-classical setting. Senecan diction is used to express Christian beliefs, such as the certainty of rewards and punishments after death. Mussato's chorus,

> Iudex rigidus, iudex placidus
> Donat iustos, damnat iniquos.
> Petit illecebras virtus superas,
> Crimen tenebras expetit imas.
> Dum licet ergo moniti stabilem
> Discite legem. . . .[4]

sounds grander, though less poignant than

> Et qui bona egerunt, ibunt in vitam eternam; qui vero mala, in ignem eternum.[5]

Mussato imitated classical models at the price of being understood only in a narrow circle of friends and of missing

[1] R. Weiss, *Il primo seculo dell'umanesimo* (Rome, 1949) 15-50; B. L. Ullman, *Studies in the Italian Renaissance* (Rome, 1955) 81-115.
[2] Guis. Billanovich, *I primi umanisti*, op. cit. 18-21.
[3] E. Franceschini, *Studi e note di filologia latina medievale* (Milan, 1938) 177-97.
[4] *Ecerinide, tragedia*, ed. L. Padrin (Bologna, 1900) 65-6.
[5] William Langland, *The Vision of Piers the Plowman*, C. Text, xiii, 118.

a wider public. His decision signified discontent with current literary modes. It caused him to break with the ingrained habit of *dictamen* and of medieval verse forms, not to mention ecclesiastical Latin. The pre-humanists were not only cultivating but preferring antiquity. Logically, their preference supposes a certain periodisation of history. The good, ancient style is dead and ought to be revived. The discovery or fresh consciousness that ancient literary culture was dead, but might live again, could widen to include politics and a whole way of life. The pre-humanists were on the brink of conceiving 'the middle age' as a period of darkness and barbarism, when antiquity had perished. They do not seem to have carried this train of thought very far; but Mussato at least reflected on the subject of periodisation. He found in his ancient authors a theory of the natural growth and decline of states and he applied it to the history of Padua to explain her loss of freedom. Further, perhaps under the influence of astrological theories, he traced a cyclical repetition of prosperity and decadence in periods of forty or fifty years.[1]

Italian history since the barbarian invasions certainly provided food for thought. An Englishman could look back on his past and see one single form of government, monarchy, continuing since the *adventus Saxonum*. He had no reason at all to imagine King Alfred as acting differently from King Edward I. An Italian could not but be aware of the gap which separated the fall of Rome from the rise of the communes within the framework of the medieval empire. The fourteenth-century emperors contrasted increasingly to their disadvantage with their ancient prototypes. Religious reformers pointed to a decline in ancient standards consequent on the Donation of Constantine and the endowment of the Church. The optimistic view of the Donation prevalent among twelfth-century theologians, who saw it as beneficial to the Church,[2] gave way to blame and grief. The Gregorian reformers had promised a moral regeneration for clergy and laity. Now the papacy presented the chief obstacle to reform. Marsilio of Padua offered an interpretation of history and a programme: the Church had gradually usurped the functions of secular government in

[1] N. Rubinstein, Some Ideas on Municipal Progress and Decline, *F.S.* 165-83.
[2] M. D. Chenu, Conscience de l'histoire et théologie au XIIe siècle, *Archives* 21 (1955) 107-33.

education, justice and politics; the State must recover its true role. Marsilio brought previous discontents and speculations down to earth.

The author of *Defensor pacis* was a friend of Mussato's in early days. The philosophic discussions centred on Pietro d'Abano made Padua a more stimulating place. Giotto's frescoes in the Arenà chapel gave a new direction to painting. Prerequisites for a new periodisation of history were present. Neither past nor current events allowed intellectuals to keep a sense of continuity or to see history in the old patterns.

When Mussato died in 1329 the pre-humanists had reached a more sophisticated stage in their approach to antiquity than English friars would ever do. The English made no attempt to imitate classical style, which would have lost them their public. The suspicion that centuries of ignorance and bad writing divided them from their dear philosophers and poets never crossed their minds. They saw nothing funny in their biblical-classical mixture. Mussato found a classical setting and style for a medieval story at a time when the English were telling classical stories in medieval idiom. The contrast will be greater still when we pass from Mussato to Petrarch.

One man's genius and long, brilliant career (1304-74) made humanism an all-Italian and international movement. Petrarch kept himself free from the chains of a profession which, as he clearly saw, had limited the achievements of Lovato and Mussato. He depended on the patronage of great noble families such as the Colonna and of princes and popes. He acted as a very superior odd-job diplomat. He took minor orders and received a prebend at Padua. Life was not easy for him. He won his freedom to write and study as he wished and to withdraw into the solitude so necessary to his inspiration at the price of restricting his wants to bread-and-butter and books and of endless journeys and removals. He would take what his friends thought was dirty money, accepting the protection of the Visconti tyrant, provided that it left him personally independent. Boccaccio (1313-75) scraped along, judging by his complaints, on less well-paid jobs and on less reliable patronage. But thanks to these struggles the next generation had a softer time. University chairs for the teaching of classical literature were founded; chanceries began to employ humanists; patronage became more fashionable. Humanism itself turned into a profession. The highbrow public was rich, exalted and big enough to support its luminaries.

Not even Petrarch could have made converts among the powers that were unless social conditions had favoured him. He would have made no headway with a northern aristocracy, which liked to identify itself with the Round Table of Arthurian romance. The Italian cities hired mercenaries to do their fighting. Wealthy citizens could devote their leisure to the arts of peace. Not only princes of the Church but lay rulers could admire and try to imitate the great civilian statesmen of antiquity and ancient generals who were also men of letters. The ideal governor and patron proposed to them by the humanists was close enough to their experience to arouse their enthusiasm, and made them long for the glory to be reflected on them by their clients. If mercenary armies spelled the political ruin of Italy, as Machiavelli thought, they were a condition for the triumph of humanism.

Petrarch and his friends travelled over a larger terrain than the pre-humanists and this had an oddly paradoxical consequence. They became more self-conscious and more aware of their mission to revive ancient letters at the same time as they entered into the full inheritance of medieval classical studies. The clerical culture of Paris and Avignon and the mixed culture of Angevin Naples both contributed to their development. Avignon served as a cultural and geographical junction, making journeys and contacts easier. The resulting interplay and enrichment appear whether we study the history of people or parchment.

The Austin friar Dionigi da Borgo San Sepolcro links up all three centres and northern scholarship with humanism in a remarkable way.[1] He studied and taught at Paris and died in 1342 as bishop of Monopoli in the kingdom of Naples. He was an intimate friend of Petrarch and Boccaccio. Intellectually he was a polymath after the manner of Nicholas Trevet, who left commentaries on both theological and classical texts. His commentary on Valerius Maximus, begun at Paris and finished at Naples, had an immense success. It was not wholly original, but seems to have depended on an earlier commentary by a mysterious Friar Peter O.P. which circulated in France.[2] A third commentator on Vale-

---

[1] For the latest information and bibliography see R. Weiss, Notes on Dionigi da Borgo San Sepolcro, *Italian Studies* 10 (1955) 40-42.
[2] M. de Marco, Un nuovo codice de commento di 'Frater Petrus O.P.' a Valerio Massimo, *Aevum* 30 (1956) 554-8.

rius was the Tuscan Dominican Luca Mannelli who died as bishop of Fano in 1362. He dedicated a *Compendium moralis philosophiae* to the poet and bibliophile Bruzio Visconti, and a *Tabulatio et expositio Senecae* to Clement VI at the Pope's request.[1] Contemporaries did not sniff at the work of these 'laborious friars' as old-fashioned, but gave it a warm welcome.

The search for manuscripts widened to include France and the Rhinelands. Here treasures lay waiting to be rediscovered for the good reason that book hunting and the collection of classical texts were nothing new in the North. The cult of the classics, which the Carolingian revival had launched, survived barbarian invasions and even scholasticism. It passed through many phases between the period of Alcuin at one end and that of Roger Bacon and John of Wales at the other. The twelfth-century Chartres period was perhaps the most relevant to the humanists' needs. Hence abbey, cathedral and even university libraries had texts which were lacking in the Italian equivalents: Italy in the early middle ages had been more devastated and education had tended to be more legal and technical.[2] It was no mere chance that Petrarch found Cicero's *Pro Archia* at Liège, though he thought it was: the cathedral had been an important centre of study in the eleventh and early twelfth centuries. Petrarch did not realise this. The story of his Chartres Livy illustrates the kind of thing that happened.[3] The cathedral library had a copy of Livy, including all three decades, dating from the time of the eleventh-century master and pioneer of classical studies, Fulbert of Chartres. A result of the system of papal provisions, so loudly denounced by contemporaries, was that the popes used to provide Italians to benefices in northern Europe. The Colonna family, one

---

[1] T. Käppeli, Luca Mannelli († 1362) e la sua Tabulatio e Expositio Senecae, *Arch. FF. Praed.* 18 (1948) 236-64.

[2] B. L. Ullman, *Studies in the Italian Renaissance* (Rome, 1955) 27-53; P. O. Kristeller, op. cit.

[3] Guis. Billanovich, Petrarch and the Textual Tradition of Livy, *J.W.C.I.* 14 (1951) 137-208; *I.M.U.* 2, 103-78.

The study of Petrarch's personal library and of his discoveries and annotations of texts is advancing so rapidly at present that it would be unwise to attempt a *résumé* of results here. E. Pellegrini, *La Bibliothèque des Visconti et des Sforza ducs de Milan au XVe siècle* (Paris, 1955) has added ten manuscripts of Petrarch to the twenty-three known to de Nolhac; she has recognised them uniquely by Petrarch's marginal notes, written in his autograph. These new discoveries are adding rapidly to our knowledge of the wanderings of manuscripts and of the history of their ownership.

of those great noble clans who, as E. Jordan put it, made it their 'secondary industry' to exploit the papacy (their primary being brigandage in the country round Rome) had an almost hereditary privilege of provision to prebends at Chartres cathedral. Landolfo Colonna, a versatile and cultured beneficiary of the privilege, took the opportunity to borrow the Livy and have it copied with other texts from the library. Another member of the family, Fra Giovanni Colonna O.P., visited his uncle at Chartres while he was studying at Paris and saw the Livy. Petrarch was a protégé of the Colonna family, thanks to his stay at Avignon, and a special friend of Fra Giovanni. He acquired and annotated the copy, so that the Chartres text of Livy passed into the textual tradition, renewed by his labours as a critic.

The humanist net spread east and south to cover Italian collections which had escaped the more local researches of the Paduans. In spite of the comparative poverty of Italy the old libraries of Ravenna, Bobbio and Montecassino, to mention some of the richest, could still produce rarities. Zanobi da Strada, a friend of Petrarch and Boccaccio, had occasion to live at Montecassino in his capacity as episcopal vicar between 1355 and 1357. He spent his leisure in ransacking the library.[1] Visits to the kingdom of Naples brought the humanists into touch with French culture grafted on to a tradition of mixed Greek, Latin and Arabic encyclopaedic learning.[2] The Greek-speaking population provided teachers who gave Petrarch and Boccaccio their first taste of Homer. The earliest Latin translation, unsatisfactory as it was, opened up the primary source of Greek poetry and myth for the first time.

Boccaccio's *Genealogiae deorum* represents an extraordinary monument to these contacts, a real Neapolitan ice. He depended mainly on the old Latin mythographers, especially Fulgentius and Alberich of London, but he also used a mysterious Greek compiler called Theodontion, who is supposed to have been a Campanian living some time between the ninth and eleventh centuries. Boccaccio may have known him at second hand through the *Liber collectionum* of the royal librarian, Paolo di Perugia. Theodontion transmitted fragments ascribed to Philochoros, a Greek

---

[1] Guis. Billanovich, *I primi umanisti*, op. cit. 30-32.
[2] R. Weiss, The Greek Culture of South Italy in the Later Middle Ages, *The Proceedings of the British Academy* 38 (1951) 24-50.

historian of the fourth century B.C. Their genuineness is open to doubt. Theodontion had probably never read the *Atthis*, where he could have found the original.[1] His Philochoros is more likely to be a forgery, a parallel to the Pseudo-Palaephatius quoted by Holcot and Lathbury. Boccaccio also took his Demogorgon from Theodontion. This progenitor of the whole race of gods is a wholly unclassical fiction.[2] The purist may feel that Boccaccio ought to have 'feared the Greeks' in this case; they did not improve on his Latin sources. But no reader of the *Genealogiae* can regret the instrusion of the pale, dank monster in its smelly cavern. It makes a magnificently romantic opening to the book.

Just as Boccaccio drew on existing compilations for his mythology, so he used the stock arguments in his defence of poetry. There was nothing new in them; they went back to patristic discussions of the use of pagan fictions in Christian education. It has even been pointed out that St Thomas Aquinas had carried the argument further than Boccaccio realised.[3] Nevertheless it would be wrong to dismiss the *Genealogiae* as unoriginal on account of its content. The earlier Latin mythographers had been theologians, though their compilations could be used for the purpose of rhetoric. Boccaccio was writing primarily for the benefit of poets and rhetors. His passionate wish to bring together the *membra disiecta* of the whole of ancient mythology puts him into a class apart from John Ridevall and his predecessors. It was a gigantic task, inspired by religious fervour on behalf of classical studies. He could not have compassed anything so grand if he had gone to primary sources and had despised textbooks.

The humanists constituted themselves the ungrateful heirs of centuries of classical culture. The only place where ancient letters had suffered neglect and needed to be resurrected was precisely northern Italy, and here the prehumanists had been at work already. The humanists' picture of themselves as the first to revive antiquity was unhistorical, a pure myth. But, like many other myths, it proved to be fruitful and stimulating, more so probably

---

[1] M. Lenchantin, Nuovi frammenti di Filocoro, *Rivista di filologia e d'istruzione classica* 10 (1932) 41-57; F. Jacoby, *Die Fragmente der griechischen Historiker*, part 3, b. suppl. vol. 1 (Leiden, 1954) 240, 242, 547, 592.

[2] Seznec, 220-22.

[3] E. R. Curtius, *European Literature and the Latin Middle Ages*, translated from the German by W. R. Trask (London, 1953) 203-27.

than the grey and complex truth would have been. The modern historian must imitate Boccaccio and treat the humanist myth as an *integumentum* or veil for a secret and true meaning. The humanists borrowed more than they would admit and more than their limited knowledge of history allowed them to grasp. On the other hand, they were also creative.

The aspect of their creativeness that concerns us here is Petrarch's discovery of historical perspective. Many shades of thought and feeling blended in his idea of the past. He hated the present. The times into which he had been born 'under an adverse star' disgusted him. His contemporaries struck him as *mesquins* in culture, politics and religion. There had never been so much talk of poets as there was at Avignon and never so little understanding of poetry.[1] Modern politics generally lent themselves to satire rather than to the writing of history.[2] His pessimism about culture and politics was partly a matter of temperament and partly reflected his prejudice against those northern barbarians who had snatched the sceptre from tired Rome. Petrarch despised both Charlemagne and chivalry as un-Roman.[3] His criticism of the Avignon papacy and of scholasticism echoed fourteenth-century commonplaces. The papacy offered a universal target. Schoolmen themselves depreciated logic. They admitted to distrust of reason in the schools and denounced sophistry when they spoke as moralists. But personal and general causes of dissatisfaction added up to something new. Petrarch condemned the whole period of years which had elapsed since Rome had fallen.[4]

This new idea of a dividing line between culture and barbarism developed slowly in his mind. He never expressed it in any precise formula. Yet he broke away from the concept of continuity as symbolised in a succession of world monarchies. 'What else then is all history but praise of Rome?': Petrarch asked the question towards the end of his life, meaning ancient Rome; the name had become exclusive. A bad, post-classical period had started at some

[1] *Fam.* xxiv, 8; xiii, 6.

[2] *De viris illustribus*, Prohem.: . . . neque enim historie sed satyre materiam stilo tribuunt. Nam etsi quosdam nuper victoriis satis insignes noverim, ita tamen aut fortune aut hostium inertie cunta cedunt, ut nullus ibi vel virtuti victoris aut vere glorie locus sit.

[3] *Fam.* i, 1, 4; *Triumphus Cupidinis*, iii, 79-81.

[4] See T. E. Mommsen, Petrarch's Conception of the Dark Ages, *Speculum* 17 (1942) 226-42.

rather vague date. Petrarch reckoned it from when the empire began to decline under barbarian rule or from when Christianity became the state religion. Both events coincided with the decline of letters.

It may seem surprising that so good a Catholic as Petrarch should have made the triumph of Christianity synchronise with decline. There was an unresolved conflict in his attitude, but it had a certain logic. He agreed with the widely held opinion that the Church had lost her purity owing to endowment with worldly power and riches. His condemnation was not all-embracing. It excluded the Fathers and those of their medieval successors, such as St Bernard, who had paid attention to style and had not gone in for logic-chopping.[1]

Later humanists developed his periodisation of history. The bad time since the decline of Rome became 'the middle age'; Petrarch himself was seen as announcing the third period, that of 'rebirth'.[2] Did he foresee it when he described himself as 'standing on the boundary between two peoples, looking backward and forward simultaneously'? Opinions differ. On the one hand, he thought of his return to antiquity as a lonely adventure and not as leading the way for a host of scholars. He made a determined escape from the present into the more congenial past, of which he felt jealously possessive. On the other hand, he dedicated his *Africa* to posterity. It seems, therefore, that he had hopes of being appreciated in a better future.

Scholarship was Petrarch's instrument in recreating the 'good' days, for he dreamed in a disciplined fashion: 'L'erudizione non è per il Petrarca solo intelligenza, ma sentimento.'[3] His researches and his sense of values enabled him to scrub off accretions. He rejected the Virgil and Alexander legends[4] and discovered to his joy that Dido was really a virtuous widow, contrary to the traditional story in the *Aeneid.*[5] He wrote the biographies of Caesar and Pompey from the primary sources, comparing them, and ignoring later chronicles. True, John Ridevall had anticipated him to some extent; but Ridevall's discoveries remained buried in a little-read commentary. Petrarch proclaimed his own as a

[1] P. de Nolhac, op. cit. 2, 189-239.   [2] T. E. Mommsen, op. cit.
[3] U. Bosco, *Petrarca* (Turin, 1936) 214.
[4] *Fam.* ix, 5; *Sen.* i, 4; P. de Nolhac, 1, 53, 94-8, 124-8.
[5] *Sen.* iv, 5; *Triumphus Pudicitie*, 10-12, 154-9.

triumph for a new method. His concentration on primary sources also gave him a deeper understanding of his authors.

The classical period uncovered by his scholarship looked different from what we have seen through the eyes of English friars. Petrarch's history was more stratified; he distinguished the biblical from the classical, and both from the post-classical. Persons from all three eras march in the processions of his *Trionfi*; but they do not mix, as they do in Lathbury's *Non sedet* passage; they keep to their own groups, like delegates at a congress.[1] Petrarch's authors have more rounded and individual characters. This was partly because he knew more about them. *Pro Archia* shocked him by disclosing a Cicero emotionally involved in politics, quite unlike the detached philosopher of the better known books. The shift in perspective also contributed. Medieval admirers of the ancient philosophers had imagined them rather as wise old relatives, who, apart from being pagans, had all the answers. They took them for granted as children do the elders of the family. Anti-intellectuals had denounced the philosophers with equal lack of discrimination, as Walter of St Victor blamed Seneca for his suicide.[2] Petrarch put himself at a distance and so felt able to converse with them as human beings. His letters to famous Romans show that he could revere them and yet see their individual faults and inconsistencies.[3]

He had made the discovery that the past and the present were different. It was not enough in reconstructing the past for the poet or story-teller to give his characters classical names. The characters must look, think and talk as they would have done, and not as though they were contemporary. The representation of bygone days demanded both scholarship and historical imagination. Petrarch had invented an eighth deadly sin, which is still with us, the sin of anachronism.

The painter Simone Martini, whom he met at Avignon, tried to please his friend by dressing the Romans in costumes other than those of the fourteenth century.[4] *Africa* strains, with inevitable mistakes, after this elusive ideal of likeness. *Gesta romanorum* and its kind look forward to our popular

[1] The chaste women are a mixed bunch, but this is exceptional; *Triumphus Pudicitie*, 136-59.
[2] P. Delhaye, *Le Microcosmos de Godefroy de Saint-Victor* 2 (Lille, 1951) 247.
[3] On these letters see Guis. Billanovich, *Petrarca letterato* (Rome, 1947) 3-55.
[4] P. de Nolhac, op. cit. 1, 23.

historical novel, a contemporary story in a pseudo-historical setting; *Africa* stands for the 'fictional biography' or the serious historical novel as we know it in the writings of Robert Graves and Hilda Prescott. The comparison sounds disrespectful to Petrarch's epic poem; he regarded *Africa* as his masterpiece and prized it far above his sonnets. In fact, it disappointed readers when it was published soon after his death, as it still disappoints the literary critic. *Africa* has more excitement in store for the modern historian. Petrarch failed to come off as a second Virgil, but read him straight after *Kyng Alisaunder*! The refined sensitivity of his attitude to the past will stagger you.

In the first place he can distinguish between different periods within ancient history. *Africa* tells the story of Scipio's conquest of Carthage at the end of the Second Punic War. Petrarch chose the republican period before Rome was corrupted by empire. He therefore brings out the austere, soldierly virtues of the early Romans as he found them described in his Livy. The Romans hired no mercenary troops, but fought themselves, and they had no poets to praise their deeds; Ennius had not yet introduced Greek literary fashions. Petrarch presents them as dignified and thoughtful, but simple in contrast to the wealthy Carthaginians. They pride themselves on action rather than words. Lelius says after the banquet given by Syphax:

> . . . Nec teste citato
> Est opus: acta patent.   Scriptorum copia nunquam
> Romano fuit in populo, quos Graius abunde
> Orbis habet. Nostris facere est quam scribere multo
> Gratius atque aliis laudanda relinquere facta
> Quam laudare alios. . . .[1]

Petrarch makes an effort to reconstruct the views that good pagans, ignorant of philosophy as well as having no intuition of Christianity, would hold on the afterlife. At least they realise that it will be more blessed and stable than mortal life, which resembles death if contrasted with the hereafter.[2] The African Massinissa, on the other hand, believes in the transmigration of souls.[3] The Roman ethic is also 'period'. When Scipio questions the ghosts of his ancestors on man's function in his sojourn on earth the answer invokes the eternal laws of God and Nature: man must live virtuously.

---

[1] *Africa*, iii, 481-6.   [2] i, 334-500.   [3] v, 670-3.

The virtues recommended are those of civic duty and patriotism.[1] Petrarch knew that the ethic of the empire tended more towards philosophic detachment, and this appealed to him in some of his moods.[2] He put into the mouth of his republican ghosts the praise of active virtues, which made their City great.

Similarly, he takes pains to provide the right setting. He avoids description of places where he has no reliable model. His famous account of the Italian coastline owes its being to the fact that natural features would not have changed since the Punic Wars. He gives a detailed picture of the topography of ancient Rome as it was shown to the Punic embassy because he thought he could reconstruct it from his literary sources. The visitors climb up and down the monuments with the weariness brought on by a conducted tour at any time.[3] Both passages stand out from their flat surroundings. The lack of equally vivid descriptions in other parts of *Africa* and the many echoes of Virgil make for dullness; but this is the penalty he had to pay for keeping within his known historical limits. The Sophonisba episode breaks through them in that medieval pathos and romance have affected the lovers' psychology, making them less classical than his other characters. This was against Petrarch's intention: relations between the sexes always present the most difficulty to a serious historical novelist, whether he faces it consciously or not. If his hero and heroine were true to their period they might lose our sympathy.

Africa, then, is an attempt at a historical novel and much more. Petrarch uses his poem as a medium for an interpretation of Roman history from start to finish. He supplements his narrative by dreams, prophecies and after-dinner speeches, so as to give his readers flash-backs and forward glances. We become increasingly conscious of Rome's distant past, of her later grandeur and of her final decay.[4] The interpretation results from both historical study and poetic subjectivism. It expresses the Petrarchan theme of transience, of glory swallowed up by time, and he puts himself into the picture. Ennius and Petrarch mark the two

---

[1] i, 489-99.
[2] See H. Baron, Franciscan Poverty and Civic Wealth, *Speculum* 13 (1938) 6-12.
[3] *Africa*, vi, 839-80; viii, 856-953; on Petrarch's knowledge of Roman topography, see *Codice topografico della Città di Roma*, op. cit. 4 (1953) 1-5.
[4] N. Sapegno, op. cit. 214.

poles of Roman literary history. The elder Scipio fore-
tells the coming of both poets. Ennius brings the rude,
inexpert Muses to Latium; Petrarch catches the Muses as
they flee. Scipio has a definite preference for Petrarch:

> Carus uterque michi, studio memorandus uterque:
> Iste rudes Latio duro modulamine Musas
> Intulit; ille autem fugientes carmine sistet;
> ... verum multo michi carior ille est
> Qui procul ad nostrum reflectet lumina tempus.

The younger poet, said Scipio, would write without any
ulterior motive. No desire to gain or flatter would move
him, but only admiration of Rome and love of truth.[1] Then
Ennius dreams that Homer appears to introduce him to his
remote successor: Ennius and Petrarch meet.[2] The latter
saw himself as ending a long line of Latin poets, sucking
the last drops from the dried-up spring of Helicon.[3]

His personal part fitted into his view of history. Rome
was never conquered; no people merited such an honour.
She fell under the weight of her own old age. Petrarch
traced her decline and saw it as a gradual process, beginning
with the rule of emperors of eastern origins. It antedated the
barbarian invasions by several centuries. Nor was the process complete in Petrarch's day. Rome had sunk into ruins
and become a mere name, but would dominate the world
as a memory until the world's end.[4] Petrarch's readers will
hear an unconscious echo of the medieval lament on the
ruins of the city by Hildebert of Tours.[5] The quality of
regret seems to be the same in both; but a gleam of hope
and pride shows in Petrarch's which is absent in Hildebert's.
Petrarch believed that he, at least, could compete with the
ancients in singing the glories of Rome. He could give fresh
content to her memory. His sadness was not only a mood;
it had purpose.

Sense of kinship with a misunderstood and neglected past
impelled Petrarch to evoke the past, and here lies his
originality. His forerunners had loved ancient philosophers
and poets and had wished to follow their examples. The
discovery that scholarship and imagination of a special kind

---

[1] *Africa*, ii, 441-454.   [2] ix, 158-289.   [3] i, 4-6.   [4] ii, 297-326.
[5] In a second poem Rome answers, saying that she is greater now as a
Christian city than she was when pagan; see B. Hauréau, Notice sur les
mélanges poétiques d'Hildebert de Lavardin, *Notices et extraits des MSS de la
Bibliothèque nationale* 28, ii, (Paris, 1878) 331-2, 334-5.

were needed before one could imitate truly was made in Trecento Italy. Rome had to die before she could live again in men's minds. The ancient City was reborn indeed; but she came back for the benefit of an *élite*. The new concept was aristocratic and subtle. Petrarch bequeathed to humanist thought his loathing of humanity in the mass. When Laura lays her wreath in the temple of Chastity, she can choose between two shrines in ancient Rome, the patrician and the plebeian; she chooses the former:

> passamo al tempio poi di Pudicizia
> ch'accende in cor gentile oneste voglie,
> non di gente plebeia, ma di patrizia.[1]

Holcot imagined the temple of Chastity differently. The goddess Vesta was painted there holding a five-leaved lily in her hand. Each leaf bore an inscription praising the virtue of chastity, which the priests of Vesta expounded to the people as they flocked to her temple. The humanists worshipped at a patrician shrine. Holcot's goddess was medieval and plebeian.

[1] *Triumphus Pudicitie*, 181-3.

CONCLUSIONS

The storie of Alisaundre is so commune
That every wight that hath discrecioun
Hath herd somwhat or al of his fortune.

Chaucer, *The Monk's Tale*, in *The Canterbury Tales*,
lines 2631-3.

CHILDREN sometimes plant orange pips to watch them sprout and are disappointed when they never see any oranges. It would be just as childish to think that the classicising movement in England could have turned into humanism. There is no point in speculating on what might have happened: suppose Waleys had kept his temper at Avignon; suppose Ridevall had been assigned to a school in Italy where he could have had the same opportunities as Waleys had at Bologna. Waleys' outburst not only cost him the best years of his life, but also proved that he cared more for theology than for classical studies. Ridevall would have had to change his Order before he could have benefited from a stay abroad: the continental Franciscans would not have encouraged him. Nor should we blame the Black Death. It may have killed off some bright young men, as it killed the elderly Holcot. D'Eyncourt, Hopeman, Ringstead and Lathbury all received their training before 1348. We should not know the names of young classicists who died before they could publish anything. But a movement which could not survive the loss of a few recruits had no future. It had never counted many members, even in the 'thirties and 'forties.

Moreover an icy wind was blowing, not from Geneva, but from Carmel. John Baconthorpe, the Carmelite friar, who probably died in the plague too, denounced from his chair the practice of using moralised fables in preaching. Unlike many reprovers of *paganica studia*, he meant business. His commentary on the first books of *De civitate Dei* tacitly rebukes Trevet, Waleys and Ridevall by omitting the explanation of classical allusions and bringing out St Augustine's anti-pagan polemic.[1] Certain English Franciscans had already turned away from the classicism of their

[1] B. Smalley, John Baconthorpe's Postill on St Matthew, op. cit. 108-13.

brother, John of Wales.[1] The defence of classical learning
added to Lathbury on Lamentations sounds like an answer
to opponents within his Order.[2] The Austin Friars in England have left little trace of any interest in the classics in the
early fourteenth century; but we may perhaps judge them
by Johann Klenkok's commentary on Acts. Klenkok came
to Oxford from Prague about 1352/3. He incepted and
taught theology in 1359 and left about 1361. His lectures
on Acts, which were given at Prague after his return to
Germany and can be dated 1369/70-1372, perhaps reflect
his earlier teaching at Oxford. They are severely theological
in character; he rarely or never quotes from the classics.[3]
The next set of lectures on Scripture to emerge from Oxford
is Wyclif's *Postilla*, given in the early 'seventies. He thought
classical allusions frivolous and moved in a wholly different
atmosphere.[4]

Perhaps the Black Death strengthened the opposition
by sobering the survivors and blinding their eyes to the
graceful and beautiful, which appealed to Holcot so strongly.[5]
Even if this could be proved, the plague of 1348/9 could not
be made responsible for the internal development of the
group between Waleys and Ridevall at one end and Lathbury at the other. The earliest stage of the classicising movement corresponds most closely to early humanism. The
turning away from scholarship to fantasy can be seen in
Ridevall and even more in Holcot. Imagination runs riot.
Lathbury proves conclusively that the classicising movement, even if it had continued instead of petering out,
would have had no point of contact with developments in
Italy. It was going in a different direction.

The scholarly type of classicism could not have matured in

---

[1] B. Smalley, John Russel O.F.M., op. cit. 315-16.

[2] See above, 228.

[3] *O.R.* 2, xix, 1057; Welter, p. 423, n. 35; Stegmüller, no. 4752, 2. I have
been able to read the lectures on Acts in MS Eichstät 204, foll. 117-92, thanks
to the kindness of the librarian. It is written in a fifteenth-century German
hand. Klenkok refers back to his teaching at Oxford (foll. 122ra, 126va), but
he seems to be addressing a German or Czech audience, since he draws his
topical illustrations from the speech and manners of the Saxons, Bavarians and
Frisians (foll. 131ra and passim). Klenkok came of a knightly family and was
born at Hanover. He may have studied canon law at Bologna before he
studied theology at Prague and Oxford.

[4] B. Smalley, John Wyclif's *Postilla super totam Bibliam*, B.L.R. 4 (1953)
186-205.

[5] See for instance M. Meiss, *Painting in Florence and Siena after the Black Death*
(Princeton, 1951).

any case so long as it was confined to friary *studia*. Teachers must be endowed or paid. Only a genius of Petrarch's stamp can achieve the barest illusion of independence. English society supported its friar doctors in order that they might teach and preach Christian faith and ethics. Their classical studies could only be marginal. It is wonderful that the margin could hold all they put there, but space was limited. Secular doctors might have gone further than the friars, since some had private means and all could look forward to provision to benefices. This allowed more freedom of choice: the friar must obey his superiors; the secular could be his own master. The seculars used their freedom to concentrate on philosophy and its subordinate disciplines and on speculative theology. Classicism left most of them cold.

The arts course at Oxford and Cambridge served to train the future philosopher and theologian. The humanist educational programme could find no place in it. Humanism in Italy developed in opposition to scholasticism, which was too lively in England to admit of any rival. The classicising friars accepted the *status quo* without protest, being school-men themselves. They had no alternative to offer, and their modest little diversions were subsidiary to the real business of academic life. The Oxford philosophers and theologians of the early fourteenth century were not 'conservatives', to be opposed to the 'progressive' humanists. A rebel against tradition could have been happy with either. All attacked established modes of thought, though the weapons varied. When Oxonians developed their new logic and discussed free will and predestination, they were handling more explosive material than the humanists could boast of inventing. New theories came up in mathematics and physics. The Merton school of logicians carried on through the mid-century in spite of the plague. It is easy to see why classicism failed to compete.

Could any other body of professional men have produced classical scholars? The early humanists in Italy were civil lawyers or notaries. The English common lawyers make an obvious parallel. Their standing, means and dignity in the early fourteenth century would bear comparison with the Italian civilians'. Justices and serjeants at law were mostly laymen by this time.[1] The more successful chief justices did

[1] T. F. T. Plucknett, *A Concise History of the Common Law*, 2nd ed. (London, 1936) 214.

well for themselves: they accumulated manors, made advantageous marriages and raised their families to high positions in the ranks of the country gentry or higher still.[1] The government used their legal experience, drawing on the Bench for supply diplomats.[2] The shapers of our common law were, as Maitland wrote, 'worldly men, . . . in their way learned, cultivated men, . . . gregarious, clubbable men, grouping themselves in hospices which became schools of law'. There must already have been some sort of grouping at headquarters which developed into the Inns of Court. The Inns would become academies of general as well as legal education.

And yet historians have found no evidence, though not for want of trying, as to how these distinguished persons were educated before they started on their professional careers. They had to know enough Latin and French to read their law books. All is guessing after that. Legal training itself was severely technical and the courts excluded rhetoric. 'True to their administrative origin, they kept themselves in a strictly business attitude.'[3] English common lawyers, therefore, differed from their Italian colleagues on two points. They had not normally attended a university; they dealt with a law which was medieval in its origins and not ancient. Civil and canon law had influenced it at an earlier stage. Some common lawyers may have learnt something of civil for purposes of government service.[4] But they took pride in the contrast between English and foreign law.

We know that the notarial course had a less formal English equivalent. Masters at Oxford received young men for training as secretaries and stewards to magnates. They taught court-keeping, heraldry, accounting, *dictamen* and a useful modicum of Latin, French and common law technique. It was freelance teaching, since no degree would be given. A similar type of training may well have existed

---

[1] W. C. Bolland, *Chief Justice Sir William Bereford* (Cambridge, 1924); B. H. Putnam, *The Place in Legal History of Sir William Shareshull Chief Justice of the King's Bench 1350-1361* (Cambridge, 1950); E. L. G. Stones, Sir Geoffrey le Scrope (*c.* 1285 to 1340), Chief Justice of the King's Bench, *E.H.R.* 69 (1954) 1-17.

[2] Stones, op. cit. 7-9; G. P. Cuttino, *English Diplomatic Administration 1259-1339* (Oxford, 1940) 93-4.

[3] Plucknett, op. cit. 199. See ibid. 195-202 for an account of the common lawyers' professional training.

[4] Cuttino, op. cit. 98.

elsewhere.[1] This, too, differed from the notarial course on the Continent in that it remained separate from the university arts course. Its practical character would make it unapt to produce bookish men.

Patronage sometimes supports a movement which has found no welcome in universities. The patrons' role in Italy raises the question why Richard de Bury's example was not followed. But what had classical scholarship to offer the rulers of England in the early fourteenth century? Scholastic learning, pre-digested, and vernacular culture met their needs. Encyclopaedias answered their questions about the world around them. Thoughtful laymen caught echoes of theological controversy. Tales of chivalry both flattered and stimulated their hearers.

Fashions rather than values changed in the next hundred years. *Dictamen* began to look silly and one had to keep up with foreign princes.[2] Duke Humphrey of Gloucester patronised and employed humanists, who coached him in the Italian Renaissance. His letters to Pier Candido Decembrio, written in 1439, express the concept clearly:

> 'We congratulate you with admiration and think ourselves happy in this one thing, that so many highly skilled men among you should flourish in our times, to revive for our own and future ages those excellent philosophers, who had once well-nigh perished.'[3]
> 'You have renewed for this age the eloquence and power of speech, ancient and worthy of the ancients, which had all but perished.'[4]

Few Englishmen would have accepted the slur on medieval culture implied by such statements. Duke Humphrey him-

---

[1] H. G. Richardson, Business Training in Medieval Oxford, *American Historical Review* 46 (1941) 259-80; Letters of the Oxford *Dictatores, Formularies which bear on the History of Oxford circa 1204-1430*, ed. H. E. Salter, W. A. Pantin and H. G. Richardson 2 (Oxford, 1942) 331-450.

[2] R. Weiss, *Humanism in England During the Fifteenth Century*, op. cit.

[3] R. Weiss, New Light on Humanism in England During the Fifteenth Century, *J.W.C.I.* 14 (1951) 25: Congratulamur autem vobis mirum in modum, et ex hoc uno nos feliciorem iudicamus, quod temporibus nostris tot floreant, quot apud vos peritissimi viri, qui florentissimos philosophos, qui quondam fere interierant, nunc aetati nostrae et posteris revivificent. . . .
On Duke Humphrey's chancery, see ibid. 22.

[4] M. Borsa, Correspondence of Humphrey Duke of Gloucester and Pier Candido Decembrio, *E.H.R.* 19 (1904) 513: . . . facundiam et copiam dicendi priscam illam et priscis viris dignam quae prorsus perierat, huic saeculo renovastis . . .

self may not have subscribed to all the implications of the *captatio benevolentiae* penned by his Italian secretary. English clerics who studied the humanities in Italy took what they found useful; they did not feel any need to reorientate themselves.[1]

Englishmen made their own discovery of historical perspective in the later middle ages. It took two distinct forms: both contrast with the Italian version. One form of the discovery took shape in the heart of scholastic Oxford of all places. John Wyclif was our terrible northern equivalent to Cola di Rienzo. The Yorkshireman and the Roman agreed in seeing the Church of their day as having broken with a desirable past. The break could only be mended by radical changes. Return to the distant past meant rejection of the present and of the immediate past. But Rienzo planned to purify the Church as part of a wider programme for the revival of Roman antiquity. He saw discontinuity in secular as well as religious life and wanted to amend both together.

Wyclif cared nothing for ancient Rome. He looked back to the Gospels and to the Garden of Eden. He contrasted the primitive Church, where Christ had restored the state of innocence on earth, with the ecclesiastical institutions of his day. The nature of his thesis forced him to be an ecclesiastical historian. His ideas on the subject are scattered through his works, and would be worth studying in detail. It is certain that he felt and registered discontinuity with a fierceness and clarity which no Italian surpassed. He periodised the history of the Church, but not that of the secular State. Secular power and its institutions remained for Wyclif on the flat level of divine remedy for sin. The State and lay culture could have no history worth speaking of. He divided life into two parts and saw one only in historical perspective of a sort.

The discovery in its second form was made later and more quietly. The honour goes to neither poets nor reformers, but to the first English antiquaries. William of Worcester and John Rous were both servants of great lords and both had studied at Oxford. Their duties as advisers and agents gave them opportunities to collect data on family history, topography and architecture. Worcester, the senior as an author, was a layman who exemplified 'the rise of the

[1] R. Weiss, *Humanism in England*, op. cit.

gentleman bureaucrat' in the fifteenth century.[1] Acting for his employer, Sir John Fastolf, in countless lawsuits,[2] he travelled round the country, reconstructing the history of family lands and drawing up genealogies as a sideline. He would record the lay-out of a town and measure buildings. His knowledge of accounting gave him a professional interest in noting what they had cost. Worcester was a practical pioneer in local researches; Rous made a theoretical advance in his capacity as chaplain and historian of the Warwick family. He recorded their history and genealogy, including mythical ancestors, on rolls of parchment, with illustrations. These drawings show that 'Rous had formed some sort of picture of past events in which people behaved with other manners and wore other clothes'.[3] It would be wrong, he felt, to show Warwick the Kingmaker's ancestors all wearing the same clothes as the earl; so he made them 'look as though they belonged to the past'. His reconstruction of the history of armour for the purpose has been passed as 'in its main principles correct'. He looked at effigies on tombs, old seals and possibly old-fashioned armour stored in Warwick castle. He even recorded changes in civilian costume for his male figures, though feminine fashions either defeated or bored him.

The Warwick Rolls and Petrarch's *Africa* have something in common, far apart as they seem. Rous resembled Petrarch in having got the feeling for historical plausibility and in trying to avoid anachronism. The fifteenth-century scholar had an advantage in the very narrowness of his subject matter. He could scrutinise the details, and he set about it practically by looking at objects instead of reading texts. It was the beginning of the antiquary's approach to history.

My post-mortem on the classicising group is closed. The failure of classical scholarship in England reflected insular conditions. There was no place for a humanist *élite*, but

---

[1] K. B. McFarlane. William of Worcester: a Preliminary Survey, *Studies Presented to Sir Hilary Jenkinson*, ed. J. Conway Davies (London, 1957) 199. See the whole paper, 196-221 for William of Worcester and also for the dates of John Rous, p. 197, n. 2. Worcester's career fell between 1415 and 1484 or a little later, Rous's probably between about 1425 and 1491; 'Most of his known works appear to date from the 1470's and 1480's.' Worcester 'had begun to form antiquarian collections' by May 1449. See *O.R.* 3, 1596-7, 2086-7.

[2] K. B. McFarlane, The Investment of Sir John Fastolf's Profits of War, *T.R.H.S.* 5th series, vol. 7 (1957) pp. 91-116.

[3] T. D. Kendrick, *British Antiquity* (London, 1950) 27. See his chapter on Worcester and Rous, ibid. 18-33.

x

new ideas about history came from Oxford and Warwick castle.

The fantasies of the group raise other questions, which call for a general view of its members. The friar doctors were aimiable storytellers: they differed from humanists and reformers alike in feeling friendly to the whole past of mankind. They did not periodise history, marking some ages 'bad', but enjoyed all equally. Their idea of the past agreed with the old recipe: a good story must begin 'Once upon a time'. They refined on the recipe by inventing sham antique settings and sham authors. A pseudo-classical library circulated, largely by means of lecture-commentaries on Scripture, which offered unrivalled scope for tales and quotations. The classicising friars produced their library with the help of anonymous compilers of *Gesta romanorum*, *Gesta grecorum* and many more nameless inventors. The 'picture' in its sham antique setting represented another brainwave. Ridevall may have thought of it first; Holcot perfected it. His stories and scenes are often pretty in their own right. His dialogue between a tearful poet and a deserted palace has pathos, which he cleverly stresses by pretending to quote from Aristotle's *Poetics*. A tale of a poet weeping over past glories *ought* to come from an ancient book about poetry! Holcot's successors, though less creative, ransacked their sources to good effect. Lathbury's forgers rise to uninhibited degrees of fancy. Lovers of Gothick twilight will enjoy his quotations from Pseudo-Fulgentius and Pseudo-Flaccianus.

All the friars are moralists, responding to public demand for new and striking *exempla*. Women in church want tales with a love interest; heraldry and lawsuits draw the attention of their menfolk. Every Englishman or woman has a stake in ancient history because Brutus came to Britain. The words 'Greek' and 'Roman' sound as magic on the preacher's lips. His tales go down better if he presents them as ancient. Fidelity to his classical sources would bore his congregation, but it takes any amount of sham. So he spreads truth and fiction about the ancients indiscriminately in such a way as to give pleasure. The mixture suited English tastes, while the French preferred scenes from everyday life and the Italians, more *blasés*, asked for simplicity.

The friars' blend of fact and fancy influenced English

literature more than their scholarship did. It is a truism to say that lay writers would replace them as storytellers and that the *exemplum* would find a new setting. Detailed study of lay borrowing from the clergy concerns the experts. More important was the friars' share in accustoming the public to listen to classical and pseudo-classical sayings and stories. Demand and supply stimulated each other. My study of the process has filled in a corner of the old generalisation: when Chaucer mocked at the friars, he was biting the hand that fed him. They educated his audience.

APPENDIX I

LATIN TEXTS IN ORDER OF QUOTATION

GERVASE OF MONT SAINT-ÉLOI, *Quodlibet*

MS Paris, Bibl. nat. lat. 15350, fol. 278rb-va

Utrum doctor vel bachelarius celans sermonem quem habet in corde suo vel in quaterno vel nolens communicare socio petenti, de quo scit probabiliter quod sine detrimento rehabebit, peccet mortaliter.

Celare sermonem suum vel in animo vel in quaterno potest fieri dupliciter, vel ex avaritia, et sic esset mortale in casu necessitatis alterius ei non communicare, quia in necessitate quilibet tenetur alteri subvenire, vel ex humana providentia, et sic potest (fieri) sine omni peccato. Verbi gratia loquor de me. Habeo tres sermones super collum meum et forte habeo multa facere. Si habeo ex providentia mea aliquid ubi potero recurrere si necesse fuerit, non video hoc esse malum, si feci sermonem labore meo apud Cartusiam vel in alio loco ubi pauci fuerunt, et cogito quod alio anno de isto sermone potero me iuvare si necesse fuerit, quia forte non vacabit michi alium facere, et veniant ad me aliqui qui habeant de qualibet die duos vel tres bonos sermones. Si non communico eis illum sermonem ad eorum petitionem, non video quod hoc sit malum, quia si communicarem, postea non possem me inde iuvare. Timerem enim michi ne posset impropriari michi sicut magnis magistris factum est: Monstrabo vobis in quaterno meo totum sermonem quem fecistis, et hoc esset contra decentiam status magistrorum, quod predicent de sermonibus qui sunt in quaternis, ex quo satis habent de tempore.

Unde dico quod licet celare ex tali providentia ne homo faciat aliquid indecens, unde status suus deturparetur.

THOMAS WALEYS, *Moralitates*

MS Oxford, New College 30, fol. 68v

Scriptori datur exemplar ut ea que in exemplari continentur in aliud pergamentum seu volumen transferat, nichil addendo vel minuendo, quia non sunt communiter scriptores (tam) scioli quod scirent addere vel minuere nisi errarent. Hiis tamen non obstantibus, scriptor falsus, quando conducitur secundum numerum linearum vel punctorum[1] que sunt in exemplari,

---

[1] Mr N. R. Ker suggests that *puncta* may refer to the prick-holes in the margin of the exemplar.

libenter aliqua transilit, quia sperat quod sua falsitas non statim deprehendetur, sed postquam fuerit sibi de suo salario satisfactum. Unde contingit frequenter quod talis non solum non est dignus mercede, sed potius dignus est pena, quia pergamentum omnino est perditum in quo scripsit, et ideo qui prudens est diligenter examinat opus scriptum, antequam opus scriptori reddat, ne in aliquo defraudetur.

fol. 41

Unde est de talibus sicut de quibusdam rusticis, de quibus audivi quod cum episcopus quidam in quodam manerio suo in Anglia vivarium fieri voluisset et ad hoc opus faciendum multi rustici vocati essent, precepit episcopus dari eis singulis diebus bonum triticum et bonos cibos ministrari, ut sic fortius operarentur et magis animarentur ad operandum, sed infra tres dies vel quatuor ceperunt remissius et lentius operari, quod advertens episcopus unum eorum corripuit, dicens eos segnitius agere quam in principio, qui respondit se non habere panem et ideo non posse laborare, et cum episcopus senescallo suo se diceret precepisse ut singulis diebus panem triticeum eis daret, respondit ille rusticus: ille panis non est pro nobis; non enim voco illum panem; sed detur nobis panis fabateus et tunc poterimus laborare; et sic faciunt (*sic*), subtracto ab eis pane triticeo.

fol. 8-8v

Dicit Sextus Iulius, lib. i de scientia rei militaris,[1] quod est quoddam explorandi (MS deplorandi) genus, quo duces exercitus per se absque aliorum adiutorio prevident, et ponit exemplum de Paulo, consule romanorum, qui in planitiem demissurus exercitum, contemplatus procul, vidit avium multitudinem festino volatu ex silva consurrexisse, et statim intellexit illuc aliquid insidiarum latere, eo quod turbate aves simul avolaverunt. Premissis ergo exploratoribus, comperit ibi decem milia latere ad decipiendum clam romanorum exercitum. Consimile narrat de alio duce, qui similiter ex avolatione avium multarum a quodam monte, et quia non residebant, deprehendit illuc insidias hostium, et sic eos insidiantes declinavit. Sic in proposito. Ex (eo) quod videmus procul tot aves, id est apostolos et discipulos et innumeros alios de mundo avolasse celeriter, nec ultra ibi resedisse, suspecte nobis deberent esse insidie illic latentes, et prudenter sunt nobis cavende et timende, Osee xi: Formidabunt filii maris et avolabunt quasi aves.

THOMAS WALEYS ON *De civ. Dei*, PROLOGUE

Fluminis impetus letificat civitatem Dei[2] . . . cives tamen multos

---

[1] Frontinus, *Strategematon* I, ii, 7-8. Waleys does not quote him verbally.
[2] Ps. xlv, 5. Waleys explains that it signifies the waters of the river of wisdom.

huius civitatis sanctissime hoc contristat, quod accessus ad eas (aquas), precipue in primis decem libris, multum videtur difficilis, nam fluvius ipse quasi puteus altus est et in quo hauriant pauci habent. Propter quod ego, frater Thomas, ordinis predicatorum, anglicus natione, cupiens prefatam difficultatem saltem pro parte auferre, et de predicto fluvio haurire volentibus accessum facilem preparare, confisus in eius auxilio, qui profunda fluviorum scrutatur et abscondita producit in lucem,[1] expositionem quandam super decem libros primos de civitate Dei, in quibus est maior obscuritas quam in sequentibus propter historiarum et fabularum multitudinem, paucis notam, composui, loca planiora transiliens. Obscuritatibus vero magis insisto, premittens quedam quasi prohemialiter, que ad intelligentiam dictorum librorum necessaria videntur.

On i, 5

Quem morem etiam Cato vel *Cesar secundum aliam litteram meliorem.* . . . Nam Sallustius in libro quem de gestis Cateline scripsit, qui vocatur Catelinarium, introduxit Cesarem loquentem in senatu de coniuratis cum Catelina[2] . . . et in sententia Gaii Cesaris ponuntur secundum Sallustium illa dicta que hic allegat beatus Augustinus, et non sunt in sententia Catonis, et tamen libri communiter habent Catonem, ubi debent habere Cesarem, et causa est, ut credo, vitium scriptorum; quia enim propria nomina consueverunt scribi per unicam tantum litteram, videlicet per primam litteram nominis, et eadem est littera huius nominis *Cesar* et huius nominis *Cato*, ideo forsan scriptores posteriores invenientes nomen Cesaris scriptum per C scripserunt ibi *Cato*. Non enim credo Augustinum in nomine errasse.

On ii, 6

Videtur quod hic debet esse *frigialia* vel *frigalia*, que vocantur festa Berecinthie, de quibus supra, cap. iv, tractavit beatus Augustinus. Festa autem illa dicebantur *frigialia*, quia fuerunt festa dee Frigie, id est Berecinthie, que prius in Frigia quam Rome colebatur; et eo modo dicuntur bachanalia festa Bachi et cerealia festa Cereris, et sic de aliis festis. Sed tamen ego diversos libros respexi in Anglia et etiam in Bononia, et in omni loco inveni *fugalia*. Crederem tamen litteram vitio scriptorum corruptam, nisi beatus Augustinus ironice et alludens conditioni gentis et convenientie nominis vocaret *fugalia* que alii vocant *frigalia*; nam secundum Hieronimum super epistolam ad galatos omnes poete vocant frigas timidos,[3] et per consequens ad fugam paratos, propter quod Augustinus eorum sacra, que dicuntur *frigalia*, hic vocat *fugalia*, et hoc est verisimile, quia postmodum

---

[1] Iob xxviii, 11.   [2] *Catilinae coniuratio* li, lii.
[3] *In Ep. ad Gal.* (*P.L.* 26) 347: Timidos Phrygas omnes poetae lacerant.

addit Augustinus sic: *et vere fugalia, sed pudoris et honestatis,* quod non esset intelligibile, si diceretur *frigalia* vel *frigialia.*

On ii, 4

Et est hic sciendum quod ista dea, quam vocaverunt matrem deorum, per quam terram intellexerunt, in tanta fuit reverentia apud romanos quod antequam eius imago esset de Pessimio Romam translata, sicut narrat Valerius, lib. i, sepius *imperatores,* id est qui imperium gesserant, sicut consules, pretores et huiusmodi, *compotes victoriarum,* id est post victorias obtentas, *suscepta vota Pessinuntem profecti solverunt.*[1]

Considerent christiani quanta sit distantia inter Roman et Pessinuntem, ut viderent quid reverentia (*sic*) debeant Matri, non falsorum, sed unius summi et veri Dei. In huius honorem etiam constructum fuit a Domitiano templum illud Rome quod Pantheum vocabatur, et postmodum Bonifacius papa in honorem beate Marie consecravit, ut habetur in legenda de omnibus sanctis,[2] et modo vocatur ecclesia beate Marie Rotunde.

THOMAS WALEYS ON Ps. viii, 2 (MS Exeter College 39)

Alio modo per magnificentiam possumus intelligere virtutem magnificentie, quam Philosophus, iv Ethic., distinguit a liberalitate. Respicit enim sumptus et dona, sicut et liberalitas, sed cum quadam magnifice(ntia), sicut docet Philosophus ibidem, et decet (MS docet) eos qui sunt nobiles ex suis progenitoribus et gloriosi. Ista *magnificentia* dicitur *super celos elevata,* quia tunc maxime apparuit quando Christus *super celos* ascendit. Magnificus etiam secundum Philosophum maxime ostendit suam magnificentiam in hiis que tangunt rempublicam. Sic in proposito, nam Christus ante suam ascensionem erat inops et pauper, unde non decebat (MS docebat) eum virtus magnificentie, quamvis liberalis (erat) et libenter conferret dona suum statum decentia, unde et apostolis ait, Mat. x: Gratis accepistis, gratis date.[3] Sed post ascensionem, ex quo apparuit nobilis et gloriosus ex linea paterna, ostendit suam magnificentiam. Tunc enim sponsam, id est naturam humanam, introduxit in domum suam primo, et ideo tunc ostendit magnificentiam suam in dando Spiritum sanctum, qui est donum maximum. . . ,[4] et fuit etiam hoc donum

---

[1] *Dict. et fact. mem.* I, i, 1. Waleys probably had a glossed text of Maximus. The commentary of Frater Petrus O.P. on this passage gives the same information, MS Rome, Bibl. apost. Ottob. 1704, fol. lv: Vocantur autem hic imperatores quicumque in dignitate officii erant constituti, sive consulatus sive prefecture.

See M. de Marco, Un nuovo codice del commento di 'Frater Petrus O.P.' à Valerio Massimo, *Aevum* 30 (1956) 554-8. The writer very kindly looked up the commentary on this passage for me.

[2] *Jacobi a Voragine Legenda aurea,* ed. Th. Graesse (Leipzig, 1850) 719.
[3] Mt. x, 8.   [4] I omit a number of biblical quotations here.

ordinatum ad reipublice utilitatem, quia eo confirmata est tota ecclesia in gratia et virtute.

JOHN RIDEVALL ON THE APOCALYPSE

V, fol. 90ra-va

Philosophi depinxerunt revelationem propheticam cum 12 conditionibus, que possunt appropriari Christo. Prima proprietas (est) quod dicitur Appollonis nata propter claritatem cognitionis, dicitur enim deus divinationis. 2°, in lecto collocata propter quantitatem dispositionis, unde ab aliquo dicebatur clinica (MS cl'enica). 3°, sopore gravata propter loquele alienationem (MS alienationis), quia occupati circa revelationes sunt alienati, sicut homo in sopore. 4°, rebus viduata propter utilitatem exproprietationis. . . . 5°, exilio dampnata propter eius ab hominibus separationem. . . . 6°, describitur cantu delectata, quia ad exequendum spiritum prophetie valet harmonia. . . . 7°, depingitur virgo depurata propter integritatem incorporationis. . . . 8°, describitur iecure vulnerata propter diligentiam cumulationis. 9°, lauro (MS laulo) coronata propter effectum comparationis, unde fingunt philosophi quod ille Apollo (MS Apollonius), deus divinationis, habet illam arborem in sua custodia, et quod de illa arbore habet (s)ceptrum in manu, et si illa arbor ponatur circa caput hominis disponit ad divinationem. 10°, osculata de facie propter munditiam generationis, quia non generatur per actum concupiscentie carnalis, sed per solum osculum. . . . 11°, oculis vallata, quia prophetia depingitur habere oculos ante et retro et a latere. . . . 12°, armis observata, quia circa eam depinguntur milites custodientes eam, ne furetur. Item dicunt philosophi omnes alias scientias esse suspectas, scilicet in pyromantia et geomantia, quia quasi fures (sunt), volentes prophetiam furari.

fol. 96vb

Pictura temporis apud antiquos vocabatur Saturnus, qui dicitur filios suos devorasse, propter temporis consumptionem. Aliter tempus depingebatur ad modum draconis habentis caudam in ore et continuo partem post partem devorantis.

fol. 92va

Nota: poete depinxerunt mortem quasi vetula rugata, in austro locata, lecto reclinata, vinculis ligata, ser(r)is obfirmata, lumine privata, viro viduata, vocis orbata, crure denigrata, carne minorata, osse desiccata, fame fedata, membris destructa.

fol. 91va

Nota: sophia a philosophis sic vocabatur quia erat depicta caput dealbata, pectus deaurata, circulo ligata, sole venustata, unde depinxerunt deam sapientie iunctam solario, facto de lumine solari, sidere depictam[1] iuxta varias proprietates sapientie, quia aliqui posuerunt in dextera sua septem stellas pliades, aliqui septem stellas errantes propter diversos effectus sapientie, voluntatem scientie et philosophie (MS phices) continentes. Sic depinxerunt eam visu concitata, quia narrat Agellius de doctrina noctium atticarum quod antiqui posuerunt imaginem sapientie ante fores omnium templorum, et hec verba posuerunt prolata ab ore sapientie:

> Usus me genuit, peperit memoria.
> Sophiam me vocant greci, vos sapientiam.[2]

fol. 93rb

Augustinus tangit contra Iulianum 5[3] . . . (quod) epicuri finxerunt voluptatem sedentem in cathedra, cui subveniunt omnes virtutes (sicut) eius ancille.[4] Stoici pinxerunt honestatem presidentem et cetum virtutum ei subvenientem (MS subventio). Peripatetici pinxerunt honestatem presidentem, in curru sedentem, et cetum alium virtutum dirigentem. Sed opinio fidelium est quod caritas est domina in ierarchia virtutum et tanquam regina optinet principatum.

fol. 90rb

Dicitur propter virginitatem meruisse revelationem de ipso Christo. Unde super pectus eius inveniebatur lamina in qua sic scribebatur: Credo in Christum, Filium Dei, nasciturum de Virgine, moriturum in cruce, resurrecturum tertia die. Iste habetur aporemo (sic)[5] in commento super Boetium de disciplina scolarium super illo verbo *probata virginitas*.[6]

---

[1] Something seems to have dropped out here.
[2] *Noct. attic.* xiii. 8. Only the verse comes from Aulus Gellius.
[3] Illegible words here seem to give some sort of reference to the text quoted.
[4] *Contra Iulianum pelagianum* iv, 3 (*P.L.* 44) 749: Quales virtutes Epicurus induxit voluptatis ancillas, quae omnino quidquid facerent, propter illam vel adipiscendam facerent vel tenendam.
[5] 'Daretis (a)porismata' occurs in the text of *De disciplina scolarium* (*P.L.* 64) 1232.
[6] The printed text has 'Platonis probata *divinitas*'; Ridevall's may have had *virginitas*. William Wheatley, who may have been Ridevall's source here, studied at Paris probably before 1305, and at Oxford or elsewhere after 1306. He was master of Stamford school about 1309 and of Lincoln school in 1316, *O.R.* 3, 2030-31. His comment reads:

> *Platonis probata deitas.* Unde narratur quod scriptum quoddam reperiebatur in sepulcro Platonis, in quo continebantur verba sequentia, aureis litteris scripta: Hic iacet Plato, qui credidit in Deum, et ipsum de Virgine nasciturum, pro humano genere moriturum et tertia die resurrecturum (MS Oxford, Exeter College 28, fol. 53ra).

Pseudo-Aquinas on *De disciplina scholarium*, the most popular fourteenth-century commentary, does not include this story.

95vb

Nota: carbuncula ponebantur in civitate romana in diversis partibus, que ita lucebant de nocte quod malefactores non audebant incedere de nocte per civitatem. Quia vero Nero imperator voluit de nocte ad maleficia sua circuire, ideo una causa fuit quare fecit civitatem romanam comburi, ut ille lampades, scilicet carbuncula destruerentur. De hoc commentator super Boetium, de consolatione.[1]

RIDEVALL ON *De civ. Dei*, PROLOGUE

S, foll. lv-3

Pro quo notandum est quod isti idolatri et cultores non unius sed multorum deorum solebant deos suos magnificare et eos magnos predicare a multiplici ratione: 1°, ex originis prioritate, sicut patet de deo Saturno et dea Cibele, qui in numero deorum sunt ab incredulis dicti magni, quia credebant quod ab istis duobus fuerunt dii alii procreati. . . . 2°, fuerunt etiam alii vocati dii magni ex culmine dignitatis, sicut patet de deo Iove, quem coluerunt idolatri tanquam deorum et dearum omnium regem et principem, et de dea Iunone, deorum et dearum omnium regina et dei Iovis coniuge et sorore, sicut tangit Augustinus et Seneca, prima tragedia.[2] 3°, sunt et alii dii vocati magni ex nimia strenuitate, sicut patet de Marte, deo belli et militie (et) de dea Bellona. . . . 4°, sunt dii vocati magni ex perfectione universitatis, sicut patet de deo Pane. Pan enim a poetis figurabatur deus universe omnis perfectionis, sicut patet ex eius pictura seu descriptione, quam tangit Augustinus et alii, scilicet Isidorus, Rabanus et Huguccio in suis derivationibus. 5°, fuerunt dii reputati magni ex affectionis familiaritate, sicut patet de diis penatibus, qui alio nomine dicebantur dii lares, quos magnificabant idolatri propter magnitudinem affectionis et familiaritatem, quam ostendebant certis personis et certis familiis; unde vocabantur dii domestici. . . .

Ista 22 genera deorum correspondent istis 22 libris, ita quod cuilibet de istis libris correspondet unus deus, cuius cultus specialiter ab Augustino reprobatur, sicut in prosecutione ostenditur.

On *De civ. Dei* i, 2 and 5

fol. 7

Hic tamen est notandum quod rationabiliter posset dubitari de processu beati Augustini, quia non videtur hic quod fundatur

---

[1] Ridevall's commentator may have been Nicholas Trevet or William of Aragon, though neither tells this story; see P. Courcelle, Etude critique sur les commentaires de la Consolation de Boèce, *Archives* 14 (1939) 5-140.

[2] *Hercules furiens.*

super veritatem historie, sed potius super fictionem poete, et per consequens argumentum quod facit foret nimis debile ad probandum propositum suum . . . (fol. 13v-14) . . . sed poeta ille more poetico finxit talia, poetice mentiendo. Notandum est hic quod ad poetam et ad rhetorem pertinet aliquando aliqua fingere vel saltem excessive dicere, ut audientes magis passionentur, modo una passione, modo alia, et ita dixerunt illi pagani romani quod Virgilius fecit. . . . Nota Augustinus arguit contra illos romanos christianos, nomini Christi infestos, ex propriis. . . . Isti etiam romani laudabant istum Sallustium tanquam nobilem et veracem scriptorem historiarum, et ideo ex dictis illorum vult ipse probare quod responsio illorum romanorum ad argumenta sua fundatur super falsum. . . . Talia enim qualia narrat Virgilius, qui fuit poeta, Eneam narrasse, talia narrat Sallustius, qui non fuit poeta, sed historiographus, Catonem consulem dixisse, periculum scilicet imminuere reipublice, nisi punirentur proditores debita punitione.

On iii, 26

fol. 150v

Dicendum est quod neuter errat, nec Augustinus nec Orosius, pro quo notandum est quod Augustinus in suo volumine non intendit texere historiam nec esse historiographus, sed bene intendit ex historiis apud romanos auctenticis probare quod cultus deorum, quem romani aliquando exercuerunt, fuit pro omni statu et tempore inutilis et infructuosus reipublice romane. De temporis autem supputatione non curat Augustinus, nisi quatenus spectat ad propositum suum, et hinc est quod Augustinus non loquitur hic de istis bellis servilibus et civilibus, nisi ad probandum per ista bella quod edes illa dee Concordie nichil valuit reipublice pro pace habenda.

On iii, 30

foll. 163-4v

Notandum tamen hic est unum dubium, nam prima facie videretur quod ista mors Iulii Cesaris computari non debuit pro infortunio; fuit enim ad magnum commodum totius communitatis occidere talem tirannum, sicut fuit iste Iulius. De sua enim tirannide loquens Marianus in suis cronicis dicit sic: Idibus Martii Gaius Iulius Cesar cum Romam venisset, insolentius agens multaque tirannica perpetrans, coniurantibus in eum 60 vel amplius senatoribus . . . confossus interiit.[1] Similiter de ista tirannide Iulii loquitur Paulus Diaconus in sua historia, dicens sic: Cesar bellis civilibus toto orbe compositis Romam rediit,

[1] Marianus Scotus, *Chronicon* ii (Bâle, 1559) 202; Ridevall had a fuller version of the chronicle than that represented in the edition.

agere insolenter cepit et contra consuetudinem romane libertatis. Cum igitur honores ex sua voluntate prestaret, qui a populo antea donabantur, nec senatui ad se venienti assurgeret, aliaque regia et pene tirannica faceret, coniuratus est in eum. . . . confossus est vulneribus.[1] Hec ibi historia, ex quo videtur quod mors Iulii non debuit computari pro infortunio reipublice, quia mors et interfectio cuiuslibet tiranni, qualis videbatur fuisse Iulius, est bonum commune, et per consequens Augustinus non habet unde posset improbare cultum plurium deorum per mortem Iulii.

Ad illud potest sic dici quod licet occidere tirannum simpliciter et absolute sit bonum et proficuum reipublice, tamen in casu potest esse malum et ad tempus et ratione alicuius circumstantie, et isto modo dixit Augustinus prius, loquens de Silla (sic) quod licet fuerit iustum et bonum quod crudelitas quam exercuerat Marius in republica fuisset punita, tamen melius fuisset quod scelus Marii mansisset impunitum quam quod fuisset per illum modum punitum quem exercuit Silla.[2] Sicut prius patuit in tertio libro, sic in casu proposito, licet Iulius iste fuerit propter suas tirannides dignus morte, tamen propter mala et incommoda in que respublica incidit occasione sue mortis minus malum (MS mala), immo melius quo ad multa fuisset pro republica quod Iulius mansisset vivus quam quod illo modo fuisset occisus. Ista enim interfectio Iulii occasio fuit et origo et seditionum et ambitionum et, quod peius est, bellorum civilium in republica romanorum; et quia talia fuerunt reipublice maius periculosa quam fuisset vita Iulii, ideo mors Iulii computatur hic ab Augustino inter (in)fortunia que acciderunt in republica.

Alia est responsio et est talis. Iulius iste, licet habuit ingressum tirannicum, contra enim voluntatem reipublica per violentiam rapuerat consulatum et dominium reipublice, postquam tamen habuit dominium Iulius iste correxit se et rempublicam disposuit cum modestia et non cum tirannide. Sed de isto videtur tangere Augustinus in littera, quando dicit quod Iulius victoriam civilem clementer exercuit suisque adversariis vitam dignitatemque donavit. Ergo videtur quod Iulius iste non exercuit pro tunc tirannidem. Igitur malum fuit eum illo modo interficere per insidias et per coniurationem; et per consequens sequitur quod mors sua fuit merito computanda (MS computandi) inter infortunia que acciderunt in republica.

Nota etiam quomodo cum ista responsione videntur concordare auctores diversi, nam et Ricardus de sancto Victore, libro

---

[1] *Historia miscella* vi, 41, ed G. Carducci, R.I.S. 1 (1900) 103-4. Ridevall quotes this work in another place as 'quedam historia romanorum, que sic incipit: Primus in Italia, ut quibusdam placet, regnavit Ianus: et ascribitur Paulo Diacono.' (S, fol. 129.)

[2] *De civ. Dei* iii, 27-8

suarum exceptionum, dicit quod romanus populus tanto fuit dolore pro morte Iulii stimulatus quod voluit incendisse Capitolium cum auctoribus cedis. Unde apud populum romanum ita postmodum Iulius postmodum memorabilis factus est ut omnes post illum romani imperatores cesares nuncupentur. Hec ille.[1] Orosius in libro suo de ormesta dicit quod diu a populo fuit deliberatum ut Capitolium cum auctoribus cedis debuit incendi. Ad locum enim illum secesserant illi duo Bruti et Gaius Cassius et alii socii illius coniurationis. Tandem vero populus, dolore stimulatus, corpus Iulii raptum fragmentis tribunalium ac subcelliorum in foro concremavit. Hec Orosius.[2] Ex ista sententia Orosii patet quod Iulius non fuit reputatus tirannus, quia non fuisset talis honor exhibitus tiranno. Accepit enim populus tribunalia et subcellia in quibus consueverant residere rectores reipublice et combusserunt ossa Iulii iuxta morem tunc circa mortuos observatum, et fuit illud a populo factum in signo subversionis iustitie in republica, quasi Iulio mortuo fuisset iustitia eversa, que in illis tribunalibus et subcelliis debuit exerceri, et sicut patet per honorificam combustionem corporis Iulii patuit eum non fuisse reputatum a populo romano tirannum, sicut idem patuit per eius honorificam sepilitionem (*sic*). Narrant enim romanorum historie et idem recitat Martinus in cronicis suis quod scilicet populus statuit in foro columpnam quandam solidam marmoream viginti prope pedum in altitudine. Supra Iulii reliquie erant intumulate, et fuit columpna illa vocata Iulia.[3] Patet igitur qualiter Augustinus habet intentum suum de morte Iulii, quando dicit (quod) fuit mors (inter) infortunia, et hoc sive teneatur responsio una vel alia.

Sed quomodo possunt salvari verba Mariani et Pauli Diaconi, qui Iulium Cesarem dicunt interfectum pro tirannide et insolentia? Dicendum est quod senatores et alii in republica potentes reputabant eum talem, quia Iulius eorum detruncaverat potestatem; et ideo machinabantur in eum (MS eis) necem. Sed tamen populus romanus non habuit de Iulio talem estimationem; et ideo historie loquuntur aliquando de Iulio secundum estimationem senatus, et tunc dicunt Iulium se habuisse tirannice et insolenter, aliquando loquuntur de eo secundum estimationem plebis et populi, et tunc dicunt Iulium egisse misericorditer et clementer, sicut patet per Augustinum in serie littere, *Tanquam regni appetitorem.*

Augustinus innuit unam rationem ad probandum mortem Iulii Cesaris fuisse reipublice romane infortunium (MS infortunia) et reducit ad memoriam causam propter quam Iulius fuit per

---

[1] *Prior excerpt.* v (*P.L.* 177, 239-40; see J. Chatillon, Le contenu, l'autenticité et la date du 'Liber exceptionum' et des 'Sermones centum' de Richard de Saint-Victor, *Revue du Moyen Age latin* 4 (1948) 23-51, 42-64.
[2] *Historia adversus paganos* vi, 17.
[3] *Chronica pontificum et imperatorum* (M.G.H.S.) 22, 406.

insidias interfectus. Causa enim illarum insidiarum fuit emulatio et invidia, sicut dicit quedam romanorum historia, prius pluries allegata. Unde de ista coniuratione in mortem Iulii dicit sic: Clementia(m) principis vicit invidia nec diutius dilatio donata est . . . ad terram datus est.[1] Istam igitur invidiam senatorum conspirantium in necem Iulii tangit Augustinus in littera. . . . Istud enim est proprium emulationis et invidie colorare malitiam suam per zelum iustitie, et sic fecit senatus in ista coniuratione. Nota istud fuit grave infortunium in republica romana, quasi dicat rectores omnes reipublice deberent laborare duplici tali vitio et tam pernicioso in omni communitate[2], quorum unum fuit vitium invidie et aliud fuit mendacium et calumpnia, nam populus romanus nec reputavit Iulium regni invasorem nec etiam libertatis subversorem. Patet igitur quomodo in Iulio non obstante cultu plurium deorum accidit duplex grave infortunium temporale. Unum fuit corruptio in moribus, vitio emulationis primo, et post(ea) vitio conspirationis. Aliud infortunium fuit iactura et amissio talis et tam probi principis. Unde de istius Iulii probitate loquitur Paulus Diaconus in sua historia, dicens sic: Nullus eo unquam . . . vicerit.[3] Hec Paulus Diaconus, cuius verbis patet quod grave infortunium temporale fuit in republica amissio talis persone. Ex quo sequitur ulterius quod deorum cultus etiam in hoc casu fuit inutilis ad declinationem infortunii temporalis.

Notare possumus pro dictis ea que tangit Iohannes Salesburiensis in suo Policratico, lib. 8°, ubi loquens de isto Iulio dicit sic: Iulius Cesar primus orbem . . . caderet.[4] Hec ille. Nota ponderando probitatem et valorem Iulii in rebus bellicis, considerando etiam honestatem eius in moribus, et pensando mala et bella que acciderunt inter cives reipublice pro sua interfectione, constans est quod melius fuisset simpliciter pro commodo reipublice quod Iulius mansisset vivus, quam quod fuisset per insidias interfectus, et per consequens Augustinus habet intentum suum, eo quod in morte Iulii accidit reipublice grave infortunium temporale.

On ii, 6

foll. 59v-60v

Augustinus probat quod doctrina poetica plus valuit ad morum informationem in republica quam valebant deorum oracula vel responsa. Nulla enim talis vitiorum reprehensio . . . facta fuit in republica per deorum exhortationem, sicut faciebat ille poeta Persius, cuius versus hic ponit Augustinus. . . . Primum

---

[1] Florus, *Epitome* II, xiii, 92-5.
[2] Something may have dropped out of the text here.
[3] *Historia miscella*, op. cit.   [4] *Policraticus* VIII, xix, 2, 365-6.

quod necessarium est homini scire causas rerum et principia;
in hoc enim puncto errabant specialiter romani, sicut patebit
per Augustinum in processu libri. . . . Ex ista informatione poete
Persii vult Augustinus concludere quod poeta iste et alii poete
potius essent colendi et honorandi quam illi dii, quia plura
honesta et necessaria ad salutem reipublice continet ista doctrina
poetica quam aliqua doctrina a diis illis vel deabus hominibus
tradita.

On vi, 2

T, fol. 41-41v

Notandum est pro mente Marci Varronis quod ipse per talia
verba non intendit excludere a scientia philosophorum delectationem, quia sicut probat Aristoteles philosophia habet mirabiles
delectationes. . . . Similiter nec Varro voluit dicere quod (in)-
utiliter omnes poete intendebant finaliter talem delectationem
carnalem, quia multi de eis intendebant reprehendere vitium
carnis, una cum aliis vitiis, sicut patet in eorum satiriis. Illi enim
poete romanorum, quos vocabant satiricos, fuerunt fortes et
acuti reprehensores vitiorum et carnalium delectationum, sicut
patet in libris Iuvenalis et Persii et poete Oratii, tam in sermonibus
suis quam in odis et epistolis suis. . . . Item etiam est ergo mens
Varronis dicere quod in hoc erat differentia inter finem intentum
a philosophis in eorum theologia et finem intentum a poetis in
theologica poetica, quia finis utiliter intentus a philosophia fuit
utilitas, id est acquisitio veritatis, que est maxime utilitatis
intellectui speculativo, quia est summa perfectio eius, et virtutis
moralis honestas, que est maxima utilitas intellectus practici.
Sed non sic fuit de carminibus poetarum, quia multi poete
fecerunt multas poeses inducentes homines ad delectationes
carnales, sicut poeta Ovidius et alii, licet aliqui, scilicet satirici,
componebant sua carmina ad reprehendendum talia vitia
carnalia . . . Nam aliqua poemata erant ordinata ad utilitatem et
aliqua ad delectationem, sicut tangit Oratius in sua poetria,
quando dicit: aut prodesse volunt aut delectare poete.[1]

On vi, 5

fol. 28v

Sed dicendum est quod non est simile utrobique, nam cultus
certus et modus determinatus colendi deos et deas in republica
romana ordinatus fuerat per imperatores et senatus consultum,
per quos etiam fuit taxatum et certo iure cautum qua pena essent
puniendi omnes transgressores et oppositum facientes, sicut satis
potest colligi ex dictis Valerii Maximi, libro dictorum memora-
bilium. Sed non sic fuit de dictis et fabulis poetarum. Eorum

---

[1] *Ars poet.*, 333.

enim dicta non erant sic auctentica quin licitum fuit cuicumque oppositum sentire et libere contradicere et etiam improbare, et hec erat ratio quare Varro dampnavit theologiam poeticam, sed non audebat reprehendere theologiam politicam vel civilem. Exemplum quomodo istud est possibile patet inter nos catholicos. Sunt enim multe questiones quas ecclesia non determinavit, et ideo licite possunt homines circa veritatem et firmitatem talium questionum habere oppositas opiniones et se mutuo improbare per argumenta et rationes, sed contraire vel contradicere sententie ecclesie, illud est illicitum cuicumque, et isto modo fuit pro parte in republica romanorum. Nam auctoritas poetica neminem ligabat, quin libere dicere poterat quod volebat. . . . Sed contra illud quod fuit decretum per senatus consultum et per imperatores eorum nulli fuit licitum venire.

On i, 2

S, fol. 7-7v

Et accipit hic Augustinus illa que poeta Virgilius dicit accidisse in excidio illius civitatis Troie, unde ponit hic versus quos dicit Virgilius 2° libro Eneydos, quando introducit Eneam narrantem Didoni, regine Cartaginis, quomodo Priamus rex Troie fuit interfectus a Pirro, qui fuit filius Achille. . . .[1] Nota: ista sunt verba Enee narrantis regine Didoni se vidisse quomodo rex Troie Priamus altaria multa diis suis erexerat et ignes accenderat pro sacrificiis intendendis et diis suis offerendis et, illo tempore, capta per fraudem civitate, intravit super regem Pirrus, filius Achillis, et regem Troie vulneravit, qui vulneratus ad aras quas erexerat fugiebat et eas sanguine fedabat, in quo facto patet quod greci locis sacris non parcebant, sed gothi pepercerunt christianis ecclesiis.

Hic tamen est notandum quod rationabiliter posset dubitari de processu beati Augustini, quia non videtur hic quod fundetur super veritatem historie, sed potius super fictionem poete, et per consequens argumentum quod facit foret nimis debole ad probandum propositum suum. Si enim eamus ad veritatem historie, Eneas nunquam vidit Didonem, que fundavit Cartaginem et fuit regina illius civitatis, quia Eneas fuit mortuus antequam Cartago fuit condita per trecentos annos et amplius. Sicut enim tangit Papias, Cartago fuit condita antequam Roma fuit fundata a Romulo per 72 annos.[2] Fuit condita Cartago tempore regis Iuda Amasie, qui fuit decimus post David, sed de isto patet per Marianum Scotum in cronicis suis.[3] Nota tamen quod Marianus in sua cronica tangit tres opiniones de fundatione Cartaginis, una quod Cartago fuit fundata tempore regis David circa annum

---

[1] *Aen.* ii, 501-5.
[2] *Vocabularium* (Venice, 1485, unfoliated) art. *Carthago*.
[3] *Chronicon* i, 17 (Bâle, 1559) 116-7.

regni sui 34 et anno 143° post excidium Troie; fundabatur vel hec civitas a Carcedone tyrio, ut dicunt aliqui, vel ut dicunt alii a Didone, filia eius; secunda opinio est quod Cartago fuit fundata tempore Salomonis et circa annum regni sui 23; tertia est opinio quod tactum est, scilicet quod Cartago fuit condita tempore Amasie, regis Iuda, circa annum quartum regni eius; sed quelibet illarum opinionum habet tenere quod Eneas non vidit Cartaginem illo tempore quando fugit de Troia, nam Eneas mortuus fuit circa annum octavum iudicis Labdon secundum Marianum Scotum,[1] et per consequens eundo ad historiam non est verum Eneam vidisse Cartaginem vel reginam Didonem.

ROBERT HOLCOT

Ecclus. lect. lxii, fol. 48vb[2]

Refert Titus Livius in libri suo de Urbis origine quod consuetudo apud romanos fuit quod quando imperator aliquam legem condere volebat, et erat sue intentionis quod solum in speciali loco servari deberet, illam publicari mandabat per nuntium. Cui legi non tenebantur nisi illius loci specialis homines in quo fuerat publicata. Sed quando sue intentionis erat quod per totum imperium servaretur, illam legem ore suo proprio publicabat, et de suo palatio ad palatium publicum et commune accedebat et ultra hec venam propriam sinebat aperiri, et sanguinem in terram effundi, ut ex hoc bene intelligeretur quod sicut ipse erat persona communis, qui proprio ore hanc (legem) publicabat, sic sue intentionis erat totum imperium ad illam obligare, et quicumque legem predictam violaret, sicut in testimonium observationis sanguinem effunderat, sic ille legem frangens eius sanguinem tangebat, et ideo sine intermissione pena mortis puniretur.

Sap. lect. clxxxii

C, foll. 268vb-269rb

Quamquam enim Christus quosdam, dum hic viveret, viros gratos inveniret, nunquam tamen tam constantem gratitudinem in Petro vel Iohanne vel Iacobo repperit quantum in mulieribus sibi devotis invenit . . . ut Christus de eis dicat illud Boetii:

> Has saltem nullus potuit pervincere terror,
> Ne nostrum comites prosequerentur iter.[3]

---

[1] ibid. i, 3, 107.

[2] The tale is omitted in MSS Bâle B.V. 11 and Royal 2.F.vii, but it is in Holcot's manner. Further research on the manuscript tradition might show whether the printed edition is correct in including it. Oddly enough, Holcot knew enough of Livy to quote *Ab Urbe condita* correctly as the source for the story of Coriolanus (B, foll. 91v, 123).

[3] *De consol. Philos.* I, metr. i, 5-6.

Harum gratitudo non solum in fidelibus elucet mulieribus, sed etiam in gentilibus satis claret. Que gratior esse potuit pudica Penelope, que Ulyxis absentiam annis 20 expers cuiuslibet virilis amoris alterius expectavit?[1] Que quantis affectionibus[2] interim angebatur explicat ipsa satis in epistola sua, dicens:

> Hanc tua Penelope tibi lento mittit Ulyxe
> Nil michi rescribas, at tamen[3] ipse veni.[4]

Que gratitudine flagrantior esse potuit Portia, filia Catonis et uxore Bruti, que viro interfecto vivere noluit, sed arma quibus se statim interemeret postulavit, famulis autem arma negantibus, prunas ardentes transglutivit.[5] De qua scribit Martialis, epigr. lib. 4:

> Coniugis audisset fatum. . . .[6]

Que[7] gratior esse potuit Arria, Peti coniuge, qui simul[8] se interfecerunt. . .?[9] Que Didone gratior esse potuit, de qua Hieronimus, Contra Iovinianum, lib. 1, et Virgilius Enead: Dido soror . . . ardere quam nubere maluit?[10] Quid de Lucretia et sabinis,[11] Iulia, filia Cesaris,[12] Sulpicia Lentuli,[13] Alcione, Ceicis[14] et aliis infinitis dici posset?

Mulier enim in regenda familia circumspecta (et) in operibus artificiosa sic se habet in domo quod omnis domus est sine ordine que mulierum caret regimine, et ideo vir et mulier non solum causa prolis coniunguntur, sed etiam propter administrationem economicam, que sine muliere compleri non potest, sicut dicit Aristoteles,[15] in cuius signum dictum est Gen. ii: Faciamus etc.[16]

. . . Sic ergo tota virorum bonitas et stabilitas (MS instabilitas) super mulierum bonarum gratiosa soliditate fundatur.

Sap. lect. i

C, fol. 3rb

Convenienter autem difficultati sacre Scripture dulcis et

---

[1] Jerome, *Contra Iovinianum* i (*P.L.* 23), 275.
[2] Bâle ed., p. 599: afflictionibus.　　　　[3] MS: actum.
[4] Ovid. *Ep. heroid.* i, 1-2.　　　　[5] Jerome, op. cit. 276.
[6] Really Martial, *Epigr.* I, xlii.　　[7] MS: Quo.　　　[8] MS: semel.
[9] Holcot here quotes Martial, *Epigr.* I, xlii.　　[10] Jerome, op. cit. 273.
[11] MS: falinis. This mistake, *f* for *s* and *l* for *b*, was an easy one. MS Laud. misc. 562, fol. 163va, has 'et Labinia'. After that all sorts of things might happen! Holcot is echoing *Valerius ad Rufinum;* see *P.L.* 30, 256: Vexilla pudicitiae tulerunt cum Sabinis Lucretia, et Penelope, et paucissimo comitatu tropaea retulerunt.
[12] Holcot probably had in mind Martial, *Epigr.* XI, civ.
[13] Martial refers to Sulpicia, *Epigr.* X, xxxv and xxxviii.
[14] Ovid, *Ep. heroid.* XVIII (XIX), line 133: 'Lucidaque Alcyone Calyceque...'. Holcot's copy of Ovid or his intermediary must have had the reading 'Ceice', which was quite common.
[15] *Œconom.* i, 3.　　　　　　　　　　[16] Gen. ii, 18.

utilis suavitas est annexa, quia secundum Horatium in Poetria et est ad propositum:

Omne tulit punctum qui miscuit utile dulci.

Omne tulit punctum, id est poeta, *qui miscuit utile dulci* in libro suo et approbationem et favorem habuit omnium romanorum. Populus enim romanus in quinque ordines erat distinctus. Erant enim patres conscripti, senatores, ordinarii, equites, plebs. Si ergo poeta quicumque aliquod nobile opus edidisset, coram populo publice legebatur. Si generaliter placuit, unusquisque ordo unum punctum apposuit in fine scripti[1] et tunc carmen illud deinceps auctenticum habebatur, et ideo docet Horatius quod qui vult opus suum omnibus placere videat quod opus suum habeat illa duo, scilicet quod sit delectabile et utile.

On the Twelve Minor Prophets
B, fol. 38

Audivi quod quidam archiepiscopus Anglie dixit se nullo modo facere regis voluntatem. Ait rex privatis suis: Pater noster archiepiscopus habet cor leoninum. Cito habebit caudam ovinam. Precepit ergo rex quod omnia bona temporalia in manus regis confiscarentur. Quo facto, optulit se beneplacito regis consentire.

fol. 20

Dicitur quod quidam rex Anglie, nomine Willelmus, misit ad omnes regiones ad inquirendum magnificum et mirificum modum in cibariis et poculis et sic luxuriam introduxit.

fol. 26v

Dicitur quod quidam rex, deditus ebrietati, dixit: Si haberem potum delectabile in manu mea et hostes regni mei essent in tali statu quod possint capi vel occidi, si dimisso potu statim sumerem arma mea, alioquin ipsi diriperent totum regnum, citius permitterem totum regnum destrui et everti quam carere potu tenerius predilecto.

fol. 129

Ideo quesitum fuit a rege Anglie Henrico, ut dicitur: Quis bene protegeret regnum? Respondit: Homo sine pelle, homo

---

[1] *Pseudoacron Scholia in Horatium vetustiora,* ed. O. Keller 2 (Leipzig, 1904) 363-4. On *Poetr.* 343: *Omne tulit punctum* . . . Puncta dicuntur populi suffragia . . . id est omnium meruit fauorem iuxta legem tabelliarum, quae cauerat non uoce, sed puncto debere ferri suffragium.

Centuriae seniorum and *equites* occur in the scholia on 341-2.

sine felle, plenus melle. Et exponendo ait: Omnia exteriora et bona mundana et laudes humane, favores et honores pelles sunt, in quibus homines inaniter gloriantur. Homo plenus melle est homo iustus, verax et humilis et mansuetus. Hoc autem dixit propter falsos, cupidos et insipientes consiliarios, qui ducunt reges et regna. Non autem a vitiis protegunt, sed consulunt potius ad peccandum, tantum commodum proprium requirentes.[1]

fol. 62v

Quidam autem advocatus in arcubus Londoniensis effectus est postea (episcopus) Cicestrensis. Dixit se aliquando accepisse centum libras uno die, ut taceret.[2]

fol. 18v

Quidam autem sacerdos in episcopatu Cicestrie tenuit concubinam et filiam procreavit, quam adultam pater oppressit, et aliam filiam generavit, et illam adultam defloravit et tenuit et priores dimisit, et hoc toti patrie notum fuit.

fol. 34

Dicitur quod quidam sacerdos apud Fromme fecit duas virgas, alligans et appendens cum corda modica pondus ferri in fine utriusque. Unam vocavit rationem et aliam iustitiam, et cum tali ratione et iustitia ipse et clericus suus de nocte in autumpno aucas vicinorum venabantur et frequentius tonderunt. Qui die dominica ad instantiam parochianorum sententiam excommunicationis protulit in hunc modum: Excommunico omnes illos et singulos qui aucas talium et talium sine ratione et iustitia rapuerunt.

fol. 44

Dicitur quod leo parcit primogenito filio regis, sicut nuper in Francia est expertum, quando regina fuerat infamata et primogenitus apud regem Francie et alios habebatur suspectus. Positus erat puer in quadam area publica leoni devorandus. Leo autem, naturali proprietate puerum legitimum sentiens, ei

---

[1] It seems clear that Henry III is meant in view of other *exempla* concerning him; see Welter, *La Tabula exemplorum* (Paris, 1927) 3, 89; *Le Speculum laicorum* (Paris, 1914) 10. The remarks on evil counsellors ascribed to him here may have originated in the memory of his revulsion from his favourites when the barons forced him to banish them in 1234; see F. M. Powicke, *Henry III and the Lord Edward* 1 (Oxford, 1947) 144-5.

[2] On Gilbert of St Lifard, bishop of Chichester, see *D.N.B.* 7, 1197-9. Holcot tells this *exemplum* apropos of Demosthenes, whose story he may have taken from John of Wales, *Communiloquium*, ed. cit. fol. 45v.

quasi domino regi reverentiam exhibuit, ludens et saltans cum gaudio coram eo.[1]

On Ecclesiasticus, lect. 1

fol. 40vb

Exemplum retulit frater Ricardus subtuler, frater admodum fidedignus, de quodam christiano qui apostavit a fide tempore regis Edwardi filii regis Henrici in Anglia, qui licet fuerit incarceratus per regem et sua conversatione diligentius informatus, tamen in sua malitia expiravit. Qui postea apparuit predicto fratri, qui prius eius notitiam habuit specialem.[2]

Sap. lect. cxc

C, fol. 280va

. . . . sicut patuit nuper nostris diebus de quodam clerico scriptore necromantico, cui demon apparens promisit quod foret rex Anglie et quod cum tanta militia duceretur in medio regni Anglie sicut unquam Edwardum filium Henrici viderat equitare. Hic tandem in Northamptona, tempore parliamenti, comitantibus totius regni proceribus, tractus fuit et suspensus quamdiu ossa ossis adherebant.[3]

Sap. lect. xi

C, foll. 19vb-20ra

Persone diversorum regnorum et diversarum terrarum faciliter ab invicem discernuntur per diversitatem idiomatum et linguarum, ut communiter, quia qui gallicum loquitur, gallicus est vel estimatur, et qui anglicum, anglicus. Sic enim arguebatur contra Petrum quod esset galileus et ex Christi discipulis, Mt. 26 . . .[4]. Sunt moraliter loquendo duo regna ad

[1] On the affair of the three princesses see L. Lehugeur, *Histoire de Philippe le Long* (Paris, 1897) 16-17; M. Boudet, Thomas de la Marche, *Revue historique* 59 (1895) 58-69. Queen Isabella, wife of Edward II, exposed the scandal while on a visit to the French court in 1314. She would have brought the news back to England, but there were many other channels of gossip between the two kingdoms.

[2] The vision showed the dead man wearing a coat which was partly white and partly blood-stained, to signify his baptism and redemption. He was being punished for having neglected the latter. On the apostate friar, John of Reading, see Hinnebusch, 32-3. The king handed him over to the archbishop of Canterbury in 1275 and nothing more is heard of him. Holcot's story suggests that he died in prison without abjuring the Jewish religion.

[3] The execution took place on July 20, 1318. Holcot may have seen it, since he came from Northampton and would be there in the long vacation. See *Chronica de Melsa* 2 (Rolls Series) 335-6; Annales Paulini, *Chronicles of the Reigns of Edward I and Edward II* (Rolls Series) 282-3; *Vita Edwardi Secundi*, ed. N. Denholm-Young (London, 1957) 86-7. Holcot's version tallies with the chroniclers' except that he gives his own account of the devil's promise.

[4] Holcot quotes Mt. xxvi, 73. It was customary to give examples from contemporary differences in dialect to clarify the meaning of this text; see *Study of the Bible*, 319.

invicem in hac vita commixta, videlicet regnum Dei et regnum mundi, et regnum Christi et regnum diaboli, regnum celeste et regnum terrestre; et sicut ista distant in regibus et legibus, ita in idiomate non concordant; nam idioma regni celestis est veritas . . . Idioma vero regni terrestris sive mundi est falsitas . . . Si ergo homo velit perpendere ad quod regnum pertineat, videat cui regno in idiomate concordat. Narrant historie quod cum Willelmus, dux Normannorum, regnum Anglie conquesivisset, deliberavit quomodo linguam saxonicam posset destruere et Angliam et Normanniam in idiomate concordare; et ideo ordinavit quod nullus in curia regis placitaret nisi in gallico, et iterum quod puer quilibet ponendus as litteras addisceret gallicum, et per gallicum latinum, que duo usque hodie observantur. Isto modo moraliter princeps huius mundi diabolus est . . . ; sed verum est quod principatum suum in mundo non habet hereditaria successione, sed violenta oppressione, et ideo non est heres, sed conquisitor.[1] Idioma autem suum proprium in provincia infernali est mendacium . . . et ideo ut concordet mundum cum provincia infernali in idiomate, ordinavit quod omnia secularia in conventionibus, mercationibus, et commutationibus utantur mendaciis; et sicut puer, docendus in scola, primo addiscit gallicum, ita iuvenis, applicandus seculo, cum studio et labore addiscit loqui mendacium.[2]

Sap. lect. xix

C, fol. 32va-b

Circa istam lectionem quero questionem: utrum resurrectio omnium generaliter sit futura; vel sic, quia dicunt quod *nemo* revertetur, quero an omnes revertentur per resurrectionem. Excipio tamen Christum cum Virgine matre sua benedicta, de qua pie credit ecclesia quod sit in ea resurrectio iam completa. . . .

Ad istam questionem sine scrupulo est dicendum quod sic, sicut evangelium et apostolica doctrina testantur, tam in locis ad oppositum allegatis, quam in multis aliis. Rationem istius resurrectionis assignat sanctus Thomas super IV Sent. dist. iv, art. 1 et 2, talem:[3] Omnes homines appetunt beatitudinem. Iste appetitus non completur in vita ista nec in vita alia nisi (?MS ubi) anima corpori sit coniuncta. Sed cum doctoris reverentia hec ratio nichil facit pro resurrectione damnatorum, in quibus oportet concedere quod appetitus beatitudinis frustratur in eternum. Et ideo alii assignant aliam rationem, sicut Ricardus

---

[1] MS Laud. misc. 562, fol. 13ra, adds 'et tyrannus' after 'conquisitor'.

[2] Welter, p. 361, n. 58, quotes this passage and notes the parallel in *Polychronicon*.

[3] The *Summa contra gentiles* iv, 79 seems indicated here rather than the *Com. in IV Sent*. dist. xliii, art. 1 and 2.

de Mediavilla, distinctione preallegata, que talis est:[1] Nulla naturalis inclinatio est frustra. Sed omnis anima rationalis habet naturalem inclinationem ad regendum et gubernandum corpus. Ergo omnis anima rationalis corpori unietur. Sed nec ista ratio cogit intellectum ad assensum, quia naturalis inclinatio voluntatis omnium hominum est ad bene vivendum, secundum Augustinum, xiii De Trinitate,[2] et in multis aliis locis; et tamen constat secundum fidem quod appetitus frustrabitur in multis, quia multi sunt vocati, pauci vero electi;[3] et ideo tenendum est quod sic, quia hoc sonat scriptura sacra expresse. Hoc etiam est sanctis patribus revelatum, et quasi infinitis miraculis declaratum, inter que est illud de septem dormientibus; nota in legenda sanctorum.[4]

Sap. lect. clv

C, fol. 231ra-b

Sed qualiter est quod philosophi ad demonstrandum Deum esse sufficientes fuerunt, cum nec christiani, qui soli unius veri Dei notitiam habent, ad hoc non sufficiant? Ad hoc dicendum, ut estimo, quod Deum esse non est per aliquam rationem demonstratum hucusque nec Deum esse creatorem mundi, sed quicumque ad Deum innocenter se habent et rationem naturalem exercent studendo, nec divine gratie obicem prebent, Deus eis sufficienter sui communicabit notitiam, sic quod eis sufficiant ad salutem. Exempla ad hoc habentur de Cornelio, cui missus est Petrus, de Paulo cui missus est Ananias, qui sic se disposuerunt quod revelationem vel inspirationem de uno Deo meruerunt habere; et ideo dicendum quod sine culpa hominis habentis usum rationis nunquam eveniet quin notitiam de Deo habeat, saltem quanta est necesse ad salutem.

Sap. lect. clvii

C, fol. 233va-b

Consequenter ostendit quomodo per ista duo media intellectus humanus ascendit in Deum, quasi dicat: hec est ratio quare gentiles ab ignorantia sua de Deo sunt inexcusabiles, quia *a magnitudine speciei et creature poterit creator rerum cognoscibiliter videri*. *A magnitudine speciei*, id est pulchritudinis *et creature*, id est mirabilis facture, debebant arguisse creatorem esse maiorem tam specie quam virtute. Sicut enim Aristoteles per viam motus nisus est probare unum primum movens esse impartibile et

---

[1] *Com. in IV Sent.* dist. xliii, q. 1 (ed. Brescia, 1591, IV, 554).
[2] *De Trinitate* xiii, 3-5, *P.L.* 42, 1017-20. [3] Mt. xx, 16.
[4] The Seven Sleepers awoke after 372 years in order to testify against heretics who doubted the resurrection; *Jacobi a Voragine Legenda aurea*, ed. Th. Graesse (Leipzig, 1850) 438.

infinitum, nullam habens magnitudinem corporalem, 8
Physicorum ...

*Si enim tantum potuerunt scire, ut possent seculum estimare, quomodo
huius Dominum non facilius inuenerunt?* ... Sed contra illud ultimum
videtur esse illud superius positus, cap. 9: *Difficile estimamus que
in terra sunt, et que in prospectu sunt invenimus cum labore, que autem
in celis sunt quis investigabit?*[1] Dicunt doctores quod aliud est
comprehendere de Deo, quia est, et aliud, quid est. Primum
potuerunt philosophi, secundum fuit eis impossibile. Sed quia
nec Deum esse hucusque demonstratum inveni,[2] aliter ad
dictam obiectionem respondeo. Dicam enim secundum mentem
beati Augustini, 18 De civitate Dei, cap. 28, quod ante omnes
philosophos grecos vel barbaros prophete sancti precesserunt,
qui tam verbo quam scripto Dei notitiam docuerunt, et ideo
Deum esse statim a principio mundi per Adam et filios suos
extitit predicatum,[3] cui dicto quidam assenserunt et quidam
dissenserunt, sicut modo de aliis articulis invenimus. Isti ergo
philosophi, audientes Deum esse et a Dei cultoribus fuisse
predicatum, poterant ex regimine mundi rerum uniformi
gubernatione rationabiliter asseruisse Deum esse; et ideo quod
erraverunt eorum vel negligentia vel malitia fuit in causa, et
quia propter antiquam revelationem divulgatum est apud
omnes gentes, legibus utentes, Deum esse, et quod est omnibus
notum, videtur ipsa natura notum. Ideo estimo Damascenum
dixisse,[4] Sent. cap. 3: Cognitio existendi Deum nobis naturaliter
insita est, quamvis non ingenii naturalis investigatione, sed
potius divina revelatione Dei notitia hominibus fuerit communi-
cata.

Unde dico quod multo facilius est Deum, id est fidem de Deo,
invenire quam *seculum estimare*, et bene utentibus naturali
ingenio Deus seipsum aliquo modo revelat vel per extrinsecam
informationem vel per intrinsecam inspirationem. Confirmatur
hec responsio, quia nec aliter astronomiam dicunt plurique (*sic*)
adinventam fuisse. Unde Magister in Historia scolis (scholastica)
super Genesim de dispersione filiorum Noe narrat Noe habuisse
quendam filium nomine Ionithum, qui accepit a Deo donum
sapientie et invenit astronomiam.[5] Sicut ergo addiscere potuerunt
ad mensurandum quantitatem terre, solis et lune, ita potuerunt
didicisse colere verum Deum.

[1] Sap. ix. 16.

[2] The printed edition has an interpolation here, p. 522.

[3] Holcot is probably referring to *De civ. Dei* xiv, 28 or to xviii, 37. He may
have had both chapters in mind.

[4] *De fide orthodoxa*, i, 3 (*P.G.* 94), 794: Velut enim iam diximus, insitum
nobis a natura est, ut Deum esse noscamus. Holcot uses Grosseteste's version,
MS. Bodl. Ashm. 1526, fol. 122va.

[5] Petrus Comestor, *Hist. schol.* in Gen. cap. xxxvii (*P.L.* 198) 1088: Centesimo
anno tertiae chiliadis natus est Noe filius ... et dixit eum Jonithum ... hic
accepit a Domino donum sapientiae et invenit astronomiam.

P, Sermo cxviii

Exemplum est unus ludus inter pastores in locis campestribus. Unus pastor cum baculo describit unum circulum et infra protrahit lineas diversas. Quo facto, colligit sibi de diversis lignis unam magnam familiam et vocat tales homines ligneos et in medio eorum ponit unum maiorem ceteris, quem vocat regem aliorum. Tunc vadit adversarius, qui ludit cum eo, et longe stans extra circulum cum baculo proicit ad homines stantes in circulo et nititur eos percutere et alium percutit modo ex una parte, modo ex alia, et quandoque ad casum pellit; sed quamdiu sunt infra circulum, quantumcumque cadant non pertinent ad dominium suum, sed vadit auctor ludi et reponit eos in loco suo; sed si poterit prosternere et ponere extra circulum rapit eos libere tanquam suos et habet sic ludum et exultat. Et quanto elongantur magis a centro, ubi stat rex eorum, et magis appropinquant ad circumferentiam, tanto minus participant de immobilitate centri et tanto minus habent de fulcimento ab extra, et per consequens tanto viciniores sunt casui et perditioni.

P, sermo xlv

Exemplum habemus Seneca, Declam. x. Narrat quod lex fuit antiquitus apud quosdam quod senior frater divideret hereditatem et iunior eligeret: et ratio est quia maioris discretionis est dividere quam eligere, et senior discretior debet esse. Alia lex fuit apud eos quod liceret filium ex ancilla tollere hereditatem, sicut filium liberum, quam legem etiam videntur habere Isaac et Iacob. Contingit ergo duo fratres, unum liberum et alium servum, hereditatem dividere. Frater vero senior sic divisit quod posuit ex una parte totam hereditatem paternam et ex parte alia matrem Othi, fratri Otho (MS Nothi, Notho) offerens optionem, qui elegit matrem, accusavitque fratrem, quia circumscripsisset, id est quod exclusisset eum ab hereditate. Responsum est quod non qui dividit, sed qui eligit circumscribit.[1]

Sap. lect. xv

C, fol. 26va

Et licet non possit forsitan ratione naturali probari, sicut satis patet per debilitatem rationum que ad hoc tam a sanctis quam a philosophis adducuntur, summe tamen convenit hoc credere, sicut multa alia sunt vera que probare nescimus.

---

[1] Trevet had told the same story in different words, without giving the name of the younger brother. Holcot's moralisation is similar to Trevet's; see MS Paris, Bibl. nat. lat. 3580, fol. 114v. Miss J. R. Dean kindly sent me her list of MSS of Trevet's *Declamationes moralisate*. The case is not to be found in Seneca.

Alterum enim istorum necessarium est: mundus incepit esse vel mundus non incepit esse; et tamen neutrum istorum demonstrative probari potest . . . Similiter quadratura circuli certa est; tamen eius demonstratio tempore Aristotelis inventa non fuit.

Ecclus lect. xix

fol. 16va

Et ideo dicitur Prov. xv:[1] Per misericordiam et fidem purgantur peccata. Unde narratur historia bene purgans, quod quidam hereticus tenuit quod anima rationalis est corruptibilis et quod unus interitus esset hominis et iumentorum, sicut dicitur Eccles. iii;[2] et solvit faciliter argumenta aliorum contra heresim quam tenebat. Tandem dixit unus conversus de ordine fratrum predicatorum quod volebat disputare contra eum, et licet de hoc esset risus, quia laicus erat et alius magnus clericus, nec boni clerici poterant contra eum prevalere, tamen sic inter cetera dixit sibi: Numquid si fides christiana sit vera boni christiani magnum gaudium possidebunt et increduli gravissima pena punientur? Qui respondit: Sic, si vera essent quod christiani dicunt. Tunc laicus: Ergo recta ratione deberes credere sicut faciunt christiani boni, quia si vera sit fides et credideris, multum lucraberis. Similiter si non sit vera et credideris, nichil perdes secundum heresim quam tu tenes, quia per te anima non manebit nec ad meritum nec ad demeritum nec ad supplicium. Ergo in omnem eventum rationabilius et securius est credere sicut faciunt christiani. Tunc hereticus, spiritu Dei motus, partim timore pene, partim spe gaudii, dimissa heresi effectus est bonus christianus. Sic igitur patet quod fides est tante virtutis quod existens in bono viro purgat peccatum malorum.[3]

B, foll. 50v-51

Quantum ad hoc, utrum ordines isti fuerint tempore illo instituti iudicetis. Videtur tamen michi quod si tunc fuerint religiosi, vel erant de secta phariseorum vel saduceorum vel essenorum. Istas tres sectas ponit Iosephus, lib. (blank in MS) Antiquitatum, et constat quod isti erant principaliter conspirantes in morte Christi, et hoc per invidiam. Ideo non est in hoc gloriandum. Ideo deberent magis dolere, si ordo illorum tunc fuisset institutus. Estimo quod milites moderni temporis non glorientur de militibus qui crucifixerunt Christum et idem de pontificibus etc. Argumenta etiam non concludunt, quia non sequitur: vidit vel instituit viros candidos vel candidis indutos (MS institutos), ergo carmelitas. Tunc enim sequeretur quod

---

[1] Prov. xv, 27.   [2] Eccles. iii, 19.
[3] Holcot tells the same tale more shortly, Sap. lect. xv, p. 56.

molendinarii vel pastores communiter essent carmeliti. Consimile argumentum de zona pellicea. Videatis etiam picturam Ioannis Baptiste et incessus.[1]

Preterea si Augustinus 18 annorum recepit habitum illum et instituit eos congregari in unum, ergo recepit habitum illum manicheus et infidelis et in habitu illo filium generavit, quia fuit 30 annorum antequam ad fidem converteretur, sicut patet.[2]

Sap. lect. xcvi

C, fol. 146ra-b

Unde fecit regulam de communi vita clericorum, que vocatur regula beati Augustini, quam multi alii religiosi postea assumpserunt, inter quos sunt fratres predicatores; et longe postea heremite sancti Guillelmi et sancti Augustini et multi alii, convenientes in unum collegium, facti sunt ex heremitis urbanite et assumpserunt regulam beati Augustini, que heremetice vite omnino repugnat; et vocatur modo ordo ille ordo heremitarum sancti Augustini, de quo ordine nunquam fuit Augustinus, quia nunquam fuit heremita, sicut patet per verba sua, 10 Confessionum in fine, ubi loquens ad Deum dicit sic: Contritis peccatis meis. . . .[3]

P, sermo xxvii

Circa primum punctum tria sunt notanda. Primo, quod ad locum celi et Dei finale iudicium omnes sunt vocati et eis expense et auxilium gratie dantur, per quod venire poterint, si voluerint. . . .[4]

Tertia ratio accipitur penes deductionem ad inconveniens, . . . quia si dicitur quod quando peccant Deus eis aliquam gratiam non dedit, et quod etiam ad hoc destinati fuerunt, concedere oportet quod nullus peccator contra Deum vel hominem peccans rationabiliter vituperari potest, quia nullus est vituperandus de hoc quod nullo modo fugere potest; sed si Deus aliquem (ad) maleficiendum destinavit, ergo gratiam ei non dedit qua tale malum fugere posset. Si ergo patrem occidat vel matrem vel quidcumque aliud malum contra Deum vel contra nos (faciat), faceret irrationabiliter qui eum vituperaret, si ad hoc esset ordinatus vel a Deo non haberet quod aliter non facere posset.

---

[1] Holcot has jotted down his argument in note form here as in other passages of his lectures on the Twelve Prophets.

[2] Holcot's source may have been the manual of his Order, written before 1291 and re-edited in 1311 by Stephanus de Salaniaco and Bernardus Guidonis, *De quatuor in quibus Deus Praedicatorum Ordinem insignivit*, ed. Th. Kaeppeli (*Mon. Ord. Fratr. Praed. Hist.* 22, 1949) 171-4, 179-81. The connexion between the Rule of St Augustine and those of the various mendicant Orders is set out clearly, but without Holcot's type of satire.

[3] *Confess.* X, xliii, 70.

[4] Holcot gives reasons to support his point.

Quod si reputaretur inconveniens, ergo et primum, scilicet quod Deus non omnes vocaret vel non daret pro via expensas . . .

Quarta ratio accipitur penes deductionem ad impossibile, . . quia aliter peccatores in morte et in die iudicii dampnandi se iustificare possent et culpam et dampnationem suam rationabiliter Deo imputare, dicendo: Nunquam vocasti nos nec dedisti gratiam veniendi. Ergo in te est causa nostri delicti et dampnationis. Sed sic hoc est impossibile, ita est hereticum dicere quod Deus talem vel tantam faceret iniustitiam.

P, sermo xlv

Est autem de Deo sicut de quodam patriarcha Ierusalem, qui iuxta fores ecclesie sive templi sibi fecit thronum sive sedem, in quo feria quarta et sexta eo zelo sedere solebat ut omnium pauperum causas audiret, ne alicui gratia negaretur. Christus autem, singulis cupiens conferre gratiam, certe non solum unam sedem vel thronum iuxta unius ecclesie ostium fecit, sed in qualibet ecclesia modo in suis vicariis thronum habet et in pluribus plures expectat (MS expectans) cum gratia penitentes, ut ad confessionem accedant cum fiducia gratiam conferendi.[1]

Sap. lect. clxxxiii

C, fol. 270ra

Bis autem dictum est ei: Pasce oves meas, ad innuendum differentiam inter doctrinam necessariam iuvenibus et senibus. Nam simplex admonitio sufficit senibus, iuvenibus vero opus est tam verbis quam verberibus, ut debite doceantur. Aliter tamen istud dicitur exposuisse quidam novitius, arguens quod iuvenes fratres debent refici bis in die et senibus convenit ieiunare; et ideo pie dixit Christus prelato bis: Pasce agnos meos, et semel: Pasce oves meas.

P, sermo xcv

Karissimi, primum quod allicit discipulum addiscere est subtilitas magistri, quia tales libenter audiuntur. Scitis quod pueri, cum primo instruuntur, non ponuntur aliquod subtile addiscere, sed tantum grossum. Ideo docuntur primo in libro cum litteris grossis scriptis, affixis alicui ligno, et postea per processum in litteris libri subtilioris . . . Secundo, reddit doctorem acceptum benignitas. Pueri enim multum amant doceri benigne. Tunc enim doctorem suum amant, et amor ille optimus est . . . Tertium est assiduitas et diligentia, quia sine hiis homo non bene docetur. Unde magni qui habent filios suos docendos faciunt quod magistri eorum morentur cum eis.

[1] This is a Lenten sermon; hence the stress on penance.

Sap. lect. liv

C, foll. 88vb-89va

Notandum ergo est quod ad statum iuvenilem, hoc est ad iuvenes, qui viriles annos attigistis quadrupliciter vos habere debetis. E(s)t enim iuventus moribus informanda, arctius castiganda, parcius sustentanda, mitius iudicanda.

Primo ergo iuventus est moribus informanda. Istud fecerunt gentiles antiqui tripliciter, scripturis librorum, picturis gestorum et figuris signorum. Exploraverunt enim nobiles antiqui (eos) qui meliores fuerunt philosophi et illis pueros suos tam litteris quam moribus imbuendos dederunt; unde Traianus Plutarchum, Nero Senecam, Alexander Aristotelem magistros habuerunt; et nec talibus magistris aliquid dissolutionis vel lubrice levitatis addiscerent summe cavebant (MS caverent); unde docuerunt iuvenes picturis gestorum; unde sicut narrat quidam expositor super Iuvenalem, libro primo satira (*sic*), nobiles romani sic disposuerunt actiones suas per singulos dies, quod summo mane omnes simul petebant vel adibant archus triumphales, in quibus antecessores sui pingebantur cum armis et cautelis, quod devicerant hostes suos, ut sic iuvenes, illis visis, attenderentur ad virtutes per imitationem gestorum.[1] Deinde templum Appollinis (MS Apposinis) petebant, qui erat deus sapientie. Postea iudices ad forum, senatores (ad) Capitolium descendebant, iudices ut causas tractarent, senatores ut de communi utilitate reipublice deliberarent; et sic tempus suum usque ad horam nonam expenderunt. Et ne iuvenes a bonis occupationibus impedirentur per totum tempus ante nonam, ordinatum erat quod meretrices nullo sensu sua prostibula egrederentur ante nonam, ne iuvenes a suis informationibus et viri a consiliis reipublice per delectationes libidinosas aliquatenus turbarentur. Et hec est ratio secundum Hugonem quare meretrices apud

---

[1] Holcot or his *expositor* could have read of the family *imagines maiorum* in the prologue to the *Liber de regno Sicilie*, where the ancient Romans are said to have kept likenesses of their forbears in their homes as a perpetual reminder to the eye; see *La Historia o Liber de Regno Sicilie di Ugo Falcando*, ed. G. B. Siragusa (Fonti per la Storia d'Italia, Rome, 1897) 4: . . . hinc nimirum antiquitus Romani patrum domi conservabant ymagines ut antecessorum eis acta semper occurrerent puderetque degenerem sequi lasciviam ac turpi languere desidia et amplectende virtutis quasi quandam necessitatem habuerunt pre oculis. This passage was 'copied between 1286 and 1297 by William of Nangis, a monk of St Denis, into the prose preface of the second edition of his life of Louis IX'; see E. Jamison, *Admiral Eugenius of Sicily his Life and Work and the Authorship of the Epistola ad Petrum and the Historia Hugonis Falcandi Siculi*, London, 1957, 370. Since the passage circulated in a well-known book of the late thirteenth century produced near Paris, Holcot may have found it in some form or other. The prologue to *Policraticus* may have suggested the triumphal arches 1, 13: Arcus triumphales tunc proficiunt illustribus viris ad gloriam, cum ex quibus causis et quorum sint, docet inscriptio. Liberatorem patriae, fundatorem quietis, tunc demum inspector agnoscit, cum titulus triumphatorem . . . indicat Constantinum.

romanos nonarie vocebantur, quia ad horam nonam licuit de suis domibus egredi et non ante.[1]

Item docebantur iuvenes ad bonos mores figuris signorum; unde narrat Macrobius, primo Saturn., quod apud romanos pueri nobilium quadam utebantur veste, que dicebatur pretexta, et inde pueri nobiles vocabantur pretextati. Habebant coram pectore suo bullam quandam auream, habentem figuram cordis humane. Bulla autem fuit semirotunde figure, quasi medietas sphere, ad similitudinem bullarum que fiunt in aqua. Pretexta erat de purpura, que est rubei coloris, ut pudore sue nobilitatis a vitiis se subtraherent, et cordis imaginem ante pectus portabant, ut se invicem intuentes, ita se fore (homines) cogitarent, si corde prestarent. Hec Macrobius.[2] Sic ergo primo iuventus est moribus informanda, Ecclesiastes xii: Memento Creatoris tui in diebus iuventutis tue.[3]

Secundo iuventus est arctius castiganda, quia. . . .[4]

Tertio iuventus est parcius sustentanda, ut in iuvenili etate assuescat sobrietati. Unde narrat Augustinus de bona matrona, ix, Confess., cap. 8. . . .[5]

Quarto iuventus est mitius iudicanda. Non est enim desperandum de eis etiam si peccent frequenter . . .[6]

The story of the daily visit to the monuments is told more shortly, but with more stress on the appearance of the monuments, in P, sermo vi:

Unde legitur de romanis quod in diversis locis civitatis romane fuerunt quedam edificia ornata et patentia toti mundo, fueruntque curiose depicta de historiis triumphalibus et bellis romanorum veterum, ordinatumque fuerat inter romanos quod omni die certa hora nobiles iuvenes romanorum ad ista loca adducerentur, ut ibi respicerent et cogitarent progenitorum suorum probitates, ut per hoc monerentur ad similia pro republica.

The moral in this case is that Christians, being the sons of the Church, should consider the deeds of the saints in order to imitate them.

[1] Huguccio, *Magnae derivationes*, MS Oxford, Bodl. e Mus. 96 (3582), p. 295: Unde *hec nonaria*, id est meretrix, quia ante nonam non licebat eis exire de prostibulo. Consuetudo enim olim erat apud romanos ut usque ad horam nonam de commodo reipublice disputarent, nec licebat alicui delectationi ante nonam vacare. Unde meretrices nonarie dicuntur, quia ad horam nonam et non ante de prostibulis exibant, ne si prius egrederentur iuvenes impedirent. See the scholia to Persius, *Sat.* 1, 133, ed O. Iahn (Leipzig, 1843) 277.

[2] Macrobius, *Saturn.* I, vi, 9-17, ed. Eyssenhardt (Leipzig, 1893), 24-6.

[3] Eccles. xii, 1.

[4] Holcot here quotes 1 Reg. ii for the story of Heli and his sons, Arist. *Ethic.* x, 9 on the need for punishment rather than argument, and Pseudo-Boethius, *De disciplina scholarium* ii, (*P.L.* 64) 1227, 'De sanguineo Lucretii filio'.

[5] *Confess.* ix, 8.

[6] Holcot goes on to mention the Feast of the Conversion of St Paul; see above, p. 140, n. 2.

Is it possible to put Holcot's morning in the life of ancient
Romans into the frame of an actual exposition of Juvenal?
Mr W. S. Anderson has recently described medieval scholia on
a Juvenal manuscript belonging to Mr Thomas E. Marston,
Curator of the Classical Collection in the Yale University
Library.[1] They are datable on internal evidence 'no earlier
than the mid-eighth century' and from the hands not later than
the twelfth century. The commentator 'regularly pauses to
fill in background with long stories concerning mythological
figures . . . or with a fanciful explanation of Roman customs:
"mos erat . . ." '.[2] I wrote to ask Mr Anderson whether the
fanciful explanations included any trace of the alleged quotation
from a commentary in Holcot and had the following very
helpful answer:

> 'The Marston MS does have fanciful explanations of
> customs, but it does not strike me as so elaborately wrong as
> Holcot's commentator. . . . The most likely place in Book I
> of Juvenal for such a discussion would have been the passage
> in Satire 1. 127, beginning

> ipse dies pulchro distinguitur ordine rerum.

> If so the Marston MS instantly becomes inconclusive,
> because it now lacks 1. 27-143. . . . The "expositor" must
> have been working from the said passage in 1. 127 ff. In
> the first place, he is describing the order of the day, as is
> Juvenal. He concentrates immediately on *arcus triumphales*,
> *templum Apollinis*, *forum*, and the law courts. Juvenal is not
> specifically talking about the young men, nor is he making
> a point of the noble moral lessons derived from their
> activities. Yet he cites familiar portions of the city, so as to
> demonstrate the depravity, the degeneracy of his day.
> It looks to me as though Holcot's "expositor" has taken
> off very imaginatively from Juvenal's words in 128/9

>   forum iurisque peritus Apollo
> atque triumphales.

> I hardly need to observe that Juvenal was not talking about
> a temple of Apollo or about triumphal arches, but about
> statues of Apollo and various triumphatores which stood
> in the forum of Augustus. . . .'

The scholia edited by Iahn would have given Holcot's *expositor*
a start:

> '*iurisque peritus Apollo*: aut quia iuxta Apollinis templum
> iurisperiti sedebant et tractabant . . .

---

[1] The Marston Manuscript of Juvenal, *Traditio* 13 (1957) 407-14.
[2] ibid., 411.

atque triumphales, id est itur ad rostra ubi habere solent triumphales statuas viri magni. . . .[1]

Thus Holcot may have been quoting from an exposition of Juvenal or he may have embroidered on the scholia himself.

Sap. lect. cxcviii

C, fol. 293ra

Dicit Papias et habetur in expositione super Iuvenalem, Satir. 2 quod Numa Pompilio sacrificante cecidit quoddam scutum de celo, quod ancile dictum fuit. Datumque est responsum quod illic foret romanum imperium ubi illud ancile foret servatum. Numa xi alia scuta fecit, ut essent xii numero et quid esset illud quod de celo ceciderat maneret occultum.[2]

Sap. lect. xlv

C, fol. 74rb-vb

Est enim uxor eligenda discrete, regenda mansuete, corrigenda secrete, et diligenda complete, ut sit electio per discretam deliberationem, directio per mansuetam gubernationem, correctio per secretam informationem et dilectio per completam communicationem. . . . Amicitia, que est propter honestum, habet istas conditiones, quod est mansiva et rara, quia fundatur super bonos mores, qui in virtuosis semper manent. Rara autem est quia pauci sunt virtuosi; et indiget hec amicitia longo tempore et convictu et experientia morum. . . . Secundo, est uxor regenda mansuete, non cum tirannica austeritate vel rigore. . . .[3]

B, foll. 137v-138

Notandum etiam quod quamdiu ecclesia fuit regulata per pauperes piscatores bene fuit et pariter (di)mensionata. Nunc autem habundantia temporalium sic occupat ecclesiam re-

---

[1] *Iuvenalis Satira,* ed. O. Iahn (Berlin, 1851) 183.

[2] Papias, *Vocabularium* (Venice, 1491) fol. 11v gives a rather more general account of the ancile shield. The *scholia vetera* edited by Iahn give no explanation and the Marston Juvenal is defective here, too. The *locus* must have been *Sat.* ii, 126. Nicholas Trevet is said to have commented on Juvenal; see J. R. Dean, Cultural Relations, op. cit. 553; G. Highet, *Juvenal the Satirist* (Oxford, 1954) 203, 315. Perhaps his lost commentary was Holcot's source for this passage. He was too scholarly to have provided the piece on the triumphal arches, just quoted.

[3] Vincent of Beauvais recommends discretion in choice and kind treatment of wives, *De eruditione* xxxvii, op. cit. Aristotle's view that friendship between husband and wife is natural and may be based on virtue if the parties are virtuous (*Ethic. nicom.* viii, 12) passed into the scholastic teaching on marriage; see C. S. Lewis, *The Allegory of Love* (Oxford, 1936) 16. Holcot goes further in transferring Aristotle's description of friendship between men as rare and of slow growth (*Ethic. nicom.* viii, 3) to friendship in marriage.

ligiosorum quod meditationes, orationes, lectiones, devotiones et contemplationes, quibus debeat principaliter sustentari, pereant in eadem. Unde officium divinum non videtur nisi tumultus et strepitus inordinatus. . . . . Nota etiam quomodo legitur in vita magni Constantini, quando datum fuit occidentale imperium ecclesie a Constantino, facta est vox de celo dicens: Hodie infusum est venenum in ecclesia Dei, quoniam ecclesiam divitiis sic ditavit. Sic nota quomodo domina in posterioribus pulcherrima et in facie turpissima apparuit sancto . . .

Sap. lect. lxi
C, fol. 100va

Fuerunt enim a tempore Silvestri pape et Constantini imperatoris, qui temporalia ecclesie primo dicitur dedisse, semper iudicia, placitationes et dissensiones inter clericos, quis eorum videretur maior ad pascendum oves Christi. Hec est causa quare volant sagitte acute, nunc regalium supplicationum ad romanam curiam, nunc accusationum, nunc diffamationum ad inferiorum iudicum audientiam, ita quod plena est ecclesia advocatis in omni causa ad defendendum iniuriam. . . . Si esset ita pauper ecclesia modo, sicut fuit quando Christus in ea vixit in terra, non haberet ecclesia tales placitores nec tales invasores. Pauper et iuvenis mercator non timet predones nec patitur insultus, sed cum est dives tunc eum nituntur spoliare etiam qui eum prius conabantur ditare. Ita est (quod) quando ecclesia studuit paupertati, bene valuit. Modo studet ditari et patitur a sagittariis.

D'EYNCOURT ON ECCLESIASTES
C, fol. 320vb

Narrat Titus Livius, prime decadis lib. i, de Tullo, rege romanorum tertio, quod cum suo tempore Urbs pestilentia laboravit. . . .[1]

fol. 325rb

Narrat Titus Livius, prime decadis lib. ii, et idem narrat Valerius de Coriolano . . .[2]

fol. 328rb

Narrat Titus Livius, prime decadis lib. vii, de samnitibus quod cum in bello tam fortiter ibi sisterent. . . [3]

fol. 356ra

Narrat Titus Livius, prime decadis lib. i, quod Numa Po(m)pilius, secundus rex romanorum, ex pietate omnium

[1] *Ab Urb. cond.* I, xxxi, 5.   [2] II, xxxiii, xl.   [3] VII, xxxiii, 16.

z

pectora imbuerat, ut fides . . .[1] Similiter hec fuit causa destructionis Cartaginis et sui impii, prout cartaginenses, a romanis devicti, confessi sunt, sicut narrat Titus Livius de secundo bello punico, secunde (sic) decadis lib. x, cum ipsi federa primo inita cum romanis iusiurando firmata violassent, et postmodum devicti et destructi. . . .[2]

fol. 370vb

Dicit enim Titus Livius, prime decadis lib. ii, quod excellentibus ingeniis citius defecit ars qua carnem regant quam qua hostem superent.[3]

fol. 349rb

Titus Livius refert (quod) cum a pireneis montibus usque ad columpnas Herculis et usque ad oceanum, devicto Hannibale et aliis romanorum hostibus, provincias subiugasset, pueros captivos et puellas egregie pulchritudinis restituit barbaris nec passus est eas in suum venire conspectum ne vel oculis eius aliquid de integritate pudicitie delibaret. Hec ille.[4]

THOMAS RINGSTEAD ON PROVERBS

L, fol. 22rb

Unde in anglorum cronicis de rege Edwardo de Karnarvan quod cum ex consilio impio pater eum abdicasset, ille patienter ferens iniuriam, cum pater eius nocte quadam equitans in hieme lutosam et periculosam viam transiret, Edwardus patris pericula timens ultro se ingerens frenum accepit, sicque incedens pedibus salvum regem eduxit, patre ignorante quis esset talis.[5] Talis filius fuit Christus. . . .

fol. 193vb-194ra

Nam et ego novi sacerdotem quendam, qui cum ad taxillos luderet cum quodam domino, in cuius patronatu ecclesia pinguis vacabat, sic proposuit domino thema suum: Ego, inquit, ponam viginti libras tecum, domine, quod lucrabis hunc ludum et tamen non dabis michi ecclesiam talem vacantem. Dominus ergo, perpendens astutiam sacerdotis, sponte ludum perdidit et vacantem ecclesiam contulit ei statim, putans per cautelam evadere simoniam. Non sic, karissimi, non sic. . . .[6]

---

[1] I, xxi.
[2] The story of Hasdrubel's saying follows; XXX, xlii.
[3] II, xliii, 10.
[4] Not in Ab. Urb. cond., but probably derived from XXVII, xix.
[5] Not to be found in any printed chronicle.
[6] Ringstead must have had secular clerks in his audience. Religious had no temptation to commit simony of this kind, since they could not hold benefices.

fol. 236va-b

Hoc siquidem videmus quod lana que colore aliquo tingitur, dum pannus est in operari vel dum lana per se est, optime durat. Si autem primo fiat pannus et postmodum tingatur, non erit ita stabilis, immo valde faciliter maculas contrahit, si liquor aliquis desuper infundatur. Sic illi qui prius ponuntur in dignitate ad alios protegendum per curam et non in adolescentia tincti fuerint virtute, non possunt stabiles portare colores. Qui vero in principio tinguntur tunc disponuntur ut alios a temptatione protegant et conservent stabiliter absque macule cuiuslibet contractione.

MS Bodl. 829, fol. 2vb; L, fol. 16rb-va

Secundo, dico quod reges nostri ad perficiendas iniurias satis sunt sensati et vigorosi, et tertio, sunt circa famam vanam, fatuorum favorem et novos apparatus nimium curiosi . . . Pro studiositate regnat rapacitas et duobus siquidem consistit studium potentum et divitum modernorum, ut pauperes rapiant et spolient impotentes. Revera, karissimi, sic est de nostris potentibus et regibus hiis diebus. Tota enim regum iustitia, et virtus principantis, que esse debent in manibus regum, constanti rapacitate et indesinenti tenacitate consistit. Ille siquidem sapientior rex et dominus nominatur, qui fraudulentius novit rapere et firmius retinere.

John Lathbury on Lamentations

E, 1, N

Similiter cur semper in cuiuslibet alphabeti qualibet clausula trini versus incipiunt ab eadem littera? Salvo iudicio (meliore) iuxta imaginem quam ego de libro concipio potest reddi talis causa moralis, quia quot capita, tot sensus, quia sanctus propheta, plangens populi infortunia, semper Trinitatem Personarum confidenter conqueritur et unitatem essentie insimul confitetur, quia iudicio meo nec littera nec numerus nec aliquid hic signatum vacat a misterio, ubi nec unus apex nec unum iota inscribitur sine stilo prophetico, et per hoc nichil aliud intelligo nisi (quod) per trinitatem versuum singularum clausularum apparet michi figurari Trinitatem Personarum et ex unitate annexe et prefixe unius littere evidenter dicitur unitas divine essentie, et ideo solum propter hanc imaginationem huius misterii assumpsi tale thema introductorium huius libri, *In nomine Patris et Filii et Spiritus sancti.*[1]

---

[1] Compare Nicholas of Lyre, *Postilla litteralis* (*Glossa ordinaria cum postillis Nicolai de Lyra et additiones etc*, 4, Lyons, 1559) 925-6: Sciendum etiam quod hic non est querendus processus artis, sed magis dolentis et conquerentis, qui lamentans aliquod factum idem repetit sub aliis verbis, sicut mater lamentans

E, 12, D

Audivi enim a quodam fidedigno, cuius dicto tantum adhereo quantum quaterno, qui firmavit se vidisse illam imaginem dolorosam, quam beatus Lucas depinxit ad effigiem Marie lamentantis sub patibulo, de qua inter alia dixit quod habet cutem claram et faciem formosam et rivos lacrimarum usque ad mentum decurrentes per declivos maxillarum, ut quasi verissime picture correspondeat prophetia scripture quod *lacrime eius in maxillis eius,* quasi diceret (Icremias): Cum tanto impetu et fervore lacrime expellerent lacrimas (quod) quemadmodum torrentis defluent per maxillas.

81, F

Unde in signum quod omnis victoria a Deo immediate dispensatur hoc michi mirabile quidam venerabilis miles, cuius sancta vita auctenticat dicta, devote retulit quod etiam occulata fide se vidisse securius asseruit. Convenerant in terra sancta septem milia fidelium, quorum ipse unus erat, ut in vindictam mortis Christi infideles debellarent. Stabant ergo in campo mortis hinc inde exercitus fidelium et infidelium. . . . Cumque more belli pars contra partem congredi deberent, stabat totus exercitus infidelium immobilis. . . . Fideles vero unanimiter et animose eos invaserunt . . . Querunt ergo fideles ab infidelibus cur nec fugerunt nec repugnaverunt. Responderunt infideles quod in procinctu congressionis apparuit in aere quidam armatus, terribilis nimis, totus candidus in armis et equo, qui etiam dextra sua comminatorie evaginatum vibrare gladium igneum et secum contra infideles innumerabilem exercitum candidum conducere omnibus videbatur . . . Hec ille.

26, C-D

Quasi enim quatuor pictores, imaginor apostolos, martires, confessores et virgines, qui suis propriis coloribus depingentes domum Dei, que est vera filia Syon, historiis effectivis varie perornant. Apostoli namque quasi primi pictores in domo Dei cum splendore decoris aurei depinxerunt voluntariam paupertatem. . . . Secundo, martires quasi contrarii pictores in domo Dei non solum cum colore sanguineo, sed cum crurore proprio igneam caritatem depinxerunt ac per imagines allectivas gesta amoris ac certamina fervoris ex caritate protraxerunt. Tertio,

---

filium mortuum aliquando nominat ipsum proprio nomine, aliquando nominat eum cor suum, et sic de aliis, et frequenter de una persona transit ad aliam magis secundum modum affectionis quam secundum ordinem rationis.

Lyre's explanation of the literal sense of the alphabet is too long to quote. Lathbury does not observe the Thomist distinction between the meaning intended by the prophet, the literal sense, and the mystical or moral sense. He includes his *moralitates* in the prophet's intention.

confessores quasi pictores curiosi cum colore virido seu verneo viridam sanctitatem multipliciter depinxerunt. Quarto, virgines, tam viri quam mulieres, quasi pictores amorosi cum colore candido in domo Dei imagines pudicitie et caracteres munditie protrahentes corporis et anime clarius depinxerunt integram virginitatem.

MS Merton College 198

foll. 191vb-192ra

Sed numquid dicta poetarum gentilium et philosophorum assumenda sunt ad sacrum usum theologorum? Videtur quod non, quia cum theologus debeat esse sciolus et solidus, solum debet uti, ut videtur, appropriatis et utilibus, sed poetica et philosophica non sunt appropriata nec videntur esse utilia, ergo non sunt assumenda ad sacra opera theologica.

Ad oppositum sic in glosa 2 Paralipomenon, xx, o;[1] Sancti doctores . . . possideant.[2] Hec ibi.

Pro responsione ad dubium, pono quatuor conclusiones. Prima est quod poetica et philosophica fidem ecclesie catholice adiuvant et doctrinam sacre scripture exornant. Secundo, dicta poetica et philosophica divine sapientie et sacre eloquentie sunt humilia instrumenta. Tertia est quod dicta illorum sunt media subtilia ad reciproce copulandum magistrum edocentem et discipulum addiscentem. Quarta est quod dicta poetica, cum sunt (*sic*) spolia nobilia, a paganis rapienda et christianis distribuenda (sunt).

Ad probationem prime conclusionis habetur sic in glosa 2 Esdre vii: doctrina philosophorum et poetarum fidem nostram per scientiam secularem adiuvat, dum per omnia adversarios plenius impugnat et doctrina(m) scripturarum per sensum moralem decentius exornat.[3] Quantum ad probationem secunde conclusionis etc. habetur expresse in glosa interlineari Levitici xx: Deleta (*sic?*) quod tales artes sunt discende, ut per ea divina scriptura quodam subtili et delectabili instrumento utilius et melius proferatur.[4] Quantum ad (probationem) tertie conclusionis etc. patenter habetur in glosa Exodi iii: . . . Hec ibi.[5]

[1] II Paralip. xx, 25: Venit ergo Iosephat, et omnis populus cum eo ad detrahenda spolia mortuorum.
The 'o' is to be explained by the contemporary method of dividing the chapters of the Bible by letters of the alphabet.
[2] *Gloss. ord.* ad loc. This is simply a variant of the theme of 'spoiling the Egyptians'.
[3] I cannot find this passage in the *Glossa ordinaria*. The *locus* may have been incorrectly given or the passage may come from an expanded version.
[4] Perhaps an incorrect reference to the *Gloss. ord.* ad Deut. xxi, 11-13: Alii putant hanc mulierem specie decoram significare rationabilem disciplinam apud gentiles inventam . . . ut ad studium veritatis assumatur.
[5] *Gloss. ord.* ad Exod. iii, 22. This is the classic interpretation of the spoiling of the Egyptians.

Quantum ad quartam conclusionem pulchre introducitur glosa
1 Machab. v, super illud: *accepit Symeon spolia eorum*: ... Hec ibi.[1]
Iterum Augustinus in glosa super illud Psalmi 105: *eduxit eos
in argento et auro*: ...[2] Iterum Augustinus, de doctrina christiana,
lib. 2: Philosophi gentium. ... Hec ille.[3] Item beatus Augustinus, de civitate Dei, in multis libris et beatus Ieronimus in suis
epistolis multum diffuse usi sunt poetis, quo ergo teneo quod
utilia sunt poetica et tam ecclesie quam scripture multum
convenientia tam testificando quam exornando, et ideo sic
transeo ad poetica. Et sicut tradit Iustinus, lib. 2, etc. Explicit.[4]

E, 1, L-M

Ergo sicut docet Lizenus in orthographia sua[5] et Isidorus,
Etym. primo, cap. 12,[6] comma est quando in metro post duos
pedes quoscumque remanet una sillaba, prout semper est in
medio versus, sicut est illud vulgare ex pede dactilo duplicato:

Omnibus omnia non mea sompnia dicere possum.[7]

Similiter ex pede spondeo duplicato est illud poeticum:

Virtus virtus supra tibi sit dilectio vita.[8]

Similiter ex pede dactilo simul et spondeo est illud in Alexandrido:

Mortem aper ictus mavult quam cedere victus.[9]

Similiter secundum Isidorum, ubi prius, lib. 1, cap. 26, metrum
est quicquid certis pedibus currit, sicut exametrum et penta-
metron, trimetrum et tetrametron, id est versus sex pedum et
quinque, nam ubi nos versus senarios (MS ydarios) ex numero
pedum vocamus, hos greci, quia gemini (MS geminos) fuerunt,
trimetros appellant. Carmen vero secundum eundem est
quicquid pedibus continetur; et carmen eroicum est tale metrum
quod virorum fortium gesta describit. Tales enim viri dicuntur
eroes, id est aerei, id est celo digni, propter facta famosa vel
propter virtutes elegantes, ut Hercules propter fortitudinem,
Absolon (*sic*) propter pulchritudincm, Ulixes propter prudentiam

---

[1] *Gloss. ord.* ad I Machab. v, 22.
[2] *Gloss ord.* ad Ps. civ (not cv), 37.   [3] *De doctr. christ.* II, xl, 60.
[4] This abrupt transition followed by 'Explicit' suggests that the *quaestio* has
been excerpted from some longer work. It is too simple in form to be a *quaestio
disputata*.
[5] 'Lizenus' may be a corruption of 'Priscianus'. Lathbury may be referring
at second hand to his *Partitiones xii versus Aeneidos*, ed. H. Keiler, *Grammatici
Latini* 2 (Leipzig, 1852) 460.
[6] Lathbury quotes Isidore, *Etym.* I, xx, 3, and xxxix, 1-11, putting it in his
own words for the most part and supplying his own examples of metre. The
list of heroes is his own, but he found the references to Moses and Job in his
source.
[7] J. Werner, *Lateinische Sprichwörter und Sinnsprüche des Mittelalters* (Heidelberg
1912) 66; N. R. Ker, *Catalogue of MSS containing Anglo-Saxon* (Oxford, 1957) 247.
[8] I have not found this quotation.
[9] This line is not to be found in the *Alexandreis*.

et Salomonem propter sapientiam, Adam propter status solempni-
tatem et Traianus propter morum nobilitatem. Et sic hoc
metrum ex dactilo simul et spondeo omnibus metris est nobil-
ius. Et tali metro metrificavit Moyses canticum Deutrono-
mici longe antequam Omerus poeta troianum excidium sub
greco prelio describebat. Eodem etiam libro Iob et Treni
Ieremie versibus exametris, dactilo simul et spondeo, dulcius
decurrunt et utriusque mixtura fit (MS sit) metrum plus ceteris
temperatum. Hec Isidorus omnia ponit preter exempla, et
consimile ponit Iunilius (MS Rivulus), de institutis, lib. 1, cap.
9, ubi dicit quod omnis scriptura aut metris hebraicis aut
simplici oratione describitur, unde Iob et Psalmi, Ecclesiastes et
Treni metris multifariis mensurantur.[1]

Ad propositum ergo non est plus ad intellectum planiorem,
nisi quod Treni Ieremie de ruina tam lugubri sub amorosiori,
subtiliori et famosiori colore metrificandi tunc inter poetas
usitato in lingua hebraica describuntur, under dicitur quod
metro saphico perornantur, id est tali metro quale adinvenit
Saffo mulier,[2] quod scilicet metrum in versibus exametris et
etiam rithmum caudatum leoninum sex pedum simul in se
claudit colorem leoninum, id est cuius metri omnes linee prime
caude, sive (MS sunt) due sive tres sive quatuor sunt, ab eadem
littera semper incipiunt et pari colore omnes linee secunde ab
alia littera oriuntur; et tale carmen est illud metricum de beato
rege Edwardo editum, excepto quod non sic incipit ab eisdem
litteris ut Treni Ieremie, nec ex tribus lineis sequitur cauda, sed
tantum ex duabus. Exemplum:

> Rex pius anglorum titulatus culmine morum
> Prepollens vernat,
> Sine crimine regna gubernat.
> Conservat regis pia mens munamina legis
> Quo iuris cernat
> Moderamina, pessima spernat.

Ecce isto modo legendi apparet rithmum caudatum sub colore
leonino, sed legatur in metro exametro et erunt versus sex
pedum:

> Rex pius anglorum titulatus culmine morum
> Prepollens vernat, sine crimine regna gubernat.
> Conservat regis pia mens munamina legis,
> Quo iuris cernat moderamina, pessima spernat.

[1] Junilius Africanus, *Instituta regularia divinae legis*, ed. H. Kihn (Freiburg-im.
Bresgau, 1880) 481.

[2] St Jerome, *Ep.* 3 (*P.L.* 22) 442-3: Habes et in Lamentationibus Ieremiae
quatuor Alphabeta, e quibus duo prima quasi Saphico metro scripta sunt:
quia tres versiculos qui sibi connexi sunt, et ab una tantum littera incipiunt
Heroici comma concludit. Tertium vero Alphabetum trimetro scriptum est,
et a ternis litteris, sed eisdem terni versus incipiunt. Quartum Alphabetum
simile est primo et secundo.

Sub tali igitur metro mirabili, subtili, simul et amabili Treni commensurantur, cum hoc tamen superaddito, quod tres linee ad quamlibet caudam concurrentes ab una et eadem littera penitus incipiunt.

DOMINIQUE DE BARTHA ON THE APOCALYPSE

MS Florence, Laurent. Plut. XII. dext. 11

On i, 1, foll. 8va-9rb: Pro almo Christi confessore Francisco thema congruum habes in hoc loco, *significavit, mittens per angelum suum.* . . . In quibus verbis attende beatum patrem Franciscum hic descriptum . . .
There is another sermon on St Francis on fol. 102va.

On iii, 8, foll. 55va-56rb: *Ecce dedi coram te ostium*, in quo themate pio almo Christi confessori et pontifici Ludovico attendere possumus . . .

On i, 3, foll. 9va-10va: *Beatus qui legit.* . . . Thema conveniens esset verbum propositum pro fabricanda collatione in principio sacrarum lectionum in auditorio theologorum studentium . . .

On i, 8, fol. 19ra-vb: *Ego sum alpha et omega* . . . In fine laboris studii esset thema congruum predictum verbum, quando ad gratiarum actiones debet consurgere. . . .

On iii, 11, fol. 57rb: *Ecce venio cito*: Collatio pro receptione alicuius novitii.

On i, 11, foll. 22va-23ra: *Quod vides, scribe in libro.* Cum predicatur pro funere, ubi esset funus notabile et laudabilis vite, esset thema congruum verbum predictum.

fol. 41ra: Collatio pro fide catholica cum heretici condempnantur.

fol. 12ra-va: *Gratia vobis et pax.* . . . Thema posset esse conveniens verbum propositum, quando persona notabilis vult facere vale alicui collegio vel alicui grosso populo, recedendo ab eo, cum ibi inter eos fuerit conversatus. In quo verbo tangitur primo munus salutaris benedictionis quod est implorandum, secundo cetus fraternalis venerationis cui exoptandum, tertio tronus supernalis dominationis a quo postulandum. . . .

PIERRE DE BAUME ON THE GOSPELS

MS Bâle B,IX.21, foll. 1-2

Magister discedens a scola consuevit dimittere talem vicarium qui sciat pueros instruere et scolares. Similiter paterfamilias recedens a domo dimittit domum in manu talis qui sciat ipsam prudenter gubernare . . . Ordinans et deputans aliquem alicui officio consuevit ei providere, demonstrans pertinentibus ad illum officium eum quem ipse deputavit, sicut rex, militans aliquem, dat ei equum et calcaria, accingens eum, sicut . . . Saul mittens David ad pugnam contra Goliam . . . et ideo iuriste, doctorantes aliquem, tradunt sibi ad manum librum.

MS Bâle B.V.6, fol. 20ra

. . . et significat quod officiales debent esse mites, benigni et seduli circa hospitium et hospitum receptionem; *et huic erat soror nomine Maria*, non domina, non ancilla, sed soror, quia officiales in claustris non deberent esse domini claustralium nec econtrario, sed omnes fratres, quia magister vester unus est Christus[1] et una mater, scilicet regula.

MS Bâle B.IX.21, fol. 93v

Nota quod electoribus data est potestas eligendi usque ad tempus tertium, puta quamdiu durat una candela. Sic eligitur rector parisiensis. Festinant et eligunt antequam extinguatur, alioquin privarentur iure electionis. . . . Nota: magister diligens respondentem arguit contra eum bis, primo ad partem et in secreto, predicendo sibi argumenta ne in presentia aliorum confundatur; secundo, arguit contra eum in scolis.[2]

PIERRE DE BAUME ON PROVERBS

MS Eton College 79

fol. 40

(dissensions rarely arise in a college) . . . nisi aliquis magnus incipiat, qui super alios vult promoveri. Illud optimum remedium sedandi tales dissensiones est abscindere alam prelationis illius.

fol. 5v

Nota: pater bene et fortiter verberat filium, sed nullo modo permitteret quod alius verberet eum. Immo si alius vellet verberare eum, ipse defenderet.

fol. 23v

Nota de advocato qui dicit in morte fratri Petro de Palude[3] quod in nullo confidebat tantum de salute sua, sicut in hoc quod semel acceperat quandam causam cuiusdam pauperis contra quendam magnum clericum, qui volebat eum exhereditare, et optinuit causam.

[1] Mt. xxiii, 8.
[2] *Rashdall's Universities of Europe in the Middle Ages*, ed. F. M. Powicke and A. B. Emden I (Oxford, 1936) 402, 452-3.
[3] *Petrus de Palma* and *Petrus de Palude* are sometimes confused in manuscript references; but it seems safe to accept *de Palude* here: Pierre de Baume refers to himself as *ego frater Petrus de Palma* (fol. 26) when he tells a story, whereas here he puts it in the third person.

ARMAND DE BELVÉZER ON ST MATTHEW

U, foll. 52v-53

Item est ibi alia beatitudo formalis in nobis, id est visio Dei, que est in nostra potentia intellectiva, et hoc est precise in essentialibus beatitudinis: sed et est etiam beatitudo in actualibus, scilicet in corporis glorificatione et omnium aliorum bonorum aggregatione. Sic intelligitur dictum Boetii quod beatitudo est status omnium bonorum aggregatus,[1] precise autem beatitudinis perfecte in homine in corpore et anima, quia visio divina est beatitudinis continualitas quantum ad glorificationem anime, que videt Deum per essentiam; sed hoc perficitur actualiter in corporis glorificatione, que ex anime glorificatione redundat in corpus, quod quidem non videt Deum, sed anima, ad imaginem Trinitatis formata, sive et cum hoc in omnibus bonis aliis aggregatis perficitur et efficitur ipsa beatitudo actualis, sive (MS scilicet) in aggregatione et societate beata omnium beatorum. De hac autem beatitudine nichil hic,[2] sed de illa que est purgatio animi, ut supra dicitur, que scilicet ponit animum in quiete, gratia divina, donis et fructibus mediantibus.

U, foll. 85v-86

Exemplum, sicut fecit ille rusticus, qui isto modo vendidit suum asinum. Dicit enim historia quod erat quidam litteratus homo, sed multum ambitiosus, qui cum audivit vacare quandam ecclesiam accessit ad eam et etiam in locis occultis, ubi tamen quandoque aliqui fratres transibant, finxit se stando, ut minus alii perciperent, multum devote orare, ita quod ex hoc quidam ex fratribus moti dixerunt in capitulo quod talis bonus esset pro eorum prelato, tum quia esset homo multum litteratus, tum quia, prout viderunt, esset homo magne devotionis et humilitatis, quia non in aperto, sed in privato, ne videretur ab hominibus, ipsum devote orare viderant. Quo audito, dixit unus qui illum melius noverat, quod vellet eis asinum vendere, secundum quod fecit semel quidam rusticus, qui cum haberet unum antiquum et vilem et omnino inutilem asinum, duxit eum ad forum (sed) vendere non potuit, quia ipse rusticus nimis lascivus apparuit, sic quod homines plene sibi non credebant. Demum duxit eum ad remotas nundinas, ubi notus non erat, et se cum asino posuit in quodam angulo et loco secreto, iuxta tamen forum et ubi multi transiebant, et ibi iuxta suum asinum stando, valde devote et aliqualiter voce elevato cepit dicere suum *Pater noster*, que(m) sic orantem cum videret quidam ibi transitum faciens,

---

[1] *De consol. Philos.* III, pros. ii, 3: Liquet igitur esse beatitudinem statum bonorum omnium congregatione perfectum.

[2] Armand stops just when he comes to the question of *when* the purged soul is to enjoy the beatific vision. It was on this point that the controversy turned.

quesivit cur instaret, cui dixit rusticus quod libenter venderet suum asinum, nisi quod adeo simplex esset, quod timeret in foro decipi, nec etiam propter hoc vellet suas orationes consuetas dimittere donec aliquis bonus homo veniret, qui sine fraude daret sibi pretium conveniens pro asino; et semper dicendo sic, pluries repetavit *Pater noster qui es in celis etc.* Quod audiens iste, et putans illum verum dicere, ait quod vellet asinum emere pro pretio quod ipse peteret, quia videretur esse simplex et verax homo, et sic tantum dedit illi pro asino quantum ille petebat, scilicet xx solidos, cum vix valuisset v solidos, qui recepta pecunia recessit et amplius non est ibi visus. Sic et iste ambitiosus, et non ita semper ut apparet, per hoc quod stetit ante angulo et oravit, vult per hanc suam apparentem simplicitatem ad nostram prelaturam anhelare, et ita suum asinum nobis vendere.

Ita etiam hodie multi ypocrite, stantes in locis occultis, ubi tamen aliqui transeunt, orant cum magna devotione exteriori, ut per hoc perfectiores ab aliis reputentur quam si in publico sic orarent.

Exemplum from notes for preachers in MS Angelica 369 fol. 24ra-rb

Tempore quo Roma dominabatur toto mundo in Roma ante templum Iovis, qui erat deus mercatorum et monetariorum, erant duo dolia diverso liquore plena, unum liquore dulcissimo et aliud liquore amarissimo. Similiter infra eiusdem templi portas erant alia duo dolia simili modo plena. Super ista duo dolia talis lex fuit scripta et constituta, quod nulli licitum erat ingredi templum nisi prius de altero doliorum qui erat ante fores gustaret et biberet. Cum ingressus fuerat templum oportebat eum bibere de altero doliorum, que erat ante portas (MS fores), sic modo econtrario, nam si in ingressu biberat de amaro, bibebat tunc de dulci, si vero de dulci, oportebat eum bibere de amaro. Spiritualiter. . . .

MICHELE DA MASSA MARITTIMA ON ST. MATTHEW
MS Angelica 369, foll. 1vb-2ra

Videmus quod quelibet natio habet in consuetudine describere generationem, modum, tempus et conditionem nativitatis domini sui, sicut in cronicis persarum et medorum legitur de generatione Ciri, qui fuit primus eorum monarcha, nam Astrages rex persarum habebat unam sororem nupta cuidam, que pluries sompniabat se videre quomodo de ventre suo exibat quidam qui co-operiebat quasi totum mundum. . . . Legimus etiam in cronicis macedonum et grecorum multa mirabilia de generatione, tempore, modo et conditione nativitatis Alexandri, filii Philippi macedonii, qui Alexander fuit primus monarcha grecorum. . . .[1] Legitur enim in cronicis gallicorum de generatione Karoli magni, qui ideo Karolus dictus est, quia conceptus in carruca est, et mirabili modo conceptus est, quia non erat legitimus filius Pippini regis francorum. Fuit etiam Karolus primus monarcha de generatione gallicorum. Et ideo rationabile fuit ut evangelista, notarius publicus christianorum, describeret generationem, modum et conditionem nativitatis Christi, qui est imperator non solum regni terrestris sed etiam celestis.

[1] Some legends concerning Julius Caesar follow.

APPENDIX II

QUOTATIONS FROM LOST OR PREVIOUSLY UNKNOWN WORKS

Arranged alphabetically according to the author's name or according to the title if the author's name is not given. Some are forgeries, but they are listed under the name as quoted.

Agellius, *De bellis Armenie*

Lathbury, E 104, A-B

De quo sic saltem sententialiter tradit Agellius, de bellis Armenie, cap. 15, rubrica de prima victoria Alexandri. Septem, inquit, (erant) duces persarum fratres gemini, septem scuta regalia curiose depicta et correspondenter descripta famose comportantes, multa regna cum regibus sibi unanimiter subiugantes, quos tandem Alexander debellavit et omnes convictos in bello prostravit atque sic regna cum regimine sibi penitus subiugavit. In quorum primo scuto depingebatur aquila volitans et predam rapiens, in signum quod hostes in pugna quasi predales aves caperet et sibi resistentes pedibus pene discerperet, et hanc picturam talis scriptura circuibat: Omnibus, ut spero, semper dissimilis ero. In secundo scuto ibi depingebatur asinus domesticus quiescens in fumo, in signum quod lento gradu fugeret, sed potenter potentibus in pugna resisteret, et hanc picturam talis scriptura circuibat: Stramina nunc stravi. Nunc sompnio dormio gravi. In tertio scuto hec tria erant inserta, vorago oceani, os medium et fundum habens apertum, cui correspondebat talis scriptura: Per tria monstrata devorabo cuncta creata. In quarto scuto erat aper dormiens, ut luto involutus, in signum quod sicut aper in estu dormiens in lutu difficulter (*sic*) excitatur, sic nec ille faciliter fugeret, immo quasi in pugno immobilis super hostes dormiret, cui talis scriptura correspondebat: Involvor luto, qui mortis dormio scuto. In quinto scuto erat lupus latens sub vellere agnino in signum quod si fortitudo deficeret prudens calliditas vinceret, cui talis scriptura correspondebat: Vincere clam curo. Satiari sanguine puro (*sic*). In sexto scuto erat leo rapax quasi rugiens in signum quod mortem minime formidaret, sed si ceteri fugerent ipse solus superaret, et ideo sibi correspondebat talis scriptura: Nulli parcetur. Summus medicus morietur. In septimo scuto depingebatur luna discolorata cuius una media erat dealbata et alia denigrata, in signum quod si pugnaret nullus ei obstaret, vel etiam si fugeret nullus eum caperet, cui

349

correspondebat talis scriptura: Et lune vento similem pugnare memento.

Audiens ergo Alexander dispositionem eorum suo depinxit in clipeo iuvenem per totum crurore conspersum, alis aquilinis alatum et unguinibus leonis armatum, in signum quod mortis periculum non formidaret, sed super superiores et inferiores dominium vendicaret, et ideo sibi talis scriptura correspondebat: Omnia transcendo. Morti mea viscera vendo. Quantum capio tantum sapio.

BEROSUS HISTORICUS ATHENIENSIS
See under Palaephatius.

BORALENSIS
This writer is also quoted as the source for three of Holcot's 'pictures'; see above, 178.

Holcot, B, fol. 7v
Potest adduci illud quod narrat Boralensis[1] de quodam qui cum ingenti gaudio occurebat Plutoni, et optulit eo Pluto pro pane (MS pace) lapidem, et accepit et comedit et factus est in ore eius amare (sic), et dedit sibi bibere de Cochito et statim cecidit in foveam.

ibid., fol. 24
Unde Boralensis querit que sit causa quare leges regni non custodiuntur nec libenter audiuntur. Respondeo. . . .
Holcot replies to the question himself.

ibid., fol. 36
Est notandum quod secundum Boralensem quidam (MS quod quidam) turpiter confusus, magnus et potens, requisitus cur tam enormiter confunderetur, respondit: confisus sum in vento, confisus sum in umbra, confisus sum in echo. . . .
An explanation follows, which may be Holcot's.

CARNOTENSIS, *Musica amoris*
Lathbury, E, Prol. QQ:
Quam auctoritatem in sua forma pertractans ille Carnotensis in libro suo de corde, qui dicitur Musica amoris, et auctor de proprietatibus elementorum, lib. 2, propr. 33, in eandem conveniunt imaginationem. Verba tamen Carnotensis sunt ista: O celum celorum et regna regnorum! O terra promissa et terra

---

[1] MS Gray's Inn 2 has 'Baralensis', 'Borlacensis' (foll. 7ra, 62vb), and the same spelling as MS Bodl. 722 in other passages.

possessa! O patria patribus perdita, sed iam filiis in fidei federe reformata, in qua sanctorum mentes quasi montes eminentes ter trino radio solis amoris omnium, supple conditoris,[1] cotidie comburuntur, quo ardore non corrumpuntur, sed perficiuntur. . . . Radios enim amoris igneos ex se exsufflat quibus omnem volentem inflamans beatificat.

5, E:

Huius ergo dilecti Dei est anima, civitas et castrum amoris, secundum quod pulchre persuadet ille scriptor in suo tractatu de corde, qui dicitur Musica amoris. O, inquit, anima mea, nonne tu es castrum amoris, cubile summi Dei et civitas regis magni? In porta enim cordis mei tres litteras difformes et dissimiles lego et intelligo, ex quibus quid et cuiusmodi es colligo et addisco. Invenio enim depingi C, litteram semicircularem, et O, litteram omnino circularem, et R, litteram triangularem; et ex hiis tribus litteris amorose legis nichil aliud concludo nisi quod tu es civitas omnipotentis regis. Hec ille.

ELIAS TRIPOLANENSIS, *De vita scholarium atque sua, contra nobilitatem*

Ringstead quotes both *De vita scholarium atque sua* and *Contra nobilitatem*, ascribing many *exempla* to the latter. John Whethamstead, abbot of St Alban's 1420-1440 and 1452 until his death in 1465, quotes extensively from *De sua scholariumque vita* in his *Pabularium*, a book of quotations arranged under subject-headings.[2] Some verses under *Stema* suggest that *Contra nobilitatem* was a *sub-title* of *De vita scholarium*: Elias argues that noble birth avails nothing and that it is better to start poor and grow rich than to be born of noble, wealthy parents and remain poor all one's life. This was an unusual point of view among medieval moralists, but it might have appealed to a scholar who had won through from poverty to riches by his own efforts. Elias wrote in mixed prose and verse, imitating Boethius in his *De consolatione Philosophiae*. He must have admired Pseudo-Boethius, *De disciplina scholarium* and set out to imitate him. Pseudo-Boethius wrote entirely in prose; Elias improved on him by adapting the alternate prose-and-verse form of the true Boethius to the subject-matter of Pseudo-Boethius. Unlike the latter, he wrote under his own (or an assumed name) instead of calling himself Boethius. The text of both Ringstead and Whethamstead is very corrupt. They or their copyists may have done Elias grave

[1] Lathbury's gloss on his text.
[2] *O.R.* 3, 2032-4. Miss Esther Hodge kindly lent me her doctoral thesis, *The Abbey of St Alban's under John of Whethamstede*, presented at Manchester University, 1933, for an account of his compilations.

injustice. If not, he was an ignorant and incompetent versifier. The following quotations are samples:

Ringstead, L, fol. 246rb (Masters today, being incompetent, compete for pupils, a conventional complaint).

Helias de vita scolarium atque sua dicit in principio: Cum olim scolares magistros pluribus sumptibus compararent, iam vice versa fit. Tales enim iam sunt magistri quod vix est aliquis habiturus auditorem nisi prece vel pretio sit conductus. Talis tibi doctor semper sit suspectus, cum scientie inopia plus conducere indiget quam conduci.

fol. 281ra ('Crime will out')

Tripolanensis de vita scolarium, lib. 4:

Facinus res promptu probat factumque perorat.[1]
Iudicis examen iuris et ordo vacat.

fol. 284rb (Slave refuses to flatter his master)

Nota Tripolanensis de vita scolarium, lib. 5, ubi de quodam servo narrat sic: Semper solitus erat, si quos viderat errores graves in domino, statim corripere.[2] Quod cum semel faceret, commotus dominus quasi prothemam (sic) famuli volens referre dixit: Sepius, inquit, frater, lingue tue lubricum nocuit tibi, pigrioremque pervenisses ad fortunam dominoque tuo commendatus esses ad gratiam si modestius esse scivisses et assentator benivolus. Cui ille: Ego, domine, dominantis nollem Iovis (MS Iovem) per sordes promeruisse gratiam nec in celum vel(lem) conscendisse per cenam.

fol. 287vb (Men are shortsighted in their fears)

Unde Tripolanensis, lib. 4 de vita scolarium:

Unus in hoc similis vite modus est animantum
Ut magis effugiant aut metuantque quod angit et instat
Quam graviora pati.
Dum sibi solamen querit, miser intrat in ignem.

fol. 185rb (*Exemplum* concerning Scipio)

. . . sicut narrat Helias Tripolitanorum vel Tripolanensis, lib. 2 contra nobilitatem. Recitat enim quod Emilius Scipio. . . .

Whethamstead, MS London, Brit. Mus. Egerton 646, fol. 6ov

Stemata nil prosunt; nil paupertate gravata
Sortes adorate confert habuisse parentes.[3]

[1] Note the false quantities.
[2] MS: in domino facere quidam statim quidam corripere (!).
[3] Should one perhaps read: 'nil paupertate gravato sortis adoratos confer habuisse parentes'? This is still very unsatisfactory.

Gloria nuda nichil cuidam tulit, excipe lucrum.
Ridiculum quod restat erit levis et sine re res.
Plus valet ut locuples vivas, de paupere natus,
Quam pauper peragas genitus de divite vitam.

Hec Helias Tripolonensis de sua scolariumque suorum vita,
lib. 2, metro primo, quasi in principio.

FLACCIANUS, De visionibus sibille

See my paper, Flaccianus, etc., op. cit.

FULGENTIUS, De gestis romanorum

Holcot, *Moralitas* XXVI in the Bâle edition, after Holcot on
Wisdom, 731.

Narrat Fulgentius in quodam libro de gestis romanorum quod
romani verum amorem sive veram amicitiam hoc modo descrip-
serunt, scilicet quod imago amoris vel amicitie depicta erat
instar iuvenis cuiusdam valde pulchri, induti habitu virido.
Facies eius et capud disco-operta erant sive nudata et in fronte
ipsius erat hoc scriptum: Hyems et estas. Erat latus eius apertum,
ita ut videretur cor, in quo scripta erant hec verba: Longe at
prope; et in fimbria vestimenti eius erat scriptum: Mors et vita.
Similiter ista imago habebat pedes nudos etc.

De ornatu civitatis

Lathbury, E, 4, C:

. . . sicut ponit Fulgentius, de ornatu civitatis, et idem habetur
5 Etym. cap. 4, civitas dicitur quasi civium unitas,[1] nec solebat
vocari civitas que non habebat simul regem ad imperandum et
pontificem ad informandum, ut sic utrobique esset unus (*sic*),
quasi unus civium; et sicut tradit Plinius de republica et tangit
Fulgentius, de ornatu civitatis, et Aristoteles et Egidius, de
regimine principum,[2] septem sunt conditiones ad civitatem
requisite, que civitatem perornant et perficiunt . . . edificia ad
hospitandum, homines ad habitandum et commorandum, quia
homo est animal civile, politicum et sociale, rex ad iudicandum,
lex ad regulandum, divitie ad invicem communicande, sapientia
ad omnia co-ordinandum.

---

[1] Isidore, *Etym.* XV, ii, 1: Civitas est hominum multitudo societatis vinculo
adunata, dicta a civibus; IX, iv, 2: Cives vocati, quod in unum coeuntes
vivant.
[2] The references are very general and cannot be found verbally in the
authors cited. 'Plinius' is probably a corruption or mistake for 'Plato'; the
Republic was known by name from Aristotle's criticism of it in his *Politics*.

AA

9, Q:

Sicut ergo tradit Fulgentius, de ornatu civitatis, et tangit Suetonius, de xii cesaribus,[1] in loco quo Nero natus est erat locus a longe quasi domus subterranea, de qua quasi subinvicem (*sic* sibi invicem or se invicem?) obiurgantium et exprobantium et quasi inter se confligentium et invadentium voces trementes audiebantur, et hoc prodigium sine quiete media continue mansit ab hora qua Nero conceptus est in horam in qua natus est, quasi pronosticans invasorem ecclesie, inimicum pacis, turbatorem imperii, filium ire et hostem nature iam ad mundum advenisse.

25, C-D:

Sic ergo tradidit ille senator romanus, scilicet Fulgentius, de ornatu civitatis: Decor et nobilitas civitatis consistit in octo conditionibus, 1, in fortaliciis sublimatis, . . . 2, in edificiis ordinatis, . . . 3, in multiplicibus militiis, . . . 4, in communibus divitiis et in metallo auri et argenti, eris et huiusmodi, ac etiam in dietis ciborum et moneta denariorum, . . . 5, in iudicibus legalibus. Apud veteres iudicia fiebant in portis civitatis, ut sic(ut) divites sic pauperes causas libere proponerent et querelas . . . 6, in sacrificiis sacerdotalibus . . . 7, in elegantia populosa, . . . 8, in politia vel communicatione artificiosa.

106, H:

Dicit ad hoc Fulgentius, de ornatu civitatis, quod trans Tiberim erat constructum palatium dedicatum militibus emerite militie pro solatio recreandis deputatum, (MS deputato) et prope palatium erat taberna in cuius medio pavimento fons aque vive perpetuo cursu effluebat, et dicta erat emerita, quia ad illam tabernam milites emeriti, qui stipendiis annonam sumpserant, illuc convenerant, ut delicate se recreantes aquam vivam cum vino salubrius temperarent.[2]

106, P:

Sicut igitur colligitur ex Fulgentio, de ornatu civitatis, et ex Martino in cronicis, parte imperiali, ex Orosio, de ormesta mundi, ex otiis imperialibus, dist. 3, et ex Beda, de imagine mundi, lib. 4, cap. 47, templum pacis dicebatur Coloseus, quod stabat ante templum solis, et erat quasi imago mundi, habens in sui (*sic*) circuitu imagines omnium provinciarum argenteas, quarum quelibet campanellam (in) dextera tenebat. Supra vero in summitate Colosei posuerant romani imaginem Romuli auream, habentem in capite coronam auream gemmis ornatam

---

[1] This is not among the portents described by Suetonius on the birth of Nero.
[2] I do not know where 'Fulgentius' found his account of a sort of Chelsea Pensioners' establishment for retired knights. Perhaps he invented it.

pretiosam (sic), in qua sic sculptum fuerat: Roma caput mundi tenet orbis frena rotundi. Tenebat hec imago pomum aureum in dextera, partim candidatum, partim rubricatum, partim viride (sic), partimque ipso sui colore aureo refulgebat, et hoc in signum dominii quatuor climatum mundi, connotando quod in Urbe romano hec quatuor precipue viguerunt, scilicet innocentia et potentia, sapientia et clementia. Tenebat etiam hec imago hastam auream in sinistra (MS sinistram), et secundum Martinum huius manus et pedes sunt Rome in Laterano.[1]

De parvo lapide
57, A:

. . . sed enigmatice quidem, (sicut) quod (MS quam) recitat Fulgentius in libro suo de parvo lapide intitulato. Tradit enim auctor ille quod cum Alexander Macedo mundum circuiret, ut omnes insulas, provincias et patrias, omnes nationes et sectas sue subderet potestati, contigit quod obsedisset civitatem mirabilem in India inferiori, cui cives pro tributo pulcherrimam virginem obtulerunt, a quibus cum quereret Alexander quale esset puelle preconium, responderunt quod prudentia et sapientia. Cum ergo Alexander ipse a virgine quereret, cum philosophus esset, quid signum sapientie et quid prudentie in aliquo sibi sciret ostendere, inter alia sic fertur ipsam respondisse: Scio solem sic reducere ut retrocedat et in sinu meo attrahere. Scio infinitum sic rapere, ut non compareat et in gremio concludere. Scio solem et lunam plenam coniungere et unica eclipsi utrumque involvere. Scio celum stellatum a raptu sistere et omnes planetas verbo revolvere. Scio fluxum maris per refluxum restringere et totum oceanum in guttam convertere. Scio spheram ignis per ignem extinguere et orbem igneum in scintillam redigere. Scio scientiam verbo brevi omnino concludere doctosque (et) scientes de verbo hoc ad plenum instruere. Alexander vero, accepta puella, a civitate recessit, placitus et placatus.

[1] Lathbury's traceable sources for this passage are (1) *Martini Oppaviensis Chronicon*, M.G.H.S. 22 (1872) 401: Item ante Coliseum fuit templum solis, ubi fiebant cerimonie symulacro quod stabat in summitate Colisei habens in capite coronam auream gemmis ornatam; cuius caput et manus sunt in Laterano (2) *Magistri Gregorii De mirabilibus*, ed. R. Valentini and G. Zucchetti *Codice topografico della Citta di Roma* 3 (Rome, 1946) 149: . . . imago Colosei, quam quidam statuam Solis existimant, alii Romae effigiem dicunt. . . . Here Lathbury could find the account of the statues of the provinces with bells round their necks and the statue at the top holding a lance. It is not said to be a statue of Romulus in either source and neither makes any mention of an apple. Lathbury perhaps found these details in Pseudo-Fulgentius. He goes on to describe the magical defence system connected with the statues, which he could have taken mainly from the *Mirabilia*. Neither Orosius nor Gervase of Tilbury says anything of the sort attributed to them. The *De imagine mundi* of Honorius Augustodunensis was sometimes ascribed to Bede, but it has only three books, not four, and does not contain this story; see *P.L.* 172, 115-88.

De secretis Virgilii

Prol., H:

Nam sicut tradit Fulgentius, de secretis Virgilii, et etiam sicut pro parte tangit auctor de proprietatibus elementorum, et sicut tangitur in primo libro qui intitulatur De xii cesaribus,[1] Virgilius arte miranda ex aere condensato et congellato palatium construxit speculare, in tantum quod civitates et homines, campi et nemora, volucres et pisces, heremi et flumina, imo quecumque res in mundo fuerant earum imago in palatio apparebat. Hec ille.

Prol. T:

... tradit Fulgentius, de secretis Virgilii, quod Virgilius librum repperit in templo Apollonis, habentem quatuor folia, et quotiescumque legebat ipse Virgilius in primo folio imperator orientis, spiritus scilicet malus, orienti presidens, Virgilio apparebat, et quoties in secundo folio rex austri sibi protinus apparebat, quoties quoque in tertio folio deus occidentis protinus apparebat, et quoties in quarto folio legebat magister aquilonis sibi apparebat et penitus obediebat.

Prol. Z:

Unde et hic in proposito alludi poterit colorate illud quod tradit Fulgentius, de secretis Virgilii. Virgilius, inquit, arte stupenda septem composuit difformia specula, effectuum omnino diversorum, sed mirandorum concausativa. Quorum unum ab effectu suo dictum est speculum voluptatis. In tantum enim intuentis voluptatem oculis ministravit quod quicquid corde optavit conspicere mox oculo speculum representa(vi)t. Hec ille.

82, A:

... per illud mirabile quod recitat Fulgentius, de secretis Virgilii. Virgilius, inquit, amore filii Augusti, arte magica cameram subterraneam condidit, que singulis septem horis se monstruosam (*sic* monstruose?) variavit. Semper enim hora lune apparuit contuentibus (MS continentibus) repleri valido murmure talium qui (MS que) operam dabant crapule et ebrietati, nec tamen quisquam videbatur, sed solum auditus. Ad talia obstupuit ascultantium[2] qualia solent audiri ex dissolutione commensantium (MS comminantium).

Semper hora Mercurii in momento consumeretur quicquid infra proiectum est. Semper hora Veneris fetor fortius inficiens (aerem?) ex inde exhalabat. Semper hora Phebi in ea quasi

---

[1] There is no *locus* for such a gloss in Suetonius.
[2] 'Ad talia' repeated in MS. A line seems to have dropped out here.

litigantium iurgia resonabant. Semper hora Martis quasi insultus viventium et gemitus morientium insimul audiebantur. Semper hora Iovis tonitrua ignea tota quasi clibanus candens videbatur. Unde quicquid tunc inventum erat, sive lapis sive metallum, calor consumpsit in cineres. Semper vero hora Saturni pacifica ut cetere domus cernebatur. Qui tamen tunc introgressus est hic ex causa incognita tristitia nimia vexabatur et tunc quasi cura omnium cogitationibus torquebatur.

Et hanc domum doloris dictam Plutoni Virgilius consecravit. Hec ille.

De tribus serpentibus

1, D:

Dicit tamen Fulgentius in libello suo de tribus serpentibus qui populum in heremo premerunt quod Ieremias in isto tormento horribili[1] erat tantum per triduum, et in hoc, inquit, Christum in lacu mortis triduane figuravit, de quo scribitur. . . .[2] Hec ille.

1, N:

Quare autem in primo, secundo et quarto alphabeto singule littere singulis clausulis, non singulis versibus ita a translatoribus preponantur et tantum in tertio alphabeto? . . . Dicunt doctor de Lira, Gilbertus et Paschasius quod summe est difficile aucenticam reddere rationem, nisi iuxta morem poetarum variam (et) curiositatem et subtilitatem in metrificando. Verumptamen causam litteralem non asserendo, sed aliquibus patribus assentiendo recitat Fulgentius in libro suo de tribus serpentibus. Iuxta enim opinionem aliquorum patrum Ieremias quasi subtilis rhetor in tertio Trenorum alphabeto sub cuiuslibet clausule singulorum versuum principio suam litteram (ponit?) in hebreo, quasi, inquit, sic diceret (MS dicens) quis languens in amore; A, amor quam invincibilis es! A, amor quam delectabilis es! A, amor quam mirabilis es!

1, P:

Hanc enim imaginationem confirmat Fulgentius, ubi supra. Si, inquit, fueris iustus vel iniustus, si perfectus vel imperfectus, si peccator vel penitens, si obstinatus vel innocens, disce quadruplex alphabetum et disce diligenter lamenta(tiones), ubi confidentia ex penitentia provocatur in peccatore, ubi clementia ex omnipotentia vendicatur in Creatore, ubi in subtili codice conscribuntur et exponuntur carmen, lamentationes et ve.[3]

---

[1] On the stoning of Jeremias see *Hist. Schol.* lib. Tob. cap. iii, (*P.L.* 198) 1440.
[2] A number of biblical quotations follows.
[3] From Ezech. ii, 9.

De vita Virginis gloriose
31, B:

Item Fulgentius, de vita Virginis gloriose: Maria omnium corpore mulierum ut rosa omnium florum pulcherrima, et citra Christum mente omnium pulcherrima creaturarum. Erat sui Filii tam divinitatis quam humanitatis similissima imago decoris. Non enim erat ei corpus carne immundum aut inflatum ventre, sed candidissimum, clarissimum (et) subtile perspicuum, ita ut corpus anime sue videretur simulacrum et ut ipsa omni oculo hominis atque Dei inclusi in utero similitudo videretur exemplum et imago. Hec ille.

Numerale
9, PP:

Nam secundum Fulgentium in suo numerali,[1] cap. 7, anima in statu innocentie septem radiis universum decorabat, qui sunt humilitas, veritas, equitas, caritas, virtuosa societas et pacis concordia; sed sicut tangit Willelmus de Montibus in suo numerali (MS mariali), cap. 26, anima per peccatum correspondenter ad istos radios septempliciter tenebratur . . . , que sunt superbia, mendacium, homicidium, invidia, iniqua stabilitas, dolorosa duplicitas et legis discordia. Et hoc probat per scripturam hoc eminente proverbio: Sex sunt que odit Deus, et septimum detestat anima eius.[2]

LIBER LEBEONIS

Holcot, B, fol. 40v:

Narratur parabolice in libro Lebeonis quod quidam erat sub duro onere et in impuro aere et in obscuro carcere, et ideo quando querebatur ab eo quali erat similis respondit: 'Similis sum talpe cece sine lumine, quia sum in obscuro carcere. Similis sum mortuo sine medicamine, quia in impuro aere nichil paret differens a morte. Similis sum celo sine iuvamine sub duro onere.' Fingunt enim poete quod celum propter onus semel periclitabatur et cecidisset nisi Iupiter (eum) sustentasset. Et quando querebatur ab eo: 'Qualis fuisti, qui (MS quia) hec pateris? Non videtur quod (est) sine causa', respondit: 'Quia tenebras quesivi, ideo sum in obscuro carcere. Gaudium odivi; ideo sum mortuus, quia tristis in impuro aere. Potentiam ambivi; ideo premor duro onere.' Quando querebatur ab eo qualem invenisset, respondit penitens et dolens: 'Inveni stellam radian-

---

[1] MS mariario. As 'mariali' is written instead of 'numerali' in the next quotation, it seems that 'mariario' is a corruption.

[2] This is a rough quotation from William de Montibus, *Numerale*, cap. cxvii. William proves his point from Prov. vi, 16, as Lathbury says he does. I have verified from the copy of Numerale in MS New College, Oxford, 98, fol. 28rb. It seems possible that Fulgentius modelled his *Numerale* on William's.

tem, auram puram et recreantem (et) virum fortem mea onera supportantem.'

MENANDER, *De figuris regum Hiram et Salomonis*

Lathbury, E, Prol., X:

Iam locum habet in proposito illud enigmaticum regis Hiram ad Salomonem, de quo sic scribit ille Menander, de figuris regum Hiram et Salomonis, lib. 1, cap. 3, parte 4: Si legis, lege. Rex enim sine regno, speculum si conspiciat, imago imaginis apparebit. Rex sine regno, desertum si inhabitaverit, lugens ledetur et vivens morietur. Rex sine regno, circulum lacteum si intraverit, perpetuo vivet et plura quam petit inveniet. Hec ille.

Prol., BB:

Secundum enigmaticum, in secundo folio libri scriptum: Rex, inquit, sine regno mellis fundum pro cibo si perfodiat, facies fellis relucebit.

Prol., RR:

De istis igitur montibus et isto sole et solis radiis iam locum habet illud enigmaticum regis Hiram et Salomonis, lib. 1, parte 4, lib. 3 (*sic*, cap. 3?): Si legis, inquit, lege. Montes quanto plus ardenti solis radio accenduntur, tanto humescunt et imbribus habundant, et quanto plus comburuntur tanto plus florescunt et fructificant.

Hoc enigma, sicut sonat, includit contradictionem. Supposito ergo, ut prius deductum est, quod iste sol sit solus Deus et quod per montes intelligantur sanctorum mentes tam in via quam in patria, tunc plenissimum et verissimum est enigma.

3, U:

Per hanc ergo conclusionem satis clare declaratur illud enigmaticum regis Hiram ad Salomonem, quod ponit ille Menander, de figuris regum Hiram et Salomonis, lib. 1, cap. 3. Si, inquit Hiram ad Salomonem, si legis, lege. Quomodo a quatuor mundi climatibus una semper omni mane simul et vespere prima vox ascendit et ultima vox descendit?[1]

5, F:

Hec ergo miseria nostre civitatis exponit michi illud enigmaticum regis Hiram ad Salomonem, quod ponit Menander, de figuris regis Hiram et Salomonis, et est lib. 1, cap. 3, partis quarti. Rex, inquit Hiram,[2] sine regno, civitatem terre si

[1] Lathbury's answer to this riddle shows that he read *vox* here, although at first sight it looks like a mistake for *nox*.
[2] MS adds 'sum'.

intraverit, experietur quod caput transit in caudam et finis in principium, quia mors transit in vitam et fortuna in infortunium. Quantum capio in hoc enigmate tanguntur quatuor quibus totus mundus. . . .

PALAEPHATIUS, *De incredibilibus*

Holcot, P, Sermo i (the text is very corrupt; some words have defeated me):

Palefatius, libro de incredibilibus, inducit Lucreonem philosophum, qui ponit et docet hominem ex tribus constitutum, scilicet ex anima, a Deo ad sui imaginem creata, que etiam ad Deum redit, ex corpore, quod de terra sumitur et etiam in terram deicitur, tertio ex umbra, quod est aer luce spoliatus ex corpore causata, que solum deficiente corpore inferni petit hostellaria. Tamen apud inferos ponit esse in ea lampades[1] secundum numerum filiorum hominum, et cuius lampas prior exit, illius corpus citius deficere et umbram infernalem petere dicit, nec tamen quemquam mori posse nisi prius Proserpina,[2] inferni regina, eius nomen apud inferos in posta notat et capillum de capite prescinderet vel lampade sua eum illustrasset. Sed quecumque de ista fabula falsa fuerint, ad moralem tamen intelligentiam et doctrina constat. . . .

ibid.:

Narrat Palefatius quod Orpheus, theologus et musicus incomparabilis, qui cithera dulcisona[3] fluvios et saxa, bestias et volucres ac arbores quaslibet dicitur movisse, quia irrationaliter viventes ex feris reddidit ipse mansuetos, E(u)ridicem, quamdam nympham, amavit, et eam sono cythare mulcens uxorem duxit, sed dum Eristeus pastor ipsam amans sequeretur, illa fugiens incidit in serpentem et mortua est. Propter quam maritus ad inferos descendit, legemque accepit ne eam conversus respiceret. Itaque conversus eam aspexit et perdidit iterato, quia a Proserpina detenta est.

Lathbury, E, 12, A-C:

Ista est prophetia ad litteram habens veritatem in Christi passionem, quando sol retraxit radios et tenebre terram occupabant tribus horis. De hac nocte trium horarum tenebrosa dicunt Palephatius, Flegon et Freculphus, Verosus (*sic* Berosus), Lactantius et beatus Augustinus eandem sententiam per omnia.

---

[1] MS in each case 'lapis' for 'lampas', except where 'vel lampade' has become 'ememdes'.
[2] MS 'Proserpentia' and later 'Proserpentina'.
[3] MS 'dulces'.

Omnes enim in hac concordant conclusione quod in hora mortis Christi tam dense erant tenebre quod stelle celi planissime videbantur. Primo enim sub istis verbis hoc ponit Freculphus, parte 2, lib. 1, cap. 6: Regnante Rome Tiberio Cesare filius Dei extra Ierusalem passus est, in quo tempore, ut in ethnicorum (MS hyncorum) commentariis et multis multorum regnorum annalibus diffuse repperimus, defectio solis universaliter facta est et terre motus immensus, quale nunquam expertus quis est super terram, quo etiam motu urbes in Bit(h)inia plurime pulcherrime corruerunt, stelleque fixe noctem illam illustrabant. Hec ille.[1] Ad hoc etiam ille eximius Flegon, qui olimpiadarum egregius erat supputator, lib. 13, scribit sic: Anno quarto ducentesimo secunde olimpiadis magis et mirabiliter, omniaque precellens que ante eam acciderant, defectio solis universaliter facta est hora solis sexta. . . . capere noctem. Hec ille.[2]

Ille vero Palephatus, 19 incredibilium, cap. 13, conscribit sic: Non, inquit, quasi credibile aut incredibile refero, sed hoc scitum a toto orbe et universis cognitum, scilicet universum commotum esse et conturbatum et solem in virtute sua virtutem suam perdidisse, lunam quoque in plenilunio e regione solis fixam situm suum subito deseruisse, ipsamque soli incidere quasi intendentem solem de celo expugnare. Sol succubuit et radios perdidit. Stelle vero noctem illius (sic) ut diem illustrabant. Hec prodigia que regnante Tiberio Cesare contigerunt sapientes conturbabant.

Ad hoc etiam ille Verosus, historicus atheniensis, lib. 3, cap. 1, scribit sic: Unum grande tibi simile non evenit. Sapientiam atheniensium infatuavit quod solem in celi medio luna plena sic obtenebraret ut nox obscura fieret et cetere stelle apparerent. Luna vero ut inopinate venerat post tres horas remeavit.

58, E:

Dicit enim Palefatus, incredibilium lib. 21, quod Lodinus erat astronomus qui, quia contemplationem stellarum neglexit et terre culture inhiabat, in vermem conversus est imbriferum (sic). Hec ille.

59, B:

Secundum Palefatum, libro incredibilium 23, virgo Rampnes sic amore deploravit amicum quendam mortuum quod ipsam ideo ponunt poete conversam esse in aquaductum.[3] Virgo vero

[1] P.L. 106, 1121. Lathbury gives the right reference to Freculph's chronicle, but does not quote his exact words.

[2] ibid. Lathbury took the quotation from Phlegon straight from Freculph. E. Grunauer, De Fontibus Historiae Freculphi (Winterthur, 1864) 41, does not seem to have found the source for this passage of the ninth-century chronicler.

[3] Could 'Rampnes' be a corruption of 'Amnis', a stream?

Noybes (*sic*) perpetuo planctu lugebat donec ipsa deficeret. Resonantibus ullulatibus merendo sic gemebat super novum sponsum coram se crucifixum[1] quod etiam ideo apud poetas fingitur conversa esse in ecco saxeum.[2] Sed virgo Cienes (*sic*)[3] iuxta patris sui sepulchrum immobilis morabatur et lacrimis cotidie conspersa tanto merore afficiebatur et tam gravi languore torquebatur quod quasi stagnum Arcadie dictum novum colorem in facie continue permutavit. Unde per fletum excessivum et quia immobilis mansit iuxta monumentum poete (MS poeta) ponunt ipsam transformari in stagnum.

82, H:

Secundum poetam Sellus (*sic*) ad distantiam stadii fingitur audisse secreta musicantium, ut tangit lib. 27 Palefatus incredibilium.

83, A:

Et hoc pulchre figuratur per illud quod recitat Palefatus, incredibilium lib. 18: In die festo Crete insula, populo in sacrificio occupato, in medio templi egressus est leo de abditis templi Apollonis, et rugiens exivit, cum impetu terram circuiens universam, cuius anhelitus quicquid tetigit infecit et infirmavit, omnemque viridum fecit marcescere et terram undique devastavit. Hec ille.

PENTASSE

Lathbury, E, 57, GGG:

Hec eadem predicta conclusio concluditur in illo libello qui intitulatur (MS instituitur) Pentasse,[4] ubi clementia Virginis gloriose Marie comparatur ad archam Noe in qua salute salvabantur omnes sublunares creature. Virginis (MS Vinide) Marie, inquit, profunditas est arche (*sic* archa?); magnitudo omnibus commensurans est amor; latitudo spiritus seraphicos scandit; altitudo perpetuis (*sic*) eternitas est vite longitudo.

> Capit animalia munda cum immundis,
> Cum sanctos exhilaret iubilis iocundis,
> Lapsos lacu scelerum trahit de profundis,
> Et puris et turbidis suprafertur undis.

---

[1] Is this a corruption of or mistake for 'occisum'?

[2] Have some lines dropped out after 'deficeret', beginning the story of Echo? If not, it seems that the metamorphoses of Niobe and Echo have been conflated.

[3] Is this a myth concerning the pool of Cyane near Syracuse? Ovid tells a different story about it, *Metamorph.* v, 412.

[4] MS Merton College 189, fol. 117vb: Pentase.

RASHI, *De Lege legenda*

Lathbury, E, 1, A: Lam. i, 1:

Et sicut plane distinguunt rabi Salomon, libro de lege legenda, et rabi Mos(es), libro de duce dubitantium,[1] ista lamentatio prophetica est liber omnino per se distinctus; pro tanto tamen annexus et inscriptus et incorporatus est prophetico primo libro Ieremie, quia quod in illo libro prophetavit futurum, in isto (MS illo) deplorat esse completum.

ibid., 13, A: i, 3:

Sicut docet rabi Salomon in libro de lege legenda, hec littera Gimel, que est tertia littera in alphabeto hebraico, nunquam in carminibus ponitur pro titulo, nisi in signum tristitie vel letitie excessive.

ibid. (on the question why the Jews departed from Babylon):

Sed causam longe mirabiliorem ponit rabi Salomon, de lege legenda, et hoc tangit Petrus Alphonsus contra Iudeos, ubi dicit quod quoddam icodum (*sic*) delusit eos.[2] Dicit ergo sic: Omnes sacerdotes iudeorum una et eadem nocte in Babilone in visione nocturna per sompnium erant decepti, tum quia dolore pene doluerunt, tum quia Deum ad vindictam provocaverunt, tum quia Caldeorum idolis adheserunt nec faciem Domini dolore debito quesierunt. Viderunt enim Moysen cornutum radiis luminosis eis advenire et post eos arguerat de legis sue transgressione, fugam indixit illis, dicens: Erit salus fugientibus a confusione Babilonis, sed ve, ve, ve remanentibus! Ille qui Saulem delusit in Samuelem (*sic* Samuele?) etiam captum populum confudit.[3] In Moysen credens ergo incredulus populus in nationes se disperserunt (*sic*). Hec ille.

23, A: i, 5:

Dicit enim rabi Salomon, de (lege) legenda, et consentit per partem Ieronimus hic in commentario, quod hebrei oppressi in Babilone ad laterales regiones undique fugiebant et ubique hostes sevientes invenerunt, et quod quandocumque fugiebant in signum ire Dei elementa eos persequebantur.

25, B: i, 6:

Sicut consentiunt Ieronimus super Isaiam et rabi Salomon, de lege legenda, et etiam magister de proprietatibus elementorum, lib. 9, cap. 36, civitas Ierusalem dicebatur *filia Syon* in prophetiis,

---

[1] I cannot find the reference in Maimonides' *Guide of the Perplexed*.
[2] I cannot find this reference in Petrus Alphonsus' *Dialogi*.
[3] Something may have dropped out of the text here; MS Merton College 189, ad loc., has 'confu' followed by a blank space in the line.

quia quasi sub vertice (MS virtutem) montis Syon erat turris et palatium ad decorem et defensionem civitatis.[1]

Dicit enim rabi Salomon, de lege legenda, quod nulla erat scientia liberalis nec ulla erat ars subtilis artificum cuius doctores non successerunt sibi in sancta civitate Ierusalem.

68, A: ii, 1:

Aleph ergo secundum rabi Salomon, de lege legenda, hic intelligitur iustitia vindicte, sicut in primo alphabeto interpretabatur negligentia doctrine.

72, A-B: ii, 3:

Nota quod sicut colligitur ex usu et auctoritatibus quod hoc vocabulum *Israel* quintupliciter pronuntiatur. Dicunt quidam *Irael*, quidam *Issrael*, quidam *Irrael* et quidam *Israel* et quidam *Izrael*. . . .[2]

(Ad) hoc rabi Salomon, de lege legenda, cap. 85, dicit sic: O, fera pessima (*sic*) peccatum, quod non solum legem nostram mortificavit, sed etiam regem nobis amputavit, dominium regni annullavit, exilium nobis incorporavit, civitatem sanctam transformavit, et captivitatem nobis appropriavit, terramque nostram alienavit et sectam Moysi diffamavit, que non est contenta, quia gentem nostram in nationes dispersit et dissipavit, quin super hec omnia scripturam a nobis abstulit et linguam nostram laceravit. Greci enim adulterant (MS adulterantur) *alleluia* et latini lacerant nomen sanctum patris nostri *Israel*.[3] Hii ultimum (MS ultimi) *lameth* tollunt, dicentes *alleluia*, isti *sin* abradunt et *res* congeminant: et sic tam hii quam isti hebraice lingue veritatem violant et scripture divine intellectu(m) impossibilitant, cum et hii laudem creature retrahunt a Creatore, et isti *principem Dei* in *palmam manus* commutant. Novimus a matris utero quod *alle* sonat *creaturam*, *lu* sonat *laudare*, *ia* vero *Dominum*. Nec nomen patris nostri (MS nostris) magis nobis remansit incognitum, cum enim *principem Dei* significat, et *ir palmam manus* manifestat. Hec ille.

Quarta conclusio que patet per rabi Salomon est quod *Izrael* per *i* et *z* et sine *s* est optime ad intellectum scripture, quia interpretatur *princeps Dei* vel *cum Deo*.[4]

---

[1] St Jerome says: Sion autem mons est, in quo Ierusalem urbs condita est; see *P.L.* 24, 37.

[2] Lathbury goes on to quote St Jerome, *De hebraicis quaestionibus super Genesim* (*P.L.* 23) 988, on the interpretations 'princeps cum Deo' and 'vir videns Deum' of Israel.

[3] The corrector has inserted *Irrael* in the margin.

[4] Mr R. Loewe kindly sends me the following comments: '*Alleluia* is a reasonably good transcription of the Hebrew *hallᵉlu-ya* (two hyphenated words). I can't think how anyone can be said to have 'removed the *lamed*', unless the writer may be thinking of some abbreviated method of writing, *such* as aia. In spite of the plea that all know from birth that *alle* means *creatura*, *lu laudare*

ROBERT GROSSESTESTE, NOTE TO ALBUMASAR'S *Introductorium*
maius

Lathbury, E, 11, H-I:

Unde ad hoc de hac virgine . . . mirabile magnum ponit
Albumasar, ubi supra.[1] . . . Hic notandum quod in libro
Lincolniensis Oxonie scribitur sic in glosa huius apparitionis:
Sciant hoc et intelligant omnes catholici quod hic non fingunt
nec mentiuntur astronomi, sed sic se habet veritas in facie
firmamenti.

THOMAS DOCKING '*Super Genesim*'[2]

Lathbury, E, 72, D: (Docking discusses the question whether
'Israel' should be pronounced without sounding the 's'.)

Dockyng super Gen.: Si hebraicam linguam et scripture
veritatem regulis latinorum subici volueris, aut tolle *s* ab[3]
utroque in hiis duobus, Esrom et Bosra, aut *s* restitue (MS
restituere) Israel, quod sine ratione rapuisti. Hec ille.

WALTER WIMBORNE, *De proprietatibus elementorum*

Holcot quotes this book as 'Tractatus moralis de elementis',
Lathbury as 'De proprietatibus elementorum'. The former
ascribes it to Wimborne; the latter quotes it anonymously. It
must be the work referred to by John Bale, who says: 'Gualtherus
Wynburne, Minorita, doctor, scripsit, Proprietates terre lib. i,
Pulsante fratrum instantia. Ex bibl. Nordouicensi.'[4] Later
bibliographers added 'sancte' to the title. This may have been
an incorrect addition, supplied to make sense. Holcot's quotations show that the work had a section called *De terra*, as might
be expected in a *De proprietatibus elementorum*. Bale may have
seen the section *De terra* with the heading *Proprietates terre*. The

---

and *ia Dominum*, only the last is correct: hall⁰lu is of course an imperative plural
masculine: *laudate.*'

On the transcription and interpretation of *Israel*: 'The interpretation of
Israel as connected with *princeps cum Deo* is an old one. . . . The operative root
in Hebrew to suggest *princeps* is *srh*, which has an *R* in it. The only way I can
account for *palmam manus* is that the writer knew just enough Hebrew to misread
the alphabet, in which *R* and *D* are easily confused; and the word for hand (not,
strictly, palm of hand) is *yad*. If the writer was capable of thinking of *yad* as
yar, I suppose that he might just possibly have recognised in *yirrael* 'hand of
God'; but the whole thing is absurd, anyway.' Mr Loewe suggests that the
discussion of contemporary transcription may have 'a mild interest' from a
linguistic point of view, but this is too technical a subject to broach here.

[1] Here Lathbury quotes from the *Introductorium maius*, ed. Venice, 1506, lib.
vi, cap. ii; see L. Thorndike and P. Kibre, *A Catalogue of Incipits of Mediaeval
Scientific Writings in Latin* (Cambridge, Mass., 1937) 50.

[2] *O.R.* 1, 580. For quotations from his biblical grammar, see B. Smalley,
John Russel, op. cit., 312-13.

[3] 'et scripture' to 'utroque' inserted by the corrector in the margin.

[4] *Index Brit. Script.*, ed R. L. Poole and M. Bateson (Oxford, 1902) 111.

book was probably a moralised account of the four elements. On Wimborne's verse, see above, 50.

Holcot, B, fol. 22

. . . et secundum Wymborne in tractatu morali de elementis, in parte de terra, amor sive dilectio est Iacob, qui xii filios genuit . . .

The names of the twelve patriarchs are then moralised. It is impossible to tell how much of the matter here is Wimborne and how much has been added by Holcot.

B, fol. 23

Habet enim amor, ut dicit Wymborne in tractatu suo morali de elementis, faciem leoninam, faciem vitulinam, faciem humanam et faciem aquilinam. Faciem leoninam habet amor sive dilectio in signum liberalitatis et fortitudinis. Quid enim fortius amor(e), qui Deum trahebat ut nos redimeret, Deum tenebat ne vindictam caperet, Deum faciendo carnem assumere (MS assumendo) Deum vincebat, quin propter nimiam caritatem, qua dilexit nos, Deus misit Filium suum ut nos redimeret et ille tradidit seipsum pro nobis?

foll. 24v-25

Super illam litteram *Ceperunt principes furere a vino*[1] notari potest secundum Wymborne in tractatu suo morali de elementis, 34, est vinum quo reprobi potantur, scilicet defectivum, vinum infectivum et vinum interfectivum, et quodlibet istorum facit principes furire. Primum vinum, scilicet defectivum, est palatium temporalis voluptatis. . . . Secundum vinum est iniquitas sive non equitas . . . Tertium vinum est ira . . .

Lathbury, E, 2, C:

Dicit enim auctor de proprietatibus elementorum, lib. 5, propr. 18, . . . sex sunt mirabiles lapides ab eadem littera inchoantes et hominem in lege sua legitime et mistice informantes.

5, D:

Quale sit hoc tributum dicit auctor de proprietatatibus elementorum. lib. 5, propr. 19: Fertur, inquit, hebreos in Babilone exulantes omne elementum dedisse in tributum.

6, K:

Et hoc est quod dicit auctor de proprietatibus elementorum, lib. 5, propr. 9: O, inquit, anima misera, cum Christum sponsum deseris devenis tributaria, nam penis infernalibus te debes pro

[1] Os. vii, 5.

tributo, malignis spiritibus opera tua omnia debes pro tributo, corpus terre et vermibus debes pro tributo et oculos eternis fletibus debes pro tributo, imo te totum debes omnibus pro tributo. Heu, inquit, misera, quam grave iugum elegisti, heu quam grave debitum introisti, O misera maledicta, redi ergo nunc, redi per amaram penitentiam, quo recessisti tam effrenate per inordinatam concupiscentiam, quia non vere vidua, sed quasi vidua[1] propheta testante diceris, si ad Christum sponsum te expectantem redire velis. Hec ille.

8, H:

. . . sicut exemplificat vel explanat auctor de proprietatibus elementorum, lib. 5, propr. 19: Plangit, inquit, sancta mater ecclesia peccatum originale in infantibus, peccatum actuale in adolescentibus, peccatum mortale in virorum effrenata malitia in semine virorum (MS vivorum) (et) femine (MS femina) natura. Hos enim quasi quatuor filios ecclesia enutrivit et exaltavit. Ipsi vero veritatem deserentes et vanitatem sectantes Deo superius comminante, conscientia interius repugnante et ecclesia quasi matre posterius reclamante, frontose corruunt in pene profundum, voluntarie enim vulnerati in hac mortis malitia nec sanati penitentia, captivi a spiritibus malis recipiuntur et pene perpetue exilio relegantur. Hec ille.

9, S:

Sicut ergo tradit auctor de proprietatibus elementorum, lib. 5, propr. 9, mons Etna flammis sempiternis inardescit, glebasque cadentes quasi ferrum sulphurei fetoris emittit. Ex una parte incavatur et sic in latere montis quasi hostium domus apertum per quod ignis interior longe distantibus manifestatur. Per hanc portam intravit Hercules rex et gigas ille famosus et amore cuiusdam virginis quam adamavit, proposito frustrato, eternis flammis illius montis se tradidit concremandum.

14, B:

Ad hanc igitur servitutem duodecim conditiones requiruntur, sicut pulchre ponit auctor de proprietatibus elementorum, lib. 1, propr. 33. Si, inquit, in curia Christi, que est ecclesia in qua serviunt christiani, cultum servi vendicas, oportet ut duodecim insignita domini tui super te habeas, que sunt humiliter et veraciter divini beneplaciti diligens perscrutatio et leta mandatorum executio, timorata subiectio, levitas animi et dulcedo verbi, tractabilis benignitas, doctrine suavitas ac patientie firmitas, labor actionis et fervor contemplationis. Hec ille.

[1] Lam. i, 1: facta est quasi vidua domina gentium.

44, A:

Expandit rete pedibus meis.[1] Notandum quod duo pedes ecclesie sunt vite sanctitas et doctrine veritas, sicut ponit auctor de proprietatibus elementorum, lib. 5, cap. 9. Duo, inquit, sunt qui quasi pedes firmissimi sanctam supportant ecclesiam, vita scilicet immaculata et esemplaris ac doctrina solida et salutaris. Uno pede mundum calcat et alio pede celum subintrat. Uno pede transit periculum, alio pede comprehendit bravium. Uno pede transsaltat (*sic*) foveas confusionis eterne, alio pede conscendit in montana societatis superne. Uno pede conculcat catervas demonum, alio pede omne malum auffugit (*sic*) et alio pede ad omne bonum currit. Hec ille.

[1] Lam. i, 13.

APPENDIX III

DESCRIPTIONS OF MANUSCRIPTS

LATHBURY ON *Lamentations*

Where an adequate description already exists, I shall refer to the catalogue and merely note points of interest.

CAMBRIDGE

Gonville and Caius College 57 (151); M. R. James, *Descriptive Catalogue of MSS in Gonville and Caius College Library* i (Cambridge, 1907) 50. English hands of the later fifteenth century. Table of contents *Ah* to *Zona*.

Peterhouse 23; M. R. James, *A Descriptive Catalogue of the MSS in the Library of Peterhouse* (Cambridge, 1899), 43-4. English hands of the fifteenth century. Two tables, one for subject-matter, as in MS Gonville and Caius 57, a second for 'textus expositi preter librum'.

LONDON

Middle Temple, unnumbered. In folio. English hands of the fifteenth century. 262 foll. Illuminated initial and border, foll. 1, 30, 231. The flyleaf has an inscription: 'Iste liber est Magistri Nichā Kempton'. Nicholas Kempston (d. 1477) was an M.A. of Oxford and owned a number of biblical works, including some by Grosseteste and Holcot; *O.R.* 2, 1034. The same or a contemporary hand has added the last words ascribed to St Bernard; *P.L.* 185, 520, also quoted by Ringstead; see above, 217. Another inscription in a sixteenth-century hand reads: 'Johannes Lathburie in Threnos sive Lamentationes Jeremie: Adiectae sunt Epistolae, altera Cyrillo Hierosolymitano attributa, altera Sancto Augustino. Item invitationes quaedam et admonitiones praeferentes nomen Beati Hieronimi. Liber Bibliothecae Illustrissimae Societatis Medii Templi apud Londoninenses. Ex dono Eduardi Smith Armigeri unius ex sociis primariis ejusdem Societatis.'

1. Table to Lathbury, foll. 1ra-29rb, headed 'Hec tabula deservit pro cota communibus nigris infra per totum librum de Lathbery'. The prologue and commentary, foll. 30ra-235v, ending '. . . Et sic explicit tertium alphabetum super litteram Trenorum secundum Lathbury'. Leaves containing the prologue, a piece in the middle and the commentary on chapter iii of Lamentations have been added to the original. The explicit of the commentary on chapter ii, fol. 230v, reads: 'Explicit

secundum alphabetum. Et sic totum opus est completum'. Erased inscription, followed by 'Anno domini m°ccccvi'. Then comes a *quaestio*, 'Sed numquid dicta poetarum', as in MS Merton College 189; see appendix i. Then the commentary on chapter iii has been added. The date has been copied from MS Merton 189.

2. *Spuria* ascribed to Cyril, Jerome and Augustine, foll. 236-248v; E. Dekkers and A. Gaar, Clavis Patrum Latinorum, *Sacris erudiri* 3 (1951) 67.

3. Another table to Lathbury, foll. 249-62, headed: 'Hec tabula deservit pro cota communibus rubris supra in libro'. The two tables refer to the two different chapter numerations used for Lathbury's commentary. The last flyleaf is blank except for the words 'Celorum cives precor ut sim mundique dives' in a tiny hand.

Sion College Arc.L.40.2/L.32: I have not seen this MS; Mr. N. R. Ker kindly allows me to quote details from his very full description, kept in Bodley. Fifteenth-century English hand. Blue initials with red ornament. 275 foll. 385×260 mm. A note on fol. 1 reads: 'Omnia probate, quod bonum est tenete Stehpen Hussam 1610', and another in the same hand: 'Iste liber è fundo Maris in Piscatoris rete ad terram productus'. The MS shows manifest signs of damp. A note inside the front cover reads: 'Purchased with the gift of Sir Henry Martin K^t, Judge of the High Court of Admiralty, and of the Prerogative Court of Canterbury, a. 1633'. The Benefactors' Book of the college records a gift by Sir Henry Martin of £15, with which this and other books were bought.

There is no title or author's name. The explicit resembles that of Gonville and Caius 57 and Middle Temple. A table A to Zona foll. 1-44 and others foll. 274-5. The end of chapter 64 has been supplied on foll. 202v-203 in a smaller hand in a space left here by the main scribe.

Oxford

Exeter College 27 (=E); H. O. Coxe, *Cat. Cod. MSS Collegii Exon.* (Oxford, 1852) 10. English hands of about the middle of the fifteenth century. Fine illuminated initials and borders for the prologue and commentary on the chapters of Lamentations. A few corrections, but no other marginalia. Two tables in different hands from the text, one for subject matter, foll. 238va-253rb, 'Explicit tabula super opus Trenorum compulatum (*sic*) per Iohannem Lathbury fratrem minorem etc.', the second, foll. 253rb-253va, headed 'Textus expositi preter librum'.

Lincoln lat. 66; H. O. Coxe, *Cat. Cod. MSS Coll. Linc.* 37. English hands of the early fifteenth century. No ornamentation, but spaces for initials left blank and red used for paragraphing foll. 123-191ra. Two tables as in MSS Peterhouse 23 and E, foll. 1ra-15rb. Very few marginal notes and corrections. Misplacement of chapters 49-60 between foll. 124ra and 129vb. Copied from MS Merton College 189 or a derivative. Not listed in the 1474 and 1476 catalogues; R. Weiss, The Earliest Catalogues of the Library of Lincoln College, *B.Q.R.* 8 (1937) 343-59.

Merton College 189; H. O. Coxe, *Cat. Cod. Coll. Merton* 75; given by Hammond Haydock (d. 1470); see Powicke, 205. The college possessed a second copy, now lost; ibid. 217. Title: 'Lectura super Trenos Ieremie prophete'. 'Explicit secundum alphabetum et sic totum opus est completum. Anno Domini millesimo cccc sexto'. The date 1406 is probably authentic, judging by the hand. There is a table A-Zona at the end and also the *quaestio* 'Numquid dicta poetarum. . . .' A scholarly hand has made an index of the authors and their works quoted in the commentary with references to the leaves on the first flyleaf. Misplacement of chapters 49-60 between foll. 120vb and 126vb, as in MS Lincoln College lat. 66. Many marginal notes and corrections in various hands.

PADUA

Antoniana 351; A. M. Iosa, *I codici manoscritti della Biblioteca Antoniana* (Padua, 1886) 93. Anonymous, lacking the prologue and ending unfinished. Part of the commentary on i, 1 has been presented as a prologue, in default of the original. 8°, North Italian hand of the fifteenth century with illuminated initial. Coat of arms, Sable an estoile gules, fol. 1. It is not a distinctive device, and would be difficult to identify. Bound in white pigskin on boards. The names of authors quoted and some of the biblical characters mentioned noted in the margins in red ink in a hand contemporary with the text.

The incipits and explicits are:

Prol. *In nomine Patris et Filii et Spiritus sancti. Amen.* Mat. ultimo. *Iuxta morem modernorum necnon et patrum antiquorum* . . . Text. *Aleph. Quomodo sedet etc.* Sub ista forma sic incipit liber Trenorum, scilicet lamentationum Ieremie prophete quia secundum Paschasium. . . .

Explicit on ii, 6: . . . habendum respectum ad Deum et hominem. *Tradidit Dominus . . . regem et sacerdotem.*

Explicit on iii, 66: . . . sicut concludit Ieremias in hoc lugubri carmine: *Thau . . . sub celis Domine.*

Only MSS Gonville and Caius 57, Sion College and Middle Temple, where it has been added later, have the commentary on iii. The others stop at ii, 6. No copy includes a commentary on ii, 7-22. MSS Lincoln lat. 66 and Merton 189 end on ii, 6:

'Explicit secundum alphabetum et sic totum opus est completum. Deo gratias'. It seems probable, therefore, that the commentary on chapter iii was added later. It is much briefer than the rest, but there is no reason to doubt Lathbury's authorship, since the same writers are quoted and there are references to earlier passages of the commentary. All copies except the Lincoln and Merton College MSS omit a section of the commentary on i, 15. The Merton MS has a note in pencil, fol. 122va: 'Alius liber non habet ab isto loco usque ad hoc signum' and a note in ink: 'Alii libri non habent hunc passum usque ad cap. 61'. The passage runs from *Sameth. Abstulit omnes . . . Sameth* interpretatur adiutorium, unde sub hac littera . . . ' to 'filie Iuda', fol. 124vb. A scribe must have omitted the passage by mistake, because the second comment on the same text begins with almost the same words: '*Sameth* in hebreo interpretatur adiutorium. . . .' The commentary after the prologue is divided into chapters of uneven length; there are generally 113 up to ii, 6. The only trace of division by *lectiones* remaining is in the prologue, marked *lectura* and *collatio* in the margins in the Gonville and Caius and Merton MSS. The chapters are divided by letters of the alphabet marked in the margin, beginning afresh with double letters, AA etc., when the chapter is longer than A to Z. Most copies are of an expensive make with illuminations; the Lincoln and Merton MSS are exceptional in being plain.

The edition published by the Oxford Press, 1482, is *princeps et unica*; a copy is kept in Bodley as Arch.G.d.38. See F. Madan, *The Early Oxford Press* (Oxford, 1895) 2-3, 240, 255-6; N. R. Ker, The Vellum Copies of the Oxford Edition of Lathbury on Lamentations, *B.L.R.* 2 (1947) 185-8. A copy was still chained in the library of All Souls in the early sixteenth century; N. R. Ker, Oxford College Libraries of the Early Sixteenth Century, *B.L.R.* 6 (1959) 478. The text of the edition includes the commentary on chapter iii of Lamentations, found only in MSS Gonville and Caius 57 and Middle Temple, and omits the comment on i, 15, found only in the Merton and Lincoln College MSS. The end of the commentary on ii, 6 has the following words not found in the MSS after . . . *sacerdotem* 'Unigenitum scilicet Filium suum Dominum nostrum Ihesum Christum qui secum vivit etc. Amen. Et sic est finis huius operis moralium super capitulum secundum Trenorum Iheremie prophete.'

Extracts

MS Paris, Bibl. nat. nouv. acq. lat. 699 (formerly Phillipps 8188), has four extracts headed 'Lathbury super Libro Trenorum', foll. 111-12. I have not been able to identify them, since the *locus* is not given, nor the chapter numbers of the commentary. They consist of quotations from pseudo-patristic works of the type found in Lathbury. The setting is a fifteenth-century miscellany of English provenance, otherwise made up of works on grammar and dictamen, including an 'Orthographia secundum usum Beverlaci', foll. 1-13v. See H. Omont, *Nouvelles acquisitions etc.* 1896-1897 (Paris, 1898) 15.

MS Oxford, Magdalen College lat. 93, has one extract headed 'De amore vel caritate. Lathbury, cap. 4 ff.' fol. 181. I have not identified this passage either. It is not in chapter 4 of the commentary, nor can I find it with the help of a table under *Amor* or *Caritas.* I looked in vain in the *Distinctiones* of his *Alphabetum morale.* A quotation from 'auctor de proprietatibus elementorum' suggests that it is genuine Lathbury. His commentary is so long that it is difficult to identify extracts without references. This one belongs to a miscellany of devotional pieces compiled by John Dygon, Bachelor of Canon and Civil Law, who retired to live as a recluse at Sheen in 1435 (*O.R.* 1, 615-16).

Alphabetum morale

CAMBRIDGE

Peterhouse 91; M. R. James, op. cit. 109. Fifteenth century. 'Ugly rough hand and rough illuminations'. Table of *distinctiones* at end.

LONDON, BRITISH MUSEUM

Harl. 4665: written in various English hands of the fifteenth century; illuminated initial fol. 1, single columns to fol. 159v then double, $8\frac{1}{2} \times 7\frac{1}{4}$ in.

1. *Alphabetum morale* without title or ascription, foll. 1-152v. Table of subject matter, giving a list of exempla under *Narratio,* foll. 153-7; another table, foll. 157v-159v; list of sermons in the *Alphabetum,* fol. 159v. Marginalia in various hands, e.g. 'nota bonam narrationem'. A note to *Excommunicatio,* fol. 34v, reads: 'De excommunicatione vide bene in tractatu Borastane, scilicet in tractatu ibi in fine libri 7b et que mala facit 24a.' On the *Distinctiones* of Simon of Boraston O.P. (d. after 1338) see *O.R.* i, 221.

2. Treatise on the Passion, foll. 160ra-201ra: '*Aspice et fac secundum exemplar* . . . Exod. 25. Etsi Christus ubique in scriptura dicitur mons . . . theoricarum ministrabit. Deo gratias. Explicit liber de 65 articulis passionis Christi.'

3. Pseudo-Origenes homily on St Mary Magdalen, foll. 201va-203vb: '*In illo tempore Maria stabat* etc. Audivimus, fratres, Mariam ad monumentum foris stare. . . . Redde itaque ei spiritum'. Breaks off because some leaves are missing.

Royal 11. A. xiii; see Warner and Gilson, *Catalogue of Western*

MSS in the Old Royal and King's Collections 1 (London, 1921), 340-41. Fifteenth-century, from Tattershall College, Lincolnshire.

1. *Alphabetum morale*, fol. 1-237: 'Expliciunt distinctiones Iohannis Lathbury de O.F.M.'

2. Sermon, foll. 237-240v: '*Amore langueo*, Cant. 3. Reverendi magistri, patres atque domini, ista verba iam dicta recitari possunt in persona Christi. . . . Dei amorem preponent'. Breaks off unfinished. This sermon was preached to a university congregation on a Good Friday, referred to as *hodierna die*, fol. 239. A date about 1355-60 is indicated by comments on the ingratitude of the English for the pleasures and honour which God has awarded them, probably a reference to the victories of this phase of the Hundred Years War, fol. 237v. The preacher occasionally speaks English and quotes a vernacular poem, fol. 239. He was probably a Franciscan, since he quotes François de Meyronnes, O.F.M. (d. 1325), referring to his compilation of quotations from St Augustine: 'Ex quo originali venerabilis doctor Franciscus de Maronis super eundum in floribus elicit duo moralia documenta', fol. 238v; see *Dict. de théol. cath.* 10, 1639-40. The sermon, though not ascribed to Lathbury, may be his or at least a colleague's.

OXFORD

Exeter College 26; Coxe, *Cat. cod.* etc., 9-10. Written in three English hands of about the middle of the fifteenth century. *Alphabetum morale* without title, foll. 1ra-214vb: 'Iohannes Latbury doctor de ordine fratrum minorum, qui fecit lecturam super librum Trenorum, compilavit istum tractatum. Deo gratias.' List of the *distinctiones*, ending 'Explicit tabula', fol. 215rb. Marginal notes and corrections in the same hands as the text, e.g. 'nota bonam narrationem', 'nota bonam moralisationem'.

The incipit and explicit are:

Abstinendum est a deliciis (quod patet per exemplum). Legitur in libro de donis. . . .

Ypocrita . . . de ave nidificante.

The *Alphabetum morale* can be dated soon after 1356 by a reference to the capture of the king of France (*O.R.* 2, 1105). The *distinctio* on *Ymago* has the words 'et nota lollardi' in the text, which must have been added in the late fourteenth or fifteenth century; the *distinctio* itself has no reference to Lollards; MS Royal 11. A. xiii, fol. 236. A. G. Little formed the impression that the *Alphabetum morale* was mainly a reshaping of Lathbury on Lamentations. There is much common matter, but it seems that a number of *exempla* have been added. Among them is a 'picture' in the *distinctio* on *Puer,* ibid. fol. 178: 'Puer potest depingi secundum 4 eius conditiones. . . '. He holds a pen in his right hand, ready to write, and his brother's hand in his left. He stands on '2 globos, videlicet *Bowlys'.* He is crowned with primroses. All four attributes are moralised. Lathbury did not introduce 'pictures' into his commentary. Two references to Waleys on the Psalter have been noted above and there is also a reference to Trevet on *De civitate Dei* iv, 10 in the *distinctio* on *Conturbare,* fol. 46; it corresponds to Trevet in MS Bodl. 292, fol. 132vb. I have not found any of these quotations in the commentary.

The most interesting feature of the *Alphabetum morale* is its sermons. Seven of them are interspersed with the *distinctiones,* beginning under *Adventus* with a sermon for the First Sunday of Advent, which refers to 'epistola hodierna', fol. 7; see also foll. 27v, 41v, 51, 58, 106v, 108. The sermon for Advent incorporates extracts from the section of Lathbury's commentary referring to prophecies of the Incarnation taken from the *Liber de testimoniis gentilium,* E, 106; see B. Smalley, Flaccianus, op. cit. The next sermon, on the text *Qui habet aures* (Lc. viii, 8), works a summary of the sibyl's vision of glass *imagines* from Pseudo-Flaccianus as described in Lathbury's commentary, E, 2 and 3, into sermon form: 'Karissimi, pro processu sermonis est sciendum quod sicut tradit Flaccianus . . . sic ergo replico thema . . .' and so on. All the sermons seem to have been designed for a university or clerical audience.

MICHELE DA MASSA MARITTIMA ON ST MATTHEW AND ST LUKE

The following represents a rough classification of MSS of the commentary on St Matthew, Stegmüller, no. 5630, 5631.

PARIS, Arsenal 1032, fourteenth-century French hand, from the Paris convent of Austin Friars (Grands Augustins), foll. 1ra-26vb. This has the complete set of prologues: 1. General prologue to the Gospels: Frater Michael super Mattheum: *Erunt fructus . . . terram.* Ezech. cap. 47. Ricardus lib. 7 super Apoc.: Sacra, inquit, scriptura arbori comparatur. . . . 2. Divisio librorum: Ex quo in verbis assumptis. . . . 3. Principium super evangelium Matthei: *Hic est sanguis meus.* Mat. 26 cap. Ex verbis Basilii tractantis. . . . 4. Exposition of Vulgate prologues: *Mattheus ex Iuda.* Duo prologi premittuntur. . . . *Mattheus cum primo.* Iste secundus prologus est sumptus de glosa . . . (foll. 1ra-18ra).

Text: *Liber generationis.* Totum evangelium beati Matthei sicut et alia evangelia versatur principaliter circa Christum . . . Explicit incomplete on Mt. i, 17: *Omnes itaque generationes . . .* de virtutibus patrum dummodo.

The rest has been lost. The remainder of the volume consists of lives of saints, etc., written in different hands.

ROME, Bibl. Apost. vat. lat. 382, foll. 1-136v. Not listed by Stegmüller; see M. Vatasso and P. F. de' Cavalieri, *Cod. vat. lat.* etc. 1 (Rome, 1902) 297. Fourteenth-century, perhaps German hand. Lacks prologues, has no ascription and ends incomplete on Mt. viii, 26: *Modice fidei* . . . perfecti in caritate, et est nondum. The rest has been lost.

PRAGUE, Univ. Libr. 1887, foll. 1-348. I have not seen this MS. It has the general prologue, *Erunt fructus* . . . as in the Arsenal MS. It ends incomplete on Mt. xxvii.

VIENNA 1512, foll. 1-259. It has the general prologue *Erunt fructus* and the *Divisio librorum* as in the Arsenal MS, but apparently not the prologue to St Matthew *Hic est sanguis*. It goes up to Mt. xxvi, 34, and therefore has the most complete version of the commentary.

Excerpts

ROME, Bibl. Angelica 369 foll. 1ra-22vb, fourteenth-century Italian hand: Expositio sive lectura venerabilis Magistri Michaelis de Massa Maritime Ordinis Fratrum Heremitarum sancti Augustini. *Liber generationis.* Titulus libri Matthei continet 8 dictiones. . . . Explicit on Mt. xxv, 41: *Discedite a me* etc. Nota pena dampnatorum que notatur in hiis versibus sequentibus. . . . Sed iusti ibunt in vitam eternam ad quem nos perducat, etc. Explicit extractio de postilla Michaelis de Massa magistri in sacra theologia super evangelium Matthei.

TROYES 827, foll. 122-38, fourteenth century from Clairvaux. Anonymous. Moralitates super Mattheum. I have not seen this MS. It has the same incipit as the Angelica, but seems to go up to Mt. xxviii, 6.

A comparison shows that these are in fact extracts from the commentary.

The Angelica MS has two sets of extracts from a lost commentary on St Luke. (1) Incipit prima expositio super Lucam ad litteram secundum Magistrum Michaelem de Massa maritime Ordinis Fratrum Heremitarum sancti Augustini, moraliter et exemplariter multum utilis . . . *Lucas syrus.* Nota quod predicator . . . *Quoniam quidam multa.* Super ista parte. . . . Explicit on xxiv, 5-6. . . . Prosequeris si volueris. (foll. 24vb-42rb). Stegmüller lists an anonymous copy at Leipzig. (2) Incipit expositio prologi super Lucam secundum Michaelem de Massa maritime Ordinis Heremitarum. *Disciplina medici exaltabit caput.* Ecclesiastici 38°. Secundum Ieronimum in epistola . . . *Lucas syrus.* Huic evangelio premittitur duplex prohemium . . . *Quoniam quidam multa.* Iste prologus qui est prologus beati Luce. . . .

Explicit super prologis. Incipit evangelium secundum Lucam. *Fuit in diebus.* Fluvius egrediebatur . . . (a *divisio libri*). *Fuit in diebus.* Iohannes evangelista suum evangelium incipiens. . . . Explicit on xxiv, 5. . . . puncti diem (?), foll. 47rb-76ra. Immediately after the explicit, which is not marked by any rubric, comes the commentary on Lc. i, 5—ii, 41, omitted in its proper place, perhaps because there were two comments beginning *Fuit in diebus*, foll. 76ra-85va. The commentary here is interrupted by the insertion of a few sermons, written in a different hand, foll. 77ra-80va; fol. 85vb is blank.

These two sets of extracts are not, as might seem at first sight, taken from a literal and moral exposition respectively. They read like two separate mixed moral and literal abbreviations of one very long commentary on St Luke, which began with a prologue to the Gospel of St Luke as in No. 2, had an exposition of the Vulgate prologues as in No. 1 and No. 2, a *divisio libri* as in No. 2, and an exposition of the text up to xxiv, 6. The two sets of extracts give comments on separate texts for the most part and contain no matter in common. Michele refers to a second work on St Matthew and on two other Gospels and also to a sermon on the first verse of St Matthew: MS vat. lat. 382, fol. 3va, ' . . . quia tamen de isto libro et duobus residuis per tractatum et in quadam predicatione ad populum in die nativitatis super isto verbo *Liber generationis Iesu Christi*, ideo ad presens pertranseo.'

Other items in MS Angelica 369 of interest for Michele are:

1. A full subject index to the volume in alphabetical order, with some additions in a later hand, fly leaves foll. 3ra-10vb.

2. Nota quedam notabilia et moralia dicta philosophorum et sanctorum de vitiis et virtutibus. Libro 2 rhetorice . . . ; see H. Narducci, *Cat. Cod. MSS in Bibl. Angelica* 1 (Rome, 1893) 182-3. This may be Michele's compilation; it has a reference to a tree *in maritima*, fol. 23va, which has been interpreted as a reference to his native city, but may merely refer to the sea-shore. The compiler was a good Roman: when his author speaks of the qualities of eastern and western nations, he lists English, French, Germans and Spaniards, adding: 'et horum medii sunt meliores, scilicet romani, unde postquam fuit natio, que presset toto mundo sicut romani?' There is also a pseudo-classical *exemplum*, beginning 'Tempore quo romani dominabatur toto mundo . . .'; see above, 347. (foll. 23ra-24vb).

3. Nota quedam moralia per figuras. This is an expanded version of Holcot's *Moralitates*, Theodosius de vita Alexandri. . . . Items 1-17, 19-22, 26, 29, 33 correspond to Holcot I, XIX, XXI, XXXVIII, II, VIII, III, XXII, XXXIII, XV, XXI, XXVI, XI, XIII, X, XL of the Bâle edition. Items 23-25, 27, 30-32,

correspond to items in the collection *Prudentia depingebatur;* see *Fulgentius metaforalis,* 53-4. Items 18, 28, 35-9 are not in either collection: (18) 'Refertur quod fuit quidam iuxta Romam . . .': four tables are found; an angel appears to explain them. (28) 'Ieronimus narrat de romanis . . .': a tales of Roman triumphs. (35) 'Narrat Egisippus in libro de supplemento veritatis evangelii . . .': apocryphal story of the shepherds. (36) A description of the milky way from Ovid. (37) Vision of a pagan priest ascribed to Suetonius. (38) Solinus on a marvellous stone. (39) A vision of heaven. (foll. 42rb-47ra.)

These *figurae* are not ascribed to Michele and can hardly have been compiled by him, since the *Moralitates* and *Prudentia depingebatur,* which quotes the *Moralitates,* probably appeared after his death. The additions are in the same spirit as the two collections drawn upon, and show the type of reader for whose benefit the compilation was made.

The other items in the volume are a treatise on the seven deadly sins, an incomplete treatise on the names of the five fingers, and two collections of sermons; see Narducci.

ADDENDA

to pp. 159, 169-70

1. Dialogue between a poet and a deserted palace.

Dr J. Engels has discovered the source of Holcot's mysterious quotation and has kindly sent me an offprint of his paper, Middeleeuwen en Latijn, *Neophilologus* (1960) 221-33. Holcot or his intermediary quoted verbally from a translation into Latin of Averroes' commentary on the *Poetics* made by Herman the German in 1256. Averroes illustrated what he took to be Aristotle's teaching by examples from Arabic poetry. He introduced the dialogue in question as an example of prosopopeia. Herman's translation runs as follows; I have used the Venice, 1481 edition, the only one available to me (fol. g, i, v), and have corrected it from MS Oxford, Bodl. 300 (2474), fol. 96rb; see G. Lacombe, *Aristoteles Latinus* 1 (Rome, 1939) 390:

> Dixit. Et est hic locus sextus famosus sive vulgatus scilicet cum rei inanimate attribuitur quod est rei animate, ut loqui vel ratiocinari, et est hic locus vulgaris quo utuntur arabes et est figura que grece prosopopeia nuncupatur, id est nove fictio persone, ut cum rebus insensatis ascribitur collocutio et responsio, ut dixit quidam poeta deplorans cuiusdam palatii habitatores, sic inquiens: O domus egregia, compungor ad lacrimas tuam intuens solitudinem. At illa contremuit, compassa michi propter lacrimarum multitudinem, cui inquit: Ubi sunt, queso, qui quondam in te habitaverunt, et iocundam vitam cum securitate et temporis amenitate duxerunt? At illa: Temporales, inquit, existentes temporaliter cum tempore transierunt, et me quoque sub sorte temporis quandoque transituram dimiserunt. Res nempe nulle stabiles, que cum fluxu huius temporis fluxibiles fluxerunt. Et huius figure plurima exempla in diversis maneriebus apud poetas arabicos inveniuntur . . .

The dialogue already had a checkered history when Holcot quoted it. Dr Samuel Stern obligingly made me a translation of the original Arabic of Averroes' commentary with a note on the context of the poem. The Arab tribes in dry weather used to camp together round a well, until the rain came, making it possible for them to disperse. It was a

379

poetic theme to recall memories of life at such an encampment, which the poet revisits and finds deserted. Averroes quotes a poem by al-Qays ibn al-Mulawwaḥ, known as Majnūn Banī 'Āmir, the madman of the tribe of 'Āmir (ed. Bulaq, Diwan, 1924, 25). He refers to a mountain called al-Tawbād:

> There is a sixth method, which is well-known and is often used by the Arabs, to make inanimate things speak and answer, as if they possessed speech. Such is for example the following poem: 'When I saw al-Tawbād, it made me weep, and when it saw me, it exclaimed: "God is great!" I spoke to it: "Where are those whom you used to know in your neighbourhood, in security and happy times?" It answered: "They have gone, and have left for me as pledge their country; who can survive the vicissitudes of time?" ' (Averroes, *Middle Commentary on the Poetics*, ed. Lasinio, 26; ed. Badawi, 228.)

The thirteenth-century translator did not know the place-name. Being ignorant of Arab custom, he naturally supposed that the poet quoted by Averroes must have been addressing a house or palace. He also embroidered a little on his original, adding some more tears and some thoughts on the passage of time. So 'the Madman's' mountain site, formerly frequented by Arab tribes, *alias* Averroes' example of prosopopeia, *alias* Herman's deserted palace, got into fourteenth-century English homiletics as an illustration of *sic transit*.

2. Gifts compared to fetters.

Dr Engels' discovery enabled me to trace another of Holcot's quotations. He ascribes to Aristotle in the *Poetics* the statement that Arabic poets compared gifts to fetters because they bound the poet to his patron. Here, too, Holcot is quoting verbally from Herman's translation of Averroes' commentary:

> . . . prout soliti sunt dicere de beneficio quoniam est torques collo, et de denariis quoniam sunt compedes ei qui bona recipit, ut dixit Abitaybi poeta: qui bona dona sive beneficia invenit, compedes invenit. Et tales metaphora quamplures apud arabes reperiuntur. (ed. cit. fol. f, viii, v, and MS Bodl. 300, fol. 95vb.)

Dr Stern tells me that the Latin translation gives the sense of the original well enough in this case. The poet quoted by Averroes is Abu'l-Ṭayyib al-Mutanabbi'.

INDEX OF PROPER NAMES

Those living before *c.* A.D. 1300 are generally listed under the first name, those living after, under the surname.

INDEX OF 'PICTURES'

INDEX OF MANUSCRIPTS